THE
HEIDEGGER
C A S E On Philosophy and Politics

TEMPLE UNIVERSITY PRESS

Philadelphia

Temple University Press, Philadelphia 19122
Copyright © 1992 by Temple University. All rights reserved
Published 1992
Printed in the United States of America

The paper used in this publication meets the minimum
requirements of American National Standard for
Information Sciences—Permanence of Paper for Printed
Library Materials, ANSI Z39.48-1984 ⊗

Library of Congress Cataloging-in-Publication Data
The Heidegger case : on philosophy and politics / edited by
Tom Rockmore and Joseph Margolis.
    p. cm.
  Includes bibliographical references and index.
  ISBN 0-87722-907-4 (alk. paper).—ISBN 0-87722-908-2
(pbk. : alk. paper)
    1. Farías, Victor, 1940– Heidegger et le nazisme.
2. Heidegger, Martin, 1889–1976—Views on national
socialism. 3. National socialism. I. Rockmore, Tom,
1942– . II. Margolis, Joseph, 1924–
B3279.H49F3413   1989 Suppl.
193—dc20   91-38166

THE
HEIDEGGER
CASE

EDITED BY

TOM ROCKMORE

AND JOSEPH MARGOLIS

Contents

v

Preface

It is always something of a marvel to send out invitations for fresh papers on a much debated topic—here, of course, that of the relationship between Heidegger's philosophy and his politics, and the larger question of the political responsibility of philosophy—and then to assemble the responses as they drift in. Authors at a distance from one another, having no clear sense of who else would be invited or what they would say, have an uncanny knack for distributing their own themes in such a way that no one really seriously invades the focused thesis of any other. Something of the sort has certainly happened here. It would be too much to say that every important point of view on Heidegger's philosophy and career has been equally represented. We did, in canvassing originally, try to include some half-dozen to ten additional voices that would have benefited an oversized collection of this kind, particularly those offering the strongest defense of Heidegger's philosophy (but hardly confined to that) that one could reasonably have expected to collect. We were turned down for various reasons—by some, it is fair to say, on the suspicion that the collection would be cooked. We are sorry to have lost the chance to include those papers, though the truth is that the added bulk alone might have made the entire venture unmarketable. In any case the ones we did receive form a lucky unity. We believe that there are no large questions regarding our topic, centered on Heidegger himself, that have not been effectively broached in the papers that follow. Inquiry will be endless here, of course. But the better strategy, now, would be to exorcise Heidegger's own case in order to recover the deeper puzzle behind it: namely, the one that confronts us as we would confront Heidegger.

Acknowledgments

We thank particularly Jane Cullen, Acquisitions Editor, and David Bartlett, Director, both of Temple University Press, for their unusually
generous encouragement and support—which by this time, frankly, we
have come to expect. The principal expenses in a project of this sort
involve, of course, translations from several languages. David Bartlett
and the Press made all of that manageable. The translations, made by
many hands, inevitably required a good deal of further editing on the part
of both of us. With the exception of Reiner Schürmann's essay, translated
by Kathleen Blamey, they were done by persons associated with the
Translation Referral Service (Center for Research in Translation) at the
State University of New York at Binghamton, under the direction of
Marilyn Gaddis Rose. We thank all these people and list them here
without matching translation to translator; it would be unfair to hold them
accountable for the changes we have made in their renderings. Here they
are: Carroll F. Coates, Giovanni Gullace, Roger C. Norton, Gustavo
Pellón, Marilyn Gaddis Rose, William Snyder. The difficulties of shep-
herding this very large text by many hands and of bringing the final proofs
into coherent order were, frankly, more onerous than the usual editorial
experience could have anticipated. We must salute with special thanks
Debby Stuart of Temple University Press, whose versatility and editorial
expertise—and generosity and labor—brought the final proofs to the clean
form we were relieved to find they could actually reach.

THE
HEIDEGGER
CASE

Introduction

The unique career of Martin Heidegger (1889–1976) poses questions of the most profound seriousness for our age and, hardly more narrowly, provokes genuine philosophical consternation. For many years, it was the practice, widespread among Heideggerians, to suggest that there was no "problem" that required discussion at all. But recently, largely through the labors of Victor Farías and Hugo Ott, it has become impossible to deny or dismiss the deep and prolonged connection between the life of the man and his philosophy, and between his philosophy and his politics. None of the tortuous efforts in the recent discussions in France, for instance, or in virtue of the sustained inaccessibility of documents under the control of the Heidegger family in Germany, has finally succeeded in concealing the personal scandal of Heidegger's life and career.

That Heidegger was a lifelong Nazi, not merely in a marginal or transient sense, is now entirely plain to all who care to read the record. But *what* that means, both in assessing *his* life and work and regarding what it exposes in *our* self-understanding, is still very much open to debate. The embarrassment of acknowledging Heidegger's eminence, his enormous influence as one of the leading thinkers of the twentieth century (according to some, one of the most original philosophical minds of all time), the indisputable connection between his philosophy and his politics, the difficulty of sorting what in his thought may be preserved free of his own Nazified orientation, the inability of the best philosophers of our day to indicate *how* to discern in the work of others the presence or absence of any threatening conceptual taint of the same sort—all this

1

clearly leads us to an existential quandary. Ironically, in putting the point thus, we are following part of Heidegger's own instruction.

We cannot escape the parallel, and we are unwilling to draw conclusions that would accord with Heidegger's own. Furthermore, philosophy is notoriously desultory in its discussion of the issues raised, in spite of the fact that the connection between politics and philosophy has played an honorable role in Western thought since Socrates' execution. Professional embarrassment, apparent everywhere, signifies an inkling of the humane importance of recovering the question of the relation between philosophy and politics, of rescuing it from its neglect within the steady routines of the profession.

Now that the first genuinely public reaction to Heidegger's story has begun to wane—a reaction often unreflective, frequently confined to the more visible aspects of the problem—we must recover its disturbing questions more carefully. We must try to penetrate what Heidegger actually thought and did, what that signifies about the world we share (with him), and what we would now reclaim as a true picture of the world in our own (corrected) image.

Heidegger's adherence to the Nazi party was quite unremarkable in the immediate German context. The famous rectoral address (*Rektoratsrede*), delivered on the solemn occasion of his assuming the post of rector at the University of Freiburg in 1933, immediately attracted the attention of his philosophical colleagues. But it is a matter of record that the ensuing discussion, which reached the attention of the (French) intellectual public only in the second half of the 1940s, did not emerge as an issue of more than transitory importance until the publication of Victor Farías's study, *Heidegger and Nazism* (1989; first edition, in French, 1987), which was rapidly supplemented by Hugo Ott's work, *Martin Heidegger: Unterwegs zu einer Biographie* (1988). Since that time, the debate about Heidegger's relation to National Socialism has elicited a wide reaction in scholarly and nonscholarly media, notably in Western Europe, where for a short time, particularly in France, it dominated philosophical and even nonphilosophical discussion.

Philosophers, Heidegger included, have often argued that philosophy needs to lift its gaze above mere temporal concerns. In Heidegger, this lofty notion took the form of claiming that philosophy should concern itself exclusively with the problem of Being. Nevertheless, his original interest in the question of the "meaning of Being"—in one formulation, the "Being of beings" rather than the actual lives of particular "beings" (human beings, of course)—led Heidegger directly to scrutinize *Dasein*, the essential Being of human being. He seems to have moved quite easily from this to defend the reform of the German university and then, after his election as rector, to assert his claim to the spiritual leadership of the

National Socialist movement—his claim to lead the leaders as the philosophical *Führer* of the Nazi state.

Plato's original turn away from "appearance" to "reality" was essentially accompanied by a Socratic expectation to return to the world of appearances (to the Cave at least), by a frank insistence on the indispensability of bringing the philosophical gaze to bear on the *hic et nunc*. Similarly, early and late, Heidegger's concern with Being was invariably combined with an insistence on its link to the historical condition of human being. The arrow of thought that wings its way from Heidegger's supposedly authentic ontology to a correspondingly authentic form of life points beyond all that to the unanswered philosophical question (which, of course, it illustrates) of just how philosophy takes account of, and applies itself to, its own historical context. That, after all, *is* the Socratic question. Philosophy has always been concerned with the relation between thought, especially its own, and the surroundings from which it emerged.

A persistent dogma of the philosophical tradition blocks the resolution of this inquiry: philosophy, it is said, is *in* but not *of* time. The notion appears in Plato's view of philosophy's ability to plumb beyond mere mutable appearance, the despised world of *doxa*—a professional skill Aristotle domesticated as the power to discern the unchangeable in real change. In different ways, Plato's perspective has been recovered again and again in modern times: in Descartes's rejection of history as a mere *fabula mundi*; in Leibniz's distinction between truths of fact and truths of reason; in Kant's reformulation of the Leibnizian distinction between *a priori* and *a posteriori* knowledge in the contrast between *cognitio ex principiis* and *cognitio ex datis*; and in Husserl's closely Kantian rejection of psychologism.

The profound question Heidegger raises which we in turn must raise about Heidegger's own life and thought, the question of the relation between thought and time or between thought and context, cannot even be rightly posed in the grand tradition of philosophy that views itself ahistorically. The atemporal vision is, in fact, the principal casualty of the growing number of historicisms and contextualisms that have appeared in the lengthening life of our century, focused more and more tellingly against all forms of foundationalism, claims of epistemological privilege, and presumptions of invariant knowledge. It threads its way through the post-Kantian world, in Fichte, in Hegel, in Marx, in Nietzsche, and, in our own century, in Heidegger and poststructuralist thought. Among other things, it makes possible—makes salient and demanding—in fact, requires, all the questions we mean to raise.

In a curious way, Heidegger's own thought and practice support the efforts of this volume to envisage the relation between thought and time and between Heidegger's own thought and the context in which it emerged. The project announced in *Being and Time*, according to which Being must now be thought as time, requires that so-called authentic ontology cannot follow the canonical figures who supposedly turned their backs on the temporal dimension. *Dasein* itself, whose ownmost capacity for Being functions as the tacit ground for interpreting in a radically historicized way whatever in the context of experience appears invariant, is meant to convey Heidegger's rejection—for instance, in the well-known analysis of the hermeneutic circle of human understanding—of all forms of foundationalism and essentialized ontology.

Three themes—Heidegger's emphasis on *Dasein* as existence, on readiness-to-hand (*Zuhandenheit*), on the hermeneutic circle—confirm the need to understand his thought in terms of the context in which it arose. Heidegger himself is particularly insistent in claiming that the proper approach to the problem of Being, the obsessive preoccupation of his entire thought, lies in recovering the pre-Socratic view of Being which, as early as classical Greece and throughout the entire later uniform history of metaphysics, was effectively suppressed and hidden from view. Heidegger insists that that tradition needs to be "destroyed" so that the saving vision it obscures may be recovered, made available once again, by and to the modern world through the destined agency of Hitler's Germany.

But it would be wrong to suppose that Heidegger means to support this argument by an ahistorical conception of philosophy. Unlike certain other thinkers (notably Husserl), who hoped to be able to begin again at the beginning of thought, Heidegger never refused the validity of the prior historical tradition, though he regarded it as effectively confined to the pre-Socratic period. Indeed, his own view of phenomenology suggests the unreliability of any version of the Husserlian claim. For, according to Heidegger, everything that is revealed is accompanied by what remains concealed. Phenomenology is said to be centrally concerned with eliciting and interpreting what thus remains concealed—an essentially inexhaustible and treacherous project. It is entirely fair, therefore, to apply the same sort of logic to Heidegger himself. Officially, the sources of his thought lie only in the pre-Socratic past, in Parmenides, Heraclitus, and Anaximander in particular; but a closer look reveals the deep influence (both positive and negative) of his reading of a considerable number of important and even unimportant thinkers, including (in no particular order) Plato, Aristotle, Kant, Schelling, Jaspers, Husserl, Dilthey, Lask, Rickert, Spengler, Jünger, Yorck, Luther, Bergson, Augustine, and Hegel at least.

As soon as we acknowledge that Heidegger's own thought arises in and responds to its surroundings—a point he makes about all thought—

we acquire a viable way to understand its relation to politics in a wider sense. The theme absorbs us in a number of respects. First, disturbing questions arise concerning Heidegger's turn toward National Socialism in 1933, shortly after the NSDAP came to power, at a time when many inside and outside the academy were also rallying to Nazism. Clearly, Heidegger took up the National Socialist cause at a time when the Weimar Republic was coming apart at the seams. At that time a conservative revolution was about to begin against the widely perceived twin evils of liberalism (or liberal democracy) and Bolshevism. What, we may ask, led Heidegger to this decision? Was the "turning" in his thought (*Kehre*) implicated in the turning toward Nazism, or did the post-philosophical turning occur only later? Whether his philosophy was the basis of his Nazi turn or his Nazism the basis of his philosophical turn, we must pose another question: what conceptual resources did he possess at the time that might have afforded him a reason for *not* turning in the Nazi direction? And we must pose another question—not often raised: did his thought provide a way to turn away from National Socialism after the turning toward Nazism?

Second, we must inquire what role politics played in the later development of Heidegger's thought. The matter has received scant attention. Heidegger's resignation from the rectorship at Freiburg in 1934, hardly ten months after he assumed the post, poses questions much easier to formulate than to answer. Did Heidegger turn his back on National Socialism when he gave up his office? How did he view the "movement" and his own relations with it after quitting the rectorship? How did all this affect the evolution of his later thought? Was the "turning" in his thought—Heidegger's term for the change in all notions that evolve in the way his own views were being transformed—a factor in his turning toward Nazism or his turning away from its official form? Did his role within official Nazism provoke a turning within the turning, leading him in a different direction after the break with the Nazi state?

In the article "Facts and Thoughts" and in the *Spiegel* interview, Heidegger admitted that for a time he thought Nazism represented an opportunity worth seizing. How did his thought change as a result of his disappointment? Beginning with the Nietzsche lectures, he developed a full-blown theory of nihilism, which was later followed by a radical theory of technology. Since he suggests, in the *Spiegel* interview, that the Nazis tried but failed to combat the hegemony of planetary technology, are we to understand that his own account of technology was actually an effort to further the National Socialist approach? If not, why not?

Third, we must inquire into the role of the wider political, social, and historical currents of his formative years in the shaping of his own earliest themes, possibly even his original philosophical orientation. With the notable exception of the work of Farías and Ott, as well as Bourdieu, most of the Heidegger discussion, like most professional philosophy, treats Heidegger's actual philosophical position as if it were a wholly autonomous creation sprung from the brow of Zeus or determined only by Heidegger's reading of other philosophical theories. But Heidegger's thought is peculiarly rooted in its environment in ways that are only now becoming known. One factor, to which both Farías and Ott refer, is the extremely conservative, virulently nationalistic form of Roman Catholicism that dominated southwestern Germany during Heidegger's formative years, the very period in which he began to develop a distinct political consciousness. Other influential factors were the many disturbing concerns of intellectuals and even ordinary Germans during the Weimar Republic, when Heidegger was writing *Being and Time*: for instance, the growing clamor for a redress of the losses of World War I, which has rightly been regarded as contributing to the genesis of World War II; also, the gathering emphasis, congruent with Heidegger's own dawning perception, on self-reliance, authenticity, resolute action, future-directedness, and the realization of what was specifically German in the most difficult and humiliating of historical circumstances. With the exception of the first item, all these concerns—which, of course, inspired many others as well—found their way into Heidegger's fundamental ontology, in the initial formulations of his philosophy. This suggests that whatever else it may be, Heidegger's thought is and remains the philosophical expression of the Weimar Republic, just as Plato's philosophy expresses fourth-century Athens, and Hegel's the formation of Prussian identity after the French Revolution. No thinker wholly escapes the period in which he or she writes, and in the final analysis each of us cannot escape coming to grips with our own time.

Fourth, we must consider the specific and unusual intellectual ethos in which Heidegger developed and to which he was particularly responsive: German neo-Kantianism—particularly the novel themes of Lask and Rickert, Spengler, Jaspers, and Jünger—and, of course, Nietzsche's thought. German neo-Kantianism exerted an early influence, although at the moment of writing the *Introduction to Metaphysics* Heidegger vehemently rejects all value theory. His lectures on Nietzsche, for instance, include a number of significant references to the rival interpretations of Baeumler and Jaspers. His unkind remarks about *Weltanschauungsphilosophie*, to which he later consigned Nazism, are partly influenced by his study of Jasper's *Psychologie der Weltanschauungen* as well as by his reading of Dilthey. Spengler is a frequent topic in Heidegger's early Freiburg lectures, and Spengler's little book *Der Mensch und die Technik* may well have influenced Heidegger's own view of technology. Jünger also attracted his attention, as providing a possible way of applying Nietzsche's analysis of nihilism to the contemporary situation.

That Heidegger's thought arose out of its own social context is hardly news; the point holds for virtually every thinker. But in Heidegger's case, even the obvious is not altogether trivial, particularly when one considers the crumbling of the official dogma, which Heidegger's own theory combats so powerfully: namely, that thought occurs in, but is not of, time. It is, then, ironic that a number of Heidegger's closest followers have tried to save his thought by employing the singularly anti-Heideggerian argument, in conflict with all he ever said or wrote, to the effect that his own thought is somehow independent of its time and place.

Our intention here is not to reduce Heidegger's position to a series of reactions to the larger influences of his world. It is rather to study his thought, against this larger backdrop but well within the conceptual space opened up by his own turning to Nazism, and sparked by recent studies about its meaning. The reevaluation entailed is both necessary and long overdue—particularly for a thinker of Heidegger's stature, a teacher whose claims are said to inform much more than the merely contingent moment in which they were made. We are perhaps still too close to Heidegger to be able to understand his position fully, much less to measure its permanent significance. But unless we make the effort to probe the full unpleasant truth, we shall never be able to decide with conviction what of his philosophy (despite that deep blemish) remains alive and worth recovering.

Any such effort is made more complex, of course, by the problems of translation—not only of the work on Heidegger published in this collection and elsewhere but of Heidegger's texts themselves. By no means all have been published; of those that have, some have not yet been translated from the German. It should be noted, then, that passages quoted here in English from sources in other languages have—unless otherwise specified—been translated by the authors (or translators) of these essays.

A final word about the discussion that follows. Our theme is plainly explosive and inherently controversial. It would be civilized if everyone who addressed the matter would proceed objectively and let the conceptual chips fall where they may. But that prospect is unlikely from the start—impossible in Heidegger's case. The stakes are too high; too many reputations are at risk; there is too close a connection between matters of personal conduct and a correct interpretation of Heidegger's life and philosophical texts. Put as simply as possible, it is an existential dilemma to which few among us are really equal. How are we to find the "objectively" valid interpretation of a body of thought—on which one's personal and professional *engagement* is based, both the original author's and our own—when that thought is already politically suspect, possibly even open to the judgment that it is evil to the core?

We believe the discussion that follows contributes to the normal intellectual reception of Heidegger's philosophy; to the attempt to come to grips with the disturbing political themes of Heidegger's life and thought; and also to the larger issue, illustrated by the Heidegger case, of the relation between thought and historical context, particularly between philosophy and politics. We have made every effort to secure a set of strong essays representing every pertinent point of view. They are certainly good specimens of the best work now available in Europe and America, and the range is as broad as we could make it. We had hoped for an even wider range of views, but unfortunately, we encountered resistance, suspicion, unwillingness on the part of a number of writers to accept our invitation, particularly among those who could be expected to adopt a protective stance toward Heidegger. We regret the refusals, but we have done our level best. More than that, we hope to have provoked the larger debate again.

I

1

Heidegger's Apology: Biography as Philosophy and Ideology

THEODORE KISIEL

Every decade since the postwar 1940s has had its public airing of *der Fall Heidegger, le cas Heidegger, il caso Heidegger,* "the Heidegger case," an international convention referring specifically to the philosopher's notorious public involvement with Nazism in the 1930s. The literature dealing with this matter records the decennial pulse of the discussion in some detail. The first round belongs to Jean-Paul Sartre's *Les Temps modernes,* as the case was initially aired under the French occupation immediately after the war; the result was Heidegger's forced temporary retirement from teaching at the University of Freiburg. The first real (albeit brief) airing in the German press occurred in 1953 with the publication of Heidegger's lecture course of 1935, in which a postwar generation of German students such as Jürgen Habermas found themselves abruptly plunged back into the thick of the 1930s through a single sentence lauding "the inner truth and greatness of this movement [i.e., National Socialism]." The 1960s began with Guido Schneeberger's privately published collections of Heidegger's statements and publicly reported activities around the time of his rectorate; these and several other "attacks" kept the case before the public eye throughout the decade. One result of this sporadic and somewhat repressed discussion was Heidegger's interview with the *Spiegel* editors in 1966, which, published posthumously upon Heidegger's death in 1976, formed the *pièce de résistance* of discussion (somewhat muted in view of the solemn occasion) in the 1970s. The next wave was also triggered by Heidegger's self-vindicative statements, this time in the posthumous publication in 1983 of his "Facts and Thoughts" on his rectorate.

Then the dam broke in 1987, and the world was inundated by the deluge bursting out of France caused by Victor Farías's book, *Heidegger et le nazisme*.[1] Now that the public storm generated by this defamatory "inquisitorial" book has subsided, with the help of more solidly founded researches such as Hugo Ott's full-length biography of Heidegger,[2] we may safely take stock of the situation from a firmer vantage and define a few future tasks. Not that all is quiet on the journalistic front. As I write these lines, I am also busy collecting the new set of newspaper clippings (that portfolio alone has expanded exponentially in the last two years), prompted by the recent discovery in the Baden government archives of a 1929 letter by Heidegger in which he complains of the "Jewification" of the German mind.[3] But it is precisely this ongoing process of archival discovery which has been fueling the discussion all along, and it is the projection of this process into the near future which I wish to attempt here.

This effort therefore might have been subtitled, to distinguish it from other assessments of the ongoing debate, "a view from the archives." Such a view looks to the supplementation and correction of current biographies of the Heidegger case, such as those of Farías and Ott, through the available evidence that is on the verge of publication. But my subtitle points instead to the need to eliminate an even greater hurdle to the full discussion of the most crucial question in the debate. It has become a virtual truism accepted by defenders and detractors alike, formulated in one way or another, that Heidegger's thought, which has become so much a part of the twentieth-century mind and letters, must be kept separate from his life—in short, that his philosophy must be kept distinct from his biography. This bit of ideology, ultimately operating as a form of intimidation and reportedly propagated by the old Heidegger himself, is now being perpetuated by his literary heirs and even conceded by many of his detractors. This position, however, flies in the face of the most unique features of Heidegger's own philosophy both in theory and in practice. For Heidegger himself resorted at times to philosophical biography by applying his own "hermeneutics of facticity" to himself, to his own situation, to what he himself called his "hermeneutic situation," precisely in order to clarify and advance his own thought. The same procedure should therefore also be applicable to the one situation to which he never adequately applied it: namely, to his rectorate of 1933–34 and the ensuing events.

The procedure involves the specification of an "ontic ideal of authentic existence" to guide one's ontological analysis. In the same vein, I have selected the well-known story of Socrates' *Apology* as my guide in the following analysis. Contrary to the usual rules of argument before the Athenian court, the core of Socrates' self-defense was a "narrative argument" in which he outlined the essential facts of his life. It is a Wisdom Story, the story of how he came to the search for wisdom and of the context and conditions in which this search was and is to be pursued, and thus a story in which autobiography itself becomes philosophy. The story of Socrates' trial in effect provides us with a striking parallel to the ongoing story of the Heidegger case in more ways than one, beginning with the continuing resistance in some quarters to the approach of philosophical biography as a way of resolving the most crucial issue of that case: Do Heidegger's political engagements mean that his thought is at bottom an expression of one of the most destructive ideologies of this century?

Bringing the Evidence Together

The current debate over the Heidegger case dates back not to Farías—he merely added journalistic ebullience to a heated but polite discussion among scholars[4]—but to the earlier appearance of Heidegger's "Facts and Thoughts" (published in 1983, written in 1945) on the rectorate. This along with the *Spiegel* interview (1966) is apparently all that we can ever expect from Heidegger himself by way of an *apologia pro vita sua*.[5] In contrast to Socrates' *Apology*, they appear at this point to have been an utter failure. But the grand jury is still out, busy gathering more facts and thus arriving at some new thoughts that perhaps did not occur to Heidegger on those two occasions. He must now be tried *in absentia* and judged posthumously, not quite yet "by history" but at least by way of a complete historical reconstruction of the case on the basis of all extant evidence. Farías's "police blotter" of evidence, by his own admission, does not even approach this, and he is still busy gathering new evidence with an eye to rounding out his case.[6] His partiality of viewpoint can in part be attributed to the partial character of the evidence available to him. The lack of complete evidence is in like fashion reflected in the subtitle of Hugo Ott's book *Martin Heidegger: On the Way toward His Biography*.

The fragmentation of the evidence, the ongoing discovery of new pieces of evidence and their concomitant instantaneous interpretation, and from this the battle lines drawn between Heidegger's defenders and detractors, ultimately stem from a polarization that separates, in view of certain barriers and restrictions, two basically different sets of evidence. On the one hand, there is the wealth of evidence of the Martin Heidegger Archive *(Nachlass)* deposited mainly in the Deutsches Literaturarchiv in Marbach but also held in the private possession of the Heidegger family.[7] On the other, there is the evidence of Heidegger's activities and literary output scattered throughout Germany and beyond, in archives both public and private. Neither side has the full story of Heidegger's complicity with National Socialism or, for that matter, of the rest of his life and thought, which is now irretrievably also drawn into the debate. Each is being exposed piecemeal, but for different reasons.

Ott and Farías exemplify the slow and painstaking resourcefulness required to locate and gather materials from the widely scattered "unofficial" *Nachlass* (government and university archives, newspaper files, Heidegger's private correspondence, diaries, and the like). Ott's researches from 1983 on, from which Farías then draws, are in fact driven by the repeated discovery of facts from such sources which suggested a "counterreading" (Ott, p. 8) to Heidegger's "Facts and Thoughts." But the success of Ott's efforts was assured when he managed to bridge the gap between the various bodies of evidence through the premature publication of large portions of Heidegger's correspondence with Karl Jaspers, which constitutes the guiding thread of Ott's book.

The extent of the unofficial *Nachlass* must not be underestimated, in spite of the ravages of World War II and its aftermath. Heidegger's prolific letter writing, with numerous correspondents scattered all over the world, is sometimes surprising in its extent and depth, as his recently published correspondence with the relatively unknown Elisabeth Blochmann indicates.[8] As a thinker, Heidegger was extremely productive; Gadamer aptly calls him a "dynamo," especially in the years that preceded *Being and Time*. Moreover, he was generous with the manuscripts thus produced, lending them out to students and later distributing them as gifts within the intimate circle of his friends. His phenomenal popularity as a teacher resulted in numerous student transcripts of his courses, which were then passed from hand to hand in a traffic that spanned the globe. For example, the very first thirty-four entries in the Herbert Marcuse Archive in Frankfurt are all typescripts of Heidegger's courses and seminars! The very magnitude of the duplication and dispersal of documents stemming directly from Heidegger's hand or voice has therefore fortunately frustrated the initial attempts of the overseers of his literary estate to gain total control over all such papers and seal them from public perusal.

Add to this the fact that Heidegger was a legend long before *Being and Time*—and thus a figure in the public eye long before his involvement with Nazism—and we come to the no less important circumstantial evidence of accounts *about* Heidegger throughout his life. As Farías's work has shown, the bureaucratic thoroughness of the Nazi regime served to preserve much such evidence, such as Heidegger's payment of party dues until 1945—which of course must be interpreted within that context of bureaucratic terrorism. Within the same context, and thus belonging automatically in the public domain, we also get some additional important documents directly from Heidegger's hand, such as the philosophically revealing plan for an academy to prepare young docents for university careers in the Third Reich, drafted by Heidegger in August 1934 (Farías, p. 197). Farías has in addition located perhaps the earliest secondhand account of significance about the public Heidegger, concerning the talented nineteen-year-old high school graduate and theology student already speaking out publicly on September 10, 1909, on Catholicism's argument with modernism, in remarks duly recorded in the hometown press (Farías, p. 34). These remarks provide a convenient zero-point in tracing the young Heidegger's intellectual development in his writings for the Catholic *Der Akademiker* (first discovered by Ott), through his avid reading of more avant-garde Catholic journals such as *Der Brenner* (not noted by either Ott or Farías), to his clearcut break with conservative Catholicism's antimodernism by 1914 (in a letter to Engelbert Krebs made public by Ott). The gathering of such independent evidence moreover brings an added dimension of completion and depth, and at times even correction, to Heidegger's own autobiographical statements, as we shall amply see.

Our present zero-point is Heidegger's major autobiographical statement, "Facts and Thoughts," regarding his rectorate, written in 1945 and left to his son, Hermann Heidegger, with instructions "to publish it at the proper time, when the occasion arises."[9] The occasion chosen was the fiftieth anniversary of Hitler's seizure of power in 1933. It was published along with Heidegger's rectoral address, also from the fateful year of 1933. The preface by Hermann Heidegger presents a brief defense of his father, who, "like many who later became resistance fighters, was at first caught up in the mood of national revolution of the day, which promised a fresh start for the nation." Hermann Heidegger goes on to explain that his father "was neither an uncritical fellow traveller nor an active party member and, from the very beginning, kept a clear distance from the party leadership." He adds other statements of apology (in the Socratic sense?) but makes no attempt to justify and support these statements from the vast documentation available to him as literary executor of the Heidegger estate. In fact, he resisted the advice from many quarters to proceed with deliberate speed to make such pertinent documentation public. It was only after the storm broke in 1987 that plans were implemented to publish some of this material. Accordingly, we now have Heidegger's correspondence with Elisabeth Blochmann, a Jewish friend of the family who spent the Nazi years in England, and with Karl Jaspers, who likewise was caught up in the mood of 1933 before becoming a "resistance fighter." We still lack the crucial correspondence with Rudolf Bultmann, as well as with Karl Löwith, Dietrich Mahnke, Herbert Marcuse, Erich Rothacker, and others—all of which is in various ways pertinent to the Heidegger case. The courses of this period are also critical. As of this date, for example, no plans have been announced to publish the course on logic given in the summer of 1934, which is known to contain a number of statements bearing on that year's political events.

Otto Pöggeler reports that "Heidegger himself, in referring to his political involvement, stressed that it must be depicted and represented exactly as it happened."[10] In view of an editorial policy that makes a public fetish of fulfilling the "wishes" of Martin Heidegger, it is to be hoped that this wish for full disclosure may soon be fulfilled by his literary executors. There should be no reason to hold back, since Heidegger obviously expressed this wish in the firm conviction that such a depiction would in the end speak in his favor. And in a related matter, he writes to Pöggeler in 1961, "With regard to the relation of my thought to Husserl, some gross errors have cropped up which can only be removed by careful philological work."[11] This concern for careful philological work belies the scorn heaped upon philology by the executors of Heidegger's *Gesamtausgabe,* an attitude that has resulted in a number of editions of poor scholarly quality and a record of misinformation on the factual context of the texts. Future editions should be equipped with at least a minimum of the traditional philological aids of biography, chronology, and doxography required by the reader to place a text in context. The contempt for philology expressed by the overseers of Heidegger's literary estate reflects a larger contempt for the painstaking scholarship required to put a reliable edition together—again in a misplaced imitation of the Master who, in one of his more poetic moods, once distinguished an "object of scholarship" from a "matter for thought" to the detriment of the former. Heidegger's motto for the *Gesamtausgabe,* "Ways—not Works," is being interpreted in this "thoughtful" way in defense of the editors' policy for the *Gesamtausgabe* without their also observing that one must get to these Ways *through* Works, cleared as much as possible of the obstacles posed to the unsuspecting reader by often hilarious errors in reading the doxographic record, as well as by chronological distortions, biographical misinformation, and other forms of bad scholarship.[12]

Accordingly, there is reason to fear that the blatantly amateurish and biased scholarship of Farías may be answered in kind by the witnesses for the defense. It is therefore fortunate for us that one of the more competent workers of the *Gesamtausgabe,* Hartmut Tietjen, has been nominated to bring the vast resources of the Martin Heidegger Archive to bear on the "Heidegger case": to wit, on his "Involvement and Resistance" (Tietjen's guiding title for his brief) in the Nazi thirties. Tietjen seems to be sensitive to the philological problems involved; he is prepared, for example, to muster the evidence to show that the parenthetical inclusion in the notorious sentence in the 1935 course on "the inner truth and greatness of this movement (namely the encounter between planetary technology and modern man)" does not constitute a chronological falsification of Heidegger's development drawn from a later period but can be "documented in the unpublished notes around 1935 and is worked out in the portions of the *Beiträge zur Philosophie* written in 1936."[13] Moreover, early in his project, Tietjen the philosopher was challenged by the Freiburg historian Bernd Martin regarding the authenticity of the documents he utilized in questioning the standard historians' thesis that Heidegger had played an active role in the summer of 1933 in changing the university constitution to bring it in line with the *"Führer* principle," and came off creditably in an archival dispute that is yet to be resolved.[14]

It is too early to tell whether Tietjen's full-length study will provide the definitive "revised standard" version supplementing the somewhat sketchy official version provided by Heidegger himself in the *Spiegel* interview and in "Facts and Thoughts." But the advance notice of themes to be treated promises philosophical depth as well as political relevance: value = philosophy and biological life-philosophy as the core of the Nazi world view; the distinction between world view and philosophy; Heidegger's phenomenology of freedom as a refutation of National Socialism; Heidegger's sense of the nation, the folk, and the homeland; how this sense of what is most one's own *(Jemeinigkeit)* has nothing to do with linguistic chauvinism regarded as a refinement of biological racism (Rainer Marten's thesis); Heidegger's critique of the Nazi sense of science and its concomitant university reform; his fundamental misunderstanding of National Socialism and how this was related to his "conspiratorial concept" of action, and so on. Tietjen's sketch of "another documentation" of the facts of the Heidegger case stops with the two "persecutions" of Heidegger during the postrectoral period and the denazification proceedings. But it does not seem to address the last and most difficult question of the postwar period, which outstrips even the fundamental deconstruction of the concept of race operative in the foregoing theses: Why did Heidegger remain silent until the end of his life about the bearing of his political complicity upon the Holocaust, which was the most gruesome issue of the regime he helped to install in power in its critical first year? Did he ever really face the full magnitude of his contribution, however unintended, to this later issue? In the end, then, Tietjen's treatise may not be the Socratic apology that the world still awaits from Heidegger and his defenders. Heidegger's silence, whether due to some mental block or to ambivalence over the core issues involved, must perhaps be left ultimately to the psychoanalysts, social analysts, and ideology critics of twentieth-century German history. Tietjen may not be the Plato that Heidegger now needs, capable of finding a vehicle by which to justify the philosopher's thought, his *raison d'être,* in its relation to his life; and by which to defend him by rebutting the charges, both old and new, brought against him in the court of public opinion.

From Life to Thought: Deconstructing Autobiography

It is by no means unusual to find that Heidegger's autobiographical statements cannot be taken at face value, that they require independent verification, supplementation, contextual qualification, and correction. This is becoming more evident with almost every new transposition of material from the archives into print. Take the long-standing footnote dating the first beginnings of *Being and Time*, in which Heidegger remarks that he has "repeatedly presented this analysis of the environing world and in general the 'hermeneutics of the facticity' of *Dasein* in his lecture courses since Winter Semester 1919–20" (H. 72n).[15] We now know that both themes were first broached two semesters earlier in the extraordinary *Kriegsnotsemester* 1919, and that there is no analysis of the world to speak of in winter 1919. The recently published correspondence with Jaspers and Blochmann dates the first appearance of *Being and Time* in late April or early May, not in February 1927, as the old Heidegger later recalls. The correspondence also presents a sequence of stages in the actual composition of *Being and Time* different from the one provided in the most recent prospectus of the *Gesamtausgabe*. This is only the most recent example of the misinformation we have almost come to expect from the overseers of the *Gesamtausgabe*, who after all these years still have not mastered and truly "overseen" their holdings to the degree needed to manage the publication of an archive with some degree of scholarly competence. Thus we read in the recently published prospectus for the second edition of volume 24 that Heidegger "completed the manuscript of the Introduction as well as the First and Second Division of *Being and Time* at the beginning of the year 1926." But Heidegger's correspondence with Jaspers in 1926 sketches a different story, virtually galley by galley, of the composition of *Being and Time:* it has the galleys of the First Division printed in April, the handwritten Second Division reworked for delivery to the printer in November 1926, along with the *revised* galleys of the Introduction and First Division, and so on and so on. The clean manuscripts of the First and Second divisions are thus finalized seven months apart. Within the accelerated time frame of composition they can be considered worlds apart, resulting in numerous discrepancies between the two divisions, despite last-minute alterations to the First Division already set in galleys. The full facts of the story are thus not without their importance in interpreting the structure of the book, especially in view of all that the later Heidegger has had to say about *Being and Time* as a failed work and all that has been written about the structure of the work. This reduction to the factual level, moreover, to the full contingency of the historical accidents of the year 1926, generates a movement of demystification that contributes to our philosophical understanding of a book rendered almost sacred by being frozen in time, as Great Books are wont to do. Essentially, this detailed tale of composition renders *Being and Time* a nonbook, a way rather than a work, and thus promotes the motto that the dying Heidegger affixed to his *Gesamtausgabe*. It provides one more example of the significance of the connection between "Facts and Thoughts" and so serves as a steppingstone to the connection between the life and the thought of Heidegger: to begin with (1) as Heidegger himself understood this connection, and then (2) as detractors such as Farías and Ott, who have written on the Heidegger case, have exploited this connection. The former is the topic of this section, and the latter that of the following section.

There is a tendency among would-be purist Heideggerians to insist on a rigid separation between Heidegger's thought and Heidegger's life, his philosophy and his biography, and so to dismiss the biographical element as fortuitous and irrelevant, perhaps even claiming the Master himself as the source for this attitude. The same attitude is reflected in the editorial policy of the *Gesamtausgabe*. Under the present circumstances, such a dismissal must be viewed with suspicion and even regarded as a form of ideological coverup, a thinly veiled attempt to insulate the purity of the thought from the "impure" events that are being dredged up from its vital infrastructure. The one verifiable context in which Heidegger himself underscored this separation confirms this suspicion: a conversation with Heinrich Petzet over the very first of the vitriolic Nazi-baiting books against Heidegger (the paradigm for the future Farías), written by Paul Hühnerfeld, which had just appeared (it was 1959): "Look here, Petzet, this Hühnerfeld wrote me a half a year ago and described a series of small monographs, 'Geniuses of the Twentieth Century'—Stravinsky, Picasso—commissioned by a respectable Berlin publisher, and asked whether I would see him and give him some biographical material. I wrote back that, as far as I was concerned, it is finally time to charge the reader less with interesting biographical tidbits than to have him concern himself *finally* with *the* matter and to ponder that to which I have devoted 40 years of long labor. *My life is totally uninteresting.*" Petzet goes on to note: "Hühnerfeld had then written a vulgar letter full of bare-faced threats: he would get even! And so here we have his 'revenge,' written in a matter of four months."[16]

And yet Heidegger, several months away from his seventieth birthday when this conversation took place, had to know that he had already prepared two very different kinds of autobiographical sketches that were to appear in print within months. And each in its own way serves to bridge the very separation between life and thought which this conversation wishes to sanction. Taken together, therefore, these documents show that Heidegger the thinker was not so much indifferent as he was ambivalent toward his *curriculum vitae*. Indeed, the earlier of these, the quasi-fictional "Dialogue on Language," written in 1953–54, is accompanied by a note seeking "to counter widely circulated allegations" that he was responsible for the deletion of the dedication to Husserl from the fifth edition of *Sein und Zeit*, which had appeared in 1942.[17] Clearly, Heidegger at this time felt himself to be under siege. The second autobiographical statement, the inaugural speech to the Heidelberg Academy of Sciences in 1957, delivered in the presence of his first two habilitation students, Karl Löwith and Hans-Georg Gadamer, who were then professors at the university, was accordingly an occasion for reunion, reminiscence—and reconciliation. Löwith, recently back in Germany after decades of forced emigration as a Jew, and one of the first to find a link between Heidegger's political involvement and his philosophy, found many an occasion in his late years to recall his time with Heidegger in the early 1920s by excerpting from their correspondence from that era. On that evening in 1957, Heidegger dwelt on his Catholic past and concluded his reminiscence with "the exciting years between 1910 and 1914."[18]

The following years brought two other accounts by Heidegger of his "path of thought" in which biography and philosophy are explicitly intercalated: the letter to William J. Richardson, S.J., in 1962; and the article "My Way to Phenomenology," in 1963. The latter is dedicated to Hermann Niemeyer and, in a brief allusion to the Nazi thirties, recounts how in this decade "every major publication was suppressed until Niemeyer took the risk of printing my interpretation of Hölderlin's 'As When on a Holiday' in 1941 without stating the year of publication."[19] In 1966 all such facts were thoroughly aired in the *Spiegel* interview. In a note prefacing his translation, William Richardson observes that "the interview takes on the quality of a last will and testament." The old Heidegger had made his peace with the journalistic world and turned his attention to the more scholarly aspects of the impending "grave stillness of God's little acre" (so in the now notorious Abraham speech of 1964).[20] For the old Heidegger—unlike Socrates, who never wrote anything—had to prepare his wealth of writings, published and unpublished, for posterity.

It would be too vast an undertaking here to analyze and assess, as well as to supplement and correct, these five major autobiographical statements. Each has its unique purpose and all are coursed by common threads. At sixty-five to seventy-five, Heidegger's repeated emphasis of his Catholic past in all five recalls the fact that he had remained a Catholic on the tax rolls all his life and in the end received a Catholic burial. One is hard put to find the slight allusions to his turn to a Protestant "free Christianity" in 1917, let alone to atheism in 1929 and to a national folk religion of his own Hölderlinized invention in the 1930s. Yet these "world views" are perhaps more influential on his turns of thought than his original Catholicism. As a result of such autobiographical slanting we have, for example, a veritable industry, among Heidegger scholars, of analyses of Brentano's dissertation on "The Manifold Sense of Being in Aristotle," Father Gröber's gift to the hometown boy in 1907, but almost nothing on Schleiermacher's "Second Speech on Religion," which sparked the breakthrough of 1919 that set the young Heidegger on the central path of his lifelong way.

Certainly the most interesting and challenging of the five statements of the period 1954 to 1966 is the first, the quasi-fictional "Dialogue on Language between a Japanese and an Inquirer"; the literary vehicle alone is noteworthy for our purposes. Looking over that decade, we thus find a reminiscence before old students, a letter to an American Jesuit (recalling Heidegger's first career goal), and a "birthday present" *(Festgabe)* for his old publisher; these are framed by two dialogues: the first cross-cultural and somewhat poetic; the other prosaic and journalistic, addressed, to begin with, to the German nation—two very different kinds of conversation. The first is based on an actual conversation of March 1954 with Tomio Tezuka, a Japanese Germanist. Dominated accordingly by aesthetic and cultural concerns common to the two former Axis powers, as well as by more sweeping East-West comparisons, the dialogue begins with a reminiscence (by way of pictures of his grave) on Baron Shûzô Kuki, Heidegger's student in the twenties, who played a major role in introducing Heidegger's thought into Japan in the thirties. The reminiscence provides Heidegger (the "Inquirer") with an opening to trace his biographical-philosophical development in the 1910s and 1920s which culminated in *Being and Time*. This extended biographical excursus, which (judging by Tezuka's independent account) was not a part of their actual conversation, yields the central fictionalized "fact" that introduces the central concepts governing the entire dialogue. When first introduced, this "fact" also allows Heidegger to parody the student traffic in his course transcripts, which literally circulated around the globe. But in actuality it involves a new fiction: the transcript in question never reached Japan; it is nowhere to be found in the Japanese archives among an otherwise abudant supply of Heidegger transcripts.

The fiction begins when the Japanese visitor tentatively recalls a course given by Heidegger in 1921, titled "Expression and Appearance," which was attended by his Japanese predecessors; they took a transcript of it to Japan, where it evoked considerable interest and intense discussion of Heidegger's "hermeneutics." Heidegger interjects a note of caution: a transcript is a "murky source," and the course itself belongs to his imperfect juvenilia. But later, he is inclined to tolerate this interest in his juvenilia, whereby one nevertheless can "easily be unfairly judged," just as the old Husserl had "generously tolerated" the young Heidegger's penchant for the *Logical Investigations* at a time when Husserl himself no longer held this early work "in very high esteem." Indeed, the allusion to Husserl's attitude toward his own work prefaces the entire discussion of transcripts in the dialogue. And when the conversation later returns to the course "Expression and Appearance," Heidegger first wonders whether the title after all was not "Expression and Meaning"—the same as Husserl's "First Logical Investigation"!²¹ But this query is immediately followed by an in-depth analysis of the "metaphysical" nature of each of the terms in the title "Expression and Appearance" in conjunction with the hidden central theme of the course, hermeneutics, even though that term was first explicitly used by Heidegger (as he recalls) in his course of summer 1923.

We now know that the term "hermeneutics" in actual fact first surfaces in the breakthrough course of *Kriegsnotsemester* 1919—Heidegger's breakthrough here to his lifelong topic richly deserves to be called his "hermeneutic breakthrough"—and that the 1921 course whose title is analyzed so meticulously in the dialogue was in point of fact held in the summer semester of 1920 and titled "Phenomenology of Intuition and Expression." Clearly then, Heidegger is construing his own biographical facts in light of the line of thought he wishes to pursue in this dialogue. Call it what you will—irony, poetic license, or whimsy—this play between fact and fiction, this creative use of biography to promote thought, suggests a whole host of structural parallels, oppositions, and exchanges (Germany/Japan, West/East, Husserl/Heidegger, Heidegger/Kuki, old/young, teacher [grown/old]/student [died young], word/picture, word/gesture, author/interpreter, original/facsimile, thought/life, philosophy/biography, intuition/expression, expression/appearance, meaning/appearance) which opens hitherto unsuspected dimensions to Heidegger interpretation. To carry the play over to our own imagined front, one wonders what Heidegger would have done had he been his own Plato with a free hand on the original transcript of the *Spiegel* interview, free of the constraints of journalistic accuracy, assuming that it would have remained under the contractual and quasi-existential stipulation of life/death—as it were, his life story in return for his death (Socrates?). Farías (p. 297) already has grounds to complain that he was not granted access to the copy heavily corrected by Heidegger, which is deposited in the archives of *Der Spiegel,* and notes the *difference* in the published interview of questions asked and questions answered, interview answers and published answers; also that "the most important and embarrassing question'' was left in the dark. What if Farías had been the interviewer? And what questions would we "journalists" have wanted to ask? what answers expected?

Tomio Tezuka's real concern was the "present state of the Japanese mind''; in this connection, he was especially eager to hear from Heidegger about the "present significance of Christianity in Europe."[22] It might have been this line of questioning that Heidegger translated into perhaps the most philosophically telling autobiographical statement in the entire "Dialogue." It occurs in the context of showing that the use of the term "hermeneutics" in his early Freiburg courses was no mere accident but rather stemmed from the fact that as a result of his earlier studies as a Catholic seminarian in 1909–11, he was still quite "at home in theology." The upshot of the story: "Without this theological provenance I would never have come onto the path of thinking."[23] This most telling of the old Heidegger's life/thought statements may now be supplemented and further qualified contextually by two key statements from the more immediate milieu of the young Heidegger, statements that have recently surfaced from the archives. In Heidegger's letter to Engelbert Krebs in January 1919 we read: "Epistemological insights bearing upon the theory of historical cognition have made the System of Catholicism problematic and unacceptable to me—but not Christianity and metaphysics (these however in a new sense)." By exploring the immediate doxographical background to this letter, we discover that Heidegger really means the *"hermeneutic* insights bearing on the theory of historical cognition" which he gleaned from Schleiermacher's and Dilthey's return to the immediacy of lived experience, which to begin with is religious experience. Such a return parallels the similar return to experiential roots pursued by radical phenomenology.[24]

But the most telling document by far, since it yields not only our third autobiographical statement but also the reason biography is indispensable to philosophy as Heidegger himself understood it, is his personal letter to Karl Löwith of August 19, 1921. In view of its importance, I dwell on this letter at some length. Löwith had just finished his second year of study with Heidegger and took the occasion to assess his relationship to Heidegger in contrast to Oskar Becker's, then also an advanced student: While Becker especially appreciated Heidegger's emphasis on science and method in phenomenological concept formation, Löwith preferred the "existentiell pathos''—in short, the "subjective" side of Heidegger rather than the "objective" aspects. Heidegger responded by noting that each student takes something from him that is not of the essence, since the two aspects belong together in a deeper motivation of his factic existence that neither one sees or would ever accept.

> I work concretely and factically out of my "I am," out of my intellectual and wholly factic origin, milieu, life-contexts, and whatever is available to me from these as a vital experience in which I live. . . . To this facticity of mine belongs what I would in brief call the fact that I am a "Christian theo*logian*." This involves a particular radical personal concern, a particular radical scientificity, a strict objectivity *in* the *facticity*; in it is to be found the historical consciousness, the consciousness of "intellectual and cultural history." And I am all this in the life-context of the university.

Heidegger a "Christian theo-logian"? The underscoring of "-logian" in fact shifts the focus to the philosophical foundations of theology in the fundamental experiences that phenomenology aims to explore—whence the importance of the phenomenology of religious life and consciousness at this stage of Heidegger's development. It involves not only the "personal concern" brought to its extremity in his personal crisis and break with the religion of his youth during the war years but also the "radical scientificity" of phenomenology's return to origins. Both are closely linked to the consciousness of an "intellectual and cultural history" in which philosophy and theology have been deeply intertwined, in which philosophy (Greek, scholastic, modern) had contributed to a degeneration of the original Christian experience while at the same time nourishing itself from that experience. His reading of Dilthey, Schleiermacher, Augustine, Eckhart, Luther, and Kierkegaard had taught Heidegger how deep the interchanges between philosophy (especially German idealism) and theology really were, up to his day, in their mutual concern for the "problem of Christianity," in particular in its relationship to history and the historical consciousness.[25] With his special background, Heidegger must have felt uniquely drawn to a history of philosophy that just happened to be thoroughly permeated by Christianity and, in Nietzsche's words, "corrupted by theologians' blood."

"I am a 'Christian theo*logian*'" (1921); "hermeneutic insights bearing on the theory of historical cognition" which yield a new sense of Christianity and metaphysics (1919): this pair of self-interpretive statements from the young Heidegger provides the historical specificity and factic articulation to the old Heidegger's confession that his "theological provenance" is the key to his philosophical beginnings. The three statements taken together reflect his biographical beginnings as a Catholic seminarian and a student of German philosophy and theology from Eckhart to Dilthey, who underwent a crisis of conversion in the shadow of the front lines of World War I. Aside from this religious substance, there is the young Heidegger's formal admission that his thoughts stem directly from the deepest motivations of his own and quite unique factic situation: in short, that his thought stems from his life. Accordingly, one cannot in principle dismiss the biographical element as fortuitous and therefore irrelevant, contrary to the pronouncements of our purist Heideggerians. The entire letter to Löwith, with topics ranging from university life to an an-archic sense of the philosophical community, is in fact an exercise in the application of Heidegger's own philosophical "hermeneutics of facticity" to himself, to his own *Dasein* and historical situation. It is therefore the very hermeneutic philosophy he is busy developing that justifies the young Heidegger's self-interpretive autobiographical statements. Heidegger's own reductive philosophy has discovered a level at which autobiography is philosophy, and it is these biographical facts internal to his philosophical development which Heidegger the philosopher feels compelled to confess about Heidegger the person. And what are these pertinent biographical facts? They are the facts that pertain to the *Jeweiligkeit* (temporal particularity) of the autochthonous "hermeneutic situation" of inherited presuppositions and interrogative motivations out of which a philosopher speaks. They might be called "situation facts" or " world facts" or even "topical facts," if we understand τόπος in its originally pregnant hermeneutic sense.

This sense of situated philosophy/philosophical situation is so important that we might dwell a bit longer on Heidegger's letter of 1921. It says very little about the substance of his being Christian but, instead, returns again and again to the stress on scientificity, objectivity, conceptual labor, and the life of research and inquiry, which is in turn equated with the personal pathos springing from his own very historical and temporally particular facticity. In this autobiographical context of distinguishing himself from his two top students, one senses Heidegger's growing sense of the unique radicality of the objectivity (*Sachlichkeit* versus *Objektivität*) of the phenomenological way of doing philosophy. The second half of the letter returns again and again to the difference between an "in-itself objectivity" and one's own temporally particularized facticity.

> You each take from me something other than what is of the essence, what I do not separate, what for that matter is never in a state of equilibrium, namely, the life of scientific research—working with theoretical concepts—and my own life. The essential way in which my facticity is existentially articulated is scientific research, done in my own way. Accordingly, the motive and goal of philosophizing is for me never to add to the stock of objective truths, since the objectivity of philosophy, as I understand it and by which I factically proceed, is something proper to oneself. This however does not exclude the strictest objectivity of explication; that for me is implied

in the very sense of my existence. Objective strictness does not relate to a thing but to historical facticity. . . .

Even in the destruction I do not want or dream of an objectivity in itself. It is my facticity which is "foisted" thereupon, if you will. It is simply a matter of whether a purportedly impersonal stance accomplishes more than going after the things directly, where we *ourselves* must obviously *be involved*—otherwise there is no engagement. We are then objectively one-sided and dogmatic, but philosophically still "absolutely" *objective and strict*. . . .

It is only crucial that we agree that what counts is for each of us to go to the radical and utmost limit for what and how each understands the "one thing necessary." We may be far apart in "system," "doctrine," or "position," and yet *together* as only human beings can really be together: in existence.

In the light of this "proper" sense of phenomenological objectivity, with its an-archic sense of philosophical community, Heidegger will in the ensuing years articulate, for example, the unique occasionality or insuperable "temporal particularity" of *Dasein* and the inescapable ontic founding of ontology (*Being and Time*, 1927). Once again, what Heidegger himself tells us here is that his thoughts stem directly from the deepest motivations of his *own* factic situation, that his thought stems from his life, and that one cannot therefore divorce the ontological (his philosophy) from the ontic (his biography). In view of this reciprocity between biography and philosophy, it is quite valid, perhaps at times even essential, on Heideggerian grounds to seek to understand philosophically Heidegger's peculiarly personal engagement with his Christianity—as well as his later engagement with an admittedly "private brand" of National Socialism. And both religion and politics are of their nature world views, basic attitudes toward life. In *Being and Time* these are described as an ontical ideal of authentic existence, "the factical ideal of *Dasein* which underlies the ontological interpretation of *Dasein*'s existence" (H. 310, 266). For on the ontic level of life, the call of conscience which summons us to our potentiality for being "does not hold before us some empty ideal of existence, but *calls us forth into the situation*" (H. 300). This exacts the demand, on the methodological level of philosophy, "to unfold with ever greater penetration" (H. 310) the "content" of this ideal (H. 266) or, more precisely, the ontic presuppositions of the hermeneutic situation that sustains the philosophically developed ontological interpretation. Put in other terms, although the primordial existentiell truth does not necessarily need the existential analysis, the latter needs the former as its ontical basis (H. 316, 312).

Jürgen Habermas, in his article "Work and World View," which prefaces the German edition of Farías's book, merely underscores the obverse side of this ontic projection into the ontological by noting the possible infection of a work of thought by elements of an "ideologically tinged world view."[26] A fundamental attitude toward life, the fundamental project that becomes the guiding "how of interpretation," whether it be Christian or tragic (as it was for a time for the later Heidegger), is not pure but is always garbled by the static of alien messages in need of demystification. Heidegger's first crisis was in fact just such a rite of passage to a more purified experiential Christianity, which in turn, as a hardening world view, itself had to be put out of play for the sake of further sallies into the full dynamics of factic life. The limpid "formally indicative" concepts needed to allude to the immediate experience of already finding oneself under way in existence stand in sharp contrast to the hardened ideological concepts that ballast such an approach. The very need constantly to outstrip one's viewpoints toward the immediacy of life's dynamics is itself an admission of the blind spots, the repressed and other covert elements, that stand in the way of such transcendence. To be already caught in existence willy-nilly means that one cannot completely escape one's roots and the trajectory into which one has been "thrown." Biography (= facticity) cuts both ways for a philosophy that professes always to be under way. Autobiography is also ideology. Though we may quibble with the specifics, Habermas performs a service to Heidegger and the Heideggerians, who are sometimes too close to their work to see such things, by pointing to the "German ideology" that secretly encumbers the argumentation of *Being and Time* and will grow rampant in the Nazi thirties: the elitist self-understanding of the German mandarin; a fetishizing of *Geist,* especially *der deutsche Geist;* idolatry of the mother tongue; the pathos of heroic nihilism in the face of "fate" and "destiny," and so on.

It is to this program, already launched by Ott and Farías, that I want to contribute in the following sections by way of supplementation and correction, with an eye especially to what the archives may yield in the near future. In view of my research interests, most of these contributions relate to the young and early Heidegger, leading up to his magnum opus, *Being and Time*. Since I build especially on the archival work of Farías and Ott, it is fitting that I first present a brief review of the essence of their work.

Beyond Farías and Ott: On Structuring a Philosophical Biography

Farías's thesis is loud and clear. Stated baldly, Heidegger's life and thought are Nazi through and through, from beginning to end. Stated in more qualified, developmental terms, Heidegger's entry into the Party in 1933 was simply the natural outcome of years of preparation determined by the attitudes he acquired from the region of his birth and youth. "As you began, so will you remain": This favorite line from Hölderlin is here turned back on Heidegger with a vengeance, to condemn him to a basically static *Bildungsroman* in life and thought. Once a peasant, always a peasant. Whatever progress he made in his vaunted "path of thought," Heidegger is irretrievably trapped "in a way of thought nourished by a tradition of authoritarianism, anti-Semitism, and ultranationalism that sanctified the homeland in its most provincial sense" (Farías, p. 4). His legacy to us is "poisoned at its roots" (*New York Times*, February 4, 1988), roots of home and country, *Blut und Boden,* that Heidegger himself never ceased to glorify.

If we begin with this thesis, willy-nilly, Heidegger's entire life from beginning to end becomes suspect and calls for the closest surveillance. Thus Farías (chaps. 3 and 18) "frames" Heidegger with the charge of anti-Semitism through his lifelong adulation of his distant relative and native son of the region, Abraham a Sancta Clara, the imperial court preacher in baroque Vienna who found a niche in German prose as the Capuchin preacher in Schiller's *Wallenstein.* The young Heidegger first broke into print with a newspaper account of the unveiling of a bust of Abraham (a good Jewish name for a rabid anti-Semite) in his hometown. And after he himself became famous, likewise finding a niche in such German classics as Günter Grass's *Hundejahre,* the old Heidegger had even more grounds to identify with his baroque role model. Thus, in a talk to the hometown folk in 1964 at the Latin school that both he and his famous relative once attended, he describes the life and times, language and thought, of Abraham in ways that are replete with parallels to his own. But Farías is too eager to get at Abraham's anti-Semitism and pogrom bellicosity—and, by association, Heidegger's latent forms of them—to take notice of the more political parallels the talk makes between the baroque period and the twentieth century, such as between treaties that brought no real peace (Westphalia, 1648, and Versailles, 1919; and, by extension, Potsdam, 1945), a parallel that could not have been lost on Heidegger's older kinsmen in the hometown crowd who had suffered that fate in common with him: "The desolation and misery left behind by the Great War were followed by new wars and threats, more hunger and poverty." Out of this tumultuous play of poverty and fortune, war and peace, "the terror of death and the lust of life," Heidegger singles out from the vast "selection of flowers" in Karl Bertsche's anthology *(Blütenlese),* one complex play on words by which Abraham describes his times, upon which the Nazi-hunting Farías (p. 289) pounces: "On a single day we find warmth, want, and wails of 'Lord, have mercy' [*warm, arm, und das Gott erbarm*], and our peace is as far from war as Sachsenhausen is from Frankfurt."[27] This is too much for Farías, for in 1964, Frankfurt, the setting for the ongoing Auschwitz trials, had to be associated with Sachsenhausen, one of the most feared concentration camps of the Third Reich. German reviewers of the French edition of Farías were quick to point out the geographical confusion between this quiet suburb of Frankfurt and the death camp near Berlin bearing the same name (it was corrected in the German but not in the English edition) and so to dismiss the association as a biased travesty of the facts, perhaps the most absurd of the surfeit of errors riddling the French edition.

But the laws of unconscious association are clearly not checked by such facts. The French press, regularly exposed to far freer poststructuralist and postdeconstructionist interpretations of texts, was more tolerant and attentive to the possibility that Heidegger on this festive occasion had perhaps slipped past his internal censor and unwittingly bared his Nazi libido. In the end, however, Farías himself does not know what to make of this Freudian slip. Was it the brief upsurge of an inner conflict secretly raging within Heidegger's repressed libido? And what exactly were the antagonistic terms of this inner polemic that was allowing Heidegger no peace? Was Heidegger, as Farías suggests, admitting the connection in German history between Abraham's anti-Semitism and Auschwitz but "without taking the risk of linking the sacred fatherland with the greatest monstrosity that mankind has ever known" (p. 290)? Was it therefore an unconscious retraction compensating for Heidegger's public silence and his stubborn refusal to criticize himself or otherwise make a "clean breast" of his complicity in this monstrosity? Or was it an expression more of resentment than of repentance, an "in" text for those "in the know," a blatant provocation by which Heidegger (not untypically) challenged postwar public opinion (typically self-righteous) on the Holocaust and "manfully" took responsibility for his part, as Himmler alone among the Nazi leaders, with their litanies of *nicht schuldig* at Nuremberg, dared to do by committing suicide instead (Farías, p. 290; this example is deleted from the German edition)? Indeed, the historical parallels between the baroque period and the twentieth century implied in the talk on Abraham a Sancta Clara, who thought in palpable images and so described the "mass deaths [*Massensterben*] during Vienna's months of plague" in terms of Death the Reaper,[28] are but one step short of the arguments used in postwar Germany's "dispute among the historians." Farías does not notice this, but Abraham's peasant realism is most likely the postwar Heidegger's "inspiration" for a series of gruesome comparisons, beginning with the substitution of the word "East Germans" for "Jews" to make the equation between postwar Russia's expulsion of refugees and the Holocaust, the only difference being that "the bloody terror of the Nazis was in fact kept a secret from the German people"; the comparison of the "fabrication of cadavers in gas chambers and extermination camps" with the motorized food industry of our depersonalized agriculture and the systematic starving of millions in the Berlin blockade; and finally the distinction between an individualized personal death and impersonal "megadeath" in a coarse description that is virtually vintage Abraham a Sancta Clara.

> Hundreds of thousands die en masse. Do they die? They succumb. They are done in. Do they die? They become items in an inventory for the business of manufacturing corpses. Do they die? They are liquidated without ceremony in extermination camps. And even without such a machinery, millions of poor souls are perishing from hunger at this very moment in China.[29]

It was not anti-Semitism that Heidegger learned from his kinsman Abraham but rather his brutally realistic way of describing plagues, wars, the siege of Vienna; a certain rhetoric and metaphorology; a thinking in images, parallels, rhymes, repetitions, oppositions, and abrupt turns of phrase that come from this preacher's mastery of the multifaceted possibilities of the German language. And how did this native son of the provinces come to master the language? Not by playing with words but by listening to the language.[30] Heidegger identifies himself with Abraham not for his crude anti-Semitism but for the sometimes equally coarse but often gently poetic sense of his native language. And though Farías (p. 295) sometimes alludes to this distinction between biological racism and the more "refined cultural fascism" or "southern chauvinism" that lauds the power and beauty of the German language, more often than not he obscures this focus by page after page of excursus into anti-Semitic smut muckraked from secondary authors writing about Abraham. In other contexts, Farías spends inordinate pages diverging into the "brown" political backgrounds of the authors who contributed to the same journal as Heidegger, or of the names on the same petition Heidegger signed, or of the members of the same committee on which Heidegger happened to serve. American readers in particular are inclined to be alienated by such an obscene and scurrilous display of guilt-by-association tactics. The reader would have been better served by a disciplined and meticulous exegesis of the entire text on Abraham a Sancta Clara, which lends itself to the same subliminal plays of oppositions and exchanges and complex overlays of associations that we found in the quasi-biographical "Dialogue on Language" of 1954: Abraham/Martin, imperial Reich/Third Reich, city/country, cosmopolitan/peasant, rich/poor, war/peace, plague's devastation/baroque harmony, life/death, coarse/gentle, fame/disgrace, freedom/destiny, call/response. The same sort of quasi-biographical analysis applies to the other "hometown" texts written by Heidegger, where we can often ask what sort of self-interpretation he is promoting or what he is revealing about himself, both wittingly and unwittingly.

But Farías did get it half right. The new witnesses in the forthcoming retrial of Heidegger will be experts not only in textual analysis of various kinds but also in psychoanalysis, likewise of various schools. This was the conclusion of Rudolf Bultmann at his postwar reunion with Heidegger. After years of separation he received a surprise phone call from Heidegger, who requested a visit with the explanation "I want to ask your forgiveness." At the end of a day of animated conversation and exchange of ideas in which old bonds were spontaneously restored, Bultmann came back to the remark made over the phone: " 'Now you must, like Augustine, write your *Retractationes*,' I said to him, 'and not only for the sake of the truth of your thought.' Heidegger's face froze into a stone mask. He left without saying a word. . . . One probably has to explain his reaction psychologically" (quoted in Ott, p. 164). The closest Heidegger came to an admission of guilt was in a letter to Jaspers on March 7, 1950, in which he explained that he had not crossed Jaspers's threshold since 1933 not because of his Jewish wife but because he "simply felt ashamed" (Ott, p. 32). The paths of the two old friends never crossed after the war.

If Heidegger was a "resistance fighter" before and during the war, he certainly was no hero, not even after the war: he was a survivor. Was he constitutionally unable to make a retraction? There is a substantial record of Heidegger's nervous breakdown in early 1946, subsequent to the stress of the denazification hearings, when he spent three weeks in a sanatorium for "psychosomatic treatment" (Ott, 300, 322); this condition is confirmed by reports, in scattered letters, of his neurasthenia throughout his life. The "existentiell crisis" (Ott, p. 70) of 1911 manifested itself through a health condition that kept him far from the front lines until the last three months of the war. The extended midlife crisis recorded in his letter to Jaspers on July 1, 1935, around which Ott (p. 42) structures his entire book (like Dante's *Inferno*!), possibly also found its climax in a nervous collapse. Socrates had more stamina. Heidegger was a stressed soul and so perhaps constitutionally incapable of Luther's "Here I stand!" A medical history and psychological profile may be the last remaining explanation for Heidegger's silence and ambivalence after the war. Or is this psychosomatic frailty merely derivative from a more basic existential frailty, as the Heidegger of *Being and Time* was wont to say? After his breakdown of 1946 Heidegger overtly cultivated an entire school of existential psychiatrists who could provide us with an answer. Medard Boss, confidant of the old Heidegger, in particular seems to hold some of the missing links to a *Daseinsanalysis* of the postwar Heidegger.[31] Was it a fatal flaw that kept him silent, or the existentiell tact of a fragile personality who opted to reserve his failing energies exclusively for his work? In October 1946 Heidegger wrote: "Intense intellectual concentration is an effort which can be maintained at the same high level in the long haul only with difficulty; but without it nothing lasting comes into being. . . . Everything must now be sacrificed to the restoration of an intellectual world."[32] Did the old Heidegger accordingly regard the rising tide of world opinion against him as a third "persecution" (already a remarkable choice of words) and therefore as life-threatening as the denazification proceedings and the paranoid "persecution" he felt from his Nazi colleagues? In his defensive posture, did he therefore feel that he did not even owe the world an Apology? Perhaps in the stress and strain he had simply forgotten the example of the old Socrates.

The preceding paragraph illustrates how indispensable Ott's book is as a reliable source and compendium of the facts of the Heidegger case. Moreover, on the basis of these facts, derived to a large degree from correspondence and private archives, Ott wants to "reveal Heidegger from the inside out" (p. 12), to fathom his "mentality" (p. 10). But as a "guild historian," he wishes to do so without getting into the problem of the relation of Heidegger's life to his thought—that is, to his philosophical works—which he would leave to the "guild philosopher." But what if Heidegger's very being, his *raison d'être,* is defined by his thought, as in fact was the case for Socrates? Precisely what mentality is reflected simply in the archival fragments that Ott manages to gather together, in particular to cross-check objectively the statements of self-vindication focused in Heidegger's two apologies, which have all too often proved to be distorted subjectively by, say, Heidegger's faulty memory of *was tatsächlich geschehen ist* (p. 212)? Ott's corrective action is in large part still a matter of Heidegger's own words, now gathered from the documents along his entire *Lebensweg* in order to "illuminate the mental disposition of the philosopher in the very specific way" that "such profound self-testimonies" allow (p. 13). Of the philosopher? In part, yes, but ultimately of the Man. This is the historian's *Ecce homo* reflected in the plethora of documents that Heidegger left behind, a Portrait of the Philosopher as a Genius but also as a very fallible human being, using that genius to win friends and influence people, learning grantsmanship and career building in order to rise out his peasant origins and "make it," so to speak, in the German "ivy leagues," parlaying his fame as a teacher and the author of *Being and Time* into a power grab for Freiburg's rectorship under Hitler and a vain attempt to become *Führer* of all the German universities. It is a story of double-crossing intrigues and petty backbiting on the level of academic politics and national politics, which in the German university system have never been unrelated, as a ready vocabulary of such basically bureaucratic German words as *Hochschul-politik, Wissenschaftspolitik,* and *Kultusministerium* suggests. Out of this story there emerges a picture of an opportunistic and pompous Heidegger, not always honest in his grantsmanship and refereeing, made vain by fame, and the like. The Heidegger who followed Hitler was, in the words of one reviewer, "ein bäuerlich-kleinbürgerlicher Nationalromantiker," a boorishly rustic, petty-minded bourgeois nationalist romantic.[33] His all-too-human self-portrait is supplemented by Heidegger's public image in the eyes of others, likewise gleaned from the archives, like the telling judgment of his old friend Jaspers: "He seemed like a friend who betrayed you behind your back, but there were unforgettable moments, which thus proved to be hollow, where he was incredibly close." Martie, we hardly knew you.

At another level, the complex self-portrait constructed from the archives yields a psychological profile that Michael Zimmerman, in a synoptic tour de force of these terms, neatly summarizes in the compass of his brief review of Ott's book: delusions of grandeur and monstrous hubris stemming from a self-mythification of his fated role as Germany's spiritual leader; the resulting "unbelievable loss of reality" (Ott, p. 22), accounting for the serious moral blindness that led him to absolve himself—and Germany!—of responsibility and to make a scapegoat of others; his increasing defiance toward his friends' insistence that he come to terms with his own guilt.[34] One could go on. For example, Jaspers (a psychologist by training) likens the postwar Heidegger to a "dreaming boy" (Ott, p. 22) in a state of shock, traumatized from reality into a fantasy world, who does not know what he is doing. He thus suggests a connection with the young Heidegger, who poetized his way through his neurosis (Ott, p. 71), except that by 1950 this "therapy" had grown into a full-fledged "self-mythicizing Hölderlin-ideology." There may have been more than philosophical reasons for Heidegger's heeding "the voice of the poet from his tower" (Ott, p. 19), with more than a measure of trepidation. Nietzsche, too, could have been an object lesson.

By now, one may wonder whether Ott's *Ecce homo* has not turned into a sheer exposé, the objectivity of which is itself in need of cross-checking.[35] But so far we have only parodied Ott and not yet come to the heart of the matter. For Ott, the real key to the personality of Heidegger is neither the surface academic-politician nor the psychologically disturbed inner life but the religious Heidegger. Taking his cue from Heidegger's own characterization of his midlife crisis in a 1935 letter to Jaspers, Ott (p. 42) organizes his factual material around two "thorns in the flesh" or two central issues that especially plagued the mature Heidegger, giving us the two longest chapters in the book: "the faith of my heritage" and "the failure of the rectorate." Of these two focuses of religious belief and political conviction, the former turns out to be the more important and in fact eventually subsumes and accounts for the latter. More precisely, it is "the conflict with the faith of my heritage," which Ott takes to be his rabid anti-Catholicism, that is troubling Heidegger; and it is this anti-Catholicism—not, as Farías would have it, his anti-Semitism—that underlies Heidegger's turn to National Socialism.

But the motivating ground is in fact a bit more complex than that. To supplement Ott, who lets his own Catholic heritage get the best of him in regarding Heidegger simply as a Catholic apostate, let us recall Heidegger's three autobiographical statements on the "theological heritage" that brought him onto the path of thinking. By 1921, when Heidegger relates this motivating ground to the fact that "I am a 'Christian theolo-gian,' " the "faith of my heritage" is not only the Catholicism of his medieval hometown but also his newfound Lutheranism. And both belong to his German heritage, since his revolt against the Italian papal line on modernism had earlier turned Heidegger from Roman Catholicism to an Eckhartian Catholicism. By 1922, when Heidegger first proclaims the fundamental "atheism" of philosophy, we can add another famous German—alongside Eckhart and Luther—to whom Heidegger is heir: namely, Friedrich Nietzsche. It will take a decade, but it will be not just an anti-Catholic or an anti-Christian but the full-blown antireligious attitude of the German *Geist* ripened from German Idealism that sweeps Heidegger into National Socialism, with all the romantic fervor of another religious conversion.[36] By 1935 he is thinking of an indigenous German *Volksreligion* of *Blut* and *Heimat* to sustain his straitened political convictions—"the failure of my rectorate"—and thus finds his way to a fourth native son, Friedrich Hölderlin. This purely German *Denkweg* needs only to be supplemented with its Greek "way markers" to provide it with a cultural infrastructure that can account for all of Heidegger's proclivities at the self-professed core of his being: namely, his thought. It is with this schematism of a philosophical biography that we can bring together the most central concerns of Heidegger's life and thought—religious, philosophical, political, poetic—to examine their underpinnings in what might be called this peasant mandarin's "German ideology" and, in turn, the complicity of the latter with National Socialism. Such a philosophical-biographical structure does not doom Heidegger to a deterministic frame, as in Farías, but allows for the freedom of both life and thought, inasmuch as "heritage always has a future."

That this religious schematism for a philosophical biography is an oversimplification of a more subtle development of Heidegger's religious-political attitudes, that Ott's jaundiced "inside story" does not take the full measure of the man, is readily demonstrable from the recently published personal letters of Heidegger to Elisabeth Blochmann, a close family friend who taught philosophy of education on the university level until her forced emigration to England during the Nazi years interrupted that career. The correspondence thus gives us entry into the intimacy of the Heidegger family circle and at the same time reveals to us not only Heidegger the man and philosopher but also Heidegger the dedicated teacher, which Ott chooses to neglect—aside from allusions to the post-war fear that Heidegger might "corrupt the youth" of Germany in view of his previous record of zeal for the "gods of the state" now defunct. The letters reveal the many faces of Heidegger. His correspondent's central interest in the education of women, for example, evokes his own deep interest in women and his thoughts on "feminine existence" along with a few erotic moments. But the unified core of fusion between life and thought is also very much in evidence, and the letters trace its shifting emphases along Heidegger's path of thought as he uses his current philosophical ideas to interpret his personal life and in turn lets the essence of that life govern his thought. The letters themselves are accordingly proof of the possibility of a philosophical biography on Heideggerian grounds which takes us to the very center of his *Denkweg* and not merely by providing us with useful chronological benchmarks, which in themselves are already indispensable for a thought that would emphasize ways instead of works. We have the young Heidegger of 1918–19 describing his personal life in the Bergsonian-Husserlian language of the "stream of experience" and its *élan vital,* and the early Heidegger of 1928 announcing a new turn in his thought, while noting that for the human being to exist is already to philosophize! One may wish to sort out biographical facts in reference to accidental or external circumstances as opposed to the more internal conditions of thought, but one cannot totally exclude these facts of life as such from an account of that thought. With the equation of existing and philosophizing, even the "external" may point to the deepest implications. Thus, if we follow Heidegger's developing "conflict with the dying spirit of Christendom" (March 30, 1933) in these letters, starting from his critique of Protestant theology in the controversial talk of 1927–28 titled "Phenomenology and Theology" (August 8, 1928), we discover within his ongoing critique of Protestantism (the anti-Greek Protestantism of the journal *Die Tat:* December 19, 1932) and Catholicism (the Jesuitism of the "Romish" Center Party, worse than Communism: June 22, 1932) the repeated expression of his highest regard for life in "Beuron," the Catholic monastery near his hometown, "as a tiny seed of something essential" (September 12, 1929); there he himself regularly spent weeks of his vacation until 1932 living the life of the monks, to the point of wishing that he too might wear the monk's robes (October 11, 1931). And what was it about the simple and primitive existence of Beuron that attracted Heidegger? We get a hint from his remarks on the matins, the night prayers of the monastery breviary: "The matins still contain the mythical and metaphysical primal power of the night, through which we must constantly break in order truly to exist. For the good is only the good of the evil. . . . The matins have thus become the symbol of existence being held into the night and of the inner necessity of the daily readiness for the night" (September 12, 1929).

Notes toward a Philosophical Biography

One can go further with this work of supplementation and correction of Heidegger's public image simply by using the new documentation indicated in the Blochmann letters: for example, Heidegger's letter of reference on behalf of his Jewish friend in a vain attempt to save her position in 1933; or the enthusiasm in 1934 for his pet project of a school for docents to prepare them for university teaching in the Third Reich. But at this point I wish to make a brief survey of the impending larger task of supplementation and correction by pointing to a few specific places in Heidegger's development where further substantial archival evidence is forthcoming for this task. Here, I am specifically interested in a philosophical biography of the formative years of Heidegger's development prior to his magnum opus, *Being and Time;* if Farías is right, it will turn out to be the biography of a proto-Nazi. In view of the grave charges mounted since Farías against the very essence of Heidegger's thought, one can no longer restrict the examination of its political implications merely to the works from 1933 on. One must also become sensitive to the seeds of any of the tares of Nazisms already latent at the very roots of this philosophy.

1909–14

Farías (p. 33) has found a zero-point for such a biography in a newspaper report of Heidegger's activity in 1909 as president of a student committee preparing for the forthcoming dedication of the monument of Abraham a Sancta Clara near his hometown. In a speech before the committee, the young Heidegger urges his fellow students to subscribe to the ultraconservative Catholic review *Der Gral* in support of its battle against the forces of modernism. Ott's discovery (pp. 62–66) of Heidegger's articles in the equally ultraconservative journal *Der Akademiker* provides the particulars of the young academic theologian's attitudes then: strict adherence to the authority of the Church against the rising tide of ethical-religious individualism based on the modern cult of personality in the "spirit of Nietzsche and Zola" (Farías, p. 42); a philosophy oriented to the objective truths of the intellect rather than to the subjective opinions derived from "inner experience" (*Erlebnis,* p. 45).

But then Heidegger went into his adolescent crisis in 1911, left theology and the seminary for other curricula, and eventually emerged in 1914 on the side of the Catholic modernists. In addition to the poetry that pulled him through the crisis, what else was the young Heidegger reading, writing, and pondering in this transition? If we are to believe Farías, he continued to imbibe deeply (if he ever did) the muckraking anti-Semitic smut prevalent in southern Germany and Catholic Austria. The old Heidegger presents us with an entirely different reading list: "What the exciting years between 1910 and 1914 brought cannot be adequately stated but only suggested by a selective enumeration: the second edition, now doubled in size, of Nietzsche's *Will to Power,* the translation of Kierkegaard's and Dostoevsky's works, the awakening interest in Hegel and Schelling, Rilke's works and Trakl's poems, Dilthey's *Collected Writings.*"[37] The remarkable thing about this list is that its content largely matches the authors that Heidegger was being introduced to through his subscription since 1911 to an avant-garde literary journal begun the year before in Catholic Austria.[38] Instead of Richard von Kralik's *Der Gral,* Heidegger was now reading Ludwig von Ficker's *Der Brenner,* in which Trakl first published his poems (thanks in part to Ludwig Wittgenstein's financial support) and Theodor Haecker was introducing Kierkegaard's critique *The Present Age* and his proposed antidotes in German translations and commentaries. In contrast to the reactionary views of *Der Gral, Der Brenner* provided Heidegger with a more sophisticated and satiric view of modern society, institutionalized Christianity, anti-Semitism, life and values in the city and country, the sham democracy of liberal individualism, the chauvinism of the German intellectual community during the war years, the sterility of scientific reason divorced from the more comprehensive *Geist.* The latter distinction would take root in the philosophical Heidegger as early as the Conclusion of his habilitation work of 1916; Kierkegaard's crowd-man makes an official appearance in the summer semester of 1923, Rilke in 1927, Nietzsche in strong doses by 1930, Trakl not until after the war, when Heidegger first meets Ficker and the two make a tour of Trakl's old haunts in Innsbruck.[39]

1917–19

The Blochmann letters provide the first truly substantial evidence of what Heidegger was thinking during the still obscure Interregnum of 1917–19, when he did not teach or otherwise go public but underwent the philosophic-religious conversion that first put him squarely upon his lifelong path of thought. In the present context, it might be described as Heidegger's conversion from Catholic to Protestant romanticism, wherein his Messkirchian nostalgia for the Latin Middle Ages gives way to a more basic Lutheran nostalgia for primitive Christianity in its Pauline Greek world. The most important moving figures are Dilthey and Schleiermacher, and Heidegger demonstrates his thorough knowledge of the latter in advising Blochmann on November 7, 1918—in the vicinity of the front lines, a few days before war's end—on how to read Schleiermacher for her dissertation. These two figures serve to bring Heidegger to a "hermeneutic breakthrough" to his lifelong topic of thought, which at this early stage centered on the question of how to articulate the immediate experience of already finding oneself already caught up in existence and under way, thus of "saying the unsayable." How to gain access to this, our most immediate experience, which *in ovo* is thus at once total and full reality and which in its immediacy precedes thought and thus is not even "given"—that is, an object standing over against a subject? For Schleiermacher, it is our fundamental religious experience, the "feeling of absolute dependence," akin to Eckhart's mystical birth of the Word sparked in our heart of hearts.[40] This Heideggerian quest for the constant background experience of all our more specific experiences is nowadays sometimes disparaged as a throwback to Romanticism (Rorty), a nostalgic quest for origins (Derrida), the quest for the ineffable sublime (Lyotard). Is this sort of romanticism and mysticism the fertile seedbed of Heidegger's alleged Nazism, pregnant with the potential for ideological and narcissistic distortion into a primitivist, neopagan, and ethnic quest for the autochthony of one's native ground and roots, as Emmanuel Levinas suggests?

German Militarism

Another set of clues to Heidegger's romantic proclivities is more overtly disturbing but traceable perhaps more to his "German ideology" than to his philosophy. The sickly "Airman" Heidegger, finally permitted to serve in a meteorological unit near the front lines in the Ardennes sector in the last three months of the war—and in this capacity reported to have done his share in poison gas attacks on the enemy—was oddly exhilarated by the "primitive Dasein" of the soldier's life, even in defeat.[41] Allusions to the war experience recur in his lecture courses, beginning with the "war emergency semester" *(Kriegsnotsemester)* of early 1919, which was designed specifically for returning war veterans. Heidegger took every opportunity to heroize Emil Lask "in his distant soldier's tomb," who "fell in the battles in Galicia, May 1915; his corpse is still missing."[42] Karl Löwith, his voice still bearing the signs of a severe lung wound received in the Italian campaign, came to Heidegger's courses in 1919 and instantly became a favored student. It should therefore not surprise us that Heidegger came to admire the much decorated Ernst Jünger, whose war novel *Stahlhelm* was a best seller in the 1920s; and later the Luftwaffe "ace" of World War I, Hermann Göring (Ott, p. 147ff.). This concern with the war experience also partly accounts for Heidegger's antipathy toward the pacifist Hermann Staudinger in 1933 (Ott, p. 201ff.). Even Heidegger's membership in 1959 on a working committee to "fight atomic death" does not really lift our wonder over his attitude between the wars.

From 1919 on, Heidegger was prone to use in his courses military examples that tend to strike the contemporary reader as odd. To illustrate the reciprocal permeation of situations in the summer semester of 1919, Heidegger mentions the coincident duration of a semester and a "year in the field," a comment reminiscent of the content of the first Blochmann letters. Just before Christmas 1919, in a course already replete with phenomenological examples, he illustrates modifications in experiential contexts by the following example: an infantry column on a forced march becomes exhausted; every man is rendered limp. Suddenly the regimental band sounds up; everyone comes to attention and is drawn along by the music. Bystanders at the roadside may perhaps coexperience this change empathetically, but they do not truly "go along" with the transition as the soldiers do. To illustrate the suddenness of approach of a fearful thing in the summer semester of 1925, Heidegger speaks of a grenade striking the ground nearby and labels the experience an everyday occurrence "with which we are very well acquainted"![43] And in a way it was a part of the everyday life of Germany between the wars and so probably accepted as a matter of course by Heidegger's students, striking as the example may seem to us. Over the years, favored examples of auditory experience are the column on the march (H. 163) and the rumbling panzer. In the winter semester of 1935–36, an example of tool use is the experience of learning how to handle a rifle as a weapon.[44]

The time has come to move from this outer perimeter of biographically tinged examples to the inner center of Heidegger's thought: The cover of the first edition (1930) of *War and Warrior* bears the portrait of a particularly vicious-looking Hun warrior complete with *Stahlhelm*, much like the caricatures of "Krauts" in American war-propaganda films. The editor's foreword by Ernst Jünger, mentioning the surfeit of war books of the previous decade, observes that "with justification, the war is the Event which has given our time its face."[45] The position Jünger assumes is called the "heroic realism" of German nationalism. The book is addressed not to its opponents in the camp of liberalism, since that is in 1930 an obsolete position, but exclusively to the German youth, "which knows its responsibility as well as the duty to implement this feeling of responsibility with a position which will define German life. The question here is no longer whether armament is necessary or not, but the space in which the renewal of armament has to unfold." To address this question, Jünger himself offers a lead essay titled "Total Mobilization." The essay focuses Heidegger's philosophical concerns in the 1930s as Jünger "expresses a fundamental understanding of Nietzsche's metaphysics, insofar as the history and present of the Western world are seen and foreseen in the horizon of this metaphysics."[46] It leads to Heidegger's reflections on the Heraclitean πόλεμος understood as a confrontation that allows those who are thus set apart to reveal themselves. Although Heidegger insists that the Greek term be stripped of all the coarse militancy and savage barbarism that "war" implies, we are nevertheless left to ponder how the pure nobility of this "heroic realism," coupled with the much-discussed "yearning for hardship and severity,"[47] can be brought together with the peasant realism that he learned from Abraham a Sancta Clara and will use to interpret the Holocaust.

Those who have compiled such military litanies in the past tend to observe with some sarcasm that Heidegger himself, small in stature, was hardly the warrior type. Such a tack is clearly an inadmissible *argumentum ad hominem* which, moreover, belies the facts about the Man Heidegger. Heidegger the peasant, like Socrates the urban proletarian, was "tough," although Socrates had a more notable war record (*Apology* 28E). Friends who went skiing with Heidegger, for example, were struck by his remarkable physical courage and endurance.[48] His stamina and endurance were of course especially manifest in his superabundant capacity for disciplined, tenacious, and frenetic intellectual work over a career of some sixty years, a capacity whose tangible proof and final embodiment lie in the staggering range and variety of thought experiments (*Denkwege*) to be found in the hundred-plus volumes of his *Gesamtausgabe*. The character and extent of this radical discipline and stamina are exemplified in the remark Heidegger made upon first hearing Hühnerfeld's scornful anecdote about how he was passed over for active duty at the beginning of the war because he was a "weakling": "Do you know why I was too weak? Because I had starved for months on end in order to at least finish the habilitation—month after month after month! I wonder whether Herr Hühnerfeld knows what hunger is when someone has no other way and no one to help him?"[49]

The Natorp Relation

Paul Natorp in Marburg (acting as it were at a distance) was just as important as Husserl (acting as Heidegger's mentor and immediate adviser on location in Freiburg) in promoting Heidegger in the German university hierarchy in the crucial postwar years, during which Heidegger quickly gained fame as a great teacher but published absolutely nothing. In fact, between the two "German mandarins" who gave him his start, Natorp had a far more developed public stance vis-à-vis the inevitable nexus within that university system between philosophy, politics, and education, making significant contributions to all three areas of German public life. The effect that this stance had on Heidegger, who would be destined to fill a similar role first in Natorp's and then in Husserl's university chair, is yet to be measured. Important in this regard, and also for the post-Versailles background against which the two older men struggled with the decisions that would right the course of a university system devastated by the war and its aftermath, is the extant correspondence among the three, which is yet to be published. The correspondence positions Heidegger in the nexus of influence and philosophical counterpoint defined by his two older mentors and provides the starting point for tracing how Heidegger exploited the career opportunities they gave him to find his own way between and beyond them. The philosophical side of this story, ending with Natorp's death in 1924, clearly marks two of the three major steps—in the years 1919 and 1922—in Heidegger's progress toward his magnum opus, *Being and Time* (1927). The ideological side is a bit more latent and elusive to track but ultimately just as essential for Heidegger's development, especially after 1927.

In an important letter to Airman *(Luftschiffer)* Heidegger "in the field" in September 1918, Husserl mentions two books by Natorp, one strictly philosophical and the other more patriotic, which he had had recent occasion to read. For the first time since its appearance six years before, Husserl had taken the time to read through the direct attack on his phenomenology contained in Natorp's *Allgemeine Psychologie;* he concludes that Natorp, despite his genial premonition of the phenomenological problem of constitution, "was completely incapable of grasping the clear and obvious sense of phenomenology as an essential analysis of pure consciousness preceding and leading philosophy and science, and to allow this sense to prevail in matters of seeing and what is given in seeing."[50] These remarks became a kind of research program for Heidegger in the first year of his assistantship under Husserl, culminating in a full-fledged "destruction"—the term is first used in this course—of Natorp's concept of constitution in summer 1920. *The* key to Heidegger's hermeneutic breakthrough to his lifelong topic in *Kriegsnotsemester* 1919 is his resolution of Natorp's double objection against the accessibility and expressibility of phenomenology's central topic of description, the immediate pretheoretical experience in which we always already find ourselves under way. As Natorp points out, intuitive reflection "stills the stream" of experience, and phenomenological expression generalizes and objectifies it. Heidegger's genial response to Natorp's equally genial objections leads him to develop a hermeneutics of "formally indicative" strategies of expression of the purported ineffability of the dynamics of immediate experience which in later years will assume more poetic forms, but take basically the same intentional tack as in 1919.[51]

In a final footnote to his 1918 letter, Husserl also mentions having read Natorp's "beautiful, heartwarming double war book," *Germany's Mission in the World,* divided into two volumes: "The Ages of the Spirit" and "The Soul of the German."[52] This rousingly patriotic and semipopular philosophical statement by Natorp, seeking to provide "guidelines from the philosophy of history" (the book's subtitle) for his fellow Germans, especially the young, is perhaps the most profound of the spate of chauvinistic war books written by philosophers (Max Scheler, for one) at that time. Natorp's justifiable pride in his "nation of poets and philosophers," his historical tracing of the German Spirit from its Greek and Judaeo-Christian roots—especially through religious figures such as Eckhart and Luther (a chapter is devoted to each)—find numerous counterparts in Heidegger's own attitudes at this time. Small wonder, then, that Natorp thinks he sees some of his own ideas on the historical development of the German Mind in the Introduction to an Aristotle book which Heidegger had sent to Marburg in October 1922 in support of his bid for a university chair.[53] A German Mind distinct, say, from a French Mind? Indeed. Let us take but one example from Natorp's "war book" worthy of further examination in the present context. The deepest experience of humankind working itself out in human history is the "eternal ground" revealing itself in the "divine spark" (Eckhart) buried deep within the human soul, which we therefore call con-science *(Gewissen)* rather than "science" *(Wissen:* 1:80, 2:51, 85). Not the superficial French foundation of clarity and distinctness governed by the Cartesian self-consciousness but this profound and dark "abyss" of the conscience is the basis of the soul's dialogue with its (not higher but deeper) self. Natorp will temper this ground of history with the universalist tendencies of the enlightened Kant; hence, history becomes "the eternal ascent from the unfathomable depths of life" (1:12) toward "the eternal future of humankind" (1:19) understood as an infinite task—a Kantian idea—to be achieved by creative human deeds (1:7). The romantic Heidegger, by contrast, will stress the more receptive moments of repeated regress to a pretheoretical abyss as the moving force of history, thereby giving priority to an undigested irrational core of history with its potential for fanaticist exploitation—whence his penchant for Schelling, for example, in his courses of the 1930s.

As a result of Natorp's powerful endorsement, Heidegger got the appointment, despite a lack of publications, and immediately became

Natorp's close associate for a scant academic year (1923–24). In the last months of Natorp's life, Heidegger taught courses pursuant to the plan, first sketched out in his Introduction, of destroying the entire history of ontology, including his summer course "Basic Concepts of Aristotelian Philosophy," in which the early Heidegger was at his most political in dealing with such texts as Aristotle's *Rhetoric* and *Politics*. In his obituary on the opening day of the following semester, Heidegger recalled Natorp's spiritual leadership of the German youth movement since 1913, and called upon his young auditors to continue Natorp's heritage of seeking to place "our German Dasein on pure foundations."

A significant aside to this story is the anti-Semitic atmospherics that worked to Heidegger's advantage in getting the appointment in Marburg. In a letter to Husserl in January 1922, Natorp considers Richard Kroner instead of Heidegger as a third nominee on the list of candidates for the chair, along with Ernst Cassirer and Moritz Geiger: "But the faculty would probably balk at having *three* Jews on the list. Even he who applies the strictest objectivity can still have second thoughts as to whether he, through the—nevertheless so 'false'—*appearance* of partiality to the other side, is merely reinforcing his resistance to even the most qualified Jews (or those of Jewish descent) and so instead prejudices the case that he would promote."[54]

University Reform

War's end brought a rash of plans for educational reform descending largely from the upper echelons of the university. Natorp, for example, developed a plan for integrating intellectual with manual labor at all levels of education which still smacks of the elitism of Plato's *Republic*.[55] A similar plan strictly at the university level would emerge later in Heidegger's rectoral address.

The Blochmann letters show us that the young Heidegger's thoughts on regenerating the German university were already incubating before war's end. The opening day of *Kriegsnotsemester* 1919 brings the first of a series of statements over the years on the "renewal of the university," typically addressing the issue of the relation of life to science in a radically phenomenological manner. Heidegger's phenomenological stress on science as an originally vital process, both personal and historical, rather than a finished theoretical product antedates by almost a half-century the same stress in recent decades by the "new philosophy of science" (Polanyi, Kuhn, Toulmin). In terms of Heidegger's everyday teaching, this translates into the effort to inculcate the personal habit of the "genuine archontic *Lebensform*" of science in those who would become active participants in the scientific lifeworld. One encounters this manifest pedagogical dedication again in the course of the winter semester of 1923–24, for example, which seeks to introduce "phenomenological research" through Aristotelian insights, sometimes turned against Aristotle. In his opening remarks Heidegger urges his students to adopt a more "phronetic" attitude toward their chosen science, contrary to the traditional equation of scientific comportment with θεωρεῖν intuitive comportment, which in fact places us closer to the finished end of science than to its interrogative beginnings. Instead, he recommends the restless passion for the genuine questions of a particular science ensconced in its situational presuppositions, as opposed to the "utopia" of presuppositionlessness. It is a matter of becoming a "native" in an ongoing science by making its presuppositional and motivational situation one's own, and so confronting its particular matters and resolutely seizing its temporally particular interrogative opportunities. All true scientists must cultivate a phenomenological sense of their motivating origins.

Heidegger's practical thoughts on the nature of science, organized around his sense of phenomenology as a pretheoretical primal science of origins, is accordingly the most important single thread from 1919 to 1933, lying at the very heart of his philosophy, as he himself observes in his "Facts and Thoughts." For there he spells out the philosophy behind his rectoral address, thereby rooting it in the central impetus of his thought by locating the essence of the university in the essence of science, which in turn is rooted in "the essence of truth," where the "original vital unity joining inquirers and scholars" is to be found.[56] Heidegger's reflections on the essence of truth, which begin in earnest in 1930, are thus preceded by his reflections on the essence of science, which begin in 1919 around the question of whether phenomenological philosophy is to be regarded as a "strict science" (Husserl) or as something more than a science in view of its attunement to pretheoretical origins and thus, as Heidegger concludes by 1928, not really a science at all.

One strand of this development significant in this context is a series of courses designed to introduce the beginning student to the university and to "academic studies," the first of which was given in the summer semester of 1919. Its tacit assumption is that the *raison d'être* of the university is the Idea of science, which in turn is rooted in the Idea of philosophy phenomenologically understood. Whence the concern for the tendency of developing sciences to depart from life ("un-living") and the repeated need to retrace the "genesis of the theoretical" back to the original life-context and life-motivations at the dynamic heart of any science. The course is accordingly interspersed with practical advice on how, in coming to scientific maturity, to keep in touch with the first spontaneity of one's original motivations in becoming a scientist, whether in the natural or human sciences—motivations so original in their dynamism that they lie on this side of any and all of those hypostatized standpoints that we call world views.

This course of 1919 may be regarded as a zero-point of development which finds a second station in a similar beginners' course on "academic studies" exactly a decade later, this time finding its focus in Plato's well-known allegory of the cave. This particular course can be understood against the background of the more public statement on university reform incorporated in Heidegger's inaugural address at the University of Freiburg in July 1929, "What Is Metaphysics?" Here, the origin of the field of sciences which constitutes the university is traced back to the *Angst* of a radical questioning challenging the extant foundations of a science, in which beings as a whole become strange and the researcher is exposed to their "nothingness," which is the topic of philosophy. It is especially in these revolutionary moments that science and philosophy are drawn together and become one in the crisis of life.

The final station in this academic series is a seminar that Heidegger gave during his rectorate. Originally announced for summer 1933 under the title "The Concept of Science," it was apparently postponed until the following semester and bore the title "Folk and Science." Heidegger tells us in "Facts and Thoughts" that this "well-attended seminar" (for which not even a transcript has yet come to public light) is to be understood against the background of his new direction toward "the essence of truth," which since 1930 was being elaborated in a series of courses and lectures focusing on Plato's allegory of the cave.[57] A topic of his courses since 1927, a central focus since 1929, this Platonic parable is undoubtedly one of the clues to the interpellation of the tripartite structure of Plato's *Republic* into the rectoral address.

Intersected as it is by so many essential strands of Heidegger's philosophical development, the rectoral address itself must be regarded as an indigenous and essential step in Heidegger's *Denkweg*. Although it may be regarded as one of the many *Holzwege* that branch off from the main path, it is nevertheless a significant part of what Heidegger himself characterized as his "turn."

Heidegger's Apology: Closet Nazi, Late Germanic, or Socratic?

The last two lecture series in particular bring out Heidegger's profound dedication to his teaching and to his students, so neglected by his recent biographers. This still does not absolve him of the charge of "corrupting the German youth" unwittingly (*Apology* 26A), willy-nilly, by infecting them with a national malady inherent in a latent ideology with deep roots in his own German past. Habermas's charges are akin to the deeply seated old charges of Mephistophelean wizardry that Socrates felt compelled to answer first in his trial. These grave issues are only clouded by the spurious charges of anti-Semitism leveled by Farías (= Meletos), whose sophistic tactics are easily exposed upon cross-examination, though his case may yet find its vestige of truth in the ongoing process of producing further facts, like the newly discovered letter of 1929. A fair weighing of the evidence is first predicated, however, upon a full disclosure of all the available evidence, contrary to the present fragmentation of the evidence due to arbitrary and thus suspiciously vested barriers. The new evidence will dictate a new trial, not before *das Man* (if that is the tribunal that *Der Spiegel* gives us; Socrates also had a low opinion of the δόξα of *hoi polloi*) but first before "the nation of poets and philosophers" which the postwar Heidegger seems to have both shunned and invoked. Heidegger must be made to speak again to answer for his life and thought in their entirety, to the extent that they can now be brought to light. I envisage a new Apology that may, like Heidegger's quasi-fictional "Dialogue on Language," take some liberties with the details but will be truer to life and thought in the structural exchanges that it uncovers. The first of these exchanges must be the open admission and understanding of the reversible Gestalt switch that is operative between life and thought, biography and philosophy—which is why even the most complete evidence would still be mixed. Accordingly, whether such a dialogue concludes in a *beau geste* or a boorish whimper would still be left to the individual narrator to decide. The less than Platonic Socrates no doubt also had clay feet.

Winfried Franzen has aptly called the dimension of biography that relates to Heidegger's philosophy "inner biography," involving those pervasive and enduring elements that dominate a life as opposed to the passing and accidental elements.[58] Socrates ultimately argued his own case not before the Athenian court, for which he repeatedly betrayed his contempt, but before Apollo, the tribunal of Truth and a spiritual court, and before his own conscience, giving a public account of how he carried out the god's mission given to him at Delphi. Heidegger, by contrast, was by nature a taciturn man. He was not a loquacious Greek prone to bare his soul so fully in public after the fashion of Socrates. We are left to eavesdrop on the private record he graciously left behind, looking for hints that will reveal the man in his innermost motivations. His worldwide influence is a final argument for full disclosure. Even Heidegger's intimacies now belong to the world.

NOTES

1. Victor Farías, *Heidegger et le nazisme* (Paris: Verdier, 1987). This French edition abounds in factual and typographical errors. The more definitive, expanded German edition, nevertheless still marred by a few serious errors in

fact, contains an important Foreword by Jürgen Habermas: Victor Farías, *Heidegger und der Nationalsozialismus* (Frankfurt: S. Fischer, 1989). The English translation, which is a hybrid of the French and German, is marred by the poor quality of the translation of the portions taken from the German (esp. chap. 4): Victor Farías, *Heidegger and Nazism* (Philadelphia: Temple University Press, 1989). Page numbers incorporated in the body of this essay refer to this English translation.

2. Hugo Ott, *Martin Heidegger: Unterwegs zu seiner Biographie* (Frankfurt: Campus, 1988); page references are incorporated in my text.

3. Ulrich Sieg, " 'Die Verjudung des deutschen Geistes': Ein unbekannter Brief Heideggers," *Die Zeit,* December 29, 1989. I am grateful to Tom Rockmore for pointing out this newspaper item, and to Alexander Masovianus and the Goethe Institute of Chicago for their speedy efforts in obtaining a copy of it for me.

4. For example, I contributed a paper (still unpublished), "Heidegger 1919–33: The University in the Service of Science," to the conference "Heidegger: From Hitler to Nietzsche. The Threat of Power and the Task of Thought," convened in Canada in August 1983 by Zygmunt Adamczewski. The papers of a conference held at the Ruhr University of Bochum in 1986 are published in A. Gethmann-Siefert and O. Pöggeler, eds., *Heidegger und die praktische Philosophie* (Frankfurt: Suhrkamp, 1988).

5. The phrase first occurs in this connection in Thomas Sheehan's review of Farías, "Heidegger and the Nazis," *New York Review of Books,* June 16, 1988, p. 42. The phrase "Heideggers Apologie" occurs in passing in Habermas's Foreword to Farías's German edition, p. 36. In view of Socrates' mortally dangerous situation, one might prefer to measure Heidegger's responses against the *apologiae* of Cardinal Newman, Beethoven, and Kierkegaard, all of which are set in the journalistic spotlight of *hoi polloi,* like the *Spiegel* interview. But the 1945 statement, made against the immediate postwar background of military occupation, contained in addition the imminent danger of confiscation of all life-support systems and at least a virtual threat to life and limb. Luther's "Here I stand!" also comes to mind as a possible measure.

6. The phrase *dossier de police* recurs in the French review of Farías. Farías's pronouncement pursuant to the discovery of Heidegger's 1929 letter (see note 3) is in *El País,* January 19, 1990: "El antisemitismo de Heidegger."

7. An overview of the holdings of the Heidegger *Nachlass*—"100 cartons"—is to be found in Ingrid Kussmaul, *Die Nachlässe und Sammlungen des Deutschen Literaturarchivs Marbach am Neckar: Ein Verzeichnis* (Marbach: Deutsche Schillergesellschaft, 1983), 181–83. There is also a substantial amount of Heidegger material in Marbach which stands outside this closed *Nachlass,* and so is publicly accessible. In addition, upon the insistence of the Archive (an institution supported by public funds), as soon as the material in the closed *Nachlass* is edited and published in the *Gesamtausgabe* or elsewhere, the underlying manuscripts of that edition become open to the qualified scholar.

8. Martin Heidegger and Elisabeth Blochmann, *Briefwechsel 1918–1969,* ed. Joachim W. Storck (Marbach: Deutsche Schillergesellschaft, 1989).

9. Martin Heidegger, *Die Selbstbehauptung der deutschen Universität— Das Rektorat 1933/34: Tatsachen und Gedanken* (Frankfurt: Klostermann, 1983); English translation by Karsten Harries, "The Rectorate 1933/34: Facts and Thoughts," *Review of Metaphysics* 38 (March 1985): 481–502. For the following citations from Hermann Heidegger's preface, see pp. 5 (Germ.)/468 (Eng.).

10. Otto Pöggeler, *Der Denkweg Martin Heideggers* (Pfullingen: Neske, 1983), p. 343; English translation by Daniel Magurshak and Sigmund Barber, *Martin Heidegger's Path of Thinking* (Atlantic Highlands, NJ: Humanities, 1987), p. 278. See also his "Den Führer führen: Heidegger und kein Ende," *Philosophische Rundschau*, 1985, p. 37.

11. Ibid., pp. 353/286.

12. A detailed critique of the *Gesamtausgabe* and its editorial principles is to be found in my "Edition und Übersetzung: Unterwegs von Tatsachen zu Gedanken, von Werken zu Wegen," Acts of the International Heidegger Symposium sponsored by the Alexander von Humboldt–Stiftung in Bonn, April 24–28, 1989.

13. Hartmut Tietjen, "Radikale Wendung gegen Wertgedanken," *Badische Zeitung*, January 17, 1988.

14. Hartmut Tietjen, "Wie das 'Führerprinzip an Badens Hochschulen kam," *Badische Zeitung*, November 10, 1988; Bernd Martin, "Das vermeintliche Schlüsseldokument war verfälscht, "*Badische Zeitung*, December 28, 1988; Hartmut Tietjen, "Viel Lärm um nichts," *Badische Zeitung*, January 17, 1989. Tietjen's treatise "Verstrickung und Widerstand" was first outlined for the Heidegger Gesellschaft in Messkirch, October 1988.

15. The "H" numbers in the margins of the English translation of *Being and Time* refer to the pagination of the original German text of *Sein und Zeit*—in this case, to the note on page 72 in the German.

16. Heinrich Wiegand Petzet, *Auf einen Stern zugehen: Begegnungen und Gespräche mit Martin Heidegger, 1929–1976* (Frankfurt: Societäts-Verlag, 1983), p. 91. The biography by Paul Hühnerfeld is *In Sachen Heidegger: Versuch über ein deutsches Genie* (Hamburg: Hoffmann und Campe, 1959). Farías, who nowhere acknowledges his muckraking precursor, does openly acknowledge his *ressentiment* against Heidegger's linguistic chauvinism (which spurred him to write his own book), stemming from remarks that Heidegger made to him regarding the untranslatability of *Being and Time* into an unphilosophical language like Spanish.

17. Martin Heidegger, *Unterwegs zur Sprache* (Pfullingen: Neske, 1959), p. 269; English translation by Peter Hertz, *On the Way to Language* (New York: Harper & Row, 1971), p. 199.

18. Heidegger's inaugural address was first published in the *Jahreshefte der Heidelberger Akademie der Wissenschaften 1957/58* (Heidelberg: Carl Winter, 1959), pp. 20ff., and immediately reprinted by Leo Gabriel in *Wissenschaft und Weltbild* (Vienna) 12 (1959): 610ff., and then in Martin Heidegger, *Frühe Schriften* (Frankfurt: Klostermann, 1972), pp. ix–xi; English translation by Hans Seigfried in Thomas Sheehan, ed., *Heidegger: The Man and the Thinker* (Chicago: Precedent, 1981), p. 21ff.

19. Martin Heidegger, *Zur Sache des Denkens* (Tübingen: Niemeyer, 1969), p. 89; English translation by Joan Stambaugh, *On Time and Being* (New York: Harper & Row, 1972), p. 81.

20. Richardson's remarks preface Martin Heidegger's "Only a God Can Save Us: The *Spiegel* Interview (1966)," in Sheehan, *Heidegger*, p. 45. For the 1964 speech, see Martin Heidegger, *Über Abraham a Sancta Clara* (Messkirch: Heuberg-Drückerei, 1964).

21. Heidegger, *Unterwegs zur Sprache*, pp. 90/51, 128/34. An initial attempt to unravel this infolding fictional structuration of Heidegger's self-image as he presents it to the world is to be found in my "Heidegger's Early Lecture Courses," in Joseph J. Kockelmans, ed., *A Companion to Heidegger's "Being and Time"* (Washington, D.C.: University Press of America, 1986), p. 24ff.

22. Citations are from Tomio Tezuka's own account of this famous conversation, now available in German translation: "Eine Stunde mit Heidegger," in Hartmut Buchner, ed., *Japan und Heidegger: Gedenkschrift der Stadt Messkirch zum hundertsten Geburtstag Martin Heideggers* (Sigmaringen: Jan Thorbecke, 1989), p. 173.

23. Heidegger, *Unterwegs zur Sprache*, pp. 96/10.

24. Heidegger's letter of January 1919 is to be found in Bernhard Casper, "Martin Heidegger und die Theologische Fakultät Freiburg 1909–1923," *Freiburger Diözesan-Archiv* 100 (1980): 541. My summary treatment of the background to this and the August 1921 letter to Karl Löwith is based on two articles of mine: "War der frühe Heidegger tatsächlich ein 'christlicher Theologe'?" in A. Gethmann-Siefert, ed., *Philosophie und Poesie: Otto Pöggeler zum 60. Geburtstag* (Stuttgart: Frommann-Holzboog, 1988), 2:59–75; and "The Young Heidegger's Phenomenology of Religion (1917–19)," forthcoming. The letter to Löwith is published in the Acts of the Heidegger Symposium, Bonn, April 24–28, 1989.

25. Karl Löwith, who learned this lesson quite well from Heidegger, summarized the philosophical history of this problem in the last chapter of his book *From Hegel to Nietzsche* (Garden City, N.Y.: Doubleday Anchor, 1964).

26. Jürgen Habermas, "Work and Weltanschauung: The Heidegger Controversy from a German Perspective," trans. John McCumber, *Critical Inquiry* 15 (Winter 1989): 431–56. This English version is slightly different from the German foreword to Farías.

27. Heidegger, *Über Abraham a Sancta Clara*, p. 5. For some odd reason, this fifteen-page pamphlet is not included among Heidegger's lesser works in the *Gesamtausgabe*, vol. 13 (1983), even though it reprints for the first time the 1910 newspaper article on Abraham, thus calling it to the attention of Farías, who uses both articles to "frame" Heidegger. The 1964 talk is reprinted, however, in Martin Heidegger, *Zum 80: Geburstag von seiner Heimatstadt Messkirch* (Frankfurt: Klostermann, 1969), pp. 46–57. See also Karl Bertsche, *Abraham a Sancta Clara: Blütenlese ausseinen Weiken* (Freiburg, 1910).

28. Heidegger, *Über Abraham a Sancta Clara*, p. 8.

29. These citations are brought together in Sheehan, "Heidegger and the Nazis," p. 42.

30. Heidegger, *Über Abraham a Sancta Clara*, p. 11.

31. For example, Medard Boss was Karl Moehling's source for original material on Heidegger's denazification proceedings, as well as its translator; see Karl A. Moehling, "Heidegger and the Nazis," in Sheehan, *Heidegger,* p. 42 n.1.

32. Petzet, *Auf einen Stern zugehen,* p. 50.

33. Mathias Schreiber, "Ein Freund, der verriet," *Frankfurther Allgemeine Zeitung,* February 4, 1989.

34. Michael Zimmermann, "Philosophy among the Ruins," *Times Literary Supplement,* May 5–11, 1989.

35. That Ott is quick to damn and loath to praise Heidegger can in part be attributed to the first reactions in Freiburg to his papers on Heidegger's rectorate. Ott himself (p. 8) tells the tale of being alienated from large segments of the university community for "profaning" the sacred precincts of Heidegger's old university. Thus, as in Farías's case, the injured sensibilities of the biographer served to fuel a hypercritical biography. The story confirmed from the American side: the American Heidegger Conference was then making plans to hold the twentieth annual meeting in Freiburg, only to be told by the reigning powers that the tenor of the place at that time spoke against such a meeting.

36. Löwith's *From Hegel to Nietzsche* and his other works amply trace this development of the "German mind" ripening from Protestantism to atheism, as Nietzsche himself foretold.

37. This selection, from the Heidelberg inaugural speech of 1957 (see note 18 above), may well have been made with Ficker's *Der Brenner* in mind, for it was about that time that Heidegger and Ficker became close friends.

38. Allan Janik, "Haecker, Kierkegaard, and the Early *Brenner:* A Contribution to the History of the Reception of *Two Ages* in the German-speaking World," in Robert L. Perkins, ed., *International Kierkegaard Commentary: Two Ages* (Macon, Ga.: Mercer University Press, 1984), pp. 189–222, esp. 220.

39. Petzet, *Auf einen Stern zugehen,* pp. 114–16.

40. The young Heidegger's reading of Eckhart, Schleiermacher, and works on primitive Christianity such as Adolf Deissmann's is explored in my article "The Young Heidegger's Phenomenology of Religion." Another strand of this early development is traced in my *"Kriegsnotsemester* 1919: Heidegger's Hermeneutic Breakthrough" (forthcoming).

41. Cf. Schreiber's review in *Frankfurther Allgemeine Zeitung,* February 4, 1989, and the Heidegger-Blochmann correspondence, *Briefwechsel,* pp. 9–12.

42. This occurs in the Foreword to his habilitation and in summer semester 1919: Martin Heidegger, *Frühe Schriften* (Frankfurt: Klostermann, 1972), p. 133; and *Zur Bestimmung der Philosophie, Gesamtausgabe,* vol. 56/57 (Frankfurt: Klostemann, 1987), p. 180. On the pivotal importance of Lask in Heidegger's early development, see my "Why Students of Heidegger Will Have to Read Emil Lask," in Deborah Chaffin, ed., *Emil Lask and the Search for Concreteness* (Athens: Ohio University Press, 1992).

43. Martin Heidegger, *Prolegomena zur Geschichte des Zeitbegriffs, Gesamtausgabe,* vol. 20 (Frankfurt: Klostermann, 1979), p. 398; English translation by Theodore Kisiel, *History of the Concept of Time* (Bloomington: Indiana University Press, 1985), p. 287.

44. Martin Heidegger, *Die Frage nach dem Ding* (Tübingen: Niemeyer, 1962), p. 55; English translation by W. B. Barton, Jr., and Vera Deutsch, *What Is a Thing?* (Chicago: Regnery, 1967), p. 71. Heidegger's discussion of ballistics here clearly takes him back to his own military experience: his lecture courses of 1919–20 were written on the backs of old gunnery ballistics charts brought back from the front.

45. Ernst Jünger, editor's foreword to *Krieg und Krieger* (Berlin: Junken und Dünnhaupt, 1930), p. 5.

46. Heidegger, *Das Rektorat 1933/34,* pp. 24/484. Harries's notes to his English translation are also helpful here: e.g., his remark on Heraclitean "polemics" (p. 488n).

47. Winfried Franzen, "Die Sehnsucht nach Härte und Schwere: Über ein zum NS-Engagement disponierenendes Motiv in Heideggers Vorlesung 'Die Grundbegriffe der Metaphysik' von 1929/30," in Gethmann-Siefert and Pöggeler, *Heidegger und die praktische Philosophie,* pp. 78–92.

48. "Ein Gespräch mit Max Müller," *Freiburger Universitätsblätter* 92 (June 1986), p. 28.

49. Petzet, *Auf einen Stern zugenhen,* p. 90.

50. R I Heidegger 10.IX.18, Husserl-Archief, Leuven. I thank Samuel IJselling, director of the Husserl Archive, for permission to cite from these letters.

51. Cf. Theodore Kisiel, "Das Entstehen des Begriffsfeldes 'Faktizität' im Frühwerk Heideggers," *Dilthey-Jahrbuch* 4 (1986–87): 91–120, esp. p. 98ff; and my *"Kriegsnotsemester* 1919."

52. Paul Natorp, *Deutscher Weltberuf: Geschichtsphilosophische Richtlinien* (Jena: Diederichs, 1918), Bk. 1, *Die Weltalter des Geistes; Die Seele des Deutschen.* Internal references in the following paragraph are to these two volumes.

53. Cf. my translation of R II Natorp 9.XI.22 in "The Missing Link in the Early Heidegger," Joseph J. Kockelmans, ed., *Hermeneutic Phenomenology: Lectures and Essays* (Washington, D.C.: University Press of America, 1988), pp. 1–40, esp. p. 14.

54. R II Natorp 29.I.22, Husserl-Archief, Leuven.

55. Fritz K. Ringer, *The Decline of the German Mandarins: The German Academic Community, 1890–1933* (Cambridge, Mass.: Harvard University Press, 1969), pp. 277–78, 350–51. This excellent book on German intellectual history needs to be supplemented by an account of "the collapse of the mandarins" in the thirties and forties, with the Heidegger case as one of its paradigms.

56. Heidegger, *Das Rektorat 1933/34,* pp. 22/482.

57. Ibid. I first attempted to trace this series of academic benchmarks from 1919 to 1933 in my "Heidegger (1919–33): The University in the Service of Science" (1983: unpublished). An error-ridden transcript of the summer 1919 course is now published in Heidegger, *Zur Bestimmung der Philosophie,* pp. 205–14.

58. Winfried Franzen, *Martin Heidegger* (Stuttgart: Metzler, 1976), p. 21.

2

Ontological Aestheticism: Heidegger, Jünger, and National Socialism

MICHAEL E. ZIMMERMAN

Martin Heidegger's recently published Freiburg lectures from the early 1920s show that as a young man he was already concerned about the phenomenon of modern technology, even though he scarcely mentioned it in *Being and Time* (composed in 1926) (*GA* 56/67, 61, 63).[1] The young Heidegger used the term "modern technology" to embrace what he regarded as the twin evils of cultural modernity and industrialism. *Being and Time*'s apparent indifference to the subject, then, is a mere appearance. Heidegger's decision to make modern technology a major topic for investigation in the 1930s was closely tied to his conclusion that only a spiritual revolution could save Germany and the West from technological technology. His decision to focus on modern technology coincided with his increasing interest in the world-forming power of the work of art, another phenomenon that he had virtually ignored in *Being and Time* but one that was obviously of great importance to him. Heidegger's investigation of modern technology, art, and their interrelation was given concrete expression in his political engagement with National Socialism. In this essay I argue that his political pronouncements and activities, as well as his philosophical utterances about art and technology, were deeply informed by his appropriation of and confrontation with the writings of one of his contemporaries, a best-selling author named Ernst Jünger.

Jünger proclaimed that modern humanity, stamped by the *Gestalt* of the worker, was destined to dominate the earth by modern technology. Jünger, Heidegger believed, showed that capitalist and communist industrialism were simply different versions of the *Gestalt* of the worker. Western humanity was destined to reduce all things to standing reserve

(Bestand) for the technological Will to Power. Regarding Hitler as the leader capable of forestalling that destiny by discovering a "third way" between capitalism and communism, Heidegger resolved to support him—and, in addition, offered himself as the spiritual *Führer* of the "revolution."

Heidegger's early confidence (1933–36) in National Socialism gradually waned. Like other intellectuals, he began distinguishing between the historical reality of National Socialism and its "inner truth." It has long been known that his lectures on Nietzsche (1936–44) were a confrontation with the crude interpretations of Nietzsche offered by the ideologues who were distorting that inner truth. Less well known is the fact that those Nietzsche lectures were also a confrontation with Jünger's Nietzsche-inspired interpretation of modern technology, nihilism, the will to power, and art. Heidegger's meditations on Nietzsche led him to conclude that only a profound work of art, such as Hölderlin's poetry, could open up a historical world in which entities could manifest themselves in richer, more diversified ways than would be possible within the technological world envisioned by Jünger. I use the term "ontological aestheticism" to describe Heidegger's view of art. For a time, at least, he believed that the National Socialist state was akin to a work of art in opening up a new world.

In 1955, Heidegger wrote "On the Question of Being," which was originally published as part of a *Festschrift* for Jünger's sixtieth birthday.[2] This essay described his debt to, but also indicated what he took to be the limitations of, Jünger's thought. While Jünger's accounts of nihilism and modern technology are often striking and sometimes bizarre, they are also governed by metaphysical categories that Heidegger himself was trying to overcome. Although Jünger was by no means the philosophical equal of Heidegger, his striking vision of modern technology nevertheless provided the optic that helped shape Heidegger's view of modern technology and Western history. In the 1950s, he convinced Jünger to republish *Der Arbeiter (The Worker)*, which originally appeared in 1932. Of this book and Jünger's essays "Total Mobilization" (1930) and "On Pain," Heidegger said: "These works will last because by them, insofar as they speak the language of our century, the discussion of the essence [*Wesen*] of nihilism, which has by no means yet been accomplished, can be newly rekindled."[3] Heidegger also remarked that his own famous essay "The Question about Technology" owed "enduring advancement to the descriptions in *The Worker*."[4] As is the case in many of his retrospective remarks about the "development" of his thought, however, Heidegger did not provide us with a complete portrayal of the extent or nature of his debt to Jünger's writings. Above all, at least in 1955, he failed to acknowledge that his support for National Socialism was greatly influenced by his confrontation with Jünger's works. In what follows I examine the intimate relationship between Heidegger's support for National Socialism, his confrontation with Jünger's concept of modern technology, and his reflections upon the nature of the work of art.

Heidegger, Jünger, and National Socialism

The question of Heidegger's relation to National Socialism has been reawakened by recent publications, including Victor Farías's *Heidegger et le nazisme* and Hugo Ott's *Martin Heidegger: Unterwegs zu seiner Biographie.*[5] Although Farías is often mean-spirited and tendentious, he marshals his sources (and the findings of the respected German historian Ott) in a way that unravels the "official story" about Heidegger's political involvement. The official story, composed by Heidegger and by sympathetic followers, maintains that he actively supported the "revolution" only during the ten months he spent as rector of the University of Freiburg in 1933–34.[6] Having resigned his position because of his refusal to fire allegedly Nazi professors, he subsequently repudiated the regime and began a series of lectures on Nietzsche and Hölderlin designed to show his opposition to Nazi "philosophy" and "poetry."

Under the scrutiny of Farías and Ott, the official story falls apart. For example, far from leaving the "revolution" in 1934, Heidegger remained a Party member from 1933 to the end of World War II. Of course, the fact that he did not revoke his membership is not in itself sufficient reason to conclude that he remained actively involved in Party affairs after 1934. Farías, however, presents documents demonstrating that Heidegger continued to be engaged in a movement to transform German universities in accordance with his own version of National Socialism. The scorn with which he was treated in the mid-1930s by such leading Nazi ideologues as Krieck and Rosenberg, then, was *not* a sign that he was regarded as anti-Nazi but instead an indication that he was involved in an interfamilial dispute about which theorist's views were to become the source of spiritual leadership for the revolution. Karl Löwith, a former student of Heidegger, who—as a Jew—left Germany in 1933, reports a meeting with his mentor in Rome in 1936. Sporting a swastika pin on his coat lapel, Heidegger proclaimed that National Socialism was the right way for Germany: one must only persevere long enough. When asked whether his allegiance to the Party was rooted in the essence of his philosophy, "Heidegger agreed with me without hesitation and explained to me, that his concept of 'historicality' [*Geschichtlichkeit*] was the basis for his political 'entry.' "[7] Although Heidegger increasingly distanced himself from the historical actuality of National Socialism, he continued to meditate on its spiritual possibilities. Some have argued that he never really abandoned his hope in those possibilities. In 1966, for example, he concluded that democracy offered no help for dealing with modern technology.[8]

Recently, Jürgen Habermas has argued that already in *Being and Time* (1927) one can discern themes that would later be utilized in Heidegger's support for National Socialism.[9] Jacques Derrida, moreover, has concluded that National Socialism is inextricably "inscribed" in Heidegger's thought.[10] But Derrida has also observed that while Heidegger's writings are deeply involved in the historical-political context of the 1930s, they cannot be *reduced* to that context. No one reading *Sein und Zeit* in 1927 concluded that six years later Heidegger would be using its language to support an authoritarian, anti-Semitic regime. Certainly none of Heidegger's Jewish graduate students, including Hannah Arendt and Herbert Marcuse, suspected such a use.[11]

In 1933, however, Heidegger the man concluded that National Socialism represented the authentic renewal of German *Geist*. Derrida has pointed out that before 1933 Heidegger had always placed *Geist* within quotation marks, almost as if to suggest that the term could be used only ironically in destitute times.[12] But in speeches supporting the "revolution," he removed the quotation marks. Convinced that Hitler's accession to power meant a glorious new dawn for Germany, Heidegger applied both his international status and his philosophical vocabulary to supporting the new regime. National Socialism offered him the opportunity of concretizing the open-ended "authentic resoluteness" of which he had spoken in *Being and Time*. Conceiving of himself as the *Führer* of the University, he maintained that the revolution had brought about "the complete transformation of our German *Dasein*."[13] In his Nazi speeches he often used Nazi political language, but he usually redefined it in order to make it consistent with his own thought. For example, in 1933 he spoke of how important it was for the German *Volk* to be rooted in "blood and soil."[14] Many Nazis interpreted "blood and soil" in a relatively coarse, biologistic, anti-Semitic sense, often appealing to Nietzsche in support of their views. While Heidegger, too, appealed to Nietzsche in an attempt to define the spiritual uniqueness of the German *Volk,* he interpreted Nietzsche's thought in nonnaturalistic, nonbiologistic terms. In 1940 he argued that "Nietzsche's racial thought has a metaphysical, not a biological sense."[15] Derrida rightly asks, however, "Is a metaphysics of race more serious or less serious than a naturalism or a biologism of race?"[16]

Of course, in light of the anti-Semitism that appeared during the 1930s in England, France, Belgium, and Spain, in light of Russia's history of pogroms, and in light of America's racism against blacks and of its genocidal campaign against Native Americans, European people and their descendants would do well to avoid self-righteous judgments about Heidegger's involvement with National Socialism. Heidegger's postwar silence about the Holocaust, however, his refusal to acknowledge the apparently inextricable relation between Nazism and anti-Semitism, angered his critics and puzzled his supporters. In only one passage that I know of, from an unpublished lecture on technology given in 1949, did he speak of the Holocaust: "Agriculture is now a motorized food industry, essentially the same thing as the fabrication of cadavers in the gas chambers of the extermination camps, the same thing as the blockades and the reduction of countries to famine, the same thing as the fabrication of hydrogen bombs."[17] Granted that there may be some validity to the suggestion that gas chambers and hydrogen bombs are both technical devices with genocidal intent, we are nevertheless right to be suspicious of someone whose explanation of the Holocaust appeals to an abstract Europe-wide event called "the history of being" and neglects the concrete determinants of the Holocaust, *including* German anti-Semitism.

Like many other Germans in 1933, Heidegger concluded that the Western world had declined to a state of commercialism, industrialism, socialism, liberalism—in short, nihilism. For him, capitalism and communism were "metaphysically" the same. The former represented the greedy, egocentric, abstract, calculating, *Geist*-destroying attitude of the English and French; the latter represented the spiritually vacant, faceless, leveling society of the Russians. Rejecting "modernity," the symbols of which were the French Revolution ("the spirit of 1789") and English commercialism ("the spirit of Manchester"), many Germans longed for a revival of the *Volksgemeinschaft*. They believed that a genuine German Reich would be founded by a divinely inspired, historical destiny that transcended the individual. During the Weimar years, Heidegger was typical of what Thomas Mann described as the "unpolitical man" who refused to sully himself by participating in the political struggle. In the early 1930s, however, as Germany's economy collapsed and the country moved toward total disarray, Heidegger became increasingly attracted to Hitler's promise of a "third way" beyond capitalism and communism.

Crucial for Heidegger's political decision was his encounter with Jünger's horrifying prophecies about the coming industrial-technological era. In a retrospective essay written in 1945, Heidegger commented:

In the year 1930 Ernst Jünger's article on "Total Mobilization" had appeared; in this article the basic features of his book *The Worker [Der Arbeiter]*, which appeared in 1932, announced themselves. Together with my assistant [Werner] Brock, I discussed these writings in a small circle and tried to show how they express a fundamental understanding of Nietzsche's metaphysics, insofar as the history and present of the Western world are seen and foreseen in the horizon of this metaphysics. Thinking from these writings and, still more essentially, from their foundations, we thought what was coming, that is to say, we attempted to counter it, as we confronted it. . . . Later, in the winter 1939/40, I discussed part of Jünger's book *The Worker* once more with a circle of colleagues; I learned how even then these thoughts still seemed strange and put people off, until "the facts" bore them out. What Ernst Jünger thinks with the thought of the rule and shape of the worker, and sees in the light of this thought, is the universal rule of the will to power within history, now understood to embrace the planet. . . .

Was there not enough reason and essential distress to think in primordial reflection towards a surpassing of the metaphysics of the will to power and that is to say, to begin a confrontation [*Auseinandersetzung*] with Western thought by returning to its beginning?[18]

Jünger helped to trigger Heidegger's meditations about the relation between Nietzsche's doctrine of the Will to Power and modern technology. In supporting National Socialism, Heidegger proclaimed that Hitler's "revolution" would avoid the "dreary technological frenzy" afflicting America and Russia (*GA* 40:40–41).[19] While using Jünger's vocabulary about work and the worker, he envisioned the possibility of a world of work that was *not* the one forecast by Jünger. Starting around 1935 he probed more deeply than did Jünger into the metaphysical essence of work. He concluded that genuine work—such as the work of art—has an ontologically disclosive function. The work of art "lets entities be." He believed that Germany's revolution could succeed only if it were guided by and founded upon a great work of art, such as the poetry of Hölderlin, that would disclose entities as other than raw material and humanity as other than a faceless mass. Eventually, he began to conclude that the actual historical movement called National Socialism would fail. Hence, not only would Jünger's prophecy come to pass, but it would *have* to come to pass if the history of metaphysics was to be completed. Only *completing* that history would make a genuine new beginning possible. We might ask whether, in Heidegger's view, Hitler was born too soon.

The importance of Jünger's writings on technology to Heidegger's understanding of National Socialism is evident in an infamous remark from the latter's lecture course *An Introduction to Metaphysics* (1935): "The works that are being peddled about nowadays as the philosophy of National Socialism but have nothing to do with the *inner truth and greatness of this movement* (namely the encounter between global technology and modern man) have all been written by men fishing in the troubled water of "values" and "totalities" (*GA* 40:208).

This statement provoked a scandal on its publication in 1953. In that same year, Christian Lewalter defended Heidegger by saying that in speaking of the "greatness" of National Socialism, Heidegger meant its status as a "tragic" symptom of the "collision of technology and man, and as such a symptom it has 'greatness,' because its effect reaches out upon the whole West and threatens to drag it into decline [*Untergang*]."[20] Heidegger agreed publicly with Lewalter's interpretation, but recently produced evidence suggests that he added the remark in parentheses— "namely the encounter between global technology and modern man"— only in 1953; hence, in 1935 he still hoped that National Socialism was "great" because it offered an authentic renewal of German *Geist*.[21] During the late 1930s and early 1940s, despite engaging in increasingly daring criticism of the *reality* of National Socialism, Heidegger retained his faith in its *inner truth*. For several years he held out hope that Hitler's Germany could provide for the West a new beginning that would be analogous to the beginning initiated by the ancient Greeks. In 1942, however, he uttered a sentence the ambiguity of which makes the reader unsure just what Heidegger's stand toward National Socialism had become: "One does not at all serve the knowledge and appraisal of the historical uniqueness of National Socialism if one now interprets Greek humanity [*Griechentum*] such that one could suppose that the Greeks have already all been 'National Socialists' " (*GA* 53:106). The course of Heidegger's engagement with National Socialism can be adequately understood only in light of his dialogue with the writings of Ernst Jünger, to which we now turn.

Jünger's Conception of the *Gestalt* of the Worker

Ernst Jünger (1895–), born to a proper Prussian family, ran away at the age of sixteen to join the Foreign Legion, before his life-changing ordeal in the trenches of the Great War in 1914–18. One of Germany's most decorated heroes for his valor as an infantry officer, he wrote several books, including a best seller, *The Storm of Steel,* about his experiences on the front.[22] His interpretation of the war as the eruption of primitive forces that purged the German spirit of its exhausted bourgeois trappings shaped the opinions of millions of the men of his generation. He viewed the war as an empirical manifestation of a nonempirical, metaphysical force: the Will to Power.[23] Critics have argued that to compensate both for his horrifying experiences at the front and for Germany's defeat, and to make sense of the titanic scale and all-encompassing character of the war, he mythologized it and elevated it to a status far higher than that of a conflict explicable in terms of "merely" political and economic categories. Other critics maintain that he coped with his war experience by depersonalizing it, primarily by turning it into an aesthetic phenomenon. Deeply affected by turn-of-the-century artistic trends, including modernism, futurism, art for art's sake, and the aesthetic of horror, Jünger used these theories as prisms through which the gruesome and gigantic events of the Great War refracted themselves as a hauntingly beautiful spectacle that symbolized the primal Will at work beneath it all.

From Spengler and Nietzsche, Jünger derived his notion that the empirical features of each particular historical epoch are governed by a particular *Gestalt,* a metaphysical "stamp" of the eternal Will to Power that imprints itself upon the character and behavior of an age. World history, then, amounts to an aesthetic phenomenon, a spectacle organized by a governing symbol or *Gestalt.* Jünger claimed that the current *Gestalt* was that of the worker who mobilizes humanity and the earth in accordance with the technological imperative. He coined the term "total mobilization" to refer to the character of the *Gestalt* shaping life in the technological era.[24] In the age of the worker there is no distinction between war and peace, soldier and worker, combatant and non-combatant. At the front, soldiers consumed the vast quantities of material produced by workers in factories. In modern war, production and consumption become completely interrelated. For the worker, everything is standing reserve *(Bestand),* a term later appropriated by Heidegger to describe the metaphysical sameness to which everything had been reduced in the technological age. Jünger claimed that total mobilization was "the expression of the mysterious and compelling claim to which this life in the age of masses and machines subjugates us."[25] The *Gestalt* of the worker called for a new *Typus* of man, one who would combine fire with ice, volcanic passion with cold precision, blood with steel. This type of man, an "organic construction," would carry out the terrible deeds necessary to respond to the claim of the *Gestalt* of the worker. Jünger's astonishing descriptions of the half-machine, half-organic worker-soldier were anticipated by the Italian futurist Marinetti, who interpreted modern war and technology as aesthetic phenomena.

> War is beautiful because it initiates the dreamt-of metalization of the human body. War is beautiful because it enriches a flowering meadow with the fiery orchids of machine guns. . . . War is beautiful because it creates new architecture, like that of the big tanks, the geometrical formation flights, the smoke spirals from burning villages.[26]

Marinetti and Jünger regarded both modern technology (with its roaring locomotives, speeding airplanes, blazing industrial furnaces) and modern technological war (with its massive and colorful explosions, gas-masked soldiers, precision-engineered weapons) as aesthetic phenomena. Only the elite, of course, were capable of peering through the apparent carnage and horror to discern the eerie beauty of a world in which life was turning itself into a machine. The attraction that this view had for right-wing and proto-fascist authors such as Marinetti and Jünger helps to explain Walter Benjamin's famous judgment in 1936 that fascism involved the "aestheticization of politics."

> *"Fiat ars—pereat mundus,"* says Fascism, and as Marinetti admits, expects war to supply the artistic gratification of a sense perception that has been changed by technology. This is evidently the consummation of *"L'art pour l'art."* Mankind, which in Homer's time was an object of contemplation for the Olympian gods, now is one for itself. Its self-alienation has reached such a degree that it can experience its own destruction as an aesthetic pleasure of the first order. This is the situation of politics which Fascism is rendering aesthetic. Communism responds by politicizing art.[27]

The aesthetic attitude toward technology adopted by Jünger and Marinetti was one of the hallmarks of certain forms of fascism, especially in Italy. George L. Mosse has remarked: "The literary tradition of the *fin de siècle* had stressed the irrational, the problems of the individual in a restrictive society. Fascism claimed to re-establish the true creativity of man which had been stifled, just as an earlier generation of men of letters had searched for the genuine beneath the façade of bourgeois culture."[28] The aestheticization of politics achieved by fascism was a specific version of a widespread rejection of philistine bourgeois life. Many people of various political stripes were attracted to one or another version of Nietzsche's overman. For some the overman, who combined personal creativity with primitive violence, reflected the mesmerizing power of the *Fronterlebnis* that made so many veterans feel that ordinary life was meaningless. Mosse has also noted that for many fascists the overman symbolized the yearning both for individual elitism and for the authority needed to renew a society weakened by leveling movements such as socialism and democracy.[29] Some proto-fascists, including Jünger, for a time regarded the Soviet Union, with its forced collectivization and industrialization, as the highest instance of a society organized by an elite corps of men stamped by the *Gestalt* of the worker. In the 1920s, Jünger was closely allied with Ernst Niekisch, a proponent of the apparently contradictory right-wing movement called "National Bolshevism."[30] Its aim was at least twofold: to renew the national identity, economic well-being, and military strength of the German *Volk;* and to reestablish organic union or *Bindung* that avoided the social problems produced by class conflict (communism), on the one hand, and individualistic competition (capitalism), on the other. Unlike those conservatives who called for the return of Germany to the preindustrial values of the family, small towns, and farms, Jünger and his friends favored a Nietzschean transvaluation of existing values in order to make way for the oncoming spectacle of modern technology. Jünger, then, represented a trend popular in certain conservative Weimar circles, a trend that Jeffrey Herf has called "reactionary modernism."[31] The history of Nazi Germany is complicated by the fact that it attempted to combine the rhetoric of preindustrial values with the *praxis* of total industrialization.

Reactionary modernists such as Jünger showed how to combine authoritarian-elitist social ideals with an economy based on modern machine technology. Unlike Hitler, however, they supported nationalism not as an end in itself but rather as an "explosive" means to give the *coup de grâce* to the remnants of bourgeois culture: nationalism would ignite the wars that would usher in the new age. Similarly, he regarded communism as a tactical ally in the attack on the existing order. Unlike communists, however, Jünger conceived of workers not in terms of the masses but instead in terms of an elite corps of highly disciplined men utilized by the Will to Power as instruments necessary to construct the artistic spectacle of the technological era. As the instruments of this higher artistic will, the members of Jünger's aristocratic corps were to live beyond good and evil. Their motto was "Live dangerously!" and their behavior was to be ruthless.

Jünger's conception of the elite, dynamic, destructive-creative worker was derived from his understanding of the bloodthirsty commando in the trenches. He regarded most soldiers, like most workers, as raw material to be shaped by the elite cadres whose behavior showed their understanding of the fact that war was the "magnetic center" of a people. Instead of explaining the world war as the outcome of competition between European capitalist powers, he made war the basis for everything, both human and natural. War is the ultimate destroyer and creator; it "is a frenzy beyond all frenzies, an unchaining that leaps all bonds. It is a fury without consideration and limits, comparable only to the violences of nature. There man is like the raging storm, the churning sea, and the roaring thunder."[32] But the overflowing passion of the modern soldier had to be combined with the calculating precision necessary to work the monstrous engines of modern warfare. Jünger's concept of the worker was based on his idea of the modern soldier. The elite worker had to combine hot blood with cold nerves, passion with technological intelligence. It was this vision of the worker that Jünger had in mind when he said that the *Gestalt* of the worker imprints or stamps on the world a character commensurate with total mobilization. Jünger defined *Gestalt* as "the highest meaningful reality. Its appearances are meaningful as symbols, representations and impressions of this reality. The *Gestalt* is the whole which embraces more than the sum of its parts. This 'more' we call totality. . . . From the moment in which one begins to experience things in terms of a *Gestalt,* everything becomes *Gestalt.*"[33]

Jünger sometimes spoke of the *Gestalt* as a "force field," a metaphysical magnet that organized human and material "filings" by invisible lines of energy.[34] But this force field cannot be understood in terms of the physical laws of cause and effect: "There is no purely mechanical law; the changes in mechanical and organic conditions [occur] through the superordinate realm [of the *Gestalt*], from which is determined the causality of individual processes."[35] Somehow the *Gestalt* "stamps" the world ontologically in such a way that ontical processes and modes of behavior change. Heidegger was to explain this stamping in terms of his phenomenological ontology and the "history of being." For Jünger, the activity of the *Gestalt* that changes historical epochs could not be understood in causal terms. Indeed, for him, "causality" was a category that belonged to the spiritless bourgeoisie, for whom explanation and control were all-important as guarantors of "security." Jünger sometimes spoke of his mythical concept of the *Gestalt* in philosophical terms, as when he claimed that the *Gestalt* constituted the very "being [*Sein*]" of the worker.[36] The power at work through the *Gestalt* was not a means to human ends; instead, humanity was a means to the goal of the *Gestalt:* to create the spectacle of planetary technology. Jünger defined technology as:

> the ways and means by which the *Gestalt* of the worker mobilizes the world. The degree to which man stands decisively in relation to technology and is not destroyed by it depends on the degree to which he represents the *Gestalt* of the worker. In this sense technology is the mastery of language that is valid in the realm of work. This language is no less important nor profound than any other since it possesses not only a grammar but also a metaphysics. In this context the machine plays as much a secondary role as does man; it is only one of the organs through which this language is spoken.[37]

Modern technology, which speaks the language of the "clatter of machine guns at [the battle of] Langemarck," could not be understood as a rational means to the end of human progress.[38] Instead, the enormous processes of production and consumption, world wars, and planetary domination had to be conceived as aesthetic phenomena, the "meaning" of which lies in their character as world-historical spectacles. The *Gestalt* of the worker was, like every artistic impulse, an end in itself. Jünger maintained that heroism was still possible for those who sacrificed themselves to and apprehended the aesthetic purposelessness animating the technological era. He affirmed:

> The last possibilities for human achievement are not excluded from our age. This is attested by sacrifices which must be valued all the more highly as they are offered on the brink of meaninglessness. At a time when values disappear behind dynamic laws, behind the compelling force of motion, these sacrifices resemble those who fall in an attack and quickly disappear from sight, but to whom nevertheless is hidden a higher existence, the guarantee of victory. Our time is rich in unknown martyrs; it possesses a depth of suffering whose bottom has not yet been plumbed. The virtue appropriate to this situation is that of a heroic realism unshaken even by the prospect of total annihilation and the hopelessness of its efforts.[39]

Jünger's aesthetic viewpoint was closely linked to his longing for adventure, by which he meant encounter with the stupendous, the awesome, the horrifying, the gruesome, and the otherworldly. To endure glimpses into the abyss, the adventurer had to develop a disinterested or even depersonalized attitude. Only such an attitude would enable the adventurer, like the worker, to will deeds that cause such destruction and pain. Here, Jünger was close to his hero Nietzsche, who observed, "Knowledge [of life's horrible truth] kills action." Only art can preserve the will: "Here, when the danger to [man's] will is greatest, *art* approaches as a saving sorceress, expert at healing. She alone knows how to turn these nauseous thoughts about the horror or absurdity of existence into notions with which one can live: these are the *sublime* as the artistic taming of the horrible, and the *comic* as the artistic discharge of the nausea of absurdity."[40]

Jünger believed that he was one of the chosen few who could penetrate beneath the violent and confusing phenomena of the early twentieth century in order to discern the elemental, metaphysical power governing all things. One critic has remarked that in the blessed moment of astonishment "there opens itself to the adventurer [Jünger] a magical perspective, there is freely given the view into otherworldly spheres . . . and grants to him insight into the meaning of existence [*Dasein*]."[41] Jünger's magical realism denied that science can tell us anything ultimate about life; scientific concepts always deal only with the *mask* of life, not with its primal essence. In an analogous way, Heidegger believed that only his own thinking was capable of disclosing the ontological movement responsible for the decline of the West into technological nihilism.

Heidegger's Appropriation of Jünger's Thought

When Heidegger's writings about technology became accessible to English-speaking readers during the 1960s and 1970s, they were received by many people as a unique insight into the technological era. In fact, however, very little that he said about technology can be construed as "original"; he was greatly indebted to Spengler, Scheler, Jünger, and many other writers who took part in the *Streit um die Technik* that occurred in Germany during the late nineteenth and early twentieth centuries.[42] The essential ingredients of Heidegger's concept of technology are found in his lectures from 1933 to 1944, when he was seeking an alternative to Jünger's vision by way of meditation on the works of Nietzsche and Hölderlin. It is helpful to view Heidegger's work during this period in three different but related phases. In the first phase, he joined the Party and used much of Jünger's vocabulary about the worker in order to *counter* Jünger's vision of the worker. In the second phase, he focused on what the work of art can tell us, both about the essence of technology and about founding a world that allows entities to reveal themselves other than technologically. In the third phase, which became increasingly important in the early 1940s, Heidegger concluded that the historical reality of National Socialism could not forestall the technological destiny forecast by Jünger; indeed, humanity must surrender to that destiny before an alternative could manifest itself. Here I have found it convenient to discuss the second phase only after discussing phases one and three.

Heidegger's infamous speeches during 1933–34, including "The Self-Assertion of the German University," are replete with Jünger's vocabulary. Apparently, in this first phase, Heidegger hoped that by using that vocabulary and by giving it a different twist, he could accomplish two things: (1) move National Socialism away from its biologism and racism toward something more authentic; (2) shape the direction of the age of the worker in a way commensurate with what he regarded as the genuine requirements of the German *Volk*. Throughout these speeches we encounter Jünger's language of *Gestalt,* imprinting and stamping *(Prägung),* work and the worker, sacrifice, courage, hardness, manliness, decision, resoluteness, surrender to higher destiny—virtually all the major categories found in *Der Arbeiter* and related works. Consider the following quotation from a lecture Heidegger gave in November 1933 in support of National Socialism.

[The new German student] enrolls himself consciously in the worker front. Followership wins comradeship, which educates those nameless and unofficial leaders, who do more because they bear and sacrifice more; they carry the individuals out beyond themselves and *stamp on them the imprint of a wholly proper stamp of young manhood* [*Jungmannschaft;* my emphasis]. With the new reality, the essence of work and of the workers has also changed. *The essence of work now determines from the ground up the Dasein of man* [my emphasis]. The state is the self-forming articulation [*das . . . sich gestaltende Gefüge*], in work and as work, of the *völkisch Dasein. The National Socialist state is the state of work.* And because the new student knows himself joined for the carrying out of the *völkisch* claim to knowing, accordingly he studies; he studies, because he is the worker; and he marches into the new order of the national *Dasein* and its *völkisch* knowing such that he himself must co-form [*mitgestalten*] on his part this new ordering. The immatriculation is no longer the mere admission in a present-at-hand corporation; it becomes decision [*Entscheidung*], and every pure decision displaces itself into acting within a determinate situation and environment.[43]

Like Jünger, Heidegger spoke of the necessity for the worker to "co-*gestalt*" or to "co-configure" the new ordering of German *Dasein*. During the 1930s he spoke as if Germans could shape their destiny by resolving to found a new world in which entities could disclose themselves in a new way. One can discern some apparent analogies between the ontologies of Heidegger and Jünger. For example, both conceived of the "being" of the worker as the ontological "field" that disclosed and shaped humanity during the age of technology. Heidegger, however, accused Jünger of failing to understand the "ontological difference" between being and entities. Jünger spoke of "being" as an elemental metaphysical power somehow related to Nietzsche's Will to Power. For Heidegger, however, such a conception reduces being to "beingness" *(Seiendheit)*, a superior kind of entity. Plato initiated this "metaphysical" conception of being as an entity with his doctrine of the eternal *eidos*. Nietzsche's doctrine of the Will to Power was, in Heidegger's view, the culminating instance of the "history of being": that is, the history of the increasing obliviousness to the original character of being as the event of unconcealment or presencing whereby an entity manifests itself *as* an entity.

Despite important differences, parallels remain between Heidegger's conception of the history of metaphysics as the manifestation of various modes of beingness and Jünger's conception of history as the manifestation of various *Gestalten* of the Will to Power. Moreover, both Jünger and Heidegger denied that causality can explain either the emergence of governing historical *Gestalten* or how they gather and shape empirical circumstances. Heidegger claimed that positivisitic science could not see that world-historical events result from the dispensation of being: "How should man, thus ensnared [in cause-effect explanations], free his heart and open his eyes to perceive this, that something can be without its effecting or being the product of an effect" (GA, 52:100–101). Despite important debts to Jünger, Heidegger distinguished between his own idea of being, which represented the possibility of a new beginning for the West, and Jünger's idea, which was indebted to Nietzsche's thought: that is, to the final stage in the nihilistic history of beingness.

Missing from Jünger's work, in Heidegger's view, was insight into the primordial ontological character of the "motion" of the synchronic event of presencing *(Anwesen),* or being, which "hardens" itself diachronically into particular historical modes of constant presence *(Anwesenheit),* or beingness. Moreover, Jünger claimed that the *Gestalt* of the worker turned humanity into a combination of the calculating, steely powers of the machine and the atavistic, instinctual energy of the Will to Power. For Heidegger, however, this view of the half-rational, half-animal man represented the culmination of Aristotle's metaphysical conception of man as the "rational animal." Far from being the sign of the end of the historical degeneration of humanity, which Jünger and Heidegger both agreed was represented by decadent bourgeois culture, the image of Jünger's iron-hard, hot-blooded worker-soldier represented the collapse of German spirit to the merely animal level. Heidegger's lectures on Nietzsche were designed to protect his thought from those who, like Jünger, conceived of the overman as the "blond beast" whose only goal was infinite aggrandizement and conquest.

Although Jünger was ostensibly unaware of the ontological difference and was thus mired within a metaphysical interpretation of Nietzsche's thinking, his doctrine of *Gestalten* nevertheless compelled Heidegger to think of this difference more radically in terms of its history and in terms of the role played by humanity in the unfolding of that history. In the late 1930s Heidegger argued that what Jünger meant by technology was the culmination of the decline from the primordial Greek understanding of technology as *technē:* that is, as the event of the disclosure of entities as entities.

> *Technē* means this: to take hold of the self-arising entity in that as which it shows itself, in its showing forth, *eidos,* idea, in order to nurture it and to let it grow according to the entity itself, namely, to arrange [it] by producing and setting up the correspondences within the entity in the whole. *Technē* is the mode of advancing *against physis* [the sheer presencing or being of the entity] but *here* still not to make the basic principle one of use and reckoning, but the other way around, in order to hold in unhiddenness the holding sway of *physis.* [GA, 45:179]

The history of metaphysics, which culminated in the technological domination of entities, began when humanity took a stand toward *physis* not to enable the entity to manifest itself in its own terms but instead to force it to reveal itself in arbitrary inspired terms that were consistent with human control-oriented goals. This desire for control indicated that humanity had abandoned its ontological calling and degenerated to the status of a "clever animal." In his lecture "The Age of the World Picture" (1938), Heidegger argued that modern humanity was governed by a radical anthropocentrism that reduced all things to the status of objects for research and technological exploitation.[44] That Jünger could derive his atavistic doctrine of the worker-soldier from Nietzsche's thinking showed the extent to which the latter's writings were in some ways influenced by a physiological interpretation of the Will to Power. Throughout his career, Heidegger remained hostile to any merely "naturalistic" interpretation of human existence.[45] And his Nietzsche interpretation aimed to discover the nonnaturalistic basis for the doctrines of the overman, of art, and of the Will to Power.

Heidegger's version of National Socialism called for an end to this hubristic human-centered domination of entities and asked instead for the reawakening of the openness to being that had characterized the existence of the early Greeks. By the early 1940s, he was still calling for the transformation of Germany (and Western) humanity, but he had apparently concluded that such a transformation was not going to happen any time soon. In the third phase of his relation to Jünger, he concluded that there was no way to stop what Jünger had foreseen:

[Today], *"the worker"* and *"the soldier"* determine the view of reality in a thoroughgoing way. These two names are not meant as names for a class of people and an occupational guild; they characterize in a unique fusion the kind of humanity which is authoritatively taken into claim by the current world-convulsion for its carrying out, and gives direction and instruction for relationship to the entity. The name "worker" and "soldier" are thus metaphysical titles and name the human form of the carrying out of the being of the entity which has become manifest, which being *Nietzsche* has conceived prethinkingly as the *"Will to Power."* [GA 51:18]

A little later in the same lecture course, Heidegger added: " 'Workers' and 'soldiers' open the doors to reality. At the same time, they carry out an imprinting of the basic structure of human making/creating, of that which up to now is called 'culture.' . . . Culture is only insofar as it remains inserted into the course of work of the securing of the condition of a form of domination" (GA 51:37–38). Put most emphatically: "Only a dreamer and a fantasizer would be able to deny that in the age now broken forth upon the whole earth, man as the worker and soldier experiences the authentic being and provides what alone should be valid as being" (*GA* 51:38). In 1942 Heidegger knew that Jünger's prophecy could not be altered by National Socialism. Using the vocabulary that would appear in his mature work on technology from the late 1940s, he said that "technology itself challenges [*fordert*] from out of itself and for itself and develops in itself a proper kind of discipline and a proper kind of consciousness of conquest" (*GA* 53:53).

Like Jünger, Spengler, and others involved in the technology debate, Heidegger noted that the character of work had changed dramatically in the technological era: "The field that the peasant formerly cultivated and set in order appears different from how it did when to set in order still meant to take care of and maintain."⁴⁶ Further, "the forester who measures the felled timber in the woods and who to all appearances walks the forest path in the same way his grandfather did is today ordered by the industry that produces commercial woods, whether he knows it or not. He is made subordinate to the orderability of cellulose."⁴⁷ In 1932, Jünger had asserted that "the farm worked with machines and fertilized with artificial nitrogen from factories is no longer the same farm."⁴⁸

In 1942, Heidegger observed that "fascination" with the process of industrialization and the "disciplines" coupled with it could "shroud the misery [*Elend*] in which technologization thrusts man. Perhaps for the wholly technicized man there is no more of this 'misery' " (*GA* 53:54). In his essay "On Pain" (1934), Jünger argued that the crucial feature of the bourgeois age was the quest to eliminate pain. While the bourgeois sentimentalist wants to be rid of it, the higher technological types defy pain by turning their bodies into objects. Jünger proclaimed that "man becomes capable of defying the attack of pain to the extent to which he is able to expose himself from himself. This exposing, this impartialization [*Versachlichung*] and objectification of life increases unceasingly."⁴⁹ He argued that the masks and uniforms worn by the technological worker-soldier were instances of the armor required in the new age.

Heidegger agreed that "a man without a uniform today [in the age of the Will to Will] gives the impression of being something unreal which no longer belongs."⁵⁰ Moreover, "it almost seems as if the nature [*Wesen*] of pain is not disclosed to man under the domination of the Will."⁵¹ He maintained that by seeking to dominate pain, technological humanity made itself ever more available to the domination of the Will to Will, for pain is capable of disclosing that which is *other than* what is made present by the Will. The Will makes present only entities as standing reserve, but pain reveals presencing as such and thus the ontological difference between entities and presencing. Heidegger remarked that "a sign of this [presencing and withholding of difference] is the metaphysico-technological reaction to pain which at the same time predetermines the interpretation of the essence of pain.''[52] As Parvis Emad has observed:

> Pain's appearance means the emergence of something which escapes Will's total control and planning. . . . Pain confronts the Will with a difference, one between its calculative arrangements and a state of being which resides outside of this arrangement. . . . Curiously enough, pain confronts the Will with the presence of something which defies it. Thus pain proves capable of manifesting a difference between the constant presence of the Will and the presence of something else.[53]

Jünger's conception of an objectified, pain-defying, and uniformly "constructed" humanity was consistent with his view that all entities become totally interchangeable in total mobilization. Heidegger remarked:

> Since man is the most important raw material, one can reckon with the fact that some day factories will be built for the artificial breeding of human material, based on present-day chemical research. . . . (Let us not flee because of antiquated prudery to distinctions that no longer exist. The need for human material provides the same regulation for preparing for ordered mobilization as the need for entertaining books and poems, for whose production the poet is no more important than the bookbinder's apprentice.)[54]

Further, Heidegger concurred with Jünger's claim that in the age of total mobilization the distinction between "war" and "peace" is no longer valid.

> The world wars are the antecedent form of the removal of the difference between war and peace. Beyond war and peace, there is the mere erring of the consumption of entities in the plans' self-guaranteeing in terms of the vacuum of the abandonment of being. . . . *War has become a distortion of the consumption of entities which is continued in peace.* This long war in its length slowly eventuated not in peace of the traditional kind, but rather in a condition in which warlike characteristics are no longer experienced as such at all and peaceful characteristics have become meaningless and without content.[55]

In an apparent turnabout from his resolute stance in the 1930s, Heidegger proclaimed in 1942 that humanity could move beyond the technological era only by *submitting* to its claim.

Technology only becomes mastered when from the first and without holding back, "yes" is said unconditionally to it. This means that the practical mastering of technology in its unconditional unfolding already presupposes the metaphysical submission to technology. With this submission in us goes the comportment to grasp everything according to planning and reckoning . . . in order knowingly and willingly to set up the durable for a longest possible enduring. [*GA* 51:17]

Hitler's quest for a thousand-year Reich revealed the distorted understanding of space and time imposed by the technological era. And so did the Soviet Union's totalitarianism.

Who has ears to hear, i.e., to see the metaphysical basis and abyss of history and to take it seriously as metaphysics, can already for two decades hear the word of Lenin: *Bolshevism is Soviet power + electrification*. This means: Bolshevism is the "organic," i.e., calculatively organized, . . . thrusting together of the unconditioned power of the party with fully realized technologization. The bourgeois world has not seen and today in part still does not want to see, that in "Leninism," as Stalin calls this metaphysics, has been realized a *metaphysical leap forward,* from which in a certain way first becomes understandable the metaphysical passion of today's Russian for technology, from which he brings to power the technological world. [*GA* 54:127]

For Heidegger, technological humanity has lost any sense of being-at-home in the world; capable of the most exacting measurements, humanity is now incapable of genuine measurement and limits. In such a condition, "Wildness becomes the absolute itself and holds as the 'fullness' of being" (*GA* 53:91). Hence, under the sway of the *Gestalt* of the worker, modern humanity becomes the "planetary adventurer," which was Jünger's interpretation of Nietzsche's overman (*GA* 53:59). In his collection of essays *The Adventurous Heart,* Jünger affirmed man's need for adventure, for going beyond established limits, for titanic suffering and destruction of the kind always required for great creation and construction.[56] His call for "adventure" was an expression of the measureless striving for power characteristic of the technological epoch. In this epoch it no longer makes sense to speak of "means" and "ends," for the technological Will to Power has become essentially goalless and thus is a kind of "game."

Who wants to deny that since all human planning and working announces with special clarity the character of a great "game," in which no individuals and also not all together are able to raise the stakes for which the "world-game" gets played? Who might wonder that in such a time, since the world up until now has gone out of joint, the thought awakens: now only the lust for danger, the "adventurer" can be the way in which man becomes certain of reality? [*GA* 51:36]

In the technological age, "adventure" had been reduced to the quest for total domination of entities, but this aim was wholly incompatible with what Heidegger regarded as genuine ontological adventure of the sort experienced by the Greeks. Such adventure required not control of entities but submission to the play of being. Jünger had some inkling of this ontological play, for he recognized that the technological era itself was ultimately purposeless—simply another spectacle brought forth by the Will to Power. Heidegger, too, saw the purposeless character of the technological era, the essence of which he named the Will to Will. Because the essence of power is the demand for *more* power, the Will to Power is essentially a Will to Will, a self-empowering process that has no "purpose" beyond its own expansion. Jünger especially was convinced that humanity was a pawn in a game that transcends human purpose and control. Heidegger, too, despite occasionally saying that technology is not an iron destiny beyond human control, also concluded that the epochmaking shifts constituting the history of being are beyond human control. Each in his own way, then, both Jünger and Heidegger were influenced by Nietzsche's conception of the world as a work of art. In Nietzsche's *Birth of Tragedy,* we read:

> Insofar as the subject is the artist . . . he has already been released from his individual will, and has become, as it were, the medium through which the one truly existent subject celebrates his release in appearance. For to our humiliation *and* exaltation, one thing above all must be clear to us. The entire comedy of art is neither performed for our betterment or education, nor are we the true authors of this art world. On the contrary, we may assume that we are merely images and artistic projections of the true author [the Will], and that we have our highest dignity in our significance as works of art—for it is only as an *aesthetic phenomenon* that existence and the world are eternally *justified*—while of course our consciousness of our own significance hardly differs from that which soldiers painted on canvas have of the battle represented on it.[57]

Ontological Aestheticism

In the first phase of his confrontation with Jünger, Heidegger appropriated his vocabulary with the aim of finding an alternative to Jünger's vision; in the third phase, Heidegger concluded that Jünger's vision would have to be fulfilled. Moreover, he also began to see the history of being (including the technological era) in a way analogous to Jünger's view of history as an aesthetic phenomenon. In the second phase, Heidegger searched for an alternative to Jünger's interpretation of Nietzsche's thought. In this phase he concluded that the artist's historical role is to bring forth the artworks that open up new worlds in which that presencing can occur. Moreover, he proclaimed that the role of the philosopher is to think the artwork that founds each historical epoch.

Though in his rector's address in 1933, Heidegger spoke of the German revolution in terms of authentic science *(Wissenschaft)*, within two years he had made art the basis of the revolution. One reason for this shift may have been, as we have already noted, that National Socialism celebrated not science but art as the means of Western culture's salvation. Recently, Lacoue-Labarthe has argued that the aesthetic dimension was so vital to National Socialism that the movement would have been more aptly named National Aestheticism. According to Lacoue-Labarthe, Heidegger shared with other intellectual Nazis the belief that the "new" Germany would be a self-producing work of art, in which the *Volk* would be simultaneously the work of art and the witnesses thereto. This self-mythologizing tendency of National Socialism, along with a profound belief in the saving power of art, was by no means foreign to Heidegger's thought.[58]

Hitler, himself a mediocre artist, conceived of his mission as saving the West from spiritual degeneration by reawakening the artistic power of the German *Volk*. In 1938 he remarked: "The world will come to Germany and convince itself that Germany has become the guardian of European culture and civilization."[59] National Socialist ideologues conceived of their political project in artistic terms: they would give a new *Gestalt* to Germany. In 1933 Joseph Goebbels wrote to Wilhelm Furtwängler:

> Politics, it too is an art, perhaps the most elevated art and the greatest that exists, and we—who give form to modern German politics—we feel ourselves like artists to whom has been conferred the high responsibility of forming, beginning with the brute masses, the solid and complete image of the people. The mission of the artist is not only to unify, but goes much further. He is obliged to create, to give form, to eliminate what is sick, to open the way to what is healthy.[60]

Albert Speer has described the gigantic architectual projects envisioned by Hitler for construction after the War.[61] But Hitler's political-artistic ambitions went far beyond public buildings to encompass the entire German landscape. Hans Jürgen Syberberg has argued that Hitler viewed the Third Reich as a total work of art *(Gesamtkunstwerk),* analogous on a national scale to the total works of art attempted by Wagner at Bayreuth.[62] Apparently, Hitler conceived of the *Autobahnen* that he built throughout Germany as akin to the paths through the gardens of French chateaux of the medieval era, or through the municipal parks of the bourgeois era. Syberberg, himself a noted German filmmaker, acknowledges that we ordinarily think of Hitler's interest in film pejoratively; still, consider the astonishing possibility that the World War II was "directed like a big-budget war film" to be viewed from Hitler's bunker! Hitler certainly understood the political power both of the titanic spectacle— such as the "cathedrals of ice" at his Nuremberg rallies—and of film. It is not impossible that he designed the great rallies with film in mind. Consider the use to which those rallies were put in Riefenstahl's famous film *The Triumph of the Will* (1936).

In light of the Nazi aestheticization of politics, and in view of Heidegger's hopes of becoming the spiritual *Führer* of the "revolution," it was no accident that he ceased to speak of his own work as a kind of science and began instead to meditate upon the work of art, especially in terms of the writings of Hölderlin and Nietzsche. He regarded the Nuremberg rallies not as political-artistic triumphs but as symptoms of degeneration and nihilism. To counter the mainstream Nazi view of art, and particularly the crude, biologistic Nazi interpretations of Hölderlin and Nietzsche, Heidegger chose "The Will to Power as Art" as the topic for his first lecture course on Nietzsche (1936–37).

If Heidegger was the leading philosopher to develop an artistic vision for National Socialism, Gottfried Benn was perhaps the leading artist to attempt the same thing. Benn was an outstanding poet who for a time had been a leading member of the Expressionist movement. Like Heidegger, he enthusiastically welcomed Hitler as the man who would save Germany from nihilism. Given the Nazi view that Expressionism was degenerate art, Benn felt compelled to defend his earlier poetry in a 1933 talk called "The Confession of an Expressionist." There, he made clear the importance of art for the Third Reich.

> The leadership of the new Germany is extraordinarily interested in questions about art. As a matter of fact, their outstanding intellectuals . . . make art almost daily a matter of extreme urgency for the state and the public in general. The enormous biological instinct for racial perfection . . . tells them that *art is the center of gravity, the focal point for the entire historical movement:* art in Germany, art not as an aesthetic achievement but *as a fundamental fact of metaphysical existence,* which will decide the future, which is the German Reich and more [my emphasis].[63]

Of course, the Nazis paid little attention to Benn's protestations. Their staging of the infamous exhibition of "degenerate art" in Munich in 1938, along with Hitler's commitment to plebeian *Volk* realism, increasingly made clear to Benn that his artistic vision was not in sync with that of National Socialism.[64]

Eventually, Heidegger also concluded that National Socialism was not on the right track, but for several years he held out what he regarded as an authentic alternative to the mediocre vision at work in the movement. While he opposed Benn's biological-racial interpretation, he remained open to the possibility of conceiving National Socialism as akin to a work of art that founds a new historical world. But for National Socialism to work, it had to conceive of art in a new way.

Heidegger saw that leading Nazi ideologues depicted art as leading the way to "lived experience" *(Erlebnis)* as an alternative to Cartesian intellectualism and mechanism. But instinctual *Erlebnis* would hardly save Germany from Cartesianism, since Descartes himself had invented the idea! (*GA* 45:149). The idea of *Erlebnis* was a metaphysical precursor to naturalism embodied in the doctrine of the "blond beast," which represented everything Heidegger regarded as wrong-headed about the Nazi interpretation of Nietzsche. He proclaimed that neither intellect nor instinct would save modern man. Instead, he had to be awakened to his profound need for what had been withdrawn from him: to wit, being as such. And he asked: "Does this need keep itself away—or is today's man already so hexed by machinization and so swept away by his lived experience that he is no longer awake to the need?" (*GA* 45:183). He sought both to preserve Nietzsche's authentic philosophical insight from its naturalistic overlay, and to show that he could derive from Nietzsche's thought a post-metaphysical conception of art that would be consistent with the "inner truth" of National Socialism. He believed that despite its preparing the way for a transformation of our understanding of art, Nietzsche's aesthetic doctrine—like all doctrines of "aesthetics"—remained within the metaphysical tradition. Because "aesthetics" originated with such thinkers as Kant, it was tied up with metaphysical subjectivism and representationalism, both of which were inimical to Heidegger's conception of *Dasein* as being-in-the-world. Aesthetic theory inquired about the relation between the perceiving subject and the material art object, but for Heidegger what the authentic work of art enabled *Dasein* to apprehend was nothing perceivable with the eyes or ears. Rather, the work of art revealed the *being* of entities. Hence, when I apply the term "aestheticism" to Heidegger's ontology of art, I remind the reader that this term is not used in its ordinary metaphysical sense.

Heidegger's confrontation with Nietzsche's doctrine of art aimed in part to provide an alternative to Jünger's reading of Nietzsche. Following

Nietzsche, both Jünger and Heidegger conceived of modernity in terms of nihilism and degeneracy (*GA* 43:105ff.). Though Nietzsche often spoke of this degeneration in terms of the decline of the instinctual potency of Germans and Europeans, Heidegger conceived of that degeneration in ontological terms. Heidegger concluded that the technological world envisioned by Jünger was the culmination of the nihilistic history of being. Hence, Jünger did not manage to surpass the naturalism at work in the final stages of metaphysics. Heidegger maintained that the essence of nihilism was modern humanity's utter obliviousness to the being of entities. Such obliviousness forced humanity to understand entities one-dimensionally: as standing reserve. The *limitless* character of the technological world revealed its nihilism: that is, its inability to provide the ontological limits necessary for entities to show themselves appropriately. The preeminence of the quantitative and measureless "is the principle of that which we call Americanism; Bolshevism is only a variety of Americanism. The latter is the genuinely dangerous form of the measureless, because it arises in the form of bourgeois democracy and mixed with Christendom, and all of this in an atmosphere of decisive historylessness" (*GA* 53:86–87).

Long after 1934, Heidegger continued to believe that the philosopher should play a leading role in shaping an alternative to Bolshevism and Americanism. Hence, he stated in 1937–38 that philosophers, though immediately useless, were crucial for the success of the revolution: "A historical *Volk* without philosophy is like an eagle without the high expanse of the glowing ether, wherein its soaring [*Schwingen*] attains its purest flight [*Schwung*]" (*GA* 45:2). He believed that overcoming the metaphysical tradition would require "a still more primordial transformation of our whole *Dasein* and knowing. . . . And accordingly we take Nietzsche's interpretation of art above all in the direction of revolution" (*GA* 43:160). For Heidegger, Nietzsche's overman was the artist who establishes the *limits* and *order* necessary to bring the overpowering presencing or being of entities to a stand. Great art is a preserving, a measuring, a shaping [*Gestaltung*] of entities as a whole (*GA* 43:105). This shaping is not to be understood as an achievement of the artist as a personality; instead, the artist is in some sense claimed by entities as the site through which they can achieve the limit necessary for them to manifest themselves. *Gestalt,* Heidegger concluded, meant the limit into which an entity *sets itself* such that it stands in itself. Humanity exists as the historical "clearing" in which this self-limiting disclosure of entities can take place (*GA* 43:138). For Heidegger, then, the overman is the artist who is called on by the overpowering to limit the overpowering. For Jünger, by way of contrast, the overman is the worker summoned by the Will to Power to overpower all entities.

Although supposedly speaking of Nietzsche, Heidegger must have had his own political decision in mind when he talked about the importance of establishing primoridal goals for humanity.

> Goal-grounding is grounding in the sense of the awakening and freeing of those powers which lend to the posited goal the all-surmounting and all-mastering force of bindingness. Thus, only in the sphere opened up and erected through the goal can the historical *Dasein* become primordially developed [*wachsen*]. Finally, and this means incipiently, *to this belongs the growing of the forces which support and enflame and take the risk of preparing the new sphere, of advancing into it, and of structuring what is enfolded within it.* [*GA* 43:194; my emphasis]

In an essay from 1937, Heidegger stated that the basic behavior and moods of a historical people "win their governing *Gestalt* and their beguiling force in great poetry, in the imaging arts, and in the essential thinking (philosophy) of a *Volk*."[65] To serve such a world-historical role, great art could not possibly be mimetic or representational. Instead, great art had to open up a clearing in which entities could manifest themselves and thus "be." As Paul Klee remarked, "Art does not reproduce what is visible; instead, it makes visible."[66] Great art is "creative" in the remarkable sense that it lets entities be: "Art itself is one, indeed the essential, way in which the entity gets made into an entity [*wie das Seiende zum Seienden geschaffen wird*]. And because this creating, limit-bearing, and *Gestalt*-grounding befalls art, the determination of the essence of art can only be achieved when it comes to the question as to what is the creative [dimension] in art" (*GA* 43:161).

Heidegger's interpretation of art borrowed from and yet also countered Jünger's concept of the *Gestalt* of the worker. At the end of "The Question concerning Technology," composed in the late 1940s, Heidegger remarked:

> Because the essence of technology is nothing technological, essential reflection upon technology and decisive confrontation with it must happen in a realm that is, on the one hand, akin to the essence of technology and, on the other hand, essentially different from it.
>
> Such a realm is art. But certainly only if reflection on art, for its part, does not shut its eyes to the constellation of truth after which we are *seeking*.[67]

Before turning to Heidegger's concept of the relation between technology and art, let us consider for a moment the relation between these two in Jünger's thought. Karl Heinz Bohrer, in *Die Aesthetik des Schreckens* (The aesthetic of horror), maintains that Jünger was one of the last representatives of an aesthetic tradition initiated by Edgar Allan Poe.[68] Later European adherents to this tradition believed that contemplation of the horrifying brought insight into the spiritual abyss and drew one nearer to the terrifying eternity of things. Such insight was accompanied by nonordinary temporality, or by the epiphany, which was such an important theme in early twentieth-century literature, especially in Germany's Expressionist poetry, to which Heidegger was attracted. In *Being and Time,* Heidegger himself argued that authenticity is made possible by a radical transformation of temporality, which he called the "moment of truth" *(Augenblick).* This authentic temporality called for a decision that could not itself be supported by existing political, moral, or institutional structures, for the epiphany revealed the relative groundlessness of such structures.

Under the spell of modern aesthetic views, including the aesthetics of horror, Jünger placed aesthetic considerations above moral or political ones. As Bohrer points out, Jünger's symbolic iconography and naive detailism turns reality into a picture that ignores the social, economic, and political realities of the twentieth century. Jünger's "magical realism" hypostatized aesthetic experience as the highest value, since in such experience one could apprehend the horrifying dimension of the eternal Will to Power at work in all things. The danger here, of course, was that he could easily affirm or even conjure up the horrible in order to discover the extent to which he could turn it into an aesthetic object, thereby ignoring the reality of the human suffering involved in such titanic "spectacles" as World War I and the transformation of the Earth into a giant factory.

At times, Heidegger spoke of his own work as an encounter with the horrifying, an encounter that required a "bearing" reminiscent of the aesthetic attitude. In the 1930s he said:

> The basic mood of *the* philosophy, i.e., the *future* philosophy, we call . . . *restraint* [*Verhaltenheit*]. Primordially unified and belonging together in it are: the *horror [Erschrecken] before this closest and most obtrusive [fact], that the entity is; and at the same time the dread [Scheu]* before the furthest, that in the entity and before every entity, being [*Seyn*] presences. Restraint is that mood in which that horror is not overcome and put aside, but instead is preserved and guarded through dread. [*GA* 45:2]

Just as Jünger maintained that insight into the Will to Power was possible only by virtue of a willingness to encounter the horror of everyday reality, so too Heidegger argued that insight into the self-concealing presencing or being of entities was possible only by virtue of a willingness to encounter the horror of the presencing of everyday entities. Heidegger spoke of the "monstrous" character of the fact that entities are. Such an encounter with the being of entities, however, required that human *Dasein* bring to a stand the overpowering "surge" of being. He described the ancient Greeks as the violent ones who ventured to bring some measure and order to the overwhelming power of being. Greek art was one of the principal ways in which the Greeks brought being to a stand. Hence, Greek existence could be described as a primal version of ontological aestheticisim: that is, the doctrine holding that an authentic encounter with entities is made possible only by great works of art that open up a delimited clearing in which entities can display themselves. In the industrial-democratic age, entities had been stripped of meaning; everything had become the same as everything else; rank-ordering and distinction had been lost. Incapable of bringing being to a stand, humanity was on the verge of being completely dehumanized, overwhelmed by the sheer indeterminate presence of entities. Heidegger believed that Jünger gave voice to the essential features of this technological nihilism and that National Socialism provided an alternative to it.

In *Male Fantasies,* Klaus Theweleit has argued that much of the imagery of reactionary German politics during the 1920s consisted of warnings about the tide of communism that threatened to flood and destroy Germany. He quotes W. von Oertzen from 1918: "The wave of Bolshevism surged onward, threatening not only to swallow up the republics of Estonia and Latvia, neither of which had yet awakened to a life of its own, but also to inundate the eastern border of Germany."[69] Theweleit claims that the right-wing German terror of being drowned in the overwhelming red tide was linked to fear of and hostility to the supposedly indeterminate and insatiable female. Yet the image of flooding was also attractive to right-wingers because it promised the destruction of the worn-out bourgeois-liberal world. Jünger's book *The Storm of Steel* expressed both the positive and the negative dimensions of the elementary natural forces at work in the Great War. For reactionary thinkers such as Jünger, the key was not to get rid of the flood but to channel it. Theweleit states that "[our soldiers] want to stand with both feet and every root firmly anchored in the soil. They want whatever floods may come to rebound against them; they want to stop, and dam up, those floods."[70]

Heidegger used a very similar vocabulary in his discussion of the founding involved in bringing forth a work of art. Consider these remarks from 1935 about the struggle to found a world:

> The struggle meant here is the original struggle, for it gives rise to the contenders as such; it is not a mere assault on something already there. It is this conflict that first projects and develops what had

hitherto been unheard of, unsaid, and unthought. The battle is then sustained by the creators, poets, thinkers, statesmen. Against the overwhelming force [*Walten*] they set the barrier of their work and capture in this the world opened up thereby. It is with these works that the elemental power, *physis* [presencing, being] comes to stand. Only now does the entity become entity as such. [*GA* 40:66]

Humanity is capable of apprehending *(vernehmen)* entities *as* entities only because humanity can delimit and thus bring to a stand their overpowering presencing. The *martial* element of this account of human existence is evident in the following passage: "To apprehend in this twofold sense [of both accepting and determining] means to let something come to one, not merely accepting it, however, but taking a receptive attitude toward that which shows itself. *When troops prepare to receive the enemy, it is in the hope of stopping him at the very least, of bringing him to stand* [*zum Stand bringen*]" (*GA* 40:146–47; my emphasis).

Like Jünger, Heidegger believed that the power at work in humanity is nothing human. Jünger conceived of this power as the primal Will to Power, whereas Heidegger conceived of it as the overwhelming presencing of being as such. For Heidegger, being compels humanity to struggle against the overpowering and indeterminate presencing of being as such. Humanity is a crucial ingredient in the very event by which entities can manifest themselves and thus "be" at all. The poet and thinker are the crucial players in this ontological game, for through them speaks the articulating word: "The word, the name, restores the emerging entity from the immediate, overpowering surge to its being and maintains it in this openness, delimitation, and permanence. . . . Pristine speech opens up the being of the entity in the structure of its collectedness" (*GA* 40:180–81).

Clearly, it takes extraordinary courage to be involved in the primordial *polemos* required to delimit the flood or surge of being in such a way that entities can show themselves. Only through such delimiting can a historical world arise. In his Nietzsche lectures Heidegger railed against Wagner's music, despite the fact that it was a favorite of Hitler's. Heidegger considered Wagner's music the epitome of degeneration, because it celebrated boundlessness, limitlessness, and the frenzy most closely associated with sexual desire. Nietzsche was right, according to Heidegger, both in regarding art as the basis of the authentic countermovement to nihilism *and* in finally rejecting Wagner for his failure to understand the need for limit and form in great art. Wagner's love for intoxicating frenzy *(Rausch)* betrayed his lack of understanding of the relation between dream and form, Dionysius and Apollo. Heidegger observed prophetically: "This opposition is no formula with whose help

we should be able to describe 'culture.' Hölderlin and Nietzsche have
with this opposition directed a questioning sign before the task of the
Germans, historically to find their essence. Will we understand this sign?
One thing is certain: History will take revenge upon us, if we do not
understand it'' (*GA* 43:122–23).

Like Nietzsche, Heidegger regarded art as being worth more than
truth, where "truth" is understood not as ontological disclosiveness
(*alētheia*) but as a body of correct propositions. Art opens up new ways
in which entities can manifest themselves; truth amounts to the hardening
of that manifesting into something fixed and determinate and useful to
humanity. Human *Dasein* exists authentically only when it wills to
confront and to delimit the being of entities. During the 1930s Heidegger
concluded that the essence of modern technology is itself nothing technical but instead involves a particular disclosure of the being of entities.
Even the technological disclosure of entities as standing reserve, however, involves a kind of "poetry" of calculating and planning: "Even if
the current and the closest humanity is technicized in the most extreme
way and is framed upon a condition of the planet for which in general the
distinction of 'war and peace' belongs to matters now set aside, even then
man still lives 'poetically' upon this Earth'' (*GA* 52:40).

Modern technology is the final, one-dimensional disclosure of being
that was initiated by the metaphysics of Plato and Aristotle. The essence
of modern technology, then, is nothing technical but instead involves
technē. For Heidegger, *technē* meant the disclosive behavior in which the
Greeks maintained their ontological wonder in the face of the sheer fact
that entities *are*. For the Greeks, *technē* meant knowing one's way about
in advancing against entities so as to let them manifest themselves. The
great art and philosophy of the Greeks were in the service of the
disclosure of the being of entities. They did not conceive of life as a
"business" to be calculated according to security and comfort. Rather,
they lived for a higher goal: to open up a world for entities to show
themselves. The struggle involved was terrifying and required the Greeks
to look into the ultimate groundlessness of things. Heidegger attempted
to dissuade National Socialism from conceiving of itself either in terms of
Jünger's technological tyranny or in terms of Nietzsche's comfort-seeking
"last man." Above all, Heidegger warned against conceiving of man as a
rational animal whose major "interest" is in survival.

> It pertains to the essence of the living to remain compelled and
> forced into its own drive. Certainly "the living," which we know as
> plants and animals, appears to find and contain in its drive its fixed
> form, as opposed to which man can elevate the living and its drive

purposely to the leading measure and can make "progress" into a "principle." If we notice only that which we use, then we are yoked into the compulsion of the unrest of mere life. This living awakens the appearance of moving and self-movement and, thus, of freedom. . . .

Man, however, is only "free," that is, movable, inside the compulsion of his "life interests." In certain respects, he is unbound in the sphere of compulsion, which is determined by the fact that everything depends on use. Slavery under the domination of the constantly "useful" . . . appears as freedom and dominance of the usufruct and its increasing. [*GA* 52:405]

In lectures from 1929–30, well before his engagement with National Socialism and his confrontation with modern technology, Heidegger concluded that life had lost its mystery, that modern humanity was subject to profound boredom, because things had lost their "weight" (*GA* 29/30). In 1933, he concluded that the rise of Hitler coincided with the possibility for things to regain their distinctiveness, to show themselves in ways that could not be reduced to commercial, scientific, or technological calculation and use. Only by surrendering to the disclosive power at work in an artist of Hölderlin's magnitude, Heidegger believed, could German *Geist* found a world that would be completely in thrall neither to the technological understanding of the being of entities nor to the animalistic craving for "experience." He urged the German *Volk* to renew the *Geist* at work in the ancient Greeks, and thus to conceive of life not in terms of usefulness but in terms of glory, play, creation, risk—and art. Jünger's conception of the worker included important elements of this artistic conception of life, but Jünger remained mired within metaphysical thinking. Hence, he could not see that the technological era was *not* a new beginning but instead the final stage of the history of metaphysics. Yet in speaking of early Greek existence, Heidegger sounded very much like Jünger and his friends who called on Germans to "live dangerously!"

The strangest [man] is what it is because, fundamentally, it cultivates and guards the familiar, only in order to break out of it and to let what overpowers break in. Being itself hurls man into this breaking-way, which drives him beyond himself to venture forth toward being, to accomplish being, to stabilize it in the work, and so hold open the entity as a whole. Therefore, the violent one knows no kindness and conciliation (in the usual sense); he cannot be mollified or appeased by success or prestige. . . . In willing the unprecedented, he casts aside all help. To him disaster is the deepest and broadest affirmation of the overpowering. [*GA* 40:72]

Is it possible that after 1945 Heidegger remained silent about the Holocaust because he regarded it as one of the terrible consequences that are often involved in the attempt to achieve something great? In condemning the Holocaust, he would have had to condemn National Socialism, including his own version of it. So far as I can tell, however, he never completely renounced the principles underlying his conception of National Socialism, which he defined as the dangerous but courageous openness to a new encounter with the being of entities. Some contemporary writers claim that Heidegger's notion of deconstructing the hardened tradition can be interpreted to mean the process of undermining the first principles or "master names" that are used to justify various forms of social domination and exploitation. Heidegger's own case, however, makes clear that the ambiguities inherent in such de-construction are very great indeed.

Despite the differences I have mentioned, Heidegger shared many of Jünger's views about the present age. Both men witnessed the extraordinary onslaught of modern technology; both were alternately fascinated and repelled by it. It may be argued that both were terrified by the prospect of the loss of measure, limit, and order, terrified by the prospect of being lost in the overwhelming flood. Jünger dealt with this terror by interpreting the flood as the latest manifestation of the Will to Power. He conquered the flood only by going with it but doing so in such a way as to channel it into the world-historical project of turning the earth into technological clockwork. Heidegger dealt with this terror by interpreting the flood as the ontological surge that he and his generation were called on to bring to a stand in order to *avoid* the technological world willed by Jünger. In the face of the "horror" of entities that no longer meant anything, both men counseled against flinching. Both believed that a man's greatness was measured by his capacity for living in *Angst,* for looking directly at what led other men to cling to the leveling values of commercialism, socialism, and positivism.

Jünger's writings on war and technology were designed specifically to evoke certain aesthetic responses in their audience. Indeed, his entire encounter with modern technology seems to have been refracted through aesthetic categories that lead us to conclude that his "observations" on technology were less phenomenological description than artistic construction. Bohrer has argued that Jünger's early writings were an instance of the literary genre of dystopia or negative utopia, akin to Huxley's *Brave New World.*

One is best convinced of the utopian character [of Jünger's work] if one recognizes its analogies to contemporary fantastic space utopia and science fiction: in Kubin's novel *The Other Side,* as also in modern technological science fiction, the superterrestrial hero is characterized by the traits of being masked, lacking in feeling, and claiming immortality, properties that make him superior to the ordinary earth dweller. Thus Jünger also distinguished as unique the *"Gestalt"* of the *Typus* from the "abstract masses."[71]

Heidegger himself concluded that Jünger understood something essential about modern technology. Those of us who contemplate Heidegger's thought in the light of his political support for a disastrous and evil political movement, however, and in the light of the proximity of his thought to a reactionary world view, may well ask whether Heidegger or Jünger really understood anything about modern technology. Can modern technology really be explained either as the latest manifestation of the eternal Will to Power or as the last gasp of the history of being? Can the economic, political, cultural, and ideological factors in history be explained as merely secondary factors that are shaped by a hidden metaphysical movement, whether it be the Will to Power or the self-concealing history of being? Is there a link between the tendency of German idealists to explain human history in terms of suprahuman forces and the German political experience in the twentieth century?

Jeffrey Herf has replied affirmatively to this last question. He argues that many Germans, including Jünger and Heidegger, rejected the political values and institutions that arose from the Enlightenment, which they regarded negatively as the triumph of a calculating rationality whose sole aim was domination and whose outcome was the destruction of European *Geist.* By failing to take seriously the possibility of an authentically liberative political dimension of the Enlightenment, many Germans—including Heidegger—scorned democratic politics as an alien system imposed by countries that had already fallen prey to technological nihilism and to rule by the masses. Lacking faith in the imperfect processes of political democracy, all too many Germans longed for the spiritual regeneration that would allegedly come to pass only by surrender to a higher destiny.[72]

Heidegger's conception of modern technology is related in a complex way to his sophisticated yet reactionary view of history and politics. Because of this fact, our reading of his interpretation of the essence of modern technology must be informed politically. Despite his reactionary attitudes and his political activities, Heidegger was a philosophical genius. His analysis of modern technology has wide appeal precisely because many people share his sense of despair regarding the ways in which modernity has transformed—and often destroyed—society, culture, and the natural environment. Apart from his explicitly political statements,

Heidegger's writings cannot be reduced to the status of mere ideological apologetics.[73] His reflections on the history of Western thought from Plato to Nietzsche repay study. Because of what we now know, we must study his writings without the hero worship characteristic of much of the scholarly work done about Heidegger's thought.[74] Nevertheless, we must also resist the temptation to move in the opposite direction and to vilify his thought indiscriminately. We must, instead, learn to read Heidegger critically but also with appreciation for what remains valid in his thinking.

NOTES

1. Passages from Heidegger's *Gesamtausgabe*, published in Frankfurt by Vittorio Klostermann, are cited in the text as *GA,* with volume and page numbers (e.g., 61:115). I cite the following volumes:

Vol. 29/30: *Die Grundbegriffe der Metaphysik,* ed. Friedrich-Wilhelm von Herrmann, winter semester 1929–30 (1983).

Vol. 40: *Einführung in die Metaphysik,* ed. Petra Jaeger, summer semester 1935 (1983).

Vol. 43: *Nietzsche: Der Wille zur Macht als Kunst,* ed. Bernd Heimbüchel, winter semester 1936–37 (1985).

Vol. 45: *Grundfragen der Philosophie,* ed. Friedrich-Wilhelm von Herrmann, winter semester 1937–38 (1984).

Vol. 51: *Grundbegriffe,* ed. Petra Jaeger, summer semester 1941 (1981).

Vol. 52: *Hölderlins Hymne "Andenken,"* ed. Curd Ochwadt, winter semester 1941–42 (1982).

Vol. 53: *Hölderlins Hymne "Der Ister,"* ed. Walter Biemel, summer semester, 1942 (1984).

Vol. 54: *Parmenides,* ed. Manfred S. Frings, winter semester 1942–43 (1982).

Vol. 56/57: *Zur Bestimmung der Philosophie,* ed. Bernd Heimbüchel, war emergency semester and summer semester 1919 (1987).

Vol. 61: *Phänomenologische Interpretation zu Aristoteles: Einführung in die phänomenologische Forschung,* ed. Walter Bröcker and Käte Bröcker-Oltmanns, winter semester, 1921–21 (1985).

Vol. 63: *Ontologie: Hermeneutik der Faktizität,* ed. Käte Bröcker-Oltmanns, summer semester 1923 (1988).

2. Martin Heidegger, *The Question of Being,* trans. Jean T. Wilde and William Kluback, with the original German "Zur Seinsfrage" on facing pages (New Haven, Conn.: College & University Press, 1958).

3. Ibid., p. 45.

4. Ibid.

5. Victor Farías, *Heidegger et le nazisme* (Paris: Verdier, 1987); Hugo Ott, *Martin Heidegger: Unterwegs zu seiner Biographie* (Frankfurt: Campus Verlag, 1988). I have reviewed Farías's book in the *Times Literary Supplement,* October 7–13, 1988, pp. 1115–17, and Ott's book in *Times Literary Supplement,* May 5–

11, 1989, p. 481. I have dealt extensively with the issue of Heidegger and National Socialism in *Heidegger's Confrontation with Modernity: Technology, Politics, and Art* (Bloomington: Indiana University Press, 1990). See also my essays "The Thorn in Heidegger's Side: The Question of National Socialism," *Philosophical Forum* 20 (Summer 1989); and "Philosophy and Politics: The Case of Heidegger," *Philosophy Today* 33 (Summer 1989).

The literature on the Heidegger-Nazism issue is now very extensive. A sampling includes Richard Wolin, "Recherches récentes sur la relation de Martin Heidegger au National Socialisme," *Les Temps Modernes* 42 (October 1987): 56–85; Richard Wolin, "The French Heidegger Debate," *New German Critique*, no. 45 (Fall 1988): 135–61; Annemarie Gethmann-Siefert and Otto Pöggeler, *Heidegger und die praktische Philosophie* (Frankfurt: Suhrkamp, 1988); Thomas J. Sheehan, "Heidegger and the Nazis," *New York Review of Books*, June 16, 1988, pp. 38–47.

6. Heidegger's version of the official story is found in "Nur noch ein Gott kann uns retten: *Spiegel-Gespräch* with Martin Heidegger, September 23, 1966,"*Der Spiegel*, no. 26 (May 31, 1976); trans. Maria P. Alter and John D. Caputo, "Only a God Can Save Us: *Der Spiegel*'s interview with Martin Heidegger," *Philosophy Today* 20 (Winter 1976): 267–84. Also cf. Martin Heidegger, *Das Rektorat 1933/34: Tatsachen und Gedanken,* published along with *Die Selbstbehauptung der deutschen Universität,* ed. Hermann Heidegger (Frankfurt: Klostermann, 1983); trans. Karsten Harries, "The Rectorate 1933/34: Facts and Thoughts" and "The Self-Assertion of the German University," *Review of Metaphysics* 38, no. 3 (1985): 467–502.

7. Karl Löwith, *Mein Leben in Deutschland vor und nach 1933* (Stuttgart: J. B. Metzler, 1986), pp. 57–58.

8. Heidegger, "Nur noch ein Gott kann uns retten," p. 206; "Only a God Can Save Us," p. 276.

9. See the essay on Heidegger in Jürgen Habermas, *The Philosophical Discourse of Modernity,* trans. Frederick G. Lawrence (Cambridge, Mass.: MIT Press, 1987); Habermas's introduction to the German edition of Farías's book, "Work and Weltanschauung: The Heidegger Controversy from a Heidegger Perspective," trans. John McCumber, *Critical Inquiry,* 15 (Winter 1989): 431–56; Habermas, "Martin Heidegger: On the Publication of Lectures from the Year 1935" (1953), trans. Dale Ponikvar, *Graduate Faculty Philosophy Journal* 6 (Fall 1977): 155–73; and *Autonomy and Solidarity: Interviews with Jürgen Habermas,* ed. Peter Dews (London: Verso, 1986).

10. Jacques Derrida, *De l'esprit: Heidegger et la question* (Paris: Galilée, 1987); Derrida, "Heidegger, l'enfer des philosophes: Un entretien avec Jacques Derrida," *Le Nouvel Observateur,* November 6–12, 1987.

11. In 1928, Marcuse wrote that *Sein und Zeit* provides the ontological foundation for Marx's theory of history. See Marcuse, "Beiträge zu einer Phänomenologie des historischen Marterialismus," *Philosophische Hefte* 1 (1928): 45–68. After fleeing from the Nazi regime supported by Heidegger, however, Marcuse became highly critical of his mentor's behavior: see his letters to Heidegger (August 28, 1947, and May 13, 1948) published in *Les Temps Modernes* 44

(January 1989): 1–4. Nevertheless, Marcuse distingushed between Heidegger's political nonsense on the one hand, and his authentic philosophical contributions on the other; see Marcuse's letter to *Der Spiegel*, no. 11 (March 7, 1966): 10–11.

12. Derrida, *De l'esprit*.

13. References to the "transformation" of German *Dasein* are found in several of Heidegger's Nazi addresses collected by Guido Schneeberger in *Nachlese zu Heidegger: Dokumente zu seinem Leben und Denken* (Bern, 1962), pp. 135–50. These essays have been translated by William S. Lewis in *New German Critique*, no. 45 (Fall 1988): 96–114.

14. Heidegger spoke of "blood and earth" in "The Self-Assertion of the German University," pp. 474–75; *Die Selbstbehauptung der deutschen Universität*, p. 14.

15. Martin Heidegger, *Nietzsche* (Pfullingen: Neske, 1961), 2:309, cited in Derrida, *De l'esprit*, p. 118.

16. Derrida, *De l'esprit*, p. 119.

17. From Heidegger's unpublished essay "Das Gestell," cited in Wolfgang Schirmacher, *Technik und Gelassenheit: Zeitkritik nach Heidegger* (Freiburg: Verlag Karl Alber, 1983), p. 25.

18. Heidegger, *Das Rektorat 1933/34*, pp. 24–25; "The Rectorate 1933/34," pp. 484–85.

19. Many of Heidegger's political pronouncements, including his rather striking claim that the United States and the Soviet Union were "metaphysically" the same, were by no means original; they were quite consistent with the Nazi propaganda of the day. On this and related topics, see Otto Pöggeler, "Den Führer führen? Heidegger und kein Ende," *Philosophische Rundschau* 32, no. 2 (1985): 26–67.

20. Christian Lewalter, "Wie liest man 1953 Sätze von 1935? Zu einem politischen Streit um Heideggers Metaphysik," *Die Zeit*, no. 33 (August 13, 1953): 6.

21. Heidegger's letter of support from Lewalter is found in *Die Zeit*, no. 39 (September 24, 1953): 18. Regarding the apparent fact that in 1953 Heidegger inserted material into what he had originally written in 1935, see Petra Jaeger's Afterword to her edition of *Einführung in die Metaphysik (GA* 40). No final determination on the matter can be made, because the page in question is missing from Heidegger's manuscript in the archives at Marbach.

22. Ernst Jünger, *The Storm of Steel (In Stahlgewittern)*, trans. Basil Creighton (London: Chatto & Windus, 1929).

23. See, e.g., Hans-Peter Schwarz, *Der konservative Anarchist: Politik und Zeitkritik Ernst Jüngers* (Freiburg: Verlag Rombach, 1962); John Norr, "German Social Theory and the Hidden Face of the Machine," *European Journal of Sociology* 15 (1974): 312–36.

24. Ernst Jünger, "Die Totale Mobilmachung" (1930), in *Werke,* vol. 5, *Essays I* (Stuttgart: Ernst Klett Verlag, 1960).

25. Ibid., p. 132.

26. Marinetti, quoted in Walter Benjamin, "The Work of Art in the Age of Mechanical Reproduction," in *Illuminations*, trans. Harry Zohn (London: Fon-

tana/Collins, 1973), pp. 243–44. An insightful commentary on futurism and politics is Marjorie Perloff, *The Futurist Movement* (Chicago: University of Chicago Press, 1986).

27. Benjamin, "The Work of Art in the Age of Mechanical Reproduction," p. 244. An excellent treatment of the relation between fascism and aestheticism is George L. Mosse, *Masses and Man: Nationalist and Fascist Perceptions of Reality* (New York: Howard Fertig, 1980), esp. chap. 12, "Fascism and the Avant-Garde."

28. George L. Mosse, *Germans and Jews: The Right, the Left, and the Search for a "Third Force" in Pre-Nazi Germany* (New York: Howard Fertig, 1970), p. 150.

29. Ibid., p. 163.

30. A helpful survey and analysis of National Bolshevism is Louis Dupeux, *Stratégie communiste et dynamique conservatrice: Essai sur les différents sens de l'expression "National-Bolschevisme" en Allemagne, sous la République de Weimar (1919–1933)*. (1974; Paris: Librairie Honoré Champion, 1976).

31. Jeffrey Herf, *Reactionary Modernism: Technology, Culture, and Politics in Weimar* (New York: Cambridge University Press, 1984), provides important insight into the context in which Heidegger developed his ideas about technology.

32. Ernst Jünger, *Der Kampf als inneres Erlebnis* (1922), in *Werke*, vol. 5, *Essays I*, p. 57.

33. Ernst Jünger, *Der Arbeiter: Herrschaft und Gestalt* (1932), in *Werke*, vol. 6, *Essays II* (Stuttgart: Ernst Klett Verlag, 1960), pp. 323, 39.

34. Ibid., p. 92.

35. Ibid., p. 137.

36. Ibid., pp. 77–81.

37. Ibid., p. 165. A significant portion (sec. 44–57) of *Der Arbeiter*, trans. James M. Vincent and Richard J. Rundell, are in Carl Mitcham and Robert Mackey, *Philosophy and Technology* (New York: Free Press, 1972); see p. 269 for the passage quoted here.

38. Jünger, *Der Arbeiter*, p. 145.

39. Ibid., pp. 187–88.

40. Friedrich Nietzsche, *The Birth of Tragedy*, trans. Walter Kaufmann, in *Basic Writings of Nietzsche* (New York: Modern Library, 1968), p. 60.

41. Helmut Kaiser, *Mythos, Rausch, und Reaktion: Der Weg Gottfried Benns und Ernst Jüngers* (Berlin: Aufbau-Verlag, 1962), p. 105.

42. Herf, *Reactionary Modernism*, discusses this dispute in some detail.

43. From *Freiburger Zeitung*, November 27, 1933; cited in Schneeberger, *Nachlese zu Heidegger*, pp. 156–57. Though this is a journalist's report of Heidegger's statement, there is no reason to believe that it does not accurately represent what Heidegger said, since it is quite consistent with remarks in his printed speeches.

44. Martin Heidegger, "Die Zeit des Weltbildes," in *Holzwege* (Frankfurt: Klostermann, 1972); trans. William Lovitt, "The Age of the World Picture," in *The Question concerning Technology* (New York: Harper & Row, 1977).

45. For an insightful treatment of the question of "nature" in Heidegger's thought, see Michel Haar, *Le Chant de la terre* (Paris: Editions de l'Herne, 1987).

46. Martin Heidegger, "Die Frage nach der Technik," *Vorträge und Aufsätze* (Tübingen: Neske, 1967), 1:14; trans. William Lovitt, "The Question concerning Technology," in *The Question concerning Technology*, pp. 14–15.

47. Ibid., pp. 17–18; p. 18.

48. Jünger, *Der Arbeiter*, p. 176; trans. in Mitcham and Mackey, *Philosophy and Technology*, p. 274.

49. Ernst Jünger, "*Über den Schmerz*" (1934), in *Werke*, vol. 5, *Essays I*, p. 196.

50. Martin Heidegger, "Überwindung der Metaphysik," in *Vorträge und Aufsätze*, 1:89; trans. Joan Stambaugh, "Overcoming Metaphysics," in *The End of Philosophy* (New York: Harper & Row, 1973), p. 108.

51. Ibid., p. 91; p. 110.

52. Ibid., p. 70; p. 91.

53. Parvis Emad, "Heidegger on Pain: Focusing on a Recurring Theme in His Thought," *Zeitschrift für Philosophische Forschung* 36 (July–September, 1982): 354–55.

54. Heidegger, "Überwindung der Metaphysik," p. 87; "Overcoming Metaphysics," p. 106.

55. Ibid., p. 84–85; pp. 104–5.

56. Ernst Jünger, *Das abenteuerliche Herz*, in *Werke*, vol. 7, *Essays III* (Stuttgart: Ernst Klett Verlag, 1960).

57. Nietzsche, *The Birth of Tragedy*, p. 52.

58. Philippe Lacoue-Labarthe, *La fiction du politique* (Paris: Christian Bourgois, 1987).

59. Quoted in Henry Grosshans, *Hitler and the Artists* (New York: Holmes & Meier, 1983), p. 27.

60. This letter to Wilhelm Furtwängler appeared in the *Lokal-Anzeiger*, April 11, 1933; cited in Lacoue-Labarthe, *La fiction du politique*.

61. Albert Speer, *Inside the Third Reich*, trans. Richard Winston and Clara Winston (New York: Macmillan, 1970). On some other aesthetic elements in National Socialism, see Anson G. Rabinbach, "The Aesthetics of Production in the Third Reich," in George L. Mosse, *International Fascism* (London: SAGE, 1979).

62. Hans Jürgen Syberberg, *Die freudlose Gesellschaft* (Munich: Carl Hanser Verlag, 1981), pp. 74–76. I owe this reference to Lacoue-Labarthe.

63. Gottfried Benn, "The Confession of an Expressionist," in Victor M. Miesel, ed., *Voices of German Expressionism* (Englewood Cliffs, N.J.: Prentice-Hall, 1970), p. 192. Else Buddeberg, in *Gottfried Benn* (Stuttgart: J. B. Metzlersche Verlagsbuchhandlung, 1961), offers an excellent treatment of the relation between Benn's artistic views and his affiliation with National Socialism. The parallels with Heidegger's case, although not explored by Buddeberg, are remarkable.

64. On the Nazi attitude toward "degenerate art," see Franz Roh, "Entar-

tete," in *Kunst: Kunstbarbarei im Dritten Reich* (Hannover: Fackeltrager-Verlag, n.d.).

65. Martin Heidegger, "Wege zur Aussprache," in Schneeberger, *Nachlese zu Heidegger,* p. 259.

66. Paul Klee, "Creative Credo," in Miesel, *Voices of German Expressionism,* p. 83.

67. Heidedgger, "Die Frage Nach der Technik," p. 35; "The Question concerning Technology," p. 35.

68. Heinz Bohrer, *Die Aesthetik des Schreckens: Die pessimistische Romantik und Ernst Jüngers Frühwerk* (Munich: Carl Hanser Verlag, 1978). This remarkable book is worthy of careful study.

69. Klaus Theweleit, *Male Fantasies*, vol. 1, *Women, Floods, Bodies, History,* trans. Stephen Conway (Minneapolis: University of Minnesota Press, 1987), p. 229.

70. Ibid., p. 230. On p. 229, Theweleit quotes an interesting passage from Bertold Brecht: "The raging stream is called violent / but the riverbed that hems it in / No one calls violent."

71. Bohrer, *Die Aesthetik des Schreckens*, p. 476.

72. Herf, *Reactionary Modernism*.

73. On this topic, see Pierre Bourdieu, *L'ontologie politique de Martin Heidegger* (1975; Paris: Minuit, 1988).

74. Cf. Sheehan, "Heidegger and the Nazis," p. 47.

II

3

Biographical Bases for Heidegger's "Mentality of Disunity"

HUGO OTT

In a preparation for a biography of Heidegger by Heinrich Petzet, published in 1983 under the somewhat pregnant title *Auf einem Stern Zugehen* (Follow a single star), the most important elements are drawn from Heidegger's selected letters and, especially, from "protocol-like" recollections. The work was quasi-authorized by the philosopher's family members and circle of friends and has, of course, no supporting framework.[1]

We read with particular interest how Heidegger describes the difficult period of his life immediately after World War II in a direct conversation in 1947:

> Back then, in December 1945, when I was brought before the faculty in the inquisition's cross-examination to answer the *twenty-three questions** and I broke down completely, Dean Beringer of the Medical School (who had seen through the whole charade and the intentions of the accusers) came to me and simply took me away to Gebsattel at Badenweiler. And what did he do then? He went up with me through the snow-covered winter forest climbing up the Blauen.

* Germans were required to answer the twenty-three questions in the *Fragebogen* concerning connections to the National Socialist Party and other Nazi activities. —Transl.

Opening address at the international Symposium "Martin Heidegger—Fascination and Terror: The Political Dimension of a Philosophy" (Marburg Debate, Hessian Radio in the City of Marburg, October 7–8, 1989). The address was broadcast as the second program of the Hessian Radio in October 1989. For publication, that version has been expanded, and notes have been added.

He did nothing other than that. But he helped me as a human being. And three weeks later I returned a healthy man.

But: What is a man? What is a human being? Is he, as an individual, the subject of psychosomatic life and, as a person, the subject of the intellectual life?[2]

No matter how the anthropologist answers such questions, every human, even the man who commands the greatest powers of thought, still remains a man—a real man; he lives a real life, and cannot be transported into inaccessibility, not even postmodern man. He must remain accessible. He possesses an intellect, a disposition, a particular manner of thinking and feeling that is generally referred to as a mentality. Let us return now to the text cited at the beginning of my remarks.

For the historian who works from biography, a presentation of existentially central events that has been formulated in such a precise manner must certainly catch his attention. Everything has pretty much been assembled in a succinct form for him: names, dates, institutions, motives, and the circumstances that led to Heidegger's mental breakdown are explained and reliably organized. The health-related physical breakdown under stress, which was the immediate consequence of the postwar period, brings to mind an earlier phase of Heidegger's biography: it reminds us of the interruption of his university studies during his third semester, in 1911, as a result of medical symptoms. At that time, a nervous heart condition with asthmatic symptoms resulting from extreme overwork had become so severe that the theology student and aspirant for the priesthood was barred from continuing his major. Heidegger was prevented by Church authorities from pursuing his studies further; as a consequence, he found himself in a serious psychological crisis from which there was no escape. He overcame it only after long months of recuperation and at the cost of psychic trauma, for others had judged him and had dismissed him from what he had clearly chosen as his course of action. Now, in 1945–46, the world-famous philosopher once again found himself dragged before a disapproving and hostile tribunal and saw himself defamed in the eyes of the world. Once again, others sat in judgment over him and turned him from his chosen course of action.

Yet this view of the circumstances turns out to be incorrect in almost every detail, particularly regarding the assignment of guilt. The faculty of the University of Freiburg, for example, was not in the least interested in Heidegger's case. On the contrary, during the months in which it had been under investigation before the inner-university *Säuberungsausschuss*,* faculty colleagues actively engaged in exerting their influence in

---

* This was the university committee set up to deal with the problems of faculty involvement in the Nazi Party. —Transl.

a positive, well-intentioned direction and in averting the worst, which would have been the loss of his *venia legendi:* that is, actual expulsion from the university.[3] What remains for us, then, is the fact that his psychological breakdown placed Heidegger in a position of extreme vulnerability, placed him even at death's door.[4] The fact is that the medical care came from Professor Beringer himself, who was then the director of the University Psychiatric Clinic: Heidegger was placed in the sanatorium Schloss Hausbaden, near Badenweiler, under the auspices of the German Caritasverband, which itself was under the direction of Victor Freiherr von Gebsattel. The therapy he practiced was much indebted to the *Dasein*-analytical tendency of Ludwig Binswanger. Or, to be even more precise, in the acute phase of his illness the patient Heidegger received his medical care from Beringer, whose orientation followed the neurosomatic approach. It was Beringer who instituted the subsequent protracted course of treatment by the anthropologically trained psychiatrist von Gebsattel. Martin Heidegger was in need of very intensive medical care, which did not last just three weeks and did not consist merely of hiking and brisk marches through the wintry Black Forest—or in climbing the Blauen, a mountain we find mentioned in the poems of Peter Hebel, for example, in "Transitoriness."

> The Belch stands all charred,
> The Blauen, too, as if they were two aged towers,
> And in between, everything is charred
> Deep into the earth.[5]

Heidegger's sojourn in Badenweiler lasted from February to the end of May 1946. After that time, the psychotherapeutic treatment continued with Gebsattel.

Let us review the facts with the help of yet another report: "The philosopher Martin Heidegger was an early student of mine and a fellow countryman. He has been given emeritus status from the university and is no longer permitted to hold lectures. He is staying at the Hausbaden in Badenweiler and has withdrawn completely from social contacts, as I learned yesterday from Professor Gebsattel. It was a great consolation for me that he came to me at the beginning of his misfortune and showed himself to be genuinely concerned for his betterment. I told him the truth, and he accepted it with tears in his eyes. I will not break off my relations with him, because I hope for a drastic change in spiritual direction for him."[6] This is what Heidegger's fatherly friend, Archbishop Conrad Gröber, wrote on March 8, 1946, in a comprehensive report to Father Leiber, a Jesuit priest in Rome. Leiber was adviser on German political affairs to Pope Pius XII; the report was intended for the hands of the Pope.

The highly gifted young Heidegger had remained sheltered, under

Gröber's wing, from his early youth onward for as long as he chose.[7] Gröber took him into his care when, in the declining days of 1945, after having strayed for decades, the professor, who now found himself in extreme jeopardy, came knocking at his door. Previously, Heidegger thought he had found understanding in the Catholic circles of Freiburg when, writing to his one-time disciple, the historian Rudolf Stadelmann in Tübingen, he said: "In the meantime I have had some second thoughts and, in the circles of the theological faculty and the Archbishop, I have come to understand that there is something entirely different behind all the apparent nihilism since even that sage Meister Eckhart had spoken of the nothingness of the Godhead."[8] Gröber was involved in efforts—entirely unsuccessful—to secure, from the French military occupation forces in Baden-Baden, through the intermediary of the military chaplain, Heidegger's continued tenure at the university. Later, when Heidegger's private library was about to be confiscated in order to begin restocking the library at the University of Mainz, Gröber's intervention finally met with success. The protector of the German Caritasverband, which at this time (after the lost war) was seen as the model of episcopal resistance,[9] worked together with von Gebsattel to see to it that after his breakdown Heidegger was adequately housed in the sanitorium of the Caritasverband.[10] Gröber, as the resident Archbishop, also functioned as Protector of the Caritasverband. Of course, they were taking care of a Heidegger who had withdrawn into himself, a man from whom there was still hope for a drastic change in spiritual direction, who had received a *correctio fraterna* from his fellow countryman and Archbishop, the penitent sinner who "showed himself to be genuinely concerned for his betterment." This is also what the fatherly friend writes; this is the way Heidegger characterized his own relationship with Gröber. It is the biblical image of the prodigal son and of the all-forgiving father for whom it is consolation enough if only the son returns, if only the long straying ends and the wanderer seeks the warmth of the bosom of the church (that is the important factor here); the image of the shepherd, the *pastor bonus,* who seeks the lost sheep until he is found and brings him back into the fold, back under his protection—that is, Gröber, now the influential leader and guardian, who even before this, as spiritual shepherd, had been so decisive for Heidegger's thought in understanding the Twenty-third Psalm. In 1907 he had handed Heidegger Brentano's dissertation "Von der mannigfachen Bedeutung des Seienden nach Aristoteles" and had thus given him with this the "rod and staff" for his first "awkward attempts at penetrating philosophy." *Virga tua et baculus tuus: haec me consolantur* (Thy rod and thy staff they comfort me). We should bear in mind the Twenty-third Psalm in discussing Heidegger—*Dominus pascit me: nihil mihi deest; in pascuis virentibus cubare me facit* (The Lord is my shepherd; I shall not want. He maketh me to lie down in green pastures)—because whatever is permanent *is* essential for him, even if such a consideration is not current in traditional Heidegger interpretations and, indeed, actually runs counter to them.[11] These interpretations will have to be revised once the actual connections to the theological sources are adequately confirmed. For Archbishop Gröber, the fatherly friend, the fellow countryman from Messkirch, the influence of the divine spirit was apparent. Heidegger's profound fall—the great Catholic opportunity! Indeed, even the Vatican would hear of this moving contrition, this overwhelming catharsis! Gröber knew Heidegger's deep-seated hatred for the papacy, whose rule was based on commands. In his opinion, this rule through command lay in the very nature of the Church. The Spanish Inquisition was a form of the empire of the Roman curia.[12] In fact, the realm of the nature of *aletheia* had been "ruined by the gigantic bulwark of a certain truth determined in a complex sense by Rome." In the future this would be different. Doesn't this echo the attitude of the former rector of the Konradihaus in Constance? This is the man who watched over his fellow countryman from Messkirch as he prepared for the priesthood, and who led him into the path of thinking, even though it was, certainly, strictly bound to Catholicism. Doesn't this sound like the sort of thing that was taken for granted in the Catholic confessional and penitential practice, a practice beginning in early childhood and repeated over a period of many years? The constant interplay between confession and penitence, the remission of sins by the priest, the making of good resolutions shattered by the sinful nature of man?

In any event, the profound discrepancy we find between the two evaluations—that is, Heidegger's own personal description and Gröber's effusive evaluation—must be obvious.

In Heidegger's description there is the pathological persecution syndrome in which the innocent victim is dragged before the inquisition to stand fully unprepared before accusers who have malicious intentions against him and who have staged the "whole charade," who want to extort a confession from an unjustly accused victim, who demand the disavowal of heresy just as the medieval Inquisition had once done. What a picture! Or, to give this a *Dasein*-analytical formulation: Heidegger answers with a complete breakdown; the physician-Samaritan rescues the victim who has fallen among thieves and provides for his care and recovery. After a short time, Heidegger returns "cured," at peace with himself, immune to further hostility which, though it may cause him pain, can no longer expose him to the same extreme suffering and danger. Heinrich Wiegand Petzet, from whose book the introductory quotation is taken, reports a significant event: on that day in November 1947 Heidegger gave him, as a going-away present, a translation of the great Chorus song from *Antigone:* "resourceful in all (resourceless he goes to meet nothing that is to come). From death alone he will procure no refuge; but he has devised escapes from baffling illnesses."*

By way of providing, in one or two short sentences, some sense of the meaning of *Dasein*-analysis—this method of scientific research and contemporary practical application in psychiatry and psychotherapy—let me offer an explanation: in this method, psychiatry is viewed as the encounter between physician and patient, in the sense of an encounter between individual and individual.[13] This explains Heidegger's description of the physician's personal care in the hike through the snow-covered forest: "But he helped me as a human being."

In Gröber's description we hear of the spiritual leader of the Catholic Church, the only true Church and the protector of truth, who has brought home the lost sheep: "I told him the truth, and he accepted it with tears in his eyes." But: What is truth? Certainly, the Archbishop did not mean the concept of truth that Heidegger had extracted from Greek *aletheia*— if he was even familiar with such a line of thought; probably not, but more likely truth in the sense of *veritas*—and then, it was a matter of opening Heidegger's eyes to the meaninglessness of his straying from the fold and of showing him the way back to the hoard of truth: that is, to the faith in the future, to the Christian credo, to the fundamental Catholic principle *a deo revelata vera esse credimus* (we believe that what is revealed through God is true); to call Heidegger's attention once again to the treasure trove of Thomistic theology that he had abandoned many years earlier—though in all probability frivolously and, in the eyes of his fatherly friend, with too little reflection.

But Heidegger did not seem to be in need of such helpful instruction. He seemed to have found, long before, the support he wanted by seeking refuge with Hölderlin, whose poetry had more than ever before become essential to him in this time of political catastrophe. His stay at the sanatorium had finally provided him the "experience of the supportable." "Support," however, is equated by Heidegger with Old High German *hut:* "Truth of Being gives 'support' for all behavior." Anyone who follows Heidegger's thinking knows that it is essential for him that "man finds the way to his abode in truth." For man is supported and bound only through such a construction—in time-space alone[14]—where, of course, he can only be grasped as Being-historically.

But what of the time of political decline? A nontime, an untime for Heidegger, for the one who thinks Being-historically. And what of space, determined by the unfathomable? Not a space in which Being can make

* *Sophocles: Antigone*, trans. Andrew Brown (Warminster, Wiltshire: Aris & Phillips, Teddington House, 1987). —Eds.

itself known by revealing itself. People had not understood what Heidegger had been up to even at the time of his inaugural lecture at the University of Freiburg, which was titled "What Is Metaphysics?" (1929): that is, nothingness was to be imagined by Being.[15] And thus in letters to his few intimates, to a few knowledgeable friends, he described the solid foundation in the contemporary bottomless abyss: "Now everyone is thinking of Germany's fall. We Germans cannot perish yet, because we haven't yet reached our full maturity, because we have first to pass through the darkness of night" (to Rudolf Stadelmann on July 20, 1945).[16] When he wrote these lines, he had already received the summons to appear before the university *Säuberungsausschuss* for a hearing. At that time he knew the serious points of the allegations against him. But, of course, his accusers were not the knowledgeable few. They were merely the calculating, the miscalculating, historians who never felt the breath of Being-history, who would never know the primitive force of Being *(des Seins)*. And thus Heidegger kept himself in the security of Being-history. The fate of the Germans, indeed the fate of mankind, in this darkest hour of the world was the concern of the few who knew that which is enduring and permanent, who could even rest within their own self-importance. Thus Heidegger writes in May 1947 to one of his disciples, whom he includes in the group of the few: "If the Germans," we read, "were still capable of turning this fate from a genuine grief into the essential, then that would be 'good': i.e., it might be difficult, of course, but it would have been deftly managed and conceived."[17] For those who are familiar with Heidegger's "Über den Humanismus" (Letter on humanism), which was written for the French public with the help of Jean Beaufret in the autumn of 1946 and which has recently been cast in quite a dubious light, the echoes are clear; Heidegger even places "good" in quotation marks in order to escape every category of ethical consideration, and interprets the colloquial "good" as meaning "difficult, of course, but . . . deftly managed and conceived."

If pastor Conrad Gröber wanted to see reflection and renewal in Heidegger, on the basis of the statement of the treating psychiatrist, this change did not correspond to the actual attitude of the patient. Worlds lay between the versions of two Messkirch figures. Heidegger had no need of renewal; he had the continuing obligation to fulfill the task of Being. For that reason, in May 1946 while still in Badenweiler, he wrote to another of his disciples, whom he also believed he could count among the knowledgeable few: "My optimism for the few knowledgeable people remains firm; they care for and increase that which endures. Their time will come, even if that which is predetermined has not yet reached its long ago predetermined form. That small-mindedness which bases its evaluation of history on the events of the present and the whim of a few

spineless representatives of the *Weltgeist* will determine the direction of
public opinion for the immediate future.''[18] What a jumble of criticism of
the times, of science (and, on yet another occasion, it is the historians
who are roasted), of the concept of predestination! The speech of the
pastor of Being, for whom the house of truth has become inhabitable!
Heidegger does not leave it at the level of general criticism in his letter
written from Badenweiler; he speaks ironically of Ernst Jünger, for
example, who has taken up theology and concerned himself with the
Church Fathers, even—*horribile dictu*—with Thomas Aquinas. Quite
clearly, Thomas Aquinas is a fighting word for Heidegger—and all this
with reference to Ernst Jünger! He comes out of the conservative revolution—a political-ideological terrain, incidentally, that was rather familiar
to Heidegger, one who, in these stormy times, seeks a safe haven with
the followers of Aquinas and a firm ground in the early Christianity of the
Church Fathers.

But hadn't Heidegger ended his own apprenticeship in this tradition
and distanced himself from the intellectual strength of Augustine and
Aquinas? We know that his biographical development led him deeper into
the concerned care of the Catholic Church and of the organizations of
Catholic sciences after the involuntary interruption of his theological
studies. Heidegger was cared for by German Catholicism, which was first
and foremost a Catholicism of specialized groups: he was nurtured and
cared for by its organizational energy. Edmund Husserl characterized
this biographical constellation quite nicely in 1917—at a time when there
was, of course, not yet any closeness between these two—when he was
involved in bringing in the young assistant professor during the search for
someone to fill the associate professorship that had become vacant at
Marburg. Paul Natorp, who had made inquiries of Husserl, judged Heidegger to be "in first place, by far," but it remained open "whether one
could be quite sure of him because of his religious allegiance." Husserl's
answer to this question: it was certain that Heidegger "was committed to
his own religion," since he was "under the tutelage, so to speak, of our
colleague Finke, our 'Catholic historian.' "

As a matter of fact, this influential historian had taken the talented
doctoral candidate into his circle and, in particular, had seen to it that
Heidegger would receive a habilitation stipend, which originated from a
foundation honoring St. Thomas Aquinas and dedicated to Catholic
scientists who wanted to work in the tradition of St. Thomas. Indeed,
Heinrich Finke had even influenced the theme of Heidegger's habilitation
research and dissuaded him from his original intention: to take up a
problem in mathematical logic. The Bishop's Council of the Cathedral of
Freiburg, which included a number of important members of the theological faculty of the University of Freiburg, accompanied Heidegger in

spirit, with sympathy and compassion, during his early career. Certainly, his course was to lead directly into the channels of the Catholic system. That is what one would have expected. And Heidegger seemed to conform to these expectations when, for example, toward the end of 1915, he wrote in his application for a stipend: "The undersigned, your obedient servant, believes he can express his continuing gratitude in the valuable confidence of the venerable Archbishop's Council by directing his scientific life's work toward making the ideas expressed in Scholasticism more accessible for the spiritual struggle of the future for the Christian-Catholic concept of life." To this, Heidegger added the information that he was just completing a study on the logic and psychology of high Scholasticism, a continuation of his work on Duns Scotus, and that the work was being prepared for publication.[19]

Certainly such statements should not be taken at their face value; there may be some trace of a feeling of obligation in them or, perhaps, a touch of opportunism or some such motive. But this is not the only evidence for Heidegger's indisputable roots in Catholic soil. This holds true even though Heidegger offered certain constructive criticism of Pius X, then pope, taking him to task for his antimodernism. We have an unbroken line, anchoring him firmly in Catholicism, which did not begin to deteriorate until Heidegger's hopes of obtaining the vacant chair in philosophy at Freiburg were shattered in 1916. The chair was designated to be taken over by a Catholic; and the historian Heinrich Finke, thanks to his influence with the Ministry of Culture in Heidelberg, managed to have the selection process drawn out until Heidegger could complete his habilitation. Throughout this whole period, Fine also nourished the expectation that Heidegger would become a full professor while still in his early years—although it became obvious that Finke had nourished these hopes only until it came to the verdict.

Whatever the reasons may have been for Finke's change of heart— the question has still not been answered—Martin Heidegger was completely shocked by the negative decision that came in June 1916. This event took its place in a chain of frustrating experiences: Heidegger's rejection at the hands of the Jesuits, who had dismissed the candidate for reasons of health after a fourteen-day trial novitiate at Tivis, in the Vorarlberg region of southern Germany; the compulsory interruption of his theological studies at the University of Freiberg in 1911, which we have already described; and now, Heinrich Finke, the Catholic, breaks his word. Since Heidegger's attitude toward the Catholic Church and the Society of Jesus appear in later remarks, we know precisely with what contempt he spoke of his former religious home; it is entirely reasonable for us to look for the causes of his bitterness in the traumatic experiences of his formative years. How else are we to understand the following verdict: "Among other things, Communism may, perhaps, be horrible, but the matter is clear: Jesuitism is diabolical, if you will excuse the expression."[20]

And Heidegger formulated enlightening statements of this sort within the framework of an intensive discussion on the current political situation which he carried on with Elisabeth Blochmann immediately after Brüning's failure. At that time the correspondents had just left one another in disagreement. For that reason, Heidegger felt obliged to formulate a political statement that was raised to a higher philosophical level—according to a practice he had adopted at the time: "In all the discussions involving Brüning and the Center Party, there was every appearance of party politics. But I do not see the Center Party *this way;* instead I see *Rome,* even *Moscow,* and, I would say, the *Greeks,* too, of whom Nietzsche said that only the *Germans* were their equals. I was not speaking out of consideration for the Center Party policies of the last two years; I meant rather the Center Party—together with the Catholic Church and its possessions, which is another matter still—which I have known from my personal experience from earliest childhood. It is unnecessary to say much about it here. Bismarck, writing about it in his *Thoughts and Recollections,* said: 'I have gotten the impression that the spirit of party and dissent *which providence has given the Center Party instead of a sense of nation which it has given other nations* is stronger than the Pope.' " Then follows the sentence cited above. Heidegger continues, exhorting: "Just consider this: where has this famous tolerance toward the Center Party led? And what has the Center Party really done as a Catholic cultural force in the last decades? It has promoted liberalism and a general intellectual leveling—whether through the *lowering* of standards or, *what is far more dangerous* because intentional, through the *lifting* of these standards to a certain level of mediocrity that is easily mastered. I know all this provokes me to anger because it immediately involves me in battles that are rarely fought through with this sort of intensity. But none of this is important. I could have brought all this out *differently.*" Without going into wording any further, let me just offer this suggestion: the continuous line of thought and attitude flowing uninterruptedly from the rectoral address through the *Beiträge zur Philosophie* (Contributions to philosophy) to the late lectures right up to the end of the war should be more closely investigated. So much lies pent up there that pours out in expressions (like the one given) as if a dam had collapsed, even though the other partner in the correspondence has no inkling at all of the hard battles being ominously hinted at.

In the summer of 1932, when the parliamentary democracy of Weimar was in its final agony, Heidegger still refrained from a clear decision about taking sides with the political party of the popular movement and chose instead to give free reign to his hatred toward particular aspects of the Catholic Church. But in a letter to Elisabeth Blochmann dated March 30, 1933,[21] he makes no secret of the "Being-historical" significance of the collapse of the national government that was gradually coming to light at that time: "Especially because so much of what is now happening remains obscure and unassimilated, I find that it offers me unusual strength to collect myself. It increases my will and confidence that I am participating in the service of a great mission and in the construction of a world grounded in the people." The destiny of the present is predicted from the future, entirely in keeping with Heidegger's way of thinking; and the language is, as always, paratheological. Then the philosopher began to sketch his new political program, which, however, he never developed at length later: "In response to this we must calmly allow the much too hasty enthusiasm for the new things that are sprouting up everywhere. This adherence to the superficial, this sudden tendency of everyone and his brother to take everything 'politically,' without realizing that this can be only one way to the initial revolution. Of course, that experience could well be and could have been, for many, a way to the first awakening, if we grant that we mean to prepare for a second and deeper awakening. The clash with 'Marxism' and 'the Center Party' must wither in its own terms if it does not mature appropriately for the struggle against the contrary spirit of the Communist world and, to no lesser extent, against the moribund spirit of Christianity. Otherwise, everything remains one great chance event burdened with the risk that we will wind up, given the appropriate changes of course, in an age like that marked off by the dates 1871 to 1900. Of course, we cannot allow ourselves to be moved by such fears to trivialize the force of these events, nor can we take this as an assurance that our nation has already come to understand its hidden mission—in which we do believe—and has found the decisive strength for its new journey."

There is yet another occasion in which we feel a mixture of the political struggle (involving the Center Party) and the inherently indicated task of providing a last salute to the moribund spirit of Christianity. Consider, in this sense, the angry letter of Heidegger the Rector (February 1934) to the Reich's Director of the German Students—it concerned the lifting of the suspension of a Catholic student fraternity imposed by the local student leader, which Heidegger viewed as a triumph for the Catholics of Freiburg: "This public Catholic victory, especially here [i.e., in Freiburg], can under no condition be permitted. This constitutes an insult to the whole effort, which *cannot be imagined to be more extreme*. For years I have been familiar with the local situation and forces even to the smallest detail. . . . People *still* just don't understand the tactics of the Catholics. One day this will take its heavy toll."[22] It is the language and recollection of someone who has been profoundly wounded and reacts aggressively to the blows he has received. We know that in 1916 Heidegger blamed the plotting between Heinrich Finke and Engelbert Krebs, Professor of Theology, for his not having been included on the list of those to be called for the professorship. He blamed particularly his close friend, the dogmatist Krebs.

For this reason, it seemed to Heidegger pure unadorned sarcasm when Finke, in congratulating him on his marriage early in 1917, wrote that he had high hopes for him because "a significant theistic philosopher" was more necessary than all the historically oriented Christian-Catholic philosophers—thereby indicating to Heidegger the direction toward the philosophy of religion in which Finke thought Heidegger would be able to make trail-blazing gains for Catholicism.

At this time, however, Heidegger had taken another direction which was to lead him ultimately and finally away from the *system* of Catholicism. He formulated it for his friend Engelbert Krebs after an inner struggle that lasted two years.[23] During this time he strove to clarify the very heart of his philosophical position and, in doing that, came to the conviction that he could no longer take up a position in a context outside of philosophy. "Epistemological reasons that extend into the theory of historical cognition have made the system of Catholicism problematic and unacceptable to me, not however, Christianity and metaphysics (this, of course, in a new sense)." He saved himself in a precautionary way from being cast in the role of the apostate. He felt that he could hold the high esteem of the Catholic world. He had felt too deeply "the sort of values the Catholic Middle Ages contained." The proposed studies in the phenomenology of religion would, he thought, strongly involve the legacy of the Middle Ages.

To his friend Krebs, the priest who in March 1914 had blessed the interreligious Heidegger-Petri marriage according to the rites of the Catholic Church, Martin Heidegger had later renounced his membership in the Catholic community, treating Krebs the priest more or less as the representative of the Catholic Church. With this, Heidegger abandoned the faith of his origins. He had become a renegade, an apostate, at least in the eyes of the dogmatist Krebs, who confided to his diary all his agony and pain over Heidegger's decision, in emotionally phrased expressions. Krebs had not the slightest suspicion that his friend had already legally dissolved his connections to the Catholic community when, in 1917, Heidegger underwent a Protestant wedding ceremony (in Wiesbaden).[24] He remembered the many conversations, the reading together, and, not least, the interest of the two friends in mysticism, their search for the immediate experience of God in the writings of Bernard of

Clairvaux, Meister Eckhart, and Theresa of Avila. But, afterward, their paths gradually separated.

For Heidegger, his work on Schleiermacher in 1917–18 assumed very great importance. Heidegger had discussed his second speech, "Concerning the Nature of Religion" *(Über das Wesen der Religion),* before a small circle in August 1917; through those encounters he arrived at the problem of irrationalism.[25] All those experiences intermingled with his readings from Meister Eckhart, Augustine, and even the mystic Theresa of Avila. Thus, for example, silence comes to play a central role as a religious phenomenon (the mystical place), especially as developed in Eckhart's eighth Tractate, "Of the Birth of the Eternal Word in the Soul": first, in the immediacy of the religious experience; second, in the specifically irrational element of mysticism. In any event, by means of this new direction in his thinking, Heidegger arrives at the realization that a "dogmatically casuistical pseudophilosophy" of "any specific religious system," such as that represented by Catholicism, is in no way close to religion or religious individuals—indeed, it actually misrepresents them, since, by way of example, the problem of the *a priori* of religion is not dealt with philosophically.

It is the system that is addressed in his farewell letter to Krebs of January 1, 1919. For Heidegger (1917–18), "system" is the antistructure of the religious *a priori,* because the ability to experience is limited by the system and within the system, and is ultimately deadened because it lacks primordial consciousness. For this reason, the system of Catholicism has to go through "a confused, inorganic, theoretically incomprehensible dogmatic preserve of clauses and proofs so that in the end, acting as canonical statutes with police authority, it can overwhelm the subject, ominously burden and oppress it."

Not the least of the effects of Scholasticism, according to Heidegger, was that it endangered the immediacy of religious life, that it lost sight of religion in pursuing theology and dogma, thus raising to a new level a development that had already begun in the early Church: "the theorizing and dogmatizing influence of canonical institutions and statutes." In this context, mysticism constitutes an elemental countermovement.

For this reason Heidegger draws personal consequences from these epistemological insights: "extend into the theory of historical cognition"—"the *system* of Catholicism" became problematic and unacceptable to him, once its destructive effect was recognized. "But not Christianity and metaphysics": that is, Christianity as Heidegger presented it in the charismatic figure of Martin Luther. In Luther, Heidegger sees the emergence of a "genuine form of religiosity" not found even among the mystics. And thus, Heidegger arrives at the analysis of the concepts and content of faith and grace and, especially, of the axiom of Catholic theology concerning the relationship between man and grace: *Gratia supponit naturam* (Grace presumes nature). Heidegger saw in Catholic faith a believing-to-be-true, which was altogether differently grounded from the *fiducia* of the Reformation. He knew the essence of Catholic faith: *a deo revelata vera esse credimus* (we believe that that which is revealed by God is true); and he contrasts it with the *fiducia promissionis* (the belief that man's salvation is assured in God's acts). Faith in tradition is traded for Protestantism's *fiducia promissionis*. Thus Heidegger ends that farewell letter to Krebs, writing that he believed he had the inner calling for philosophy, and that in fulfilling it in research and teaching, he would do all in his power to achieve the eternal destiny of the inner man and in this way to justify his existence and actions even before God. A grand gesture!

After this, Heidegger came to be considered the Protestant who had come from Catholicism, the authority on Luther who was also familiar with Scholasticism, an intermediary between theology and philosophy, as Rudolf Bultmann wrote at the end of 1923 after participating in the St. Paul seminar that Heidegger offered following his call to Marburg. Heidegger, he thought, was also fully familiar with modern theology of the kind developed by Gogarthen and Barth.[26]

But were Christianity and the corresponding metaphysics that accompanies it still essential and thus, too, unproblematical and acceptable for the professor from Marburg (and later from Freiburg)? Not one bit. Christian faith is "wooden iron" for a philosopher who is given to radical thought, who again and again poses the decisive philosophical question "Why is there any existent at all, rather than nothingness?" Christian faith is the mortal enemy of the thinking philosopher, if he is not merely a scientific artisan. For this reson, Heidegger declared the God of Jews and the Christians to be finally dead; and, often enough, he proclaimed anew this philosophical abolition of a personal God, of a Creator-God, of a Savior-God. In so doing, he emphatically denied, of course, the need for an ethic based on the Decalogue. " 'Monotheism' and 'theisms' of every sort exist only since the Judaeo-Christian 'apologetic,' which counts metaphysics as a prerequisite to thinking"—so we read in *Beiträge zur Philosophie*.[27] And further: "With the death of this God, the end of all theisms has come. Their multiplicity is not limited by number but by the inner resource of soil and chasms among the momentary places of the flash and concealment of the last God's sign."

While Heidegger was expressing sentiments of this sort (c. 1936) and similar opinions in the *Introduction to Metaphysics* (1935) he was struggling with the faith of his origins in a way that could hardly be conducive to its recovery. The struggle was tied up with the failure of his political efforts; all this came together for him in an atmosphere of loneliness.

"For loneliness is nearly perfect," he confides to Karl Jaspers, in Heidelberg, in a letter on July 1, 1935. He goes on to say that now, after just a few months, he has managed to get back to the work he had broken off in the winter of 1932-33. "But it is a thin scaffolding which supports, where I usually also have two thorns*: the conflict with traditional faith, and the failure of the rectorate—just enough for such things as do have to be overcome."[28] We must look beyond the almost complete textual isolation and focus on the central theme—which, significantly, was drawn from St. Paul (2 Cor. 12:7). The connection becomes particularly relevant if we are mindful of the echoes of Kierkegaard's speech "The Thorn in the Flesh," which had been translated by Theodor Haecker in 1914. Here, by way of a hint, we can afford to identify no more than one important component of Heidegger's sources: his inner conflict involving Theodor Haecker and the *Hochland Kreis* (Highland Circle): that is, specific variants of intellectual German Catholicism.[29]

In any event, in the middle of his life, basking in the glow of world fame, Heidegger had not yet overcome or gotten over the turnabout in religion and *Weltanschauung* which had come so much earlier. A stigma cannot be eradicated. It continues to make itself felt even when it seems to have been vanquished. Karl Löwith has skillfully highlighted this existential feature of Heidegger's personality: "By education a Jesuit, he became a Protestant out of indignation, a Scholastic dogmatist in his training and an existential pragmatist through experience, a theologian by tradition and an atheist as a researcher, a renegade from his tradition in the garb of being its historian. As existential as Kierkegaard but with a mind like Hegel's for system, as much a dialectician in his mthodology as he was single-themed in content, apodictic in his assertions in the spirit of negation, with others laconic but as inquisitive as only a very few, ultimately radical but penultimately inclined to compromise."[30] Such was the contradictory effect the man had on his disciples, who nevertheless remained loyal because he far surpassed all other university professors in the intensity of his philosophical commitment.

But the wound keeps reopening. The thorn in the flesh remains virulent. How else are we to understand the passage in a letter, written in 1935, in which Heidegger, sobered, descending from his soaring and deluded flights into the realm of political philosophy, gradually back in touch with firm ground, comes into conflict with the religion of his origins? Many a statement of Heidegger's about the Catholic Church, about meaning and nonmeaning or, rather, about justifying the assignment of academic teaching positions for Christian-oriented philosophy,[31] may strike us as crudely polemic, even spiteful in its exposition, more

---

* The word here is *Pfahl*, which means both "post" and "thorn." —Transl.

like the concealing, the touching-up, of diseased tissue. But behind all that, the wounded areas burned painfully and could hardly be eased with the Band-Aids of existential thought. The question of Heidegger's Catholic origins, of the faith of his origins, remained open without being even slightly contained.

Had Heidegger resolved the question, written himself free of it in 1936–38 in the *Beiträge zur Philosophie?* For instance, in that central chapter "Der letzte Gott" (The last God), to which he gave the motto "That which is utterly unlike what formerly was, i.e., the Christian"? Or had he, speaking historically, declared God dead only to remain caught in his thrall, caught by this *deus creator mundi* who had created man in his image and likeness, the beginning and end of all that exists, Being itself—*ipsum esse*—toward Whom the whole of creation, *omnis creatura,* moves?

But there was still another thorn in the flesh to be overcome: the failure of the rectorate, understood here as *pars pro toto*—that is, the failure of the political structure of his thinking. The contemporaneous emotional wording of a statement in a lecture in the summer semester of 1935 parallels the admission in the letter of July 1, 1935, to Karl Jaspers, Heidegger's longtime companion in philosophy: "What is being passed around today expressly as a philosophy of National Socialism has absolutely nothing at all to do with the inner truths and greatness of National Socialism, that is fishing in the muddy waters of 'values' and 'integrities.' " The concepts "inner truth" and "greatness" conceal the amplitude of Heideggerian thought: the inner truth of National Socialism signifies the instant and ceaseless limitation and decrees by *aletheia,* of the disclosure of truth, the revelation and illumination of submerged Being that shows itself thus to the knowing few, that makes itself theirs, that happens.

Hadn't the students listening in the audience remembered what Rector Heidegger had promised them and had proclaimed to all the world scarcely two years earlier? "May your courage to sacrifice for the salvation of the essence and for the elevation of the innermost strength of our people in its nation grow unceasingly. Let not the 'dogma' and 'idea' be the rules of your Being. The *Führer* himself, and only he *is* the present and future German reality and her law. Learn to know more profoundly: From now on, everything demands decision, and all action demands responsibility. Heil Hitler!" The visionary strength and unconditional authority raised in this language cannot be detached from the prophet. First and foremost, the messenger of Being-destiny is still on duty, still in service, still in intellectual service, still responsible, especially for the future! Because: Heidegger himself politicized his philosophy and, with the *auctoritas* of his own person, he bound—indeed he chained—others to the *Führer* and the movement.

We must ask—the question is not at all motivated by self-righteousness blessed with the good fortune of being born late—was it enough to acknowledge, in *forum internum,* the failure of the political mission? That is no admission of guilt: to confess to a onetime friend, to patient paper, to pages not destined for publication. We now read in the *Beiträge:* "The fear of Being has never before been as great as it is today. The proof: the massive measures for overcoming this fear. These are not the essential signs of 'nihilism': whether churches and cloisters are destroyed, whether people are murdered, or whether 'Christianity' may go its way. This is what is decisive: whether we know or want to know that all the widespread talk of 'providence' and 'the good Lord,' honest as it may seem to each, is no more than excuses and embarrassments in *that* sphere that people do not want to recognize as *that* sphere in which decisions must be made about Being and Not-Being, or even to take them into account" (p. 139).

Against the background of the historical events of the time—the Spanish Civil War, the enormous preparations for the Olympiad in Berlin, and the convention of the Reich party in Nuremberg—Heidegger imposes a harsh judgment on the *Führer*—the one who and only who *is* the present and future German reality and her law—because this *Führer* had given in to the fear of Being and had evaded "every decision to set goals." The movement had deteriorated into a "noisy adventure" sort of drunkenness, a "strength through joy" organization. It had plunged into the abyss. The people who bore within themselves a distant directive—that is, to accept the mission of Being, to find the Being-historical verdict and to execute it—betrayed themselves and so had failed. Heidegger, however, had remained faithful to his Being-historical mission, so he was not to blame before Being. But in 1945 his accusers knew nothing of this, pausing on the stage of the world theater where the main performance involved a distributed, redeeming assignment of blame, with the image of man before them as one in need of salvation. For Heidegger, this was tantamount to subjugation under one God, the same as self-abasement. They did not know the night of the world that had to be traversed if, like the sun, the Germans were ultimately to rise again.

When, in November 1945, Heidegger's real existence fell into a *peripeteia* and it seemed prudent to take the difficult road to Archbishop Gröber, the fatherly friend he had avoided for years, he reached for the deliverance that seemed intended for him like a drowning man grasping at straws. It came from France—though not from Jean-Paul Sartre, as he first hoped it might, but in the person of Jean Beaufret (a sort of second choice). He wrote to Beaufret on December 23, 1945, that although he had known his name for only a few weeks, nevertheless he sensed what a large command Beaufret had of the nature of philosophy: "Here there remain still-hidden realms that will not come to light until the future. . . . For fruitful thought, one needs more than writing and reading; one needs the *synousia* of conversation and the symbiosis of learning and teaching." This community of thought lasted until Heidegger's death. His letter *Über den Humanismus* (Letter on humanism), which he gave to Beaufret on December 12, 1946, is a symbol of this *synousia*. This is the letter in which he announces his emphatic renunciation of philosophical ethics, but also where, especially "at the present moment in this world," Being "announces itself in the crisis of the existent." He who is mindful of Being has no need of ethics in the traditional sense as defined since Plato, because it has found its home in Heraclitus's ηθοζ for "that thinking which construes the truth of Being as the inceptive element in man as existing Being is already, in itself, the original ethics."

One issue remains. Heidegger's persistent silence regarding the crimes committed in the name of the German people is always a central theme. Indeed, it has even been characterized recently as a genuine dimension of Heidegger's hermeneutics: the dimension of silence. However one may decide that question, Heidegger did refuse to come to grips with the crimes of National Socialism. There is just one privately offered reference to all this in what were less than accessible circumstances; the relevant comment was made public in 1983. Heidegger had given a lecture on modern technology "Das Gestell," for a select group of guests from Bremen: "Agriculture is presently a motorized industry of food production; it is essentially the same as the production of corpses in the gas chambers of concentration camps, the same as the blockage and starvation of countries, the same as the production of hydrogen bombs."[32] Such thinking, seen from Heidegger's point of view, signifies the indifference of the phenomenal world, which the demon of all up-to-date technological and environmental destruction produces: Agriculture as a motorized industry for the production of food is "essentially the same" as genocide.

As has been known for some time now, Jean Beaufret has identified himself with Faurisson's "Studies" and has in effect authorized them. Was Faurisson right, then, in claiming Heidegger, as well as Beaufret, as his predecessor? Did the exchange between them also touch on this question, or did it go unmentioned? Didn't the "dimension of silence" risk dissolving into nothingness? Of course, not Nothingness, in Heidegger's sense of the word.

NOTES

1. Heinrich Petzet, *Auf einen Stern zugehen: Begegnungen und Gespräche mit Martin Heidegger, 1929–1976* (Frankfurt: Societäts-Verlag, 1983), p. 50.

2. I allude to Theodor Haecker, *Was ist der Mensch?* (Leipzig, 1933), a book that Heidegger did not easily come to grips with.

3. Cf. my detailed study "Martin Heidegger und die Universität Freiburg nach 1945: Ein Beitspiel fur die Auseinandersetzung mit der Politischen Vergangenheit," *Historisches Jahrbuch* 105 (1985): 95–128.

4. "Death is Dasein's *ownmost* possibility. Being towards this possibility discloses its *ownmost* potentiality-for-being, in which its very Being is the issue." This is how Heidegger formulated it in *Being and Time* (1927). In 1946, it was a matter of life and death.

5. Cited from *Johann Peter Hebel Werke* (Frankfurt, 1986), Insel-Verlag, 2:122ff. The poem bears the subtitle "Conversation on the road to Basel between Steinen and Brombach, at night." Heidegger had struggled mightily with this profoundly meaningful poem. He evaluates it in, e.g., a letter to Ernst Jünger on November 7, 1969; cf. Ernst Jünger, *Shuttlecocks*. parts. 1 and 2 (Zurich, 1980), pp. 71ff.

6. Quoted in Hugo Ott, *Martin Heidegger: Unterwegs zu seiner Biographie* Frankfurt (1988), p. 323, from Gröber's *Nachlass* in the Archives of the Archbishopric in Freiburg.

7. See my study "Der junge Martin Heidegger: Gymnasial-Konviktszeit und Studium," *Freiburger Diözesan-Archiv*, 3d. ser., 104 (1984).

8. Bundesarchiv Koblenz, Nachlass Rudolf Stadelmann.

9. See my biographical article in *Zeitgeschichte in Lebensbildern* (Mainz) 6 (1948): 65–75.

10. The concept of a psychosomatically oriented sanatorium (with a Christian basis) had been developed only in the fall of 1945 and was built entirely around the person of von Gebsattel. For von Gebsattel's intellectual environment, see *Quis est homo? Victor Emil Freiherrn von Gebsattel zum 75. Geburtstag von seinen Freunden and Schülern, Jahrbuch für Psychologie and Psychotherapie* 6 (1958). Of special interest is the article by Igor A. Caruso, "Excerpta anthropologica," which attempts a thorough evaluation of Gebsattel.

11. His Catholic roots, which were such a determining factor in Heidegger's life, have not been traced nor the extent of their efficacy measured; e.g., no consideration whatsoever has been given to how strongly the performance of the Catholic liturgy had marked the young Heidegger. One might have examined the "Magnificat," which had been introduced into the Archdiocese of Freiburg. The Psalm translations, which originated in this Wessenberg period, also belong here; these set the tone and direction for the *volks*-piety of the German Vesper. Let me give you just one example, the initial verses of Psalm 23: "Thou most holy, sent from God / Thou art my shepherd and my provider. / Thou leadest me to pasture in lush meadows, / Thou leadest me to pure streams. / In your care I shall not want. / Abundance in everything pours out to me. / And should I walk in the Valley of Death. / I shall walk joyfully, without trembling, / for thou, my shepherd, are at my side, / Thou art my staff and my support. / In your hand I can not go astray. / Thou art the true way to life" (*Magnificat* [Freiburg, 1908], p. 714). Cf. my article "Zu den katholischen Wurzeln im Denken Martin Heideggers: Der theologische Philosoph," in *Akten des römischen Heidegger-Symposions* (forthcoming).

12. Martin Heidegger, Parmenides lectures, 1942–43, in *Gesamtausgabe,* vol. 54 (Frankfurt: Klostermann, 1982), pp. 26ff., 78.

13. See e.g., *Lexikon der Psychiatrie: Gesammelte Abhandlungen der gebräuchlichsten psychiatrischen Begriffe,* ed. Christian Müller (Berlin, 1986), pp. 129ff.

14. These passages are taken from Heidegger's "Letter on Humanism," first published in German (Bern, 1947), based on the version of 1946, which appeared in French; it is quoted here from *Brief über den "Humanismus"* (Frankfurt: Klostermann, 1949), p. 45. I want to emphasize in particular the weight Heidegger attaches to the term "security." "Being is the security, which protects man in his ek-sistent essence for her truth in such a way that she accommodates ek-sistence in language." (ibid.) Notice, too, the connection to his Catholic roots, which I have indicated above.

15. Cf. Heidegger's letter to Herman Zelter (August 2, 1950), which has been published in facsimile in Hermann Zelter, *Existentielle Kommunikation,* vol. 24 of *Erlanger Forschungen Reihe A. Geisteswissenschaften* (Erlangen, 1978), following page 116.

16. See Ott, *Martin Heidegger,* pp. 19ff.

17. In private possession.

18. In private possession.

19. See for these events, my study "Der Habilitand Martin Heidegger und das von Schaezlersche Stipendium: Ein Beitrag zur Wissenschaftsförderung der katholischen Kirche, *"Freiburger Diözesan-Archiv* 106 (1986): 141ff.

20. Letter to Elisabeth Blackmann, the social pedagogue, of June 22, 1932, in Martin Heidegger and Elisabeth Blochmann, *Briefwechsel 1918–1969,* ed. Joachim W. Storck, Marbacher Schriften 33 (Marbach: Deutsche Schillergesellschaft, 1989).

21. Ibid., pp. 60–61.

22. See Ott, *Martin Heidegger,* pp. 95–96.

23. For the following, see ibid., pp. 106ff.

24. According to the most recent information, which confirms the tawdry gossip current for some time, the Protestant ceremony was performed by Pastor Lieber of Wiesbaden, where Heidegger's in-laws (General Petri and his wife) had taken up their retirement. Cf. correspondence in Heidegger and Blochmann, *Briefwechsel,* p. 148 n.20.

25. For the following, see my "Zur den katholischen Wurzeln."

26. See Ott, *Martin Heidegger,* p. 123.

27. Martin Heidegger, *Beiträge zur Philosophie,* ed. Friedrich-Wilhelm von Hermann (Frankfurt: Klostermann, 1989), p. 411; henceforth cited by page number in the text.

28. Ott, *Martin Heidegger,* p. 42.

29. The overdue investigation of the intellectual relationship between Haecker and Heidegger will prove how closely Heidegger followed Haecker's publications.

30. Karl Löwith, *Mein Leben in Deutschland vor und nach 1933. Ein Bericht* (Stuttgart 1989); cited here from the pocket edition (Frankfurt, 1989), p. 45.

31. Cf. my study "Die Weltanschauungsprofessuren (Philosophie und Geschichte) an der Universität Freiburg, besonders im 3. Reich." In *Historisches Jahrbach* 108, *Jg. I. Halbbd.* (1988): 157–73.

32. Quoted in Wolfgang Schirmacher, *Technik und Gelassenheit: Zeitkritik nach Heidegger* (Freiburg, 1983), p. 25.

4

Heidegger, Nietzsche, and Politics

OTTO PÖGGELER

In 1964, Heidegger gave a lecture titled "The End of Philosophy and the Task of Thinking." He did not intend the formula "the end of philosophy" in a negative sense, since he pointed out that the philosophical tradition had never reached to its own roots: "Philosophy does speak about the light of reason, but does not heed the opening of Being." There must be an event, he believed, and an appropriation of an opening if Being is to be open to men, and reason is to discern the distinct Being of beings. The end of philosophy represents the possibility of a new beginning: "We may suggest that the day will come when we will not shun the question whether the *opening*, the free open, may not be that within which alone pure space and ecstatic time and everything present and absent in them occupy the place that gathers and protects everything."

The end of philosophy is not the concern of a few philosophers only. According to Heidegger, it is the end of the West: the West—that is, Greek and modern European culture—which relies on "philosophy." This tradition, only this European tradition, is rightly characterized by a dualism: the religious and political sphere is mediated by an orientation toward Being reflected or grounded in reason. Orientation and reflection lead, finally, to mere values. It was for that reason that Nietzsche proclaimed his diagnosis of nihilism. Perhaps the "metaphysical" attempt

Parts of this paper were delivered in speeches at a conference of the John M. Olin Center for Inquiry into the Theory and Practice of Democracy of the University of Chicago in Paris (June 1989) and at Duquesne University, Pittsburgh (October 1989). I thank Elisabeth Brient for reading through the manuscript.

to find an all-encompassing orientation is a negation of the many-sidedness and openness of life: hence, nihilism. In any case, not only did the philosophical tradition and the orientation of the West suffer a great decline, but those philosophical attempts of the century that were meant to recover a measure of order could not fail to be deeply ambivalent. Politically engaged philosophers and scientists such as Georg Lukács, Martin Heidegger, and Albert Einstein, however much against their own intentions, paved the way to the Gulag, to Auschwitz, to Hiroshima.

The West: that means the Occident. In his lectures on the philosophy of history, Hegel compared the history of mankind to the course of the sun: the sun rises in the East and sets in the West. In history, the sun—the idea of the Good and the Divine—sets in the hearts of men, and this path finds its fulfillment in the "West." When Hegel went to Berlin, he learned that Prussia was not only a *parvenu* but a state built on intelligence (as the Prussian reformers said). After the Congress of Vienna, Prussia was the fifth and youngest member among the great states. Hegel discerned the reason of history deployed in the community of European states. He also realized that America and Russia—the wings of Europe with their vast territories and their enormous resources—might well become the leading powers of the future. But if so, then the civil society of America would have to evolve into a suitable state, and the despotism of Russia would have to be complemented by civil society and its doctrine of rights. Hence, it would still be true that nothing other than European reason would govern history, even in the future.

When Hegel's orientation toward Europe was abandoned, the meaning of the expression "the West" was changed: the great states of France and England (and, in the past, Spain), which had been compared with Russia, were now also distinguished from Central Europe, where a great many different peoples lived in close quarters and where no national state had yet been founded. Jacques Derrida, who discusses Heidegger's inaugural address as rector at the University of Freiburg (1933) in *De l'esprit*, pertinently cites (in note 73) the English essayist Matthew Arnold. In a letter *Arminius and "Geist,"* Arnold theatrically presents a Prussian (or German) carrying on as follows: " 'Liberalism and despotism!' cried the Prussian; 'let us go beyond these forms and words. What unites and separates people now is *Geist*. . . . There, you will find—in Berlin—that we oppose *Geist*, *intelligence*, as you or the French might say, to *Ungeist*. The victory of *Geist* over *Ungeist* is, we think, the great issue of the world. . . . We North Germans have worked for *Geist* in our way. . . . In your middle class, *Ungeist* is rampant; and as for your aristocracy . . .' "[1] Was it the task of Central Europe—of Austria and, especially, of Prussia and Germany—to find a way between Western liberalism and Russian despotism? The attempt to found in Central

Europe states suitably capable of leading the others led to the catastrophe of the two world wars. Was the failure due to resisting the Western tradition? Or was the acceptance by Central Europe of the nationalism and imperialism of the great Western states a false path as well?

Tocqueville learned considerably from his experience in America; he became concerned about the future—that effectively means: about the possibilities and the dangers of America and Russia. By contrast, the great historian Jacob Burckhardt perverts this kind of reflection because he considers only the dangers. Burckhardt saw the ineptness of mass democracy in the context of small Swiss communities and its ambivalence in the fact that Napoleon III was able to gain power by elections in a plebiscitarian democracy. In 1974, after the death of the "great European" Carl Jacob Burckhardt, Heidegger quoted Burckhardt's letter to Max Alioth, from 1833: "With growing age I become more and more one-sided in my convictions, for instance, in the conviction that the day of the decline of Greece came with democracy." Concerning this passage, Heidegger made the following remark: "Our Europe is destroyed by 'democracy' from below (and the tendencies of this Below) against a numerous (and therefore weak and invalid) Above."[2] In the 1930s, in favor of this conviction, Heidegger cites the more radical remarks of a friend of Burckhardt's: Friedrich Nietzsche. In any case, this critique of "democracy" (the term is in quotation marks!) is not Heidegger's critique alone; it claims a long European tradition.

The English, of course, not only conquered Scotland and Ireland; they established an empire. So it was that Franz Rosenzweig was able to distinguish between the British Empire and Europe. In 1917, following the wake of Hegel's philosophy of history, Rosenzweig wrote his essay "Globus" (he had also in mind Friedrich Naumann's book *Central Europe*). Rosenzweig regarded World War I as a war between culture (Germans) and civilization (represented by England, with France playing the role of England's agent). Great Britain, Central Europe, and Russia represented the three forms of empire or future empire. Then there were Japan, North America, and the Islamic States to consider.[3] In the second half of the nineteenth century, the image of England and America declined in Germany; writers became suspicious of that sort of "West." In his first lecture course after World War I, Heidegger distinguishes philosophy from *Weltanschauung* (world view). The pious peasant in the Black Forest, for example, says Heidegger, has his *Weltanschauung* as well as the worker who is without a religious tradition; in the same sense, "The word has been spoken concerning the contrast between the Anglo-American and the German *Weltanschauung*." Obviously, Heidegger has in mind such writers as Max Scheler (and Scheler's friend Werner Sombart).[4] Scheler used Nietzsche's concept of *ressentiment*, but without the anti-Christian polemic: it is the bourgeois who is characterized by *ressentiment*—toward status, toward historical difference and tradition. (Scheler, who never visited England or America, proved to be much more polemical than Max Weber, writing his famous account of the Calvinistic roots of capitalism in England and America.) During World War I, Scheler was prepared to permit his ideas to be used to serve the ends of nationalistic propaganda. But at least from 1916 on, he saw that the war—hence, also, nationalism and imperialism—were the "bankruptcy" of Europe. Scheler wanted to establish a European orientation toward "solidarity," by means of a religious renaissance, as a way of navigating between capitalism and communism. (Already, the French socialist Leroux, a pupil of Schelling, had interpreted Christian love as human solidarity.) Scheler was of the opinion that this new orientation toward solidarity must arise out of a new unity between France and Germany. The most horrifying vision, he thought, would be of Europe being torn to pieces between capitalist America and communist Russia.

Thus, the expression "the West" could come to mean: England and the United States, as opposed to Continental Europe. Today, "Continental philosophy" signifies a philosophy with speculative, existential, and hermeneutic elements—a philosophy perhaps as modest as a Continental breakfast. (Because of Kant's relation to Hume, and because of the Vienna School, Königsberg and Vienna do *not* belong to Continental Europe!) But in the 1960s, a time of crisis, Continental philosophy influenced the American universities—not only the divinity schools and the humanities but also the philosophy departments. Might then such issues as "civil society and state" and "religion and art in the time of technology" be dealt with effectively by means of this Continental philosophical tradition? Or has the victor of the war already been subverted by the spirit of the conquered—that is by German historicism in the guise of French existentialism and deconstructionism?

Of course, the East-West distinction may refer to the Western nations that share the European tradition and are drawn to the political leadership of the United States on one side and the Soviet Union on the other. Even so, writers like Scheler were of the opinion that America and Russia, or capitalism and communism, did have common roots. Also, is there not an enormous gap between the great traditions of the West (that is, Europe, America, and the Soviet Union) and those of East Asia? Keiji Nishitani (Heidegger's most important pupil at the Kyoto School, who was also, as it happens, involved in the Japanese war party) cites Toynbee in support of this very opinion; for, even the Iranian religion, like the Mediterranean and European cultures, is concerned with the self—and therefore with history—whereas Taoism and Zen Buddhism, for example, are able to accept as meaningful what must be described as wholly anonymous structures.[5] Heidegger, who entered into a dialogue with Taoism and the Japanese tradition, has today gained a new influence in China. Hegel was studied in China, after the end of the Cultural Revolution, as the proper representative of reason and the philosophical tradition. But now Heidegger prevails, and *Being and Time* has been translated and distributed throughout the country in some ten thousand copies. Perhaps Heidegger's thinking will serve to actualize China's own traditions, especially Taoism; perhaps through such a "destruction," philosophy in China may find its way into the future.[6]

The expression "the West" denotes a number of different constellations: the political thinking developed in France and England (democracy as well as imperialism); the bourgeois spirit (according to Weber and Scheler, characteristic of England and America); the United States and Europe as opposed to the Soviet Union; and finally Europe, the United States, and the Soviet Union together as opposed to East Asia. Heidegger considered all these distinctions. He also began a dialogue with the East, but he was of the opinion that the "West" (Western thinking and behavior since the time of the ancient Greeks) had lost its roots and needed a new beginning. Isn't it possible, therefore, to treat Heidegger as a "modern" thinker who pursued a new future? For him, however, European modernity was nothing but the consequence of our having lost our roots in antiquity; for already, he believed, classical philosophy had lost sight of the oldest task of thinking. It was not Heidegger but others who favored the concept "postmodernism." It may be used polemically, of course, but does it actually have clear limits?

When we restrict ourselves to architecture, we may perhaps distinguish fairly easily between the modern and the postmodern architecture. Sullivan (with his formula "form follows function"), Gropius, Mies van der Rohe all had enormous success: an international "modern" style raced through the world. For many, successful though it was, modernity became a nightmare; hence, they applauded the coming of postmodernism—for instance, in Hollein's forms and soft materials, in Stirling's hints of different traditions. But in philosophy we face a different situation: there never was an international modern style of philosophy. Just thirty years ago, in fact, one could distinguish at least three quite different spheres of influence in philosophy: Continental Europe addressed the great metaphysical and existential questions and stressed the historicity of thinking; the English-speaking world relied instead on the nominalistic and analytical traditions; the politically installed Marxism of the Soviet Union and its satellites was more politically minded and attracted to materialism. In the last few decades, however, the situation has changed entirely: all these tendencies are now found on all the continents and in all the countries of the world. Because there never was a unified international modernity in philosophy, postmodernism has found it difficult to make its distinction from modernism. There are many postmodernisms, and there are postmodern tendencies that had already appeared before its time. Of course, one may say: postmodernism denies that there can be one entirely adequate system of thought or one inclusive course of history or world history. (We may recall Hegel, who already had his many critics.) A question arises as to whether in gaining its advantage over modernism, postmodernism eliminates such central notions as those of the subject of responsibility, of truth in general. The polemics of modernity and postmodernity seem to proceed best in onesided maneuvers only or in a sort of totalitarian criticism that overlooks the pertinent details.

I intend these remarks as a preamble for reviewing Heidegger's concern with the decline of the West. I want to examine how this concern takes form during three phases of Heidegger's historical path: the first culminates in *Being and Time*; in the second, between 1930 and 1940, Heidegger was decisively influenced by Nietzsche; and in the third, the decades after about 1940, Heidegger developed a critical attitude toward Nietzsche, in a search for a new understanding.

Decline and Destruction

Martin Heidegger was born the son of a sexton at Messkirch. Of course, it was decided that the gifted boy should study theology: according to his mother's wishes he was to become a bishop, or at least a suffragan bishop. The Church's support guaranteed his studies. The new theology student began to lend his voice, in short articles, to the fight against modernism in Catholic teaching. After only two years, Heidegger gave up the study of theology (because of weak health, he said). He went on to philosophy, mathematics, and the natural sciences. When the Pope issued a *motu proprio* ("in his own concern") against modernism, Heidegger wrote to his older friend, the theologian Krebs (July 19, 1919): "Perhaps as an 'academic' you could apply for better treatment: all who succumb to having independent thoughts could have their brains taken out and replaced with Italian salad." After his habilitation, Heidegger offered courses in theology at Freiburg. But in January 1919 he wrote to Krebs that he had cut his ties to the Catholic *Weltanschauung*—though not to the Christian faith and not to metaphysics if taken in a new sense. He now became an assistant to the phenomenologist Edmund Husserl, who had come to Freiburg in 1916.[7]

The most important students who came to study phenomenology at Freiburg found their way to Heidegger. This rebel in the academic sphere was able to win the friendship of another outsider, Karl Jaspers. Heidegger was not concerned with the fight against mere decline; he wanted to achieve a radical "destruction" of the tradition—a destruction that would reopen the forgotten questions concerning human being in the world. In 1920, he wrote to one of his first pupils, Karl Löwith: "Instead of abandoning oneself to the general need to become cultivated, as if one had received the order to 'see culture,' it is necessary—through a radical reduction and disintegration, through a *destruction*—to convince oneself firmly of the 'only thing' necessary, without paying attention to the ideal task and agitation of enterprising and intelligent men. . . . My will at least is directed toward something else, and it is not much: living in the situation of de facto upheaval, I am pursuing what I feel to be 'necessary' without worrying whether the result will be a 'culture' or whether my quest will precipitate ruin." Heidegger also wrote that he could not be compared with "philosophers like Nietzsche who sought to decide about new 'values.' " He saw himself as a former Christian theologian, but now the accent was laid on the second part of the word "theology": it is not the task of philosophy to decide religious (or political) questions; the task of philosophy (as phenomenology) is to unfold a new philosophical logic in paving the way towards these questions.[8]

In 1919 Oswald Spengler published the first volume of his famous book *The Decline of the West*. Spengler construed great human questions as questions regarding different historical cultures and epochs. Already in his lecture course of the winter of 1919–20, however, Heidegger objected that Spengler's book was unable to grasp its own position (that is, by way of hermeneutics of historical facticity). With its skepticism, Spengler's book would contaminate the life of an entire generation. In his lecture course "Ontology or Hermeneutics of Facticity" (summer 1923), Heidegger takes Spengler's book to represent the historical consciousness of "Today," an approach he severely criticizes: the history of art (for instance, the work of Riegl and the Vienna School) may take art as the history of style and expression, but history in general cannot simply copy or ape this approach. Yet this was the method of Spengler, who offers (in his inauthentic historical consciousness) even a prophesy of the future. According to this lecture course, the philosophy of "Today" either returns to Hegel's dialectics or is merely a Platonism of barbarians: a supposed way to superhistorical ideas through historical consciousness, and a mere mediation between them.[9] Heidegger fights against all such attempts, the old-fashioned remnants of the liberal epoch—in neo-Kantianism, in Hegelianism, in the school of Dilthey, among historians. In pursuing this criticism, he finds an opponent in the new theology of Barth and Gogarten.

In 1920, Gogarten published a manifesto titled *Between the Times*. The formula "between the times" also became the title of the journal of the Barth-Gogarten group (the journal was abandoned in 1933, when Gogarten took up with the revolutionary party). Gogarten asserts that it was not for the well-known teachers such as Troeltsch (Gogarten's own teacher) to be the real instructors of the time but for thinkers such as Nietzsche and Kierkegaard, Meister Eckhart and Lao Tzu. Nobody likes to live among corpses, and so Gogarten writes: "We are jubilant over the Spengler book. It proves, whether one agrees with its details or not, that the hour has struck in which this fine, clever culture discovers, out of its own cleverness, the worm that is eating it; where trust in the development of culture received its deathblow. And Spengler's book is not the only sign." There was, of course, the dream of a new culture, but that was gone ("Aber dieser Traum ist ausgeträumt"); the same formulation finds its echo in Husser's remarks on the crisis of the European sciences—but in bitter mockery of his contemporaries.[10] Already in August 1917, Heidegger gave a private speech on Schleiermacher's *Reden über die Religion*, especially the second speech, which abandons metaphysical theology, the crown of philosophy since Aristotle. Apparently, only a cautious hermeneutics can lead into the religious sphere of life—and finally, also, to concepts like "God." But Heidegger agreed with those theologians who treated the eschatology of the early Christian community quite seriously (J. Weiss, Schweitzer, Overbeck) in critizing idealistic and liberal theology. In the winter of 1920–21, in a lecture course titled "Introduction to the Phenomology of Religion," he criticizes Ernst Troeltsch, for instance, who was unable to formulate the problems of historians but who tried to return to a metaphysical or speculative theology—not only in the manner of Schleiermacher but also in the manner of Hegel. According to Heidegger, the logic of philosophy is not speculative dialectics but formal, indicative hermeneutics. Philosophy may interpret life, but it cannot decide the religious (or political) questions of life itself. A formal indication can only point out that there *is* a religious (or political) sphere in our life, posing its own distinctive questions.

In the second part of the course, Heidegger presents an interpretation of eschatology in the letters of St. Paul, especially in the first letter to the Thessalonians (the oldest document in the New Testament). Nothing is said there about the question of whether or not this theology can be accepted as theology, but the faith of the early Christian community is presented as a model for the experience of the facticity and historicity of life: Jesus taught the acceptance of the task of the unique moment; as Christ, he became the measure of history, but his coming (*parousia*) can be characterized only by kairological, not chronological, concepts (a prediction, after all, is not possible). There is no "idea" of the Christian life (as Harnack and Troeltsch taught); true religion can only accept the task of the unique moment, from situation to situation. When Heidegger

accepted a philosophical chair at Marburg, he took part in Rudolf Bultmann's seminar on the ethics of St. Paul, and Bultmann was then able to
write to a friend (on December 23, 1923): "This time the Seminar is
especially instructive for me, due to the participation of our new philosopher, Heidegger, a student of Husserl. He comes from Catholicism, but
is entirely Protestant. . . . He has an extraordinary knowledge not only of
Scholasticism but also of Luther. . . . It is of interest that Heidegger—
who is familiar with modern theology and has a special respect for
Herrmann—knows Gogarten and Barth as well. The former he values
above all, exactly as I do. You can imagine how important it is for me
that you come and join the discussion. The older generation is unable to
participate, as its members no longer even understand the problem to
which we are lending our efforts."[11]

Bultmann was correct in saying that a new generation sought to
clarify its own experiences with the help of Heidegger's philosophizing.
Heidegger's thought was convincing because his hermeneutic phenomenology was developed in terms of a reception and criticism of the leading
philosophies of the time. The problems of these philosophies—especially
those of Bergson, Dilthey, and Husserl—was to find an answer in the
lived experience of Heidegger's approach. In 1921, Edmund Husserl
published a dissertation on Bergson by Roman Ingarden, in the yearbook
of phenomenology. As Husserl's assistant, Heidegger was asked to
correct the style of the Polish student. Of course, Ingarden was able to
talk with Husserl about Bergson on several occasions. In fact, Bergson's
books lay for a time on Husserl's bedside table; today we can see these
books, with Husserl's own markings, in the Husserl Archives at Leuven.
Bergson's thoughts needed to be submitted to a phenomenological critique, and yet Husserl rediscovered his own thoughts in Bergson's
writings as well. But didn't Bergson challenge the approach of Husserl's
phenomenology when he pointed out the relativity of perception to
action? In the ensuing years, Heidegger had intended to start his destruction of the philosophical tradition by writing a chapter on Bergson's
concept of time. Indeed, the decisive issue common to Bergson and
phenomenology was time and time-conscousness. In the nineteenth century not only was a new cosmology being developed, which vastly
lengthened the time of the origin of the universe, but a theory of evolution
and prehistory was also being elaborated according to which human and
other life forms must have existed for millions of years—though of course
even this expanded interval represents only a short time in the total
history of the universe. And so time and finitude became the main
problems of philosophy. If philosophizing is embedded in the contingency
of human life, then philosophy itself is challenged: is it still able to speak

about the substance or essence of entities? Can philosophy claim to discover the essential order to the universe?

Philosophers went their different ways in an effort to rescue the task of philosophy. In its English and German translations, Bergson's *Essai sur les données immédiates de la conscience* bears the title *Time and Free Will*. Indeed, the essay points out that lived time (*durée*) is not measurable like space; only through an intuition can we get an experience of lived time. A genuine experience of time resists causal explanation and calculation; in this openness, then, time makes free will possible. In his later books, Bergson deals not only with the connection of perception and action but also with the problems of the evolution of life and with the origins of metaphysics, ethics, and religion. Bergson's work was crowned with great success because it coincided with the leading tendencies of the epoch. But phenomenologists like Scheler, Ingarden, and Heidegger were set to ask the question whether the intuition of time leads to an intuitionism that then abandons conceptual knowledge. In a review of Jaspers's *Psychology of World-Views*, Heidegger mentions Bergson's opinion that human language depends on one's view of space but that it is unable to articulate a genuine experience of lived time. Heidegger calls this opinion an old drug on the market; he demands a new theory of conceptual work.[12]

Meanwhile, Wilhelm Dilthey had begun to work out his *Introduction to the Human Studies*. The peculiar character of the humanities—for instance, jurisprudence and theology—posed the following epistemological question: Are there different forms of conceptual knowledge? And, assuming an answer in the affirmative: How are these forms of understanding taken together with practice and art rooted in the totality of life? Dilthey's justification of the human studies was pursued from two different directions; first, by way of a descriptive psychology, supposed to make intelligible the process of education or the connection between need and labor, the presupposition of economy; second, by way of a hermeneutics, a reexperiencing and interpretation of other lives, the presupposition of a historical understanding that is itself founded in history. A theory of cognition and logical reflection was supposed to show how to combine these two approaches, but Dilthey never published the pertinent books (4 and 5) of his *Introduction to the Human Studies*. Some fragments and essays start with the thesis of phenomenality: we can speak about entities only insofar as they become phenomena for us. According to a second thesis, consciousness of lived experience is a totality—including not only perception and representation but also feeling and desire or striving after a good. In spite of his doctrine of phenomenality, Dilthey distinguishes between an outer and an inner world. The feeling of resistance points to the reality of an outer world; the inner world of lived experience is given only in time, and there, the process of time and its discontinuity points to the experience of other lives. Therefore, descriptive psychology ends in hermeneutics. But Dilthey never developed a founding theory of time consciousness or of individualization in space and time. Instead, he conquered himself with how the modern scientific approach destroys metaphysical illusions. He was also interested in how the specific human studies might be justified in terms of their distinctive character.

Dilthey was of the opinion that transcendental consciousness needed "blood": that is, the totality of life. In attempting to analyze this totality, he came across Husserl's phenomenology. Husserl himself confirmed in a letter: "What we strive for, coming from different studies, being determined by different historical motives, having passed through a different development, harmonizes and belongs together: on the one hand, a phenomenological analysis of elements, and on the other, a phenomenological analysis on a large scale—as disclosed in your morphology and typology of great cultural formation.[13] Husserl wrote this letter, in 1911, after long reflection. When in his youth he had attempted to formulate a philosophy of arithmetic, his view was criticized (for instance, by Frege) for being a kind of psychologism. Partly because of the need to overcome this criticism, Husserl developed his phenomenological point of view: in particular, the concepts of intentionality and categorical intuition, in the fifth and sixth of his *Logical Investigations*. In a famous lecture course in the winter of 1904–5, Husserl also analyzed the lower cognitive faculties, including time consciousness. Might not this analysis of time consciousness, then, serve to integrate Bergson's analysis of lived time and evolution and Dilthey's analysis of historical understanding? Might not Husserl be able to overcome historicism and relativism, the abyss of philosophy? Dilthey's understanding of the task of philosophy was much more cautious and limited: he saw philosophy as being finally confronted by the facticity of cultural formations, by the facticity of life itself. He used the term "facticity," for instance, when he wrote (in his essay on Novalis, the romantic poet) that if one applied its norms, Christian dogmatics offered an interpretation of the facticity of Jesus' appearance, an interpretation for a specific historical community. Is philosophy, then, limited simply in being hermeneutic? That is, is it limited to an interpretation of what ultimately remains factical? In an essay on philosophy as rigorous science, Husserl saw in opinions of this sort the decline and fall of philosophy. In his letter to Dilthey he wrote that the facticity and historicity of life and cultural formation can only supply examples for a philosophical analysis—which is itself concerned with essences and *a priori* structures. The restriction of philosophy to a kind of hermeneutics must and can be overcome by this transcendental approach.

What Husserl knew of theology was limited to what might be learned in confirmation classes. Could he then plausibly insist on a clarification of the essence of religion in such a way that the different historical religions could be construed as examples only—the Jewish, the Christian, the Buddhist, the Taoist? Or is history itself constituted by the discontinuity of a lived time that ends and begins again and again in ever new ways? Is history uniquely individualized so that there is no bridge between one life and another? In any event, human history is embedded in the lived time of human lives irreversibly propelled into the future. But does it follow that time itself is irreversible? A new philosophy should address these questions radically as well as universally. According to Husserl, phenomenology would become radical in addressing the problems of conceptual knowledge and time consciousness, and could become universal by linking the natural sciences and the human studies. In this spirit, Husserl published in his 1927 yearbook two different studies by his best pupils: *Being and Time* by Martin Heidegger, and a contribution to the ontology of mathematics by Oskar Becker. Since the volume was to deal with nature and history, with mathematics and historical understanding or theology, Husserl agreed to publish the first two parts of *Being and Time* without the important but problematic third division—on time and being (or temporal interpretation as hermeneutics).

But already in July 1919 (in the regular Saturday discussions), Heidegger had criticized Husserl's transcendental approach: he argued that if we are to speak of a transcendental or primary ego, we must interpret this ego as itself historical. The pure ego, the subject of objective-theoretical acts, is derived from this primary ego by the repression of all historicity and quality. Heidegger adopted Dilthey's view here: philosophy construed even as transcendental phenomenology must lead back to its origin, but that origin is factical, historical life. The foundation of philosophy itself is historical: therefore, its method must be hermeneutical. Of course, Heidegger was of the opinion that there is a theoretical or theorizing dimension to human life, which philosophy must penetrate. But he had grave reservations about the traditional preponderance of theory. From Parmenides to Husserl, he observed, philosophy had treated knowledge as a kind of seeing: what is "present-at-hand," for instance, is directly assigned additional value in the context of practice—"usefulness" perhaps. By contrast, Heidegger insists that in an originary way we are already familiar with the environing world of the "ready-to-hand"; theory begins only in an emancipation from this life-world. Similarly, in the sphere of religion, human life goes back to its origins and restores a meaningful life—but only in a *kairos*, in a unique moment (for instance, according to genuine Christian faith).

Augustine had already pointed out that thinking-as-seeing was the lust of the eyes or mere curiosity. When Heidegger gave a lecture course on Augustine and Neoplatonism (in the summer of 1921), he began five years of intensive research on Aristotle. Remember that *Being and Time* took its motto from Plato's *Sophist*. In that dialogue and in the *Parmenides*, Plato develops the logic of philosophy as dialectic: "suddenly" the main concepts change. In a famous note to his book on the concept of anxiety, Kierkegaard interpreted this suddenness (*exaiphnes*) as the unique moment, the *kairos* of Christian eschatology. Kierkegaard used St. Paul's "poetic" expression "ripe *ophthalmou*," *Augenblick*—the short, fugitive "twinkling of an eye," the unique moment of decision (1 Cor. 15:52). In that moment of decision, dialectic (the logic of philosophy) becomes an experimental dialectic, also an introduction to faith—to a formal, indicative hermeneutics, according to Heidegger. Aristotle, read through the eyes of Luther, may be said to point to the same sort of hermeneutics. In the first half of his lecture course on Plato's *Sophist* (winter of 1924–25), Heidegger dealt with the sixth book of the *Nicomachean Ethics*. There, he says, *phrōnesis* (as "resoluteness") gives an orientation in different situations and points to *kairos*. But an ontological prejudice destroyed this disclosure of *kairos*: hence, a destruction of the philosophical tradition also becomes necessary.

With Aristotle, the philosophical tradition comes to explore a multitude of senses of being (grasped, for instance, by the categories). The tradition held this multitude together in terms of analogy—as the coordination of all possible senses in terms of a simple leading meaning. That leading meaning was found in the idea of being as *ousia* or substance: namely, as a persistent presence. If presence is construed as the present—that is, as a dimension of time—the established tradition will be seen at once to approach time unilaterally, from only one of its many dimensions. A full inquiry into "being and time" would, therefore, have to acknowledge that limitation and move on to explicate the meaning of being more adequately in terms of the full play of time. In his lecture course for the winter of 1925–26, Heidegger had planned to deal with Aristotle; but in midsemester he suddenly switched to work on a new interpretation of Kant. He no longer planned to begin his destruction with a critique of Bergson's concept of time, for he began to see that Kant's schematism provided a way of structuring the manifold senses of being and distinguishing them from one another. The multitude of those senses of being must, it seemed, be open to *Dasein*, existence. Existence is temporal, carried toward different horizons of time, toward the ecstasies of existence. Every horizon has its own schema; for instance, the authentic future has, as its schema, "for the sake of." When this schema comes into play, the religious dimension of life is opened to us. From the "for the sake of" also springs a "for which," the schema of the inauthentic future. For instance, the craftsman working in his working environment does not as such try to find his way back to life for the sake of life. He does not anticipate death and so-called last things; he reckons only with specific goals. (In that way too, of course, he can reckon with his death—for example, by buying life insurance.) If, then, the "for which" is put out of play, a scientific point of view may arise, an inclusive theoretical view of things lacking any of the specific interests of the craftsman, or of public interests. The connection between time and being, between the horizons of time (that is, their schematization), and the different senses of being enables us to distinguish between practice and theory, between the religious dimension of life and the environmental world of craftsmen, between physics and the humanities, between historical understanding and theology.

Time has different dimensions: historicity, for example, with its tendency toward the unique moment, or, in a given moment of time, the self-forgotten and "wordless" reckoning of a mathematician. Heidegger wanted to be able to enter into dialogue with Bergson and Dilthey, of course, but also, for instance, with Einstein. In 1922, in fact, Bergson and Einstein discussed the problem of time at a conference in Paris. Einstein argued that the concept of lived time depended on a metaphysical illusion and that Bergson's adherence to it was based on an unscientific intuition. Indeed, Bergson could not justify his intuition by means of modern physics, or by a criticism of the dogmatism of physicists. *Being and Time* wanted to be able to respond to such matters. (The interpretation of *Being and Time* as a kind of existentialism by the way, or a mere historicism, is of course sheer nonsense, but it has been the fashion for several decades now.)

For the author of *Being and Time*, philosophy is not *Weltanschauung*. Scheler's political opinions belonged to *Weltanschauung*, not to philosophy. Not only Scheler and Simmel in Germany but also Bergson as well as Claudel in France wrote during World War I in support of their nation's interests. Thus, in his lecture course in 1919–20, Heidegger could say that Bergson's nationalistic opinions had nothing to do with his philosophy: that is, with the analysis of time consciousness. But *Being and Time* itself cites the polemics of Count Yorck of Wartenburg against public opinion. Do these polemics, then, belong to philosophy or to *Weltanschauung*? Whichever way we decide, *Being and Time* suddenly connects the individual and his or her fate to history and an encompassing community: that is, to the destiny of a generation and a people. It could not be avoided, but was the concept "a people" (used since Herder and

Hegel) not already obsolete in 1927? In his theological discussions, Heidegger was in the habit of quoting Franz Overbeck, Nietzsche's friend. Some decades later Heidegger published his lecture "Phenomenology and Theology" (written in the 1920s as part of a book originally planned to be published with Rudolf Bultmann). The introduction gives an appraisal of Nietzsche's *Untimely Meditations* and their reference to Hölderlin, and also appraisal of a booklet by Overbeck that "confirms the world-negating expectation of the End as the basis of primordial Christianity." Did not *Being and Time* itself use similarly one-sided theological presuppositions (for instance, the world-negating expectation of the End, criticized later on)? Heidegger intended his destruction to counteract all the idle talk about the decline of the West through a new unfolding of the task and logic of philosophy. But did that destruction perceive the real task of our time? Could it possibly supply philosophy with an adequate logic? Part III of *Being and Time* was intended to lay out an account of temporal interpretation as hermeneutics and schematization, but it was never published (and Heidegger burned his various drafts).

Nihilism and World Revolution

In the winter of 1929–30—that is, at the beginning of the great economic crisis—Heidegger gave a lecture course on the fundamental notions of metaphysics. He said that Kierkegaard's concept of the unique moment leads to a new philosophy of the future, which was unknown to the Greeks. Once again Heidegger stressed that formal, indicative hermeneutics could indeed be the logic of philosophy. He pointed to the Nietzscheanism of the time; philosophers and historians such as Scheler, Spengler, Klages, and Leopold Ziegler were following Nietzsche, he claimed, when they spoke of the antagonism of life and spirit. Nietzsche himself was of the opinion that historical greatness requires that a people have a myth, a "tragic" experience of life and world; he saw the underlying law of European history (from Aeschylus to Richard Wagner) as an articulation of the antagonism between Dionysian and Apollonian tendencies. Heidegger wished to present Nietzsche's critique in its most redical form; therefore, he too quoted the formula of the later Nietzsche: "Dionysus against the Crucified."[14]

Heidegger brought his lecture course to a close with a poem by Nietzsche which spoke of enjoyment as a desire for eternity. Jaspers had, in fact, already cited the text in his *Psychology of World Views* and had compared Kierkegaard's approach to weakness with Nietzsche's approach to strength. In the following years, Heidegger attempted to edit

Scheler's posthumous works with the help of the Nietzsche Archives (of course, this was impossible during the time of National Socialism). Later, Heidegger gave up discussing such "academic" philosophers as Husserl, Dilthey, Scheler, and Jaspers (Husserl himself, in a famous speech in 1931, had condemned Dilthey and Scheler—hence, Heidegger too—as anthropologists and historicists). Heidegger, however, did wish to discuss Nietzsche, because Nietzsche seemed to be in conformity with the spirit of the time. In his first lecture course on Nietzsche, in 1936–37, he said about Spengler: "What a revelation that was, two decades ago, for the multitude unfamiliar with genuine thought and its rich history: Spengler believed himself to have found out for the first time that every age and every culture has its own *Weltanschauung*. However, this was all just a very skillful and spirited popularization of thoughts and questions that had long ago—most recently by Nietzsche—been more deeply thought through. Nevertheless, those thoughts were by no means mastered, and to this hour have still not been mastered."[15]

The lecture course from the winter of 1929–30 points to the many problems of the time: poverty, political confusion, the vanishing strength of science, art, religion, and so on. There were many groups fighting this or that specific problem, but there was nobody who grasped the one, the unique overarching problem, the emergency of the time—nobody who sought "inner greatness." Heidegger said: "We must again call him who is able to threaten our *Dasein*. For: how does it stand for our *Dasein* if such an event as the World War leaves no trace?" What kind of shock, what sort of trace should World War I have left? Scheler spoke of the bankruptcy of Europe: nationalism and imperialism, which had enlisted God for their cause, had destroyed Europe and European reason. But at least for a period of a few years, Scheler had hoped for a religious renewal. Against such hopes, Heidegger took up Nietzsche's critique of Christianity. The lecture course on Heraclitus in the summer of 1943 once again mentions the "historical bankruptcy" of Christianity in modern history, and asks: "Is a Third World War necessary to demonstrate this bankruptcy?" "Christianity" here means the interpretation of the Christian faith by an Aristotle, whose philosophy has been transformed by Jewish and Arabic thought translated into Latin; it also refers to Hegel's speculative philosophy. Now, Heidegger claims, the two world wars would have warned us of our obliviousness to the truth of being.[16]

In his final lectures, Scheler had called for a time of balance and reconciliation between life and spirit, between the Dionysian and the Apollonian, between the East and West, between woman and man. According to Scheler, spirit is capable of saying "No!" to life, hence capable of grasping "ideas," the suprahistorical in life and history. Opposing Scheler's "metaphysical" presuppositions, Heidegger was concerned, rather, to explicate the *problem* of metaphysics—the event of the plurality of the modes of being and of *logos*. Man in his particular form of life, Heidegger affirmed, is open for a world—*is* spirit therefore; but spirit is historical, at least in certain of its dimensions. (This was also the critique of Plessner, who fled the Third Reich; and of Gehlen, who in 1933 and 1934 attempted to write a philosophy of National Socialism but, after 1936, took up Scheler's project of a philosophical anthropology.)

Scheler developed two kinds of metaphysics: the first was concerned with metaphysical perspectives in the various sciences—for instance, "metanthropology"; the second was a speculative metaphysics concerned with the ground of the world. Heidegger was of the opinion that the second sort of metaphysics unwittingly incorporated many of the presuppositions of the philosophical tradition: for instance, that of the distinction between essence and existence. For his own part, Heidegger went on to connect his fundamental ontology with the first kind of metaphysics—with "metaontology." It is true that only man asks the question "Why?" and it is true that this question leads to fundamental ontology. But the questioning itself, which constitutes the spirit of man, finds its presuppositions in life (man's place in the cosmos, as Scheler had said). The world of man is grounded by "earth," and this grounding must already be indicated in the transcendental or ontological sphere— well before the unfolding of special or regional ontologies. Men understand themselves as mortals in contrast to gods: that relation—whatever it means—must also be suitably indicated, but it must be analyzed by means of reflecting on the traditions of myth and great poetry, not in a mere speculative or metaphysical theology. With the help of Scheler's important article "Knowledge and Labor" (*Erkenntnis und Arbeit*), Heidegger was able to grasp the connection between history and the schematization or unfolding of ontologies. Scheler had pointed out that mathematical physics and capitalism were motivated by the same schema of world access, a technical interest (analogous to the way parent birds and nestlings are said to be driven by a schema in accord with which the parent birds search out and find food for their young).

Heidegger's new encounter with Max Scheler also led to a confrontation with Nietzsche that began in the winter of 1929–30. In his attempt to develop the problem of this new metaphysics (proclaimed by Scheler), Heidegger had to deal with the great beginnings of metaphysics, with Plato and Aristotle in particular. The central problem of Plato's *Sophist* concerned how, in fact, antithetical concepts such as *stasis* and *kinesis* are related. Heidegger discussed the same dialectical issue in Aristotle: How do *ousia* and *kinesis* relate? Heidegger was concerned with Aristotle's notion of orientation within a given situation (according to the sixth book of the *Nicomachean Ethics*) and with "substance" (according to his *Physics*). Heidegger offers a "destruction" of the concept of being (*Metaphysics* 9.10), but he does not discuss the problem of *kinesis* and time and its relation to book 12 of Aristotle's *Metaphysics*: that is, in terms of its relation to the theology of Aristotle. After the publication of *Being and Time*, Heidegger abandoned medieval Aristotelianism (also, Brentano's approach). He no longer posed the question of how *ousia*, understood as essence and substance, could belong to the different dimensions of time. His new concern was with the dimension itself—in which *ousia* and *kinesis* do belong together. Thus *energeia* becomes the leading concept of being: that is, *energeia* understood in terms of *dynamis* or open possibility (not *energeia* as *entelecheia*—as, for instance, in Hegel's sense). Heidegger construed *dynamis* as qualification and appropriation (*Eignung*); hence, *energeia* could be understood as *Ereignis*, the event of appropriation. In *Being and Time* (also in his lecture course from the summer of 1927), Heidegger had used Latin expressions to formulate his own claims (*essentia* and *substantia* as equivalents for *ousia*, and similarly for conveying the sense of "temporal," "interpretation," "presence"). He also made use of certain technical terms formed in the seventh century from Greek roots, such as "hermeneutics." After the publication of *Being and Time*, however, Heidegger was of the opinion that one should not present the leading concepts of Greek philosophy through their Latin translations: for example, one should avoid using *actualitas* for *energeia*. The German, it seems, is closer to the Greek language. *Energeia* (connected with *ergon*), for instance, means *Wirklichkeit*: that is, "to be at work." The origin of the "work" of art, thus, points to *energeia* and *Ereignis*.

Together with Nietzsche, Heidegger wished to return to the "tragic" age of Greece, when philosophy and poetry seemed to be close neighbors. The *energeia* of Aristotle was no more than an echo of a more originary *physis* (Heidegger was of the opinion that not only in Hellenistic times was a concept like *peri physeos* used; even Heraclitus used *physis* to convey his conception of an all-encompassing nature). Heidegger pointed to the fact that the verb *esse* or *sein* takes such forms as *fui, ich bin*, "to be"; in other words, besides the root *sein* there is a root *bhu*, signifying becoming. Nietzsche succeeded in formulating the old problem of becoming and being, but he remained deeply entangled in the ideologies of the nineteenth century. (Heidegger pressed the point against Nietzsche, after his first political disappointment [in 1934–35] at the end of his first lecture course on Hölderlin.) Hölderlin was able to draw the problem out more clearly: see, for example, Heidegger's remarks on the categories of modality in his essays on the Empedocles project. The problem concerns the salvation of European *Geist* in a time of decline. Nevertheless, Heidegger's first lecture course on Nietzsche takes this project of salvation to be the task of the Germans: "The varied conflict we know between the Dionysian and the Apollonian, between holy passion and sober exposition, is a hidden law of the style of the historical determination of the German people, and one day must find us ready and prepared for it to take its form. This antithesis is not just a formula with the help of which we may only describe our 'culture.' With this conflict, Hölderlin and Nietzsche have set a question mark in front of the task of the Germans, to find their essence in a historical way. Will we understand the question mark? One thing is certain, history will take its revenge upon us if we do not understand it."[17]

In his inaugural address as rector in 1933, Heidegger claimed that Nietzsche was the last great philosopher, considering his remarks about the death of God, that is, considering his diagnosis of nihilism. The political dimension of this diagnosis was formulated in Nietzsche's conception of great politics, a politics based on philosophical foundations. Still, in the summer of 1936, in his lecture-course on Schelling, Heidegger declares: "The two men who, each in his own way, have introduced a countermovement to nihilism—Mussolini and Hitler—have learned from Nietzsche, each in an essentially different way. But even with that, Nietzsche's authentic metaphysical domain has not yet come into its own."[18] In the circumstances permitting such an utterance in 1936, Heidegger affirmed that Mussolini and Hitler appeared to rely on Nietzsche, yet they did not understand Nietzsche's confrontation with the metaphysical tradition. In later lectures Heidegger finally tried to show that Nietzsche's diagnosis of nihilism was itself the strongest kind of nihilism. But at least the first lecture course on Nietzsche, from the winter of 1936–37, makes clear just who Heidegger had construed Nietzsche from 1929–30 on (these passages were silently omitted by Heidegger in the 1961 edition!). Heidegger said: When Nietzsche spoke about the death of God or the death of the God of morality, he was not only standing before the "event of the dying God"; he was also waiting for the coming (Dionysian) God. During Nietzsche's lifetime (after 1871, in the *Gründerjahre*), conjuring with phrases like "God, Liberty, Fatherland," the Germans were able to co-opt God for many ends; that mendacity reached its summit in World War I, in which each of the European nations in turn claimed God for its undertakings in the war. Nietzsche experienced the death of this "God." Besides Hölderlin, Heidegger says, Nietzsche was the "only believing man who lived in the nineteenth century."[19]

In an additional passage of this lecture (not written down in the manuscript), Heidegger says that he used Nietzsche's phrase about the death of God in his rectoral address of 1933 "with full consciousness." That means that he also relied on Nietzsche's "great politics"—on the diagnosis of a world revolution and the necessity of the fight against so-called democracy. "Europe tries to cling to 'democracy' and will not admit that this 'democracy' will be Europe's historical death. For democracy is—as Nietzsche clearly saw—only a kind of nihilism." Democracy merely tries to reestablish the old values—in a leveling of all differences between men. Here, Heidegger has in mind Nietzsche's teaching about the revolt of the slaves in Hellenistic Christianity and construes liberalism and socialism as secularized forms of this revolt. Those who experience the Dionysian depth of life must defend status and difference. Nietzsche did not speak about Marxism, of course, but Heidegger freely translated Nietzsche's diagnosis so as to apply to the time after the revolution of Russia: "According to Nietzsche, Christianity is as nihilistic as Bolshevism and therefore as nihilistic as mere socialism." Heidegger also links this diagnosis of the time of world revolution to the beginning of philosophizing; that is, he links it to the teaching of Heraclitus on war as the father of all things, on the depth of *physis*, and on the difference between master and slave. Contrary to the opinion of Hannah Arendt, therefore, it was precisely the study of the Presocratics in the lonely hut at Todtnauberg, joined to the study of Nietzsche, that led Heidegger to choose National Socialism.

It may suffice to quote from one of the documents concerned with Heidegger's political path after 1929. At the end of 1931 Hermann Mörchen, in a passage in his notebook about a visit to Todtnauberg, observes that Heidegger and his wife had become National Socialists: "He does not understand," Mörchen writes, "much about politics. And therefore it was especially his disdain for mediocrity and for doing things by half measures that made him expect something from the Party, which had promised to do something decisive and to contradict communism effectively." Democratic idealism, and the conscientiousness of men like Brüning, could do nothing in this situation. Heidegger was not afraid of dictatorship as a political means, for "only by means of such a dictatorship could one avoid a much worse communist dictatorship that would extinguish all culture of individuality and personality and, therefore, all culture in the Occidental way." This means that Heidegger had wanted to save Europe by his political choice: in this conviction, he was only radicalizing his former position. (Afterward, he himself said that he had relied on the political judgment of Friedrich Naumann.)[20]

After discussing Nietzsche's statement that "being" had become a mere haze, Heidegger said in his lecture course *Introduction to Metaphysics*, in 1935: "This Europe, which in its ruinous blindness is forever on the point of cutting its own throat, lies today in a great pincers, squeezed between Russia on the one side and American on the other. From a metaphysical point of view, Russia and America are the same:

the same dreary technological frenzy, the same unrestricted organization of the average man.''[21] Heidegger does not use Nietzsche's and Scheler's term *ressentiment*, but he delineates the conception of *ressentiment* as an attack at all levels. He also uses Ernst Jünger's notion of Americanism: America, he claimed, was able to win the Great War because Americanism is merely effective organization without traditional restrictions (restrictions imposed, for instance, by an aristocracy or a monarch's ideals). In Germany, there had been a revolution in 1933, but things ended up much the same: in Marxism, the organization of economic relationships; in the West, the organization of the given "positive"; in National Socialism, but it amounted finally to nothing more than the organization of the "race" or the vital energies of a people. In each case, spirit or the spiritual-historical Dasein had become mere "intelligence." Here, Heidegger adopts Scheler's term (not, of course, his idealism). Scheler had used the results of Wolfgang Köhler's famous intelligence tests with apes in order to distinguish between spirit and intelligence (a mere technical faculty). Scheler was able to claim, therefore, that even an Edison, with his "intelligence" as an inventor, differed from brute animals only in a quantitative, not a qualitative, sense. That is to say: in Bolshevism, Americanism, and National Socialism, men behave like animals.

In the years 1936 through 1938, in total seclusion, Heidegger wrote his main work, *Contributions to Philosophy*—a final attempt, in the company of Nietzsche and Hölderlin, to search for a "revolution"; it offers a sharp criticism of National Socialism, and of "Liberalism" and Bolshevism as well. (The fragmentary manuscript was published some fifty years later, in 1989.) Because he confronts here the totalitarian attempt to mobilize all resources for a new world war, Heidegger now points out that all the sciences are now in the service of these tendencies; that is, he abandons his former attempt to distinguish between physics, history, and theology—between the different modes of *logos*. Only one great drama remains: totalitarianism versus the search for new and original beginnings. Heidegger thus begins to develop his later opinion that the universal technology of our time is only the end of the metaphysical attempt to grasp the being of all beings. Heidegger regards Max Weber's disenchantment (*Entzauberung*) with the European form of rationalization as itself a great enchantment (*Verzauberung*); but for Heidegger it is only the enchantment of metaphysics, the European tradition that had remained unchanged ever since Plato's theory of ideas. Here, Heidegger follows Dilthey and Nietzsche, who viewed the metaphysical tradition as a totality: that is, as an illusionary search for ultimate foundations. This search for grounds, this totalitarianism of universal technology, reveals itself as European rationality, because *logos* and *ratio* mean reason but also ground.

Now when Heidegger uses the term "metaphysics," he is talking about the leading tendencies of our history, not just philosophical theories. He was of the opinion that great philosophers had found the apt term for their times, the name for their leading tendencies. Nietzsche, the last of the great philosophers, had (according to Heidegger's interpretation) to find the right term for the totalitarian "will to power." Heidegger confirms that Nietzsche had indeed grasped the truth: metaphysics, now, as totalitarian technology. Thus, following the defeat of France in June 1940, Heidegger could say, in a lecture that draws a continuous line from the Cartesian ego to Nietzsche's will to power: "These days we are witnesses to a mysterious law of history, which states that at a certain point a people no longer measures up to the metaphysics that has sprung from its own history; this happens when, precisely, that metaphysics is transformed into the absolute." A few weeks later, when the British fleet destroyed the French fleet after its capitulation, Heidegger found an apt example of Nietzsche's concept of the "justice" of the will to power: "When the British recently blew the French fleet docked at Oran to smithereens, they found the action 'justified' from *their* point of view, for 'justified' merely means 'what serves the enchantment of power.' At the same time, what this suggests is that *we* dare not and cannot ever justify that action."[22]

By the 1940s, Heidegger no longer regarded Nietzsche as the philosopher who had seen the measure of Occidental history and had given an answer to the Greeks. In fact, he no longer viewed Nietzsche as having anything to do with the Greeks, because Nietzsche thought in the manner of Machiavelli and the Romans. Since Herder and Hegel, the Romans had been regarded as the representatives of totalitarian politics. Hegel had illustrated Roman history with a reference to Napoleon's sentence to Goethe: "Now politics is destiny." Against this, Heidegger, affirms in his lecture course on Schelling: "Spirit is destiny." Nietzsche's biologism is made responsible for the National Socialistic conception of *Zucht*, and Heidegger stresses that Nietzsche necessarily pointed the way to the "*blonde Bestie*." In 1942, Richard Kuhn (biochemist at Heidelberg and Nobel prize winner) received the Goethe prize of the city of Frankfurt; and Heidegger writes that (under the protection of Goethe) *Schrifttumsführung* (the propaganda and censorship of Dr. Goebbels) may now be combined with *Schwängerungsführung*, decisions concerning the desired number of male and female children in the time of the war. The superhuman *Führer* are nothing but agents of a total mobilization, organizing with their "instinct" a mere animality well below humanity. Heidegger's study of Nietzsche was hardly easygoing reading; he himself said, later, that he had suffered a physical breakdown during his Nietzsche lectures: "Nietzsche hat mich kaputt gemacht."[23]

End and New Beginning

In his lecture course on Parmenides, in the winter of 1942–43 (during the battle of Stalingrad), Heidegger wanted his students to learn what "victory" means for the "metaphysical" nation of the Germans: "It is important to realize that, when it comes to 'victory,' this historical people has already won and is unconquerable so long as it remains the people of poets and thinkers that it is in its essence, so long as it does not fall victim to the ever-pressing and thus fearful threat of straying from, and thereby misunderstanding, its essence." In the next term, the summer of 1943, Heidegger gave a lecture course on Heraclitus ("The Beginning of Occidental Thought"). He closed the course with remarks about decline and fall, the confusion of modernity, and the greatest and truest task of the Germans: against their will, the Germans might well be tested by those who know nothing; are they strong enough (above mere readiness for death!) to "rescue beginning and origin from the small-mindedness of the modern world"? Heidegger wanted to educate students so that, discerning the truth of being, they would be able to fight at the age of thirty or forty against mere "modernity." That would place them, as thirty- and forty-year-olds, between 1953 and 1963, at a time the Americans (knowing nothing about beginning and origin) would "test" the Germans during the years of occupation.[24]

In a memorandum written during his denazification hearings, Heidegger said that not only today but even "then" (in the years after 1938) he saw the rule of the will to power in global history: "Today everything stands within this reality, whether it is called communism or fascism or world democracy. From the standpoint of the reality of the Will to Power I saw even then what *is*. This reality of the Will to Power can be expressed, with Nietzsche, in the proposition: 'God is dead.' . . . This means: The supersensible world, more specifically the world of the Christian God, has lost its effective force in history. . . . If that were not the case, would World War I have been possible? Even more: If that were not the case, would World War II have become possible?"[25] When Heidegger speaks of "world democracy" and not simply of "democracy," he obviously means to convey his conviction that democracy is only one tendency within the world revolution and the struggle for world domination. He always viewed political undertakings directed against the so-called underdeveloped countries as a kind of imperialism. He also insisted that democracy in our time remains an illusion: were there, for instance, democratic decisions made about the use of atomic energy in war and peace, he asks, or about the traffic and information systems? In 1966 Heidegger clearly stated in his *Spiegel* interview: "For me, today, it is a decisive question as to how any political system—and which one—

can be adapted to an epoch of technology. I know of no answer to this question. I am not convinced that it is democracy."[26] Of course, this interview was the greatest disappointment for those of his pupils who had taken up Heidegger's criticism of totalitarianism, beginning in 1942, and who had tried (at least in Germany) to rehabilitate practical philosophy.

To what political and historical context did Heidegger's search for new beginnings belong? After 1945 he began a dialogue with the French (for instance, in his letter on "humanism"). Of course, there was no dialogue with the Americans. Only very late did Heidegger give up the term "Americanism" and his judgment about "the" Americans, for instance in his *Spiegel* interview: The Americans "are still caught up in a thought which, under the guise of pragmatism, facilitates technical operation and manipulation but at the same time blocks the way to reflection on the genuine nature of modern technology. At the same time, here and there in the U.S.A., attempts are made to become free from pragmatic-positivistic thinking." In the next sentence Heidegger (in his youth a passionate reader of Dostoevski) looks to the East: "And who of us would be in a position to decide whether or not one day in Russia or China very old traditions of 'thought' may awaken that will help make possible for man a free relationship to the technological world?" There is a dialogue with a Japanese—not a member of the Zen Buddhist Kyoto school but a translator of Hölderlin; Heidegger has in mind Shintoist Japan, the "way of the gods"—and in 1946 and 1947 he tried to read and translate Lao Tzu.[27] With the end of the West and its domination of the world, Europe will be able to see that it is only a part of the world and that the world has different great traditions. Therefore, dialogue is necessary, but Europe must find its own way out of its own tradition. Heidegger again claims "inner" greatness as a resistance to modernity. Hence, he says in his *Spiegel* interview: "Recently I had a long dialogue in Provence with René Char—a poet and resistance fighter, as you know. In Provence now, launch pads are being built and the countryside laid waste in unimaginable fashion. This poet, who certainly is open to no suspicion of sentimentality or of glorifying the idyllic, said to me that the uprooting of man that is now taking place is the end, unless thinking and the poetic imagination once again regain nonviolent power."[28]

Can Heidegger, who celebrated Albert Leo Schlageter, be allowed to stand beside René Char? Hans-Georg Gadamer reports that as early as 1923 he missed one of Heidegger's lectures: Heidegger had gone to the train station to witness the return of Albert Leo Schlageter for burial. After engaging in terroristic acts, Schlageter had been condemned to death by the French occupation troops, and his body was transported to his birthplace near Freiburg. Not only the nationalists but the communists as well wanted to celebrate Schlageter as a hero (also, in fact, the Catholic

Church and the universities). Afterward, however, the National Socialists succeeded in adopting Schlageter as a martyr to their cause; hence, as rector, Heidegger was able to give his speeches about Schlageter (who, as it happened, had attended the same school Heidegger did). Already in 1933–34, National Socialists such as Jaensch and Krieck were condemning *Being and Time* as "Jewish" and "schizophrenic."[29] Was it merely an irony that French resistance fighters relied on this book and therefore found their way to Heidegger? Around 1938, Heidegger had no *political* alternative to National Socialism; nevertheless, he condemned this totalitarianism in formulations that might well have cost him his life, had they come to light in the darkness of those days. After 1945, resistance against the occupation became the aim of many colonies as well, but now such fights and such wars had to be allowed through the silent agreement of the new superpowers. So "resistance" could be directed against the madness of the new technologies drawn into the service of the struggle for world domination.

For more than twelve years, also, Heidegger exchanged books and articles with Paul Célan, the translator of Char's notebooks beginning with the resistance. He read Célan's poems from a point of view focused in a particular poem dedicated to René Char; that poem, "Argumentum e silentio," speaks about the word "resistance." When Célan visited Heidegger for a second time, he did not visit Hugo Friedrich, who was the author of a famous book on modern lyric poetry. Obviously, he would not have visited Paul de Man either, if he had read de Man's famous article on modern lyric poetry or on Hölderlin or Célan. After the discovery of the nationalistic and anti-Semitic articles written by Paul de Man in his youth, Geoffrey Hartman wrote: "Once again we feel betrayed by the intellectuals. The accusations we bring, however, are a warning to ourselves." But that betrayal can and must be criticized without reference to any controversial biographical facts. Hartman also mentions the historical context of the activities of de Man in 1941, the "passing enthusiasm for Mussolini on the part of such figures as W. B. Yeats and Emil Ludwig," but also the existence of "a large group of fascist intellectuals active in France and Belgium" (for instance, Maurice Blanchot).[30] Lyotard now relies on Blanchot's opinion that anti-Semitism was directed against people lacking "myth" and that Heidegger was also unable to recognize such people. But already in 1933–34 Heidegger defended Jewish colleagues such as von Hevesy and Fraenkel as "noble Jews" with "exemplary characters."[31] Obviously, they seemed "noble" in the sense defined by Nietzsche: out of their tradition and destiny they built their "exemplary characters." But what about the Jews who were not "noble" in this sense, ordinary assimilated Jews, Zionists, Jews without Lyotard's quotation marks, and the real historical person Célan?

In his *Contributions to Philosophy* Heidegger repeats: "This is the time of *Untergang*." He understands *Untergang* in terms of the fall of the hero in Greek tragedy. According to Hölderlin's and Heidegger's interpretation, the fall and death of Antigone signify a new age, an epochal change; her death has something new to say—it "teaches" us. This *Untergang* is not only decline and fall but also the setting of the sun—a setting into an element that does not vanish (*to me dunon pote*, as Heidegger says, with Heraclitus, in his lecture course of the summer of 1943). Nietzsche seems to be of the opinion that metaphysical and poetic conceptions concerning such an *Untergang* must be taken ironically—not only as tragedy but also as comedy. Heidegger treats this *Untergang* as tragedy alone (perhaps such tragedy was at times also comedy, but only against his will).

NOTES

1. Matthew Arnold, cited in Jacques Derrida, *De l'esprit: Heidegger et la question* (Paris: Galilée, 1987), n. 73.

2. Quoted in Heinrich Wiegand Petzet, *Auf einen Stern zugehen: Begegnungen mit Martin Heidegger, 1929–1976* (Frankfurt, 1983), p. 232.

3. Franz Rosenzweig, *Zweistromland*, vol. 3 of *Gesammelte Schriften* (Dordrecht, 1984), pp. 313–68.

4. Martin Heidegger, *Zur Bestimmung der Philosophie* (Frankfurt, 1987), p. 7. Cf. my essay "Scheler und die heutigen anthropologischen Ansätze zur Metaphysik," *Heidelberger Jahrbücher* 33 (1989): p. 175–92.

5. Keiji Nishitani, *Was ist Religion?* (Frankfurt, 1982), p. 310. Cf. Otto Pöggeler, *Heidegger und die hermeneutische Philosophie* (Freiburg, 1983), pp. 362–64.

6. Wei Hsiung, "Chinesische Heidegger-Rezeption," in *Zur philosophischen Aktualität Heideggers*, vol. 3, ed. D. Papenfuss and O. Pöggeler (Frankfurt, 1990).

7. Hugo Ott, *Martin Heidegger: Unterwegs zu seiner Biographie* (Frankfurt, 1988), pp. 83, 106–7.

8. Three letters by Heidegger, published in Papenfuss and Pöggeler, *Zur philosophischen Aktualität Heideggers*, vol. 2.

9. Martin Heidegger, *Ontologie (Hermeneutik der Faktizität)* (Frankfurt, 1988), § 11.

10. Cf. *Anfänge der dialektischen Theologie*, ed. Jürgen Moltmann (Munich, 1987), pt. 1, pp. 95–101; trans. Jeffrey A. Barash, *Martin Heidegger and the Problem of Historical Meaning* (Dordrecht, 1988), p. 149.

11. *Rudolf Bultmanns Werk und Wirkung*, ed. Bernd Jaspert (Darmstadt, 1984), p. 202. Cf. also Otto Pöggeler, *Martin Heidegger's Path of Thinking* (Atlantic Highlands, N.J., 1987), pp. 24–26.

12. See Otto Pöggeler, *Bergson und die Phänomenologie der Zeit*, in *Aratro Corona Messoria: Festgabe für Günther Pflug* (Bonn, 1988), pp. 153–69.

13. *Materialien zur Philosophie Wilhelm Diltheys*, ed. F. Rodi and H.-U. Lessing (Frankfurt, 1984), p. 117; Otto Pöggeler, "Heideggers Begegnung mit Dilthey," *Dilthey-Jahrbuch* 4 (1987): 121–60.

14. Martin Heidegger, *Die Grundbegriffe der Metaphysik* (Frankfurt, 1983), pp. 225–27, 103–11.

15. Martin Heidegger, *Nietzsche* (Pfullingen, 1961), 1:360.

16. Heidegger, *Die Grundbegriffe der Metaphysik*, pp. 243–45, 255–56; Martin Heidegger, *Heraklit* (Frankfurt, 1979), pp. 209, 74, 84.

17. Martin Heidegger, *Einführung in die Metaphysik* (Tübingen, 1953), pp. 54–56; Martin Heidegger, *Hölderlins Hymnen "Germanien" und "Der Rhein"* (Frankfurt, 1980), pp. 294, 122–23; Heidegger, *Nietzsche*, 1:124.

18. Otto Pöggeler, "Den Führer führen? Heidegger und kein Ende," *Philosophische Rundschau* 32 (1985): 26–67, 56–57; Martin Heidegger, *Schelling: Vom Wesen der menschlichen Freiheit* (Frankfurt, 1988), pp. 40–41.

19. Martin Heidegger, *Nietzsche: Der Wille zur Macht als Kunst* (Frankfurt, 1985), pp. 190–92; for the following passages, see pp. 193, 31.

20. Hermann Mörchen, in *Der Zauberer von Messkirch* (Westdeutsches Fernsehen, 1989); Martin Heidegger, " 'Only a God Can Save Us': The *Spiegel* Interview (1966)," in *Heidegger: The Man and the Thinker*, ed. Thomas Sheehan (Chicago, 1981), p. 48.

21. Heidegger, *Einführung in die Metaphysik*, p. 28.

22. Heidegger, *Nietzsche*, 2:165, 198.

23. Ibid., pp. 144, 221, 200, 309; Martin Heidegger, *Vorträge und Aufsätze* (Pfullingen, 1954), pp. 91–97.

24. Martin Heidegger, *Parmenides* (Frankfurt, 1982), p. 114; Heidegger, *Heraklit*, p. 181.

25. Martin Heidegger, *Die Selbstbehauptung der deutschen Universität: Das Rektorat 1933/34* (Frankfurt, 1983), p. 25.

26. Heidegger, "The *Spiegel* Interview," p. 55.

27. Ibid., p. 61; Otto Pöggeler, *West-East Dialogue: Heidegger and Lao-tzu* (*Heidegger and Asian Thought*), ed. Graham Parkes (Honolulu, 1987), pp. 47–78.

28. Heidegger, "The *Spiegel* Interview," p. 56.

29. See Ott, *Martin Heidegger*, p. 244.

30. Geoffrey Hartman, "Blindness and Insight: Paul de Man, Fascism, and Deconstruction, *New Republic*, March 7, 1988, p. 26; Otto Pöggeler, "Passing-by and Trace: Hölderlin and Celan" (Yale Colloquium on Speculative Philosophy and Hermeneutics: Hegel and Hölderlin, New Haven, Conn., 1990); Otto Pöggeler, *Spur des Worts: Zur Lyrik Paul Celans* (Freiburg, 1986), pp. 259–71: "Todtnauberg."

31. J.-F. Lyotard, *Heidegger et "les juifs"* (Paris, 1988); Ott, *Martin Heidegger*, p. 199.

5

Heidegger and Hitler's War

DOMENICO LOSURDO

I

The enthusiasm aroused by the outbreak of World War I among German intellectuals is well known. To quote one among them, Max Weber, "This war, whatever its outcome may be, is truly great and marvelous beyond any expectation."[1] That was a moment when not even the theorist of "disenchantment" could escape the "fascination" of war. Even after Germany's defeat, self-criticism was very slow to blame German culture as a whole. The general assessment seemed to imply that it was not so much the war that was to be questioned but the divisiveness and the crisis of the West.

In 1931 Jaspers observed: "Politics, as the *egotistical calculation of a state and territorial unit*, considers all others as allies or enemies, according to the context in which they belong. A country allies itself with strangers against those with whom it has a historical and cultural affinity. . . . England and France used Indian and black troops on the Rhine front. Germany would not refuse an alliance with Russia, if such an alliance offered the possibility of recapturing its freedom."[2] The West, then, was in the process of destroying itself. On the one hand, as Spengler emphasizes, the use of colored peoples to quell domestic conflicts was not entirely new in the West. The English made use of Indian tribes to subdue the rebellious American colonies. And later, during the French Revolution, "the Jacobins utilized the Haitian blacks in order to promote the 'rights of man.'" But the mass use of colored peoples during World War I brought about a change in quality—one that implied a radical power change detrimental to the West: "World War I was lost not by Germany but by the West, when it lost its respect for colored people."[3] Indeed, Jünger insisted, the Western democracies risked the loss of their colonial dominions in order to repay the debt "in blood and work force" which they contracted with colored peoples in 1914–18.[4] The country that emerged victorious, Spengler complained, was Russia, which, with its October Revolution, put down the "white mask" to become "again a great Asiatic, 'Mongolian' power," an integral part of the colored populations, and animated by fierce hatred for Europe."[5]

To remedy the dangerous division that developed in the course of World War I, Jaspers proposed "a policy *founded on the historical consciousness of totality*, which would be . . . in a position to perceive, beyond each single state, the future interests of human existence as it emerges from the antagonism between East and West, between European freedom and Russian fanaticism. Such a policy would not ignore the profound human and spiritual bond between the German and the Anglo-Saxon and Latin peoples, and would regard with horror the treason many times perpetrated to date against their affinity."[6] Against this background, and always keeping in mind the tragic experience of the discord in the Western world, Jaspers complained that the war was "no longer a conflict between different faiths, but a struggle of interests, a conflict not between authentic civilizations but between administrative entities. . . . It [did] not reach a historical conclusion, such as, for instance, the victory of the Greeks over the Persians, which is still the foundation of Western man's personality, or even the victory of the Romans over the Carthaginians, which consolidated the Greeks' conquest."[7]

Clearly, the new Persia that threatened the West was represented by the Soviet Union. Jaspers assumed an apocalyptic tone: "Today *the last campaign against nobility* begins. . . . Past revolutions could take place without destroying man; if this one should succeed, it would annihilate man."[8] In a recent work, Ernst Nolte wrote that the Jaspers' text from which I have quoted (whose title translates as "The Spiritual Situation of the Time") was not suited to dissuade the Germans from joining Nazism.[9] Jaspers, however, never adhered to the Nazi regime—"for reasons of a private nature," Lukács writes, alluding to the philosopher's Jewish wife.[10] But these "private reasons" are also linked to his philosophical outlook: in the origin of the West, there are not only the "Greek philosophers" but also the "Jewish prophets."[11] The contrast with Nazism is evident, and Jaspers declared that he had already begun, in 1933, to hope for a military intervention by the Western powers against the Third Reich[12]—even if there is no public record of his hope in this regard.

At any rate, the East-West opposition and the renewed appeal to save the West, following the example of the Greeks, constitute a theme also found in Heidegger. The reference to "Grecism" is not and cannot be a unifying element for all of humanity, but it serves to define the conflicting parties: "Heraclitus's name" is not "the formula of a thought of humanity embracing the whole of mankind [*Allerweltsmenschheit an sich*; it is rather the name of the original force of the Germanic-Western race in its first confrontation with the Asiatics."[13] Heidegger constantly returns to this confrontation between the West and Asia, to this *Auseinandersetzung* that led Greece to establish colonies on the coast of Asia Minor. "We must not forget," the philosopher writes in 1937, that "the Greeks would not have become what they will forever be, if they had closed themselves within their own 'space.' Only through the harshest yet creative clash with elements foreign and hostile to them—the Asiatic elements—did they rise to the apex of their uniqueness and historical greatness."[14] Heidegger hopes that the "great decision concerning Europe" will not come about "through annihilation [*auf dem Wege der Vernichtung*]"[15] and that there will therefore be no repetition of the brotherly bloodshed of World War I. But mutual understanding among the European peoples is possible only if each acquires consciousness of its "historical mission": "The fundamental character of their mission is defined for Western peoples, the creators of history, by the current international moment as the salvation of the West." Only through "radical decisions" can "the menace that threatens the West with total eradication and general disarray" be foiled.[16] And, in this context, an important role must be assumed by Germany, which is at the "center" of Europe (and the West): Germany is the "country richest in neighbors and, therefore, most threatened," the one that feels most deeply and painfully the "pincers" that the Soviet Union and the United States (two countries that represent, on the philosophical level, the very same principle—that of the explosion of technology and the "massification" of man,[17] bring to bear on Western Europe.

During the same period, referring to the "great speech at the Reichstag" on March 7, 1936, in which "the *Führer* and the *Rechskanzler* Adolf Hitler" spoke of the European nations as a "family," and of Europe as the "home" of this family, Carl Schmitt underlines "the national and *völkisch* kinship among the European peoples"—in contrast, however, to the peoples foreign to Europe and the West: for example, Ethiopia (where fascist Italy rightly refused to recognize a "homogeneity on the level of civilization") and the U.S.S.R. (unfortunately added to the "community of Western states" by the enemies of Germany).[18] Schmitt protested the pact of May 2, 1935, that France had concluded with the Soviet Union, which had joined the League of Nations and its council; he protested, that is, the deterioration of the *cordon sanitaire* applied to Russia after the October Revolution. It is in this context that Heidegger's observation

during the summer semester of 1935 must be read. Heidegger notes that
Europe "in its regrettable blindness is always on the point of stabbing
itself."[19] But there is no historical sense in trying to find, in Heidegger's
texts of this period (which underline the necessity of comprehension
among European peoples), utterances and programs opposed to Nazism.
The pathos of the European and Western community, and even the appeal
for respect for the peculiarity of each European people, are themes that
figure conspicuously in Hitler's speeches in those years—aimed at undermining Versailles and at remilitarizing Germany in the name of equal
dignity with the victors of World War I.[20] Hitler was cautious, however,
fearing their military intervention. It was not by accident that Jaspers
declared that his own hope, after 1933, for an Anglo-French intervention
in Germany seemed to acquire some consistency in 1936 (on the occasion
of the entry of German troops into the Rhineland, out of spite not only
for Versailles but also for the Locarno Pact, freely negotiated by Germany
in 1925).[21] European and Western passivity in diplomacy involving the
Reich and the public pronouncements in those years offered, therefore,
no peaceful approach. Its further evolution would have confirmed that.
But Jaspers observes that, already, "everybody sensed—including, of
course, Heidegger—that in the end the situation would lead to war."[22] On
the other hand, as early as 1933, hailing Hitler's ascent to power, Spengler
saw the foreshadowing of the outbreak of World War II.[23]

II

The war that many expected from the East broke out, instead, in the
West (with France and England allied with Poland, which was itself
quickly destroyed). It was not the "historical" war on which Jaspers
pondered in 1931. He now hoped for the defeat of Germany, whose anti-
Semitic frenzy foreshadowed the "final solution." But the vast majority
of his countrymen, even his "old friends," Jaspers adds, were hoping, of
course, for a "German victory."[24] Doubtless, among those was Heidegger. Is there perhaps a moment of embarrassment for him in the presence
of a conflict arising from an unexpected turn of events? World War I, he
observed in his course of lectures of 1936–37, had shown the validity of
the Nietzschean thesis about the death of God, the moral God of Christian
tradition: in fact, both opposing armies at war in the "Christian West"
appealed, in their merciless struggle, to the same "benevolent God."[25]
Was the new conflict not the confirmation of the spreading of nihilism in
the West? Germany, which stood as a defender of the West, had in the
meantime concluded an alliance with Japan and a nonaggression pact
with Bolshevik Russia. This is a point on which Thomas Mann exercised

his irony in a radio broadcast addressed to a hypothetical German public.[26] And in 1935, had not Heidegger himself urged Europe, squeezed between U.S.A. and U.S.S.R., not to stab itself? What had determined the outbreak of the conflict, according to Heidegger, was the will to power that permeated the history of the West as a whole. Specifically economic factors, including the "population increase," had played only a secondary and casual role; therefore, not even the search for *Lebensraum*, to which official German propaganda referred, would supply an adequate explanation. Heidegger did not by any means subscribe to the accusations leveled at the Third Reich and its expansionistic policies; on the contrary, he was quick to reject them: "When one interprets the fulfillment of the metaphysical will (to power) as the 'result' of the selfishness and arbitrariness of 'dictators' and 'authoritarian states,' there is no other motive than calculation and political propaganda, or a lack of metaphysical awareness of a thought fallen for centuries into a blind alley, or both."[27] Indeed, "for the living being, to ensure its 'vital space' is never an end, but only a means to expand its power. Following such an expansion, the need for more space necessarily grows in turn." The insatiability of Nazi expansion is here described with utmost precision, and its aggressive character is explicitly recognized. But such determination has no critical aim, since Heidegger repeats again that all this constitutes "a fundamental metaphysical law of power itself" and therefore cannot be attributed to particular governments or political-social regimes.[28] Indeed, this unrestrained will to power is nihilism, but every attempt to criticize it on the basis of moral or juridical norms, as we shall see later, is itself incomplete nihilism and thus worse.

During the same period of time, Thomas Mann contrasts Germany's "politics of power" with the "humanity" and the "values and goodness of the soul" that he saw embodied by England.[29] But for Heidegger, Germany's enemies are moved by the same will to power that they insist on attributing exclusively to the Third Reich. To confirm the point, he offers a significant example. Soon after the defeat of France and the signing of the armistice, England proceeded to destroy its ex-ally's fleet in order to prevent the ships from falling into the hands of Germany and reinforcing German naval and military power. Here is Heidegger's comment: "When, as now, the English bomb and destroy the French naval units anchored in the port of Oran, it is perfectly right from their viewpoint as a political power: *right* is, in fact, that which serves to increase power. But this, at the same time, signifies to us that we can in no way lawfully justify a similar behavior; every power, metaphysically conceived, has its right [*Recht*]. And only through impotence does it fall into illegality [*Unrecht*]. However, it is a part of the metaphysical tactics of every power to consider the opposing power's behavior not from the viewpoint of a power as such; rather, the adversary's behavior is evaluated from the viewpoint of a universal, human morality, which has simply propagandistic value."[30] Therefore, the explanation of the genesis and meaning of the conflict, as well as the determination of its course, rests entirely with the Nietzschean *Gerechtigkeit*, a "justice" that rewards the stronger, which Germany at that moment doubtless appeared to be. The identification with Germany is clear, as is demonstrated by that "we" (*wir*) just mentioned. Still, consider this question: if in the war being fought only the will to power is at stake—the will to power that has nihilistically dissolved any other consideration—what is the sense of taking sides with one or the other of the parties in the struggle?

At this point, Heidegger introduces an important distinction: "The Nietzschean concept of nihilism does not have a 'negative' character at all; only incomplete and passive nihilism is negative, the arid aspiration to replace current values with values that are similar but of a weaker nature, and to point, for instance, to 'socialism' and 'universal happiness' as the ideal rather than 'Christianity.' . . . When Nietzsche repeatedly defines himself as a 'nihilist,' he does not mean collapse or annihilation and fall; rather he thinks of nihilism as *positive and pointing to the future*."[31] Socialism and democracy, on the contrary, have "retarded the resolute rejection of current values. Nihilism remains incomplete, for to become complete it must go to extremes. *Extreme nihilism* recognizes that there is no eternal truth in itself, that truth must be conquered and posited over and over again. Thus, active nihilism, which does not confine itself to witness the slow collapse of the existent, intervenes actively to reverse the process."[32] In this sense, nihilism "means not simply collapse [*Einsturz*] but cessation [*Wegfall*], insofar as it is *liberation* and therefore the beginning [*Beginn*] of something new."[33] Active nihilism, with which Heidegger clearly identifies himself at this moment, is represented by Nazism, which is driven by the will to power and is on its way to realizing the "new order" with its dazzling victories. The allusion to the *Neue Ordnung* resounds more than once in the course of lectures from the second semester of 1940: the ruthlessness and brutality with which the Third Reich was achieving its goals were philosophically described and transfigured by Heidegger as complete and active nihilism, which contains nothing decadent, because it accelerates and completes the collapse of decaying values that are devoid of credibility. In fact, the double negation of the existent and the ought-to-be of any normative view is the presupposition of the "new order, which only the (complete) nihilist can realize."[34] In conclusion, "Nietzsche demands a clear look at the advent of nihilism, not for the purpose of spreading the belief in the 'decline of the West' but to effect a complete reversal and to introduce a new beginning unhampered by half measures."[35] It must be noted that it is not properly the "beginning" (*Anfang*) that presupposes the definitive over-coming of the metaphysics of the will to power; only the *Neubeginn* discloses "*the unconditional domination of nihilism*."[36] But it is this disclosure alone that makes the "new beginning" possible.

At any rate, the denunciation of the nihilism that permeates Western history does not in the least imply a detached attitude. On the contrary, "the consciousness [*Besinnung*] of nihilism cannot signify a mere histo-riographical consideration of the present epoch and of its 'historical' presuppositions; it is in itself not necessarily a decision as to what the humanity [*Menschentum*] on this earth is to become in the future."[37] "Nihilism and nihilism are not the same thing."[38] And here Heidegger is following with passionate involvement the vicissitudes of the war, seeking to interpret philosophically the dashing victories of the Third Reich. These are the victories of complete and active nihilism over incomplete nihilism. The disastrous defeat of France is not accidental; it is the result of a "mysterious law of history": the country that gave birth to Descartes is crushed by a country that, thanks to the completeness of its nihilism, has gone far ahead in the organization of the "machine economy," from which a "new humanity" (*neues Menschentum*) has emerged victori-ously, moving beyond present-day man. In fact, "only the superman is capable of an unconditional 'machine economy' and vice versa: the one needs the other in order to establish an unconditional domination over the earth."[39]

Now Heidegger's attitude does not move away from that assumed by Jünger in *Der Arbeiter*, a work which, at this very time, the philosopher discusses and comments upon "among a small circle of university profes-sors."[40] For Jünger, "a new world order is the outcome of world domi-nation," which will in turn be the result of a gigantic armed confrontation under the banner of the will to power: "This must determine which of the many manifestations of the will to power, answering the call to dominate, possesses the legitimacy to do so. The certification of such a legitimacy consists in mastering the things that have become preponderant, in being able to control the absolute movement, which can only be the work of a new humanity. We believe that such humanity already exists."[41] The *neues Menschentum* prophesied by Jünger demonstrates concretely its own existence and its own superiority through the invincibility of the war machine of the German Third Reich.

Heidegger's admiration for the efficiency of this war machine, during the first phase of the war, is evident. With transparent allusion to the occupation of Scandinavia, in one of his first lectures of the second trimester of 1940, he observed: "When, today, on the occasion of the most audacious military operations by the airborne landing troops, an aircraft also participates to film the launching of the paratroopers, this has nothing to do with 'sensationalism' or 'curiosity'; the diffusion, after a few days, of the consciousness and vision of these actions is itself an element of the global activity and a factor of the armament. Such 'filmed reporting' is a metaphysical procedure and will not be subjected to the judgment coming from daily representations."[42] This theme is taken up again at the end of the course, in which Heidegger outlines an assessment of a year of German victories culminating in the invasion of France: "Starting from the perspective of bourgeois 'spirituality' and culture, one would like to consider total 'motorization' of the *Wehrmacht*, from top to bottom, as unlimited 'technicism' and 'materialism.' In reality, this is a metaphysical act."[43] Heidegger is concerned with dispelling the suspicion of the "materialism" and even "technicism" of the efficient German war machine.

German victory is metaphysically necessary; it concludes one epoch of Western history and prepares another. Metaphysics as the will to power reaching its limit is ready to reverse it course. This scheme is still present in the summer semester of 1941, during which, by implicitly referring to Jünger, he now considers as "decided the fact that the shaping of reality is brought about by the 'worker' and the 'soldier,' " regarded as representative figures of the new "humanity" that is called to realize the Nietzschean will to power.[44]

III

At this point it would be appropriate to dwell a bit longer on the assessment Heidegger makes of the war during this first phase. As with Nietzsche, the "new order" that Germany has realized with triumphal victories in the name of the will to power, openly displayed, is also to be interpreted as an end and, at the same time, as a passage to a new beginning. In this sense, there is no perfect identity between the "new order" and active nihilism and the will to power. These accelerate and mark the end of a historical epoch, clear away hypocrisy and the half measures of incomplete and still unconscious nihilism (democracy, socialism, and so on). But by themselves, active nihilism and the will to power—that is, Nietzsche—are not yet the new beginning. On the contrary, as Heidegger declares at the culminating moment of the Third Reich's military might, "the metaphysics of the will to power goes in step only with 'Romanism' and Machiavelli's 'Prince.' "[45] To stop at this stage or perspective means to remain precluded from the new Greek-German beginning. After the American intervention in the conflict, Heidegger asserts that "Romanism" continues to live in Americanism: they are brought together by a "monumentality" alien to German authenticity (*undeutsche Monumentales*).⁴⁶ The tendency to move away from Nietzsche's "Romanism" is further accentuated in the course of the war. Hölderlin is the one who represents authentic Grecism and therefore the possibility of the *Überwindung* of modern metaphysics, and he must not be confused with Nietzsche, from whom he is separated by "an abyss."⁴⁷ The Grecism that Nietzsche pretended to have discovered is in reality "absolutely Roman: that is, modern and Greek at the same time"—and "Roman" is here synonymous with "imperial."⁴⁸ The criticism of the Nietzschean will to power, in the last analysis considered imperial and Roman, reemerges here. Are we then in the presence of a Heidegger in the process of distancing himself from the Nazi regime? Did not Hitler pose, at least in private conversations, as a reborn Roman emperor?⁴⁹ And was not the same Nietzsche, whom Heidegger criticized for being Roman and imperial, widely publicized as the precursor of the Third Reich?

In the meantime, we must consider the faulty notion according to which all the more or less Nazi ideologists would have massively and unequivocally drawn inspiration from Nietzsche. On this topic, too, it is possible to note different views and even contradictions.⁵⁰ Certainly, there is in Heidegger a polemical attitude with regard to the *Nietzsche-Bewegung* (strongly felt in the Third Reich)—particularly toward Baeumler, who sees Nietzsche as the interpreter of Grecism struggling against the "Romanism" typical of the modern world. But at the same time, there is a convergence of negative judgments both on "Romanism" and the modern world. For Baeumler, "Romanism" is synonymous with intellectual order, which destroys national peculiarities; it is synonymous not only with cosmopolitanism and imperialism but also with a philistine vision of life—in contrast to the agonistic spirit typical of the Greeks: *pax romana* and *imperium romanum* appear thus with a distinctly negative meaning.⁵¹ These themes, with considerable variations, are also found in Böhm, a most authoritative Nazi ideologist, who contraposes, in turn, the celebration of the "original Grecism" to the "two thousand years of universalism" of Western history, reinterpreting Grecism in a *völkisch* key as the celebration of the "Greek state with its popular foundation," which is then lost with Aristotle and still more with the "Roman empire" and the modern world.⁵² Even in Rosenberg one can find attacks against "the world a-racial imperialism of Rome."⁵³

It would be hasty to see in Heidegger's criticism of Nietzsche's "Roman" and "imperial" will to power a camouflaged censure of German imperialism. Carl Schmitt, who denounces "Versailles imperialism,"⁵⁴ contrasts *Reich* with *imperium*: while the latter, beginning with "Romanism," has tended to have a universal meaning and has therefore shown little respect for the peculiarities of individual peoples (in this sense, the term fits "the empires of Western democracy" and the "universalism of the Bolshevik East tending toward world revolution"), the German *Reich* has an "ethnic [*volkhaft*]" foundation and implies "a juridical organization essentially nonuniversalistic and respectful of every people."[55] We are in 1939. The *Anschluss* and the subsequent dismembering of Czechoslovakia are behind us: "The center of Europe [*die Mitte*], which was weak and impotent, has become strong and unassailable," capable moreover of penetrating "the space of central and southern Europe" with "the great political idea" which is "respect of every people, as a reality of life determined by race [*Art*] and origin, blood and land," and of defending it against the intervention of foreign powers.[56] In fact, the expansionistic offensive of the Third Reich develops in the name of "great space" and "vital space," reorganization and unity of *Mitteleuropa*, sometimes even with "antiimperialistic" slogans and, at any rate, claims of "Europe for the Europeans": a sort of Monroe Doctrine for Europe, with Germany obviously as the power leader.[57]

Heidegger, for his part, whenever he speaks of "imperialism," alludes explicitly to England[58] or indirectly to America—identified, as we saw earlier, as Romanism, which had become synonymous with *imperium*. *Reich*, on the contrary, has for him a positive meaning.[59] On this point, therefore, it is impossible to draw a clear line of demarcation between the position taken by the philosopher and the views expressed in publicity more or less connected with the regime. Hitler himself loved to pose as a Roman emperor, although he also celebrated Greece (Athens and, above all, Sparta) and a presumed Greco-Nordic race.[60]

These are the contradictions in the German *Kriegsphilosophie* that had already been manifested during World War I. In the dazzling victories of William II's army, Spengler already sees the new Rome in victorious Germany, called upon to contruct a new world empire. There, the role of Greece (more exactly, that of Athens) is taken by France, bound to be dismembered and substantially incorporated into Germany, which would then triumphantly bring the war (or a series of wars) to a conclusion at Zama—a Zama, of course, located not in Africa but in the heart of England.[61] Spengler's analogy between the age in which he lived and the age that witnessed the irresistible ascent of the Roman empire stimulated, even forced, him to establish an explicit analogy between *Imperium Romanum* and the future *Imperium Germanicum*,"[62] between Prussians and Romans.[63] In 1933 Spengler still calls upon Germany to realize the *Imperium mundi*.[64]

On the other hand, in the course of World War I a view arose that, though directly opposed to the one just examined, enjoyed a period of extraordinary success. It can be analyzed by beginning with Thomas Mann's *Considerations of an Unpolitical Man*, in which the 1914–18 war is interpreted as the highest moment in "the struggle of the Roman world against stubborn Germany." Not only does Mann dwell repeatedly on the "Roman West" in opposition to Germany; he points out that the Roman West already extends "beyond the Ocean, where rises the new Capitol."[65] And Weber in his turn, at the moment of the crumbling of Germany, compares the "world domination" already gained by America to the domination gained by Rome after the victorious conclusion of the Punic wars.[66]

During the Third Reich, too, the struggle between the "Roman option" and the "Greek option" continued.[67] The latter clearly prevailed, notwithstanding the alliance between the Third Reich and the "Romanizing" Italian fascism. During World War II the reference to the Greeks was so widespread, even in the academic world, that Heidegger was forced to resort to an ironical warning: "In most of the research works the Greeks appear as pure National Socialists. In this excessive zeal the scholars do not seem to realize that such works do not serve the cause of National Socialism and its historical uniqueness, the more so since it does not need such a service."[68]

Yet Heidegger's position is not so far removed from that of Spengler as might appear. It is true that Spengler likens Prussia and Germany to imperial Rome, but the characterization he makes of the latter is quite interesting: "Let us not forget that the *Imperium Romanum* was solely a business enterprise devoid of scruples, and that the great Romans were all speculators. . . . The Roman expansion was simply a financial seizure slightly camouflaged in military terms." On the other hand, contemporary Germany which, in the conquest of the Empire, followed in Rome's footsteps, is "a second America," Spengler writes in 1915.[69]

Here one finds all the terms of the Heideggerian equation: Rome equals unscrupulous will to power equals America. In opposition to Greece, Spengler characterizes Rome as the kingdom of money, of prosaic practicality, of the supremacy of economics—in short, of *Zivilisation*.[70] The same theme, though profoundly transformed, is present in Heidegger. The difference is that for Heidegger the new *Imperium* that Germany was able to conquer was not necessarily a manifestation of decadence, the decline of *Kultur* and *Zivilisation*, but could and ought to be the premise of a new beginning: the revival that Germany would have brought about in an authentic Grecism by breaking with modernity (of which Romanism and the will to power were the expression) and giving a new turn and imprint to Western history. His criticism of the Roman will to power was at times rather harsh, and perhaps Heidegger's "Greek" option was, in the last analysis, a "Western" option that looked with uneasiness at the war within the West. Indeed, his metaphysical justification of Germany's victories in 1940 also seemed to be falling step by step into oblivion, because of the concrete developments of the war. It was the Nietzschean *Gerechtigkeit*, understood as a "fundamental image of the will to power," which resolved, in Germany's favor, the clash with England and France—or so it was in 1940. But in the winter of 1942–43 Heidegger insists that this *Gerechtigkeit* is a Roman principle that seals the loss of the original Grecism and the ruinous crumbling of the West.[71]

Perhaps the exacerbation and the diverse configuration of the polemic against Spengler are not incidental. Spengler, as we know, represents the "Roman option." In 1940, Heidegger contrasts him with Nietzsche. Let us go back to a passage already quoted: "Nietzsche demands a clear look at the advent of nihilism, not for the purpose of spreading the belief in the 'decline of the West' but to effect a complete reversal and to introduce a new beginning unhampered by half measures."[72] Contrary to Spengler, Nietzsche knows how to distinguish complete nihilism from incomplete nihilism.[73] This was the case at the time of Germany's triumph in the West. The shadow of Stalingrad, however, projects itself into the course of the winter semester of 1942–43, which Spengler views "exclusively from the viewpoint of Nietzsche's metaphysics": that is, the will to power.[74] In 1940, Spengler is also condemned because, unlike Nietzsche (and Jünger), he was not in a position to furnish proofs for the metaphysical justification of the German victory. In 1942–43, Spengler is condemned as an expression of the will to power: that is, the Roman option that had such tragic consequences for the West. Once the distinction between complete and incomplete nihilism has disappeared, there remains the comprehensive condemnation of the will to power itself (Nietzsche's and Spengler's) as the nihilistic oblivion of Being. As we shall see, after the war moved to the East, it is, for Heidegger, precisely Being (and therefore Greek-German and Greek-Western "historicity") that is truly at stake.

The increasing uneasiness about the war in the West was tied to the ever transparent intolerance of the "measurement of skulls" and racist biologism.[75] The latter's naturalistic determination of the patriotic and the national thwarted or made impossible the self-comprehension of Germany as the heir of Greece and the vanguard of the West. For this reason, some listeners in Heidegger's courses during the last years of war had the impression of being in the presence of a sort of Fronde against the regime,[76] even if up to the end he identified himself with the fate of Germany at war.

IV

With the extension of the conflict beyond the "West," as Heidegger understood it, the interpretation of the war begins to reacquire that pathos of European and Western "historicity" characteristic of the texts appearing between 1933 and the outbreak of the war. When the United States, which represented a "lack of historicity" (*Geschichtslosigkeit*) and "self-destruction," joined the war coalition against the country that was the heir of the great Greek "beginning" of Western history, then Germany could simply take "scornful note" of the event and confidently await the "decisive moment" of victory.[77] A few months later Thomas Mann, ironically commenting on "the discovery of Europe through the Nazis," quoted the speech by Baldur von Schirach, who, at the "Congress of European Youth" in Vienna, turned to America and exclaimed: "Where are your Praxiteles and Rembrandt? . . . From where do you draw the audacity of taking arms in the name of a sterile continent against the divine inspiration of European genius?"[78]

That Germany would lose "appeared to us to be certain since the fall of 1941," Jaspers writes with reference perhaps both to the bogging down of the *Blitzkrieg* in Russia and to the intervention of the United States.[79] But Heidegger thought otherwise. Certainly, the American intervention would cause the war to be harder and bloodier; perhaps only through "suffering and sacrifice" could Germany, "the historical humanity" representing the Greek Western beginning, become "mature" for this very "beginning."[80]

The interpretation of the war as the clash between incomplete and complete nihilism (the latter being the only one capable of fully mastering technology and resolving the struggle for planetary domination, thus preparing the conditions for the new beginning) could not survive after the end of the dazzling victories of Germany's *Blitzkrieg*. In this context, the philosophical interpretation of the battle for Stalingrad is significant: the Soviet victory is the victory of "complete technicalization" and industrial and social planning; thus, the U.S.S.R. "has realized a metaphysical advantage."[81] At this point, Germany's victory cannot be envisioned in the name of the "new humanity," of the German "superman," the only one capable of dealing with modern technique and metaphysics. The battle of Stalingrad represents not only the turning point of World War II; it is perhaps also a turning point in Heidegger's evolution. One notes how the official propaganda moderated expressions of admiration for the efficiency of the Third Reich's war machine and spoke with terror of the "robot motorized divisions" fielded by the Soviets. So Goebbels contraposes "Eastern Bolshevism" and the "historical dangers" it brings to bear on Europe, and "European humanity" and Germany's "historical mission" for the salvation of Europe.[82] In this case, the question is not to liken the positions of a great intellectual to those of the official manager of government propaganda; the contradictions continue to be considerable and evident (for example, the furious anti-Semitism Goebbels vents, also on this occasion, when he speaks of the "Judaic-Bolshevik" danger).

The fact remains that, beginning with the campaign against Russia and increasingly after the defeat at Stalingrad, members of some circles not always close to Nazism (sometimes even opposed to it) increasingly called for the salvation of the West. A case in point is the Catholic Archbishop Franz Joseph Rarkowski whose appeal of June 29, 1941, soon after the beginning of the "decisive great battle in the East," speaks of the German people as the "heart of Europe,"[83] echoing the Hölderlin formula so dear to Heidegger, who evokes it repeatedly and warmly. The Third Reich's official propaganda, which presented the war in the East as the fatal clash of the West with "Central Asia," was also, as Thomas Mann noted immediately after Stalingrad, aimed at breaking the anti-Nazi alliance in the name of the struggle against the "Red and Asiatic danger."[84] Perhaps a similar theme is also present in Heidegger.

At any rate, one thing is certain: the interpretation of the war is radically changed from that of the initial phase of the Western campaign. No longer are wills to power contraposed to wills to power (even if the preference is given to the will to power expressing complete nihilism). Instead, Being is now directly at stake, or perhaps *Being*: "There approaches a historical moment whose uniqueness is not determined only by the condition of the existing world and by our history in it. 'The stake' involves not only the Being or not-Being of our historical people; it does not concern the Being or not-Being of a 'European' culture, for at that level one has always to do only with Being. But before all this, and originally [*anfänglich*], the decision concerns Being and not-Being as such, Being and not-Being in their essence, in the truth of their essence. How could Being be saved and kept in the freedom of its essence, if the essence of Being is undecided, noninterrogated, and even forgotten?"[85]

From this moment on, Germany no longer represents active nihilism, which fights for a different configuration of Being, but is the country that fights and sacrifices itself for the "truth of Being." In this context, "sacrifice is the farewell to be-ing [*Seienden*] on the way to preserving the favor of Being."[86] The German combatant is no longer the *Übermensch* capable of mastering technology better than his enemies; instead, he is now the desperate custodian of the truth of Being. He can sacrifice himself and die for Being, since he has profoundly renounced any selfish calculation. In the desperate endurance of Germany there is the last glimmer of Greece and the truth of Being. The more clearly defeat looms, the more tormentingly resounds the pathos of Thermopylae, which Germany defended first against the irruption of a new Persia, represented by the Soviet Union.

In this context, the change in the evaluation or, at any rate, the distinct shift of emphasis in the evaluation of Nietzsche is understandable. This emerges with particular clarity from the lecture courses of 1944–45.

In 1936–37, Heidegger saw in Nietzsche, if not the standardbearer of the struggle against nihilism, in any case a countertendency or a possible aspiration toward a countertendency: "Europe always wants to cling to 'democracy' and refuses to realize that this would constitute its historical death. In fact, as Nietzsche clearly saw, democracy is only a variety of nihilism."[87] "Both men who have introduced a countermovement in regard to nihilism, Mussolini and Hitler, have been at Nietzsche's school, though in an essentially different way."[88] This theme is no longer present in 1944–45. The course in 1937–38 insisted on the fact that Nietzsche was to be understood not only as an "end" but also as a "passage," the "end of the first beginning of Western philosophy" and a passage to the second beginning. To neglect the moment of passage and, therefore, of the announcement or the presage of the new beginning meant, in Nietzsche, to proceed "to a philosophically inessential and misleading" interpretation.[89]

In the course of the war in the West, Nietzsche indeed stood for complete nihilism: that is, the complete nihilism considered to be superior to the incomplete (democracy and socialism). This theme now also disappeared. Particularly enlightening is the comparison between the two comments, in 1940 and in 1944–45, accompanying the same central thesis as that of the later Nietzsche: classical nihilism as the "ideal of *ultimate power*." In 1940 Heidegger writes: "This nihilism exceeds ordinary life and opens the way to 'a new order,' and to those who want to waste away, it suggests also the 'wish to end.' Under this double aspect, nihilism clears the ground and at the same time opens new possibilities."[90] Clearly, at that moment, classical nihilism was embodied in the army of Nazi Germany, which was sweeping away the decadent Western democracies and creating the "new order," a new order that was certainly not the end of nihilism but seemed equally rich in promises. In 1944–45 the shadow of defeat is cast over Germany and all this has disappeared: with its "ideal of *ultimate power*, Nietzsche's metaphysics . . . corresponded to the utmost form of nihilism."[91]

It is understandable that this interpretation would conflict, if not with the regime, then certainly with the common view held by National Socialism. The fact remains that Heidegger to the end continued to identify himself entirely with Germany at war. As a result, his criticism of Nietzsche's nihilism seemed at times to envision a new ideological platform to justify the desperate effort of the German army in the East: "The sacrifice is inherent in the essence of the event in which Being claims man for the truth of Being. This is the reason why the sacrifice does not tolerate any calculation on the basis of which, in each instance, one counts as useful or useless high as well as low purposes. Such a calculation deforms the essence of sacrifice."[92] The sacrifice continued to impose itself, or imposed itself most at a moment when every plausible calculation led one to believe that the balance of forces was already turning against Germany. And so, the insistence on sacrifice became "the purest experience of the voice of Being." It was natural that the "first to feel the voice of Being" was the German "historical humanity, called together with the Greeks to poetize and think."[93] Hence, the sacrifice of Germany, its constant bleeding in the East: it was only to be hoped that other peoples would hear the voice of Being.

V

The consummation of Germany's defeat stimulated a new phase in Heidegger's reflection: now the war and the will to power themselves became expressions in their own right of the technical "massification" of the modern world. The way in which Heidegger tried to exculpate himself, soon after the end of the war, before the occupation authorities is surely significant. The Nazis, he declares, "related themselves to Nietzsche, according to whose doctrine 'truth' has no autonomous foundation and content but is only an instrument of the will to power: that is, a mere 'idea,' a subjective representation. And what was and still is grotesque in this is that such a 'political' concept of science coincides with the 'idea' and the theory of the Marxist and Communist ideology." Against this theory shared by Marxists and Communists, Heidegger boasts of having pronounced his rector's speech in 1933.[94]

In reality, such a speech polemicizes against the reduction of the "*spiritual world* of a people" to the "superstructure of a culture," but only to assert that "the spiritual world of a people . . . is the power to keep its forces tied to the land and blood." Not only is there no assertion of the autonomy of culture and science, but there is a decisive rejection of the vision of knowledge as the "easy comfort of an occupation free of dangers for the promotion of a mere progress of knowledge."[95] Two years later, referring explicitly to his rector's speech, Heidegger goes so far as to denounce the new "propaganda tactics" of "Russian Communism" for its attempt to reduce spirituality and culture to a heap of "ornamental and decorative objects," with no relation to the "historical mission of our people, placed at the center of the West."[96]

But this is not the essential point. In the course of 1940 and of the first phase of the war, the complete nihilism of Nietzsche (and of Nazism) was favorably contraposed to the incomplete nihilism represented by democracy, socialism, and communism. Now, after Hitler's defeat, likening Marx to Nietzsche and communism to Nazism (in the name of the will to power) permits Heidegger to implicate both Marx and the revolutionary tradition in his assessment of the catastrophe of the West (of which the two world wars and Nazism are an integral part). Indeed, it is now precisely Marx who represents "the position of extreme nihilism,"[97] rather than that of incomplete nihilism. But if complete nihilism (Nietzsche and Nazism) had, in 1940, a positive meaning, for the reason that it put an end to hypocrisy and "half measures" (democracy, socialism, and so on), it was preparing the ground for a "new beginning"; now, complete or extreme nihilism has a meaning univocally and exclusively negative, because it serves to indicate the lowest point in the ruinous decline into which the oblivion of Being has caused the West and the entire planet to fall.

In the assessment outlined by Heidegger, there is no place for "moral indignation" with regard to the *Führer* (the term is always used in the plural): moral indignation was considered to be misleading and ridiculous because it failed to take into account that it was no more than the "necessary consequence" of the oblivion of Being.[98] This theme was already present, as we have seen, in 1940–41, within the context of a "metaphysical," indirect justification of the expansionistic policy of Nazi Germany—a justification now giving way to a condemnation that involves and submerges everything and everybody. In 1940–41 there was room for distinctions: only Germany, contrary to its enemies, was in a position to express complete nihilism, free of hypocrisy and half measures. Now, there is no room for distinctions (it is impossible to identify favorite targets in the act of condemnation): "communism," "fascism," "world democracy" are just different names for the "universal domain of the will to power."[99] The *Führer* and their very *Führerschaft* are, as an expression of events that infinitely transcend them and that have made the entire planet homogeneous and uniform, rendered substantially uniform and homogeneous (*gleichförmig*), beyond "national differences."[100]

And the gas chambers and the extermination of the Jews? In his January 1948 response to Marcuse's query about this problem, Heidegger says that the Allies treated the "Eastern Germans" in the same manner as Hitler treated the "Jews."[101] The planetary heights from which he judges centuries and millennia of history do not prevent Heidegger from taking a position on well-determined events that would seem to be of lesser significance—for example, the West Berlin blockade decreed by the U.S.S.R. in 1948 and immediately reinterpreted "metaphysically" in a speech of 1949: "Agriculture is now a motorized food industry, essentially the same thing as the production of corpses in the gas chambers and in the extermination camps, the same thing as the 'blockade' and the reduction of countries to hunger, the same thing as the construction of the hydrogen bomb."[102] The insertion of the military "blockade" in this global overview is particularly interesting and not devoid of political skill.

It permits the indictment not only of the Soviet Union (the Berlin blockade ended in May of that same year) but also of the Western democracies. Already in the course of the debate on "culpability" following World War I, Weber had spoken of "about 750,000 men" that the "English blockade," "openly illegal," had cost Germany.[103] Now the debate on "culpability" was resuming with greater vigor: Jaspers's self-critical assessment of 1946 (which need not be examined here), *Die Schuldfrage*, was (not by accident) translated into Italian, with the author's consent, as *La colpa della Germania* (The fault of Germany).[104] And it is also from Jaspers that Heidegger distances himself with the assessment that subsumes genocide, military blockade, and mechanization of agriculture under the terms of a single planetary event—in the name of technology and the will to power.

The self-criticism solicited by Marcuse is, at any rate, disdainfully refused. Indeed, even before receiving that request, Heidegger had counterattacked: if we must talk of "culpability" in regard to his attitude toward Nazism, "is there not also a fault of essential omission [*wesentliches Versäumnis*]"? Would it not have been better "if around 1933 all the capable forces had been put to work to purify and moderate, slowly and in secret accord, the movement which had come to power?"[105] This is the same fundamental thesis as that of 1936: to Löwith, who points out to his teacher or former teacher (standing before him with his Nazi badge) the most disgusting aspects of the Third Reich, Heidegger responds with a harsh attack against the intellectuals who had stood aside: "If these gentlemen had not held themselves to be too delicate to commit themselves, things would have gone differently; but I was completely alone."[106] Here the year 1933 appears more as a missed opportunity than the beginning of the catastrophe: and this assessment has not changed substantially nine years later, despite all the tragedy experienced in the meantime.

Among the intellectuals too delicate to soil their hands with the Third Reich, to whom Heidegger alludes with disappointment, there was perhaps also Ernst Jünger, who had contributed to the ideological preparation of the victory of Nazism. And it is interesting to note his evolution. During the Weimar Republic, in a reference to World War I, he had gone as far as to celebrate the "voluptuousness of blood."[107] But here is the assessment Jünger made, after 1945, of war and massacre: "The Greeks fighting against the barbarians and the Christians fighting against the pagans adopted the most cruel norms. In the last war the Germans conducted a campaign in the East different from that in the West, and not only because of the difference in the character of the territories."[108] "Clausewitz's prescription to spare the people from useless bloodshed appears then quite without validity: it is, in fact, valid only when one fights an enemy who in war accepts certain rules. Long ago Xenophon showed the panic of an army at the prospect of falling into the hands of an Oriental victor." "In the military clashes with the East, the rules, which are valid in the battlefields of the West, are disregarded."[109] One almost hears the echo of the directives given by Hitler on the eve of the aggression against the Soviet Union: "We have to depart from the viewpoint of military comradery, . . . in the struggle against Bolshevism we cannot count on an enemy's behaving according to the principles of humanity or of international law."[110] And so . . .

Jünger's criticism seems to strike at Hitler, principally because in "the last years of war" he would have wanted to "notify the Western powers of the discontinuance of the Geneva Convention: this would have meant the extension to the Western front of the conduct of war adopted on the Eastern front." But what *is* the cause of this barbarization of the war looming also in the West? Jünger blames the revolutionary political tradition more than Nazism: if "the war among peoples becomes more horrible," it is because of the irruption of the "world civil war," which "has assailed and corrupted military traditions" and "above all cancelled the difference between those who are armed and those who are unarmed. . . . the great moments that have brought us where we stand are three: the Reformation, the French Revolution of 1789, and the Russian Revolution of 1917, which is still going on."[111] The same theme is developed particularly by Carl Schmitt, for whom it is the political tradition from the French Revolution to the October Revolution, and above all Lenin and Bolshevism, which built "absolute enmity"—this new figure unknown to the *jus publicum europaeum*—and in which the origin of the massacres and the catastrophe of the West is to be sought.[112]

Heidegger, Jünger, Schmitt, these three great twentieth-century German intellectuals so different from one another, nevertheless have a trait in common: they looked with sympathy, at least at the beginning, on the crumbling of the Weimar Republic and the advent of Nazism; around 1933 they took part in the fierce polemic, typical of those years, against democracy, socialism, and the revolutionary political tradition. This is the context in which the "revisionist" historiography of our time must be set: it is not by accident that the historian Ernst Nolte, a Heidegger disciple, more openly than anybody else attributes genocide and holocaust to "Asiatic" barbarity, imitated by Hitler with an eye to the October Revolution.[113] At this point everything is clear: the West can recover its good conscience. Toward the end of World War I the theme of the decline of the West made its appearance and enjoyed an enormous popularity, but the decline of the West is now reversed in its final and dazzling transfiguration.

NOTES

1. Quoted in Marianne Weber, *Max Weber: Ein Lebensbild* (Tübingen, 1926), p. 536. On the war as a rediscovery of the "authentic," see D. Losurdo, *La catastrofe della Germania e l'immagine di Hegel* (Milan, 1987), pp. 61–65.

2. K. Jaspers, *Die geistige Situation der Zeit* (1931; Berlin, 1947), p. 97.

3. O. Spengler, *Jahre der Entscheidung* (Munich, 1933), p. 151.

4. E. Jünger, *Der Arbeiter* (1932; Stuttgart, 1982), p. 254.

5. Spengler, *Jahre der Entscheidung,* p. 150.

6. Jaspers, *Die geistige Situation der Zeit,* p. 97.

7. Ibid., p. 82.

8. Ibid., p. 174.

9. E. Nolte, *Der europäische Bürgerkrieg 1917–1945: Nationalsozialismus und Bürgerkrieg* (Frankfurt, 1987), p. 416.

10. G. Lukács, *Die Zerstörung der Vernunft* (Berlin, 1954), p. 415.

11. Jaspers, *Die geistige Situation der Zeit,* p. 174.

12. K. Jaspers, *Philosophische Autobiographie* (Munich, 1984), p. 76.

13. M. Heidegger, *Gesamtausgabe,* vol. 39 (Frankfurt, forthcoming), p. 134.

14. Ibid., vol. 13, p. 21.

15. Ibid., vol. 40, (1983), p. 42.

16. Ibid., vol. 13, p. 16.

17. Ibid., vol. 40, pp. 40–42.

18. C. Schmitt, "Die siebente Wandlung des Genfer Völkerbundes," and "Sprengung der Locarno-Gemeinschaft durch Einschaltung der Soviets," *Deutsche Juristen-Zeitung* 41 (July 1, March 15, 1936): 785–89, 337–41.

19. Heidegger, *Gesamtausgabe,* vol. 40, p. 40. The philosopher followed political events with the utmost attention: e.g., he mentions the "attempt on the life of a king in France" immediately after the murder of Alexander of Jugoslavia on a visit to Paris, October 9, 1934. And in his subsequent courses of lectures the reference to political life is constant. (See the important essay by N. Tertulian, in *La Quinzaine Littéraire,* December 15–31, 1987.) This frustrates the attempt of those who would pretend to place Heidegger's theoretical elaboration in a rarefied sphere of absolute transcendence in relation to political contingencies.

20. As far as the Heidegger-Hitler relation is concerned, see H. Crételle, "Heidegger contre le nazisme," *Le Débat,* no. 48 (1988): 125, which discusses above all the speech in which the philosopher and rector of Freiburg calls for support of Hitler's decision to take Germany out of the League of Nations (cf. G. Schneeberger, *Nachlese zu Heidegger: Dokumente zu seinem Leben und Denken* [Bern, 1962], pp. 144–46). In his appeal, Heidegger declares that the German will to affirm its own "autonomous *völkisch* responsibility" does not mean "aloofness from the community of peoples." And Hitler on March 21, 1933, said that the German people "have never dissociated the sentiment of their power from the profound responsibility for the community of European nations." Heidegger speaks of "an open and virile relationship of autonomy and reciprocity of peoples and states." And here is how a propaganda publication of the Third Reich sums

up a passage from Hitler's speech of May 17, 1933: "The very National Socialism which, as a national movement, has sworn loyalty to its own people [*Volkstum*] shall respect the national rights of the other peoples, according to its own vision of the world" (cf. *Zeitgeschichte in Wort und Bild: Vom Alten zum Neuen Reich,* 2d ed. [Oldenburg, 1942], 4:38, 71). Obviously, the point is not to flatten the philosopher's position to the level of that of politicians also expert in the art of lying; but it is absurd to insist on seeing in the appeal of the former in support of the latter, who was struggling against the League of Nations, an opposite political program. On the other hand, it is significant to note the presence, always in Heidegger's text in question, of a scornful liquidation of the ideal of an "inconsistent and uncommitted universal fraternization."

21. Jaspers, *Philosophische Autobiographie,* p. 76.

22. K. Jaspers, *Notizen zu Martin Heidegger,* ed. H. Saner (Munich, 1978), pp. 180–81.

23. Spengler, *Jahre der Entscheidung,* p. 11.

24. Jaspers, *Philosophische Autobiographie,* p. 76.

25. M. Heidegger, *Gesamtausgabe,* vol. 48, p. 191.

26. Th. Mann, "Deutsche Hörer!" (April 1941), in *Essays,* ed. H. Kurzke (Frankfurt, 1986), 2:265.

27. Heidegger, *Gesamtausgabe,* vol. 51, p. 18.

28. Ibid., vol. 48, pp. 141, 264.

29. Mann, "Deutsche Hörer!" (October 1940, August 1941), pp. 263, 267–68.

30. Heidegger, *Gesamtausgabe,* vol. 48, pp. 234–35.

31. Ibid., p. 168.

32. Ibid., p. 138.

33. Ibid., p. 51.

34. Ibid., p. 139.

35. Ibid., p. 73.

36. Ibid., p. 16.

37. Ibid.

38. Ibid., p. 87.

39. Ibid., p. 205.

40. Ibid., vol. 9 (1976), p. 390; and M. Heidegger, *Das Rektorat 1933–34: Tatsachen und Gedanken,* app. to the re-edition of *Die Selbstbehauptung der deutschen Universität,* ed. Hermann Heidegger (Frankfurt, 1983), p. 24.

41. Jünger, *Der Arbeiter,* p. 79.

42. M. Heidegger, *Gesamtausgabe,* vol. 48, pp. 94–95.

43. Ibid., p. 333.

44. Ibid., vol. 51, pp. 36–38.

45. Ibid., vol. 48, p. 297.

46. Ibid., vol. 53 (1984), p. 191n.

47. Ibid., vol. 52 (1982), pp. 143, 78.

48. Ibid., vol. 54 (1982), p. 63.

49. Cf. E. Nolte, *Der Faschismus in seiner Epoche,* 2d ed. (1965).

50. There are even frontal attacks against Nietzsche by, e.g., Ch. Steding,

Das Reich und die Krankheit der europäischen Kultur (Hamburg, 1938); cf. G. Penzo, *Il superamento di Zarathustra: Nietzsche e il nazionalsocialismo* (Rome, 1987), pp. 341–51. Also significant is the reservation formulated by F. Böhm (*Anti-Cartesianismus: Deutsche Philosophie im Widerstand* [Leipzig, 1938], p. 2), who criticized the "ideal of power" sought by Nietzsche as *volklos*.

51. A. Baeumler, *Nietzsche, der Philosoph und Politiker* (Leipzig, 1931), esp. pp. 67, 92–94.

52. Böhm, *Anti-Cartesianismus*, pp. 38–39, 49, 189.

53. A. Rosenberg, *Der Mythus des 20. Jahrhunderts* (1930; Munich, 1937), p. 87.

54. C. Schmitt, *Nationalsozialismus und Völkerrecht* (Berlin, 1934), p. 11.

55. C. Schmitt, *Völkerrechtliche Grossraumordnung mit Interventionsverbot für raumfremde Mächte* (Berlin, 1939), pp. 70–71.

56. Ibid., p. 88.

57. See the texts quoted in R. Opitz, ed., *Europastrategien des deutschen Kapitals 1900–1945* (Cologne, 1977). The first to theorize about the European Monroe Doctrine was Schmitt, *Völkerrechtliche Grossraumordnung;* it then met with remarkable success, sometimes with specific reference to Schmitt. See Opitz, *Europastrategien*, pp. 630, 641ff., 688. On the "European" passwords of Nazism, see also H. W. Neulen, *Europa und das 3. Reich: Einigungsbestrebungen im deutschen Machtbereich 1939–1945* (Munich, 1987).

58. Heidegger, *Gesamtausgabe*, vol. 48, p. 18.

59. Ibid., vol. 51, p. 5.

60. Cf. E. Nolte, *Der Faschismus in seiner Epoche*.

61. Letter to H. Klöres, December 18, 1914, in O. Spengler, *Briefe,* ed. A. M. Koktanek with M. Schröter (Munich, 1963), pp. 32–33.

62. Letter to H. Klöres, July 14, 1915, in Spengler, *Briefe*, p. 44.

63. Letter to H. Klöres, January 9, 1918, in Spengler, *Briefe,* p. 108; O. Spengler, *Der Untergang des Abendlandes* (1918; Munich, 1980), p. 36.

64. Spengler, *Jahre der Entscheidung*, p. 41.

65. Th. Mann, *Betrachtungen eines Unpolitischen* (1918), ed. H. Hebling (Frankfurt, 1988), pp. 40–43.

66. Quoted in W. Mommsen, *Max Weber: Gesellschaft, Politik und Geschichte* (Frankfurt, 1974), p. 93.

67. Cf. L. Canfora, *Ideologie del classicismo* (Turin, 1980), pp. 133–59.

68. Heidegger, *Gesamtausgabe*, vol. 53, p. 98.

69. Letter to H. Klöres, July 14, 1915.

70. Spengler, *Der Untergang des Abendlandes*, p. 49.

71. Heidegger, *Gesamtausgabe*, vol. 54, pp. 78, 137.

72. Ibid., vol. 48, p. 73.

73. Ibid., p. 137.

74. Ibid., vol. 54, p. 82.

75. Ibid., vol. 52, p. 131

76. Cf. O. Pöggeler, "Heideggers politisches Selbstverständnis," in A. Gethmann-Siefert and O. Pöggeler, eds., *Heidegger und die praktische Philosophie* (Frankfurt, 1988), p. 61 n.17.

77. Heidegger, *Gesamtausgabe*, vol. 53, p. 68.

78. Th. Mann, "Deutsche Hörer" (October 24, 1942), p. 271.

79. Jaspers, *Philosophische Autobiographie*, p. 77.

80. Heidegger, *Gesamtausgabe*, vol. 53, p. 68.

81. Ibid., vol. 54, p. 127.

82. Joseph Goebbels, speech of February 18, 1943, reported in the *Völkischer Beobachter* the following day. For the *motorisierte Roboterdivisionen*, see also Neulen, *Europa und das 3. Reich*, p. 38.

83. Reported in *Dokumente zur deutaschen Geschichte, 1939–1942*, ed. W. Ruge and W. Schumann (Frankfurt, 1977), p. 75.

84. Reported in *Dokumente zur deutschen Geschichte, 1942–1945*, ed. W. Ruge and W. Schumann (Frankfurt, 1977), p. 31.

85. Heidegger, *Gesamtausgabe*, vol. 54 (1982), p. 241.

86. Ibid., vol. 9 (1976), pp. 309–10.

87. Ibid., vol. 53, p. 193.

88. As in a passage of the course on Schelling (summer 1936) not included in the subsequent publication, *Schelling: Abhandlung über das Wesen der menschlichen Freiheit (1809)* (Tübingen, 1971). Cf. letter from Carl Ulmer to *Der Spiegel*, May 21, 1977; and O. Pöggeler, *Heideggers politisches Selbstverständnis*, pp. 37, 59 n.11. Cf. also *Gesamtausgabe*, vol. 42, pp. 40–41.

89. Heidegger, *Gesamtausgabe*, vol. 45 (1984), pp. 133–35, 196–97.

90. Ibid., vol. 48, p. 102.

91. M. Heidegger, *Nietzsche* (Frankfurt, 1961), 2:339.

92. Heidegger, *Gesamtausgabe*, vol. 9, p. 311.

93. Ibid., vol. 54, p. 250.

94. We refer to Heidegger's text as reported by H. Ott, "Martin Heidegger als Rektor der Universität Freiburg 1933–1934," *Zeitschrift für die Geschichte des Oberrheins* 132 (1984): 350n.

95. Heidegger, *Die Selbstbehauptung der deutschen Universität*, pp. 14, 13.

96. M. Heidegger, *Gesamtausgabe*, vol. 50, pp. 52–53. The new "tactic" is the position adopted soon thereafter by the Seventh Congress of the Communist International. Heidegger's polemical allusion is perhaps aimed particularly at the anti-Nazi congress "For the Defense of Culture" (Paris, 1935), in which, among others, Ernst Bloch participated. Besides the intellectuals tied to "Russian Communism," it is the very *freischwebend* intellectual, dear to Mannheim, whom Heidegger violently aims at. The polemic against the *"freischwebend* speculation enclosed in itself" (*Gesamtausgabe*, vol. 29/30 [1983], pp. 258, 261) must be interpreted in this sense. It is a course of lectures of 1929–30 which immediately follows the publication in 1929 of Mannheim's *Ideology and Utopia*.

97. Heidegger, *Gesamtausgabe*, vol. 15 (1986), p. 393.

98. M. Heidegger, "Überwindung der Metaphysik" (these notes, which Heidegger declares he took between 1936 and 1946, with no further details, were consequently published only after 1945; they must therefore be placed within the postwar production), in *Vorträge und Aufsätze* (Tübingen, 1954), p. 93.

99. Heidegger, *Das Rektorat 1933/34*, p. 25.

100. Heidegger, "Überwindung der Metaphysik," pp. 96–97.

101. See Marcuse's letter to Heidegger of August 28, 1947; Heidegger's response of January 20, 1948; and Marcuse's reply of May 13, 1948, in V. Farías, *Heidegger und der Nationalsozialismus* (Frankfurt, 1989), pp. 372–75.

102. It was thus in the first draft of a lecture published in 1949, according to W. Schirmacher, *Technik und Gelassenheit: Zeitkritik nach Heidegger* (Freiburg, 1983), p. 25.

103. M. Weber, *Zum Thema der "Kriegsschuld"* (1919), in *Gesammelte politische Schriften* ed. J. Winckelmann (Tübingen, 1971), p. 494.

104. K. Jaspers, *La colpa della Germania,* Ital. trans. R. De Rosa (Naples, 1947).

105. Heidegger, *Das Rektorat 1933/34,* pp. 25–26.

106. Cf. K. Löwith, *Mein Leben in Deutschland vor und nach 1933: Ein Bericht* (Stuttgart, 1986), p. 58.

107. E. Jünger, *Der Kampf als inneres Erlebnis* (Berlin, 1922), p. 9.

108. E. Jünger, *Der gordische Knoten* (1953), in *Sämtliche Werke,* vol. 7 (Stuttgart, 1980), p. 412.

109. Ibid., pp. 417, 450.

110. Quoted by Nolte, *Der europäische Bürgerkrieg,* pp. 465–66.

111. Jünger, *Der gordische Knoten,* pp. 412–13, 420–21.

112. Cf. esp. S. Schmitt, *Theorien des Partisanen* (1963; Berlin, 1975).

113. E. Nolte, "War nicht der 'Archipel Gulag' ursprünglicher als Auschwitz?" *Frankfurter Allgemeine Zeitung,* June 6, 1986.

6

Heidegger and the Greeks

RAINER MARTEN

Just so we understand each other, I will be quite direct right from the start. You must revise your views, your views on philosophy, that is. I would suggest that you see in it an intellectual institution that governs the universal as the universal: the whole—the entirety of the intellect as man actually possesses it—of man's existence and practices, of his world and history, of his beyond and timelessness. But this is a wrong view of philosophy. Every philosophy is provincial and contemporary; it proves itself the master of the "small view" and the limited perspective; it aims at the specific and the unique. In its own way, of course, it creates its entirety out of such things. It never concerns itself with anything less than the "whole," but this is defined each time in what is only a relatively narrow and also socially very exclusive framework.

Heidegger's great theme is the relationship between man and Being. "A broad field" you might suppose. But you are wrong! This relationship cannot possibly be conceived narrowly enough: narrow in its subject, narrow in its conception.

"Man": this does not extend any further than Western civilization. True, Heidegger does occasionally speak of the "mankind of the earth" (*Menschentum der Erde*)[1] but he does this only to give his purely Western perspective the appearance of its broadest possible historical reality. For him, mankind itself means only the West.[2] Anyone who rejects this notion completely misses his thought. But it gets even narrower.

An address delivered on June 19, 1989, in the Studium Generale of the University of Freiburg.

Western man represents the human race, because Western man is the only one with a history.[3] And what about the Egyptians and Indians, the Sumerians, the Chinese, and the Aztecs? Without question, they have no history at the point where history is defined narrowly and "rigorously" enough. In Heidegger's thinking, one constraint follows hard on the heels of another. History: for him this is only the history of philosophy. But do we not read, too, of Indian philosophy? Of course we occasionally do. Heidegger, however, is concerned with *philosophia*, pronounced, conceived, and realized in Greek φιλία της σοφιας (*philia tis sophias*). If man is only Western man, because he alone is historical, then his history can only be that which begins with (*beginnt*) and has its inception in (*anfängt*) ancient Greece. "Heidegger and the Greeks": this "and" is inescapable for Heidegger whenever he is contemplating the relationship between man and Being. Man is Western man, historical man, philosophical man—or else he is simply "Being-historical" (*seinsgeschichtlich*). This "essential" (*wesentlich*) man begins with the Greeks. Do not feel offended if you happen to come from somewhere else and have just failed to fit into this—imagined (*gedachte*)—constraint. Of course, I cannot promise that I will strike some sort of blow for freedom that would remove this hindrance, nor can I argue away this "eye of the needle" definition of true mankind; it is implicit in Heidegger. But I can offer an explanation that ought to make clear how Heidegger comes to draw limitations that exclude so many, and how at the same time he still manages to inspire far more people than do his rivals, to make them feel that they are the best, if not the only, ones of their kind, as soon and so long as they just "think."

Man; Western man; historical, philosophical, originally Greek man— where is he? "The Greeks" now exist only in old books, aside from antique buildings, statues, and vases. But we must not imagine this sort of ("ontic") "being" if we wish to stay on course with Heidegger's thoughts on "Being." The ancient Greeks *are*; they have not passed away but *have been*, and in such a way that they are just now coming into their own: in the Germans, in German. Man, as Western man, historical, philosophical, and originally Greek, appears ultimately as German: that is, at the historical time that Heidegger regards as his own and even at this still enduring hour! German man—that is, "universal" man (the distinction is added in the editing of a lecture course from the summer of 1933)—that is the new constraint.

With this constraint, reality has been left completely behind. German man is even supposed to be the one who discovered "the German." But this discovery, as Heidegger conceives it, has at this hour not yet arrived, because he is the culmination, the *eschaton* or, more precisely, the eschatologically predetermined essence-event (*Wesensereignis*)—an event that has been postponed *per definitionem ad kalendas graecas*, although Heidegger himself thinks of three hundred years (this ominous number last emerged in the *Spiegel* interview).[4] For him, on the other hand, there are thinking, and *Dasein*, which *as* thinking and *as Dasein* are German.[5] But then, that means nothing truly ultimate but only contemporary.

This thing that is Western, historical, philosophical, originally Greek, and ultimately German—as long as it is just listed this way—is still without life. It lacks the one thing that most concerns mankind: it lacks meaning. That is because Heidegger takes for granted that this question has already been settled: only Western man has human and historical meaning.[6] For him this meaning of the West coincides with its eschatological salvation: the West and only the West is in danger.

Danger and salvation: only these give to what is imagined to be the only relevant mankind its imagined life and its imagined nearness to death. Anyone who wants to be within the span of the originally Greek and finally German man, and is capable of becoming man (historically as well as philosophically), must be prepared to sacrifice his or her life, has to be prepared for death. Whatever particular historical part of mankind (persons like the ancient Greeks) possesses this intellectual calling must accede to death, which "sacrifices Being-man [*Menschsein*] for the preservation of the truth of Being."[7] You heard it right: to sacrifice Being-man for Being! Heidegger says of this sacrifice that it has "its own essence within itself" and "has no need of goals or purpose."[8] (And that, by the way, is the first new thought on man as his own goal since Kant!) Before this self-sacrifice there will be a struggle: "When we fight the battle of the ancient Greeks, we do not at the same time become Greeks but Germans."[9]

Who is actually doing the fighting here; from whom is the willingness for self-sacrifice demanded? Heidegger sees this "Greco-German mission"[10] literally signaled in the fact that the Greeks and the Germans are the only two peoples who can be regarded as the people of "poets and philosophers." Philosophy and the struggle that must be fought out historically are thus entrusted to the poets and philosophers.

If Vergil, Horace and Ovid, and Dante and Petrarch do not make a people into a nation of poets, and if Marsilius Ficinus, Pico della Mirandola, Bruno and Vico do not even make a people into a nation of philosophers, then we may suppose that methodological education, which we have been pursuing for some time now, does not stop even at philosophy and poetry. And so it is. For Heidegger, philosophy and poetry worthy of the name are exclusively the "inceptive" philosophy and poetry of the Greeks and their original "repetition"[11] in the poetry and philosophy of the Germans.

This affords us the occasion to seek out the essential poets and

philosophers among the Greeks and the Germans who do full justice to
the narrowly Western definition of this action. Is it—on the basis of
common nationality and language—every one of them or just a few, a
very small few?

As you may have noticed, Heidegger distinguishes between beginning (*Beginn*) and inception (*Anfang*). At the beginning of philosophy
there are many thinkers, but only a few of them, very few, think
"inceptively." For him, there are precisely three, no more: Anaximander, Parmenides, and Heraclitus.[12] After them—in Greece—come only
Plato and Aristotle, who, though they are no longer at the beginning of
philosophy, are still involved with it in an exceptional way. Of Aristotle,
Heidegger says quite literally that he is "one of the Greek thinkers who
was far removed from inceptive philosophy, in whose thinking, however,
Greek philosophers reached their culmination."[13] In the subsequent lecture period he described Aristotle, by way of a slight variation, as "that
philosopher in whose words Greek philosophy reaches its culmination."[14]

What we are to understand, then, is this: inceptive mankind has its
abode in the "thinkingdom" of Greekdom. Xenophanes, Anaxagoras,
and Empedocles do not belong to this group, however, not to mention
Zeno, Protagoras, and Democritus. The poets do not fare any better.
Addressing himself to Pindar's poetry, Heidegger at one point speaks of
"actual Greekdom."[15] Clearly, an Archilochus who, in his poetry, describes throwing away his shield because it was too much of an encum-
brance in his flight, only to purchase a new one at the first opportunity,
or a Euripides who understands the psychology of women, is not the kind
of poet who belongs to inceptive poetdom: these are not poets at all.
Anyone who in his "poetic creation" is seen by Heidegger as "destructive" is referred to as a writer.[16] Thus, for Heidegger, there are in
actuality only two Greek poets: Pindar and Sophocles. True, he does cite
Homer, and he shows as well an understanding of Sapphic verse; but, as
Heraclitus recommends, Homer and Archilochus deserve to be thrashed
with rods (*rhapizesthai*).[17] Laughing gods, cowardly warriors, homophile
women—the poetic criticism of Heraclitus, of Plato, and of Heidegger is
open to considerable challenge.

The inceptive, essential, and actual Greeks do not number a dozen,
even if we are permitted to count ghosts. Among the Germans there are
still fewer. Heidegger deems Leibniz, Schelling, Hegel, and Nietzsche to
be German philosophers, even "most German" ("one of the most German philosophers of the Germans, Leibniz").[18] Only the "writer" Schopenhauer is expressly excluded from this company.[19] But even though
Greek philosophy is very much alive in them, they are for Heidegger
committed to oblivion. He who understands inception as inception is the
only correct choice; as for the poets, there is only Hölderlin. The

recurring exclusion of Goethe from historically relevant Western "poet-dom" suffices to exclude as well Schiller and Lessing, Wieland and Büchner. Also excluded from the essential poetdom as the founding force (founding "that which is German"), each for reasons that apply to him alone, are—especially—Georg Trakl and Rilke.[20] Only Hölderlin thinks, in Heraclitus's sense.[21] Not even Hebel, who ranked so very high in Heidegger's esteem, can stand before the judgment seat of the essential: he is far too onesidedly involved with the Christian god.

No more than the number of the Muses and no fewer than the Graces: the circle of true mankind has been assembled, the time-tested number for conversation. Let us take our leave of the poets now, since they are not our topic for now. We have left to us only the true thinking beings, who have that understanding that is actually in danger and must be saved; just three or (with Plato and Aristotle) five Greeks and one German. But we must not count this way. Heidegger is concerned with true mankind and thus with true "Greekdom" and true "Germandom." Heraclitus is just one name, but it stands for "Greekdom." When Heidegger says "the Greeks," he frequently means no more than Hera-clitus or Aristotle: that is to say, no more than his interpretation of the one or the other.

If any of you believe that Heidegger would find himself alone in the cold if he pursued German philosophy further, then you are on the wrong course. "Heidegger and the Greeks" is no real relationship, not a historical relationship, but rather an essential relationship conceived for its own purpose. We must change our intellectual level in addressing it. From this point on, only the essence, the intellectual essence—as Heidegger would say—counts.

To simplify this shift in intellectual levels, let me surprise you with two "essence-ideas" (*Wesensgedanken*) of the purest sort. Thought number one (I quote):

The nature of power is alien to this πόλις [*polis*].[22]

Thought number two:

The Greeks are simply the unpolitical nation, which they are by their nature; . . . their humanity is inceptively and exclusively determined . . . by Being itself.[23]

Power was alien to the Athenian ἀρχή! The Greeks were unpolitical in the times of a Solon, or of a Pericles! But, then, these are no objections at all. Judged historically, certainly, Athens was a power that was second to none in terror and violence in her time; Athens was politicized to a high degree. But Heidegger emphasizes, as you heard, "nature": power was alien to the nature of the *polis*; the Greeks were unpolitical according to their human nature (*menschentümlichen Wesen*).

If we have arrived with Heidegger at essence (*Wesen*), then we have also arrived at intellect: the "inceptive" intellect. Everything that Heidegger takes in view in thinking is subject to a peculiar "intellectualization." "The Greeks" become intellectually *wesenhaft* and thus unpolitical, alien to power. He sees nothing in the Romans but the imperial *gestus*, which renders them incapable of being a part of Western man in a positive way.[24] "Humanism" today, for Heidegger, would be nothing but an institution for the third-class burial of the "great Greekdom," since, "of course, it is a notorious fact that the Romans understood nothing more for the Greeks"—a true Heideggerian expression.[25]

Christians fare no better. Historically, Christianity is of no more worth than Rome, because it is equally incapable of paying heed to incipient "Greekdom." (The god of creation is a technological concept: "Replenish the earth and subdue it!" is a command to lay waste the earth; the Curia is a stronghold for the exercise of power; salvation of the soul is a subjective concern.)[26] Greek gods are the only things that have essence. Only that which is exclusively Greek, which is akin to a god, can stand at the side of the Germans, who at this hour, in their national spirit and their language spirit, alone em-"body" mankind. These are, of course, the inceptively conceived Greek gods who are clearly derived from the inceptively Greek "experienced" Being,[27] not just any gods, such as we meet in Homer and Hesiod, Euripides and Aristophanes.

The truly Greek-experienced man corresponds to the truly Greek-experienced god of the truly Greek-experienced Being. He is "in his essence and in accordance to the essence of ἀλήθεια [*aletheia*: the truly Greek-experienced truth] the author of god."[28]

No wonder that "we" Germans are in need of the Greek gods, in order to rescue and to be rescued. Listen to any one of the truly outrageous wordings of the choices offered here: "But it is an entirely different question whether the concealed essence of history in which we belong has been forced from an essential need for a dialogue with that which was the θεοί of the Greeks. The real answers to the questions 'Who is Artemis?' and 'Who is Zeus?' are concealed in our future history to the extent that this itself responds to what has been."[29]

Artemis and Zeus *ante portas*? Do not worry, this is meant only intellectually. It is a pure conceptualization of Being-history, which is not, was not, and never will be any part of true human history. Artemis and Zeus, too, are meant only intellectually: inceptively *wesend*, not some sort of Zeus with the glitter of power and sexual desire; not an Artemis who lets fly the deadly arrow because of a personal grudge; not even the buxom Asian Artemis of Ephesus at whom Heidegger expressly aims his Heraclitus interpretation (even though he was ignorant of the object of his criticism).[30] If Artemis and Zeus are imminent in the future of "the Germans," this just means that they are imminent only in the Being-thinking (*Seinsdenken*) of the only essential German thinker at the present time. As Heidegger says: "This 'Greek thinking' which is constantly demanded here is experienced and perfected as the means of a dialogue [!] with inceptive thinking which alone will lead us into proper German thinking."[31] And earlier: "To what extent the fate which befell the Greeks . . . [is] one which is yet to come, that we, the Germans, after a long period of time, can and must anticipate."[32]

The view of man has become incomparably narrow in its object and in thinking: mankind is reduced intellectually to the true Greeks and the true Germans who are essentially intellectual in nature. Some time ago I suggested that this view of the nature of man be termed *intellectual racism.* Heidegger's thinkers (and poets) are a unique race—an intellectual race. Of course, in their purely intellectual definition there is no precise conclusion drawn to the effect that they are the only ones who deserve and are capable of life. But neither is this excluded—even though the "thinker" automatically allows all of mankind to live—because, for him, human beings are not simply *living* beings. When in *Mein Kampf* Hitler recognizes the Aryan race (as represented by the German people) as the true human race and, in contrast to the Jews, as the image of God, he has already defined the intellectual concept of nation and blood in such a way that it also means quite particularly real physical life on earth.[33] Thus his racism (that is, "German" as synonymous with "Aryan": a radical concept!) should be termed biological, together with the appropriate predicates "capable of life" and "deserving to live."[34] But Heidegger suggests only such predicates as "capable of having a nature," "deserving of nature," "capable of having a history," "capable of sacrifice," "worthy of sacrifice," "capable of truth," and "deserving of truth"—indeed, even "capable of Being" and "deserving of Being."[35] Dignity itself is extended to man only out of the Greco-German Being-history.[36] And remember (just as an observation): this is the first new concept of the dignity of man since Kant.

This is profoundly disturbing: the one (Heidegger) who, by his own admission, is the true intellectual man eradicates the nonintellectual man (as having never possessed Being) whom he himself had construed as man coming to awareness through him. If ordinary man is not deserving of Being, then he is in a strict sense without Being, unworthy of Being. This is not something arbitrarily read into Heidegger but rather something received from him with horror. Blacks, as he determines in his lectures of the summer semester of 1934 (edited into the notes), have in common with minerals that neither think. Because they are incapable of thinking, it is impossible that they could be worthy of Being. This is no intellectual naiveté. It is intellectual racism, a philosophical scandal that cannot be called anything the least bit paler or less precise.

"German man" as the intellectual elect is not Heidegger's invention. For example, in his fragment "Über das Wesen deutscher Wissenschaft" (1811), Schelling writes: "Should it not be the lot of the Germans that they alone pass through all of the various stages, the general lot of all man which all other nations represent as separate, in order to represent in the end the highest and purest unity of which human nature is capable?"[37] But even if Schelling's potential for discrimination were comparable with that of Heidegger, surely we must agree about a kind of thinking that occurred around, during, and after the time of Hitler— during the Holocaust and after Heidegger's "calling," not during and after Napoleon. That is a new (intellectual) situation that cannot be deprived of its uniqueness and incomparability by any tradition. Intellectual racism—the apt offensiveness of this word is effective precisely because it cannot be dulled by the excuse that it was all intended only intellectually. It is precisely against this conviction, and nothing else, that my choice of the term is directed.

That was not meant to be the final word. We are just at the beginning of "Heidegger and the Greeks." Just as in Heidegger's first work *Being and Time* (pt. I, 1927), the "and" does not separate and bind together two essentials but instead is meant to reveal the concept of the one to be that of the other. Thus we have before us the task of making the thematic "and" disappear, at least to the extent that we recognize in Heidegger's Greeks the intellectual blueprint on which he models himself. To this end, let us read his Greeks, his three or five Greeks. We begin with the fifth.

Heidegger was very familiar with Aristotle, as they say; a favorite saying in his seminars was "Let us begin by reading Aristotle for fifteen years!" But then he interprets Aristotle in such a way that no one who has delved deeply into Aristotle would recognize him again. In the naive perspective of the historian of philosophy and the scholar of Greek, everything is seen incorrectly, right down to its very foundation. It is a question neither of trivialities nor of different possibilities of interpretation. Being (οὐσία), time (χρόνος), nature (φύσις), truth (ἀλήθεια), language (λόγος)—every one of the essential concepts of Aristotelian philosophy is "interpreted" against its letter and its spirit.

In his lectures on Heraclitus (summer 1943), Heidegger defines Aristotle's entity (*das Seiende*) as that which has its future in οὐσία as γένος'.[38] In his *Beiträge zur Philosophie* and in *Grundfragen der Philosophie*, we already read how Heidegger has begun to get into an awkward position in the definition of γένος and τὸ τί ἦν εἶναι.[39] This is a fundamental position of the Aristotelian ontology: precisely, that Being is not to be considered a genus. (One need only study B.3 and Γ.2 of Aristotle's *Metaphysics*, and *Being and Time*, chap. 3!) Being is special (*jegeartet*) and, at any one time, uniquely bound. With Aristotle there is no general (κοινόν, καθόλου) "Being" from which the entity could derive as if from a family tree and from a source. It was his own philosophical good fortune that kept Aristotle oblivious of Being, at least to the extent that he had not exactly thought of Heidegger's "Being itself," had not even begun to think of it, not even of its pale shadow.

In his 1924 lecture "The Concept of Time" (*Der Begriff der Zeit*), presented before the Marburg Theological faculty in 1924, Heidegger begins his interpretation of the Aristotelian concept of time, which he repeats in *Being and Time* and repeats again at every opportunity up to his latest works (*Time and Being*, 1962).[40] The central point of his interpretation is τὰ νῦν, the now, to which he attaches calculated time: the oblivious-of-Being now-time (*seinsvergessene Jetzt-Zeit*) as a human appointment-time (*Verabredungszeit*). But in so doing, Heidegger has fallen into a fundamental misconception of the twofold nature of the νῦν as we find it in Aristotle. Heidegger always emphasizes that τὰ νῦν, the "immediates," are the enumerated elements and never a unit of time. For this reason, too, the plural cannot be added to time. This is no small error: it renders Heidegger's interpretation of the Aristotelian concept of time entirely worthless. Other errors build on this: for example, the notion of the homogeneity of enumerated time, even though homogeneous time alone is enumerating time.

In his essay "On the Nature and Concept of φύσις [*physis*]: Aristotle's *Physics* B.1," Heidegger reads a sentence incorrectly and, in so doing, inverts the entire understanding of nature and Being in Aristotle.[41] But it is precisely this sentence that Heidegger makes the basis of the whole of his interpretation; he views φύσις as ὑποκείμενον (*hypokeimenon*): that is, nature as an independent being (*Vorliegen*). The accurate meaning in Aristotle is just the opposite. Nature is never independent Being. It is never a *hypokeimenon* but in each case only *in* a ὑποκείμενον; it is only the Being (that is, a principle of movement and form) *of* something. There is no essence for-itself, but only the essence in and of things. Heidegger has thus gotten rid of the "in," in that he has set it doubtfully in italics in his first translation; in his second edition he has it in quotation marks; and, even later, he simply does not mention it. This (incorrectly understood) "Greek" concept of nature as the basis of the "Greek" understanding of Being haunts his entire later philosophy. The fact that an important comma is missing in the edition Heidegger used (Greek-German, Prantl, 1854) cannot excuse the matter. The error had been corrected in 1863. It was never really a problem.

In his seminar on Aristotle in the winter of 1951–52, Heidegger tries to convince the seminar participants that of the four interpretations of Being that Aristotle discusses, Being as Being-true was philosophically the most important. To this end he supports his arguments with Θ.10 of the *Metaphysics*: τὸ δὲ κυριώτατον ὂν ἀληθές (*to de kyriotaton on alethes*).[42] But this says only that the truth of judgment is the most frequent interpretation of Being, not that what is judgmentally true is of preeminent ontological interest. For Aristotle, in fact, it is precisely the opposite, since being true or being false is not *in* the thing but only in the judgment of the thing. Philosophy has no interest in this particular Being.[43] Where Aristotle goes beyond "true" in the sense of "it is so," "it behaves so" (in Θ.10), and speaks of the truth of the "unconnected essence," Heidegger becomes silent. The terms "disclosedness" (*Unverborgenheit*) and "the present" (*Anwesen*) with which he is accustomed to operate in explaining "Greek-experienced" truth are truly out of place here. Moreover, using the text and the significant secondary literature, virtually every student, even a beginner, can form the well-founded conclusion that the definitive concept of Being for Aristotle reads τὸ τί ἦν εἶναι (*to ti en einai*), "that peculiar essence of each individual thing," which makes itself known in its essential form or in its purpose.

In his interpretations of Heraclitus, Heidegger asserts:

> According to an ancient Greek definition, man is the ζῷον λόγον ἔχον (*zoon logon echon*)—the ζῷον is defined by ζωή (*zoe*), this, however, by the ψυχή (*psyche*), that which surging out fetches in [because of the breathing and the living breath]. The ψυχή of man, whose surging out and fetching in is like λέγειν (*legein*) in the sense of ὁμολογεῖν (*homologein*)—that which is gathers within itself, gathers that which, as the original gathering, as 'the λόγος', originally, i.e., preserving essence-origin, en-trusted itself to man. Man *is* the locality of the truth of Being.[44]

But let us listen to this "ancient" Greek definition as Aristotle originally thought and formulated it:

> Of all living creatures only man possesses speech. Language, however, serves to reveal that which is beneficial and that which is harmful. . . . Unlike other living creatures, it is peculiar to man that he alone disposes over the perception of good and bad. . . . The community [in perception] of these things creates the state.[45]

The ζῷον λόγον ἔχον is *political* man, humans who must always seek anew among themselves an understanding of the basic values of their political constitution. Therefore, this "ancient" definition of man stands together with another equally ancient one: man is the ζῷον πολιτικόν (*politicon*), the politically constituted living creature. Ζῷον πολιτικόν and ζῷον λόγον ἔχον—the one is explained by the other. The first book of Aristotle's *Politics* cannot be read any other way. Yet for Heidegger there can be absolutely no question of any discussion among human beings as a potential that could derive from a human essence. The human being speaks and "gathers" only the language of Being, and that in such a way that it responds to Being ("co-responds"). In interpreting "Greek" λόγος, Heidegger is concerned not with living and social man but with his essence, conceived in terms of his history of Being. Seen this way, man ("Greek man") is, as you will recall, quite simply apolitical. Thus Heidegger burdens the ζῷον λόγον ἔχον with nature (φύσις), turns it into the very epitome of human nature—via the breath of life, which is then sent off with the blessing of the perfect harmony of the inceptively conceived being: homology, agreement ("saying the self" *das Selbe sagen*). Ζῷον λόγον ἔχον—the conjoint merging into the truth of Being. This has to do with Aristotle only insofar as it completely perverts his definition of man (not to mention, here, the further problem of interpreting Heraclitus in the same way).

For his own ontological concept Heidegger uses the notion of Being, from which everything that exists originates as such; he uses, as he believes, as a counternotion to essential time, the entire enumerated now; he uses the notion of nature that shows nature as a rising (*Aufgehen*), a revealing-itself (*Sichentbergen*), an illuminating-itself (*Sichlichten*), a concealing-itself (*Sichbergen*). He uses the precedence of truth (as that which is open); he uses the notion of the λόγος of Being as that which gathers and preserves all; and he uses Aristotle to confirm all this. Judged scientifically, whatever has been translated incorrectly and has been incorrectly reconstructed accommodates whoever has his own essential notions and thinks them first. Only *that* Aristotle who confirms Heidegger's interpretations of the history of being is the true Aristotle: the perfecter of the "Greek inception." You will notice that the "lever effect" of such a hermeneutics cannot sustain any reliable reading.

Should we just shake our heads and stand there in amazement? But wait: do you really know what essential standing-in-amazement is? The word comes, as you know, from Plato; standing in amazement, τὸ θαυμάζειν (*to thaumazein*), is the beginning of philosophy.[46] Heidegger often returns to this standing-in-amazement. In his lecture course "Basic Questions of Philosophy" (winter 1937–38), he expressly dedicates a good thirty pages to it.[47] Let me cite its quintessence:

> Now and thus the standing-in-amazement [*Er-staunen*] discloses its standing-in-aweness [*Er-staunliches*]: that is, the whole as the en-

tirety, the whole as that which exists, that which exists is the whole, *that* it *is what* it *is*, the ens qua ens, τὸ ὄν ᾗ ὄν (*to on e on*).[48]

In the winter semester of 1942–43 it sounds like this:

> For the Greeks, that which is amazing is that which is simple, the invisible, Being itself. The amazingness, revealing itself in being amazed, is the enormous [*Un-geheure*] which belongs so immediately to the strange [*Geheure*] that it can never be explained from the strange.[49]

"The Greeks" come from Plato and Aristotle, who alone explain philosophical θαυμάζειν;[50] we understand it—the essential and inceptive—within the horizon of Heidegger's plan for Being-history. No wonder that it is not the same amazement of which the Greeks themselves speak.

Herodotus writes his histories "in order that whatever has come about through human actions will not be lost with time, not even the great and amazing works [μήτε ἔργα μεγάλα τε καὶ θαυμαστὰ (*mete erga megala te kai thaumasta*)]."[51] Whatever is human is regarded with "Greek" amazement, not Being itself. All that which irritates reason: the paradoxes, the *aporiai*, again amaze Plato and Aristotle. Whatever is amazing is exclusively contradictory to reason. In any elucidating, edifying, and responsible exercise of reason, it should be reduced as such to the point of disappearing. Reason becomes calm again. Heidegger, on the other hand, had his imaginary Greeks stand in amazement in order to remain in that state, has them be amazed, moreover, at such things as had never occupied the Greek intellect, neither as an irritation nor in contemplation: at the *that* (conjunction) of the entity in its entirety and at Being *itself*.

How, now, are we supposed to be amazed at Heidegger's Greek interpretations—"inceptively" or in good Greek? I suggest that we try to be amazed at Heidegger's kind of Greek, at least for the moment. But to do that, we have to submit ourselves to his sort of thinking. "Heidegger and the Greeks": without his own (German) thinking, that relationship would be suspended in midair.

Heidegger's thinking follows an unambiguous and simple purpose: the intellectual dissolution of the subject-object relationship. Because, in it, the event of modern times with which intellectual history has been pregnant since "ancient Greece" manifests itself for him: man has become the subject. But that means that in his imagining and calculating, man takes everything in reference to himself in order to deal with it as something objective. That is intended as an intellectual attitude and as real behavior: man soars upward as the subject, which he is, to be the master and executor of reality. The devastation of the earth through "technology," which—according to Heidegger's words from the summer semester of 1928—"rages about in the world today like an unchained beast," is for him an actual expression of the intellectually predominating subject-object relationship.[52]

What is to be done? One must think!—that is, think *essentially*. Heidegger imagines man as *being*—that is, as human-*being*—and, in so doing, imagines an intellectual attitude for him, which in a significant way promises the preservation of the life-bearing world and of the gifts that strive for Being. For these thoughts he needs "the Greeks," who, as the "inceptive" ones, convert his own thinking into an "ultimate" thinking.

Heidegger adopts as his own an ancient bit of philosophical good sense: it is better not to begin literally with the so-called subject-object relationship that one means to reformulate. So, instead of saying he is reformulating the subject-object relationship, he introduces in its place other linguistic expressions. There are four in all:

Man and Being,
Thinking and Being,
Speaking and Being,
Word and Thing.

For Heidegger, the important thing is to rethink the relationship between man and Being and thus the attitude of both, which bears this relationship as an intellectual one. With this intent in mind, we see him de-substantialize man and Being, de-anthropologize man at the same time, and also de-ontify Being. "Both" in their relationship to each other are no longer related things. They are the relationship itself. Heidegger succeeds in this by raising "both" to the level of essence (*Wesen*): man is raised to the thinking Being (*Denkwesen*); Being is raised to the present (*Anwesen*).

Thus the relationship between man and Being is not only made essential but also inverted: it is not man who turns to Being but Being that turns to man. Heidegger elucidates this in his use or, more precisely, in his inversion of *uti et frui*. It is not we who use Being and make it bear fruit; it (*Es*) uses us: for its revelation, for its preservation, for its structuring, as he says.[53] Language for Heidegger, however, is nothing alongside Being. He imagines Being as language, and speaks in this sense of word and Being.[54] Language now exists only in the relationship between thinking-being (*Denkwesen*) and present-being (*Anwesen*). Here, it appears as command, instruction, demand, dictate.

Heidegger does not want to see mankind (*das Menschentum*) use anything more, but he wants everything for Being, for language. Herein lies the inversion of hermeneutics. True hermeneutics does not explain, does not translate or interpret, but becomes instead the courier for the message of Being. Man is co-opted to proclaim by word—the message of Being itself, of the language of Being. The essential language is the mistress; she needs man. Essential man does not master language, does not use language.

With this in mind, we are, I think, now adequately equipped to turn, in an "inceptively" thinking fashion, to "inceptive 'Greekdom.' " This time, it is to be the third of the "inceptive" three: a "word," a "saying" of Heraclitus, something that needs *us*. I have selected Fragment B.123, whose interpretation Heidegger gave me to read in unpublished form (it was in the Black Forest in 1949, and I was just a third-semester student in Munich).

φύσις κρύπτεσθαι φιλεῖ[55]

If we were still naively scientific, the translation and comprehension of the text would be no problem. The words and syntax are clear:

> nature—conceal itself—(he/she/it) likes: that is, nature likes to conceal herself.

Herodotus speaks of the "nature" of the Nile, of the periods of its inundations and the origins of its waters.[56] In its calm and sluggish periods one does not see the power it has when, for no known reason, it suddenly brings huge floods. Nor can one tell immediately just by looking at a plant (*Gewächs*) whether it is poisonous or palatable, good or bad. Gemokedes, who had successfully operated on the Great King of Persia for a breast tumor (φῦμα), knew of this. "Physiologists" who wrote in the sixth and fifth centuries B.C. spoke continually about how many things are inaccessible and concealed from man: from his eyes and his intellect. Nature, too, conceals itself, eludes—us. That she "loves"—as philologists translate this term (according to Heidegger "a thoroughly old maid concept of φύσις")[57]—although "welcome," is for naive scientists without any anthropologizing or psychologizing tone. They read Fragment B.87:

βλὰξ ἄνθρωπος ἐπὶ παντὶ λόγῳ ἐπτοῆςθαι φιλεῖ

An idiot usually stands there shocked at every word. You hear "usually" (as the translation of φιλεῖ). This applies also to Fragment B.123: "Nature usually conceals herself." That is the rule; it usually works. At least φιλεῖ seems clear.

If a philologist wants to know how Heraclitus uses the word φύσις (nature) elsewhere, there is little to be found. Twice he would find κατὰ φύσιν, "naturally." That is all. To classify a thing naturally means to divide it up according to its behavior (ὅπως ἔχει), as it actually is (Fragment B.1); to treat the thing naturally, and thus exercise the virtue of truth, in the sense of truthfulness (Fragment B.112). Or, summing up: the correct διαίρεσις and the true λόγος adhere to the φύσις and, in so doing, adhere to that which professes and portends reality.

This explains everything in a naively scientific manner. But for those of us who are now trying to think "inceptively" and "essentially," this jumbles everything into confusion, unclarity, the unintellectual, the ahistorical—in a word, the un-Greek. Whoever translates and reflects, betrays Western humanity (we might say, echoing Heidegger), does not let the Greeks be the true Greeks and does not let us find the true Germandom.

Starting over from the beginning then (ἐξ ἀρχῆς):

Φύσις κρύπτεσθαι φιλεῖ

Let us just try this in sequence: φύσις. This is quite clear (speaking in essential clarity, now); it cannot possibly mean something objective; it cannot be the Being of something (like the force of the Nile or the malignancy of a tumor), it cannot be the objective, theoretical basis of a cosmology either; it affords no basis for Being, no principle for explanation, no element (not even if the "inceptive thinkers," scientifically well read, understand τὸ πῦρ [to pyr: fire] to be one principle among others—as Parmenides, for instance, speaks of fire and earth, fire as the active demiurgical element, earth as the shaping element) (Fragment A.1). No. For Heidegger, the historical beginning of thinking belongs to the past and to oblivion (and thus, experimentally, for us, too). What is left? That is quite new and clear: φύσις as a *pure* Being-word (*Seinswort*).

Our preference would be to say "Being" for φύσις. But we have to proceed "literally." Why? Because the possibility that one would understand something objective by this must be eradicated. Good, then we will verbalize: presence (*Anwesen*), appearance (*Erscheinen*) become unconcealed (*Sichentbergen*), clear (*Lichten*), stepping-into-the-open (*Insoffenetreten*), rising (*Aufgehen*), loom (*Ragen*). Imagined "inceptively" and "essentially," all these are tight on the mark. There is no trace left of an objectivity that stands in opposition to subjectivity.

We continue: κρύπτεσθαι. Fortunately, this is already "of itself" a verb. We need only to understand this word as an intellectual response to becoming-unconcealed and opening-up: rising conceals itself. This is imagined purely: pure Being and presence in pure isolation. This, too, is without any subjective—without man's—calculation or dominion, without his imagining or involvement. Pure rising appearance and pure concealing-itself belong together. But how?

Now we come to love: not that urgent, longing, enthusiastic, erotic love but love that is completely free of subject, experience, dominance. But that's—well, what is it? Just imagine "loving" without any volition or desire. Indeed, you can see for yourselves what this means: it is a granting and giving and offering-of-oneself, a free-wheeling live-and-let-live. Now, you can listen to Heidegger. You will be amazed at how well he captures the subject and how close you were to it:

φύσις κρύπτεσθαι φιλεῖ: The (always present) rising gives its favor to the self-concealed.

Now that is thinking "inceptively" and "essentially"! But what does it have to do with what, for us, has been the oh-so-bitter and yet-so-sweet discovery of "the German?" Superfluous question: And now we have found our way to the German "word"—not the scientifically supportable one but the "essential" word. This is precisely what happened, what Heidegger indicates in his Heraclitus lectures in the summer of 1944.

It would be well, indeed, uniquely necessary, for us to take these German words seriously now—"literally" at their word. We would then be standing in the very middle of the territory which the Greeks intended but never ever specifically discussed.[58]

The German word—taken literally—is just what the "real" Greeks intended. When Heidegger says that the world-historical attitude can come *only* from the Germans,[59] he had entered into this awareness, as we have just witnessed for ourselves; indeed, we were co-conspirators. The Germans have the word—for example, the word "rising" (*Aufgehen*: this is the self-explanatory word "rising," which says that it offers its favor to self-concealment)—and this *in the middle* of what was "Greekly" imagined and said. This attitude, once initiated, succeeded thus as the original repetition of the "essential," of the beginning of the beginning of the West, bereft of all history and reality.

You know already the "ancient" Greek definition of man that Heidegger derives from the φύσις of Aristotle—via Heraclitus and Parmenides. But I will let you hear it, differently, from Heidegger just one more time:

According [to the Greek definition of man], man is: to ζῷον λόγον ἔχον—that entity rising out of itself, rising in such a way that it has the word in this rising (φύσις) and beginning.[60]

This interpretation already misses Aristotle. And fifteen pages later:

For this reason the destiny "to have the world," λόγον ἔχον, became the essential characteristic of mankind which became historical as Greekdom.[61]

"German thinking,"[62] and only this, has speech. It has the language of Heraclitus, whose name, Heidegger says, is "the name of a primitive force in the Western-Germanic historical *Dasein*."[63] Heraclitus's German-imagined and German-expressed word reads: "The (perpetual) 'rising' gives its favor to the self-concealed." It is historically destined exclusively and solely for the German nation of thinkers to say and think this in order to give to it (the history) its own dimension—"Greekdom: Germandom"—and at the same time to speak the word for its salvation from danger. To interpret philosophical amazement thus as pure amazement at Being is reserved for German thinking, which has found its German purpose in keeping with its "Greco-German mission": that is, to interpret οὐσία as the pure stem of Being, χρόνος as pure presence of Being, φύσις as pure rising of Being, ἀλήθεια as pure clearing of Being, λόγος as pure collection of Being.

The danger awaiting the "inception," which Heidegger continually conjures up, consists especially of what is Roman and Christian, of what is mathematical and technological, of what is without roots and basis— where roots and basis are to be understood as that "inceptive" Greek intellect that rests in "final" German custody. As Hölderlin and Heidegger "have" the German word, and with it the "inceptive" Greek word, this and only this is supposed to promise salvation, or at least the preparation for it. As Heidegger says in his late utterances (1966), only a "god" can save us[64]—an ultimate and German god, that is understood, who "repeats" the "inceptive" Minerva and the "incentive" Zeus, and also repeats originally "inceptive" ᾿Αλήθεα (*Aletheia*) and Δίκη (*Dike*).

The Greeks whom Heidegger constructs, in order to find through them the way to that which is "German," never existed—not their language, not their thinking, not their *polis*, not their amazement, not their gods. No more so than there will be Germans for whom Heidegger's Hölderlin and Heidegger's Greek gods are about to appear. But Heidegger's thinking is capable even of an inversion of the utopian idea. He says literally:

> According to this, Being ought also be a "Utopia." In truth, however, it is Being and Being alone which is the τόπος for everything which is. Plato's *Politeia* is not a "utopia" but precisely the opposite: that is, the metaphysically determined τόπος of *the nature* of the πόλις.[65]

Thus, *per definitionem*, that which is intellectually essential is not Utopian because it is the *topos* of the—imagined—essence. But the Greeks who existed, who lived and worked, who spoke and thought, acted in politics and religion, and the Persians and Egyptians, too, the Romans and Christians, the scientists and technologists, the Jews and cosmopolitans—indeed, all of you—we are all Utopian because none of them and none of us are at the scene of essence. The intellect alone, the true Western, Greek intellect, is "topical" Western reality, however, and everything else—measured by that—is "Utopian": that is, without ground or roots, without home or essence.

There are many reasons why it is expressly "the Greeks" that Heidegger needs for his design for an inverted Utopia of Being itself and of an intellectual, German definition (of essence). To return, eschatologically, to the German intellect, this must be reflected in an inceptive destiny. And where could this reflection better succeed than in the beginnings of philosophy when the imagined intellect is one that is through and through philosophical? Add to this that Heidegger envisions technology as deriving intellectually, exclusively, and alone from philosophy, for which reason obliviousness-of-the-self can, for him, be overcome only via "inceptive" Greekdom. This follows the principle ὅμοια ὁμοίοις φρονεῖν (homoia homoiois phronein): similia similibus conari.[66] For my own part, I would like to propose for your consideration four reasons for Heidegger's Greek option.

First of all, Heidegger needs "the Greeks" for the creation of a historical dimension by means of which a Western Being-history (Seinsgeschichte) and a Being-historical (seinsgeschichtliche) mission for "the Germans" could be represented.

Second, he needs them in order to obscure and to legitimize his "essential" "German word" and his "essential" "German thinking."

A third reason for his making it seem that he has believably employed "the Greeks" lies in Heidegger's intention, never concealed, to make his Being-thinking seem indisputable and irrefutable.

Fourth, and I give this for your consideration as a final reason, "the Greeks" serve as a dramatization of his own attempts at thinking. The persuasiveness of his Being—thinking is indebted in no small measure to the way it is staged as a struggle with the insuperably great thinkers of "inceptive" intellect.[67]

Heidegger's interpretation of "the Greeks" has a fascinating and stimulating effect on us. It is always new and convincing (and not just here) as thinking that is great and bold, original and genuine, profound and farsighted. Here the intellect shows itself to be at home; history and destiny announce themselves; nothing falls from the essential into the commonplace. Thoughtfulness, piety, power, and infallibility, all succeed it. But, especially, it radiates the certainty to tell us just where we are and what lies before us. For many people, it is *the* prescription for moving to counter the perceived reflection of human man: one has to raise intellectually the objectively calculating, resolute, and dominating subject that represents the modern form of placeless (ortlos), "Utopian" man. Naive-scientific and "realistic" doubts cannot touch it. It has already seen to it that things of this sort remain beneath its greatness and dignity.

"Heidegger and the Greeks"—in a most curious way this relationship, when it is read critically, always causes amazed amazement anew among not a few of our contemporaries, even though others are increasingly alienated and horrified.

NOTES

1. Martin Heidegger, *Heraklit* (1943–44), vol. 55 of *Gesamtausgabe* (Frankfurt: Klostermann, 1979), p. 219.

2. Martin Heidegger, *Beiträge zur Philosophie (Vom Ereignis)* (1936–37), vol. 65 of *Gesamtausgabe* (Frankfurt: Klostermann, 1989), p. 100; idem, *Wege zur Aussprache*, in *Alemannenland: Ein Buch von Volkstum und Sendung*, ed. F. Kerber (Stuttgart, 1937), p. 135.

3. Martin Heidegger, *Grundfragen der Philosophie* (1937–38), vol. 45 of *Gesamtausgabe* (Frankfurt: Klostermann, 1982), p. 215.

4. Martin Heidegger, "*Spiegel*-Gespräch mit Martin Heidegger am 23. September 1966," *Der Spiegel*, May 31, 1976.

5. Martin Heidegger, "Germanien" (1934–35), in *Hölderlins Hymnen "Germanien" und "Der Rhein,"* vol. 39 of *Gesamtausgabe* (Frankfurt: Klostermann, 1980), p. 123; idem, *Deutsche Lehrer und Kameraden! Deutsche Volksgenossen und Volksgenossinnen!* Nationalsozialistischer Lehrerbund Deutschland/Sachsen (Dresden, 1934), p. 14.

6. Martin Heidegger, *Parmenides* (1942–43), vol. 54 of *Gesamtausgabe* (Frankfurt: Klostermann, 1982), p. 83; cf. p. 241.

7. Ibid., p. 50.

8. Ibid.

9. Martin Heidegger, "Der Rhein" (1934–35), in *Hölderlins Hymnen*, p. 293.

10. Heidegger, "Germanien," p. 151.

11. For this choice of words, see Heidegger, *Beiträge zur Philosophie*, p. 73.

12. Heidegger, *Parmenides*, p. 2; idem, *Heraklit*, p. 4; idem, *Grundfragen der Philosophie*, p. 222.

13. Heidegger, *Heraklit*, p. 54; cf. idem, *Parmenides*, p. 131.

14. Heidegger, *Heraklit*, p. 72.

15. Heidegger, *Parmenides*, p. 100.

16. Heidegger, "*Spiegel*-Gespräch"; see also *Heraklit*, p. 20.

17. Heraclitus, *Fragmente*, in *Fragmente der Vorsokratiker*, ed. H. Diels and W. Kranz (Berlin, 1951), vol. 1, frag. B. 42.

18. Heidegger, *Wege zur Aussprache*, p. 138.

19. Heidegger, *Heraklit*, p. 20.

20. Heidegger, *Parmenides*, p. 226.

21. Heidegger, "Germanien," p. 123.

22. Heidegger, *Parmenides*, p. 135.

23. Ibid., p. 142.

24. Ibid., p. 57.

25. Heidegger, *Heraklit*, p. 20.

26. Ibid., p. 209; idem, *Grundfragen der Philosophie* p. 141; and cf. idem, *Parmenides*, p. 67.

27. Heidegger, *Parmenides*, p. 89.

28. Ibid., p. 166.

29. Heidegger, *Heraklit*, p. 15.

30. Ibid., pp. 18, 25.

31. Ibid., p. 366.

32. Ibid., p. 204.

33. Adolf Hitler, *Mein Kampf* (Munich, 1927), pt. 2.

34. On this see Rainer Marten, *Leben und Vernunft: Thesen zur Ideologie menschlicher Selbsterhaltung und zur Neubestimmung menschlicher Selbstbestimmung, Zeitschrift für Philosophische Forschung* 38 (1984): 24–27.

35. Heidegger, *Grundfragen der Philosophie*, p. 140; idem, *Parmenides*, p. 4; idem, *Brief über den "Humanismus"* (1946), in *Wegmarken* (Frankfurt: Klostermann, 1967), pp. 160, 161, 172.

36. Heidegger, *Parmenides*, p. 4.

37. F.W.J. Schelling, *Über das Wesen deutscher Wissenschaft* (1811), vol. 4 of *Schellings Werke* (Munich, 1927), p. 389.

38. Heidegger, *Heraklit*, pp. 56, 73.

39. Heidegger, *Beiträge zur Philosophie*, pp. 66, 75, 116; idem, *Grundfragen der Philosophie*, p. 59.

40. Martin Heidegger, *Sein und Zeit* (1927) (Tübingen, 1953), p. 81.

41. Martin Heidegger, *Vom Wesen und Begriff der* φύσις: *Aristotles Physik B. 1* (1951–52), in *Wegmarken*.

42. Aristotle, *Metaphysics*, ed. W. Jaeger (Oxford, 1957).

43. Ibid., E. 4.

44. Heidegger, *Heraklit*, p. 375.

45. Aristotle, *Politics* (German and English), ed. H. Rackan (London, 1950), A. 1. 1253a10–18.

46. Plato, *Theatet, Platonis opera*, ed. J. Burnet (Oxford, 1900), 1:155d.

47. Heidegger, *Grundfragen der Philosophie*, pp. 151–81.

48. Ibid., pp. 168–69.

49. Heidegger, *Parmenides*, p. 150.

50. Aristotle, *Metaphysics*, A. 2. 982b12,, 983a12–21.

51. Herodotus, *Historiae*, ed. C. Hude (Oxford, 1927), A.

52. Heidegger, *Metaphysische anfangsgründe der Logik im Ausgang von Leibniz* (1928), vol. 26 of *Gesamtausgabe* (Frankfurt: Klostermann, 1978), p. 279.

53. Heidegger, "*Spiegel*-Gespräch," p. 209.

54. Heidegger, *Einfuhrung in die Metaphysik* (1935) (Tübingen, 1953), p. 131; cf. p. xx.

55. Heraditus, *Fragmente*, frag. B. 123 (henceforth cited by fragment number in text).

56. Herodotus, *Historiae*, B. 19; cf. B.5.

57. Heidegger, *Heraklit*, p. 127.

58. Ibid., p. 366.

59. Ibid., p. 123. For the "only," see Heidegger, *Parmenides*, p. 114; see also idem, *Heraklit*, pp. 180–81, 189, and *Parmenides*, p. 250.

60. Heidegger, *Parmenides*, p. 100. Cf. *Grundfragen der Philosophie*, p. 21: "Ζῷον λόγον ἔχον" (man—that whole which perceives the whole).

61. Heidegger, *Parmenides*, p. 115.

62. For this figure of speech see Heidegger, "Germanien," p. 134.

63. Ibid.

64. Heidegger, "*Speigel*-Gespräch."

65. Heidegger, *Parmenides*, p. 141.

66. Empedocles, *Fragmente*, in Diels and Kranz, *Fragmente der Vorsokratiker*, vol. 1, Fragment A.10; cf. Fragment B.109.

67. For a discussion of the "great ones" see Heidegger, "Germanien," pp. 144–46.

7

Heidegger and *Praxis*

J A C Q U E S   T A M I N I A U X

Well before the stir caused by Farías's book, the Philosophy Department at the University of Essex invited me to take part in its colloquium "Reading Heidegger." They left the topic up to me.

At that time I was captivated by the work of Hannah Arendt, who, I was well aware, had been Heidegger's student and an intimate at Marburg—that is, during the years when Heidegger began to articulate a field of investigation which he called "fundamental ontology"—his famous inquiry into the horizon of intelligibility of the meaning of Being, the horizon (as *Being and Time* would soon try to demonstrate) formed by the finite temporality constituting the beings we are. The Arendt work that captivated me especially was the one on *vita activa*, *The Human Condition*.

In that work Arendt distinguishes three degrees of active life or, rather, three forms of hierarchized activity. The first is *labor* (*animal laborans*): that is, activity conditioned by *life* in the biological sense. The maintenance of life among the members of the human species, and the species itself, requires of humans (as of all living creatures), an activity that wrests from nature whatever can support their vital needs. Because this labor is conditioned by the necessities of life, it remains a prisoner of the eternal return of those vital cycles and is incapable of making its titulars anything more than representatives of a species or, as Marx would say, generic beings.

The second activity is that of producing works or artifacts, broadly defined. This activity, Arendt says, is conditioned not by life but by *belonging-to-the-world*, a function not simply of being-*in*-the-world but

of being-*of*-the-world. Beyond the biological environment, the least arti-
fact institutes a properly human habitat, which has a duration that
exceeds a mortal span of life. At the same time, this activity transcends
biological life only to substitute another form of anonymity for species
anonymity. It is not in its singularity that the referent of this activity can
emerge, but only as an exemplar of general aptitudes which others could
just as well have also. Moreover, this activity transcends life only to
substitute another form of eternal return for the vital cycles. "Fabrication" means "achieving an end which is this or that product with the help
of adequate means." But as soon as the product is completed, it becomes
in its turn a means for other ends, which in their turn become means for
ulterior ends ad infinitum. This circle of utility is no less futile than that
of vital cycles—with the result that the very mentality of those who
institute a world as a properly human habitat—a utilitarian mentality—is,
paradoxically, also a threat to the security of that habitat.

For such security, only a third activity will suffice: action proper,
which the Greeks called *praxis* (πρᾶξις), different from *poiesis* (ποίησις),
the making of works or definite effects. Action proper is the activity that
binds humans not to life (like labor) or to things (like fabrication) but to
other humans. The condition of action, Arendt says, is *plurality*, the fact
that humans are simultaneously similar and different: in short, they
impose and affirm themselves as individuals, instead of being multiple
copies of a single and same model. Because they resemble one another,
they can understand one another; because they are all different, they
must show who they are and make their difference manifest. Showing
and expressing to others the new capacity for initiative that they have or
what they are *by birth*, by natality, Arendt says, constitutes action.

Since such activity is as much interaction as interlocution, since the
activity is inscribed in a prior network of acts and words which the acting
individual cannot rise above, it makes everyone who acts (is active) as
much a patient as an agent. The result is that, strictly speaking, an action
resists the distinction of proper and improper. It is through this activity,
Arendt insists, that the category of *meaning* emerges, beyond the categories of necessity and utility to which the activities of labor and fabrication are bound. It is this activity, she adds, which, by its link to meanings
debated with others, permits the security of a common world. It is
through this activity that individuation is constituted, not by a withdrawal
to self but at the heart of a plurality. It is through this activity that
artifacts which are not utilitarian but works of art bear witness. It is in
fact this activity that is the condition *per quam* of the political—if it is
true that the very institution of the Greek *polis* refers both to *philia*
(attraction between like and like) and *eris* (rivalry between like and
unlike), if it is true that the Greek city-state, at its apogee in its democratic

and isonomic form, took extreme care to relegate the solitary activities of labor and fabrication of artifacts to a nonpublic sphere, so as to guarantee the sharing of acts and words.

It seemed to me that such an analysis invited a critical, even hostile, examination of Heidegger's fundamental ontology. In any case, it was this sort of consideration that drew me to the problem of *praxis* in Heidegger.

Arendt's analysis, I said to myself, puts dualism on trial, the alternation of the proper and the improper, the authentic and the inauthentic, which governs Heidegger's existential analytic. Indeed, it follows from this alternation that the "world" in its most properly existential quality *could in no way be common*, because it is disclosed only in the nothingness that a radically separated existent might experience through anguish. From this it also follows that the world could not be a habitat, since the Being-in-the-world called *Dasein* is, by definition, *unheimlich*: that is, "having no home." It follows further that there is no other individuation than the Being-toward-death, and since men and women cannot unload their deaths upon someone else, it is therefore not vis-à-vis others that individuals declare who they are but only vis-à-vis themselves in the solitude of their inner selves, in a profound absence of relationships.

In short, I was saying to myself, if I reason according to the distinctions Arendt laid out—and I found them phenomenologically pertinent—I could say that in *Being and Time* there is a thought of fabrication but not of action or *praxis*. There is certainly a notion of fabrication there, since all the everydayness in toto from which *Dasein* must detach itself in order to exist in itself is governed by a preoccupation with goals, effects, or products to be gained by means of suitably manipulative things. There is not, I said to myself, an insight into praxis, since plurality, far from constituting individuation, is opposed to it and is reduced by Heidegger to what he calls "Man," the neuter, the leveled human referent; and also since, generally speaking, "the sharing of deeds and words" picks up by definition from the daily waste and routine of life, from a mode of Being governed by the fabricating and utilitarian mentality.

This very clear contrast between Arendt's analysis of the *vita activa* and Heidegger's analysis seemed to me all the more surprising, however, because Arendt and Heidegger—at least during the period of Heidegger's work on fundamental ontology—both claimed a Greek inspiration, more precisely an Aristotelian inspiration.

Such was my quandary when I received the British invitation. That invitation gave me the opportunity to examine more closely the Heidegger texts on fundamental ontology to see whether they actually do neglect the form of activity that is action (Greek *praxis*) or, what amounts to the same thing, whether fundamental ontology simply conflates *praxis* with fabrication, the activity the Greeks called *poiesis*.

In his letter prefacing William Richardson's *Heidegger: Through Phenomenology to Thought*, Heidegger claims that he rediscovered *aletheuein* in the Greek sense, because of a study, nurtured by Husserl's teaching, of the ninth book (Theta) of Aristotle's *Metaphysics* and the sixth book of the *Nicomachean Ethics*. Now if there is a distinction illuminated and emphasized by these Aristotelian texts, it is certainly—though I will not say it is the only one—that of *poiesis* and *praxis*, of fabrication and action. It seemed to me highly unlikely that a reader as vigilant and penetrating as Heidegger could have carelessly conflated what Aristotle separated. At any rate, I felt it incumbent upon me to consider more closely what could have caught Heidegger's attention in those texts of Aristotle's.

So I began to reread Aristotle with Heidegger's notion of fundamental ontology in the back of my mind. And here is what I noticed. Not only does Heidegger pay heed to Aristotle's distinction and careful clarification between the activities of *poiesis* and *praxis*; he even makes it the framework for the first stage of his fundamental ontology: that is, his existential analytic. At the same time, Heidegger appropriates Aristotle's distinction in his ontological terms (not Aristotle's), which results in a genuine transformation of the Aristotelian notion of *praxis*, an obliteration or a rejection pure and simple of a certain number of traits Aristotle considered essential to *praxis*, just those that Hannah Arendt wished to feature in her work.

Let me explain.

Book 6 of the *Nicomachean Ethics*, which Heidegger highlights, takes up dianoetic excellences, which translators have usually called "intellectual virtues." Aristotle divides these into two groups corresponding to two aptitudes of the soul: epistemic or scientific, and logistic or deliberative. It is the second aptitude, the deliberative, that *poiesis* and *praxis*, fabrication and action, correspond. There were grounds, then, in my opinion, for me to examine Aristotle closely and to compare Aristotle and Heidegger.

The activity of *poiesis* in Aristotle's sense is an action that does not achieve its goal—for example, victory for the strategist, recovery of the patient's health for the physician, or some construction project for the building contractor—unless the action is based on a disclosive aletheic disposition which is its alone. This disposition is *technē*, a word we can translate as *savoir-faire* (knowhow). This knowhow is the dianoetic excellence or virtue of fabrication. Where fabrication is concerned, the absence of savoir-faire signifies a blind, ineffectual groping; knowhow is a virtue just to the extent that it exerts a discerning function. Those endowed with knowhow knowingly deliberate, and so discover with precision the means, materials, apparatus, and measures that assure the completion of the product they propose to make or the appearance of the effect they seek.

Action, the activity of *praxis*, is also an activity based on a discerning or disclosing disposition which is its alone. This disposition is not know-how, however, because unlike *poiesis*, which reaches its fulfillment, its entelechy, in the production of things or effects outside the agent, *praxis* has no fulfillment outside itself: it aims at nothing beyond acting well, the *eupraxia* of the agent. In other words, while *poiesis* is exteriorized in things or effects, *praxis* is an activity that strictly concerns the manner of being of the agents themselves, the very life of humans as individuals capable of excelling in their own individuality and of leading, in dealing with others and living among them, a good and appealing life. The discerning disposition corresponding to *praxis* is *phrōnesis*, a word traditionally translated as prudence or practical wisdom. It involves foresight or sagacity in judging what is appropriate to the requirements of a good and attractive life at any moment in situations that are always particular and changing. *Phrōnesis* is the dianoetic virtue of *praxis*.

In the *Nicomachean Ethics* as well as Book 9 of the *Metaphysics*, the other text Heidegger cites as essential, Aristotle emphasizes the structural differences between the two activities of *poiesis* and *praxis*. The difference is striking if we view each of these two activities (which are movements, processes) under the notions of *archē* and *telos*: that is, under the notions of principle and goal. The principle of the activity of fabrication is in the fabricator: it is the plan that the producer has in his head, the model he aims at and wishes to realize. But the goal of this activity is beyond the activity itself: the work or the effect to be produced. On the other hand, *praxis* has both its principle and its goal in itself. Its principle is the prior option in favor of acting well. And its goal is the quality of the action itself. It is therefore an activity that is its own end, performed for its own sake.

Accordingly, these activities are also distinguished if they are envisaged with respect to the notions of *dynamis* and *energeia*: power (or potentiality) and effectivity. In the case of fabrication, since what is to come to pass—for example, a certain building—is something other than the process of fabrication itself, *energeia* is in the thing built, *and* in relation to that object, the building activity is a *dynamis* or potentiality. The completeness of that activity, its entelechy, falls outside it, in its product, signifying that the *dynamis* and *energeia* are outside each other. But since *praxis* in no way has its fulfillment outside itself, such exteriority has no place there. The agent himself contains the *energeia* of *dynamis*, the second being internal therefore to the first.

Accordingly, these two activities differ finally with respect to time. Since fabrication finds its fulfillment in a product that emanates from it, a person cannot be at one and the same time the one who makes and the one who *has* made, the one who builds a certain building and the one who built it. On the other hand, since *praxis* has simultaneously *dynamis* and *energeia* in the agent, the agent is here simultaneously the one who acts and the one who has already acted. And since the agent's *praxis* is this person's very way of living and of responding to each instant of changing and particular circumstances, since the agent's *praxis* is therefore continually being started up again and always in the future, the perceptive function adjusted to that *praxis* (to wit, that *phrōnesis*) is not innately discerning and sagacious (that is, is not excellent) unless *phrōnesis* is applied to a past and is opened to a future. It requires a prior disposition in favor of acting well and a persistent pursuit (*epidioxis*) of the good and appealing life.

Aristotle repeatedly says that it is *praxis* thus defined—and not *poiesis*—which permits life to be properly human. To exist as a human consists not in producing but in acting. *Poiesis* involves things, *praxis* concerns human affairs, and the virtue of *poiesis*, *savoir-faire*, is inferior to the virtue of *praxis*, *phrōnesis*. And this is why: not only does *poiesis* have its product outside itself, but once this product is produced, it is viewed relative to other ends for which it serves as a means: it is for this or that, for this purpose or another. Consequently, if human activity were only production, it would be a prisoner of the infinite circle of means and ends. Nothing would ever be selected except for something further; and this endless process without a sense of actual use would render all desire futile and vain, as Aristotle insists at the beginning of the *Nicomachean Ethics*. This vanity does not affect *praxis*. The *pros ti* is something else, the for-this-then-for-that to which *poiesis* is linked and submits. Instead, *praxis* is *on eneka*, "for the sake of," the good and beautiful life worthy of being sought for itself. *Poiesis* is servile; *praxis* is oriented to living well, free, because it liberates desire from necessity and utility and renders an individual existence worthy of being remembered or taken as an example.

I shall provisionally stop this review of the Aristotelian analysis at this point. As I was reading the analysis with Heidegger's fundamental ontology in mind, it struck me that Heidegger had reappropriated that analysis as the very heart of his own existential analytic and, more broadly, in his fundamental ontology, in the famous opposition between proper and improper, between authentic and inauthentic.

Heidegger's fundamental ontology—his first philosophical project— aims at finding a response to the question of the locus (*foyer*) of intelligibility of the meanings of Being in the being we ourselves are, *Dasein*, the being that understands what Being means but understands it usually and at first in an inauthentic mode. To understand Being inauthentically is for *Dasein* to understand its own being starting with the mode of being of mere things involved in everyday usage, fabrication, and production. But to understand Being authentically is for *Dasein* to understand itself starting with its most singular being-able-to-be (*pouvoir-être*). In looking at the matter closely, I thought that with all the oppositions specifying it—on the one hand *Umwelt* (one's daily environment), on the other hand the world (*Welt*) proper to *Dasein*; on the one hand man (in the abstract: *man, le On*), on the other hand self (*Selbst, le Soi*); on the one hand preoccupation, on the other hand care (*Souci*); on the one hand foresight and prospective circumspection, on the other hand resoluteness; on the one hand *wozu*, on the other hand *worumwillen*—it appeared to me, I was saying, that this contrast which permitted Heidegger to articulate his problematic question of Being resulted from his reappropriation of Aristotle's distinction bewteen *poiesis* and *praxis*: that is, between an active behavior whose end is other than this behavior, and an activity deliberately exercised for its own sake, *praxis*.

Suddenly the clouds lifted on Heidegger's later statements regarding the role his study of Aristotle had played in his own discovery—going beyond Husserl—of truth as inherently revelatory, not simply in consciousness (*Bewusztsein*) but in existence, in *Dasein*. Husserl had shown that truth is not solely located or "domiciled" in judgment, since there are antepredicative truths; he had also shown, more profoundly than in adequation or coincidence between intellect and thing, that truth consists in exhibiting (*Aufweisen*), for each mode of intentionality its specific correlative. If the Aristotle of the *Nicomachean Ethics* could seem to Heidegger more original than Husserl on the question of truth, it is because Heidegger attributes the capacity for exhibiting or disclosing not to consciousness but to activity—more precisely, to comportment, notably to *poiesis* and *praxis*.

From there, we may establish certain strict parallels between Heidegger and Aristotle.

When Aristotle takes up *poiesis*, he assigns it a specific mode of disclosing: *technē*, knowhow. In a parallel way, when Heidegger analyzes daily behavior, in *Being and Time*, the way we act "proximally and for the most part," he maintains that this behavior is ruled by productive activity, broadly conceived—*Herstellen* ("to place here, create or establish"), which is the literal German translation of *poiein*. Heidegger claims that production, which governs ordinary preoccupations, is animated by a specific sort of circumspection, *praktische Umsicht*, knowing how to proceed, an inclusive view of the environs and networks of means and ends indicated. The affinity between this analysis and Aristotle's analysis of *technē* is obvious.

When Aristotle takes up *praxis*, he shows that it has no end apart from itself. Similarly, when Heidegger takes up the mode of Being proper to *Dasein*, existing, he emphasizes that it consists in being concerned with itself: "Das Dasein existiert umwillen seiner." Foresight fitted to *praxis* is, according to Aristotle, *phrōnesis*, which, vis-à-vis the moment of decision that particular situations require, consists in making a preliminary option converge with acting well and the pursuit, always in the future, of *eupraxia*. Bearing this in mind, we may observe in Heidegger the transposition of his famous analysis of the mode of disclosure proper to existence: that is, *Entschlossenheit* (resoluteness), decision, which consists in a particular existent being's reclaiming what he is already and anticipating in a glance (*Augenblick*) his innermost being-able-to-be—in short, fully assuming his own finite temporality.

It seemed clear from these parallels (which we could certainly pursue further) that there was indeed, in Heidegger, contrary to what I first thought, a view of *praxis* and that there was no confusion whatsoever between *praxis* and *poiesis*.

Still, a number of features of Heidegger's reappropriation of Aristotle surprised me. Indeed, it is futile to look in the *Nicomachean Ethics* for the equivalent of such themes as being-toward-death, the anguish of nothingness, existential solipsism, homelessness (*estrangement, Unheimlichkeit*), and the unrelatedness of existence (*Unbezüglichkeit*). Heidegger's insistence on these themes, I said to myself, is equivalent to extracting *praxis*, metamorphosed to the finite existence of *Dasein*, from human plurality and from every form of one's appearance before another (*autrui*). Whereas Aristotle basically teaches that *praxis* individuates someone at the heart of plurality, Heidegger teaches that *praxis* individuates solely in face-to-face confrontations with the self. This metamorphosis of the very notion of *praxis* brings with it, I said to myself, an absence of emphasis (in Heidegger's analytic of *phrōnesis*)—having favored being-toward-death—regarding a certain number of features essential to Aristotle's *phrōnesis*, notably the features concerning plurality, particularly in political life. Aristotle, to be sure, is careful to emphasize, in opposition to Euripides, that it would not be possible to be *phrōnimos*—that is, endowed with *phrōnesis*—if one were concerned only with self. This is why Pericles, in virtue of his wisdom and sense of proportion concerning the business of the isonomic city-state, seemed a model of *phrōnimos*. In this case it is hard to see the equivalent in *Being and Time*, since there, the resoluteness is, by and large, radically private, opposed to whatever is public, private in such a way that it relegates opinion to fallen everydayness, that it raises resoluteness above opinion, whereas

Aristotle says expressly that *phrōnesis* is a doxastic excellence. In the same way, it is hard to find in *Being and Time* the equivalent of these two traits (connected with human plurality), which, according to Aristotle, qualify *phrōnesis*: *synesis*, understanding the other; and *syggnome*, indulgence of the other.

As to the question of what motivated Heidegger to divert *praxis* toward a solipsism profoundly alien to Aristotle's views, it seemed to me that the answer was to be found in Plato. The relationship to death and the solitary dialogue of self with self are Plato's themes long before they are Heidegger's. They are introduced in Plato, as in Heidegger, to overvalue the excellence of a very special style of life, the philosopher's life-style, the *bios theoretikos* entirely given over to the task of unveiling Being from the totality of distributed things, the task that after Plato and Aristotle is designated by the name of metaphysics.

Earlier I pointed out that Heidegger's reappropriation of Aristotle's analysis of *poiesis* and *praxis* is inscribed in the context of forming a fundamental ontology: that is, the reappropriation is motivated by the fundamental ontological question of designating the unique focus for understanding the diverse meanings of Being. Since at first sight the question is not practical but theoretical—it asks not how to act but how to understand Being as such—this motivation leads us to ask whether Heidegger describes *praxis* phenomenologically for what it itself is, or whether he does so only to the extent that it is capable of providing the ground for the science of Being: metaphysics. And since this science mobilizes all efforts of thought and imposes on thought the unceasing pursuit of its solitary dialogue with itself, we may well wonder whether metaphysics does not lead to construing the activity of thinking Being as the sole authentic form of action, of *praxis*. It is at that point, it seemed to me, that an attempt had to be made to understand—not just anecdotally but philosophically—Heidegger's Nazi commitment. For in the end it is undeniable that Heidegger's Nazi proclamations are expressed in the language of fundamental ontology, first of all in the famous address as rector, "Die Selbstbehauptung der deutschen Universität" (Self-affirmation of the German university). This address is profoundly continuous with the sense of the inaugural lesson of 1929 "Was ist Metaphysik?" And its claims derive neither from *Mein Kampf* nor from Alfred Rosenberg's *Der Mythos der zwanzigsten Jahrhunderts*, still less from the writings of Abraham a Sancta Clara, but from a text founding the entire metaphysical tradition: Plato's *Republic*.

It was from this perspective at the Essex colloquium that I formulated a certain number of questions for Heidegger's project, to which I am going to return in more detail. But now, in order to give these questions more specificity, I must refine the description I have just offered of Heidegger's reappropriation of the *Nichomachean Ethics*. Indeed, until now I have acted as if only the Aristotelian distinction between *poiesis* and *praxis* had inspired Heidegger. I have realized since that Heidegger's reappropriation—deeply metamorphosed—involves not only the two activities that derive from what Aristotle calls the deliberating part of the soul but also, no less profoundly metamorphosed, what Aristotle calls the epistemonic part of the soul: *theoria*. This is what I learned from my recent reading of the unpublished transcripts of the two courses at Marburg: "Fundamental Concepts of Greek Philosophy" (1926), which takes up an interpretation of Aristotle as a whole; and "The *Sophist*" (1924), which devotes the first third to an overall interpretation of the *Nicomachean Ethics*. I should like to pinpoint briefly how these lessons cast a sharper light on Heidegger's concept of *praxis*.

On Heidegger's reading, all of Aristotle's philosophical research is animated by a single question, that of Being, in the sense in which Being is not itself a being. When Aristotle takes up physics, it is to find a point of departure for his ontological theory of nature, particularly regarding the problem of movement. When he takes up life, it is to establish an ontology of life. When he takes up *logos* and concept formation, he takes up some modalities according to which Being is revealed by saying and speaking and is included in them. When he finally takes up ethics, it is to establish (and I quote from the course "Fundamental Concepts") "an ontology of *Dasein*: that is, of human life."[1]

At the same time, this ontology, according to Heidegger, suffers from two defects: equivocation and indetermination. It is equivocal because the question of Being, in Aristotle, tends to be confused with the question of those beings that are most properly denominated as such. In Aristotle, therefore, ontology tends to be confused with theology, the science of the supreme being, which for Aristotle is the *primum motor immobile* of movements of *physis*. It is also indeterminate because when Aristotle indicates that he is concerned with the be-ing of things, which arises in many ways, he does not expressly inquire what assures us of the unity of this multiplicity. He does not expressly pose the question of the meaning of Being.

Heidegger's praise of Aristotle's ontological power is associated with his highlighting of the two defects he obviously thought it was his project to correct, by removing the onto-theological equivocation and by removing the indeterminacy of the meaning of Being. Aristotle himself showed the way in correcting the second defect. To be sure, he does not expressly pose the question of what unites the four respects in which Being is defined, but he does answer it implicitly and in a single word: *ousia*— which, according to Heidegger, means *Vorhandenheit des Vorhandenen* or *Anwesenheit der Gegenwart* (presence of what is present). The "Fundamental Concepts of Greek Philosophy'' course ends with these words: "Greek ontology is an ontology of the world in the sense of *physis*. Being is interpreted as presence and constancy (*Beständigkeit*). Being is understood in the present as a point of departure—naively, through the phenomenon of time in which, however, the present (*Gegenwart*) is simply a *single* mode. Question: How does the present acquire this privilege? Why do the past and future not have the same rights? Shouldn't Being be understood through temporality as a whole?'' (transcription p. 102). To take away the indeterminacy of Being means therefore to understand Being not solely in the light of the privilege of the present but in the light of temporality as a whole: that is, a temporality in which future and past take precedence over the present. Such temporality is no longer that of *physis* but of *Dasein*, a temporality that throws light on the foundation of the beings we are, the ontology of *Dasein* explored in *Being and Time*.

Now, I have just reminded you that at that time, Heidegger also characterized the *Nicomachean Ethics* as an ontology of *Dasein*. In order to juxtapose the two *Dasein* ontologies profitably and understand the metamorphosis that Heidegger's ontology of *Dasein* imposed on Aristotle's ontology of *Dasein*, we must take into consideration not simply what Aristotle says about *poiesis* and *praxis* but what he says about *theoria*. We find, in effect, that Heidegger's intended removal of the onto-theological equivocation and the indeterminacy of the meaning of Being is articulated at the expense of a metamorphosis not only of Aristotle's concepts of *poiesis* and *praxis* but even of his concept of *theoria*. This is obvious—if we interpret ever so little in the light of Heidegger's reading of the *Nichomachean Ethics* in the introduction to his course on Plato's *Sophist*.

Theoria in Aristotle's sense has two excellences or hierarchized epistemonic virtues: *epistēmē* and *sophia*. In these two cases, *theoria* bears on what is not perishable. In the case of the *epistēmē*, the view or perspective of *theoria* (*theorein* means "to look") bears on immutable beings: for example, mathematical entities. In the case of *sophia*, this view bears on Being and on the highest being, the first *primum immobile*, which is at the origin of the movements of *physis*. That view on the part of mortals is, for Aristotle, the highest way of life humans can attain, inasmuch as *praxis*, in this view, transcends itself, approaches the eternal that is divine, and escapes (as long as *theoria* lasts) the fragility that affects existence when it is embodied in the movement of human affairs. To these human affairs, Aristotle says, no *sophia* could correspond, because they do not derive from first principles; only the inevitably provisional judgment of *phrōnesis* applies to them.

These Aristotelian views set up a double-edged reaction from Heidegger: first, a critical thematization on its most obvious side; and then, a metamorphosed reappropriation on its more circumspect side. When Heidegger thematizes these views, he criticizes them for not recognizing, because of privilege they concede to eternity, the originariness of the finite time of *praxis* itself, understood as the mortal existence of humans. For Heidegger's deconstruction, this privilege of the eternal in Greek *theoria* is due (in spite of its claiming to have escaped both *poiesis* and *praxis*) to its entanglement in the prospects of everyday engagements: that is, the prospects of *technē*, which, in order to guide the production and use of tools (in short, *poiesis*) needs to rely on the stable persistence (*Vorhandenheit*) of Nature. Aristotle's *primum mobile* would therefore be only a hypostasis of *Vorhandenheit*: that is, the presence-at-hand of entities offered to ordinary preoccupation. But this critical thematizing is accompanied by a transformed reappropriation.

As I have said, it is from Aristotle's confrontation between *poiesis* and its *technē* on the one hand and *praxis* and its *phrōnesis* on the other that fundamental ontology borrows—at the price of a considerable metamorphosis—its distinction between the inauthentic everyday comportment of concern (animated by circumspection) and an authentic manner of Being (animated by the resoluteness to be a self). It is Aristotle also— this is what the courses I am referring to suggest—who inspires Heidegger when the latter says and repeats that the highest form of existence or *praxis* is *theoria*, understood as the thinking of Being. But Heidegger departs from Aristotle radicallly—or, if you prefer, metamorphoses Aristotle from top to bottom—when he assigns to this thinking of Being a role not of dissociating itself from *praxis* and its *phrōnesis* but of reinforcing them (which means reflecting in an ontological grounding the finite movement of resolute mortal existence). To think Being is from now on to think the finite time of *praxis*. Reciprocally, the thinker of Being is the ultimate judge of human affairs.

What does all this have to do with Heidegger's compromise with Nazism in 1933 and the years following?

To reply to this question I shall make three points corresponding successively to the source of the Nazi engagement, its center, and then its outcome.

The source of this engagement is fundamental ontology itself— *grosso modo*, *Sein und Zeit*, 1927. It seems to me totally inadmissible to claim, as Adorno did, that this text is already deeply Nazi and that there is a necessary link betwen it and the engagement of 1933. I say this for the simple reason that one searches this text in vain for a political philosophy. Nevertheless, one can find in *Being and Time*, and in the related courses, conditions of the possibility for being blind where political judgment is concerned.

Let us note first that Heidegger's very selection of what is promising for reappropriation in Aristotle's doctrine of *praxis* and *phrōnesis* seems to indicate a Platonic bias. If it is conceded that it is *Entschlossenheit* that radicalizes Aristotle's *phrōnesis*, then isn't it surprising that neither opinion nor plurality belongs to his concept of *Entschlossenheit*? In its essence, *Entschlossenheit* is linked to what Heidegger calls "existential solipsism."[2] *Doxa*, the relationship to the other (*autrui*), and plural debate are all excluded from it and relegated to the orbit of preoccupation; that is, of the inauthentic behavior of *Dasein*. As a result, the very distinction between authentic and inauthentic seems to coincide with the distinction between public and private. We are justified in suspecting here an echo of Plato's disdain for human affairs. Such disdain comes through as early as the introduction to *Being and Time*, in which Heidegger opposes Plato's "unheard-of formulations" (in *Parmenides*) and Aristotle's *Metaphysics* to the "flatness" of Thucydides' narratives, thereby overlooking the admirable account of Pericles' city-state (*Sein und Zeit*, p. 39). Indeed, even the way Heidegger describes everydayness as subject to the weight of productive mentality and the equivocations of *doxa* is quite compatible with Plato's description of human affairs and Plato's depreciation of it so as to justify the *bios theoretikos* as the highest activity, the sole activity that is the soul's dialogue with itself. His insistence on the preponderant role of the "they" (*Man*) in the public character of everydayness echoes Plato's disdain toward *hoi polloi* in the *Republic*. And the very reappropriation of the notion of *doxa* to characterize inauthentic comprehension and speech, which are alleged to govern everydayness certainly, owes more to Plato's critique than to Aristotle's justification of *doxa* with respect to *phrōnesis*. There is no place in fundamental ontology for what Aristotle called right opinion. But there are many echoes of Plato's division between *sophia* and sophistic, between science and rhetoric.

This Platonic tendency, which Hannah Arendt insisted on, deserves more attention than it usually receives. We must ask whether Heidegger's reappropriation is a radicalization of Aristotle's teaching, or an impure mixture of radicalization and obliteration. To be sure, Aristotle and Plato were in agreemnt in thinking that the *bios theoretikos* is the highest form of *praxis*. But at the same time there is hardly any doubt that Aristotle rejected Plato's ambition to put the entire field of *praxis* under the role of the *bios theoretikos*. The *Nicomachean Ethics* (1094b) in fact shows his disagreement with Plato on this point. After having indicated at the beginning of the work that his study "is in a sense a study of politics," Aristotle emphasizes that, contrary to Plato's, his own treatment of political science will be adapted to his subject—which implies "considerable difference of opinion and uncertainty," and which for that very reason is not capable of the *akribeia* (exactness) that "should be expected in other sectors of philosophy." As a consequence, he says, "it is the mark of an educated mind to expect from each discipline the degree of exactness the subject allows. It is equally unreasonable to accept from a mathematician merely probable conclusions and to require of an orator rigorous demonstrations.'' What resonates in these remarks is the mentality of the city-state of Pericles. Difference of opinion and uncertainty are inherent in *praxis*. There are grounds for accommodating them but none for getting rid of them. Aristotle's political philosopher is not a rhetorician, but, unlike Plato's, he is certainly closer to the public orator than the mathematician or metaphysician. And the reason for this proximity is the essential link between *praxis* and plurality. In virtue of plurality—this *plethos* which he opposes in his *Politics* to the monist and unanimist views attractive to Plato—*praxis* in Aristotle's sense is essentially ambiguous and, for that reason, cannot be the subject and basis of a science devoid of ambiguity. But is not this essential link and the ambiguity that results from it precisely what the attempt to build a fundamental ontology on the basis of *praxis* obliterates, when *praxis* means the free transcendence of *Dasein*, which understands Being in the exact measure where it exists resolutely and for its own ends? In fundamental ontology, the concept of transcendence is totally dominated by the resistance of the ''own'' against the improper, or, in Platonic terms, by the resistance of the One to the Many. This prevents inscribing *praxis* in a common domain of shared acts and words, as occurred in the Greek city-state, and in Aristotle, who captures its spirit.

The deliberate orientation of Heidegger's reappropriation of *praxis* to the sole and solitary comprehension of Being bears witness therefore to a rejection of Aristotle's resistance to Plato. In fundamental ontology, everything happens as if the *bios theoretikos* completely incorporated and governed *praxis*. Everything happens as if this *bios*, definitively solitary, were the sole authentic form of individuation. ''Philosophy,'' Heidegger writes in his 1928 course on Leibniz, ''is the central and total concretion of the metaphysical essence of existence.''[3] Or again, in the course on the *Sophist*, specifically on Aristotle: ''It is in *theorein* as pure research of Being as such that man conquers the greatest possible proximity with regard to the highest mode of Being that is accessible to him. This mode of Being, Aristotle did not merely teach; he also lived it: philosophy at that time had no need to get close to life.'' In short, to live truly was to philosophize. So much for the source (of the Nazi engagement). What is there at the center?

Heidegger's famous rectoral address can be considered a confirmation of this same Platonic bias. The theme is the normative position of metaphysics as queen of the sciences. The theme of this discourse in which Heidegger treats public affairs, is borrowed from Plato's *Republic*, which, to remove the pain, ambiguities, and multiple tensions inherent in the democratic city-state and its *praxis*, proposed to transform the state into a kind of vast workshop wherein each would have a defined role at the heart of a defined organ of the body politic. We find an echo in Heidegger's image of a corporatist state wherein each of the bodies, the *Stände*, provides a distinct service: service of work, service of defense, and, at the summit, the service of knowledge.

And a propos of the Greeks, responding to a question of what *theoria* was for them, Heidegger writes: "It is said that the only consideration is that it remain linked to the thing in its plenitude and exigency. It is in making an appeal to the Greeks that this contemplative behavior is presumed to emerge by itself. But this appeal is wrong. Because, on the one hand, *theoria* cannot emerge for itself, but only in the passion of remaining close to beings-as-such, under their constraint. On the other hand, the Greeks struggled precisely to understand and carry out this contemplative interrogation as the high style, even as *the* supreme modality of *energia*, proper to man's being-at-work. Their intention was not to equate Praxis and Theory but, on the contrary, *to understand theory itself as the highest realization of true praxis*. For the Greeks, science was not a cultural good, but the milieu determining at the most intimate level the *Dasein* of the people and the State.''[4]

No need for a special analysis to see in this text the repetition and accentuation of what has been noted up to this point. The concept of *Dasein*, applied to a people organized into a state, does not lose the traits it had in *Being and Time*. It preserves them. The *Dasein* of the "people-state'' is a *praxis*, and the highest actualization of *praxis* is the comprehension articulated of beings-as-such: that is, the science of the Being of beings, metaphysics. The *Dasein* of the people-state accentuates these traits as well, because applying the concept of *Dasein* to a people-state is equivalent to intensifying the monadic traits noted above: it is equivalent, in other words, to making the state (and its leader), not its citizens, the sole true individual. To claim that the people-state is a *Dasein* is equivalent to denying plurality, to denying the sharing of speech and acts, or— what comes to the same thing—to replacing the plural debate on what appears to each (*dokei moi*) by a unanimous passion for the Being of the beings. The Platonism of these lines is obvious and in strict conformity with the disdain that *Being and Time* displayed for Thucydides. Everything transpires here as if Heidegger—who relies on Greek authority throughout his speech, without bothering to ask himself about the fact that the birth of the science of the Being of beings beginning with Plato, far from accompanying the flowering of the Periclean city-state, watched its decay—wanted to believe that the Greeks invented the *polis* for speculative reasons. He does not seem to suspect that the Greeks of the city-state at the time of its glory regarded the *nomos*—that is, the legal management of the debate relative to the pluralism of their *doxa*, and not at all the science monitored by the sages and experts—as the true pivot of their Being-together (*isonomia*). Like Hegel, when in the preface to the *Philosophy of Right* he interprets the Greek city-state in the light of Plato's *Republic*, Heidegger takes for granted that the Platonic image of *politeia* reflects exactly the essence of the *polis*. It seems therefore as if, hearing the word *Kampf*, so terribly charged in Hitler's Germany, he translated it unthinkingly into the *gigantomachia peri tēs ousias* which Plato discusses in the *Sophist*. There is no doubt, finally, that the rectorial address is in close agreement with the Platonic concept of the philosopher-king. Nor is there any doubt that it is very far removed from the pluralist mind-set of the Greek city-state which still animated, contrary to Plato, Aristotle's concept of *praxis*.

What about the period after 1934, after June 1934, when Heidegger resigned as rector? Heidegger's readers, attentive to the explanations he gave, after the war, of his compromise with the regime, might have expected to find in the courses following the resignation an expression of his disillusionment and a recognition of his error. More precisely, they might have expected to find in those lessons the first indications of the famous turn (*Kehre*) from the fundamental ontology project—from the science of the meaning of Being—toward the meditation on the historical withdrawal of Being in the age of technology and nihilism: the first clues, therefore, of an overcoming of metaphysics, of heeding Hölderlin, the poet of finitude and the sacred, rather than Nietzsche, the philosopher of the will to power. But things are never so simple.

If we consider more closely the first course on Hölderlin (1934–35), the course *Einführung in die Metaphysik* (1935), and the documents now available regarding the genesis of the famous essay *Der Ursprung des Kunstwerks*, we notice that the project for completing metaphysics continues to inform these undertakings, and even that Heidegger is more of a metaphysician than ever. These texts show therefore a continuity with fundamental ontology.

This project is totalizing (*totalisant*). It means extracting from "beings-in-totality"—a syntagm that functions like a refrain in the texts from 1934–1936—the secret of their Being. The project is voluntarist: to think, to question in the direction of Being, is *to want to know*; Prometheus is the first philosopher. However, the locus of this willing, which is deeply historical, is not longer the resolute existing of the singular *Dasein*, for its own sake alone, as was true in *Being and Time*. This locus is now the singular *Dasein* of a singular people, the Germans. *Being and Time* taught basically that singular *Dasein* is a metaphysical being. The writings of 1934–36 teach that the German people is the metaphysical people; and since metaphysics is of Greek origin, the project that is the German people must claim its heritage both from the Greeks and from the two German thinkers who had claimed such rights before Heidegger: to wit, Hegel and Nietzsche. The essays of this period celebrate the "grandeur of German Idealism": we can see in them Hegel's *Grundlinien der Philosophie des Rechts* taking the place of Plato's *Republic*; as for Nietzsche (the only philosopher, we may note, who is cited without criticism in *Being and Time*), this work already claimed its roots in the second "Untimely Meditation" in developing an existential notion of historicality, and the first course on Hölderlin is filled with Nietzschean words: the superfluous, power, superpower, will, superwill, creation, superman. At the same time that the first reading of Hölderlin claimed Hegel and Nietzsche as forerunners, it enlarged the terminology of fundamental ontology for the Being-toward-death of an entire people.

If I recall this course in the context of an exposé of Heidegger's thought of action, it is because it provides an important correction to the theses argued in *Being and Time*. This correction concerns *poiesis* and therefore *technē*, which is its disclosive or aletheic function. Let us remember that according to *Being and Time* and the related courses, *poiesis* (that is, activity concerned with means and ends) and *technē* (that is, practical circumspection) are relegated in their entirety to the inauthenticity of everydayness. Everydayness is in the position of fallenness with respect to what *Dasein* properly is. What appears with the first course on Hölderlin—and holds steady in the *Einführung in die Metaphysik* and "Der Ursprung des Kunstwerks"—is, above this *poiesis* (fallen in everydayness), a nonfallen *poiesis* that can assume three forms: that of the workmanship of the thinker, that of the workmanship of the poet, and—alas!—that of the workmanship of the founder of the state. These forms raise workmanship to the rank of creation. Indeed, the property of a people's authentic time entails that only certain individuals, the creative ones, are up to its measure. The thinker by his work—which is a mixture of *theoria* (the culmination of *praxis*) and *poiesis*, since not only does he think but he writes texts—calls together his *Volk* to confront its historical Being at the heart of beings-in-totality. The poet by his work summons the people to welcome its gods. As for the founder of the state—he is referring to *der Führer*, of course—the opposition between the fallen everyday *poiesis* and an authentic and creative *poiesis* permits Heidegger blindly to wash away any mud and filth and send all that back *en bloc* to the fallenness of everyday babble: the Führer above racism, *Volkstum*, culture and science for the people, the slogan *Blut und Boden*, organization, and the normalization of the masses.

Of course, any voluntarist and totalizing pathos relative to the destiny of the metaphysical people is effaced in Heidegger's thought of the retreat of Being in an age of technology and nihilism. But it is by no means sure that the speculative and Platonic bias I evoked a little while ago, with all the blindness it carries concerning human affairs, their plurality, their ambiguity, has vanished as well. Ten years after the rectoral address, in a seminar of 1942–43 titled *Parmenides* in which Heidegger refers copiously to Plato's *Republic*, we find the following definition of the Greek city-state: "What is the *polis*? The word itself turns us toward the answer, provided we mean to gain an essential view of the Greek experience of Being and truth—an essential view that illuminates everything. The *polis* is the *polos*, the pivot, the locus around which gravitates, in a specific way, all that appears to the Greeks, including beings. The pivot is the locus toward which each being turns in such a way that it shows in relation to that locus what implied link it has with Being. To the extent that it is such a locus, the pivot lets beings appear in their Being according to the totality of their implication. . . . Between *polis* and Being reigns an originary relationship."[5]

These lines seem strictly in accord with the rectoral address regarding the concept of the city-state. In making the city-state the locus of the disclosing of beings-in-totality and their Being, these lines state, by and large, that the essence and foundation of the political domain are of a speculative order. These lines suggest as a consequence that those who devote their lives to thinking the Being of beings are best qualified to rule human affairs, or at any rate to be the counselors of the prince. They are in conformity with Plato's views in the *Republic*, and are not without some traces reminiscent of Hegel. It seems to me extremely significant in this respect that, shortly thereafter, in the same seminar, Heidegger continues thus: "Germans would not be the people (*Volk*) of thinkers if their thinkers had not thought the same: Hegel says in the foreword of the first edition of his *Logik* in 1812 that 'an educated people devoid of metaphysics is like a richly decorated temple without a Holy of Holies' " (*GA* 54:148). In the same seminar we find a passage no less significant on *phrōnesis*. Plato says in the *Republic*: "Those who are not saved by *phrōnesis* drink beyond any measure" (621A.7ff.), which Heidegger glosses as follows: "*Phrōnesis* is the penetration of this power of sight, which has a view of what is authentically visible and disclosed. The sight to which Plato refers is the sight of essential seeing: that is, philosophy. *Phrōnesis* means philosophy, and the word says: having an eye for the essential" (*6A*. 54:178). If these lines interpret the Platonic concept of *phrōnesis* correctly, we may suspect that they are very far removed from the Aristotelian understanding of the same word. We may similarly take Heidegger's agreement with the Hegelian concept of "educated people" to be no less removed from the Aristotelian notion of "education" regarding human affairs (see above).

It is not clear that this Platonic bias ever disappeared from Heidegger's view when his meditation on the history of Being was definitively substituted for the project of fundamental ontology. On this subject, let us limit ourselves to recalling the beginning of the "Letter on Humanism," the first text published after the war, in which Heidegger gives up any further pretense of completing metaphysics as a science of Being. "We are still far," he says, "from pondering the essence of action decisively enough. We view action only as causing an effect. The actuality of the effect is valued according to its utility. But the essence of action is accomplishment. To accomplish means to unfold something into the fullness of its essence, to lead it forth into this fullness—*producere*. Therefore only what already is can really be accomplished. But what 'is' above all is Being. Thinking accomplishes the relation of Being to the essence of man."[6] Here the Platonic penchant reappears: the accomplishment of action is none other than thinking—which Heidegger repeats in 1950, in a lecture on the *Kehre*: "Thinking is acting in what is most proper."

To be sure, this thinking no longer aims at a science of Being. It is no longer metaphysical. But isn't it a sign of Platonism to treat action— "*engagement*," according to Beaufret's question—without paying the least attention to its insertion in the context of human plurality (as the word action connotes), and to orient the sense of the proposition at once toward a mode of *bios theoretikos*? Even if Heidegger takes care not to confuse the thought of Being and a knowledge of the same (a confusion made by fundamental ontology), even if he takes care to dissociate thought from willing and, above all, from willing-to-know, we cannot say that he takes the same care not to confuse the thinking of Being and judgments relative to human affairs. What was in play in *praxis* in the eyes of the Greeks of the isonomic city-state was the goal of excellence strictly conditioned by the free participation of individuals, by their sharing deeds and speech in a common world the identity of which was not separable from the plurality of perspectives directed upon it. This is the plural and ambiguous manifestation Aristotle wanted to preserve against Plato, when in his *Ethics* he warned against any absorption of *phrōnesis* by *sophia*. In this sense, *phrōnesis* was, by and large, the aptitude recognized (in each, not in professionals alone) to judge competently in public and in private matters. But if the sole manifestation to which *praxis* essentially refers when it is confused with the activity of thinking is the disclosure of Being, then, whatever may be the ambiguity of this disclosing, it marginalizes the original agents of human affairs. The plural and ambiguous manifestation of these affairs deserves no further attention than in Plato: with respect to the history of Being, the peripeties of these affairs are like the futile agitation of a foam hiding the essential to which a few of the rare elect—thinkers and poets—are alerted.

In the sixth book of the *Nicomachean Ethics*, so dear to Heidegger, there is a passage in which Aristotle says, apropos of Anaxogoras and Thales, that a person may be *sophos* without being *phrōnimos*, that a person may attain the summit of *theoria* without being capable of judging. This means that the young Thracian girl was right to laugh at Thales. I am not sure that Heidegger ever succeeded in reappropriating this passage.

NOTES

1. Martin Heidegger, *Grundbegriffe der antiken Philosophie,* ed. Franz-Karl Blust (in preparation). Quotations are taken from the transcription by Hermann Mörchen.

2. Martin Heidegger, *Sein und Zeit* (Tübingen: Max Niemeyer, 1963), p. 188. Page numbers are hereafter cited in the text.

3. Martin Heidegger, *Metaphysische Anfangsgründe der Logik im Ausgang von Leibniz,* ed. Klaus Held (Frankfurt: Klostermann, 1978), app. to sec. 10.

4. Martin Heidegger, *Die Selbstbehauptung der deutschen Universität,* ed. Hermann Heidegger (Frankfurt: Klostermann, 1983), pp. 11–12.

5. Martin Heidegger, *Parmenides,* ed. Manfred S. Frings (Frankfurt: Klostermann, 1982), pp. 132–33; hereafter cited as *GA* 54 (*Gesamtausgabe,* vol. 54).

6. Martin Heidegger, "Letter on Humanism," trans. Frank A. Capuzzi with J. Glenn Gray, in *Martin Heidegger: Basic Writings,* ed. David Farrell Krell (New York: Harper & Row, 1977), p. 193.

8

The History of Being and Political Revolution: Reflections on a Posthumous Work of Heidegger

NICOLAS TERTULIAN

The sixty-fifth volume of Martin Heidegger's complete works contains a study of more that 500 pages, the most important work the philosopher produced after *Sein und Zeit:* it is the *Beiträge zur Philosophie.* Written between 1936 and 1938, therefore after Heidegger's resignation from the rectorship and at a moment when, through disappointment with that experience in the real world, he was devoting himself entirely to developing his conceptions, this work had to wait for the centenary of the philosopher's birth in order to be published.[1] Did its author consider it too critical of the dominant ideology to be published in Nazi Germany? And afterward, did he think it was too marked by its time, or simply unfinished, to allow it to be published?

In any case, the important place *Contributions to Philosophy* reserved for the theory of truth and the Heideggerian vision of the history of the Occident can only raise once more the fundamental question underlying current debates on the philosopher: is there a link between the inner direction of Heidegger's thought and his temporal commitment, *in saeculo*, in favor of National Socialism?

Halfway between *Being and Time* and the "Letter on Humanism," the *Contributions to Philosophy* makes it possible to measure Heidegger's course since his first great work, and to form a more accurate picture of the turning-point (the famous *Kehre*) that his thought presumably took toward the end of the 1920s.

When he was beginning to write his *Contributions* in 1936, he alluded, in the introduction to his course on Schelling, to what Napoleon said to Goethe at Erfurt in 1808: "Where are we headed now with destiny? Politics is destiny. Come to Paris; I categorically demand it of you. Here, there is a vaster conception of the world.''[2] By praising the anti-French resistance and those who embodied it, like Hardenberg and Scharnhorst—especially their will to make a *Staat der Intelligenz* of the Prussian state—Heidegger imagined that he had categorically refuted Napoleon's claim: "No, spirit is destiny and destiny is spirit.''[3]

Schelling's *Of Human Freedom* (1809), which Heidegger took to be "one of the profoundest works written in Germany and thus of occidental philosophy,''[4] was, in his opinion, one of the best replies the German mind could offer to the challenge implied in the French emperor's words.

In another text from the same period, Heidegger praised the idea of revolution. He did not hesitate to place his philosophical meditation under the sign of a revolution in thought and to condemn the forces of conservatism. The polarity between revolutionary and conservative forces running through all of politics did not fail to gain a certain resonance when thus transposed to the field of philosophical reflection.

Heidegger of course justified the necessity of revolution (or of revolutions) on the basis of the great historical drama of *Seinsgeschichte* (history of Being). Since the great Greek beginning of philosophy had been hidden from sight (*Verschüttung*) in modern thought, through a degradation of the original conception of truth, the inception of a new beginning quite naturally became, in Heidegger's eyes, a perfect revolutionary gesture capable of eliminating habits deep-rooted for centuries.

The legitimacy of revolution is defended in the introduction to his course *Grundfragen der Philosophie* (winter semester 1937–38). Stressing the necessity "of changing what had become overly habitual—[the necessity] of revolutions," he wrote that "the original and authentic relationship to the beginning is the revolutionary spirit, which, by overturning ordinary life, once more liberates the invisible law that held at the beginning. . . . [The conservative spirit] remains the prisoner of past history; only the revolutionary spirit grasps the profound dimension of living history.''[5] This praise of revolution, quite unusual in Heidegger's characteristic philosophical texts (and, by contrast, very much in evidence in his 1933 political speeches), evokes a central thesis of *Being and Time*: the preeminence of the future with respect to the two other temporal extases, the present and the past. "The path and the events of history are to be first of all and ever the future. . . . The future is the beginning of every event.''[6] The spokespersons of the future (*die Zukünftigen*) are designated in the *Beiträge* as the figureheads of the revolution to come.

It is interesting to recall here that Sartre, in his polemic with Lukács in *Search for a Method* (1956), says quite forcefully: "Heidegger has never been an [activist]—at least insofar as he expressed himself in his philosophical works.''[7] One may wonder what Sartre's reaction would have been regarding this praise of revolution and of "future man" (*der zukünftige Mensch*) in the Heideggerian texts of 1936–38, whose "activist" tone cannot be doubted.

The point of departure of Heideggerian reflection in the *Beiträge* as in his courses of the same period—we could say his *Grunderlebnis* (his rock-bottom experience)—is the state of distress of the world: such expressions as uprooting (*Entwurzelung*), desacralization (*Entgötterung*), and the darkening of the world (*Weltverdüsterung*) flow repeatedly from his pen. He says, on the other hand, that disenchantment (*Entzauberung*) is in fact a perverse enchantment (*Verzauberung*). The Nietzschean analysis of nihilism regarded as a constitutive condition of the modern world—Nietzsche defined it nonetheless in terms of value: "the devalorization of all values"—is taken up by Heidegger in his own account, where he tries to give it a more profound dimension by pointing to the abandonment of Being (*Seinsverlassenheit*) as the origin of nihilism. In his course on Schelling, he explains that nihilism, denounced with foresight by Nietzche, is markedly evident in the transitional period from the nineteenth to the twentieth century (in his eyes, it represents a distinct age, *ein Zeitalter*). By evoking in rather striking terms the decline of Europe at this period ("That which belongs to the lower domain is assigned to the higher level; that which is merely an adroit invention is made to pass for creative work; absence of reflection is held to be energy, and science assumes the appearance of essential knowledge"), Heidegger designates Nietzsche as the only thinker who began a "countermovement." The essence of nihilism requires, in his eyes, the most rigorous reflection: "Thus, reflect and reflect with increased perspicacity! Know, and know with ever more pitiless rigor!" It is in this context that Heidegger brings into his discourse the figures of Hitler and Mussolini, whom he presents as two political personages acting under the essential impetus of Nietzsche's message and activating, each in his own way, "countermovements" destined to curb the dominant nihilism. The passage in question was suppressed in the edition of the course on Schelling published in the form of an autonomous work by Max Niemeyer in 1971. (The omission was noted for the first time by Karl Ulmer, a former philosophy student, in a letter addressed to *Der Spiegel* in May 1977.) It may now be found once more in the text reproduced according to the original manuscript in volume 42 of the *Gesamtausgabe*: "It is known, moreover, that the two men who launched countermovements in Europe based on the political organization of the nation, that is, on the people—in a different manner, to tell the truth—[I mean] Mussolini and Hitler were, by reaction and in different ways, influenced by Nietzsche in an essential manner and this, without the specific metaphysical sphere of Nietzschean thought being implicated directly."[8]

The reservation expressed in the last part of the sentence does not attenuate the impact of the initial affirmation: the action of the two dictators was clearly placed by Heidegger under the sign of a great historical movement directed against the decadence that, according to him, afflicted Europe. Formulating his reservation, he assumed a certain distance with respect to the two politicians, the latter not having succeeded in encompassing the total profundity of Nietzsche's thought: this mission could only return to a far more radical interpretation, which was to localize the origins of nihilism in *Seinsverlassenheit* and to point out, in Nietzsche's thought, the end and the goal of the history of metaphysics.

Central to the philosopher's considerations on *Seinsverlassenheit*, in the *Beiträge*, (proficiency of a practical sort), is the concept of *Machenschaft* which has, for Heidegger, the sense of an artificial construction: the person who has always declined to play a role as *Kulturkritiker* (critic of a culture) does not hesitate to heap all sins on the reign of *Machenschaft* in the modern world. On a first level, *Machenschaft* designates taking possession of the real in order to dominate it and to subject it to goals sought by the subject. Waxing ironic about the conviction that the world may become translucid and that "problems" merely wait to be resolved, Heidegger does not find sarcasm enough to condemn the reign of calculation and utility: foresight (*die Berechnung*), swiftness (*die Schnelligkeit*), and the emergence of the masses (*der Aufbruch des Massenhaften*) are the most glaring symptoms of decadence. But his demonstration hinges primarily on the attempt to project this phenomenology of decadence, which coincides essentially with romantic criticisms where modernity is concerned, onto the grandiose screen of *Seinsgeschichte*. He traces the origins of the technico-instrumental conception of the world to the Platonic conception of truth: at the moment when Being, in its original plenitude and truth, was submitted to the searching examination of the philosopher, who had begun to find therein "ideas" and "essences" (*eide*); and when *ousía* was interpreted as *substance* and *physis* was understood as *techné*, the premises of the technico-instrumental conception of the world were first posited. Beginning with this process, understood mainly as precision or exactitude, he does not hesitate to bring into question the nature of the truth of modern science taken as a whole. If the latter is stricken with fundamental indigence with respect to the truth of Being, it is because its inspiring principle must be precisely that technico-instrumental manipulation of *das Seiende* (the Be-ing). One has the impression that, by a sort of shortcut, Heidegger projects the neo-Kantian or neopositivist conception of science onto the very origins of the principle of reason. It is by establishing a short circuit between the extremely negative results of the technico-instrumental manipulation of reality (*Machenschaft*) and the principle of reason, which by its self-legislating nature supposedly renders *Machenschaft* possible, that Heidegger manages to bring *ratio* into question. The categorial apprehension of Being, whose origins are found in the thought of Plato and Aristotle, may thus be held responsible in the final analysis for all the misdeeds of modern civilization, for the primordial function of *ratio* is, according to Heidegger, to ensure the mastery of the existent (*étant*) and to obstruct the route toward the truth of Being. "What usually happens with Plato, which is interpreted especially as primacy of being (*l'étant*) based on *technē*, is so aggravated today and has become so exclusive that the fundamental condition is created for an age of humanity in which "technic"—the *primacy* of artificial construction, of the measures taken, of the process over *what* [really] enters into all that and is affected by it—assumes dominance."[9]

One can only subscribe to the vigorous denunciation of the extent of the manipulation of the real in the modern world, and also to the challenge to its foundations: the neopositivist conception of science and its extreme indifference with respect to Being. Georg Lukács noted in his *Ontology of Social Being*, moreover, that a revolt against the manipulation of the real is still present in the thought of Heidegger during the period of *Being and Time*.[10] There is, nevertheless, no reason to reduce the practice of science and its search for truth to a single merely functional conception of the real that would ensure its instrumentalization and its manipulation. The purely theoretical aspects of scientific process and search for truth beyond any immediate finality (tangible "results") are completely obscured by Heidegger's reasoning. He treats the principle of causality itself as a simple projection of the utilitarian apprehension of the world and deprives it thus of any real ontological import. Here, he adopts all the neopositivist prejudices on the subject without noticing that he's doing so.

Heidegger rightly questions the autonomization of logic and the hegemony of theory of knowledge (of *Wissenschaftstheorie*) on the philosophical scene—the two disciplines that tend to eliminate fundamental ontological problems (this is what he calls the *Fraglosigkeit*, the absence of questioning in the current world, to which he opposes the obligation of *Fragwürdigkeit*, of original questioning); but there, too, his construction—*seinsgeschichtlich*—sees the origins of the logicist debasement of thought in the traditional conception of truth as *certitudo* and *aedequatio*, managing to bring into question categorial thought itself, and thus thinking as such. The mechanization of life in the modern world, with its negative consequences (the proliferation of manipulation, of leveling, of massification, and so on) is attributed to the hegemony of the spirit of calculation (*Berechenbarkeit*), whose origins are sought in Cartesian *mathesis*, and even further in the Aristotelian theory of categories: "With the Presence [*Anwesenheit*], *peras* is posited, *periehon*." This point of departure and its interpretation remain; they do not allow turning back toward something more original, which is possible only through the questioning *of the truth of Being*; on the other hand, for Aristotle, *poū*, *potē* (where, when)—are determinations of being, *oùsía*!

"Whatever the adjunctions that take place in neo-Platonism, in Saint Augustine, in the Middle Ages, beginning with eternity, the object of Christian faith, and with the *summum ens*, the principle remains and is the foundation of the *mathesis* that comes into force as the essential element for the determination of being [*Seiendheit*]. It is thus that rationality comes into force through pure and simple mechanism, and that space and time fortify their position in this interpretation with as much insistence and obviousness as the notion [*Vorstellung*] one has of being [*Seiendheit*]."[11]

It is in the same spirit that the mathematical apprehension of the real is held responsible for the expansion of mechanism and "technicism": the eminently contestable thesis of a manipulative and pragmatic nature of science brings Heidegger to deny autonomy and ontological dignity to mathematical knowledge by reducing it to a mere instrument for manipulating reality. Since the objective conception of time and space is considered as the foundation of mathematical knowledge, the radical challenge of that foundation becomes as necessary for Heidegger as that of thought based on *certitudo*: "But the matter of knowing how one gets to what is *allowed* by mathematicization in space and time remains decisive. The answer lies in understanding what results when the abyss, barely justified, is covered up by the ground-less [*dass der Abgrund, kaum ergründet, schon durch den Un-grund verschüttet wird*]."[12]

The void and monotony of existence controlled by the *Machenschaften* find their natural complement in the cult of sensations and the "experienced" (*der Erlebnisse*): a life dominated by the generalized manipulation of things would need endless stimulants and new sensations—Heidegger will denounce inebriation through the "experienced" (*Erlebnistrunkenboldigkeit*) as the inevitable concomitant of the reign of *Machenschaft*. From the point of view of the *conditio humana*, *Erlebnis* is, in his eyes, merely an excrescence of the individual and monadological conception of the human personality whose origins go back to the Cartesian ego: "The experienced is only the evil descendant of the Cartesian *cogito ergo sum*."[13] But already, beginning with his course on Hölderlin, the philosopher will point an accusing finger at the "liberal" conception of man that had dominated the nineteenth century and that was the home of the *Erlebnisse*. By vigorously challenging the conception of poetry as "the appearance beneath which the soul, the experienced, is expressed [*Ausdruckserscheinung von Seele, Erlebnis*]," Heidegger goes on to indicate that it comes from a more general view of the world, which he identifies under the name of "liberalism": "That manner of thinking is in itself merely the realization of a very precise manner of being, that of the [liberal] man."[14] His hostility toward that style of life sometimes takes a virulent form, like the condemnation of great cities, the milieu par excellence for the proliferation of sensations and "great spectacles." As he wrote to Julius Stenzel in August 1930: "The great city, as characterized, yields nothing but sensations and excitement—the appearance of being in a waking state. The strongest will is itself stifled in sensation and representation—something monstrous for all philosophy."[15]

In the same context, Heidegger inserts a negative reference to the *Bekenntnisfront* (that is, the Front for the [Christian] Confession, an anti-Nazi association), whose very name seems to be an illustration of the manipulative character of the *Erlebnis* that inspired it. In his course for 1937 he writes regarding this matter: "The experienced becomes a mechanistic process; let us simply reflect a moment on what is brought together in that expression, 'Front for [Christian] Confession,' and on the fact that we have come to that expression, not simply what it implies in practice."[16]

The disavowal of liberalism, which was, it should be remembered, a *Leitmotif* of the conservative ideologies of the time and of course one of the pillars of the National Socialist ideology, was associated by Heidegger with the challenging of the reign of world views (*Weltanschauungen*) and of *Weltanschauungsphilosophie*. As concerns the free confrontation of world views, regarded as one of the characteristic aspects of the liberal era, Heidegger sees nothing there but a manifestation of the arbitrary and the loss of authentic philosophical meaning. "For even in the [liberal] conception of the world . . . there is still that mania for caviling, in the sense that it requires that each person be allowed his own opinion. Nevertheless, this carelessness is enslavement to mere chance happenings."[17]

As early as his rectoral speech, Heidegger had expressed his scorn for the university tradition of "academic freedom" by denouncing its sterility and approving its abolition by the Nazi power: "Academic freedom, whose praises have been sung, is banished from the universities, for this freedom was inauthentic, since it was merely negative. It meant primarily lack of concern, carelessness about intentions and inclinations, irresponsible freedom to do or not to do."[18]

Conceptions of the world are only emanations of man's thought as an autonomous subject, and their degraded forms—"ideologies"—are implicated in the same fundamental error: a conception of the world, or an ideology, is a "perspective" through which the subject looks at the world by organizing his vision about a central nucleus. Subjectivism is thus consubstantial for them. Modern theory of ideologies, of which Marxism is the most recent expression, is considered by Heidegger to be one of the latest embodiments of the Platonic doctrine of Ideas, which supposedly inaugurated the eclipse of the originary truth of Being by instituting the "yoke of ideas." By means of a spectacular *seinsgeschichtlich* derivation, a page figuring in the appendixes of the 1932 course on Plato's *Theaetetus* locates (within the Platonic theory of Ideas) the origin of a vast movement of thought, which passes through Christianity, modern rationalism, the Enlightenment, and Hegel's thought and arrives at Marx, with his system of thought and his doctrine of ideologies. In 1932 Heidegger explicitly sets for himself the problem of an *Überwindung des Marxismus* (overcoming Marxism). For the first time, to the best of our knowledge, he cites a passage from Marx taken from the *Poverty of Philosophy* (in the edition of the *Early Writings* published the same year by Siegfried Landshut). Along with his reflections on the *Platonische Ideenlehre* and on its posterity, he remarks: "*Theory of Ideas*, presupposition for Marxism and the theory of ideologies. 'Conception of the world' as ideology, abstraction, superstructure or social relations with production. Surpassing Marxism?!"[19]

It must be remembered that in his letter of January 20, 1948, to Herbert Marcuse, replying to his correspondent's request for a clarification of his position with respect to Nazism, Heidegger specified the reasons for his support of National Socialism as follows: "A propos of 1933: I was expecting from National Socialism a spiritual renewal of all life, a reconciliation of social antagonisms, and a rescue of occidental existence from the perils of Communism."[20] Alongside democracy and liberalism, communism and the thought that inspired it (Marxism) surely figure among Heidegger's obsessions in the 1930s.

It seems obvious to us that he could not have seen in National Socialism "a *spiritual* renewal of all life" [emphasis added] if he had not considered other currents of thought and forms of civilization that were dominating the historical stage as manifestations of the *Un-geistes*, forces hostile to spirit (*Geist*). He should have rejected them as expressions of a reduction of the spirit to impotence *(Entmachtung des Geistes)* on the premises of his own thought and of his own vision of the originary meaning of the word *Geist*.

His severe condemnation of democracy was based on the conviction that democratic egalitarianism necessarily leads to the annihilation of the highest values of the spirit. He thought that the philosophy of values at the basis of the democratic movement was the antipodes of a true comprehension of history and of the creative powers that control it. He completely shared Nietzsche's convictions on this subject, as well as his critique of nihilism—the epoch of the degradation of all values: "Europe wants to cling to democracy and does not want to discover that the latter would be its historical death," he wrote in 1937, in his first course on Nietzsche, "for democracy, as Nietzsche has clearly said, is nothing other than a variety of nihilism: that is, of a devaluation of the highest values, and this to such a point that they are only simple 'values' and no longer formative forces." He then cited Nietzsche's scornful formulas for democracy ("the rise of the populace," "the social game," "equal men"), which would merely be the perpetuation of "ancient values." (It should be mentioned that this passage, along with similar ones, was suppressed by Heidegger in the two-volume edition of his Nietzsche, published in 1961, which can only be considered an unspecified concession to the new social-historical conjuncture.) Heidegger also repudiated Christianity (which according to Nietzsche was at the origin of the democratic credo), as well as socialism and of course Bolshevism, each incriminated in turn as equivalent expressions of the same nihilism: "A profound knowledge is needed and an even deeper seriousness in order to understand what Nietzsche designated as nihilism. For Nietzsche, Christianity was as nihilist as Bolshevism and, thus, as much as simple socialism."[21]

We may note in passing that Heidegger is committing a strange anachronism here by attributing to Nietzsche a critique of Bolshevism. In 1961, this sentence was also suppressed.

In his course on Aristotle in 1931, Heidegger explicitly defended the legitimacy of an "aristocracy of the spirit" and derided the claims of the "university proletariat" of the time; the real proletarians were, in his eyes, "those who have had their subsistence for a long time [die längst Versorgten], who, in respect for the aristocracy, are at ease with their weakness [in der Ohnmacht zur Aristokratie wohlfühlen], "and not those who have no work; the notion of "university proletariat" needed to be revised then, he noted ironically, for, in fact, it could concern only "those who have no particular intuition for the most elevated elements in the realm of the spirit—in other words, for combat itself—or the inward strength that is indispensable to give it supremacy."[22]

To show the decrepitude of old conceptions of the world and to awaken the sinking feeling of distress (der Not) by demolishing everything that could hide it, according to Heidegger, were the primordial conditions for preparing future historical decisions. Harsh expressions such as "the distress of the absence of distress [die Not der Notlosigkeit]"[23] or "what is depressing . . . is the absence of essential depression [das Bedrängende ist . . . das Ausbleiben der wesenhaften Bedrängnis]"[24] fully convey the affectation of his thinking.

When he ridicules the sufficiency "of the normal and honorable man [*des heutigen Normalmenschen und Biedermanns*]," who is afraid to have his self-assurance shaken and who holds on desperately to his ancient idols; or when, in the footsteps of Nietzsche, he sets "radical nihilism" (active and extremist, having lost all confidence in old values) against "unrealized nihilism" (still believing in the virtues of social reform and in political programs capable of curbing decadence), his goal is to inspire dread (*der Schrecken*) and to stimulate distress (*die Not*) in order to prepare the great leap into the future. "First, we must once more invoke that which is capable of casting terror over our existence," he wrote in *Die Grundbegriffe der Metaphysik*, his course for 1929–30.[25] The hunt for illusions, alibis, substitutes was in his eyes the necessary condition for interrupting the current path of Occidental civilization and for instituting a "new beginning": "The other questioning comes from dread faced with the groundlessness of the existent [*Grundlosigkeit des Seienden*]. . . . The most hidden misery, and thus the deepest of this century, and only that is what is required."[26]

The role that the critique of "security" and of reassuring ideologies played in prefascist and fascist thought is familiar. A book such as Ernst Jünger's *Der Arbeiter* puts security (thematized as the "insufficiency of bourgeois security") at the heart of his polemic. Numerous writings of the period glorify distress, despair, and "heroic realism." And, as early as 1929–30, Heidegger himself had already criticized complacency in the absence of danger (*sattes Behagen in einer Gefahrlosigkeit*) and praised strength in confronting danger (*stark zu sein und uns der Gefahr entgegenwerfen*—"to be strong and to set out to encounter danger") as the sign of true thought.

In the *Beiträge,* he took up this theme again and gave it a *seinsgeschichtlich* dimension. "Liberalism" remained one of the principal targets of his attacks, of course. To shake self-assurance (*Selbstsicherheit*) (which he calls "the most profound essence of 'liberalism' [*das innerste Wesen des 'Liberalismus'*]" and the Cartesian conception of the subject, "that *clara et distincta perceptio* in which the *ego* is born for itself and acquires certainty") is a primordial condition for the revolution of the *conditio humana* of which this great, posthumously published work is the sign and the foundation, at least in the eyes of its author. We must note that Heidegger himself established parallels and even direct connections between the radicalism of his philosophical questioning regarding human essence (*Wer sind wir?*) and the goals of the German revolution. The doctrines that he abhors, as we have already seen, are the same as those denounced by National Socialist ideology. In the text cited above from the *Beiträge* (*Philosophie: zur Frage: wer sind wir?*), he insists on the eminently *dangerous* nature of his philosophical questioning, which abolishes all traditional doctrines, and he adds that not only does the fate of the Occident depend on the answer to his question but, despite appearances (he insists on specifying this), there is a deep convergence between his approach and the new German will (*neue deutsche Wille*).

> But the dangerous nature of the question "who are we?" is at the same time, if danger can require [of us] what is most high, the only road toward ourselves and, thus, the original salvation, that is, the [way] to prepare the justification of the Occident on the basis of its own history. The dangerous nature of this question is so essential for us that it loses the appearance of hostility to the new German will.[27]

In the same context, he opposes an exception to Marxism as well as to Christianity, both relegated to the camp of nihilism. But he wants to stress that "Bolshevism," which he identifies with Marxism, has Occidental (*westliche*) and European origins and, consequently, is neither Russian nor Jewish. He takes a stand, thus, against Nazi propaganda, which identified Marxism and Judaism. As a product of mass industrial and technical civilization in western Europe, Marxism, according to Heidegger, would not have any tie to the Russian spirit (*das Russentum*), in whose depths he finds an unexhibited spiritualism (*einen unentfalteten Spiritualismus*); he thus rediscovers the Spenglerian thesis of "pseudo-morphoses," which denied any claim of universality to Occidental rationalism. It does not exclude, however, a possible filiation between Bolshevism, Judaism, and Christianity, for the glorification of the realm of reason (*die Vernunftherrschaft*) in Marxism fits in with the egalitarian morality of Christianity. Now, as Nietzsche showed, Christianity was rooted in Jewish morality, a product of the revolt of slaves.[28] The conclusion is that from the point of view of essential decisions, these doctrines lead to nothing ("And what decisions become necessary starting there?") and that "the new German will" must reject them as enemy thoughts and look elsewhere for its foundations.

It is the fury against Christianity that is striking in the Heideggerian discourse of this period. In the *Beiträge* he affirms—clearly inspired by the Civil War in Spain—that, like assassinations, the destruction of churches and monasteries does not represent the essence of events. He addresses a sort of warning to those who might be tempted to back the Christian camp and to forget that Christianity is in itself a form of nihilism. He states that even if one can concede to Christianity that its fight against vulgar nihilism (*den groben Nihilimus*)—that is, against Bolshevism—is justified from the standpoint of the "truth of Being," those two opposed camps are akin to each. He thus places Christians and their adversaries back to back, for victory by one or the other would simply consolidate nihilism: "If the two extreme and adverse forms of nihilism struggle against each other, and, in fact, do so necessarily, that combat leads, in any case, in the most obvious way toward the *victory* of nihilism: that is, to its renewed reinforcement."[29]

This example clearly shows that the judgments of the philosopher about contemporary history stem rigorously from his fundamental thought on "the truth of Being." Even the struggle of the Spanish Catholic Right against its mortal enemies, the Communists, cannot find grace in his eyes, for its doctrinal foundation is still located in the sphere of the forgetfulness of Being (*Seinsvergessenheit*). According to Heidegger, theological or onto-theological thought, and Christianity in particular, is essentially anchored in Platonism and, especially, in a species of causal thought. For the relation between the *summum ens* and the *ens creatum* is described as a cause-and-effect relationship. But access to the truth of Being requires, in fact, the abandonment of the causal sphere and the principle of sufficient reason (*der Satz vom Grund*): "Necessity in its greatest form always does without the crutches of 'why' and 'because' and without the support of 'to what end' and of 'for that.' "[30] It requires a transition from a categorial or thematic apprehension of Being (in which the Christian faith also participates) to a far more original apprehension based on a new beginning (*ein anderer Anfang*). This is the transition from the *Leitfrage* to the *Grundfrage,* from the "directorial question" to the "fundamental question" of philosophy. Only the latter is capable of preparing the coming of future man (*des zukünftigen Menschen*).

Heidegger's posthumously published work contains, as we have noted, critical remarks directed at the official ideology of the Third Reich, at certain of its slogans, and especially at biologism and race theory. The philosopher sometimes takes care to answer those who detected in care (*Sorge*) or in *Seinsverlassenheit* the expression of a pessimism or a defeatism incompatible with official doctrine. By not holding back in his sarcasm concerning noisy "heroism" (*der lärmende "Heroïsmus"*), he tries to emphasize that his thought about fear (*das Erschrecken*) and the reserved attitude (*die Verhaltenheit*) are fundamental moods (*Grundstimmungen*) opening the way to a "new beginning"—the expression of a more original and more authentic "will" than that glorified by contemporary propaganda. He denounces the elucubrations of "Aryan" science and pokes fun at those who contrast the "North German" character of the "experimental research" with the strange (*fremdartig*) nature of rational thought: "We must decide then," he exclaims ironically, "to consider Newton and Leibniz among the Jews."[31] But it is especially the disavowal imposed on the idea of *totale Weltanschauung* that must hold our attention: the hegemonic claims of official thought are profoundly unacceptable to Heidegger, for they imply the refusal to problematize the foundations and the so-called certainties—specifically, the theory of races and the omnipotence of the "political"—of Nazism. May we conclude from this, together with the weekly *Rheinischer Merkur* (which added an extra lead to an article by Alexander Schwan), that *"The Contributions to Philosophy [Beiträge]* imposes a radical exception to National Socialism"? or with the author of the article himself, who says in a more nuanced manner that the *Beiträge* is "an unequivocal renunciation of the embarrassing implications of 1933, which are revealed as the result of infelicitous confusion between ontological thought and political activism"?[32]

It is difficult for us to share such peremptory judgments, for things seem to us a little more complicated. In a passage already cited, Heidegger proposed to eliminate the misunderstanding that remained between his thought and the "new German will"; refusing the idea of disparity and, all the more so, that of opposition, he demonstrated, to the contrary, the existence of a deep convergence. It must be added that most of the critiques he formulated against *völkisch* thought, the reliance on the idea of race, or the "conception of the total world" criticized these forms of thought for their lack of radicalism in respect to the basic requirements of true revolutionary thought. In his opinion, they remained attached to the molds of the old "liberal" thought and could not succeed in detaching themselves from the categories of subjectivism or from *Weltanschauungsphilosophie*.

Could we more reasonably say, then, that the *Beiträge* represents a withdrawal in respect to immediate history, a renunciation of political ambition, and even an "uncontestable resignation" in respect to the historical efficacy of philosophy?

The philosopher's fits of ill temper in regard to his "contemporaries" (*die Heutigen*), explicitly aimed at the current ideological practices of the Nazi regime, led certain commentators to see in Heidegger's *opus postumum* the expression of a profound disappointment and even a farewell to National Socialism. "As for the contemporaries, whom one can barely mention in order to turn away from them," he in fact wrote with acrimony, "they remain excluded from knowledge about the paths of thought; they take refuge in 'new' contents and, having recourse to concepts of 'the political' and 'race', they procure themselves superficial ornaments, hitherto unknown, [dredged up in] the apparatus of school philosophy."[33]

On the contrary, it seems to me that far from expressing alienation from or renunciation of historical action, the *Beiträge* glorified it more than ever—at least in the first part, "The Decision" (*Die Entscheidung*), by explicitly investing philosophy with the mission of providing its foundation. Heidegger even feared that decadence might carry the day over the power of decision and dreads "the destruction of the possibilities for decision by the irresistible course of the uprooting [*Entwurflung*] that threatens us."³⁴

The paragraphs devoted to "decision" outline for the first time the Heideggerian charter for the future and the profile of those who will embody it. These chosen persons carry the mark of a particular vocation; they bear no resemblance to the human type that has long dominated the historical scene. Heidegger calls them "those beings predestined by their excellence" (*jene ausgezeichnete Gezeichneten*) or "the future men" (*die Zukünftigen*) and distinguishes three hierarchical categories: those rare individuals (*jene wenigen Einzelnen*), those more numerous members of the alliance (*jene zahlreicheren Bündischen*), and those numerous adepts of the unified community (*jene vielen Zueinanderverwiesenen*). Thus, in the avant-garde, there is a very restricted elite, composed of rare and solitary souls who have access to the "nobility of Being" (*der Adel des Seyns*). "The understanding that unites those who are very few, those who are more numerous, and those who are in large number is hidden; it is not artificial; it is sudden and organic." The moral or existential-anthropological categories are declared inoperative in order to apprehend the very particular quality of that fighting elite. Its primordial mission is to found the *community of the people* by sharing with them the truth of Being.

A *sui generis* aristocratism permeates this Heideggerian vision of the great turning (*der Kehre*). Historical decisions must be taken in solitude and in "invisibility," far from the noisy scene of "public opinion," beyond the grip of the crowd—protected, according to the expression, from the "plebeian touch" (*pöbelhaften Betasten*) and directed against "that which is common and low" (*das Gemeine und Niedrige*), against mass character and the comfortable (*das Massenhafte und Bequeme*).³⁵

The fundamental categories of his philosophy, as they were formulated in the period of *Being and Time* and "What Is Metaphysics?"—for example, resoluteness (*die Entschlossenheit*), being for death (*das Sein zum Tode*), nothing in its nothingness (*das nichtende Nichts*), the singularity of being (*die Einzigkeit des Seins*)—are taken up again and converted into a thought for action and a historical dynamism. If the philosopher does not hide his scorn for the common interpretation of National Socialism, for its slogans and its clichés, it is because he intends to found the revolution on an incomparably loftier vision. Behind the stylized design of this vision, however, we find his structural affinity for the revolution taking place. The disdain for the lukewarm and the indifferent (*die Gleichgültigen*), the stress on the state of extreme urgency (*Not*), the suspension of reflection in favor of determination (*keine Reflexion, sondern das Gegenteil davon*),³⁶ the celebration of sacrifice (*die wenigen*

Einzelnen und die Seltenen sind die "verschwiegenen Opfer"), the praise
of the unconditional, the necessity of self-deprivation in order to receive
the impulse (*den Stoss*) of Being and the will to destroy the old categories
of the liberal individual (*Persönlichkeit, Subjekt, Individualität, Genie,*
and so on)—these terms cannot fail to evoke, in a sublimated form, the
spirit of the movement of 1933.

When Heidegger objects, in a 1942 course on Hölderlin, to the forced
"politicization" of the history of ancient Greece by Nazi researchers, is
it, once again, really a disavowal of National Socialism? Here is the
passage in question: "This excess of zeal in erudite individuals seems to
ignore completely that with such 'results' it renders absolutely no service
to National Socialism and to its historical uniqueness; that service is
strictly unnecessary to the latter [National Socialism], moreover."[37] Is
this critique not directed rather against the vulgarization of National
Socialism, with the intention of conserving authenticity in opposition to
a compromising practice?

Karl Löwith was even able to say (in a text of 1940, repeated in 1960
in his study on Carl Schmitt) that "Heidegger's decision to join Hitler
goes far beyond agreement with the ideology and the party's program.
He was and remains a 'National Socialist' on the fringe and in an isolation
that is in any case not at all ineffective." Heidegger could, Löwith
continues, "take the risk of some bitter remarks in his courses, which
was nonetheless not contrary to his substantial adherence to National
Socialism as a movement of protest and negation animated by belief. For
the spirit of National Socialism had less to do with the national and the
social than, rather, with that resolution and that dynamism which rejected
any discussion or understanding because they trusted uniquely and solely
themselves, the specific (German) power to be."[38]

Even as it contributes to qualifying this judgment, the *Beiträge* does
not seem to invalidate it. In this work, the philosopher unveils with a
clarity not found in his earlier writings the scope of his commitment to
history. The most "speculative" concepts of his thought, beginning with
the differences between Being (*Sein*) and the Entity (*Seiendes*), are
directly implicated in his resolve to shake the very foundations of the
Occident. The integral secularization of life and thought by means of a
pure philosophy of immanence, which does not recognize the autonomy
of Being and tends to annul the latter in the autosufficiency of the
existent, continues to be his hobbyhorse. And he himself mentions both
world war and world revolution as great challenges hurled against Occidental thought, challenges for which he tries to furnish the epochal
answer. By deploring the fact that for two thousand years Occidental man
has been unable to create any God ("der abendländische Mensch seit
zwei Jahrtausenden keinen Gott mehr zu schaffen vermochte") and by

expressing at the same time his scorn for religions and existing churches, which only drag the Occident down in its "fall," he intends to make of the "rapprochement and the distanciation of the gods from the existent [*die Näherung und Entfernung der Götter am Seienden*]" and of the opening toward "the passing of the last God [*der Vorbeigang des letzten Gottes*]" the crucial experience for the future history of the Occident. The explicit finality of this process is to divest man of the insane illusion of his autonomy and to inculcate in him the sense of being in dependence on Being, by making—of a transcendence that is at once unveiled and hidden—the power that regulates the course of history.

When Heidegger disavows, some years after having concluded the *Contributions*, the theologians favorable to the regime (the *Deutsche Christen* sphere of influence) as well as the opposition (*die Bekenntnisfront*) and Catholic theologians in general for their inability to accede to the sacred nature of the fatherland (*das Heilige des Vaterlandes*), and when he associates with them the biologists and specialists of prehistory who are supposed to divulge the theory of races, he brings together all these somewhat heteroclite groups under the sign of a common sin, "the intellectualism . . . that not even the quite denigrated nineteenth century succeeded in introducing—[the century] that they carry on in a blind manner." His reproach aimed at the debasement (*Herabsetzung*) of what he called "the hidden dignity of the most specific being of the fatherland" in order to arrive at the conclusion that "at any rate" none of those persons "think German."[39]

This convergence between *Seinsphilosophie* and the exaltation of Germanness (*des Deutschtums*), especially present in the courses given during the war, should keep our attention for a moment more. Heidegger makes incursions into contemporary history rather often in his courses on Hölderlin (1941–42), Parmenides (1942–43), and Heraclitus (1943–44). His judgments on current events are formulated on the basis of his fundamental concepts: the philosophical reflection of the *Beiträge* thus finds some surprising applications *in politics*. For example, he occasionally stigmatizes thought based on "values," his old hobbyhorse, as belonging to the "sphere of freemasonry": "Yet, when we speak of the true, the good, and the beautiful, we are, whether we know it or not, in the sphere of the spirit of the Enlightenment and of freemasonry."[40] By holding up the thought of the Enlightenment as well as of freemasonry to public obloquy, Heidegger fell in with the spirit of the time.

The entry of the United States into the war gave him the occasion to show his resentment with respect to "Americanism." The American initiative would be "the last American act of that America that has no history and is destroying itself." At an earlier time he had already alerted his compatriots to the menace imposed on them by the modern spirit, of which Americanism was the most corrupt form: "The sacrifice of German being to Americanism already goes so far sometimes, unhappily, that certain Germans are ashamed that their people was once called 'the people of poets and thinkers.' "[41]

Now, he projects Germany's combat, which bathes in the aura of the beginning (*das Anfängliche*), onto the great stage of the history of Being. The Americans represent in his eyes "those who are deprived of beginning" (*das Anfanglose*), for their civilization is only a mixture of "bourgeois democratic spirit" and "Christianity," while the German people can "await in the calm inspired by the peace of beginning its hour of plenitude."[42]

There is no doubt that Heidegger invests his thought with a historical vocation: to express Germany's destiny in order to ensure as a consequence the salvation of the Occident (*die Rettung des Abendlandes*). The thinking on Being, as it was inaugurated by *Being and Time,* is, according to his own words, only "the allusion to the event that allows Being itself to endow Western humanity with experience closer to origins."[43]

The great danger was to see the original essence of the German people led astray, turning away from that vocation, and falling back into the traps laid by other forms of civilization, which are only the product of ancient metaphysical thought. During the most difficult moments of the war, and on the very eve of catastrophe, the philosopher continues to glorify Germany's invincibility, to adorn it generously with the fundamental concepts of his reflection, and to point out, on that basis, the road to follow: "We must realize," he said in 1943, "that this historical people, is after all a 'victory' is at stake, has already vanquished and is invincible."[44] Almost to the end of the war, he follows the inexorable course of events imperturbably, delivering the same message of salvation and uttering the same vaticinations: "The planet is in flames," he says at one point in his 1943–44 course on Heraclitus. "The being of man has come apart. It is only from the Germans that the historical awakening can come, provided that they find the German specificity and conserve it."[45]

The conception of the "political" is endlessly connected by Heidegger to his fundamental thesis on "the essence of truth." If, in turn, he disavows the *imperium romanum* (and thus the "imperial" conception of politics), the *res publica,* the *Civitas Dei* of Augustine and the political organization of the Roman Curia, the State and the organization of modern society with their different components—liberalism, democracy, socialism—it is because all those forms of political organization represent in his eyes a conception of truth, the one established for the first time in antiquity with the "Romanization" of the Greek spirit: truth as "appropriateness" (*Richtigkeit*) and as *certitudo*. As did others at the same time, he projected onto the stage of history the dream of the resurrection of a mythical *polis* founded on the presence of the Gods—*der Vorbeigang des letzten Gottes* is the culminating idea of the *Beiträge*—and whose "German essence" would be the sole legitimate heir. Even German classicism (that of Goethe and Schiller) and the great German idealism (Hegel in the forefront) failed to escape banishment. "Goethe is a disaster [*Goethe ist ein Verhängnis!*]," he said in a course of that period,[46] speaking also of the "form deprived of form in the so-called pagan classicism of Goethe and Schiller"[47] and the metaphysics of Hegel appeared to him to achieve, in the nineteenth century, along with Nietzsche, "Roman truth in its essence,"[48] which in his eyes signified the degeneration of truth.

With only a slight exaggeration, it could be said that the defeat of Germany in World War II was also a defeat for Heidegger's thought: victory returned to the forms of life and civilization against which he had, in conformance with the history of Being (*seinsgeschichtlich*), opposed his demurrer—to democracy and liberalism, to Americanism and socialism, to Christianity and the messages of the churches. If he never renounced his political views, it is because they were too connected to the foundations of his thought: in his first course given after the war, "What Is Called Thinking?" the earlier attacks against democracy and against the liberal spirit can be found in the quotations from Nietzsche, along with barely concealed praise for the authoritarian state and charismatic figures (associated with the *Übermensch,* the Superman, of Nietzsche).

Karl Jaspers wrote to Hannah Arendt on September 1, 1949: "[Heidegger] is totally engulfed in speculation on being; he writes [this word] *'Seyn'* [instead of *'Sein'*]. Two decades and a half ago he insisted on 'existence,' and he distorted the essence of the problem. Now, he insists in an even more essential manner, and that does not leave me indifferent either. Let us hope that he will not distort the questions once more. But I suspect he will. Can one, with an impure soul . . . can one in insincerity see what is most pure? Or will he live yet another revolution? I am more than skeptical."[49]

Karl Jaspers, like Karl Löwith, had the precise intuition of a profound convergence between Heidegger's *Seynsspekulation* and his views on the society of his time, including his political views. Today, with much richer documentation, it is no longer possible to dissociate these two aspects by pretending not to notice that the deepest thrust of Heidegger's thought implies a precise attitude toward contemporary history.

NOTES

1. Martin Heidegger, *Beiträge zur Philosophie (vom Ereignis),* in *Gesamtausgabe,* vol. 65 (Frankfurt: Klostermann, 1989).

2. Martin Heidegger, *Schelling: Vom Wesen der menschlichen Freiheit*, in *Gesamtausgabe*, vol. 42 (Frankfurt: Klostermann, 1988), p. 2.

3. Heidegger, *Schelling*, p. 3.

4. Ibid.

5. Martin Heidegger, *Grundfragen der Philosophie, Ausgewählte "Probleme" der "Logik,"* in *Gesamtausgabe*, vol. 45 (Frankfurt: Klostermann, 1984), pp. 37, 41.

6. Ibid., p. 3.

7. Jean-Paul Sartre, *Questions de méthode* (Paris: Gallimard "Idées," 1960), p. 55.

8. Heidegger, *Schelling*, pp. 40–41.

9. Heidegger, *Beiträge*, p. 336.

10. Georg Lukács, *Zur Ontologie des gesellschaftlichen Seins* (Darmstadt: Luchterhand, 1984), 1:381ff., 395; cf. p. 64.

11. Heidegger, *Beiträge*, p. 376.

12. Ibid., p. 387.

13. Heidegger, *Grundfragen*, p. 149.

14. Martin Heidegger, *Hölderlins Hymnen "Germanien" und "Der Rhein,"* in *Gesamtausgabe*, vol. 39 (Frankfurt: Klostermann, 1980), p. 28.

15. Letter cited by Hugo Ott in his *Martin Heidegger: Unterwegs zu seiner Biographie* (Frankfurt: Campus Verlag, 1988), p. 194.

16. Heidegger, *Grundfragen*, p. 42.

17. Heidegger, *Beiträge*, p. 38.

18. Martin Heidegger, *Die Selbstbehauptung der deutschen Universität* (Breslau: Verlag Wilh. Gottl. Korn, 1933), p. 15.

19. Martin Heidegger, *Vom Wesen der Wahrheit: Zu Platons Höhlengleichnis und Theätet*, in *Gesamtausgabe*, vol. 34 (Frankfurt: Klostermann, 1988), p. 325.

20. The letters of Marcuse to Heidegger and Heidegger's reply are in the Herbert Marcuse collection at the University of Frankfurt.

21. Martin Heidegger, *Nietzsche: Der Wille zur Macht als Kunst*, in *Gesamtausgabe*, vol. 43 (Frankfurt, 1985), pp. 193, 30–31.

22. Martin Heidegger, *Aristoteles: Metaphysik, IX*, in *Gesamtausgabe*, vol. 33 (Frankfurt: Klostermann, 1981), pp. 82–83.

23. Heidegger, "Woher die Notlosigkeit als die höchste Not?" in *Beiträge*, p. 125.

24. Martin Heidegger, *Die Grundbegriffe des Metaphysik: Welt-Endlichkeit-Einsamkeit*, in *Gesamtausgabe*, vol. 29/30 (Frankfurt: Klostermann, 1983), p. 244.

25. Ibid., p. 255.

26. Heidegger, *Grundfragen*, p. 198.

27. Heidegger, *Beiträge*, pp. 53, 54.

28. See Nicolas Tertulian, "Histoire de l'être et révolution doctique," *Les Temps Modernes*, January 1990, pp. 124–25.

29. Ibid., p. 140.

30. Heidegger, p. 144.

31. Ibid., p. 163.

32. Alexander Schwan, "Verliebt in Untergang und Abgrund," *Rheinischer Merkur/Christ und Welt*, no. 17 (April 28, 1989): 15.

33. Heidegger, *Beiträge*, pp. 18–19.

34. Ibid., p. 97.

35. Ibid., p. 96–97, 103.

36. Ibid., p. 102.

37. Martin Heidegger, *Hölderlins Hymne "Der Ister,"* in *Gesamtausgabe*, vol. 53 (Frankfurt: Klostermann, 1984), p. 98.

38. Karl Löwith, *Sämtliche Schriften* (Stuttgart: J. B. Metzler, 1984), p. 8:67.

39. Martin Heidegger, *Hölderlins Hymne "Andenken,"* in *Gesamtausgabe*, vol. 52 (Frankfurt: Klostermann, 1982), p. 33.

40. Heidegger, *Hölderlins Hymne "Der Ister,"* pp. 108–9.

41. Heidegger, *Hölderlins Hymne "Andenken,"* p. 134.

42. Heidegger, *Hölderlins Hymne "Der Ister,"* p. 68.

43. Martin Heidegger, *Parmenides,* in *Gesamtausgabe,* vol. 54 (Frankfurt: Klostermann, 1982), pp. 113–14.

44. Ibid., p. 114.

45. Martin Heidegger, *Heraklit* in *Gesamtausgabe*, vol. 55 (Frankfurt: Klostermann, 1987), p. 123.

46. Heidegger, *Parmenides,* p. 108.

47. Heidegger, *Hölderlins Hymne "Der Ister,"* p. 94.

48. Heidegger, *Parmenides,* p. 86.

49. Hannah Arendt and Karl Jaspers, *Briefwechsel, 1926–1969* (Munich: Piper, 1985), pp. 176–77.

IV

9

Philosophy, Politics—and the "New" Questions for Hegel, for Heidegger, and for Phantasy

HANS-CHRISTIAN LUCAS

The tranquil waterway . . . seemed to lead into
the heart of an immense darkness.
—JOSEPH CONRAD

This study examines the relationship between Heidegger and Hegel under three headings. (1) Hegel's relationship to the authority of the state, especially in Prussia, is portrayed by some critics primarily from the point of view of suspicion of an *accommodation*. Thus, the same suspicion would fall on Hegel's philosophy as well and, from there, on all thinking obligated to his philosophy. (2) For Heidegger there is an unambiguous identification with National Socialism, which is clearly documented, at least for a certain period of time. Nevertheless, there is still disagreement on the extent to which Heidegger's personal involvement in the movement during 1933–34 can also be claimed to include his thinking (if not his philosophy)—or whether his thinking might have its foundations in this involvement. In particular, Heidegger has attracted criticism because he trivialized and misrepresented this association in his autobiographical reflections.[1] (This is especially evident in Hugo Ott's research.)[2] But Heidegger also cloaked himself in silence regarding the multimillionfold murder of Jews and the political opponents of National Socialism.[3] (3) This critical, admittedly incomplete retrospective on Hegel and Heidegger is intended to promote our present-day understanding of philosophy; it thus takes the "classical" philosophical route of self-awareness of our own history, in which, of course, every form of dogmatism is to be excluded from the very outset. We can infer its critical power from its inquiry into its nongenesis from *reality*, on the one hand, and, on the other, from its potential for affording a transcendent basis of philosophy for the "new." Given the debatable thesis of the end of philosophy, or the end of metaphysics, which can be traced back to Marx, Nietzsche, Heidegger, and others, we have to ask whether that significant and perhaps even decisive potential of philosophy for critique should also be dismissed.

Perhaps the prerequisite of this necessary consequence also needs to be reexamined along the lines of the maxim "Those given up for dead live longer." Or should we begin instead by recognizing that philosophy in our century finds itself in a continuing state of crisis, the resolution of which is still entirely uncertain. This crisis is very much like the crisis of modern times, perhaps like the *conditio humana* itself, and probably has been going on since the French Revolution, whose two-hundredth anniversary has recently been celebrated, although under very different portents. If we could answer our question, we should have to assume that certain "farewells" have been somewhat prematurely concluded. To the farewells to philosophy and modernity, let us add, then, the farewell to Substance, to Subject, to Enlightenment, to Humanism, to metaphor, and so on.[4]

Hegel: Reality and History

In virtually every recent assessment of the relationship between philosophy and politics in Hegel and Heidegger, Hegel's philosophy is reconstructed and condemned as the intellectual source of National Socialism; yet at the same time and even in some of the same places, attempts are made to play down Heidegger's demonstrable involvement in National Socialism or at least to construe as insignificant its effect on his philosophy. Condemnation of Hegel generally rests on his high estimation of the state and on his assessment of reality as rational. But in assessing both these points, we should take notice of the way Hegel's thesis fits his perspective on world history and, even more fundamentally, his dynamically conceived ontology. In point of fact, these two theses refer only to the Prussian state of Hegel's own time—hence, to its particular reactionary and authoritarian form. According to Hegel, however, *that which is* must always be a stage in the process of progress in the awareness of freedom, and must therefore be understood in the sense of the actual process of the development of political freedom.

We may assume that during his lifetime Hegel was concerned with the political implications of his philosophy. His first, anonymously published work and his very last were both concerned with political themes:

that is, the "Confidential Letters Concerning the Earlier National Law Defining the Relationship between the Watland and the City of Bern" (so-called *Cart* letters) in 1798, and his 1831 text, *On the English Reform Bill*. The points of reference in the political situation at that time may be succinctly said to include the French Revolution, the post-Napoleonic developments in Germany (especially constitutionalism in southern Germany), and the reactionary political attitude of Prussia. The material on which he based his arguments is drawn from the Europe-wide constitutional debate.[5] The political categories between which he moved are revolution and reform as forms of political development. A number of his critics (for example, Rudolf Haym) accuse him of making himself useful to (Prussian) reactionary politics in order to gain personal advantages for himself.[6] But much of the criticism directed against Hegel has its basis in the relationship, in his thinking, between philosophy and politics, even though it should have been directed against his entire philosophical system. It focuses chiefly on several points made in the notorious Introduction to his *Philosophy of Right* (*Grundlinien der Philosophie des Rechts*).[7]

1. Defining the identity of reality and reason, an issue frequently criticized and almost always misunderstood: "*What is rational is actual; and what is actual, rational*" (GH, p. 10; original emphasis).
2. Linking (or limiting) philosophy to its own time: "To comprehend *what is*, this is the task of the philosopher, because what is, is reason. Whatever happens, every individual is a *child of his own time*; so too *philosophy is its own time apprehended in thoughts*" (GH, p. 11).
3. Claiming the *belatedness* of philosophy as well as the negation of the "rejuvenating" (that is, renewing) power of philosophy: "When philosophy paints its gray in gray, then has a shape of life grown old. By philosophy's gray in gray it cannot be rejuvenated, but can only be understood; the owl of Minerva spreads her wings only with the falling of dusk" (GH, p. 13).

These *dicta* attracted critics, especially because they appeared shortly after the infamous "Karlsbad Decrees." Those critics hoped to find in Hegel someone who, in abject servility, tried to fit his philosophy of justice, his theory of the state, even the whole of his philosophical system to the reactionary politics of the Prussian state.

In a letter of August 8, 1821, a former student of Hegel's—in fact, a friend—Nikolaus von Thaden, assembled a number of critical objections that have since reappeared with great regularity.[8] Von Thaden had already begun, then, to trace the arguments of the *Philosophy of Right* back to the review of the *Verhandlungen der württembergischen Landstände*:

that is, to a constitutional dispute that more recent research has come to include in the discussion of the *Philosophy of Right* under the title "Southwest German Constitutionalism."⁹ Von Thaden summarizes the anticipated effects of the *Philosophy of Right*: "We are no longer discussing philosophy without any sort of attribute, since this has been vigorously rejected—one moment as the work of a royalist philosopher, the next, as that of a philosophical royalist; for which reason a part of this brave little book has become a philosophical-historical pamphlet." He takes up this issue of "that, which is": "They insist especially and rightly on insight into the matter, but insight into a bad matter—for example, into the politics of the Turkish state—still does not make the matter good." He restates the "identity sentence" in a form in which it has since frequently been quoted: "The grandest and most important sentence of all, 'The *ens* is the good and the rational,' is *philosophically* true, but *politically this sentence is false*" (italics added). We will need to discuss this argument further, but with the condition that reality be placed together with truth. Von Thaden notes the possible connection between Hegel's theoretical position and the politics of the Prussian state: "You have represented the state as the reality of justice, as the realization of freedom; but for what state are your doctrines an institution?"¹⁰ The question is meant purely rhetorically: von Thaden does not regard Hegel's theory as having been realized in Prussia at all.

A reviewer signing himself only "Z. C." begins his account by assuming that philosophy is "its time captured in thought"; he sees a danger there: such a philosophy would be nothing more than "a mere abstraction of the state of the world and the situation in it at that particular time, and thus it would necessarily be changeable and changing." Philosophy is measured here against an eternal claim to the truth thought to be derivable from it; the thesis regarding Hegel's accommodation views Hegelianism as a sort of reversible jacket. "Such a philosophy can obviously accommodate itself to anything that is the order of the day. If it is the liberals who rule the world, then it is liberalism that philosophy will proclaim; if despotism has the upper hand, then philosophy will preach this." Despite these objections, this critic does concede the "vanity and arrogance that so dominate the present and want to know something better than that which is in it."¹¹

Reviewing this criticism, Rudolf Haym promises once and for all to create a historical Hegel: "We want to inter him in a bigger, less temporary tomb; we hope to preserve him in the great edifice of eternal history, to give him a place, in truth, in a place of honor in the history of the development of the German spirit." But, the twofold statement (that is, regarding philosophical and political truth) becomes, for Haym, the "classic word of the spirit of restoration"; it expresses "the absolute formula of political conservatism, quietism, and optimism." Correspondingly, Haym sees a "double cult of what is actual and what is comprehensible" pervading the entire system.[12]

In a footnote to paragraph 6 of the *Encyclopedia of Philosophy* (*Enzyklopädie der philosophischen Wissenschaften*) in 1827,[13] Hegel offered a defense of his twofold statement which he retained in the 1830 version. His definition referred to the conceptual differences he had noted in his *Science of Logic* (*Wissenschaft der Logik*), where he made a distinction between actuality and existence and phenomenon, and so on. He also designated "the actual" and "actuality" as "emphatic names" essentially different from contingency and possibility.[14] The progressive character of the identity of reality and reason makes a mere "shall," which opposes reality, appear "impotent."

Only after the publication of the *Philosophy of Right* did Hegel develop his specific philosophy of history. In his lectures on the subject the progressive character of reality is specified as *progress in the awareness of freedom*.[15] The certainty about the identity sentence now appears as the "belief that world history is a product of eternal reason, and reason has determined its great revolutions" (GH, p. 46). In contradiction to the dictum of the "owl of Minerva," in which it is also clearly stated that philosophy cannot rejuvenate reality, the image of rejuvenation no longer suffices for Hegel. He reintroduces the "image of the Phoenix," which he views as appropriate only for "natural life," or for the body: it remains an "image of the orient." "What is occidental is that the spirit does not merely emerge rejuvenated but elevated, transfigured" (GH, p. 35). The result is a "new formation." Hegel had earlier, in the famous prologue to his *Phenomenology of the Spirit* (*Phänomonologie des Geistes*), represented his time as one of crisis and revolution: "Moreover, it is not difficult to see that our time is the time of birth and transition to a *new* period" (emphasis added).[16] Then follows the oft-cited sentence about the *qualitative leap* paralleling the process leading to the birth of a child. There, the newborn is the "new," announced in "portents" appearing as "premonitions of something unknown . . . that harbors something different in its direction." This "thing that is different," the *new*, announces itself like a severe storm, like an event to be feared. The present (*das Bestehende*), which, according to his critics, Hegel wishes to support at all costs, he views as inevitably collapsing, decaying: "This gradual disintegration, which does not alter the physiognomy of the whole, is interrupted by a dawning; this, a flash of lightning, abruptly reveals the form of the new world [Dies allmählige Zerbröckeln, dass die Physiognomie des Ganzen nicht veränderte, wird durch den Aufgang unterbrochen, der ein Blitz in einem Male das Gebilde der neuen Welt hinstellt]" (GW 9:15).

The appearance of the *new* is endowed with an irresistible force; the fear, the lecherousness, the stench of blood of the French Revolution gather in our memory here, although Hegel had long since come to think of Napoleon as the real "enactor" of that event. The metaphor of *lightning*, which Hegel uses later in another place in his completed system, signifies an insuperable vestige of irrationality that he was unable to overcome here or in the transition from natural philosophy to the philosophy of the spirit.[17] This does not prevent him, however, from greeting the lightning. His enthusiasm for revolution marks two significant poles of thought that must somehow be reconciled. For Hegel, unlike virtually any other thinker, the eruption of the new is linked to the concept of permanence. In his "Lectures on World History," of all places, there are statements that must be read in the sense of *nunc stans*: "Whatever is true, is eternal in and of itself—not yesterday or tomorrow, but entirely in the present, 'now' in the sense of an absolute present" (GH, p. 150). Platonism? Perhaps we should also listen to the following: "But what the spirit is now, it has always been" (GH, p. 151). Between the *one* that always remains the same and the *new* (or other) that is generated by disruptive change, Hegel acknowledges, in various places in his system, millennia of effort. In the "Lectures on the Philosophy of World History," for example, he mentions "6,000 years of effort . . . of world history" (GH, p. 150).[18]

But it is not clear how the enduring identity of the spirit is supposed to fit the euphoric description of the emergence of the new. Whether it is to come from the world spirit, or from various peoples (*Völker*), or from world-historical peoples, or from world-historical individuals, the "effort" still seems more apparent than real: the *new* seems to be merely a pretense. The required explanation is supposed to be afforded by the "dialectical" conception of negation that Hegel calls *sublation* (*Aufhebung*). If the effort is to be negated, preserved, and elevated to a higher position, then there is in "reality" nothing new, nothing old. Perhaps there is a renewed old, but not the *new* shrouded in the murkiness of the approaching storm—as Hegel describes it in the Prologue to the *Phenomenology*.

It is a well known that the unity of Hegel's system proved fragmentary; as a consequence, philosophy after Hegel took a number of conflicting directions. In the revolution of 1848, for instance, disciples of Hegel apparently fired at other disciples. It is reported that V. Griesheim, one of Hegel's eager students, had rioters in Berlin shot down with case-shot. Marx and virtually all Marxists manifest a considerable friction between themselves and Hegel, but this hardly constitutes a part of his legacy. Nazi legal minds have often cited Hegel as a favorite authority (Binder, Dulckeit, Larenz, to mention a few), and other theorists have tried to reconstruct a path from Hegelian idealism to National Socialism (Popper, Topitsch, Kiesewetter, for instance). In France, Hegel was finally accorded the stature of a "master thinker" after he became well known—and thus he was eliminated. We do not necessarily need to take André Glucksmann as paradigmatic of a collective national thinking, but his renunciation of the so-called *master thinker* as a guide regarding the *shoah* or Holocaust does have its chilling effect. I refer to a parenthetic remark in his book: "Paradoxically, we had to wait for Heidegger to find a German philosophy that was not anti-Semitic; on the path to Greece it was Rome, not Judea, that blocked our way: the *imperium romanum*, its revised versions just as devastating as its times of peace."[19]

Let me juxtapose here a remark of Toni Cassirer's, taken from an admittedly unreliable statement in which she personally recalls the famous meeting between Heidegger and Ernst Cassirer in Davos (in 1929, though she recalls it as having occurred in 1931): "His rejection of all social convention was familiar to us, just as was his hostility against the neo-Kantians, especially against Cohen. His inclination toward anti-Semitism was also not unfamiliar to us."[20] Even if we cannot give complete credence to this source, it conveys the compelling impression that many of Heidegger's contemporaries were convinced quite early that he was ideologically very close to National Socialism. We are of course no longer obliged to rely on dubious sources. Hugo Ott's research, the much-discussed book by Victor Farías, and a number of more recent publications have amassed a good deal of information about Heidegger's personal career.[21] Apart from all that, however, philosophical research is now in a position to examine the extent to which Heidegger's political *engagement* extended beyond purely personal activity into his philosophical work and thinking—thanks to the publication of texts that have hitherto not been generally known, especially the *Contributions to Philosophy (Beiträge zur Philosophie)*.[22]

Heidegger: Entanglement and Silence

The evidence now emerging from inquiries into Heidegger's appointment as rector at the University of Freiburg, 1933–34, clarifies not only his engagement in the cause of National Socialism but also a number of events in his personal life. He made a sensational entrance into the Party on May 1, 1933; his activities reveal some shameful traits of the thinker as a person. There is no question that Heidegger identified himself with the political aims of the National Socialists. But we must ourselves question when or whether he ever turned away from its political goals—also, whether his later behavior is to be construed as repudiating Nazism altogether or whether—as Farías and others have claimed—it is more likely linked to factional disputes within the Nazi movement.[23]

Before we pursue these questions, a general observation is in order. The career of National Socialism was inextricably bound up with its perception of the causes of World War II, including its reactive brutal persecution of political opponents—exemplified, preeminently, in the Holocaust. Of course, we understand Nazism better in retrospect. But even in the early days, it was possible to predict many of the disastrous events that were to occur, given the goals the Party had set for itself and the actual behavior of the National Socialists. Certainly, everyone who supported the Party and contributed to its developing authority in the days following the seizure of power helped to make these events inevitable.

In any case, the considerable number of political texts from the period of Heidegger's rectorate which are characterized (as George Steiner correctly points out) by "inflated brutality" and "macabre kitsch"[24] would have to count as "overproduction" if, after the fact, Heidegger had really wanted to prove himself a sort of fellow traveler.[25]

Do Heidegger's predominantly political texts (which almost always betray some philosophical implication) constitute a sort of isolated cluster in the collected opus, or should they be completely integrated into the entire body of his work, as Philippe Lacoue-Labarthe and Jacques Derrida intend?[26] Even if George Steiner protests convincingly against such an integration, we must still heed the reasons that speak in favor of so proceeding.[27] If the philosophical texts do have political implications (which remains to be demonstrated), and if the political texts do have philosophical implications, then between them there may obtain what Heidegger might have termed a "correspondence" (*Entsprechung*). Heidegger apparently proceeds entirely from the concept of a continuing development in his thinking. For example, the *Spiegel* interview of September 23, 1966, refers back to his inaugural address, "What Is Metaphysics?" (delivered at the University of Freiburg), for the basic thematic content of the rectoral address. That alone confirms the fact that Heidegger's famous statement on "academic freedom" was still valid for him in 1966.[28] But it is just that statement, so profoundly linked with Heidegger's introduction of the *Führer* principle at the University of Freiburg, which promoted the principle's spread throughout the German university system. Heidegger strongly supported its adoption at Freiburg because he hoped to bring about, by means of the principle, an extension of the sphere of influence of his thinking to include the upper echelons of National Socialist politics: in a way, he wanted to lead the leader (*Führer*) philosophically—or, to put it better, to lead him in thinking.[29]

Evidence for the two polar elements of our account may be found in

Karl Jaspers's *Notizen zu Martin Heidegger:* (a) Heidegger "in 1933 knew as little as any of the rest of us what the outcome of all of this would be. This much was certain, however: laws were being broken, there was discrimination against the Jews, theft of positions. . . . He did not suspect (any more than did the rest of us); murder, systematic killing"; and (b) "He hoped, as a philosopher, to educate the *Führer.*"[30]

Jaspers also calls attention to nonpolitical elements in Heidegger's political behavior.[31] That sort of mixing of elements in the political context can, as Ernst Vollrath and Hanna Arendt have remarked, engender its own particular dangers. Thus, if a political situation is perceived not as distinctive and authentic but only as some banal phenomenon or other, then its perversion may also go recognized. Perhaps we may find here an explanation of Heidegger's aforementioned *silence* regarding the emphatic perversion of Nazism: "He neither recognized nor acknowledged that his error was one of politics, and all because of a philosophical adherence to the priority of pure thinking."[32] We are reminded of von Thaden's caution to Hegel (cited above) that the theory of identity was philosophically correct but politically wrong.

Another parallel to the dispute about Hegel obtains at the very point at which one begins to suppose that there is no conceptual affinity between *Being and Time* and the ideology of National Socialism. C. F. Gethmann goes so far as to suggest that Heidegger's concept of action (at least, in *Being and Time*) contains "no political or theoretical political affinities." From this he infers that "the philosophy of *Being and Time* could, in principle, be connected to almost any political theory" which brings to mind Z.C.'s evaluation (above) of Hegel's *Philosophy of Right:* that is, that Hegel's philosophy could accommodate itself to any political practice. Gethmann therefore considers it impossible that Heidegger's philosophy could become a "dike" against "the swiftly rising flood of some obscure nationalism."[33]

Even though there are some facts that might argue for political indifference in *Being and Time* (this, in itself, dangerous enough), still, Winfried Franzen must be taken quite seriously when he says that there is "in the diction, at least, and in parts of the vocabulary and in the whole atmosphere created by the language of the writing, a striking continuity . . . between *Being and Time* on the one hand and the rectoral address of February 1934, as well as the shorter political appeals, on the other."[34] Franzen has summed up this tendency in Heidegger's diction with respect to the themes of "harshness and severity" (*Härte und Schwere*); Hugo Ott has also taken up these themes in the political context of the rectoral address.[35] Franzen sees the lecture "The Basic Concepts of Metaphysics" (1929–30) as a link between *Being and Time* and the texts of 1933–34.[36] There are, however, more substantive arguments, such as those developed in the expanded version of his book *Politische Philosophie im Denken Heideggers* (Political philosophy in Heidegger's thinking).[37] There, the argument leads through the notion of "setting-in-motion" and Heidegger's concept of freedom. We are pursuing a different line of analysis.

In *Being and Time*, care (*Sorge*) is shown, on the one hand, to be the being of *Dasein* and, on the other, "the most original [*ursprünglichste*]— because it is the authentic [*eigentliche*]—truth of *Dasein* gained through decisiveness."[38] But as the "authenticity" (*Eigentlichkeit*) of care, decisiveness is bound to it (p. 301). Furthermore, the "they" (*das "Man"*) remains in a state of "indecisiveness" (*Unentschlossenheit*), characterized by its "mundane indifference" and "mediocrity" (p. 43). This "mediocrity" Heidegger shows to be the enemy of the "primordial" (*das Ursprüngliche*), of "what has been gained through struggle [*das Erkämpfte*]" (p. 127). The radical quality and originality of the decisiveness of *Dasein* is, therefore, lost to the "they" (ordinary man) in "everydayness," mediocrity, timidity. The excision of that decisive radicality obtains an anxiety that is deprived of its generality (*Depotenzieren*) and becomes mere fear: "In the fear before death, *Dasein* is brought before itself as convicted and sentenced to insuperable potentiality. The 'they' carries out the inversion of this anxiety into the fear of an approaching event." Here the discussion moves on to "courage" instead of decisiveness: "the 'they' does not let the courage for anxiety emerge in the face of death" (p. 254).

It is known that this discussion of the "they" is not easily reconciled with that of *Volk* and "generation," which also appears, briefly, in *Being and Time*. In this same context there follows a discussion of the common origin of "death, guilt, conscience, freedom, and finiteness" (pp. 384–85; Otto Pöggeler calls attention, in particular, to the erratic quality of this discussion).[39]

If we may presume that the lecture course of 1929–30, "The Basic Concepts of Metaphysics" (world—finiteness—isolation) is, in a pedagogical sense, an explication of *Being and Time*, then § 38 of that lecture, certainly contributes to an appreciation of the link between *Being and Time* and the rectoral address.[40] In the lecture of 1929–30, Heidegger begins primarily with the *problems of existential need (Not)*, not care, taking into account difficulties that are not confined to Germany alone: "Everywhere there is despair, crisis, catastrophe, distress: today's social suffering, the political confusion, then impotence of science, the hollowness of art, the baselessness of philosophy, the inadequacy of religion." (GM, p. 243). Individual political experts, collective groups, or organized seers who oppose this diagnosis need not apply to Heidegger for favor. He views all such opposition as "attempts and efforts at confirming these problems of existential needs, at putting an end to them, at bringing them straight away into order and calm"; in that regard, Heidegger sees that there are "not just individuals but groups, clubs, classes, parties, everyone and everything at work everywhere, organized against the problems of living, and every organization with its own program." One might conclude from this that Heidegger will have nothing more to do with the usual parties and classes. In such situations, a fascist program seems indicated. But, then, the efforts of democratic parties must be made to seem ridiculous when they fail, or, where efforts to bring about their failure through talk also fail, then their failure must be achieved through force: "This fidgety self-defense against the problems of living *prevents an existential need in particular from emerging in its entirety.*" Just as in *Being and Time* the radicalization of care is hindered by the "they", so it is now, here, the insistent problem of existential need that is compelled (by social groups and parties) to fade gradually from the scene. In essence, a fundamental ontological category reappears here in the form of a politico-sociological one.

Philosophical radicalism, which, politically, could only be pseudoradicalism, expresses itself in the call for actual distress (*Not*): "It is not a problem in existential need that this problem or that oppresses in this way or that; the very deep and hidden problem which oppresses far more is *the absence of an essential torment for our Dasein in its entirety*" (GM, p. 244). The terror that is supposed to "distinguish" Germany soon was invoked quite literally by Heidegger. Here, too, it is important to emphasize that philosophical radicalism promptly becomes a political pseudoradicalism. "Our *Dasein* lacks secretiveness and, given this, the inner terror is lacking, which every secret carries with it, the terror that gives to our Dasein its greatness." What Heidegger is calling for he names specifically "strength and power" (*Kraft und Macht*; GM, p. 245).

In the rectoral address, "The Self-Assertion of the German University" (*Die Selbstbehauptung der deutschen Universität*), Heidegger apparently had in mind the solution to the desperate situation he announces.[41] The National Socialist movement, which was even now beginning to assert itself, he described as "the young and most recent power of the people, which already extends above and beyond us" (Rr, p. 19). At the start of the text he speaks at once of the "clarity, position, power" that the "essential character of the German university" should achieve. Its fate, however, must be determined by *leaders* in circumstances where "the *leaders* themselves are being led." The necessary condition for such *leadership* is the "severest sort of self-contemplation" (Rr, p. 9). The purpose of such power and *leadership* is to stand up to "the fate of Germany in her extreme distress." Thus, the motif of existential need and of extreme radicalization is taken up again from the lectures of 1929–30. Just how this idea of the "power of the beginning" and the "predominance of fate" is to be linked to the notions of *Volkstum*, of "the whole strength of concealment," and the motif of the "highest defiance" will not be considered here (Rr, p. 11). There is, however, an especially precarious constellation linking "spirit" (here used by Heidegger without quotation marks)[42] and the "powers that are in the blood." This is just the sort of language that suggests the all-too-familiar Nazi drivel about *Blut und Boden*. Spirit is supposed to be separated from *spirit* in the sense of *esprit* or of "intelligence": "Spirit is the primordially defined, knowing determination for the essence of Being." That is, an essentially ontological "category" is more or less transformed into a political-sociological phenomenon. The spiritual world of a people (*Volk*) is apparently just as little the superstructure of a culture as it is a repository for useful knowledge and values; it is instead the power of the profoundest preservation of the strengths of the earth and of blood as the power of the innermost fury and deep disruption of *Dasein*. Here, everything lies packaged together: primordiality, resoluteness, radicalized distress *qua* broadest disruption—but also the power and strength of *Blut und Boden*. Then, on the same page, there follows a discussion of the "elite" (*Auslese der Besten*)—in every close connection with the call for "true allegiance" (Rr, p. 14). The identification of "leaders and protectors," and the call for "leaders and protectors of the fate of the German people," appears as a curious anticipation of Heidegger's later writings. Could the identification of the "protecｏrs of fate" and the "shepherd of Being"[43] be merely contingent when we are dealing with a philosopher as linguistically acute as Heidegger?

We should also call attention to a short publication by Heidegger in the *Freiburger Studentenzeitung* (Freiburg student newspaper) of November 1933. It has the character of an appeal to the German students. Apart from the typical preaching about clarity, hardness, power, and struggle, it is the first and next-to-last sentences of the text that are of particular interest to us. (1) "The National Socialist revolution produces a radical change in our German *Dasein*." It is clear enough that when Heidegger thinks of revolution, he thinks of a National Socialist revolution. In his view, such a revolution would entail a radical change in then-current circumstances. (2) "The *Führer* himself and only he *is* the present and future German actuality and law."[44] It has already been pointed out that only the *is* in this sentence is emphasized. Establishing identity, therefore, takes on a certain fundamental significance. For Heidegger, the *Führer* is, in a clearly defined Being-sense (perhaps, with Hegel, we may say an "emphatic" sense),[45] *the* actuality and the law. Existential need, in its extreme formulation, undergoes an alteration. Later, Heidegger called this "necessity." The formulation "theories and 'ideas' should not be the rules of your Being" strikes one as being directed not in any way against the party apparatus of the NSDAP but against university teaching that fails to place itself in the service of the intended "revolution."[46] In this setting, Hitler assumes an importance exceeding all else.

On April 23, 1934, Heidegger resigned as rector of the University of Freiburg; this means as well that he withdrew from all political activities of a public character. How this conforms with his personal political views and their realization or reworking in his philosophy cannot be deduced from the fact alone. We need only think of that much discussed sentence from the "Introduction to Metaphysics" (1935, and still included in the 1953 and subsequent editions) with its parenthetical expression that speaks of "the inner truth and greatness" of "the movement" (*die Bewegung*). In the later publication the expression becomes "this movement" (*diese Bewegung*), which noticeably softens unambiguous identification of "the movement" as "National Socialism."[47] According to Karl Löwith, Heidegger wore his party badge in Rome, in 1936, at a meeting to which he presented a paper on Hölderlin. In answer to Löwith's question whether "his partisanship lay in the nature of his philosophy," Heidegger (favoring the verb "was" over "had been") agreed "without reservation" and went on to explain "that his concept of 'historicity' was the basis for his political 'engagement' " (again preferring "was" to "had been"). To Löwith, Heidegger left no doubt about his faith in Hitler; he also expressed his conviction "that National Socialism was the predestined path for Germany."[48]

Heidegger's fundamental options continue relatively unchanged at least until 1936. Philosophically, he had turned, first to Hölderlin and then to Nietzsche—that is, to a poet and a thinker who, each in his own way, no longer belonged to the sphere of metaphysics—in order to begin work, in 1936–38, on the *Beiträge*, which bears the "essential" title *Vom Ereignis* (The event).[49] A rethinking of Heidegger's ideas up to this time may be found in the *Beiträge*, as Otto Pöggeler has explained it in his summation: "If existence becomes Ek-sistence, then the center of gravity within the self-sameness of Being and thinking moves from the existent to the particular unclassifiable occurrence of truth."[50]

In a sense, in the *Beiträge*, one confronts the beginning of the *silence* that Heidegger sustains after the end of the War and after the end of the Nazi regime. This silence has brought upon Heidegger a great deal of criticism. The *Beiträge* was never published by Heidegger himself, although in later lectures and in published texts he clearly took up its themes—retrospectively, as it were. And now, since the centennial celebration of his birthday, it is available to the public. Here, however, I address only the lectures of 1937–38, which bear the title "Basic Questions of Philosophy" (*Grundfragen der Philosophie*), and the "Letter on

Humanism" (*Brief über den Humanismus*) insofar as they bear on the thought of the *Beiträge*. This philosophical rethinking obviously includes an ex post facto "rationalization" or "explanation" for the political activities of 1933–34.

In the lecture of 1937–38, the idea that philosophy is never useful is closely connected to the entry into the *new*: "Genuine philosophical knowledge is never the lame addition of the most general representations of something familiar." (This sentence may be regarded as a fundamental rejection of Hegel's formulation of the "Owl of Minerva".) "Quite the opposite," the lecture continues, "philosophy is that knowledge which leaps ahead, opening new areas and directions for inquiry into the nature of things which, in its turn, is constantly concealing itself."[51] But it is precisely this extension into new areas that explains why philosophy is not useful and yet is still dominant: its knowledge "is always effective when it works indirectly, where philosophical reflection readies new prospects for all conduct and new standards for all decision-making." When it does that, philosophy establishes "philosophically" the "goal of all reflection for man's *Dasein*"—and thus establishes "in the history of man a concealed dominance." Once again, taking up a formulation of the *Beiträge* (BzP, p. 43), Heidegger conceives this in a most emphatic way: "Philosophy is that knowledge of things which is not immediately useful yet nevertheless dominant." The sciences and scientists—we probably should include the representatives of more "traditional" philosophy: that is, those oriented toward modernity—are, for Heidegger, "the most miserable of the slaves of the latest period" (which he explains, moreover, by reference back to the rectoral address: GdP, pp. 4–5). In this new dominance of knowledge, Heidegger finds a special significance for the German people: "If the Germans seek this goal and so long as the Germans seek this goal they have also already found it. Because *our goal is this seeking itself*." And yet here the treatment of the "new" seems still to move on the terrain of philosophy, even if political parallels may be drawn.

But, if we admit the statement made to Löwith in Rome—that *historicity* is the basis for Heidegger's "intervention" in the sense of National Socialism—then the way in which Heidegger develops the connection between historicity, the *new*, and revolution in the context of the lecture proves particularly revealing.

His starting point is this: "Man *has* history, because he alone can *be* historical."[52] This Being-historicity is clarified in that man alone "stands and can stand in that open area of goals, standards, motives, and strengths and he endures and overcomes it in his manner of forming, of directing, of acting, of effecting, and of tolerating." For Heidegger, the determining dimension of time for the pertinent "event and the history" thus conceived is definitely not the past of the usual historical sense (the sense in which the early Nietzsche meant it, mere antiquarian history); instead, it is the *future:* "The *future* is the *beginning* of *everything that occurs.* In the beginning everything remains already concluded." Measured in the dimension of the inception of the future, Heidegger calls the *new* "unessential, but still unavoidable." In his view, in order to get through to the dimension of the *new*, there must be "a turning away from what has become commonplace—[there must be] revolutions." The revolutionary is expressly set in opposition to the conservative. This makes sense only if "revolution" is conceived not in any way in accord with the tradition of the French Revolution and the Enlightenment but rather in the narrow political sense in which Heidegger had previously used the word. Still, the fascist or National Socialist revolution is so similar to conservatism that some sort of new distinction between the two is needed: "The original and true connection to the beginning is . . . the revolutionary which once again places in the open the hidden law of the beginning through a radical change in the commonplace. The beginning is not preserved . . . by the conservative precisely because it has not been achieved" (GdP, pp. 40–41).

For Heidegger, revolution, beginning, history constitute an intimate philosophical context from which one may finally come to understand greatness. Greatness is also to be effected at the cost of force: "In order to rescue the beginning and in so doing to rescue the future, too, the dominance of the usual and of the all-too-customary must from time to time be broken. The radical change of the customary, the revolution, is the true connection to the beginning." In this text, Heidegger also draws a distinction between the revolutionary and the conservative; for him, it is not merely an illustrative example but an essential distinction. "The 'conservative' is mired down in the historical; only the revolutionary achieves the peak in which revolution is not a mere toppling and destroying but a recreating radical change in the usual so that the beginning once again takes shape."

On Heidegger's view, the *new* certainly can't be introduced into philosophy as just a "compulsion for something new"; nor does it appear adequate to him "if we are only to add on the racial question, thus putting an outright political face on the whole thing." (GdP, p. 143; cf. p. 53). On Heidegger's view, it is important not just to meet political demands in a genuinely philosophical way but to open up the truly necessary perspective to the political element. The text is almost topically filled with references to existential need resulting from the lack of that necessity out of which the necessity of philosophy gains its meaning. That which determines everything else, however, also poses the "theme" of the end of the beginning. We cannot discuss this concept here, but we should at least note that *an* end to philosophy is definitely formulated in the *Beiträge* as well as the lectures of 1937–38: "The age of the 'systems' in philosophy has finally passed."[53] It is a familiar fact that this is just one of the many farewells proclaimed by Heidegger.

The farewell that interests most of us here is the farewell to humanism, which, in turn, is very closely connected with the farewell to metaphysics: "Metaphysics conceives of man from the perspective of *animalitas* and does not take into account his *humanitas*."[54] This thinking, opposed to metaphysics, is subjected to unexpected strain in the composition of the "Letter on Humanism" (*Brief über den Humanismus*). For, quite unexpectedly for Heidegger, a new direction in philosophy was creating a furor in France at the time, a new direction that claimed him as its inspiration—in his opinion without the slightest justification. I am thinking here of Sartre and his reflections on the question of whether existentialism is humanism.[55] Behind the formulations of the "Letter on Humanism" lie once again the thoughts of the *Beiträge*: "Self-reflection has put all subjectivism behind it, even that subjectivism which conceals itself most dangerously in the 'personality' cult" (BzP, p. 52). ("Personality cult" is an expression that has come to have a special meaning since the time of Stalinism and Maoism; it is more likely that Heidegger was thinking of individualism.) Here, in a somewhat disguised way, the thread leading from Hegel to Heidegger is revealed, for Hegel rejected atomism in the context of natural philosophy and, also, politics (that is, with respect to natural right).

Here, too, we find a further manifestation of Heidegger's lengthy hostility toward the public, extending back to his period of political engagement. He speaks of the "dictatorship of the public," of "enslavement to the public," of the "dominance of subjectivity which presents itself as the public."[56] He directs these comments against the form of democracy that issues from the Enlightenment. It is quite clear to Heidegger that he is exposing himself to a host of objections. The form his self-defense takes confirms that his commitment reaches back to the period of *Being and Time,* when he opposed "humanism" and stated that in humanism man's nature "has not yet experienced the true dignity of man." To this extent the thinking in *Being and Time* is opposed to humanism. But contradiction does not mean that such thinking would strike at reciprocal humanness and affirm inhumanness, defend inhumanity and denigrate the dignity of man. The opposition to humanism is conceived because it does not value the *humanitas* of man highly enough.[57] In the aftermath of the coldly organized debasement of inhumanity and the unparalleled massive indignities people suffered at the hands of Heidegger's fellow Party members (surely, Farías has proved by now that Heidegger was and remained a dues-paying member of the Party right up to its wretched end),[58] these sentences must certainly sound like either some scarcely credible naiveté or some unbelievable cynicism. Heidegger speaks of the "just silence" and of the "path of silence," and overtaxes the written word.[59] This may well have been the starting points for a strand of Derrida's thinking.

Heidegger's silence in the face of the horrors of Nazism has been much lamented and blamed,[60] but now we can confirm it just as concretely as he presented it to us. He followed the common trend of silence during the Adenauer era of the Federal Republic of Germany: that is, at a time when the new generation was continually confronted with the horrors of the Nazi period. Their urgent questions about such horrors were met by a wall of silence when their grandparents were in a position to make the decisions, and when their parents were reaching maturity. No one had done anything; no one know anything; but everyone had known a nice Jew who was carried off by magic.

Despite all his struggles against mediocrity and the commonplace, by virtue of his silence, *Heidegger had returned home to the bosom of the usual and customary.*

The End of Philosophy as an Open Question

Our field is a very peculiar one. Anyone who has studied chemistry and works at the profession may call himself a chemist without shame or blushing. The same applies to members of all professions, even to theologians. Only those who have studied philosophy and who work at it need be concerned. *Philosopher* is a name still held in high esteem, much too high esteem.

If we are not philosophers, then, and if we are not even certain whether what we do should be called science unless it proceeds in a narrowly historical manner, does this not imply a disturbed self-awareness in the individuals involved, and in that which is called (or was called) philosophy?

May we say that philosophy, whatever it may be, resembles a mother from whom the umbilicus must be severed but toward whom we have certain complexes of which we need not be ashamed? For my generation, getting involved with philosophy includes a desire for a catharsis of something for which we were not to blame, something we had not even experienced, though it profoundly influenced our lives. Often enough, this entanglement has occurred in unusual ways even through Heidegger.

Even before we were able to read about it, we had often tried to do something that Michel Foucault had urged in discussing the *Anti-Oedipus* of Gilles Deleuze and Félix Guattari: "Deleuze and Guattari," he says, "pursue even the slightest traces of fascism in the body." This, too, leads to antiindividualism, but in the sense, of course, of "multiplicity and displacement by means of diverse combinations."[61] We too may do something like this, by way, however, of a "philosophy of the *we*" that expressly takes into consideration the otherness of the other and builds on conviction rather than allegiance.[62]

It is still an open question whether Hegel and Heidegger comply with the interests of reason that Kant formulated in three questions at the end of his *Critique of Pure Reason:* "What can I know? What should I do? What can I hope?" The second question is answered by an imperative. I should like to augment that imperative with another, which Foucault formulates in his discussion of the *Anti-Oedipus:* "Don't you become enamored of power yourself."[63]

Both Hegel and Heidegger, politically ignorant and in their political ignorance, had a distinct tendency to support reactionary political ideas. The moral corruption of the political situation at the particular time each wrote played no great role in that. They followed their respective courses of action with very different measures of intensity and clarity. In reality, Hegel did not do what his critics have accused and still accuse him of: he was not the "philosopher of the Prussian state." Heidegger did *far more* for the cause of National Socialism (largely because of his personal interpretation of National Socialism and Hitlerism) than his apologists are yet prepared to admit. Both, in very different ways, had extremely unpolitical conceptions of earthshaking "new" ideas. Both had fundamental reservations about democracy. There is a very great difference, however, in their attitudes toward *political institutions*. Hegel (in *The Philosophy of Right*) expressly dedicates the systematic chapter "Objective Spirit" to the thematization of political institutions; it is democratic institutions that fall before Heidegger's judgment, in favor of something new that is completely undefined.[64]

Hegel once said that countries and people could fall out of history, and that one might live quite comfortably in one of these countries.[65] Apparently he did not anticipate that in such decentralized places a peculiarly free strength of morality and of imaginative criticism might obtain. In his concept of necessary (*not-wendige*) loneliness, Heidegger may have been thinking of something of this sort in praising the provinces.[66]

What remains then of the earth-shaking *new*? Well, if we insist that the world remain as it is, we will only be the cause that it will not do so.[67]

NOTES

1. M. Heidegger, *Das Rektorat, 1933/34: Tatsachen und Gedanken* (Frankfurt, 1983).

2. Hugo Ott has written a series of separate articles that deal critically with Heidegger's autobiographical descriptions of his controversial political involvement. Heidegger wrote these in 1945, and they were published in 1983, along with the rectoral address (ibid., pp. 21–43). The results of Ott's research have been collected in H. Ott, *Martin Heidegger: Unterwegs zu seiner Biographie* (Frankfurt, 1988).

3. With regard to Heidegger's silence on these issues, see J. Altweg's synopsis, "Heidegger in Frankreich und zurück?" in *Die Heidegger Kontroverse,* ed. J. Altweg (Frankfurt, 1988), pp. 14–25, esp. 19, 23. For other comments on this silence, see esp. Jean-Michel Palmier, George Steiner, Philippe Lacoue-Labarthe, and Jacques Derrida (see notes 26 and 28, below).

4. I have prepared my own essay on the connection between the "overcoming" of metaphysics, metaphor, and humanism: H.-C. Lucas, " 'Worte, wie Blumen': Metaphern und das 'Neue' in der Philosophie," in *Philosophie und Poesie: Otto Pöggeler zum 60. Geburtstag,* ed. A. Gethmann-Seifert, 2 vols. (*Spekulation und Erfahung,* II, 7–8) (Stuttgart, 1988), 2: 169–94.

5. See H.-C. Lucas and O. Pöggeler, eds., *Hegels Rechtsphilosophie im Zusammenhang mit der europäischen Verfassungsgeschichte* (*Spekulation und Erfahrung,* I, 1) (Stuttgart, 1986).

6. The book R. Haym, *Hegel und seine Zeit* (Berlin, 1857), is discussed below. With regard to the "thesis of discrediting," see my "Wer hat die Verfassung zu machen, das Volk oder wer anders?" (Who should write the constitution, the people or someone else?). On Hegel's understanding of the constitutional monarchy between Heidelberg and Berlin, see Lucas and Pöggeler, *Hegels Rechtsphilosophie,* pp. 175–220.

7. In the original the work appeared with a double title page: G.W.F. Hegel, *Naturrecht und Staatswissenschaft im Grundrisse,* for use in his lectures (Berlin 1821); *Grundlinien der Philosophie des Rechts* (Berlin, 1821). (Actually, the book appeared at the end of 1820, but for purposes of the book trade the publication date was given as 1821.) Citations in the German text follow the edition from J. Hofmeister (Hamburg, 1955); quotations in this translation follow the translation by *Hegel's Philosophy of Right,* trans. T. M. Knox (London: Oxford University Press, 1952); cited as GH).

8. See Nikolaus von Thaden in *Briefe von und an Hegel,* ed. J. Hoffmeister, 4 vols. (Hamburg, 1953–), 2:279.

9. Cf., e.g., K.-H. Ilting's introduction "Die neue Quellenlage," in G.W.F. Hegel, *Die Philosophie des Rechts,* (Heidelberg, 1817–18; Berlin, 1818–19), ed. K.-H. Ilting (Stuttgart, 1983). See also Lucas, "Wer hat die Verfassung."

10. Von Thaden, *Briefe,* p. 279.

11. See M. Reidel, ed., *Materialien zu Hegels Rechtsphilosophie,* 2 vols. (Frankfurt, 1975), 1:101.

12. See Haym, *Hegel und seine Zeit,* pp. 2, 365, 387.

13. G.W.F. Hegel, *Gesammelte Werke,* vol. 19, *Enzyklopädie der philosophischen Wissenschaften im Grundrisse* (1827), ed. W. Bonsiepen and H.-C. Lucas (Hamburg, 1989); trans. G. E. Mueller, *Encyclopedia of Philosophy* (New York: Philosophical Library, 1959).

14. G.W.F. Hegel, *Enzyklopädie der philosophischen Wissenschaften im Grundrisse*, ed. F. Nicolin und O. Pöggeler (Hamburg, 1959); trans. G. E. Mueller, *Hegel Encyclopedia of Philosophy*, (New York: Philosophical Library, 1959).

15. G.W.F. Hegel, *Vorlesungen über die Philosophie der Weltgeschichte*, vol. 1, *Die Vernunft in der Geschichte*, ed. J. Hoffmeister (Hamburg, 1955), p. 63; cited as VG).

16. G.W.F. Hegel, *Sämtliche Werke*, vol. 9, *Phänomenologie des Geistes*, ed. W. Bonsiepen and R. Heede (Hamburg, 1980), p. 14; cited as GW 9.

17. Cf. G.W.F. Hegel, *Sämtliche Werke*, Jubiläumsausgabe in zwanzig Bänden, ed. H. Glockner; based on *Werke* (Stuttgart, 1927–), vol. 10, *System der Philosophie* (i.e., *Enzyklopädie der philosophischen Wissenschaften* of 1830 with editor's additions), par. 113, p. 254.

18. These ideas, which I can only suggest briefly here, are discussed in my article "Kontinuität, Einheit und das Neue: Überlegungen zu Hegel and Thomas S. Kuhn," in H.-C. Lucas and G. Planty Bonjour, eds., *Logik und Geschichte in Hegels System (Spekulation und Erfahrung*, II, 10) (Stuttgart, 1989), pp. 259–92.

19. A. Glucksmann, *Les maîtres penseurs*, cited here from the German translation *Die Meisterdenker* (Hamburg, 1978), p. 97. See p. 190 for an example of Glucksmann's downplaying of Heidegger's Nazi involvement.

20. T. Cassirer, *Mein Leben mit Ernst Cassirer* (Hildesheim, 1981), p. 182. Cf. also Husserl's letter to Dietrich Mahnke on May 4, 1933; quoted by H. Ott, "Martin Heidegger und der Nationalsozialismus," in *Heidegger und die praktische Philosophie*, ed. A. Gethmann-Siefert and O. Pöggeler (Frankfurt, 1988), p. 69.

21. See Ott, *Martin Heidegger;* Ch. Jambet, Preface to V. Farías, *Heidegger et le Nazisme* (Lagrasse, 1987); V. Farías, *Heidegger und der Nationalsozialismus, with Foreword by von J. Habermas* (Frankfurt, 1989); further, J. Habermas, *Martin Heidegger: L'oeuvre et l'engagement* (Paris, 1988).

22. M. Heidegger, *Beiträge zur Philosophie (Vom Ereignis)*, ed. F.-W. von Herrmann, in vol. 65 of *Gesamtausgage* (Frankfurt, 1989); cited as BzP.

23. Cf. esp. Farías, *Heidegger und der Nationalsozialismus*, pp. 40–41.

24. G. Steiner, *Martin Heidegger: Eine Einführung* (Munich, 1989). The English edition, *Martin Heidegger* (New York, 1978), was expanded with an extensive introduction, Steiner's "Prologue: Once More Heidegger" (1989), pp. 9–43, from which the comments cited here are taken.

25. One should bear in mind the following formulation, in *Das Rektorat 1933/34*, p. 2: "Immediate opposition and mere opposition did not conform to my convictions at any time (they were never party loyalty) nor would this have been prudent." Cf. "When I assumed the office of the Rectorate, I dared attempt to salvage, to reform, to affirm what was positive."

26. P. Lacoue-Labarthe, *La fiction du politique* (Paris, 1987); J. Derrida, *De l'esprit: Heidegger et la question* (Paris, 1987; German translation, *Vom Geist: Heidegger und die Frage* [Frankfurt, 1988]). Both authors deal with the text of the rectoral address as one Heidegger text among several. This also applies to J.-F. Lyotard, *Heidegger et "les juifs"* (Paris, 1988; German translation, *Heidegger und "die Juden"* [Vienna, 1988]). In favor of this proposal is the fact that

Heidegger himself in the recently published *Beiträge zur Philosophie* and in subsequent texts also follows this procedure.

27. Steiner, *Heidegger*, p. 33. The protest is in a certain sense counterproductive, since other texts confirm what Steiner considers to be abstruse (cf. n. 28).

28. See *Spiegel-Gespräch mit Martin Heidegger* (1966): "The basic reason that prompted me to assume the Rectorate at all was already indicated in my inaugural address 'What Is Metaphysics?' at the University of Freiburg, p. 8: "The fields of science are widely separated." In answer to the question about his precarious statement on the repudiation of academic freedom (in the rectoral address), Heidegger confirms, on September 23, 1966: "Yes, I still stand by it. Because this 'academic freedom' was basically purely negative; freedom from work . . . I saw no other alternative at the time [we need to explain here that this means no other than the eruption of National Socialism.] At a time when there was general confusion of opinions and the political direction of the 32 political parties, it was important to find a position on national and, especially, on social questions, somewhat in the sense intended by Friedrich Naumann." Responding to questions about the period after 1930, of course, Heidegger answers: "At this time I was still completely caught up in the questions which are developed in *Being and Time* and in the writings and the lectures of the following years. These were basic questions of thinking which, when communicable, also touch on national and social questions." Quoted from *Antwort: Martin Heidegger im Gespräch,* ed. G. Neske (Pfullingen: Kettering, 1988), pp. 83ff.

29. See the review article by O. Pöggeler, "Den Führer führen? Heidegger und kein Ende," *Zeitschrift für philosophische Forschung* 32 (1985): 27.

30. K. Jaspers, *Notizen zu Martin Heidegger,* ed. H. Saner (Munich, 1978), pp. 180, 183. See also W. Franzen, *Die Sehnsucht nach Härte und Schwere.* Concerning a disposition toward involvement with the NS as reflected in motifs in his lecture "Die Grundbegriffe der Metaphysik" (1929–30), see Gethmann-Siefert and Pöggeler, eds., *Heidegger und die Raktische Philosophie,* p. 79.

31. Jaspers (*Notizen zu Martin Heidegger,* p. 183) comes to the conclusion that Heidegger "had not a trace of clever politics. . . . Heidegger's mentality had nothing in common with this method." Paraphrasing a formulation of Max Weber's, Jaspers goes on to say: "He comes out of this like the foolish child that has stuck his arm into the machinery of history and has had the good fortune not to get himself crushed by the wheel of history but to come out of it instead with only a few scratches."

32. E. Vollrath, "Hanna Arendt und Martin Heidegger," in Gethmann-Siefert and Pöggeler, *Heidegger und die praktische Philosophie,* p. 362.

33. V.C.F. Gethmann, "Heideggers Konzeption des Handelns in *Sein und Zeit,*" in ibid., pp. 142, 170. With reference to the openness or indifference of *Being and Time* with regard to politics, Gethmann points to Marcuse (through Habermas) as a "Heideggerian Marxist"; cf. J. Habermas, *Theorie und Praxis: Sozialphilosophische Studien* (Frankfurt, 1969), p. 330: "Herbert Marcuse was the first 'Heidegger Marxist.' "

34. Franzen, *Die Sehnsucht nach Härte und Schwere,* p. 82; for the following citations, see pp. 78, 83.

35. Cf. Ott, *Martin Heidegger,* pp. 146–66.

36. M. Heidegger, *Die Grundbegriffe der Metaphysik: Welt—Endlichkeit—Einsamkeit,* in vol. 29/30 of *Gesamtausgabe* (Frankfurt, 1983); cited as GM.

37. Cf. A. Schwann, *Politische Philosophie im Denken Heideggers,* 2d. ed. of 1988 (Opladen, 1989); idem, "Zeitkritik und Politik in Heideggers Spätphilosophie," in Gethmann-Siefert and Pöggeler, *Heidegger und die praktische Philosophie,* pp. 93–107.

38. M. Heidegger, *Sein und Zeit* (Tübingen, 1963), pp. 18, 297; hereafter cited by page number in text.

39. I refer here to unpublished texts by Otto Pöggeler, whom I wish to thank for allowing me to make use of them.

40. Cf. Franzen, *Die Sehnsucht nach Härte und Schwere;* and GM.

41. M. Heidegger, *Die Selbstbehauptung der deutschen Universität* (1933; Frankfurt 1983); cited as Rr.

42. *De l'esprit,* Derrida examines how Heidegger first avoids *spirit,* then reintroduces it in quotation marks, and, finally, allows it to reappear without special marking of any kind. The rectoral address is of particular importance in this regard. In "spirit" Derrida sees metaphysics more or less returning to Heidegger's text, and it is precisely in this return that Derrida finds the disposition for Heidegger's political engagement. We must ask, though, whether a study carried out in such intense earnestness might not have the effect of turning these relationships upside down.

43. See M. Heidegger, *Über den Humanismus: Brief an Jean Beaufret* (Paris), published together with *Platons Lehre von der Wahrheit* (Bern, 1947; Munich, 1975), p. 0. Cf. the Frankfurt 1949 edition, p. 32 and elsewhere.

44. G. Schneeberger, *Nachlese zu Heidegger: Dokumente zu seinem Leben und Denken* (Bern, 1962), pp. 135, 136. In Farías, *Heidegger und der Nationalsozialismus,* p. 176, the text is printed in its entirety. Ott offers an extensive critical analysis on this formulation of Heidegger's; see Ott, *Martin Heidegger,* pp. 160ff. See also B. Martin, *Martin Heidegger und das "Dritte Reich": Ein Kompendium* (Darmstadt, 1979), p. 17.

45. In the *Spiegel* interview Heidegger clearly distanced himself from this formulation: "Today, I would no longer write those sentences cited here. I have not said things of this sort since 1934" (cited from Neske, *Antwort,* p. 86).

46. Schneeberger, *Nachlese zu Heidegger,* p. 135. For these sentences, see O. Pöggeler, "Heideggers politisches Selbstverständnis," in Gethmann-Siefert and Pöggeler, *Heidegger und die Praktische Philosophie,* pp. 31–32.

47. M. Heidegger, *Einführung in die Metaphysik* (1953; Tübingen, 1976), p. 152: "What is being passed around today [i.e., in 1935] as the philosophy of National Socialism, but has nothing whatsoever to do with the inner truth and greatness of this movement (that is, with the confrontation of a planetarily defined technology and modern man), this is only its fishing in muddied waters." With regard to this controversial sentence, cf. the epilogue to the second edition of O. Pöggeler's *Der Denkweg Martin Heideggers* (Pfullingen, 1983), pp. 340–43. See

also Pöggeler, "Heideggers politisches Selbstverständnis," p. 59 n.11, citing a communication from Walter Bröcker: "Heidegger did not use the term 'the NS' in conversation but referred instead to 'the movement.' And only the Nazis themselves used the expression 'the movement' when speaking of the NS. For this reason Heidegger's use of 'the' was unforgettable for me." Cf. also J. Habermas, "Heidegger: Werk und Weltanschauung," foreword to Farías, *Heidegger und der Nationalsozialismus.*

48. Cf. K. Löwith, *Mein Leben in Deutschland vor und nach 1933: Ein Bericht* (Stuttgart, 1986), pp. 56, 57.

49. For the question concerning this title, see BzP, p. 3.

50. O. Pöggeler, *Der Denkweg Martin Heideggers* (Pfullingen, 1963), p. 173. Heidegger himself speaks of a "turnabout" (BzP, pp. 23, 407).

51. M. Heidegger *Grundfragen der Philosophie* (Basic questions in philosophy, vol. 45 of *Gesamtausgabe* (Frankfurt, 1984), p. 3 cf. pp. 5, 50); cited as GdP.

52. The citations in this paragraph and the next are from GdP, pp. 36ff.

53. GdP, p. 144. Cf. BzP, p. 5: "The time of the 'systems' has passed."

54. Heidegger, *Über den Humanismus,* p. 66 (Bern and Munich), p. 15 (Frankfurt).

55. Cf. J. P. Sartre, *L'existentialisme est un humanisme?* (Paris, 1946); German trans. *Ist der Existentialismus ein Humanismus?* (Zurich, 1946); republished in *Drei Essays* (1960) with an epilogue by W. Schmiele (Frankfurt, 1989).

56. Heidegger, *Über den Humanismus* pp. 58ff. (Bern and Munich), pp. 21, 36–37 (Frankfurt).

57. Ibid., p.75, and cf. pp. 95, 98 (Bern and Munich), p. 21, 36–38 (Frankfurt).

58. Farías, *Heidegger und der Nationalsozialismus,* pp. 41, 137.

59. Heidegger, *Über den Humanismus,* p. 92 (Bern and Munich), p. 34 (Frankfurt).

60. Farías, *Heidegger und der Nationalsozialismus,* p. 41.

61. M. Foucault, "Der *Anti-Ödipus:* Eine Einführung in eine neue Lebenskunst," in *Dispositive der Macht: Michel Foucault, Über Sexualität, Wissen und Wahrheit* (Berlin, 1978), p. 228.

62. Cf. H. Kimmerle, *Entwurf einer Philosophie des Wir,* Schule des alternativen Denkens (Bochum, 1983).

63. Foucault, "Der *Anti-Ödipus,*" p. 230. (Recall G. Deleuze and F. Guattari, *L'anti-Œdipe,* expanded ed. [Paris, 1972]; *Anti-Ödipus* [Frankfurt, 1974]).

64. Regarding Heidegger's erroneous assessment of political institutions, cf. G. Schmidt, "Heideggers philosophische Politik," in Martin, *Martin Heidegger und das "Dritte Reich,"* pp. 51–56.

65. In his lectures on the philosophy of world history, Hegel compares the death of a people with the death of an individual and then concludes: "In a moribund state such as this, a nation may even prosper, although it no longer participates in the life of the idea" (VG, p. 60).

66. E.g., in text 5 of the *Beiträge,* Heidegger refers to "the greatest courage

of loneliness" placing it, moreover, in the immediate proximity of "the last god" and of "silence"). Cf. further M. Heidegger, "Schöpferische Landschaft: Warum bleiben wir in der Provinz?" (Creative landscapes: Why do we stay in the provinces?) (from 1933). In idem, *Denkerfahrungen* (Experiences in thought) (Frankfurt, 1983), pp. 9–13. Along with other sentences, which, because they are so anti-urban, seem to have been formulated even more unambiguously, the following must seem striking to us: "In the deep winter night, when a wild snowstorm roars about the house, assails us with its blasts, and covers everything with snow, this is the best time for philosophy."

67. Homage to Eric Fried, who once said in a lecture: "Whoever wants the earth to remain as it is, does not want it to remain."

10

A Comment on Heidegger's Comment on Nietzsche's Alleged Comment on Hegel's Comment on the Power of Negativity

L E S Z E K   K O L A K O W S K I

This is no more than a footnote to one subchapter of the first volume of Heidegger's lectures on Nietzsche.[1] The footnote, however, deals with an issue of some importance to the understanding of both Heidegger and Nietzsche.

In the interview published in *Der Spiegel* just after his death, Heidegger asserted that whoever had ears to hear knew that he had criticized the Nazi regime in his Nietzsche lectures.[2] It probably takes an ear subtler than mine to hear this criticism, even if it is true (as Alexander Schwan points out in the second edition of his excellent book *Politische Philosophie im Denken Heideggers,* 1989) that he was reluctant to interpret or to voice his nationalist feelings in biological terms, as the official Nazi ideology normally did. My intention is to suggest, on one small point, that Heidegger employed his peculiar reading of Nietzsche to express—obliquely but clearly—his political commitment to German imperialism.

The object of his reflection is the "essence of power" in Nietzsche's sense. (*Die Macht,* as we know, has no precise equivalent in English; depending on the context it could be translated variously as power, might, domination, strength, authority; "power" admittedly comes closest to the original meaning, and is used in the English translation of the famous posthumous collection of Nietzsche's aphorisms; the actual order of the sentences given is unimportant.) Heidegger argues (rightly, it seems) that according to Nietzsche's meaning, the word "power" in the expression "will to power" adds nothing to the notion of "will"; it just helps to explain it. This is because every will, every act of willing, is nothing but a will to power: that is to say, a will "to be more," to grow, to lift oneself up, to rise ("Im Willen als Mehr-sein-wollen, im Willen als Wille zur Macht liegt wesentlich die Steigerung, die Erhöhung"). This is explained by the fact—though Nietzsche does not say so in so many words—that to remain permanently at the same level of power is bound to result in exhaustion; therefore the will, if it is not to collapse, must strive unceasingly toward an ever higher achievement. It can never be satisfied with the range of domination it has already acquired; it must—by its very nature—want more and more power.

The will to power is the will to have more and more power, to be stronger and stronger. Every will consists precisely in that: to gain more strength. This is the very principle of life, nay, the principle of Being, its inherent nature. Life's purpose is not merely to preserve itself—as Darwinism would have it—but to assert itself; self-assertion amounts to the will to be at the top of or at the head of ("Selbstbehauptung, d.h. Im Haupt, d.h.oben bleiben wollen," as Heidegger says in one of his typical untranslatable word plays). Self-assertion is the never-ending return to the "essence," to the source; the will to grow and to expand is no less than existence itself, the essence of what *is*.

The will to power is creative, but the point of the creation is not just to make or produce something but to lift something higher to transform its essence (not *das Hervorbringen* but *das Hinaufbringen und Verwandeln*). Consequently, destruction, the power of negativity, belongs to the essence of creation, hence to the will, hence to Being itself.

That Being itself—or the very act of being—includes negativity is an idea that belongs to the heritage of German idealism, Heidegger says. He supports it by quoting the famous fragment on the power of negativity from the preface to Hegel's *Phenomenology of Mind*.

> The tremendous power of the negative; it is the energy of thought, of the pure "I." Death, if that is what we want to call this non-actuality, is of all things the most dreadful, and to hold fast what is dead requires the greatest strength. Lacking strength, Beauty hates the Understanding for asking of her what it cannot do. But the life of Spirit is not the life that shrinks from death and keeps itself untouched by devastation, but rather the life that endures it and maintains itself in it. It wins its truth only when, in utter dismemberment, it finds itself. It is this power, not as something positive which closes its eyes to the negative, as when we say of something that it is nothing or is false, and then, having done with it, turn away and pass on to something else; on the contrary, Spirit is this power only by looking the negative in the face, and tarrying with it.[3]

Thus, Heidegger goes on, German idealism had the courage to attribute Evil to the very nature of Being. Nietzsche himself had noticed that in German pantheism, in particular in Hegel, "evil, error and suffering are *not* perceived as an argument against divinity," whereas Schopenhauer's moralism resulted ultimately in his denial of the world. Schopenhauer's popularity in the second half of the nineteenth century, according to Heidegger, was not a testimony to his victory over German idealism; it resulted from the fact that the Germans were not "any more" up to the level of this idealism; it is only now, by a circuitous route, that the German spirit is extricating itself from this mode of decline.

The will to expand and to dominate (*Über-sich-hinaus-Herrsein*) always and inevitably includes destruction. Being is the will to power. By proclaiming this idea, Nietzsche revived, perhaps unknowingly, the genuine Aristotelian insight obscured by the scholastic theory of *actus* and *potentia*. This Aristotelian-Nietzschean notion of Being belongs to the very foundation of Western thinking and therefore is capable of providing an essential impulse to the spiritual challenge of the twentieth century.

So far Heidegger. It can hardly be doubted that his analysis of Nietzsche's thought was *not* intended as a purely historical interpretation. (Heidegger neither was, nor pretended to be, a historian, only a philosopher of "historicity.") His endeavor was to shape an ideological appeal, to find in the tradition of German thought a powerful source that would legitimate the effort to meet the challenge of modernity. Nietzsche, he supposed, revealed himself as a font of strong energy from whose source the German spirit, hence German self-affirmation in the will to power, could be resurrected.

Here, then, is the comment on Heidegger's comment:

First of all, it is quite clear that the quotation from Hegel supports neither the Nietzschean nor the Heideggerian theory of the "will to power"; in fact, it has nothing to do with that theory. It was exploited by Heidegger for a philosophical or ideological purpose quite out of keeping with its original meaning. Real substance, or the subject—says Hegel, somewhat earlier in the same text—"is in truth actual only insofar as it is the movement of positing itself, or is the mediation of its self-othering with itself. This substance is, as Subject, pure, *simple negativity,* and is for this very reason the bifurcation of the simple; it is the doubling which sets up opposition, and then again the negation of this indifferent diversity and of its antithesis, [the immediate simplicity]."[4]

The sentences quoted by Heidegger continue along the same line of thought. Spirit, by its very nature, has to reach and discover itself afresh, time and time again, in the "absolute split": that is to say, it is bound to produce its own negation unceasingly, and is capable of persisting in this self-denial. What is meant is neither death, in the sense of total annihilation, nor evil or error. Nor is there reason to suppose that Nietzsche, in praising German pantheism, had in mind the fragment of the *Phenomenology* under scrutiny here. Moreover, there is nothing specifically Hegelian or pantheist in the belief that evil, error, and suffering are not to be construed as an argument against divinity: they have never been thus construed in the entire history of Christian philosophy (St. Augustine included). On this point, therefore, Nietzsche is wrong, and Heidegger is twice wrong: first, in repeating Nietzsche's mistake; second, in suggesting that when Hegel originally featured the "power of negativity," he had in mind the same creative (hence, destructive) "will to power" that Heidegger conceived as the principle of Being.

True, according to the Hegelian account, Spirit proves its "truth" historically by being victorious. This sounds sinister and suggests that in every struggle the winners are right by definition, right by the mere fact of having won. One must remember that Hegel is addressing himself to the phases of cultural history. His thesis is not meant to signify that any victory, no matter how unimportant or accidental, confirms the "rightness" of the victor. For example, it is certainly not the case that any boxer who happens to knock his opponent out thereby proves that he is the bearer of the "truth of Spirit." These questions are meant to be distinct. Still, we can hardly find (in Hegel) clear criteria by which to separate the historically significant victories from the merely contingent ones, the real self-assertions of historical Reason from merely trifling accidents. It is for this reason, of course, that Hegel's philosophy could be so easily used (or misused) to glorify the rightness, as such, of every victor.

Apart from that, however, the Hegelian speculation neither implies nor in any way endorses or suggests any (universal) metaphysics of the "will to power." That doctrine, taken in the Nietzschean sense, simply assumes that there is nothing in the world except the centers of will, each of which attempts endlessly to expand at the expense of others, to command as much room for itself as it can, and to enfeeble or destroy as many other centers of power as possible. Although Hegel believes that— on the largest historical scale—Spirit proves or displays its truth by victory (which inevitably also anticipates a subsequent intrinsic split within itself), he by no means assumes that the whole of reality is anything more than an irrational collection of discrete centers of will, each of which strives blindly and separately to expand its power. For Hegel, no expansion of power could be "right" unless it was embedded in an all-encompassing historical plan, so that the meaning of particular events would depend upon the absolute meaning of the universal "becoming" of which they were a part. "Right" obtains only as a component of the grandiose march of the World-Spirit toward self-reconciliation through

a series of self-denials and "mediations." Consequently, even though
Spirit dispenses with moral criteria in the process of growth, its energy
comes from the universal goal that it aims at. All this is utterly alien to
the Nietzschean world view, in which there is no room for goal, plan, or
progress.

Moreover, although he mentions Hegel, Nietzsche as the author of a
theodicy (or a historiodicy) does not affirm his own metaphysics of the
will to power (he does not call it a "metaphysics," but what else is it?) to
be a Hegelian provenance, and we should not assume that it is. On this
score, Heidegger commits three further blunders. First, in wrongly asso-
ciating the Hegelian "negativity" with the Nietzschean will to power,
Heidegger imputes (no less wrongly) the same blunder to Nietzsche.

Second, he suggests that the evil, error, and suffering of which
Nietzsche speaks in the Hegelian context, is both the Hegelian "negativity" and a sign or expression of the Nietzschean will to power. But for
Nietzsche, the natural expansion of the centers of will cannot be equated
with evil, error, or suffering. The very idea of evil proves meaningless in
Nietzsche, especially in the last collection of aphorisms prepared for
publication by his sister (prepared, as Schlechta proved, with an ulterior
ideological purpose in mind).[5] The will (for Nietzsche) is what it is, and
to measure it by moral rules would be futile; such rules never arise from
an unprejudiced perception of the world; they arise only from human
weakness; The universe produces neither good nor evil.

Third, Heidegger falls victim to a self-contradiction. On the one
hand, he associates negativity with evil, error, and suffering; on the
other, he seems to perceive in the expanding will to power not—like
Nietzsche—the very nature of reality but rather a mark of a special
dignity, a particular splendor, an eminent value, which the German spirit
is manifestly called on to embody.

Moreover—and this is directly relevant to his political ideology—
when he praises the will to power and declares that it is the task of the
German spirit to awaken it, Heidegger seems to make of Nietzsche the
herald par excellence of just that historical mission. Is his reading of
Nietzsche valid? Well, of course, the question is part of that more general
time-honored question: What *was* the relationship between Nietzsche's
philosophy and Nazi ideology? Was the Nazi assimilation of Nietzsche
legitimate and credible? I shall venture no more than a brief remark on
the issue.

Schopenhauer voices a quasi-Buddhist intuition: the world is horrible. There seems to be something pathological in the very particulariza-
tion of existence; the individual is, so to say, a sickness of Being. But the
principal human virtue remains compassion. Nietzsche heaps scorn on
such moralizing: the virtue of compassion, he holds, is hostile to life; and

the law of life consists in expansion as an end in itself. Is there, then, any practical conclusion to be drawn from this metaphysics of power? Apparently there is at least this: fight on and fight on! For what? For power, for the sake of further power. Whatever there is either asserts itself through expansion or destroys itself with its own sting like the mythical scorpion.

It is a widely held and well-grounded opinion—supported by Schlechta's analyses—that Nietzsche was neither a German nationalist nor an anti-Semite (one finds in his writings some nasty comments about the Jews, but there are even nastier ones about the Germans). It is quite unreasonable therefore to suppose that the Nazi ideology, of which those two components—German jingoism and anti-Semitism—were obviously the main pillars, was either potentially or explicitly in accord with Nietzsche's philosophy or could have been extrapolated from his intellectual message without severe distortion.

On the other hand, the Nietzschean *Weltanschauung* assumed a kind of universal imperialism, embracing all aspects of reality and explaining virtually everything: the basic law of Being is expansion, and Being knows neither good nor evil. In other words, whatever expands, destroying or absorbing the environment, not only cannot be judged by mere moral rules—by the norms of civilization or custom, by the principles of decency or of human rights or of similar pathetic figments of human imagination—but, through expansion, reveals only its vitality: it is real, and it is therefore valid and legitimate.

I was once asked by students, during a seminar, the following classic question: "What do you think Nietzsche would have said if he had had the opportunity to see the Nazi regime in action?" I repeat here my answer roughly as I phrased it then: "Granted the inevitable uncertainty of counterfactuals, expressed in the *modus irrealis* of the past tense, I think we can give a reasonable answer. (It would make no sense, of course, to ask 'what would Aristotle have said?' but in Nietzsche's case the temporal distance is not too great; we still share the same cultural reality; his sister after all lived long enough to become a Nazi.) My guess is that had he survived until World War II, Nietzsche would have utterly despised the Nazis—but for the wrong reasons. In terms of his own philosophy, there cannot be anything intrinsically wrong or reprehensible in genocide (including, presumably, the gas chambers), in the extermination of other nations, in imperialist expansion, in the search for *Lebensraum*, in martial cruelty. The point is not that, in these regards, the *Germans* would have been entitled to special rights and privileges or that the Jews and the Slavs would deserve to be destroyed. The point is rather that Germany's expansion and the extermination of foreign tribes would not be qualitatively different from a shark's swallowing smaller fish. In both cases, we are faced with the law of life, to condemn which would be as silly as to condemn Being itself. Nevertheless, I think Nietzsche would have looked at the Nazis with utter contempt; in his eyes they would have been a rabble without dignity, miserable parvenus lacking altogether the aristocratic virtues he loved and praised so effusively, not just a bellicose tribe but a gang of sadists.''

It is quite incredible that the Nazi ideology could have sprung fully armored from Nietzsche's head. Nevertheless, the Nazi assimilation of his philosophy cannot be discounted as a careless reading of his work or as a merely insolent distortion of its meaning. Nazi ideals were well settled in this tradition of the master race: by efficiently enslaving and destroying other peoples, it proves that it *is* the master race. The Nazis enriched that doctrine with some supplementary ideas of their own, in particular with the bogus biological definition of superior and inferior races. For, to gain practical application, the idea of an all-embracing ontological imperialism had to be suitably incarnated in a politically specific, well-defined imperialism.

Let us return to Heidegger, then. Heidegger's attempt to harness the Hegelian philosophy to the chariot of the German spirit is, as we have seen, full of errors and confusions. Nonetheless, he did absorb the Nietzschean metaphysics in its original meaning and supplement it with the notion of a particular mission of German culture. Certainly, there was nothing new in this idea. But *in* the historical context within which it was uttered, its message (never of course spelled out in so many words in the text under scrutiny) was unmistakably clear: encouragement and praise for German imperialism then and there.

It is worth noting that apart from jumbling together three different ideas of negativity—the Hegelian (negativity as an internal split of Spirit in progress), the Nietzschean (the expansive energy of any particular being), and the traditional (evil, error, suffering)—Heidegger adds to the confusion by introducing a fourth sense of negativity: he insists that creation—always and unavoidably—is destruction. In the latter sense, however, negativity becomes an empty tautology: whatever happens, whatever changes, one condition is replaced by another. When I move my finger, for instance, one arrangement of the molecules of the air is disturbed and supplanted by another. What is created entails the "destruction" of what it replaces. Once this barren meaning is added, without further differentiation, to the other three, the glory of German imperialism begins to seem indisputably self-evident.

It is not my intention to claim on the basis of this fragmentary criticism, however, that Heidegger's philosophy was entirely propelled, as it were, by the ideologically focused will to strengthen National Socialism, or that that had been its intended meaning from the very beginning. Nevertheless, certain of its essential, hardly secondary, themes did turn out to be remarkably well-adapted to that particular task. This does not imply, of course, that the entire philosophy is to be condemned, or held to be a product only of a sick mind. Heidegger was beyond doubt a *Bahnbrecher*, as the Germans like to say. He opened new avenues to our eternally uncertain exploration of the meaning of what it is "to be," and he was not the only thinker whose work could have been employed for evil purposes without distortion, while at the same time it actually advanced in a seminal way the work of civilization.

NOTES

1. See Martin Heidegger, *Nietzsche,* 2 vols. (Pfullingen: Neske, 1961), par. 11.
2. See "Nur noch ein Gott kann uns retten," *Der Spiegel,* no. 23 (1976): 193–219.
3. G.W.F. Hegel, *Hegel's Phenomenology of Spirit,* trans. A. V. Miller (Oxford: Oxford University Press, 1977), p. 19.
4. Ibid., p. 10.
5. See "Philosophischer Nachbericht," in *Friedrich Nietzsche Werke,* ed. Karl Schlechta (Munich: Carl Hansen Verlag, 1972), 5:35–84.

V

11

Heidegger's Scandal: Thinking and the Essence of the Victim

JOHN D. CAPUTO

"Why has Martin Heidegger always refused to make an explicit critique of the monstrosities of the Nazis?" Farías asks. His silence can be explained, the author continues, by Heidegger's boundless attachment to the inner truth of the movement, whatever criticisms he may have made of the Party itself. An anecdote from Rudolph Bultmann proves the point, Farías thinks. When Bultmann suggested after the war that, like St. Augustine, Heidegger write his *Retractiones,* not waiting like the saint until the end of his life but doing so now and for love of the truth of his thought, Heidegger's face froze over and he left Bultmann without saying a word.[1]

Like everything in *Heidegger et le nazisme,* Farías's report is biographical, journalistic, anecdotal, and devoid of any attempt to confront the thought of Heidegger, to situate what Heidegger did or did not say within the context of what Heidegger called again and again "the matter for thought" (*die Sache des Denkens*). This is not to say that Farías does not pose a good question. The silence is indeed scandalous. One could have been mistaken about the Party's intentions in 1933, but after 1945 it was no longer possible to mistake who the Nazis were and what they had done. It would have been dangerous to speak out during the war, but after the war nothing prevented one from speaking.

Indeed, when the silence is broken, the scandal worsens. For the fact of the matter is that a few years after the war, Heidegger did advert to the Holocaust in a passage from an unpublished lecture, "Das Gestell" (The enframing), part of the 1949 lecture series held at Bremen upon which "The Question concerning Technology" was based.

> Agriculture is now a motorized food industry—in essence, the same
> as the manufacturing of corpses in gas chambers and the extermina-
> tion camps, the same as the blockading and starving of nations, the
> same as the manufacture of atom bombs.[2]

The comment is baffling: Is something very "deep" intended here? Or
does it betray a shocking insensitivity to mass murder? Is it "damning
beyond commentary," as Thomas Sheehan says, who brought it to the
attention of American readers?[3] What does it even mean? Of what was
Heidegger thinking when he compared modern methods of farming with
the Holocaust? In what possible sense are tractors and farm equipment,
which make it possible to feed thousands of hungry people in underdeveloped nations, to be compared with the gas chambers in which millions
were ruthlessly murdered? Is the remark a work of thought or an obscene
comparison? Philippe Lacoue-Labarthe, in a sensitive and penetrating
study of Heidegger's politics, grants that there is a grain of truth in the
comment, but he regards it nonetheless as "scandalously insufficient."[4]
The scandal of the silence is deepened by the scandal of the speech.
    What does it mean to say that such incommensurables—motorization
and murder, technology and the victim—are essentially the same? What
does "essence" mean here? What is the essence of essence (*Wesen*)?
What is the essence of the "victim"—an unheard-of question, a question
never asked by Heidegger himself—if the mass production of victims can
be essentially the same as motorized agriculture?
    In this study I undertake a close reading of this passage in connection
with two other equally unsettling texts from the postwar period in an
effort both to understand this text and to insert the question of the
meaning of the "victim" within the question of the meaning of Being. In
so doing I hope to take up the issue raised by Farías's question in a
manner which reflects a sense of the matter for thought, a sense which it
seems to me Farías is entirely lacking.

One might suppose that this is an offhand comment, strange and atypical.
Actually, the opposite is the case. Heidegger says things of this sort with
disturbing regularity. The passage obeys the deepest laws of Heideggerian
discourse. It is heavily coded, almost formulaic, a profoundly typical
gesture on his part. The passage is written from the standpoint of
"thinking" (*Denken*). Thinking is always a scandal and a stumbling block,
not only to common sense, which is satisfied with the banalities of what
"they" say on television and in the newspapers, but also to scientific
reason, for science does not think. The thinker means to offer a deeper
reflection (*Besinnung*), to cut beneath the superficiality of everyday
observation, to say something more "essential" (*wesentlich*): "in es-

sence, the same . . ." (*im Wesen das Selbe*). Journalism and political science, which are concerned with concrete events, with entitative goods and evils, literally give no thought to what is coming to pass in essence, in the *Wesen* of things. *Wesen* is to be understood verbally: as that coming to presence which governs the appearance of everything present (*Anwesendes*), which puts its stamp upon everything which is.[5]

The thinker is engaged in a meditation on the "essence" of technology, not on this or that technical thing, this or that piece of technological equipment. This remark has a parenthetical quality, like an aside. The thinker pauses for a moment to swing back over the concrete and entitative, to show with a passing glance how the meditation upon the *Wesen* can throw light on the *Anwesendes,* on what is all around us, all over us, today. The task of thought is to uncover what is really and authentically happening in the technological world, which thinking determines as the age of the "enframing" (*Gestell*).

Something deeper is going on in the mechanization of agriculture than first meets the eye. Motorized farming, making a technological industry out of it—complete with an "agricultural science" that actually passes itself off as university or college education today—is not neutral. It is not a mere technological means which can be used for good (to provide food for the hungry) or for ill (to exploit underdeveloped nations, to poison the earth with pesticides). What is coming to pass in the phenomenon of modern agriculture runs so deep that it is comparable to the most momentous events. For the same thing—"in essence the same"—is going on elsewhere: in the Russian blockade of Berlin and in the American manufacture and deployment of the atom bomb over Japan. (It was 1949, the same year as the former and four years after the latter). The tractors of modern agriculture belong together with the two notorious "pincers" (*Zange*)—Russia and the United States—described in the famous prewar lecture course *An Introduction to Metaphysics*. Russia and America "are both, metaphysically speaking (that is, in essence), the same; the same dreary frenzy of unleashed technology and of the groundless organization of normal man."[6] Tractors and pincers, bombs and blockades, airlifts and air raids—in essence, the same.

But the difference now, after the war, is that Germany—the homeland itself, "our people"[7]—lying in the middle of the middle land (Europe), has itself been swept up in the same groundlessness and unleashed technology that Heidegger warned against in 1935. The gas chambers of the Holocaust—which are neither Russian nor American—are in essence the same as pincers. The revolution has failed. Everything that Heidegger hoped for has been ruined. Far from serving as the antidote to global technology, far from asserting its metaphysico-spiritual greatness, far from assuming its destiny in the history of Being, Germany capitulated;

and this defeat is of greater consequence for the history of Being than its capitulation to the allies. Germany succumbed to the same massive technologization which it was its historic mission to offset and resist. The Third Reich, the much-longed-for new beginning, has served only to scar Hölderlin's "skies" with aircraft; to erode his "earth" with tractors and fertilizers; to drive his gods to flight; and finally—this is the horizon of the remark—to replace his "mortals" with the mechanical production of corpses in gas chambers. The inner truth of the movement—that means its vocation as the eschatological agent, as the vehicle of the German repetition of the Greek beginning, as the occasion of the New Dawn of the West, now in the endtime (*eschaton*)—has been destroyed. The Party, its ideologues and political hacks, devoid of thought and of a thoughtful poetic guide, have plundered the "world" of the "fourfold" and have tragically betrayed the "movement." Russia, the United States, the Third Reich: in essence, the same.

There is moreover a semantic rhythm in the passage, a rhetorical play of opposites, that we must not miss. What specifically is coming to presence (*west, an-west*) in the agricultural industry? What "is" there, really, authentically? Nothing less than the rape of soil and field (*Acker*) by automatized equipment, a violent assault upon an earth that was once tended by the loving hand of the farmer (*Bauer*). Where once farmers waited upon the heavenly gifts of rain and sun, now vast irrigation systems and fertilizers push the soil beyond its natural yield, maximizing crop production and multiplying the food (*Ernährung*) supplies. Now all of that is in essence the same as what takes place in the death camps and the gas chambers, even though the one produces life and the other produces death. For there holds sway in both the same essence of technology, the rule of the *Gestell*, the darkening (*Verdüsterung*)[8] of the earth. The same *Wesen* comes to presence in the filthy smokestacks of modern food processing factories and in the smokestacks of Auschwitz. Tractors and gas chambers, artifically fertilized crops and mechanically produced corpses: in essence, the same. How so? Because whether what is produced is nourishment or a corpse, a nourished body or a dead body, life or death, Being is nonetheless understood as raw material (*Bestand*), and the same rule of the *Gestell* holds sway. For coming to presence (*Wesen*) is not measured by life or death but by the stamp that Being bears at any given moment in its history.

The same essence prevails, too, in the blockade of a city: a massive military technology surrounds a city, squeezes it to near death with its lethal pincers, and produces starvation (*Aushungerung*). The production of food and starvation; nourished bodies and starving bodies: in essence, the same, the same fury of unleashed technology. What happens when the tending of the field (*Ackerbau*) becomes a motorized industry is the same, in essence, as technologically enforced hunger.

Finally, the will that sets upon earth and field with unrelenting harshness in modern industrial agriculture is the same will that is unleashed in the production—and let us add, the detonation—of the bomb. The earth is destroyed not merely in fact (August 1945) but in essence. Automatized farm equipment and nuclear bombs, nourished bodies and incinerated bodies: in essence, the same.

The massive power of the *Gestell* levels, abolishes, transcends the distinction between nourishment and starvation, life and mass death.

But one could object—the ethicist, the political scientist, the journalist, people of common sense, the hungry people in the underdeveloped nations, the people being sent to the gas chambers—they might all object that there is a vast difference between using technology for good and using it for evil, for preserving life and for killing people. That is a literally thought-less objection, arising from the bankruptcy of metaphysics, which assumes that the essence of technology is neutral. The *Wesen* of technology is nothing technological, nothing we use, nothing we can master, but something that needs and uses the essence of man.

The thinker is by no means unaware that thinking is a scandal and a stumbling block to science and common sense.[9] Indeed, one senses that he takes a certain delight in this scandal, a pleasure in the order of rank that has always separated thinkers from Thracian maids and made a mystery out of Heraclitus to the curious tourists who were out to catch a glimpse of a thinker at work. In itself, there is nothing inherently scandalous about the fact that thinking should throw those who do not think into confusion. That is an old gesture on the part of thinkers, a structural feature of thinking (which is never loath to assume the mantle of something extraordinary and great).

Still, we ask, is it possible for thinking to raise itself to so sublime a point that it neutralizes the distinction between life and death, between feeding people and murdering them? We are still troubled by this discourse on essence, still scandalized. Is this because we do not hear what is calling in the thinker's words, do not hear that more essential call to which the thinker himself responds? Have we failed to hear the thinker? Or has the thinker failed to hear everything that calls, failed to respond to everything that addresses him, failed in his responsibility?

Let us proceed slowly. Let us turn to two other passages—in fact, there are many others—that obey the same formula.

The first passage: In an address to an architectural society, in the midst of the postwar housing shortage, Heidegger remarks:

On all sides we hear talk about the housing shortage [*Wohnungsnot*], and with good reason. Nor is there just talk, there is action too. We try to fill the need by providing houses. . . . However hard and bitter, however hampering and threatening the lack of houses remains, the *real need* [*eigentliche Not*] *of dwelling* does not lie merely in a lack of houses. The real need of dwelling is indeed older than the world wars with their destruction, older also than the increase of the earth's population and the condition of the industrial workers. The real plight of dwelling lies in this, that mortals ever search anew for the nature of dwelling, that they *must ever learn to dwell*. What if man's homelessness [*Heimatlosigkeit*] consisted in this, that man still does not even think of the *real* plight as *the* plight? Yet as soon as he *gives thought* to his homelessness, it is a misery no longer.[10]

The passage is governed by the axiomatics of authenticity, of what is genuinely and really (*eigentlich*) needy, the "real plight" (in Hofstadter's translation), as opposed to what is not the authentic need, what is less than a real plight, what is "merely" (*erst*) a lack (*Mangel, Fehlen*). A more primordial neediness (*Not*) cuts deeper than mere lack, which is derivative, secondary, not so needy, somehow or other inauthentic, not a real plight. Those who are really needy, who have needs of a more profound sort, they are *not* (Heidegger makes a liberal use of italics to emphazie his point here) those who have been victimized by world wars (Heidegger uses the plural; there have been two of these, so far) and their destructiveness. Homes have been destroyed; people roam the streets by day, sleeping without shelter by night. Indeed, we do not require a world war to bring this about. In every major city the homeless seek out the cavernous hollows of urban subway systems, huddle against the sides of buildings for protection against the wind. The sprawl of poverty, laborers crammed into substandard housing—these are phenomena of war *and* peace.

The misery such people endure is, to be sure, "hard and bitter," "hampering and threatening," but it is not authentic need, not *eigentlich*. Such people are not really needy. Let us say that they are in pain, that they suffer, but that their pain is not essential enough, not old enough, not primordial enough. The valorization of authenticity communicates with the valorization of *Wesen*. The authentic need for dwelling consists in this, that mortals must seek the essence of dwelling, must search for what is really and truly coming to presence in dwelling. The authentic need is to need (*müssen*) to learn the essence of dwelling. Indeed, this need is of an even finer and more subtle essentiality, and this in keeping with the dynamics of "oblivion," of the forgottenness of the forgottenness. For the really real need (to learn to think), the authentic neediness of this need, is that men do not yet grasp that this is *the* need, that there is one need above all, that all needs are gathered together in(to) the site of one need, the really essential need, the essence of real need.

The need for dwelling is not merely that we do not know the essence of dwelling but that we do not know that we do not know, that we do not know that this is necessary, what is needed most of all. What we really lack is thought, not shelter; what we really need to provide for is thinking, not housing. But then, *as soon as* (*sobald*) one gives thought to this essential neediness (*Notwendigkeit*), the lack of *Heimat*, as soon as one begins to *think* on what is truly coming to presence in homelessness, this essential homelessness is over and all its misery (*Elend*) is ended. The thinker can put an end to this misery, or can at least prepare for it, by lending the weight of thought to the essence of dwelling. The lack of dwelling units (*Wohnungsmangel*) threatens to blind us to the deeper need of *Heimat* (*Heimatlosigkeit*), which is the dwelling that is built by thinking. The house that we really lack is the house of Being; the home we really need is to make our home in a thoughtful poetic language in which we can ponder the essence of dwelling and of the true *Heimat*.

Finally, there is one last connection to be made, one more link in the axiomatics that links *Eigentlichkeit* with *Wesen*, and that is the valorization of the "call"—which raises the question of responsibility, of responding to the call. For from this essential homelessness, this lack of thinking on the essence of dwelling, there issues the address, the summons (*Zuspruch*) which *calls* (*ruft*) to us, which calls us into dwelling. In responding to this call, mortals can bring dwelling into the fullness of its essence, and they can do this by building out of authentic dwelling and thinking for the sake of dwelling, so that dwelling is tied to thinking and thinking to dwelling. For real building, essential authentic building is really (*eigentlich*) dwelling, which is what calls to us in the old word *buan*.[11] Hence, the building that understands itself as and in terms of dwelling unfolds into the building that builds buildings. So the *fullness* of dwelling will *also* include actual buildings, places where people will come in off the streets and into shelters. Answering the call of homelessness will bring the essence of dwelling into its full complement. Dwelling in its proper essence—as thinking the essence of the home and the homeland—is to be supplemented by the inauthentic, improper actuality of actual housing units that will fill the need for shelter. The authentic neediness of thinking the essence of dwelling calls mortals into dwelling and also, as a supplement, unfolds into actually building houses. To the thought of authentic dwelling, which meets the need for the *Heimat*, there comes the afterthought of filling the lack of actual dwelling places, the inauthentic, mere lack of a place to sleep and live. The concrete work of building houses that will bring people in out of the cold is, from the point of view

of thought, an afterthought. It must come after thought, not chronologically but essentially; it must be led into its essence by the essence of
thought, which must itself follow after (*nach-denken*) the essential direction given to thought by the essence of dwelling.

But what if—at the risk of thoughtlessness—one were simply to question this order of essence, the before and after of *Wesen*? What if one
were to say that what essentially calls to us in homelessness is not the
essence of dwelling but the cries of those who suffer from the lack of
shelter? What if the call were really the cry of grief? What if the call were
the appeal for help of those who suffer? What if the summons by which
we are summarily called were the summons for aid by the victim? What
if responding to the appeal of the victim were the oldest responsibility of
all? What if the poor were the oldest of all, those who are always around?
What if the pain of those who cry out in homeless nights were older,
more authentic, more primordial, more essential than the call to think the
essence of dwelling? What if the "neighbor" were not the nearby *Bauer*
in the Black Forest but the homeless ones who roam city streets, *not* the
one whose home is nearby but the one who has no home at all? Would
that be to reinstate a biblical as opposed to a Hellenic horizon in this
discourse, to shift the discourse on the home from a Greco-German
Heimat to a biblical neighbor?[12] What if the neighbor were to be thought
of in terms not of nearness but of otherness, that other one who needs
shelter? What if the entire discourse on dwelling, *ethos*, building, and
Heimat were to displace the Greco-Germanic rhetoric of the Fourfold and
everything were reorganized around the call of those who suffer? What if
the homeless were no longer an afterthought who must *also* be provided
for in order to serve the needs of the essence of dwelling, in order to
bring it into its fullness; what if, rather, thinking would become thoughtful
concern for the Other, responsiveness to the call of the Other?

What if one were to question the hierarchical impulse that leads one
to distinguish the more essential essence of what is coming to presence
in dwelling from the concrete need for shelter? We see the profoundly
disturbing analogy of this passage with the passage on the Holocaust:
thinking can distinguish the essence of homelessness and hunger in such
a way that the authentic and essential thing would not be that people are
actually homeless or hungry. Even if we understand *Wesen* verbally, as
what is coming to presence, is there not something profoundly Platonic
in thought's step back from the lack of housing to the essence of dwelling?
For *Wesen* understood verbally—even written in Middle High German—
wants to be uncontaminated by that of which it is the *Wesen*. The essence
of technology is nothing technological; the essence of language is nothing
linguistic; the essence of starvation has nothing to do with being hungry;
the essence of homelessness has nothing to do with being out in the cold.

Is this not to repeat a most classical philosophical gesture, to submit to the oldest philosophical desire of all, the desire for the pure and uncontaminated, not to mention the safe and secure?

What if, in short, the entire axiomatics of *Wesen* and *Eigentlichkeit* were to be displaced, so that one could no longer be drawn into devalorizing world wars and their victims as inauthentic, nonessential, and into hierarchizing thinking and suffering? What if the entire problematic of responsiveness and responsibility were to include the victim?

The second passage: In his essay "The Thing," Heidegger remarks as follows upon the prospect of a nuclear conflagration that could extinguish all human life:

> Man stares at what the explosion of the atom bomb could bring with it. He does not see that what has long since taken place and has already happened expels from itself as its last emission the atom bomb and its explosion—not to mention the single nuclear bomb, whose triggering, thought through to its utmost potential, might be enough to snuff out all life on earth.[13]

In a parallel passage, he remarks:

> Man finds himself in a perilous situation. Why? Just because a third world war might break out unexpectedly and bring about the complete annihilation of humanity and the destruction of the earth? No. In this dawning atomic age a far greater danger threatens—precisely when the danger of a third world war has been removed. A strange assertion! Strange indeed, but only as long as we do not meditate.[14]

The thinker is menaced by a more radical threat, is endangered by a more radical explosiveness, let us say by a more essential bomb, capable of an emission (*hinauswerfen*) of such primordiality that the explosion (*Explosion*) of the atom bomb would be but its last ejection. Indeed, the point is even stronger: even a nuclear bomb, or a wholesale exchange of nuclear bombs between megapowers, which would put an end to "all life on earth," which would annihilate every living being, human and nonhuman, is a derivative threat compared to this more primordial destructiveness. There is a prospect more dangerous and uncanny—*unheimlicher*—than the mere fact that everything could be blown apart (*Auseinanderplatzen von allem*). There is something that would bring about more homelessness, more not-being-at-home (*un-heimlich*) than the destruction of the cities and towns and of their inhabitants. What is truly unsettling, displacing (*ent-setzen*), the thing that is really terrifying (*das Entsetzende*), is not the prospect of the destruction of human life on the planet, of annihilating its places and its settlers. What is more, this truly terrifying thing has already happened and has actually been around for quite some time. This more essential explosive has already been set off; things have already been destroyed, even though the nuclear holocaust has not yet happened. What then is truly terrifying?

> The terrifying is that which sets everything which is outside [*heraus-setzt*] of its own essence [*Wesen*]. What is this displacing [*Entsetz-ende*]? It shows itself and conceals itself in the *way* in which everything presences (*anwest*), namely, in the fact that despite all conquest of distances the nearness of things remains absent.[15]

The truly terrifying explosion, the more essential destruction is that which displaces a thing from its *Wesen*, its essential nature, its ownmost coming to presence. The essential destruction occurs in the Being of a thing, not its entitative actuality; it is an event that befalls Being, not beings. The destructiveness of this more essential destruction is aimed not directly at man but at "things" (*Dinge*), in the distinctively Heideggerian sense. The *Wesen* of things is their nearness, and it is nearness that has been decimated by technological proximity and speed. Things have ceased to have true nearness and farness, have sunk into the indifference of that which, though at a great distance, can be brought close in the flash of a technological instant. Thereby, things have ceased to be things, have sunk into indifferent nothingness.

Something profoundly disruptive has occurred on the level of the Being of things, something that has already destroyed them, already cast them out of (*herauswerfen*) their Being. Beings have been brought close to us technologically; enormous distances are spanned in seconds. Satellite technology can make events occurring on the other side of the globe present in a flash; supersonic jets cross the great oceans in a few hours. Yet far from bringing things "near," this massive technological removal of distance has actually abolished nearness, for nearness is precisely what withdraws in the midst of such technological frenzy. Nearness is the nearing of earth and heavens, mortals and gods, in the handmade jug or the old bridge at Heidelberg, and it can be experienced only in the quiet meditativeness that renounces haste.

Thus the real destruction of the thing, the one that abolishes its most essential Being and *Wesen*, occurs when the scientific determination of things prevails and compels our assent. The thingliness of the jug is to serve as the place that gathers together the fruit of earth and sun in mortal offering to the gods above. But all that is destroyed when pouring this libation becomes instead the displacement of air by a liquid; at that moment, science has succeeded in reducing the jug-thing to a non-entity (*Nichtige*). Science, or rather the dominion of scientific representation, the rule of science over what comes to presence, what is called the *Wesen* which is at work in science and technology—that is the truly explosive-destructive thing, the more essential displacing. The gathering of earth and sky, mortals and gods, which holds sway in the thing—for "gathering" is what the old high German *thing* means—is scattered to the four winds, and that more essential annihilation occurs even if the bomb never goes off.

> Science's knowledge, which is compelling within its own sphere, the sphere of objects, already had annihilated things long before the atom bomb exploded. The bomb's explosion is only the grossest of all gross confirmations of the long since accomplished annihilation of the thing.[16]

When things have been annihilated in their thingness, the mushroom clouds of the bomb cannot be far behind. So whether or not the bomb goes off is not essential, does not penetrate to the essence of what comes to presence in the present age of technological proximities and reduced distances. What is essential is the loss of genuine nearness, authentic and true nearness, following which the actual physical annihilation of planetary life would be a "gross" confirmation, an unrefined, external, physical destruction that would be but a follow-up, another afterthought, a less subtle counterpart to a more inward, profound, essential, authentic, ontological destruction.

But what if we were simply to resist this hierarchizing of inward and outward destruction and run the risk of another bout of thoughtlessness? For where are we in truth to locate the distorted, the displaced, the terrifying? Where the thinker does, in that which sets the thing outside the *Wesen* upon which thought would meditate? Or rather, precisely in the prospect of the nuclear omnicide, the loss of all, the universal incineration, *holos-caustos*, the holocaust to end all holocausts, the war to end all wars? Or, to aim the question at Heidegger himself: is there not something deeply unsettling in a thinking that is anesthethized before unspeakable suffering, deaf to the cries of the victim?

Having taken into account Heidegger's critique of biologism, must we not now begin to reconsider the implications of the prioritizing of Being (*physis*) over life (*bios*) and of Heidegger's denigration of the formula that describes man as the *zoos*, the living thing, endowed with *logos*, with speech and thought? For does not this subordination of life in the order of *Wesen*, of what comes to presence, not imply the unsettling valorization of things, "compliant and modest" (*ring und gering*) in number, as measured against the all-too great mass of living beings with which Heidegger ends this essay?[17] Is there not rather an incommensurability, a lack of common measure, which forestalls this hierarchy, which allows us at once to be "vigilant"[18] about the "thing" even while we are not less vigilant about the life of living beings, the shelter and the nourishment they require, and the threat to life on earth? Has not the time come to rethink the relationship between the Being of the thing and the Being of living things, between what was once called the ontological and the ontic?

It is now possible, I believe, to understand Heidegger's troubling assertion about the Holocaust, his association of modern agricultural technology with the gas chambers and extermination camps. The statement is governed by the rigor of "thinking," and it is made possible by the axiomatics of *Wesen*, authenticity, and nearness. It is possible to understand what Heidegger is saying, but I do not believe it is possible to remove the scandal. The remark becomes intelligible once one sees that it is the issue of "thought," but it does not become less problematic. On the contrary, I think the remark serves to draw thinking into its problematicity. I should like in the space that remains to offer an explanation of just what is so problematic about "thinking."

I would say that Heidegger's path of thought has been governed from the very start by what I would call here a certain "phainesthetics." His thinking has always turned on the experience of Being as *phainesthai*, as the self-showing of the *phainomenon*, as that which shows itself from itself as it is in itself (*Being and Time*, §7a). Being means the appearing (*Erscheinen*) of what appears, the shining gleam (*Scheinen*) of beauty (*Schönheit*). His thought has been guided by an axiomatics of the beauty and simple splendor of what shines forth and radiates. *Axiom*: that means neither the assumptions needed in an axiomatic system nor the "values" of modern axiology but that which overtakes and overwhelms the thinker, that whose shining aspect we are bound to hold in regard.[19] Being is primal presencing, the interplay of presence and absence, rising up and passing away while lingering for a while, the gentle play of the four together. *Phainesthetics*: that means Being is such as the poet (which poet?) experiences, and thinking is such that it must be conducted in the closest cooperation with the poetic experience of the Fourfold.

What calls to us above all in Heidegger's thought, what calls the thinker into thought, what calls human speaking into language, is that address which calls upon the help of thought to bring the essence of what shows itself into its self-presentation. The task of thinking and speaking is to be responsive to this primordial call, to let it come to presence (*west*), to let it come toward (*an*) and overtake us. Thus, when Heidegger undertakes essential thinking (*wesentliches Denken*), to think on things in terms of what is coming to presence in them (*wesen* in the verbal sense), what he means is something phainesthetic. Presencing (*wesen*), coming to presence, coming toward us and concerning us (*An-wesen*), means above all self-showing, shining with a primordial, gleaming radiance.

Shining with an early Greek glow: like a gleaming Greek temple, its white marble flesh glistening in the sun, towering toward a brilliant blue sky, the open and the free (das *Freie*) proudly overlooking the rich blue Mediterranean waters below. Everything blue and white, shining and glowing. The place is filled with gods—and mortals too, lifting gifts of bread and wine, the fruit of earth and sun and soil, in humble gratitude for the giving of what gives, for what is given here, for a now forgotten but aboriginally unforgettable gift.

But, as Lyotard has argued, there is a singular "anesthesia" in this Greco-German *phainesthai*, a forgetting in all this recalling, a deafness in all this hearing and hearkening. To pursue the Kantian analogy of which Lyotard is so fond, if there is a recalling of the beauty of being, there is a profound insensitivity to the sublime.[20] It is precisely what is forgotten which lets thinking run amiss, precisely this other kind of oblivion which stirs within these strangely skewed and scandalous accounts of the truly authentic danger, of the real loss of home, of the truly unsettling and terrifying—and above all of the gas chambers. For nowhere in the call of Being is the cry of the *victim* to be heard, nowhere the plea for mercy, the summons for help. The silent peal of Being is deaf to the appeal of suffering. The assault upon the earth which turns the soil into an object of agricultural engineering is more primordial than the ravages of hunger, than ravaged bodies. The matter to be thought is not hunger and starvation but whether one works the land with hand and oxen instead of with motorized equipment. Hungry and undernourished bodies do not figure in the account, do not come to presence; hunger is (*west*) not, it simply is (*ist*).

That is a valorization which is possible only on phainesthetic grounds, on the constriction of experience to "world and thing," on reducing everything which *is* to the call of Being, to shining glow and gleaming beauty. It is a world in which a wholly *other* kind of responsiveness and responsibility has been silenced, a responsibility to those who live and die, to those who are embodied, who suffer or are in pain, who grow old and infirm—above all, to innocent victims. The thinker leaves no room at all for the victim in the history of Being's self-showing.

This is a Greek world or, more accurately, a world of Greeks invented by Germans, a Germanico-Greek world of the innocence of becoming, of the lack of all guilt, where *dike* and *adikia* have to do strictly with the play of presence and absence.[21] Nothing or no one is guilty; there are no victims in the epochal play, no dead bodies, no spilled blood, no incinerated flesh, no death camps—or, at least, they are not essential, not what is really happening. The dark night of the oblivion, of the withdrawal of Being—that does not mean the rule of injustice and murder any more than the primordial call of Being has anything to do with justice. The ethical has been not "naturalized" in the sense of naturalism or materialism but rethought in terms of *physis*, of emerging into presence. The only *ethos* permitted is a more essential, originary *ethos*, an early Greek poetic *ethos*, which dictates a more poetic mode of dwelling on the earth. There is no call of conscience, no response that says "guilty,"[22] and so there are no victims. There is/it gives only the epochal shifts which have fallen into an escalating history of oblivion from *eidos to Technik*. Now, in the endtime (*eschaton*), Hölderlinian skies are marred by industrial smoke. The tranquillity of hillside farms has been disturbed by the roar of motorized equipment which drowns out the tinkle of the cowbells. It gives/there is everything, all beings—except victims.

The victim never comes to presence, never makes an appearance on the scene of the history of Being. There are no victims in the first beginning, in the great early Greek epoch before metaphysics, no women, slaves, non-Greeks who figure at all in that glorious first start where all is still well with *Wesen*, understood verbally. Neither do the victims figure in the endtime of the history of metaphysics, when they are gassed to death by motorized equipment. For that is not the matter of concern (*die Sache*); they are not the task for thought.

That is why the gas chamber is the same as the tractor, as motorized farm equipment. The victim is invisible in the history of Being, is not a matter of concern, is not what is at issue. The victim does not come toward us and concern us (*an-wesen, an-gehen*) in the history of Being, does not call to (*an-rufen*) us. The victim has no voice in the call of Being, cannot speak, cannot be heard. The victim is thus a *différend* in Lyotard's sense. He (or she) has been robbed of his voice, does not have the means to register a protest on his own behalf about the damage that has been done to him.[23] Victims do not make their appearance on the register of Being. Their cry has no say (*Sage, sagen*); they are not an appearance, do not reach the level of *Wesen*, cannot show themselves from themselves. What is a matter of concern is the manner of their death—gas chambers, a motorized technological means—not the matter itself, the *Sache selbst* of murder.

Let us cite another, even more scandalous saying about gas chambers, one mentioned by Lyotard.

> I have analyzed thousands of documents. I have tirelessly pursued specialists and historians with my questions. I have tried in vain to find a single deportee capable of proving to me that he had really seen, with own eyes, a gas chamber.[24]

Faurisson wants to doubt that the gas chambers existed. Heidegger does not doubt their existence but wants to think through to their essence. The gas chamber merely is (*ist*), but the more important issue is how it comes to presence (*west*). So when we want to talk about what really is, what is really essential, when we make the step back to the difference (*Unterschied*), then there is no difference between tractors and gas chambers. Now it is part of the idea of victim "not to be able to prove that one has been done a wrong." It is impossible for the wrong to make an appearance. That is what Faurisson has done, for he demands that the victims of the gas chambers testify to the wrong that has been done to them. He requires a resurrection for proof.

But the thinker has made the proof of the victim almost as difficult. The victim does not have to prove that he or she is (*ist*), but that he or she is (*west*): that is, attains the level of *Wesen* and so matters a little. Victims must show that they are essential, that they belong to the essence of what is calling us to think and speak and act. (Or rather that they are a matter of concern, for this whole axiomatics of essence and authenticity is at the root of the trouble, the source of Heidegger's thoughtlessness.) But that is what the victim cannot do. The victim is a matter of indifference for the matter of thought, a matter of phainesthetic indifference. It makes no difference to the history of Being, of *phainesthai*, whether there are or are not victims. In the history that runs from shining Greek temples to industrial pollution, there is no place for victims.

Die Sache des Denkens: that means *phainesthai* and shining appearance, coming into presence and lingering for a while, *An-und Ab-wesen, Wesen. Thinking*: that means a responsiveness to that which calls for thought, calls upon us and asks to be thought. What then of the appeal of the victim, the silent peal of the starving and homeless, or the still deadlier silence of the murdered? Do they not call for thought? Do we simply need to amplify thinking so that thinking *also* includes the call of the victim? Is it a matter, as I once suggested, of needing to extend Heideggerian *Gelassenheit* to other people instead of restricting it to jugs and bridges?[25] Or must the matter for thought (*die Sache des Denkens*) and the task for thought (*die Aufgabe des Denkens*) be more profoundly disrupted by an otherness to which it has systematically made itself deaf? Would the opening of thinking to the victim undo the very notion of "thinking"? What must the victim do to gain a voice in the call of Being? Is it possible to ask about the essence of the victim, the victim's coming to presence? Or are we left with one final, ironic Heideggerian reversal, that the essence of the victim is a victim of essence—understood verbally?

N O T E S

1. Victor Farías, *Heidegger et le nazisme* (Paris: Verdier, 1987), p. 289. The Bultmann anecdote that Farías uses is from Hans A. Fischer-Barnicol, "Spiegelungen-Vermittlungen," in *Erinnerung an Martin Heidegger,* ed. G. Neske (Pfullingen: Neske, 1977), pp. 95–96.

2. I use the translation of Thomas Sheehan in "Heidegger and the Nazis," *New York Review of Books,* June 16, 1988, pp. 41–43. Sheehan is translating the German as it appears in Wolfgang Schirmacher, *Technik und Gelassenheit* (Freiburg: Alber, 1983), p. 25, who himself cites p. 25 of a typescript of the lecture. The first part of the sentence also appears in "The Question concerning Technology," in *Martin Heidegger: Basic Writings,* ed. David Krell (New York: Harper & Row, 1977), p. 296. The attempt to determine the "essence" of technology in terms of the *Gestell* is the context of Heidegger's remark. The German is as follows: "Ackerbau ist jetzt motorisierte Ernährungsindustrie, im Wesen das Selbe wie die Fabrikation von Leichen in Gaskammern und Vernichtungslagern, das Selbe wie die Blockade und Aushungerung von Ländern, das Selbe wie die Fabrikation von Wasserstoffbomben."

3. Sheehan, "Heidegger and the Nazis," p. 41.

4. Philippe Lacoue-Labarthe, *La fiction du politique: Heidegger, l'art et la politique* (Paris: Christian Bourgeois, 1987), p. 57ff. It is right, as far as it goes, for Heidegger to situate the Holocaust within modern technology, according to Lacoue-Labarthe. This reading of the remark is criticized by Jean-François Lyotard, *Heidegger et "les juifs"* (Paris: Galilée, 1988), p. 137ff.

5. On understanding *Wesen* verbally, see "On the Essence of Truth," in Heidegger, *Basic Writings,* pp. 139–41.

6. Martin Heidegger, *Gesamtausgabe* (henceforth *GA*), vol. 40: *Einführung in die Metaphysik* (Frankfurt: Klostermann, 1983), pp. 40–41; trans. Ralph Mannheim, *An Introduction to Metaphysics* (New Haven, Conn.: Yale University Press, 1959), p. 37 (translation modified).

7. *GA* 40, p. 41; *Introduction,* p. 38.

8. *GA* 40, p. 41; *Introduction,* p. 38.

9. Martin Heidegger, *Gelassenheit,* 2d. ed. (Pfullingen: Neske, 1960), pp. 26–27; trans. John Anderson and E. Hans Freund, *Discourse on Thinking* (New York: Harper & Row, 1966), pp. 55–56.

10. Martin Heidegger, *Vorträge und Aufsätze* (Pfullingen: Neske, 1959), p. 162; trans. Albert Hofstadter, *Poetry, Language, Thought* (New York: Harper & Row, 1971), p. 161.

11. Heidegger, *Vorträge,* p. 147; *Poetry,* p. 147.

12. Jacques Derrida, "The Politics of Friendship," *Journal of Philosophy* 85 (November 1988): 644.

13. Heidegger, *Vorträge,* p. 164; *Poetry,* p. 166.

14. Heidegger, *Gelassenheit,* p. 27; *Discourse,* p. 56.

15. Heidegger, *Vorträge,* p. 164; *Poetry,* p. 166.

16. Ibid., p. 168; p. 170.

17. Ibid., p. 170; p. 182.

18. Ibid., p. 180; p. 181.

19. *Der Satz vom Grund* (Pfullingen: Neske, 1965), pp. 34–35.

20. Lyotard, *Heidegger et "les juifs,"* p. 15.

21. See Heidegger's reading of *dike* and *adikis* in "The Anaximander Fragment," in *Early Greek Philosophy,* trans. David Krell (New York: Harper & Row, 1975), pp. 41–47.

22. Guilt and conscience were essential features of the analytic of *Dasein,* but they have disappeared from the history of Being.

23. Jean-François Lyotard, *The Différend: Phrases in Dispute,* trans. G. Van Den Abbeele (Minneapolis: University of Minnesota Press, 1989), nos. 9–27.

24. Robert Faurisson, in Pierre Vidal-Naquet, "A Paper Eichmann," trans. M. Jolas, *Democracy* 1, no. 2 (1981): 81, cited in Lyotard, *The Différend,* no. 2.

25. See my *Radical Hermeneutics: Repetition, Deconstruction and the Hermeneutic Project* (Bloomington: Indiana University Press, 1987), pp. 266–67.

12

Heidegger and Politics: Some Lessons

FRED DALLMAYR

"Why is it that you don't engage in polemics?" Foucault was asked shortly before his death, to which he replied: "It is true that I don't like to get involved in polemics. If I open a book and see the author is accusing an adversary of 'infantile leftism,' I shut it again right away. That is not my way of doing things; . . . I insist on this difference as something essential: a whole morality is at stake, the morality that concerns the search for the truth and the relation to the other." In the same interview, Foucault distinguished sharply between interpersonal discussion or conversation, on the one hand, and polemical strategies or methods, on the other. In a discussion, he noted, each partner takes pains "to use only the rights given him by the other"; the polemicist by contrast proceeds "encased in privileges that he possesses in advance and will never agree to question." Thus, instead of treating the other person as a partner in the quest for "a difficult truth," the polemicist reduces him to an adversary, an enemy "who is wrong" and "whose very existence constitutes a threat"; in doing so, the polemicist relies on "a legitimacy that his adversary is by definition denied." To underscore his point, Foucault drew a parallel between intellectual polemics and certain inquisitorial, judicial, and ideological tactics. As in the case of heresiology, he wrote, polemics establishes "the intangible point of dogma, the fundamental and necessary principle that the adversary has neglected," and denounces this negligence as "a moral failing." The judicial analogy resides in the polemicist's acting as judge and jury: instead of dealing with an interlocutor, he is "processing a suspect." The closest parallel, however, exists with ideological partisanship: like the latter, polemics "defines alliances, recruits partisans, unites interests or opinions, represents a party; it establishes the other as an enemy, an upholder of opposed interests, against which one must fight until the moment this enemy is defeated and either surrenders or disappears."[1]

These comments seem apropos with regard to the book published by Victor Farías in 1987 and subsequently translated into English. By all standards, the book is an intensely polemical work, exuding a prosecutor's zeal; although based in part on historical and archival research, the presentation of findings has the character of a police blotter or criminal indictment. Since its first publication, the aura of polemics has steadily deepened, as has the range and intensity of charges. In fact, the book and its effects have the earmarks of a publishing event (or media event)—a rare occurrence in the philosophical domain.[2] The target of the book is Martin Heidegger and particularly his political thought or orientation. The thesis advanced by Farías is that Heidegger was predisposed toward National Socialism by his background and origins; that his involvement in the regime in 1933 was complete and unqualified; that this engagement persisted unchanged throughout the Hitler years; and that it remained intact even after 1945—as shown by the lack of a clear retraction of Nazi views and the continued talk about a "spiritual rebirth" of Europe. In reading this general indictment, one can hardly avoid thinking of Foucault's statements. Throughout the book, Heidegger is never treated as a partner in any common search but only as "an enemy who is wrong" and "whose very existence constitutes a threat." In line with the practice of heresiology, the book proceeds from a superior position or principle which is never fully articulated or defended but whose accuracy is presupposed and in whose name the adversary is judged. Following the prosecutor's model, Farías is content with "processing a suspect" and collecting "proofs of his guilt." As in all polemical battles, the goal (in Foucault's words) is the moment when the enemy is "defeated and either surrenders or disappears." One of Farías's strongest complaints is the absence of a univocal retraction or surrender on Heidegger's part. But would such a retraction—and I mean a complete reversal, since nothing else would do—really have served anyone's purpose? Western intellectual history, from Galileo to Helvetius to Lukács, is replete with recantations—but cast in a manner hardly comforting to defenders of free thought (or the freedom of "spirit").

My point here is not to vindicate or exonerate Heidegger prematurely but simply to raise the issue of fairness. As most commentators agree, the book is a jumble of truths, half-truths, insinuations, and innuendoes—all presented with the same conviction and endowed with the same unquestioned authority.[3] This aspect is particularly disturbing, given the general standpoint from which the indictment is launched—which (if I am not mistaken) is that of liberal democracy. A basic pillar of such democracy, however, is respect for due process—which is sorely lacking in Farías's book. Nowhere in the text is an effort made to uncover not only evidence speaking against Heidegger but also testimony speaking in his favor or at least mitigating his case. Nowhere is there an attempt or even an inclination to interrogate Heidegger himself as to the motives (or to simply the nature) of his views; whenever these views are considered, they are quickly dismissed as tainted, while credence is accorded to every accusing voice. Given the gravity of the indictment—unqualified attachment to National Socialism—more surely would have expected a careful definition of terms, but there is none. As it seems to me, National Socialism as a doctrine includes two basic ingredients: first, belief in the absolute superiority of the Aryan race; and second, advocacy of the exercise of world dominion (*Weltherrschaft*) predicated on this racial superiority. Yet as most observers concede even those sharply critical of Heidegger, he subscribed to neither of these tenets. In recognition of this fact, nuanced critics resort to a variety of alternative labels: "conservatism, "ultraconservatism," "cultural elitism." Whatever the merit of these labels—and I consider them at best only partially correct—none of the views they designate are commonly considered indictable offenses (at least in a democracy tolerant of a certain measure of dissent).[4]

One of the chief defects or incongruities of Farías's book is its general inattention to Heidegger's philosophical opus—as if the latter were immaterial to the investigation at hand. I do not see how thinker and opus can be disconnected without subverting the book's objective. The fact is that, without his opus, Heidegger is simply not the *cause célèbre* presented by Farías. As Heidegger has cogently remarked (commenting on the nature of art), the artist is not an artist prior to or independently of his artwork; on the contrary, it is the artwork that constitutes its maker an artist. The same consideration applies to the philosopher and his work. Viewed independently of his opus, Heidegger is simply one of thousands or millions of German *petits bourgeois* who managed to conform to the Nazi regime; thus seen, *l'affaire Heidegger* hardly generates special interest. Thus, in an important sense, the prominence or event-character of Farías's book depends on Heidegger "the philosopher," on his philosophical opus—which is completely slighted in Farías's account.[5] My argument is not that Heidegger and his work are indistinguishable, that we cannot differentiate between the "philosopher" and the "man." On the contrary, there is good reason to believe that Heidegger—like so many other authors—fell, at crucial junctures of his life, well below the level of his philosophy. Even without a detailed personality study (which I leave to others), I suspect that Heidegger's conduct betrays certain character flaws (aggravated by the context of the totalitarian regime in which he lived): for instance, fits of megalomania, occasional vindictiveness, a frequent lack of civic courage (*Zivilcourage*). My point is only that biographical knowledge of this kind is no substitute for familiarity with the philosophical opus.

What particularly chagrins me in this matter is the counterproductiveness of the chosen procedure: its inability or unlikelihood to generate new thought or some kind of learning process. To quote Foucault again: "Has anyone ever seen a new idea come out of a polemic?"[6] The only likely outcome of the book is to confirm Heidegger's accusers in their pristine rectitude or correctness—while driving his defenders into stubbornness. In my view, there is still a great deal to be learned from *l'affaire Heidegger* and Heidegger's involvement with National Socialism—whose specter is even yet far from banished. Precisely because Heidegger exposed himself at one point to the virus of fascism, he was constrained to wrestle in a concrete way with this infection and to search for an antidote. On my reading, Heidegger's work after 1933 is best seen as a prolonged struggle to expel or subdue the virus—without returning to philosophical orthodoxy. For this reason, at least, his work is instructive. As I see it, a central issue of our time remains the frailty of traditional world views—ranging from conservatism to liberalism to socialism—all of which are linked, one way or another, with a humanist metaphysics. The question is whether a path can be forged beyond inherited ideologies—a path that does *not* end up in fascism. The question was not resolved in 1945 and is not likely to be resolved in the foreseeable future. To make some headway in this area—and to counterbalance Farías's account—I want to turn to two writers who are well known for their intimate familiarity with Heidegger's opus and for their interpretive skills: Otto Pöggeler and Jacques Derrida. Both have written broadly and extensively on Heidegger's thought. In fact, both have commented on Heidegger's politics in publications that appeared at roughly the same time as Farías's book. My guiding concern is neither acquittal nor condemnation. Can anything worthwhile be learned, I want to ask, from this politics and these commentaries—anything beyond the bounds of vengefulness and the solidification of ill will?

I

Before interrogating these two authors, I want to invoke briefly some comments by another philosopher and leading Heidegger scholar: Joseph Kockelmans. In 1984, Kockelmans published an important study on Heidegger's "later philosophy," on the central themes of his thought that emerged after *Being and Time*. Kockelmans felt it important to include in

this study—essentially focused on theoretical themes—a chapter dealing
with Heidegger's political outlook or, better, with the relation between
his philosophy and his politics. He sensed a difficulty straightaway, the
difficulty of placing Heidegger's outlook within a traditional political
vocabulary. "On the one hand," he wrote, "in order to be able to relate
critically to Heidegger's ideas, one must already have a conception about
what ideally the relationship between philosophy and politics should be.
On the other hand, in formulating these ideas, one must formulate and
justify this conception with the help of a metaphysical philosophy, which
Heidegger precisely tries to overcome." The difficulty is compounded by
another dilemma: the seeming political aloofness of much of Heidegger's
philosophizing (as well as his protestations against being viewed as a
"political" thinker), an aloofness that stands in stark contrast with his
active engagement around 1933. Was it possible to treat Heidegger's
philosophy as "pure" thought, as somehow completely uncontaminated
by political concerns; or conversely, could Heidegger's thought be reduced to his involvement in 1933 (whatever its true nature)? Neither of
these alternatives appeared sensible to Kockelmans. The chapter distanced itself from the notion that there could be a "genuine form of
thinking which would be totally 'apolitical,' " but it was also unwilling to
surrender philosophy, particularly Heidegger's philosophy, to partisan
politics or ideological platforms. Kockelmans observed that with regard
to Heidegger's opus, conflicting claims have been advanced: either, it
appears, there is "no concern with politics" at all or else Heidegger's
thought is "really no more than an attempt to justify National Socialism
as a political movement. It does not take much reflection" Kockelmans
goes on, to realize that neither of these claims can be correct or even
remotely relevant to the state of affairs and the actual historical events."[7]
    Kockelmans's observations are still pertinent and worth pondering,
even in the face of recent findings. Clearly, Heidegger's opus is not
"political theory" in any conventional sense (or as practiced by professionals). In particular, it can scarcely be compressed into a compact
ideological formula—given Heidegger's persistent attempts to escape
from all "world views" (metaphysical or other). By the same token,
Heidegger's work offers no purely speculative retreat, as is evident from
the stress on "being-in-the-world" and the "worldliness" of human
experience (where "world" is a "political" world—in a sense still to be
explained). In the rest of his chapter, Kockelmans examined various
broadly construed interpretations of Heidegger's politics, among them
some that anticipate Farías's approach—which Kockelmans described as
"tendentious and sometimes even defamatory." In these writings, he
noted, Heidegger's rectoral address and other speeches during 1933 and
1934 are said to express "a deep-seated and long-lasting affiliation with

the National Socialist movement, taken in its worst possible interpretation, and a clear sign of Heidegger's insincerity and irresponsibility."
Moreover, this affiliation is said to be unambiguously rooted in *Being and
Time* as well as a permanent fixture of the later work. None of these
charges were persuasive to Kockelmans. "It seems to me," he wrote,
"that anyone who defends the view that there is an intrinsic link between
Nazism and Heidegger's later philosophy or between Nazism and the
ideas proposed in *Being and Time* is simply mistaken." The point, he
emphasized, was not "to condone Heidegger's behavior in 1933 and
1934" (or afterward), because his behavior was "indeed unacceptable on
several counts." Nevertheless, one could not, on that evidence, defend
"the thesis that this behavior merely made manifest a political philosophy
that had always been there and always would remain there."[8]

In support of his arguments, Kockelmans relied on a number of
earlier analyses, particularly that of Otto Pöggeler. Pöggeler is renowned
for his comprehensive and detailed study of the development of Heidegger's thought, in his *Der Denkweg Martin Heideggers (Martin Heidegger's Path of Thinking)*. In its original edition of 1963 (when Heidegger
was still alive), the book virtually bypassed political issues and political
implications. However, less than a decade later, Pöggeler remedied this
gap by publishing a monograph specifically devoted to political issues.
Building on the structure of the preceding study, the monograph traced
the unfolding of Heidegger's thought through a number of major stages,
highlighted by such labels as "meaning of being," "truth of being,"
"topology of being." In each instance, Pöggeler explored the political
relevance of Heidegger's outlook, paying close attention to the linkage
with National Socialism as well as to affinities with French existentialism,
neo-Marxism, and related movements. As Pöggeler noted in the opening
pages: "Even an initial glance at his work shows that Heidegger did not
elaborate a political philosophy but that, in various stages of his thought,
he nonetheless was in diverse ways a politically engaged philosopher."
Observations on Heidegger's politics, partially gleaned from the monograph, were incorporated into the second edition (1983) of the *Denkweg*
study (which became the basis of the English translation).[9] For present
purposes I want to concentrate on a still more recent and more detailed
essay by Pöggeler, "Heidegger's Political Self-Understanding," which
appeared in a volume titled *Heidegger und die praktische Philosophie*
(Heidegger and practical philosophy) in 1988. The objective of Pöggeler's
essay (and of the other papers collected in the volume) is not to engage in
partisan polemics or recriminations but rather to explore the difficult
nexus of politics and Heidegger's opus. What is at issue, states the book's
introduction, are the thoughts and perspectives that "guided the *philosopher* Heidegger in such a manner as to motivate his political options and
his articulation of goals or aspirations."[10]

Pöggeler's essay at once sets the discussion in the global context of our century, the context of the political and ideological struggle for "world dominion" (*Weltherrschaft*), particularly as seen from the vantage of a disoriented Europe. As Pöggeler notes, the elements of this background always permeated Heidegger's political thought, overtly or covertly. Heidegger's persistent concern he writes, was "to respond philosophically to the crisis of Europe as it had been revealed by the First World War. For Heidegger that war meant the senseless self-destruction of Europe, triggered by the fact that—instead of trying to solve their problems creatively—European nation-states threw themselves into the external battle for world dominion." The task facing Europe in our century, in Heidegger's view, was to reconsider its position in the world and to exert its cultural leverage—a task "perverted" by global military ambitions. On occasion Heidegger was fond of citing the lines penned by Stefan George during and about the First World War: "These are the flaming signals—not the message." Heidegger shared with many observers the sense of a "crisis of Europe" that had its intellectual roots in the progressive sway of "nihilism" and that surfaced politically in successive military conflagrations. He asked himself whether Europe, which had spawned its own nihilism, would find the strength to reverse its anticipated decay. Heidegger assigned a crucial corrective role to "Germans" or the "German people." These terms should not be taken in a simple ethnic or racial sense: partly because of Germany's central location in Europe, partly because of her own contribution to modern "nihilism" and the cultivation of the "will to power," partly because of the assumed affinity between German and classical Greek culture. As he remarks in his lectures on Heraclitus (in the midst of the Second World War): "The planet is in flames; human nature is out of joint. A reflective world-historical reorientation can come only from the Germans—provided that they discover and preserve 'the German' " (or what "German" means).[11]

Heidegger's commitment, involving the cultural revival and perhaps political hegemony of Europe, went through a number of changes. During the Weimar period, no doubt, his commitment was still largely embroiled in the question of the struggle for world dominion, which, in the long run, he himself bemoaned and sought to avoid. That is the phase for which the label "cultural elitism" (specifically: cultural elitism under German leadership) would probably be most appropriate—the same elitism that led Heidegger into the proximity of National Socialism, from which he sought subsequently to extricate himself, with ambiguous and uncertain success. In the essay cited, Pöggeler offers a condensed tour through the major writings and lectures from the Weimar period to the end of the war, always focused on the relation between philosophy and politics. Very early on, as he points out, Heidegger nurtured sympathies for Naumann's vision of a restored "Middle Europe" under national and social auspices. With the impact of the depression and the malaise of Weimar institutions, however, Heidegger's thinking was radicalized in an extraparliamentary direction. At this point (around 1930), he fell under the spell of a stark "Nietzscheanism" that viewed the world as the arena of irresoluble conflicts and antagonisms—the contest between Dionysus and Apollo, between life and "spirit," between nihilism and the overcoming of nihilism (achievable only by a cultural elite). This was the time, also, when Heidegger was influenced by Ernst Jünger, especially by his essay "Total Mobilization" (1930) and his book *The Worker* (1932). What Jünger tried to show was that World War I had ushered in an era of world revolution, a struggle for world dominion, in which the total mobilization of all available resources (material and human) alone could promise victory; instrumental-industrial labor, rigorously disciplined in a military fashion, was said to be destined to spearhead the struggle. As Pöggeler reports, Heidegger discussed these writings "in a small circle" and "sought to grasp [the significance of the fact] that planetary history now was placed under the universal sway of the will to power—whether this occurred under the auspices of communism or fascism or world democracy."[12]

From this radical Nietzschean and Jüngerian conception the path was not long to an embroilment with Hitler's movement, which Heidegger greeted as a possible ally and instrument in effecting the cultural revival of Europe (as distinct from Russia and America). As for his motives, Pöggeler mentions national-patriotic sentiments regarding a German "resurgence," as well as social concerns about overcoming large-scale unemployment in the wake of the great depression; he also points to certain speeches of Hitler—especially the so-called "peace talk" of May 1933—which were likely to encourage illusions about is goals. "The 'resurgence' [*Aufbruch*] which Heidegger joined in 1933," he writes, "was nationalist in character, designed to restore the dignity of Germany and . . . to be part and parcel of the Wilsonian program of the self-determination of nations." In his rapprochement with National Socialism, Heidegger was guided in part by the belief that he would surely be able to steer Hitler and his movement in the appropriate (cultural-elitist) direction. Here, apparently, Heidegger's personal megalomania emerges, which subsequently exacted its own heavy price. In his reminiscences after the war, Karl Jaspers expressed the view that it was Heidegger's ambition to guide or lead Hitler (*den Führer Führen*)—probably an accurate assessment, which, if true, reveals Heidegger's immense political naiveté as well as his lack of modesty. His own speeches and pronouncements during this time were more idiosyncratically Heideggerian than indicative of any strict adherence to party ideology. This is especially true of the rectoral address, "The Self-Assertion of the German

University," which inaugurated his ill-fated service as rector at Freiburg. As Pöggeler reports, relying on Heidegger's own post-war elaborations, immediately after the address the National Socialist minister in attendance chided Heidegger for cultivating a "private (or idiosyncratic) National Socialism," an idiosyncrasy evident in his not adopting the racial idea and in his rejecting the complete politicization of the university.[13]

The content of the rectoral address has been the target of many analyses and interpretations. Although brief on the matter, Pöggeler makes some important points. He observes that the theme of university reform had been a persistent concern of Heidegger's since at least 1919 (when he first lectured on the topic)—but that the 1933 address greatly accentuated the element of structural or administrative elitism. Pöggeler also remarks on the favorable reception of the address among intellectuals, including Werner Jaeger and Karl Jaspers (who, in August of that year, praised the speech as "so far [the] only document of a contemporary academic willpower").[14]

The address bore the distinct imprint of Jünger's "total mobilization"; however, whereas Jünger extolled the importance of "labor service" and "military service," Heidegger added a third co-equal pillar, the function of "knowledge service" (Wissensdienst) to be performed chiefly by universities.

The rectoral period following the address is a dismal story on the whole and the hub of the polemics surrounding l'affaire Heidegger. In Pöggeler's account, the evidence is bleak, at best deeply ambivalent, a mixture of subservience and partial nonsubservience to the dictates of the regime; his general conclusion: "precisely as a leader [Führer] Heidegger was a complete failure." After resigning the rectorate in the Spring of 1934, Heidegger began the difficult process of disentangling himself not only from his involvement with Hitler's movement but also from some cherished beliefs—particularly his infatuation with Jünger and an extreme Nietzscheanism. In his turning to Hölderlin and the pre-Socratics, Pöggeler sees Heidegger moving "beyond the horizons confining Jünger's attempts to conceptualize his age." Five years later, in fact, in his lecture script for the summer of 1939, Heidegger castigates "total mobilization" as "the organization of absolute senselessness on the basis of the will to power and in the latter's service." During the winter of that year, at the beginning of the war, Heidegger discussed Jünger's The Worker, with a small group and complained that the book "fails entirely to grasp Nietzsche's metaphysics philosophically. It does not even point the way; on the contrary: instead of treating it as questionable [fragwürdig], it renders this metaphysics self-evident and thus apparently redundant."[15]

The departure from Nietzsche proved to be more complicated and halting than the rejection of Jünger's work—mainly because of the depth of Nietzsche's insight. Immediately after resigning the rectorate, in the summer of 1934, Heidegger offered a lecture course on Heraclitus with a focus on *polemos* and conflict—a treatment in which Nietzsche's "agonistics" was curiously distanced or rendered in alien garb (*verfremdet*), facilitating a certain ontological or metaphysical scrutiny. Subsequent lecture courses on Nietzsche bear the earmarks of intense personal struggle. The lectures of 1936 and 1937—on "the will to power as art" and "the eternal recurrence of the same"—still present Nietzsche's thought as a viable and innovative critique of Platonism, though a critique still formulated in traditional metaphysical terms. By contrast, the course on European nihilism—offered in 1940, after the outbreak of the war— exudes a somber, even hostile mood: Nietzschean "will to power" is now portrayed as an outgrowth of an aggressive anthropocentrism in which "man" or the human is reduced to the level of "brute animality" or "bestiality." As Pöggeler indicates, the progressive distantiation from Nietzsche was paralleled by the steady growth of Hölderlin in Heidegger's work: that is, by the accentuation of poetic "world disclosure" (which eludes human control or manipulation) as opposed to radical conflict and willful self-assertion. A lecture course of the winter of 1934 was devoted to a discussion of Hölderlin's hymns "Germania" and "The Rhine"— seemingly straightforward patriotic themes. Instead of serving as a chauvinistic symbol, however, "Germania" became in Heidegger's lectures a synonym for the reflective turn toward the disclosure (or truth) of being and the origins of Western culture; in Hölderlin's own vision. Germany was meant to be not an imperial power but an unarmed, defenseless "heartland" preparing the ground for a cultural or spiritual renewal. These themes were intensified in courses on Hölderlin offered during the war years. Thus, in lectures presented during the summer of 1942, Heidegger differentiated sharply between the classical conception of *polis* and the ideological "politicization" of life in general in contemporary politics. Whereas the classical *polis* was a place of questioning and unsettled openness, modern politics aims at the implementation of specific historical plans: "Since it denotes the technical-historical certainty of all action, politics or 'the political' is marked by its own absolutely unquestioned status. This status of politics and its totality go together."[16]

Throughout these years, Heidegger's political thought was more and more preoccupied with the issue of world dominion as the common goal of competing global ideologies. The lecture course of 1935, *An Introduction to Metaphysics*, turned philosophical attention to the pre-Socratics and also to Sophoclean tragedy (as interpreted by Hölderlin). But the political focus was entirely contemporary: human destiny in a world steadily instrumentalized, closing in on itself. Heidegger talked at the time of a "darkening of the world" (*Weltverdüsterung*) connected with the crisis or decay of Europe, a crisis induced or generated by the European "spirit" itself, especially by Western metaphysics. "This Europe," he asserts, "which in its ruinous blindness is forever on the point of cutting its own throat, lies today in a great pincers, squeezed between Russia on one side and America on the other. From a metaphysical vantage, Russia and America are the same: the same dreary technological frenzy, the same unrestricted organization of the average man." Similar assessments of Russia and America recur in Heidegger's writings and lectures of the period—always with an edge against technology and mass organization (united through the will to control). Generally speaking, he distinguished three major instrumentalizations of culture or "spirit": Marxism, positivism, and fascism. The first relegates culture to a redundant "superstructure"; the second (prevalent in America) is content with the scientific replication of given states of affairs; and the third aims at the organizational control of a people under racial auspices. That picture, to be sure, is quite different from the conception that led Heidegger into the proximity of National Socialism. As the same lecture course affirmed (in its printed version): "The stuff which is now being bandied about as the philosophy of National Socialism—but which has not the least to do with the inner truth and greatness of this movement (namely, the encounter between global technology and modern man)—is casting its net in these troubled waters of 'values' and 'totalities.' " More than any other passage, this one has been strongly attacked by critics—understandably so, given its reference to "inner truth and greatness." Moreover, research has shown that the parenthetical phrase was not part of the original lectures but a later addition, perhaps inserted to attenuate the harshness of the claim. However that may be, one can hardly deny that Heidegger's concern with planetary strategies and the struggle for world dominion antedates 1935 and can be traced to his involvement with Jünger.[17]

Pöggeler's essay also discusses at some length the so-called *Beiträge zur Philosophie* (Contributions to philosophy), written between 1936 and 1938 (which has only recently been published). Pöggeler describes it as Heidegger's crowning work. According to his report, the *Beiträge* is a philosophical depth inquiry seeking to uncover the truth of being as a "happening" (*Ereignis*) not amenable to human control, as a "clearing" leading toward spiritual recovery. The treatise outlines in stark contrast with this clearing the dominant features of our age, concentrating on mass organization, the unleashing of technology, and the general instrumentalization and ideological politicization of life. Among the ideologies criticized are Bolshevism with its planned social progress; liberalism with its treatment of ideas and culture as "values to be implemented"; and "folkish" ideology with its focus on political training and racial breeding. At the time, Heidegger argued that the term "folk" should refer not to a given race or empirical entity but to a common search or aspiration. The general goal of the *Beiträge* was to encourage a renewed philosophical reflection, particularly a recollection of buried cultural origins that heralded or held the promise of a better future. As Pöggeler points out, philosophizing in Heidegger's sense is "authoritative" (*herrschaftlich*) because it turns back to origins as opposed to the decay of later times; "authority" in this case is said not to signify dominion, because its chief exemplars are not rulers but marginalized thinkers and artists (such as Hölderlin, Nietzsche, and van Gogh). Philosophy of this kind, Pöggeler comments, is "useless in that it cannot be placed in the service of historical self-assertion (as Heidegger had still assumed in 1933). Such philosophizing means opposition and resistance to a National Socialism which at that time was preparing for the struggle for world dominion and which, in lieu of reflection, was seeking the unquestioned sway of a total ideology and total politics."[18]

By way of conclusion, Pöggeler points to some of Heidegger's writings and statements after the war. At that time, Heidegger disengaged almost entirely from political orientations and ideological formulas, including the restorative tendencies promoted in postwar Germany. Increasingly and stubbornly, his thinking focused on the effects of modern "nihilism" and on the prospect of technology as global human destiny. In this respect, World War II appeared to him not as an end or a turningpoint but only as a stepping-stone to planetary instrumentalization. As he observed in *What Is Called Thinking?* (1951–52): "That world war has not decided anything, provided we take decision here in that broad and crucial sense where it concerns the basic human destiny on this planet." Similar sentiments were echoed in the *Spiegel* interview of 1966. In response to questions about global trends, Heidegger said the past several decades had shown "that the planetary movement of modern technology constitutes a power whose determining historical significance can hardly be underestimated." In the same context, he pondered the question of the political order appropriate to this technological age—and doubted that it would be democracy (as commonly understood). A striking feature of the postwar years was the appropriation of Heidegger's thought by various intellectual movements—French existentialism and Western neo-Marxism, for instance—developments that Heidegger observed with curiosity but without engaging or lending support. While not discouraging adjustments to political trends, Heidegger—in Pöggeler's account—persisted in his ontological-metaphysical "radicalism," seeking the antidote to modern nihilism in recollective-meditative thinking, in poetic world-disclosure, particularly in Trakl's postmetaphysical (or postmodern) poetry. Pöggeler himself suggests a counterbalance to this radicalism: the importance of practical-political judgment, which Heidegger generally lacked, and the need for a nonradical, prudential politics. "If there is a European responsibility—as Heidegger insisted in his own way—then", Pöggeler says, "this responsibility (after the self-destruction of Europe as former heartland) must reside in the effort to accentuate the limited chances of a prudent politics which still remains possible."[19]

II

As can be seen, Pöggeler's account accords major weight to political factors and particularly to the struggle for planetary dominion—sometimes in a manner that overshadows philosophical issues. Although probing the nexus of philosophy and politics, his essay alludes only briefly (if at all) to certain key Heideggerian themes—the "overcoming" of metaphysics, for instance. Virtually the reverse is true in Derrida's interpretation in *De l'esprit*, subtitled *Heidegger et la question* (1987). There, political struggle, though not entirely neglected, takes a back seat to philosophical and "deconstructive" queries. Derrida was never formally a student or disciple of Heidegger's, but he explores "sympathetically open" issues in Heidegger's work that remain "suspended, undecided, and thus in movement" in his texts. One such issue is the meaning and status of "spirit" (*Geist*), a topic Derrida finds surprisingly neglected in the massive secondary literature. His study aims to remedy this inattention. On the one hand, Derrida finds that the theme of "spirit" enjoys an "extraordinary authority" in the tradition of German philosophy, especially in German idealism, which reverberates through Heidegger's account of the "path of thinking." On the other hand, he finds the theme inscribed in Heidegger's writings in "politically charged" contexts surfacing in discussions of such topics as "history, nation, gender, the Greek or the German." The linkage is not accidental. "Perhaps this thinking (of spirit)," he writes, "determines the sense of politics or the political itself; at least it can indicate the locus of such a determination (if one is possible). Hence the not yet fully recognized privilege which the theme enjoys in all matters relating to the question of politics or the political."[20]

De l'esprit offers a tour through Heidegger's successive writings and lectures, this time, like Pöggeler's essay, featuring the shifting role of "spirit" and spirituality. Derrida takes his point of departure from *Being and Time*. He notes that Heidegger emphasized at the time the need to avoid or bracket the term "spirit" (*Geist*), together with such related terms as "subjectivity" and (transcendental) "consciousness." In his comments on Trakl's poetry some twenty-five years later, Heidegger resumed this counsel, observing that Trakl had always steered clear of *Geist* and *geistig*, preferring the word *geistlich* (spiritual) instead. Nevertheless, in the interval between *Being and Time* and these comments—a period that was not "just any time span"—Heidegger repeatedly contravened his own counsel. Not only did he not avoid the term; he explicitly invoked *Geist* and related expressions. "What has happened?" asks Derrida. "How can we explain that in the time period of twenty-five years which lies between the two counsels of *warnings* [of avoidance], Heidegger himself frequently, regularly, and even emphatically used this vocabulary, including the adjective *geistig*? How do we account for the fact that he often spoke not only about *Geist* but also in the name of *Geist*, occasionally carried away by his emphasis?" In Derrida's view, both the use and the non-use, or attempted avoidance, of *Geist* are symptomatic of Heidegger's philosophical development: they demarcate a "nodal point" at which different strands of Heidegger's thought are interwoven in a particularly dense and revealing fashion. Among the intersecting strands, Derrida mentions four: the issue of "questioning" in its relation to being; the status of technology in its contrast to thinking; the meaning of "animality" as compared with *Dasein*; and the epochal character of the history of metaphysics. "As we shall see," he writes, "these epochal divisions may be tied up with the kind of 'difference' which . . . separates the Platonic-Christian, metaphysical or onto-theological definition of *Geist* from another thinking which surfaces in the dialogue with Trakl: the thinking of the spiritual (*des Geistlichen*)."[21]

Turning back to *Being and Time*, Derrida reminds his readers that Heidegger tried there to extricate himself from traditional metaphysics, particularly from subject-object or mind-body dualism—which surfaces also as the opposition between spirit and matter (or thing). His "existential analytic" sought to rescue *Dasein* not only from various sorts of objectification but also, explicitly, from a "*subjective* definition of spirit." In traditional metaphysics, spirit (*Geist*) belonged to a string of "non-objects"—that is, what opposed to material reality—such as consciousness, soul (or *psyche*), subjectivity, personhood, and reason. The attempt to elucidate *Dasein* nonmetaphysically required an effort to avoid or bracket that entire string of non-objects, "including particularly the concept of spirit." According to Heidegger, the defining characteristic of *Dasein* was not so much consciousness or spirit as its openness to being or to the "question of being"; among other entities, *Dasein* must be differentiated as that mode or modality for which its own being (being as such) is "questionable," raised to the status of a question. From this vantage, *Dasein* is not an objectively given or ascertainable entity (in the sense of *Vorhandenheit*), but neither is it merely a non-thing. Categories such as spirit and consciousness prove to be obstructions to understanding *Dasein* as the locus of the questioning of being. Heidegger uses expressions such as "existence" and "being-in-the-world" to obviate misunderstanding: that *Dasein* is an inquiry signifies that "the 'substance' of man resides not in spirit construed as synthesis of soul and body but in his existence." Heidegger distanced his work from every Cartesian metaphysics as well as from cognate disciplines: "mental sciences" (*Geisteswissenschaften*), for instance, and philosophical anthropologies and theories of personality animated by the traditional vocabulary.[22]

Before he leaves *Being and Time*, Derrida turns to the later chapters concerning space and time, especially Hegel's conception of history. At this point, Heidegger reintroduces the concept of spirit but places it in quotation marks. Apparently, "something signified by *Geist* in quotation marks can be salvaged"; *Geist* is simultaneously distanced and reappropriated. Regarding space, Heidegger insists that *Dasein* is not spatial in an external sense: that is, due to the spatial character of the body (as part of extended matter). By the same token, *Dasein* is not an inner mental quality (after the fashion of *res cogitans*). Rather, *Dasein* has a distinctive mode of spatiality; not being a mere object, *Dasein* is *geistig*—although the term now appears in quotes. "Precisely because it is '*geistig*' (the word now obviously in quotation marks)," Derrida remarks, "*Dasein* is spatial, endowed with an original spatiality, *only* because of this kind of '*Geistigkeit*'—Heidegger underscores the point—is *Dasein* a spatial being." The issue recurs in the discussion of Hegel's conception of time and history. Though he presented history as the history of spirit (unfolding in time). Hegel nevertheless also maintained that spirit "falls into" time, lapses into something mundane or sensual. Here, according to Heidegger, Hegel himself lapsed into something nonphilosophical: the "vulgar" notion of temporality construed as external clock time—which shows his indebtedness to modern (Newtonian) physics. Only if one were to cling to the notion of clock time could temporality and history be opposed to spirit; only then could spirit be said to "fall into" time. In seeking to overcome this opposition, Heidegger invokes the term *Geist* again—again in quotation marks. In his own words, " '*Geist*' does not merely fall into time, but exists as the original temporalization of time itself." To the extent that there is still a "falling at all, the term denotes a lapse from one time into another, from "original" into "vulgar" temporality—an inherent possibility of "spirit" construed as temporalization. In this way, Derrida explains, *Geist* is only halfheartedly accepted; with a "reticent hospitality" it is greeted at the door—and kept there in quotation marks.[23]

Leaping ahead six years, Derrida turns to the rectoral address, and discovers a surprising fact: the return of *Geist*—this time in full regalia, no longer constrained by quotes. Suddenly, "the curtain rises," he writes, "the quotation marks disappear—making room for a powerful effect: *Geist*, itself comes on stage." Undisguised, spirit now asserts itself as an integral part of the "self-assertion of the German university." What induced this change, asks Derrida, this "passionate rhetoric" in the name of spirit? Self-assertion in Heidegger's usage involves a *geistig* order supported by a leadership (*Führung*) that is itself guided by a *geistig* mission or commission. As Heidegger puts it in the opening paragraph: "Assuming the post of rector means to take on the task of the *geistig* leadership of this high school of learning." That leadership is possible only if the leaders (*Führer*) permit themselves to be led—, "by the inescapability of that *geistig* mission that molds the fate of the German people into the distinctive shape of its history." Overstepping his usual caution (and certainly his earlier counsel of avoidance), Heidegger proceeds later in the address to offer a definition of spirit in which certain crucial elements of his thought are conjoined. As opposed to mere cleverness, wit, analytical intelligence, he asserts, *Geist* "is the originally tuned and knowing resoluteness in the pursuit of the essence of being." Accordingly, the *Geist* or "*geistig* world" of a people is not a mere cultural superstructure or an arsenal of usable values but an existential "power" (*Macht*) arising from chthonic forces and the deepest testing of its historical *Dasein*. As Derrida comments, the definition and its elaboration combine the highest and the lowest, spirit and chthonic yearnings. He points to its evident philosophical ambivalence. For *Geist*, treated as a concrete historical force, no longer fits the metaphysical model governing modernity; *Geist*, in accord with *Being and Time*, is "not equated with subjectivity, at least not in its psychic and egological construal." At the same time, the "massive voluntarism" of the address still seems hostage to the age of subjectivity.[24]

There is a more important political ambivalence lurking behind this philosophical quandary. One could perhaps suppose that Heidegger, in invoking *Geist* and the *geistig* mission, "spiritualizes National Socialism," Derrida observes, and legitimates its policies thereby (even its worst). On the other hand, in shouldering this burden of spiritualization, Heidegger may have intended to cleanse and thus salvage National Socialism (from its worst inclinations). In that case, Heidegger's address opens a breach between *Geist* and biological racism or naturalism; then, the address *appears* no longer to belong to an ideological discourse that "relies on dark forces—forces that are not *geistig* but natural, biological or racial forces (corresponding to a non-*geistig* construal of the 'blood-and-soil' theme)." But then, Heidegger's spiritualization exacts its own price: the price of a relapse (at least in part) to a traditional metaphysics rooted in spirit and subjectivity. In Derrida's view the cost is unavoidable, because "one can extricate oneself from or *oppose oneself* to biologism, naturalism, or racism in its genetic form only by stipulating spirit as the opposite pole, by equating the latter again with subjectivity (if only a voluntaristic mode of subjectivity)." Derrida observes that the pressure exerted by this dualism is "very powerful: it affects most of the discourses that today—and probably for a long time to come—oppose themselves to racism, totalitarianism, National Socialism, fascism, and the like, and that do so in the name of *Geist*, in the name of freedom, or in the name of axioms directly or indirectly indebted to the metaphysics of subjectivity (such as the axioms of democracy and the 'rights of man')." On Derrida's view, the alternatives available in this scenario— the options for or against *Geist*—are all "frighteningly impure and contaminated." One has to ask oneself which option or "type of complicity" is the least grievous; in any event, "the urgency and importance of the question cannot be taken seriously enough."[25]

As far as the rectoral address is concerned, Heidegger mixes the two options in a number of ways, compounding their ill effects: he "vouched" for National Socialism by invoking what is "still [a] metaphysical gesture." The same ambivalence persists however modified, in the *Introduction to Metaphysics* (1935). Heidegger himself alludes to it in the opening pages: "Every essential form of spirit hovers in ambivalence." The treatise was meant as an introduction (*Einführung*) into philosophy construed as a mode of questioning more specifically, as the "questioning of the basic question." It was meant not to lead to a substantive domain of inquiry or to yield specific useful information but only to arouse wonder and questioning: furthermore, the guidance intended could not rely on any other form of external leadership (*Führung*) but had to entrust itself entirely to self-questioning. Thus unguided and free-ranging, a questioning guidance forms the gateway to philosophical questioning: "This is precisely what characterizes spirit; it is the nature of *Geist* itself." By using the vocabulary of leadership, Heidegger seemed to accede to the dominant fascist formula. But, as Derrida remarks, "one should be honest enough to admit: at the very moment when he seems to place the theme of *Führung* in the service of a certain kind of politics, Heidegger shows that he entirely distances himself from this politics, that he cancels his service." To be sure, this distancing was neither complete nor unambiguous. For one thing, questioning is still connected here with the "will-to-know," and thus with assertive "resoluteness" (familiar from earlier writings). And for another, the *Introduction* does locate itself in a new geopolitical context, the planetary context of the struggle for world dominion. According to Heidegger, Europe and Germany in particular are held in "a great pincers," threatened on two sides by Russia and America (both, technological powers bent on global mastery). The question posed is this: whether Europe would be able to recover the strength of her origins, which required the "unfolding of new historical-*geistig* forces from the middle" (or heartland-Germany). Here, Derrida remarks, geopolitics takes the form of a "world politics of the spirit," meant to counter the "darkening of the world (*Weltverdüsterung*): flight of the gods, destruction of the earth, massification, rule of mediocrity."[26]

In the *Introduction to Metaphysics*, the darkening of the world is equated with a progressive loss of power or "disempowerment" (*Entmachtung*) of the spirit—a process that is not an external accident but a feature endemic to spirit itself. In Heidegger's account, this disempowerment takes a number of forms, including the misconstrual of spirit as wit or intelligence, its reduction to a "superstructure" (as in Marxism) or to a formula for racial mass organization (as in fascism). Countering this process of decline, Heidegger presents spirit as a source of strength or force, as "an originally unifying and obligating power." The *Introduction* reinvokes the definition of *Geist* offered in the rectoral address, adding these comments: "Spirit is the empowerment of the powers of being as such taken as a whole; wherever spirit rules (*herrscht*), being as such becomes steadily more essential." Heidegger's formulations here, as Derrida notes, are still distinctly (if ambiguously) indebted to traditional metaphysics, to its focus on spirit as self-possession and self-identity (or *logos*). Later, these moorings are considerably loosened. In his lecture course on Schelling (1936), Heidegger still emphasizes the gathering nature of spirit, calling *Geist* the "originally unifying unity." But he also says that that unifying "spirit is *pneuma*," a wind or breeze, a mode of respiration or aspiration. Whence does the wind arise? Following Schelling, Heidegger points to the potency of love: "For even *Geist* is not the highest; it is only the spirit or breeze of love. But love is the highest." The same Schelling lectures broach the topic of "evil" (*das Böse*), the falling away and self-enclosure of existence in rebellion against the unifying spirit of love. Derrida refers in addition to some of Heidegger's lecture courses on Hölderlin, particularly "The Ister" (1942). There, Heidegger construes the "soul" (*Gemüt*) of the poet as the receptacle and nourishing soil for spirit. Spirit or *Geist* is now seen as a fire or flame, as in the opening of Hölderlin's hymn "Come now, fire!" As fire, spirit no longer denotes self-possession of self-identity but rather a continual yearning, a perpetual process of expropriation and reappropriation. By offering his soul, Hölderlin the poet is put afire; he is "almost incinerated, turned to ashes."[27]

The last stage reviewed in *De l'esprit* concerns Heidegger's intense postwar engagement with language, particularly his commentary on Trakl's poetry (1953), in which he raises again the question "But what is spirit?" Now replies: "*Geist* is the flaming (or enflaming)," or more simply, "*Geist* is flame." *Geist* is both what enflames, by putting to fire, and what goes up in flames. The passage does not merely paraphrase Trakl, Derrida believes, but captures Heidegger's fresh thought as well: *Geist* no longer belongs to traditional metaphysics (and thus, need no longer favor a strategy of avoidance). This is made clear in Heidegger's comments on Trakl's verse: "But the soul is a stranger-sojourner [*ein Fremdes*] on earth." Here, Heidegger insists, the term "stranger" does not mean that the soul is banished to an alien bodily or earthly prison, in accord with an old-fashioned Platonism. It signifies rather a wayfaring-sojourning quality, the truth that the soul is "in search of the earth" which it still does not yet rightly inhabit. The yearning of the soul points to the future—not in the sense of ordinary clock time but by way of a different mode of temporality where the "later" anticipates the "earlier" or earliest, where evening is prior to morning, and death prior to life. For this same sort of temporality (and its earth world), Trakl employs the term *geistlich* (spiritual)—as when he writes of the "spiritual twilight," of the "spiritual night" as the concealing disclosure of the sun's path. In pointing forward, *geistlich* temporality has the character of a promise—the promise of morning or dawn before night and day, before evening-land and morning-land construed as Occident and Orient. "Evening-land" (*Abendland*) in Trakl's poems must, Heidegger affirms, be carefully distinguished from Western civilization or the "idea" of Europe in Plato's sense (largely assimilated by Christianity). Trakl's evening-land, he writes, is "older, namely earlier and thus more promising than the occident conceived along Platonic-Christian and especially along European lines."[28]

In adopting Trakl's use of *geistlich*, Heidegger distances himself again—as in his early work—from traditional metaphysics and its vocabulary. As Derrida observes: "Although after 1933 the term had been employed regularly and for a long time without question marks, the adjective *geistig* is now brusquely rejected"; Heidegger acts as if, for twenty years, he had not eloquently "celebrated the *Geistigkeit* of *Geist*." Instead, these terms are now relegated to the "Platonic-metaphysical tradition"—or, rather, the Platonic-Cartesian tradition—of the West. In his commentary on Trakl, Heidegger is quite explicit on this point. Why, he asks, does Trakl "avoid the term *geistig*? Because *geistig* means the opposite of the material. This contrast highlights the difference between two spheres of being and, in Platonic-occidental language, designates the gulf betwen the supersensual (*noeton*) and the sensual (*aistheton*)." Understood in this way, *Geist* and *geistig* have, in the meantime, been leveled to the "rational, intellectual and ideological," and thus belong, together with their opposites, to a decaying age. Their condemnation, Derrida notes, corresponds roughly to the views voiced in the

Introduction to Metaphysics, but the critique proceeds now from the vantage of *Geistlichkeit* (not *Geistigkeit*). Still, as Derrida concedes, the distinction does not amount to a radical dismissal, for *Geistlichkeit is* earthly temporality illuminated by *Geist* (fire or "flame"); and fire is the source of spirit (as *pneuma* or *spiritus*, as well as *ruah*). Hence, even under the auspices of *Geistlichkeit*, Heidegger does not abandon the unifying or gathering quality of *Geist*; as in his commentary on Trakl, *Geist* remains "as such the gathering." By way of conclusion Derrida returns to the political connotations of the reviewed journey, of the various options for or against *Geist* (with or without quotation marks). "What is at issue here," he writes, "is not something abstract. Rather we are dealing with past, present, and future 'events,' with a constellation of forces and discourses that seem to wage a merciless war (roughly in the period from 1933 to today)." Strictly speaking, "no discourse that participates in this power struggle can be described as innocent."[29]

III

So far, I have juxtaposed two accounts of the trajectory of Heidegger's thought. In many ways, the two authors—Pöggeler and Derrida—complement each other, the one by accentuating more overtly political (or geopolitical) issues; the other more, subterranean metaphysical issues. Although different in style and general orientation, both accounts link politics and philosophy, interpret Heidegger's political views in the light of his opus. In doing that, they add new aspects or dimensions to *l'affaire Heidegger*—by counterbalancing Farías's polemical approach. Pöggeler's account is particularly helpful in recovering concrete historical contexts and background factors which (while not explaining or justifying) do render some of Heidegger's motivation more plausible. The following are particularly important: Heidegger's disaffection with the stalemate of Weimar politics (a disaffection shared by many intellectuals at the time); the fascination exerted by an extreme Nietzscheanism (as articulated chiefly in Jünger's writings); the concern with the fate of Europe in the midst of the struggle for world dominion (a concern promoting cultural revivalism and elitism); the attempt to "guide" Hitler's movement in the direction of a cultural or *geistig* resurgence (an attempt giving rise to an idiosyncratic or "private" National Socialism); the progressive disenchantment with the biologism and racism of Hitlerism and with the growing brutalization of the anticipated resurgence (a disenchantment entailing, at least philosophically, a kind of "inner emigration"); the preoccupation with the "darkening of the world" under the onslaught of planetary technology (a decline sealed by the outcome of the Second

World War). Pöggeler also points to reasons bearing on Heidegger's aloofness (from concrete politics) after 1945: a distrust in merely "restorative" tendencies (reminiscent of the Weimar period) as well as Heidegger's absorption with issues of planetary technology. Regarding the recanting of earlier pro-Nazi views—a prominent point in the accusations leveled at Heidegger—Pöggeler offers some personal testimony: "By stating forcefully at least in conversation that he was completely wrong in 1933 and that nothing could excuse this mistake, Heidegger also supported efforts to avoid such mistakes in the future."[30]

To be sure, all the foregoing cannot (and is not meant to) exculpate Heidegger's conduct in 1933 and later, on both a personal and a broader intellectual level. In personal terms, there are too many manifestations of pettiness, immodesty, occasional vindictiveness on Heidegger's part. There are also important acts of omission to be tallied: for instance, his persistent silence on Auschwitz and the Holocaust. Pöggeler correctly states that the comparison of Auschwitz with wartime mass killings neglects the fact that the inmates of the concentration camps were "killed before their death, namely, by being stripped of human dignity." I am also troubled by Heidegger's continued self-distantiation from modern democracy—although on this score, one may speculate responsibly about his reasons for being silent. From Heidegger's vantage, democracy or "popular rule" very likely signified a collective anthropocentrism or a collective will to power along humanist-metaphysical lines. Perhaps his scruples might have been eased by recent "nonfoundational" postmetaphysical conceptions of democracy. The issue of anthropocentrism was at the very heart of Heidegger's complaint against planetary technology, which he probably construed too readily in monolithic terms. One sees this in his assessment of America and Russia as purely technological powers. In my own view, Heidegger was largely ignorant of America and its culture—where the fascination with technology is clearly circumscribed by a great many historical and *geistig* factors. I tend to agree with Pöggeler's assessment regarding the deficiency of prudential judgment in Heidegger's outlook—although cultivating prudence need not (I believe) conflict with philosophical radicality.[31]

I also believe (with Pöggeler) that we should not be too quick to pronounce a verdict. Is not political invective also, Pöggeler asks, an attempt "to escape from those questions that Heidegger effectively posed for our time?" Here, polemics is decidedly counterproductive—or productive only of self-congratulatory conceit while undercutting the task of learning (even, and especially, from mistakes). Regarding world politics, how can one be sanguine about planetary technology at a time when through "star wars" (or Strategic Defense Initiatives) the struggle for world dominion is extended into outer space? For what purpose is this contest being waged? In the name of what spirit or nonspirit, *Geist* or *Ungeist?* As we know, Heidegger's philosophical animus was often directed against modern ideologies and "world views." Was he simply mistaken in regarding these as attempts to transform the globe into an instrument of human satisfaction and self-aggrandizement, or into an arena for implementing a master plan (or competing master plans)? Has the situation really changed that much since the time he wrote? More likely, problems have been aggravated by the linkage of Western ideology, particularly the ideology of rapid global "development," and worsening ecological conditions. Is there not good reason to be troubled by the reduction of nature and the global environment to a human tool, to the kind of "standing reserve" Heidegger always deplored in his comments on technology and "technicity" (*Technik*)? Is it reasonable to put Heidegger summarily aside here? Can we not learn from his reflections? Can we afford to ignore them?

Sometimes Heidegger is chided for having initiated or invented "nihilism"—or at least for having compounded Nietzsche's nihilistic outlook. But is this not blaming the messenger for the message? Are there not grounds for holding that if transformed into "values," goals to be implemented, traditional metaphysics must progressively deplete itself and create thereby an existential or ontological void? For both Nietzsche and Heidegger, nihilism was not a simple fact to be accepted but something to be wrestled and overcome. For both, nihilism could not be wished away. Contemporary assaults on nihilism would be well advised to heed Heidegger (and Nietzsche): they have, after all, mapped the problem and its solutions so tenaciously. Nihilism is also closely linked to the question of metaphysics and its standing in our time. For instance, certain of the "foundational" pillars of traditional metaphysics—consciousness, subjectivity, reason or *Geist* (in the sense of *logos*)—have become extraordinarily problematic. Heidegger struggled throughout his life with this sort of metaphysics and with the possibility of "overcoming" it. He wrestled with the question in a way that still remains challenging and instructive, far beyond the clamor raised by *l'affaire Heidegger*. In departing from foundational moorings, he ventured, however cautiously, into uncharted waters fraught with promise and peril. By center-staging this departure, Derrida's comments (in *De l'esprit*) accentuate a "nodal point"—perhaps the crucial thread—integrating Heidegger's sprawling opus; his comments also signify that Heidegger's departure was not willful, not merely a headlong plunge into irrationalism (as so many of Heidegger's critics have claimed).[32]

One of the chief merits of *De l'esprit* rests with its attention to the political implications of traditional metaphysics and the attempt to overcome it. As Derrida insists, the option for or against *Geist* is never politically risk-free; accordingly, Heidegger's halting (always ambiguous) distantiation from *Geist* was not simply a fall from innocence—say, from the presumed innocence of humanism or humanist liberalism. Derrida considers the *geistig* aura surrounding modern humanism and remarks: "It is not my intent to criticize this humanist teleology. It seems to me more urgent to realize that regardless of attempts to avoid or deny it, this teleology is *until today* (until Heidegger, but time and circumstances have not drastically changed) the price one has to pay for the ethically and politically motivated denunciation of biologism, racism, naturalism, and the like. I analyze this 'logic,' its aporias and limits." Given the linkage between *Geist* and ascendancy over nature (and otherness), the price is not politically negligible: in any event, one must weigh the gain and loss entailed in questioning a *Geist*-centered metaphysics: "What is required is a hitherto entirely unknown responsibility of 'thinking' and 'acting'— especially with regard to the future where the issue remains for us an imminent or impending dilemma." From Derrida's perspective, that dilemma—focused in Heidegger's thought—cannot be exorcised through *bonhommie* or a return to time-honored formulas. Only a steady probing could possibly make headway, although the prospects for resolving it are slim enough. As Derrida remarks: "Are we up against a fatality; can one escape it? Nothing speaks for the latter; there are no indications in its favor—either in the discourses of the 'Heideggerians' or in those of the 'anti-Heideggerians.' Can the dilemma be changed or transformed? I do not know."[33]

Though I endorse Derrida's account, I do not accept it altogether. For instance, I am not persuaded that Heidegger's statements on the so-called crisis of Europe were separated by any radical gulf (excluding even "analogies") from Husserl's nearly contemporaneous observations or from Paul Valéry's earlier reflections, particularly Valéry's complaint (in 1919) of an impending *capitis diminutio* of Europe. On my view, many of Heidegger's writings around 1935 were precisely motivated by concern about such a *capitis diminutio,* although his account of Europe obviously differed from Valéry's *geistig*-humanist conception. I am also uneasy about the treatment, in *De l'esprit,* of the matter of overcoming metaphysics, which occasionally suggests a simple exit from tradition: for instance, in the discussion of Heidegger's departure from Platonism and a Platonically inspired Christianity in the direction of an "earlier" promise (beyond morning-land and evening-land). Heidegger's direction is said to be "radically different" from that of traditional metaphysics, especially historical teleologies of the kind formulated by Hegel, Marx, and "some other thinkers of modernity." Heidegger's departure promises "more," something completely "other," than what metaphysics offers, but according to Derrida, it does so only because the conceptual passage is blocked (*ungangbar*): "What is dissimilar from origin in foundation appears from this vantage . . . as foundation, as *Geist* and as essence of Christianity." But these comments by Derrida neglect the complex interweaving of departure and continuity, of surpassing and preservation, which is the hallmark of Heidegger's path—which Derrida himself has so eloquently portrayed elsewhere. The same dichotomizing operates in the concluding imaginary dialogue, in *De l'esprit,* between Heidegger and "certain Christian theologians." Clearly, the postmetaphysical reading of Christianity (and the broader Judaeo-Christian tradition) does not mean a negation or denial of Christianity or Western civilization—any more than Heidegger's critique of Platonism means a "destruction" of Plato's teachings.[34]

More important there is a certain muffling of politics: an occasional tendency to separate texts from their contexts. We see it, for instance, in the discussion of Heidegger's reinvocation of *Geist* (its invocation without quotation marks) in violation of his earlier counsel of avoidance. But are not dates essential here? The quotation marks are first dropped in the rectoral address (1933), a public speech held in an atmosphere of rampant political rhetoric. Quotation marks are nuances, marks of subtlety— which would only have been wasted on Hitler's movement. By emphatically invoking the tradition of *Geist,* Heidegger deftly distanced himself from Nazi biologism. The appeal was intensified in 1935, in the *Introduction to Metaphysics,* when the last remaining quote marks were lifted. By that time, the Nazi regime had become firmly entrenched, and Heidegger had began the difficult process of political disentanglement.[35] Incidentally, apart from the rectoral address, Heidegger's use of *Geist* never signaled a simple return to the Platonic-Cartesian metaphysics. *Geist* was also prominently celebrated in the Schelling lectures of 1936, precisely as an antidote to biologism and militarism; but the term was reinterpreted as *pneuma* (rather than *logos*), as an agency subservient to love. From there, it was not far to the Hölderlin lectures and the portrayal of spirit of flame or fire or the outgrowth of fire—and with that, the way was cleared to construing *Geistlichkeit* (in the Trakl commentary) as a modality of time (or space-time) suffused with spirit as fire. Derrida fails to mention, however, that during the Nazi years Heidegger did not simply abandon quotation marks in discussing *Geist.* In his lectures on "The Ister" (1942), for instance, he often sets the term *Geist* in quotation marks in order to designate both the "spirit" of modern technology and the dominant category of German idealism. By this time, Hitlerism was clearly beyond salvage, beyond the pale of *geistig* rhetoric. My point is not to dwell on the role of quotation marks (to compound Derrida's strategy) but to suggest a closer link between Heidegger's rhetoric and the political context in which he spoke and wrote.[36]

I do not mean to "politicize" Heidegger's opus narrowly. In my opinion, ever since *Being and Time,* Heidegger's path was marked by an intensive labor: the struggle with the "overcoming" of metaphysics *and* with the political implications of doing so. His early counsel of avoidance and the later temporary suspension of this counsel testify to his effort to move beyond a *Geist*-centered metaphysics (*Geist* = *logos,* intellect, subjectivity) without lapsing into *Ungeist* or irrationalism. It is helpful, here, to recall Heidegger's indebtedness to Husserl, his former teacher and mentor, particulary the latter's warnings against the perils of "naturalism" and "historicism." Heidegger's departure from Husserl and transcendental idealism—in *Being and Time* and subsequently—should not be construed as repudiating these warnings. Alternatively put: the turn to the "question of being" (Heidegger's postmetaphysical thinking) must be read not as a relapse into objectivism but as an attempt to rethink the relationship between consciousness and phenomena, between spirit and world. Derrida links the dismissal of naturalism necessarily with the endorsement of *Geist* as transnatural spirit. He apparently despairs of Heidegger's transcending that bifurcation. I take a more hopeful view. On my view, the alternatives posed are not obligatory. On the contrary, Heidegger rules out naturalism and biologism, because they are only the correlates of intellect. Translated politically, the critique of modern ideologies (derived from metaphysics) cannot possibly support National Socialism or any kind of "naturalist" politics (neither nature nor human nature is merely "given"). *This* may well be the most urgent lesson to be drawn from *l'affaire Heidegger,* despite Heidegger's own meanderings.

This learning experience of Heidegger's is my central concern here. Safely ensconced ideologically, contemporary readers may consider themselves above the fray of political learning—mistaking thereby (I fear) their own condition and the point of *l'affaire Heidegger.* For Heidegger, the Weimar and Hitler years must have been a time of agonizing soul-searching. Reared in a Eurocentric (perhaps Germanocentric) culture— Europe having been for some two thousand years the very heart of the universe—he must have been deeply troubled by Europe's crisis and decentering. His initial response was a rallying call: a call for the "resurgence" of the *Geist* of Europe, the reassertion of European hegemony in the struggle for world dominion. Only slowly did he realize the futility of that pursuit: not merely because of Hitler's perversion of the European spirit (admittedly a major factor) but also (at a deeper level of analysis) because of the incompatibility of *Geist* and the drive for world dominion. Progressively, in his lectures on Hölderlin, Schelling, and Nietzsche, Heidegger turned away from the hegemony of power toward an acceptance of the disempowerment (*Entmachtung*) of spirit—not only as an external calamity but as the indigenous path of spirit itself. In doing so, he turned against the long-standing Western preoccupation with dominion, particularly with the spirit's right to rule (epitomized in the model of the Platonic philosopher-king). Only by abandoning mastery or the right to rule, only by enduring dispersal and submission, he realized, could spirit subsist as a generous source of human empowerment. Given his initial bent for leadership, this must have been a painful lesson—something akin to *metanoia* or the internal "highway to despair" described in Hegel's *Phenomenology*. In fact, this supplies one of the chief meanings of Heidegger's *Kehre,* which has been the target of so much speculation.

This turning has (I believe) general significance, particularly when reviewed against the struggle for world dominion. Given the prospect of a technological Armageddon, are there not good reasons for such a turning? And is not such a turning bound to be painful? On my view, one of the most dangerous effects of the (polemical) dismissal of Heidegger is the resulting silence about the need for *Kehre* (as sketched in his opus). In Heidegger's work, the turning involves first of all a move away from anthropocentrism and an anthropocentric will to power, as those are reflected in global politics and planetary technology. It involves a stand against the domestication of the earth, done in order to save some native or national culture. For Heidegger, the "native culture" in question was of course the German world. He has often been accused of harboring an extreme nationalism. But we should recall that during the Nazi years the Nazis themselves, and with growing urgency, Heidegger, portrayed the "homeland" as a promised land only at a distant horizon—far beyond the reach of any managerial mastery. In his lectures on Hölderlin, for instance, he compared German and Greek culture, assigning the former a special capacity for clarity and organization and assigning the latter an openness to the "fire from heaven." The task for Germans, he insisted, was not to be satisfied with their native endowment but to venture abroad—into the disapora of spirit as the only path for reaching something like home. "The finding of the proper in the encounter with the alien," the lectures of 1942 state, "is the path of homecoming," Heidegger subsequently expanded his horizon, beyond the German-Greek encounter, in a search for a new future beyond morning-land and evening-land. Should we silence this search for an alternative to the quest for world dominion? We still have the opening lines of Hölderlin's "The Ister" (together with Heidegger's comments): "Come now, fire! Anxious are we to see the day."[37]

NOTES

1. See *The Foucault Reader*, ed. Paul Rabinow (New York: Pantheon Books, 1984), pp. 381–82.

2. See Victor Farías, *Heidegger et le nazisme* (Paris: Verdier, 1987); and,

for the English version, *Heidegger and Nazism*, ed. Joseph Margolis and Tom Rockmore, trans. Paul Burrell and Gabriel R. Ricci (Philadelphia: Temple University Press, 1989). The book has been reviewed in leading newspapers by (among others) Thomas Sheehan, Richard Rorty, Michael Zimmermann, Jacques Derrida, and Jean Baudrillard. In large measure, it relies on research done by Hugo Ott and Berndt Martin. In the meantime, Ott has published his findings in a comprehensive work titled *Martin Heidegger: Unterwegs zu einer biographie* (Frankfurt: Campus, 1988). More judicious and sober than Farías's book, Ott's study is a less likely media event.

   3. Philippe Lacoue-Labarthe, who by no means exonerates Heidegger, is blunt on his score: "This book is profoundly unjust and I even consider it—weighing my words carefully—dishonest [*malhonnête*]" (*La Fiction du politique* [Paris: Bourgeois, 1987], p. 178). Unfortunately, not all commentators share this sense of fairness. While acknowledging the deficiencies in much of the accumulated "evidence," Thomas Sheehan proceeds to subscribe basically to the accuracy of Farías's account; he certainly makes no effort to sift the evidence or to introduce additional or countervailing evidence. See his "Heidegger and the Nazis," *New York Review of Books*, June 16, 1988, pp. 38–47, esp. p. 23 n. 5, where he speaks of the "sloppiness of Farías's notes" and the "tendentiousness of the French translations of Heidegger's statements."

   4. As Sheehan ("Heidegger and the Nazis," p. 44) writes: "Although he never accepted the party ideology in its entirety, particularly its racism and biologism, he did see Nazism as a movement that could halt the spread of Marxism and realize the ultraconservative vision of one of his favorite political theorists, Friedrich Naumann (1860–1919): the vision of a strong nationalism and a militantly anticommunist socialism, combined under a charismatic leader." Pierre Bourdieu describes Heidegger as one of the many German intellectuals or radical conservatives during the Weimar Republic calling for a "conservative revolution" that would offer a "third way" between Bolshevism and American capitalism: *L'ontologie politique de Martin Heidegger* (Paris: Minuit, 1975). Michael Zimmermann argues that Heidegger's "conservatism" was based on two interrelated beliefs: "(1) that the West was in the final stages of a long decline into industrial nihilism, and (2) that only a radical change could save Germany from this dreaded fate"; but he also adds that "there is no *necessary* relation between the conservative Heidegger's philosophy and the violent racism which we associate with Nazism": "*L'affaire* Heidegger," *Times Literary Supplement*, October 9–13, 1988, p. 1116.

   5. In the words of Lacoue-Labarthe: "Where is the 'philosophy' of Heidegger, or rather his thinking, if not in his texts? And what is at issue here: Heidegger's thinking or something else? If there is a '*cas Heidegger*'—which is not distinguished (to my knowledge) by any 'crime against humanity,' even though his silent complicity is terrifying—it is because there is the 'thinking of Heidegger,' " (*La Fiction du politique*, p. 187).

   6. *The Foucault Reader*, p. 383. As Foucault adds: "And how could it be otherwise, given that here the interlocutors are incited, not to advance, not to take more and more risks in what they say, but to fall back continually on the

rights that they claim, on their legitimacy, which they must defend, and on the affirmation of their innocence? There is something even more serious here: in this comedy, one mimics war, battles, annihilations, or unconditional surrenders, putting forward as much of one's killer instinct as possible. But it is really dangerous to make anyone believe that he can gain access to the truth by such paths.''

7. Joseph J. Kockelmans, *On the Truth of Being: Reflections on Heidegger's Later Philosophy* (Bloomington: Indiana University Press, 1984), pp. 262–63.

8. Ibid., pp. 264–65. Among the more "tendentious" works cited by Kockelmans are Paul Hühnerfeld, *In Sachen Heideggers* (Hamburg: Hoffman & Campe, 1961), and Guido Schneeberger, *Nachlese zu Heidegger* (Bern: Suhr, 1962).

9. See Otto Pöggeler, *Der Denkweg Martin Heideggers*, 2d ed. (Pfullingen: Neske, 1983), trans. Daniel Magurshak and Sigmund Barber, *Martin Heidegger's Path of Thinking* (Atlantic Heights, N.J.: Humanities Press, 1987). See also Pöggeler, *Philosophie und Politik bei Heidegger* (Freiburg: Alber, 1972), pp. 15–16.

10. See Annemarie Gethmann-Siefert and Otto Pöggeler, eds., *Heidegger und die praktische Philosophie* (Frankfurt: Suhrkamp, 1988), p. 8. The editors add: "From this vantage it would be misguided to equate Heidegger's philosophy substantively with certain political consequences: that is, to hold his thinking as a whole rather than the 'man' Heidegger responsible for the debacle whose scope and duration occupy most inquiries."

11. Pöggeler, "Heideggers politisches Selbstverständnis, in Gethmann-Siefert and Pöggeler, *Heidegger und die praktische Philosophie*, pp. 20–23; Heidegger, *Heraklit*, vol. 55 of *Gesamtausgabe* (Frankfurt: Klostermann, 1979), p. 123.

12. Pöggeler, "Heideggers politisches Selbstverständnis," pp. 27–29.

13. Ibid., pp. 19, 31–32. On Karl Jaspers, see his *Notizen zu Martin Heidegger*, ed. Hans Saner (Munich: Piper, 1978), p. 183; and Otto Pöggeler, "Den Führer führen? Heidegger und Kein Ende," *Philosophische Rundschau* 32 (1985): 26–27. For the rectoral address, see Martin Heidegger, *Die Selbstbehauptung der deutschen Universität* (1933), republished with *Das Rektorat 1933–34* (Frankfurt: Klostermann, 1983); trans. Karsten Harries, "The Self-Assertion of the German University," *Review of Metaphysics*, 38 (1985): 470–80, and "The Rectorate 1933/34: Facts and Thoughts," *Review of Metaphysics* 29 (1975–76): 481–502.

14. Letter from Karl Jaspers to Martin Heidegger, August 23, 1933, in Martin Heidegger and Karl Jaspers, *Briefwechsel 1920–1963*, ed. Walter Biemel and Hans Saner (Frankfurt: Klostermann and Piper, 1990), p. 155.

15. Quoted in Pöggeler, "Heideggers politisches Selbstverständnis," pp. 21, 30, 32–33. For a perceptive interpretation, see Graeme Nicholson, "The Politics of Heidegger's Rectoral Address," *Man and World* 20 (1987): 171–87.

16. Pöggeler, "Heideggers politisches Selbstverständnis," pp. 33–35, 39. Cf. also Martin Heidegger, *Hölderlins Hymne "Der Ister,"* vol. 53 of *Gesamtausgabe* (Frankfurt: Klostermann, 1984), p. 118. Regarding the lecture course on "Germania" and "The Rhine," see my "Heidegger, Hölderlin and Politics,"

Heidegger Studies 2 (1986): 81–95, reprinted in slightly revised form in *Margins of Political Discourse* (Albany: State University of New York Press, 1989), pp. 207–20. According to Hannah Arendt, Heidegger's so-called *Kehre* (turning) surfaced primarily in the shift of mood separating the Nietzsche lectures of 1936–37 from the wartime lectures on nihilism; see Arendt, *The Life of the Mind*, vol. 2, *Willing* (New York: Harcourt Brace Jovanovich, 1978), pp. 172–73.

17. Pöggeler, "Heideggers politisches Selbstverständnis," pp. 35–38; Martin Heidegger, *Einführung in die Metaphysik* (1935) vol. 40 of *Gesamtausgabe* (Frankfurt: Klostermann, 1983), pp. 40, 208, trans. Ralph Manheim, *An Introduction to Metaphysics* (New Haven, Conn.: Yale University Press, 1959), pp. 37, 199.

18. Pöggeler, "Heideggers politisches Selbstverständnis," pp. 42–47.

19. Ibid., pp. 23–24, 48–51, 54–57. See also Martin Heidegger, *Was heisst Denken?* 3d ed. (Tübingen: Niemeyer, 1971), p. 65, trans. J. Glenn Gray, *What Is Called Thinking?* (New York: Harper & Row, 1968), p. 66; and "Only a God Can Save Us: The *Spiegel* Interview (1966)," trans. William J. Richardson, in Thomas Sheehan, ed., *Heidegger: The Man and the Thinker* (Chicago: Precedent, 1981), p. 55.

20. Jacques Derrida, *De l'esprit: Heidegger et la question* (Paris: Galilée, 1987), pp. 16–19, 23. The title is adapted from Helvetius's well-known work, burned in Paris in 1759, regarding which Helvetius subsequently wrote an elaborate retraction or recantation (as Derrida mentions, p. 14 n. 1). The subtitle refers to the "question of being" and the shifting role of "questioning" in Heidegger's opus.

21. Ibid., pp. 11–12, 24–29. The translation is complicated by the fact that the English "spiritual" can stand for both *geistig* and *geistlich*. The difference might be elucidated as follows: If *Geist* captures the Greek *logos, geistig* might be rendered as "logical" or "*logos*-related." In contrast to the coincidence of *logos* and being in *Geist* and *geistig, geistlich* expresses the openness of thinking to the disclosure and otherness of being. In the following, I use "spiritual" for *geistlich* and "spirituality" for *Geistlichkeit*.

22. Derrida, *De l'esprit*, pp. 33–36, 40–42; Martin Heidegger, *Sein und Zeit*, 15th ed. (Tübingen: Mohr, 1979), par. 25, p. 117.

23. Derrida, *De l'esprit*, pp. 44–52. See also Heidegger, *Sein und Zeit*, par. 82, pp. 428–36.

24. Derrida, *De l'esprit*, pp. 53–58, 60–61; Heidegger, "The Self-Assertion of the German University."

25. Derrida, *De l'esprit*, pp. 63–66. The reference to spiritualization is a straightforward translation of the French (*spiritualiser*); it should not be taken in the sense of "spiritual" as *geistlich*.

26. Ibid., pp. 67–73.

27. Ibid., pp. 102–5, 107–8, 122–29. Derrida also alludes to Heidegger's Nietzsche lectures, but without pondering their progressive shift of accent. "During these same years (i.e., 1930s)," he writes (p. 117), "Heidegger's interpretive strategy is also concerned with Nietzsche. Its goal is to extricate Nietzsche

from biologistic, zoologistic, or vitalistic appropriations. This interpretive strategy is also a mode of politics; the extreme ambiguity of the gesture resides in the attempt to salvage a thought by surrendering it [to metaphysics]." See also Heidegger, *An Introduction to Metaphysics*, pp. 37–41; *Schellings Abhandlung Über das Wesen der menschlichen Freiheit (1809)*, ed. Hildegard Feick (Tübingen: Niemeyer, 1971), pp. 153–54; and *Hölderlins Hymne "Der Ister,"* pp. 150–70. Regarding the Schelling lectures, cf. my "Ontology of Freedom: Heidegger and Political Philosophy," in *Polis and Praxis* (Cambridge, Mass.: MIT Press, 1984), pp. 121–27.

28. Derrida, *De l'esprit,* pp. 131–35, 138–41, 145; Martin Heidegger, *Unterwegs zur Sprache* (Pfullingen: Neske, 1959), pp. 35–77, trans. Peter D. Hertz, *On the Way to Language* (New York: Harper & Row, 1971), pp. 159–98.

29. Derrida, *De l'esprit,* pp. 153–57, 175–76, 178–79. See also Heidegger, *Unterwegs zur Sprache,* pp. 59, 66; *On the Way to Language,* pp. 178, 185.

30. Pöggeler, "Heideggers politisches Selbstverständnis," p. 52.

31. Ibid., pp. 52, 56–57. Invoking a distinction familiar in French discussions, one might say that prudential judgment operates on the level of *la politique* (politics as policy), whereas philosophical radicality is more appropriate to *le politique* (politics understood as polity or as paradigm or framework). Regarding post-metaphysical conceptions of democracy, see, e.g., Claude Lefort, *Democracy and Political Theory,* trans. David Macey (Cambridge: Polity Press, 1988); and Ernesto Laclau and Chantal Mouffe, *Hegemony and Socialist Strategy: Towards a Radical Democratic Politics,* trans. Winston Moore and Paul Cammack (London: Verso, 1985); on the latter, cf. my "Hegemony and Democracy: A Review of Laclau and Mouffe," *Philosophy and Social Criticism* 13 (1987): 283–96.

32. For a critique along these lines, see Jürgen Habermas, *The Philosophical Discourse of Modernity: Twelve Lectures,* trans. Frederick Lawrence (Cambridge, Mass.: MIT Press, 1987), pp. 131–60.

33. Derrida, *De l'esprit,* pp. 66, 87–88.

34. Ibid., pp. 176–84; regarding the "crisis of Europe," see pp. 94–97. Heidegger refers explicitly to Valéry's "La crise de l'esprit" (1919) in "Hölderlins Erde und Himmel," in *Erläuterungen zu Hölderlins Dichtung,* vol. 4 of *Gasamtausgabe* (Frankfurt: Klostermann, 1981), pp. 176–77.

35. Derrida (*De l'esprit,* pp. 106–7) makes much of the fact that the definition of *Geist* in the rectoral address places the term in quotation marks but that these marks disappear two years later when Heidegger cites his own earlier definition.

36. *Hölderlins Hymne "Der Ister,"* pp. 66, 157–64. Actually, Heidegger uses *Geist* in these passages with and without quotation marks (virtually interchangeably).

37. *Hölderlins Hymne "Der Ister,"* pp. 6–9, 155–59. Cf. also these comments in the lectures of 1941–42: "The own or proper cannot be proclaimed like a dogma whose dictates can be implemented on command. The own is something that is most difficult to find and most easy to miss." See *Hölderlins Hymne*

"Andenken," vol. 52 of *Gesamtausgabe* (Frankfurt: Klostermann, 1982), p. 123. Two years later, in 1943, Heidegger spoke openly of the importance of emigration and diaspora for homecoming (*Erläuterungen zu Hölderlins Dichtung*, pp. 29–30).

13

Riveted to a Monstrous Site: On Heidegger's *Beiträge zur Philosophie*

REINER SCHÜRMANN

> . . . the as yet unnamable that announces
> itself—and cannot but announce itself that way,
> as is necessary each time a birth is in progress—
> in the species of a nonspecies, in the formless,
> mute, and terrifying form of monstrosity.
> —JACQUES DERRIDA,
> *L'écriture et la différence*

In what follows, I should like to glean from Heidegger's *Contributions to Philosophy*[1] some evidence for reading that text, just as well, as a monstrous "Contribution to Politics."

Why this text rather than another? Not, to be sure, because—following certain commentators—I consider it his masterwork.[2] Far from it. But, in a sense, *because* of this "far from it." First, these *Contributions* date from the years when Heidegger was painfully working through what he would later call his greatest blunder, committed a few years earlier; when, circumspectly, he dared in his courses to distance himself from the regime; and when he was writing under the most intense, combined influence of Hölderlin and Nietzsche. Next, this text deserves one's attention for the overdetermined legacy it bears. It is a disconcerting document indeed. The elevated tone easily veers toward exaltation: "No one understands what 'I' am *thinking* here" (BzP, p. 8). The language is more ponderous than in any of his other writings; at times one may think one is reading a piece of Heideggerian plagiarism, so encumbered is it with ellipses and assertoric monoliths. The uneven treatment of the trivialities—in the sense of the *trivium*: grammar, logic, rhetoric—makes for difficult reading. An atrophy of grammar (undernourishment of the sentence, often stripped of its predicate) and a cacotrophy of logic (misnourishment of the rules of discourse so as to make them perish) serve a hypertrophia (overnourishment) of rhetoric. Litotes, hyperbole, sentence fragments, questions left open, nouns reduced to their verbal origins: these and other rhetorical devices are meant, it seems, to undo in philosophical discourse the work of construction.

The masterwork of the thinking of being? Far from it—but doubtless Heidegger's most significant effort, because symptomatic. Far, as the center in the metaphysical arena is from the periphery. The text begins by tracing this periphery: we are living "the age of the transition from metaphysics to the historical thinking of being" (BzP, p. 3). Thus is traced the closure of an epoch, which it is impossible to leap over in order to place oneself abruptly outside it and so make an absolute break.[3] Centripetal forces, however, which there is reason to believe are not foreign to those that drew him to the administrative center of a model university, never cease to pull Heidegger's thinking back from the periphery. From the viewpoint of epochal history, the line of embarment that encloses our site accounts for all the embarrassments of this text. It is the schema of an epochal closure, just as much as the attempts to think otherwise, that makes it significant, monstrous.

Conventional wisdom holds that phenomenology remains incapable of any critical discourse, particularly as political regimes are concerned. Its method, it is claimed, condemns it to mere descriptions, whatever the political reality. Thus it would exclude itself from current debates around liberalism and democracy, to say nothing of socialism and its still viable forms.

In Heidegger's case, this objection is just not pertinent. His phenomenology is one of "worlds"—of economies, regions of manifestation, constellations of presencing, games of gathering (*legein*), contexts. We always stand inscribed in many such worlds, each of which is phenomenalized according to its own law (about which, more below). Now, to free these irreducibly plural worlds, Heidegger has to argue against all ultimacy claims based on the representation of some one covering law. The most enduring among such representations, maximized into ultimate referents, have been the Greek *cosmos*, the Latin *natura*, and modern subjectivity. Their epochalization provides Heidegger with a powerful tool for criticizing totalitarianism. Indeed, *totalitarianism conflates the ultimate referent constituting modernity with a regional referent constituting a given political world.* More precisely, National Socialism conflates subjectivity, our epoch's standard sense of being, and the subject

"German people." What makes the *Contributions* symptomatic is that in them, Heidegger, while denouncing it vehemently, also yields to the impulse of such conflation. To understand his philosophical reaction, after 1934, to the ideology of his day—and to sort out elements of collusion from elements of critique—one must inquire into the many places and postures in which the subject appears in his attempt at thinking being without maximizing representations: that is, at thinking it as event.

I first give the *Contributions* a topological reading, spelling out in a four-point inventory some of the gravitational forces that carry it toward the center of the very arena it seeks to delimit and to work to its very limits. After each such sketch of a focalizing strategy, I indicate in a few words the dispersive counterstrategy monstrously allied with it. Than I give the text a nomological reading, approaching the political from the point of view of the law. Through his understanding of *the law as broken from within*, Heidegger eliminates the very possibility of maximizing this or that representation as an ultimate standard, and hence of identifying it with a given collective subject. I ask: Under what law do the counterstrategies so indicated place our historical site—that is, us?

Embarments (Topological Reading)

What we found and create . . . alone will be true.
— MARTIN HEIDEGGER,
Beiträge zur Philosophie

Who?

The center where, as Heidegger never stops repeating, metaphysical strategies have from all time been interwoven, was and remains "man": the concept of representable beings endowed with attributes and capable of perfecting themselves, be it by ascending toward the universal, by entering into themselves, or, yet again, by progress. Now, in these pages, Heidegger just as tirelessly repeats: Who? who are we? A question not to be confused, to be sure, with that other one: What? what are we? The What ends up pointing toward the archive of humanist idealities; the Who, toward the self understood as a possible *gift of the times*. But this other response—other than humanist—appears only at the end of a complex series of detours, of decelerations and accelerations, in an itinerary of utterances that still issue from the most solid center of entitative doctrines regarding man, where the technique of representation and the logic of attribution sustain the thesis of perfectibility. "No one understands what 'I' am thinking here": the I who is thinking and who signs with his initials *M.H.* is still placed within a pair of quotation marks, holding the hegemony of the subject at bay; at that distance, that is, which is to separate the thinking that traces the history of the being-event from all historicist representations of entities. Elsewhere, the quotation marks disappear. Here is one specimen of that more ancient cloth, forming a text with the logic of things and the thesis of perfectibility that this logic helps to weave: "decision."

In the phenomenology of historical destiny, this word is to be taken literally. It designates the epochal breaks "severing" (*caedere*) eras of truth. The question Who? does not arise there, since such a (protostructuralist) phenomenology is concerned with processes of concealing-unconcealing, not with agents.

But it happens that alongside this aletheiological semantics of decisions-caesurae, one reads for instance: "Who decides? Every one." To the question Who? suddenly answers the sum total of humans capable of taking a decision. The persistence of the subject in its most entitative form is flagrant indeed. And what is at stake as a result of *this* decision, posited as one posits an act? "The *rescue* of beings"—that is to say, the rescue of a collective subject, for these beings are "the West." It is difficult not to construe a decision such as this after the modern paradigm of consciousness. Decision so recentered appeals most obviously to an agent and to effects emanating from him, when formulated as an alternative: either "found *truth* and recreate beings," or else succumb to "anesthesia," to the lack of creative and founding efficacy, which carries the gravest consequences (BzP, pp. 100–101). Whence the call, also reiterated, for creators (*die Schaffenden*) and founders (*die Gründer*).

The few who are to create and found the site from which the many will then decide where to go: this model of decision is generally "political" and doubtless more specifically "populist." What does it presuppose here? One might well believe oneself in the thick of an anthropology of capacities or faculties, where the possible denotes acts in our power: "Who is capable [*wer vermag*], and when, and how?" (BzP, p. 353). *Being and Time* had taught us to inquire about ourselves (and about the possible) in another way than in accordance with our powers (*Vermögen*). In addition, action is to be focused on an aim, on an end, on a founding. "Why? (an appeal to grounding)" (BzP, p. 258). *Kant and the Problem of Metaphysics* had taught us to understand groundings, too, in another way. Furthermore, in order to "overthrow today's man," the latter "must step out of his current basic constitution." Is this not asking the utmost of freedom as the seat of acts *in potestate nostra*? Last, the anthropologism is patent when Heidegger suspects his contemporaries of not measuring up. To step out of his mode of being "is perhaps already asking of today's man something impossible" (BzP, p. 248). *On the Essence of Truth* had taught us to understand freedom in another way.

Counterstrategy, now, concerning the Who: The self will be inscribed in discordant times and will thereby be wrested from the grasp of the modern hegemony of self-consciousness. The double bind of appropriation and expropriation will constitute it as tragic.

"The Last God"

The final section of the *Contributions* (at least prior to the trustees' editing)[4] is titled "The Last God." The phrase recalls first of all the theology of salvation as it was practiced by Heidegger (and Rudolf Bultmann) in their weekly sessions in Marburg a decade earlier: a theology of *eschata* (last things), not in the sense of an outcome to occur at the end of time but in the sense of the fullness of salvation offered in the instant. The phrase is overdetermined, however, by an intimation of essence. It connotes the possibility that widely differing experiences of the divine found in both the Greek and the biblical traditions can be gathered together in a single nucleus (*das Gottwesen*; BzP, p. 406) and extracted from their speculative and religious gangue. This resurgence of Husserlian idealist essentialism in the notion of *Wesen* is as provisional as it is unexpected. Finally, there occurs a return of the theory of *kairos* (the opportune moment) which Heidegger, in the early 1920s, had hoped to make the core of a study on Aristotle that never got written. The word "last" is indeed to be understood in a temporal sense, designating not, to be sure, the endpoint of some time span but an instant marking an epoch. Everything which, for the past two and a half millennia, has been held to provide salvation would then be reduced to its quintessence, as it were, and gathered together in a now. This critical moment, when the phenomenological truth of the divine in its numerous past acceptations could become the "own" (*eigen*) of a historical human type, would be the event (*Ereignis*) to come. It was thought to be a possible event, for which Heidegger during the mid-1930s was attempting to prepare the way. Concerning the last god, he takes up an expression of the prophet Elijah (1 Kings 19:11), and speaks of this god's "passing" (*Vorbeigang*).

Counterstrategy, now, concerning the divine: Heidegger suggests (but without providing any definite outline) a more pagan god, one that he does not name: a god venerated since remote antiquity for his resistance (through flexibility) to all forms of representation and co-optation— Proteus. Given his tenacious labor of decentering, Heidegger may well have meant to say, toward the end of his life: Only Proteus can save us now.

The People

This becomes an issue for Heidegger as a direct consequence of the being question. In the first beginning—the Greek—where they become problematical, the phenomena of the city and of being overlap in many ways. They share the same "poietic" and linguistic characters (in its gathering, being utters itself and sets itself to work, just as the city is, above all, the space instituted by the word); the same "technical" manifestation of *phusis* (*technē* of inscribing within bounds whatever shows itself); the same agonistic character due to the undertow affecting the city (its archaic past in the sense of the pre-Doric: that is, the heroic) as well as being (its "expropriation"). Last, they share the same nomic essence, as both are sites of a gathering (*legein*, whence a certain redundance in defining man as a living thing either "endowed with *logos*" or "political"). These are but so many intersecting meanings reflected by the proximity of words (*polis-pelein*). They are so many features, too, connecting "the act that founds a political state" with the act that produces a work of language.[5] In the Greek beginning, there is being as both extradiscursive and discursive gathering together: the kinship of Solon and Homer.

The same features—obviously neither exhaustive nor systematic—would also mark the rebeginning, the repetition, the retrieval, the refounding after a long history of forgetfulness. Now one must take a good look at the role assigned to Germany in this other beginning. As the young Hegel as well as Marx had first observed, followed unanimously by the subsequent tradition, nineteenth-century Germany had no being of its own. Heidegger shares this view: Germany still has no being in accordance with any of the features just mentioned.[6] In Hegelian terms (turned, however, against the system of objective Mind), the state remains for Heidegger a *notion*, something abstracted from everydayness. But only a concrete gathering, in the sense of the everyday, can become phenomenal. The properly political phenomenon will therefore be not the state but the people. Put the other way around: It will be termed "people," the sort of gathering capable of becoming a phenomenon in accordance with the features mentioned. The philosophical impetus behind Heidegger's administrative commitments is to be found in the kinship these features suggest between the question of being and that of politics, a kinship rooted in *legein*.

The founding in the realm of language, responding to the Greek epic, then bears the name of Hölderlin. For a few months, Heidegger also thought he could name the new Solon. The *Volk*,[7] at any rate, is to be understood as a gathering brought about by a founding utterance (*technē* assigning its limits to "natural" language), in ceaseless struggle with the concealment traversing from within and dispersing every poetic, as well as every political, configuration.

The return of representational thinking is no less obvious here than it was in the case of the Who? and of the last god. One cannot help feeling disturbed as one recalls that the step beyond *Being and Time* was meant precisely to disencumber thinking from the remnants of subjectivism that still burdened the Existential Analytic. In the *Contributions,* those remnants appear in Heidegger's oscillations between the particular (which always results from an operation of individuation starting out from a referent posited as universal) and the singular (a referent that lies outside all positions, universals, and individualizing operations). He rehabilitates the same old prestige of the particular for the Who? and the god and the people, while attempting to retain the singular more firmly than ever—more pathetically, as we shall see. There is the universal "people," particularized in the Greek, the Roman, the German, and so on. Contrary to what one might believe at first sight, it is not with his attention to entities that Heidegger invalidates the very phenomenological project he unrelentingly claims for himself (singular beings alone—the temple of Paestum, this pitcher, that bridge, to cite some well-known examples—allow one to *diasozein ta phainomena* [Eudoxus of Cnidus], "to save and preserve what shows itself"); it is with the representation of ideal entities. Germany must fulfill the idea. This collective subject must step into the *topos* historically occupied by ultimate referents, a *topos* Heidegger otherwise *denounces* as the nest of all metaphysical illusions.

Counterstrategy, now, concerning the "people": Heidegger will never undo the tie linking *pelein* to *polis* (which is not to say that he will keep conflating ultimate [i.e., metaphysical] with regional [e.g., political] referents; he will, on the contrary, work through the first so as to overcome them, and fracture the second so as to destabilize them). The questions of politics and of being will always raise for him one and the same problem of "gathering." A thought of being, however, which has been freed from subjectivism—if such a thinking is at all to come within our reach—forces one to think of politics in another way. The strategy of decentering in the *Contributions* struggles with this transition. The gathering can then no longer take place around, or by, or on a self-conscious subject such as the people. It will place every *single* phenomenon within the normative double bind of gathering and dispersion, of unconcealing and concealing, of appropriation and expropriation.

The Contingency of Being-There

The task of particularizing the idea remains, for "the 'people' is *not yet* the essence of the people [*das* noch nicht *volkhafte 'Volk'*]" (BzP, p. 398). The quotation marks signal Heidegger's disenchantment with the movement of the day. In 1936, the essence of the people—without quotation marks this time, as one commonly speaks of things common—remains as yet to be established. As previously, the mutation in being-man remains in arrears, since the uprising (*Aufbruch*) of 1933, it can be conjectured, had not fulfilled its promises. The "principle of the people" (*ein 'völkisches Prinzip'*; BzP, p. 42) will still have to provide the standard for the wholly other being-man, but one has henceforth to await the domination by the founders to come. What would these have to found? With the people, Heidegger removes to the sphere of the not-yet the *there* by which, in the earlier Existential Analytic, he had sought to break up subjectivist solipsism. The postponement of the *there* holds the Who? in suspension, just as it delays the passing of the last god and puts off, until some remote tomorrow, the popular uprising. "*Man* transmutes himself by founding being-there" (BzP, p. 230). Only when the "people" will have become a people (no more quotation marks, for we "dare [to use] immediate speech"; BzP, p. 239), being-there shall be. "*Being*-there is nothing but *moment* and history" (BzP, p. 323): moment, as it finitizes human gathering as never before; history, as it thereby founds a beginning other than the Greek. The *there* remains thus still "to be prepared" (BzP, p. 231), and being-there—in an explicit critique of *Being and Time*—"the ground of a determinate being-human: of the one that is yet to come" (BzP, p. 300). Such is now the surprising contingency of being-there. It may, and it may not, come to be.

With this ontic singularization of the *there*, the historical or destinal obviously collapses onto the historiological or historicist. The historical is always measured in Heidegger by the scale of being as it gives itself to and at the same time withholds itself from thinking. The modes of these gifts and these withholdings spell out the epochs in our destiny, thereby determining what at any given time it is possible and impossible for humans to do, to will, to experience. The historiological is measured by a different scale, one that is just the converse of epochal concealing and unconcealing. Here, facts such as inventions, revolutions, and other seizures of power—the will of leaders, the consensus of rational agents, and so on—determine the periods of history. Thus, each time Heidegger ventures in subsequent writings to *date* the beginning (for instance, with Parmenides) and the end (for instance, "in three hundred years")[8] of the history of being's self-withholding, there lurks a risk of succumbing to a second-order positivism where acts, including philosophical acts, mark turning points in history.

Now if January 30, 1933, did not start the hoped-for renewal, the breakthrough to a new type of man still remains possible at a later date. Heidegger does not hesitate to describe the forms of power, both exoteric and esoteric, capable of leading us there. In order to stand up to the isomorphism that has come to envelop the planet, "the dominion over the 'freed' (that is to say, uprooted and egotistic) masses is to be established and maintained through the constraints of 'organization.' " This seems to be what he has to say about government. Simultaneously, another, more hidden domination is needed for the sake of the renewal ahead. "Here it is a matter of preparing the future [founders] who will create new sites on which to stand within being itself." And he adds that both forms of domination, the exoteric and the esoteric, "have to be willed by those who know" (BzP, pp. 61–62). Willed to what end? To found *Da-sein* understood as an ontic possibility.[9]

Reading *Being and Time*, who would ever have thought that a few years later Heidegger would submit being-there to the will of a few? This establishment of a contingent will ruling over the *there* determines the anthropologism, the theologism, and the populism we have just seen.

Counterstrategy, now, concerning that contingency: Heidegger will remove the *there* from the hegemony of self-consciousness. The *there* arises as a possibility, he will say, from the *fractured instant*. The temporality (*Temporalität*) of being, out of reach for an analytic starting from ecstatic temporality (*Zeitlichkeit*), will then become thinkable by means of the double bind of a given phenomenalization and, within it, a singularization to come: that is to say, as tragic temporality.

Such is the profound ambivalence of the contributions to politics operative in the "contributions to philosophy." It results from the monstrous overdetermination of being's event-historical sense by a subjectivist-epochal sense.

Concerning an analogous shift in another text of Heidegger's, written during the same years, that contamination of deconstruction by subjectivity has been judged fatal.[10] Fatal, yes, if *fatum* is meant to render *Geschick*: destiny, sending, "mittence" (an awkward Latinization, though). But fatal in the sense that the persistence of the human, divine, national, historical subject would lead to the ruin, even the death of the deconstructive project, that this project would thereby suffer a fatal blow—that seems to me much more difficult to argue. One might as well assert that attributive grammar is itself harmful or deadly for thinking (and indeed it is, for a thinking—not Heidegger's—that claims to implant itself firmly outside the metaphysical closure). What could be more "metaphysical" than to determine a grammatical subject by means of a predicate? It is therefore indispensable to grasp the "destinal" necessity which, after 1934, continues in Heidegger to encumber the *other* thinking by the system of the *same*.

The double level of writing (for the public and for the initiate), the tactics for mastery on both levels, the calculation of dates, the conjunction of preparatory knowledge and will, the creation (not the reception, as he will later say) of sites in being, and, finally, the kerygma announcing a type of humanity to come: all of these obviously form a system, and a "system" in just the sense Heidegger has tirelessly sought to dismantle. Does one not hold with the eidetics of the Who?, of god, of the people, and of factual history the branches of a tree-diagram modeled on Porphyry or Descartes, only revised on the drawingboard of historical consciousness?

Perhaps so, at least if the trunk of this new *arbor Porphyreana* were to promise in its turn some eidetics of being. Only then would the totalitarian impulse—the conflation of the German collective subject with subjectivity as the modern standard sense of being—triumph. On this point, however, there is no compromise, no contamination, no hesitation at all. Being, in the *Contributions,* is understood as "event." It can be said in many ways—for example, in the singular and in the plural—but never as the starting point of a dieresis. The event like tree trunk grafted with eidetic branches remains monstrous: it possesses that monstrousness which Jacques Derrida himself, in the lines quoted in the epigraph above, has so pertinently shown to be an epochal necessity; a monstrousness which never ceases to turn Heidegger's contribution to politics into claudication.

The Integrative Violence of the Law (Nomological Reading)

As regards the founding of the essence of
being's truth, "logic" itself is an illusion,
though the most necessary illusion that the
history of being has known up to now.
    —MARTIN HEIDEGGER,
        Beiträge zur Philosophie

It remains to be shown how, in the *Contributions to Philosophy*, Heidegger moves away from the conflation of regional and ultimate referents: that is, away from the totalitarian impulse. The book indeed provides also contributions to politics in a sense other than crypto-subjectivist. This other sense has to do with the law. It denatures the genealogy of *logos-lex* legitimacy and renders the law itself monstrous. What is said of *logos* in the lines quoted above applies also to the law. *Logos* and *lex* designate functions of any focal meaning of being: *logos*, its function of gathering phenomena into a constellation; *lex*, its function of subsuming them under one principle or referent.

In those lines Heidegger states one feature common to all ultimate representations. The Greek *cosmos*, Latin *natura*, modern subjectivity, and all other archic representations hinge on this "most necessary illusion," logic, itself understood as the corpus of norms for truth. Heidegger's critique of those representations supposes that with regard to the principial—in particular, transcendental—*logos*, he takes a step back toward the tragic *logos*. This distance alone allows him to describe logic as "an illusion whose essence lies even deeper than the 'dialectical illusion' made visible by Kant" (BzP, p. 461). He could not state better the radicalization he inflicts on the modern critique of totalizing speculations. For Kant, their illusion unceasingly mocked and tormented (*zwackt und äfft*) reason.[11] Their megalomania kept the natural metaphysician in us alive, as every search for conditions necessarily postulated the unconditioned. If, in Heidegger, postulates *per thesin* trick us out of a "more necessary" historical necessity, it is because they bear upon being independently of its fixation around the normative ego and its antecedents. Here, necessity results not from a system of *a priori* acts but from the tragic double bind of life-death (better: natality-morality).[12] How, now, does the logical illusion with its nomic function arise from this double bind?

In epochal history, one phantasm of the universal always commands any given economy of present beings. "Commanding" here means that logic proves to be illusory in its *work of subsumption*. To show how, it may suffice to point out in the logic of the same (a) the interest that speaks through it and (b) the understanding of being that is reflected in it, as well as (c) the originary conflict that it covers up. These incursions into "metaphysical" territory—which constitute its terrain as such (but that is another problem)—aim at anything but bringing in some verdict on the past. What is at stake each time is rather our own historical possibility carved out indirectly by these incursions.

Interest

In logical subsumption (a redundancy, anyway) an interest declares itself. Heidegger suggests this first, speaking as a symptomologist of modern times. "The dread before being has never been as great as today. The proof: the gigantic staging by which we attempt to surmount this dread" (BzP, p. 139). He describes the gigantic therapeutic contriving as an all-pervasive "operative machination" (*Machenschaft,* a word that expresses at once making [*poiesis* and *technē*], sinister maneuvering,[13] and the collapse of *physics* into "that which produces itself"; BzP, p. 126). Later he was to describe the same thetic contriving as "positional enframing" (*Gestell*). Both descriptions suggest one and the same phenomenon. The dread that has become unbearable hints at it, for all to feel; the most rigid institutionalize fixity (which, in these late 1930s, has thus become one instance of a planetary development) displays it for all to see; it is called need for security. In the logical fixation of being, conceived to make true the phenomena so fixed, "the unwavering assurance against all insecurity" (BzP, p. 203) is sought. In what attracts us as logically true, the interest in safety grips us from within (by the need for consolation) and from without (by the need for consolidation). It also drives the entire history of truth from the time *physis* came to denote self-production up to the global reach of contemporary technicity. The referents supported by the historical illusions have thus nothing disinterested about them. If they have been able to maintain themselves over quasi-pharaonic millennia, it is because they have served as our bearings for damming up anguish in the face of instability. Whence a first indirect feature of "the essence of the truth of being" as event: it will have to be thought of otherwise than as guaranteeing stability (otherwise too, obviously, than as the determinate negation of the stable, such as flux, becoming, or movement).

Understanding

The understanding of being reflected in the logic of subsumption can only have been fashioned so as to satisfy, without remainder, the need for assurance-security-safety. Without remainder—whence the attraction (and the word) of the universal. The illusion, one and unique in this, arises as one "posits something before oneself, in its *koinon* and its *katholou*" (BzP, p. 477); as one turns an aggregate of "this" and "that" toward what is common to them from one general point of view (*ad unum vertere*: to "universalize"). Whether such positing of the universal, the common, and the general operates through defining, predicating, or naming, it always results from inflating one phenomenon beyond the limits of manifestation. Standards such as the *cosmos, natura,* and subjectivity has been "maximized" (*aufgesteigert;* BzP, p. 246) out of one finite experience. The operation of standard-setting cuts philosophy loose from any attachment to phenomena. This observation allows Heidegger to argue against the very posit of ultimate referents, hence also against their—totalitarian—conflation with regional referents. Yet it also prompts a most troubling question: On what basis have the universal, the common and the general "assumed [*angemasst*] an eminent rank" (BzP, p. 477)? What has been the impetus behind the hubris (*Anmassung*) of the universal posited as the sole standard (*Mass*) for the true? The question is one of phenomenology, not of some explanatory etiology. If the illusion vitiates our languages, then the *regional* games of singulars and their phenomenalization open the space for all speech and hence for words. What falls victim to critique, however, are ultimate subsumptions as well as the law they impose. In what way has their hubris come to us? From a historical point of view, one would have to answer: through the ancient construction of causes and the modern construction of conditions. From the point of view of being, the answer would be: through the representation of a true beingness, cause as well as condition of beings. The sway of the illusion is only secondarily due to the concatenation of epochs. It is due first of all to the fact that the truth of being has been cleansed of its intrinsic discord (which cleansing is nothing other than *epechein*): that is, of the concealment-unconcealment that the step back toward the event is to restore. Being could turn into a reliable ground only once purified of everything recalling tragic antagonisms. It could come to render services of assurance only once reduced to the same, integrating all otherness within the empire of a *logos* more powerful than which nothing could be conceived.

Ordinary Conflict

Normative maximization is an illusion because it covers up the originary strife of appropriation-expropriation. Yet both everydayness and our historical site make us more familiar with that strife than with anything else: everydayness, through the double bind of life and death (natality and mortality), and history, through that of modern pathology (archism and anarchism). Everydayness and history thereby manifest truth in its conflict of unconcealment-concealment. How does the logical illusion arise from that double bind? Answer: by the manic denial—the thought-lessness, in other words—of life posing as if the expropriating, conceal-ing, mortal, anarchic undertow were not. I take Heidegger to state the one issue that guides his critique of totalitarianism as he asks: "Entering into being-there, its instant and its place: how does this occur in Greek tragedy?" (BzP, p. 374). Answer: always through assenting to the double bind by which, in Aeschylus and Sophocles, the law of the family lineage undermines the law of the city, and conversely.

For Heidegger, the task of thinking amounts to retrieving this poly-morphic undertow. The task is complicated by its polymorphism. Thus he speaks of the event at times in the plural, designating the openings of epochs, where being refuses itself (*epechein*), all the while granting an economy; and at times in the singular, designating the disparity that "*keeps* the standard" (BzP, p. 510) in such refusing and such granting. If the reversals in our past have displaced the logical illusion in accordance with some hegemonic hold, in retrospect their consecution signals in the direction of a forgotten, entirely other hold. Phantasms have been able to rule as law, only inasmuch as they have been kept by being itself as event (*das steht beim Seyn selbst;* BzP, p. 492). A thinking that acquiesces in the double bind may be nihilist, relativist, and anything else one likes to show upon epochal phenomenology; it is all this in that it recognizes the historical differing that opposes points of reference lacking any common name. But such a thinking is, first of all, tragic in that it recognizes the differing within the event, which opposes concealment and expropriation in the condition of being to unconcealment and appropriation. Again, it takes a manic denial of tragic truth to cry nihilism in reading Heidegger. The strife between normative referents for the true only reflects the strife within originary truth itself, a strife for which "being qua being" is bound to remain nameless.

Acquiescence to originary discordance summarizes all of Heidegger's efforts after 1934. To suggest its an-archic "contribution to politics," it will have to suffice to sketch the archic concordance forced by normative phantasms. Such concordance results from the integrative violence of the law, spreading isomorphism.

In jumping from strategy to strategy, the *Contributions* not only thematizes the monstrous passage to the normative limits; it carries it to completion. Thus, Heidegger first speaks *under* the rule of self-consciousness. Then all of a sudden he speaks from somewhere else, pointing to the transgressive strategy in every argument for ultimacy. Whence is he speaking then? Where is he who says: Ultimate norms are illusions whose legisltive institution and whose transgressive destitution depend on being itself? Clearly, a discourse such as this no longer issues from the epochal ascendancy of consciousness and subjectivity. If it still did, how could it render that ascendancy problematical? The enterprise may rather be compared to the question "What is metaphysics?" To raise it, he was to say later, "is, in a sense, to have left metaphysics."[14] In a sense. The same is true here. He asks: What are the phantasmic illusions that are more necessary than the transcendental? The question can no longer be raised in the broad daylight of transcendental subjectivism. From what place, then? Not, to be sure, from some extrametaphysical satellite or some new wave washing beyond the antisubjectivist tidal wave. These are but so many reactive effects to that last "old sun" (unless it is the worldnight's moon), the ego. Heidegger does not leave the terrain where the substitutes for the Platonic sun continue to rule. He speaks instead from the blank place (*offene Stelle*; BzP, p. 510) that has been gaping in consciousness from the time of its normative institution. He speaks from the place of the innermost rent (*der innigste Riss*) in the modern theticism of the same, a rent first apparent in Kant in the disparate modes of positing (being as *Setzung* and as *Position*)[15] where night turns into twilight the leaden evidence of noon. This is something quite different from declaring cheerfully that metaphysics has ended and that one has only to decide to change terrain by brutally placing oneself outside.

Principal theticism becomes problematical from the site, our own, where the fragility of the modern normative posits has become the most widely spread piece of information in the Western world. Just like the experience of Oedipus, this new evidence may open one's eyes. From the blank place in pathetic consciousness Heidegger will end up being able to describe the discordance that rends the event and that has broken all epochal referents. But—and this alone is important here—speaking from that blank rent, he can describe those referents themselves both in their subsumptive effectiveness and in their hubris. With a strong dose of polemics he traces them back to Greek key concepts such as *harmonia, eudaimonia,* and *entelecheia:* "The fissuring of being must not be patched up by the fabricated semblance of compromises, of "happiness' and of false accomplishments" (BzP, p. 406). So much for the equalizing beginning. Allusions to the Stoa, to Plato and Aristotle, are barely concealed. Beingness has been phantasized to reconcile what being as event fissures. Then, here is what he has to say about the normative force of these illusory reconciliations: the subject runs "the danger of revolving around itself and of idolizing what are only conditions for its permanence, to the point of turning them into its *unconditioned*" (BzP, p. 398). This time, Heidegger reads the genealogical history from its end, where the subject revolves around itself, literally making a world of its own representations. Whether it designates the individual or the people, the ego raises its own identity to the level of an idol, postulating it as the ultimate condition for the sake of consoling and consolidating itself. The description of idolization is obviously pertinent for every equalization posited as normative. Heidegger does not hesitate to name a few of these illusions—one and all, versions of logolatry—which have served to force the tragic disparity within the event into some guarantee of the same.[16] How is being understood if it is to lend itself in this way to the phantasms of the same? "Only that properly is which endures in being present" (BzP, p. 115). Hegemonic phantasms invade thinking only after all topological incommensurability has been smoothed over by *commonplaces:* only after the discordant event has been leveled off into the universal as what remains identical and common. The agent of such leveling-off is the law.

What indeed is a representation to be called whose job it is to force into isomorphism all other representations measured by its yardstick? What is of its essence *the same* for an entire class of cases, and before which all are *equal?* Such a representation is called a law. To speak of equality before the law amounts then to yet another redundancy. The law is defined by the equality it imposes on subjects and cases, just as its subjects and cases are defined by the law that equalizes them. "All men are mortal"; "The square of the hypotenuse is equal to the sum of the square of the other two sides of a right triangle"; "Oviparous animals

reproduce by means of eggs hatching outside the female's body; vivipa-
rous, by bringing forth living young"; "Thou shalt not kill"—in every
case, a law gives a figure to the same, and it always makes equal the
cases, the facts, particulars, subjects, human practices, and natural
processes for which it "obtains." Without integrative violence there is
no law, and without the law, no isomorphism. To obtain, to be valid and
fit: all this means to be strong—to exercise integrative violence. What
then is more violent than a "value" posited in order to impose on
disparate singulars some figure of the same, turning them into *affinitive
particulars?*

Such is at least the work of the law as it appears through the strict
reciprocity between a standard and the standardized. It appears in an
entirely different light from the perspective of the event that breaks an
opening, not for the universal concordance among particulars, but for the
conflictual discordance among singulars. This is tragic law, thinkable by
mortals who have unlearned to philosophize death away manically.

NOTES

1. Martin Heidegger, *Beiträge zur Philosophie* (1936–38), vol. 65 of *Gesamtausgabe* (Frankfurt: Klostermann, 1989); cited hereafter as BzP. The present
article is fully understandable only in conjunction with three related papers of
mine: in K. Harries, ed., *Heidegger on Art, Politics, and Technology* (New
Haven, Conn.: Yale University Press, forthcoming); in M. R. Zinman, ed.,
*Science, Reason, and Modern Democracy: The Problem of Technology in the
Western Tradition* (Ann Arbor: University of Michigan Press, forthcoming); and
in *Graduate Faculty Philosophy Journal* (forthcoming).

2. For a quarter-century, Otto Pöggeler has kept his readers in suspense;
the *Beiträge* alone, he claimed, contains Heidegger's genuine thinking, which the
lectures and public courses merely make accessible to a more general audience:
Der Denkweg Martin Heideggers (Pfullingen: Neske, 1963), p. 145. The *Beiträge*
is said to constitute his "major work proper [*das eigentliche Hauptwerk*]":
"Heidegger und die hermeneutische Theologie," in *Verifikationen: Festschrift für
Gerhard Ebeling* (Tübingen, 1982), p . 481.

3. Jacques Derrida's strategy has been "to decide to change terrain, in a
discontinuous and irruptive fashion, by brutally placing oneself outside, and by
affirming an absolute break": *Margins: Of Philosophy,* trans. A. Bass (Chicago:
University of Chicago Press, 1982), p. 135. This might be read as a description of
events in France at the time the essay was finished—"May 12, 1968" (p. 136)—
were the proclamation of a future "which breaks absolutely" not a leitmotif in
Derrida; cf. the "Exergue" to his *Of Grammatology,* trans. G. C. Spivak
(Baltimore: Johns Hopkins University Press, 1974), p. 5.

4. See the editor's postscript, BzP, p. 514.

5. Martin Heidegger, *Poetry, Language, Thought,* trans. A. Hofstadter (New York: Harper & Row, 1971), p. 62.

6. The modern national states seem to be taken by Heidegger as avatars of Roman republicanism, if not of Caesarism: "The Roman relation to beings is managed by the *imperium,*" he wrote in 1942–43; from this imperial conception of being stems Roman law (*ius,* deriving from *iubeo,* "I command"). Now this "Roman essence of truth finds its completion . . . in the nineteenth century": *Parmenides* (lecture course of 1942–43), vol. 54 cf. *Gesamtausgabe* (Frankfurt: Klostermann, 1982), pp. 65, 86. On Heidegger's deliberate obliteration of the concept of state, see the following note.

7. It is needless to set one's nerves on edge over this word. Its theoretical usefulness goes back a long way: it has to do with German quarrels over the concept of state. From at least the time of Friedrich List, "political economy" has been rendered in German as *Volkswirtschaft;* the League of Nations was the *Völkerbund;* since Kant, "international law" has been *Völkerrecht,* and so on. Among German theorists of the eighteenth and nineteenth centuries, the word "people" had no ethnic connotations; it was a terminological choice due primarily to negative motives. One has only to open Adam Smith to see how fluid the concept of "nation" was at the time. The concept of state was no better suited to the Germans by reason of their *Kleinstaaterei* and their *Vielstaaterei*—the proliferation of their mini-states. In the social sciences and philosophy, *Volk* was used to avoid these semantic difficulties. In the mid-1930s, in opposition to the word's univocal use under National Socialism, Heidegger appeals to its polysemy. The "abandonment by being," he writes, appears in particular in the "total insensitivity to polysemy [*Vieldeutigkeit*]." Thus the word "people" evokes at once that which characterizes "the community, the race, that which is low and inferior, the nation, that which endures" (BzP, p. 117). This *pollachôs legetai* is instructive, since the last of these ways "the people" is said, barely conceals a polemic against what does not endure: the state—from which Heidegger had just withdrawn his services. Neither in *Being and Time* (§ 74) nor in BzP can the word *Volk* be taken without some *argumentum baculinum* to support the thesis of a persistent ultranationalism on Heidegger's part.

8. "Only a God Can Save Us Now" (interview with *Der Spiegel*), trans. D. Schendler, *Graduate Faculty Philosophy Journal* 6 (1977): 21.

9. The "there" (*da*) thus takes the place of what in *Being and Time* Heidegger had called *eigentlich,* usually translated as the "authentic"; the "not-there" (*weg*) takes the place of the "inauthentic" (BzP, p. 323ff.).

10. Derrida deems "fatal" the removal of quotation marks from the word 'spirit' (*esprit, Geist*) in Heidegger, after *Being and Time: De l'espirit* (Paris: Galilée, 1987). He insists heavily on this (pp. 24, 65, 66, 87, 90, 100). There may be something of a rhetorical tactic in both the charge and his insistence, since they obviously serve to distance him from Heidegger. They also seem to serve the more astonishing tactic of stepping out of "metaphysics": a tactic for which, Derrida declares, one needs only to "decide [*sic*] to change terrain" (see above, note 3). This candor has something perplexing about it. What could possibly guide one in such a decision? What would be its conditions and its means? Has

not Derrida himself reiterated the extent to which *logos* ties every statement back to the "old ground"? Doubtless a more local quarrel is also being carried out behind the scenes: Derrida is obviously demarcating himself from French philosophy, which (as every handbook tells it) was spiritualist until the arrival in France of Marx, Freud, and Nietzsche. So be it. This rattling of axes to grind should not, however, obscure the fact that Derrida, seeking to inscribe National Socialism within the spiritualist tradition—in order to place himself abruptly, irruptively, absolutely outside—*responds poorly*. I find the responsibility regarding the monstrous site that is ours better kept by the Derrida who observes that the "the simple practice of language ceaselessly reinstates the new terrain on the oldest ground" (*Margins,* p. 135). The subjectivist allegiance commanded by Heideggerian "spirit," just as by Derridean "decision," "choice" (*Margins,* p. 135—without quotation marks), and so on, must be viewed as an object lesson demonstrating the impossibility of jumping over our epochal closure. No text administers this lesson more harshly, however, than Heidegger's *Beiträge*.

11. Immanuel Kant, *Critique of Pure Reason,* B.397.

12. The originary double bind in Heidegger—i.e., the tragic condition of being—is discussed in the articles cited in note 1; for the distinction between natality and mortality, cf. Hannah Arendt, *The Human Condition* (Chicago: University of Chicago Press, 1958), pp. 9, 117, 247.

13. The word obviously alludes to maneuvers (*mechanêma*) such as the ones to which Agamemnon fell victim (Aeschylus, *The Libation Bearers,* p. 981). The victim of these machinations is bound in "toils no bronzesmith made" (p. 492), caught in a net that is also a trap. In the German vocabulary of hunting, one would say he is *gestellt*. The two words Heidegger uses to describe contemporary technology, *Machenschaft* and *Gestell,* connote the hunting trap and the tracking-down of prey.

14. Martin Heidegger, "The Way Back into the Ground of Metaphysics," trans. W. Kaufmann, in *Existentialism from Dostoevsky to Sartre* (New York: New American Library, 1975), p. 208. According to the *Contributions,* the "questioning conversation" with the Greeks "already requires the leap" into the other beginning (BzP, p. 169).

15. This disparity is already operative in the *Critique of Pure Reason,* in the distinction between being as givenness and as category; it becomes explicit in the *Critique of Judgment,* sec. 76.

16. E.g., "the Suprasensory World, the Ideas, God, the Moral Law, the Authority of Reason, Progress, the Happiness of the Greatest Number, Culture, Cilization": Martin Heidegger, *The Question concerning Technology and Other Essays,* trans. W. Lovitt (New York: Harper & Row, 1977), p. 65.

VI

14

Foreword to the Spanish Edition, *Heidegger and Nazism*

VICTOR FARÍAS

I

When the appearance of my book aroused controversy first in France and then in Italy, Brazil, and Holland, I not only wanted my response to answer adequately the objections it raised; I also wanted it to reflect the suppositions, motivations, even the implications involved in my having written it in the first place.

Until now, the fundamental discussion has been carried out in Europe and the United States. The criticism, of course, has addressed the content of the problems set forth, but at the same time—and surprisingly—it has also focused on the specific manner in which the debate began to take shape.

The first attitude with respect to the set of objective problems raised by the book was to avoid them and to displace the fundamental issue with what became a typical series of reciprocal accusations. For my German critics first and foremost, it was to show how "the French" had been so naive as to make Martin Heidegger the most important "French philosopher" without having noticed that the Germans, of course, had long ago discovered the full extent of his involvement with Nazism.[1] For some Italians, like Umberto Eco, the issue clearly centered on the following: that the scandal was actually a problem for the French and North Americans since only they—unlike the Germans and Italians—confused

This essay was first published as the Foreword to Victor Farías, *Heidegger y le Nazismo* (Barcelona: Editorial Muchnik, 1989).

fashion and philosophy.[2] For other, more reactionary Italians—Gianni Vattimo, for example—it became a worrisome issue whether Third World philosophical pretentions lay hidden behind my book.[3] For the French, the second time around, the principal issue was to underscore the need to rethink Heidegger—this time seriously—from the essence of Nazism: that is, from the point of view of a relevant question of German history that had not been previously appreciated by those pertinently concerned. This is the opinion of Jacques Derrida.[4]

The controversy concerning the results of my research has been marked—in effect—by an element of surprise, especially in France (the school of Derrida and Jean Beaufret), in Italy (Vattimo and the crystallizations of "weak thinking") and in the philosophical and literary circles of West Germany and the United States that are under the influence of postmodernism. Under the banner of escaping from all forms of historical or social commitment, there was a move to opt for a notion, which, like Heidegger's, seemed to offer every possible guarantee for a more or less lucid reflection that would even open the door to the disappearance of a responsible "subject" capable of carrying out a rational dialogue. Losing touch with all "reality" seemed to permit the single-minded pursuit of composing and decomposing "texts." The discovery of the essential link between Nazism and both the thought and the person of Heidegger, the documented study of his deep commitment and of his background, the evidence of his essential fidelity—until the end of his life—to the generic postulates of Nazism, the demonstration that the philosophy of Heidegger is unthinkable (above all, Heidegger for himself) without the fanatical and xenophobic commitment to the alleged spiritual superiority of Germans— all this came inevitably, above all in the "periphery," as a considerable surprise. The inescapable problem of responsibility was reopened precisely with regard to one of the fundamental figures of the privatization of thought, and this in relation to the most virtuously (*virtuosamente*) monstrous crime known to history. The effect produced in many colleagues has really been one of surprise and not wonder. Wonder leads to reflection, and it is said to be the starting point of philosophy. Surprise, on the other hand, usually provokes a defense to the death and even bewildered insults. Thus it was that the defensive strategy took shape and structure. Rainer Marten was therefore right in speaking of the transformation of the *affaire Heidegger* into the *affaire Farías*. To that end a rhetoric was deployed that was at times as violent as it was vulgar. E. Martineau called me "the Chilean Zorro, just down from the Andes, who sought to destabilize the Western democracies by making Heidegger pay for the C.I.A.'s debts."[5] H.-G. Gadamer could find in my work only "ignorance," "grotesque superficiality": in sum, a "mental muddle."[6] Jacques Derrida even went so far as to affirm that I had not read Heidegger "for even one hour."[7] A "progressive" German critic compared me to a "bulldog"; a less progressive one compared me to Judas. While some serious German historians explained my being able to make discoveries in the archives of the German Democratic Republic by the fact of my being Chilean,[8] others excused their inactivity in a much more original manner: because they were German they had been denied access to the North American archives of the Document Center in West Berlin. This affirmation was officially denied by the Foreign Office, which at the same time verified my information regarding Heidegger's militant involvement in the Nazi Party.

Despite the satisfaction I have gotten from the opinions of such scholars and thinkers as Habermas, Marten, Faye, Ferry and Renaut, Levinas, Todorov, Rossanda, Eco, Goldschmidt, Jambet (among others),[9] it was actually an almost anonymous testimony that led me to rediscover with greater force and transparency the seriousness of the problem to which my study refers. After my book appeared, a young student at the Latin American Institute of the Free University of Berlin, where I work, came to speak to me about himself—hoping for a helpful word from me. He told me that as long as he could remember, he had never had a loving relationship with his parents. Only his grandfather offered affection. He had told the boy bedtime stories and played with him in the country; he was at his side through all those moments of insecurity in childhood and adolescence. A few days before our talk, his grandfather had died, and he alone accompanied him to the cemetery. Back home, he began to put his grandfather's things in order. Among them he found his grandfather's diary, and read with horror that his grandfather had been a member of the SS, had taken part in the killing of Jewish children, and, what was certainly worse, had died with the conviction that he had acted well. My student's question was what he should do now and where he could find a reason to go on living. His question was on a much higher plane than any occasional intellectual polemic between philosophers or historians, because it was grounded in the only context in which a responsible scholarly discussion is possible. His question diluted neither the function nor the relevance of scholarly discussions, but it did place them on a plane of seriousness that does not always constitute the principal motivation of quarrels among different groups, trends, or schools.

II

The purpose of my work, although complex, is simply to expose the germ of discriminatory inhumanity without which the philosophy of Heidegger is as such unthinkable, but only insofar as this denunciation manifests— at the same time—the intention of contributing toward the safeguarding of humanity assaulted precisely by one of the so-called philosophical "lights" (*cúspides*) of the century. This hope of mine—which, as R. Maggiori has remarked, calls into question the very era that chose such "lights" (*cumbres*)—has for the most part been ignored. Instead of discussing my central thesis and seeing in it the fundamental key to understanding, first, Heidegger's adherence to Nazism and, later, his curious relationship to it until his death, some critics have tried to establish as dogma the separation between an admittedly despicable "person" and a great, untouched, and untouchable "philosophy."

The defense of that "greatness" has plotted various many-colored strategies. The most primitive one—that of the guardians of the Grail—has chosen to deny the facts and to attribute my work to a simple desire to harm and to cause a scandal (F. Fédier) or to create "sensational material" (E. Nolte). This strategy has been answered brilliantly by Rossanda. Another strategy has held that "all this was common knowledge," but it has also urged paradoxically and, precisely, only after my book's appearance—that it was now necessary to think "all anew," vaguely and frivolously referring to the relevant facts as "fascinating abysses" without proposing anything more concrete than variant "readings" (Derrida). Confronted with an ineliminable mass of evidence, other coverup attempts here chosen to dissociate "the person" of the philosopher from his "work" (Vattimo, R. Rorty)[10]—all this, by the way, without taking notice for an instant that Heidegger's political activity (on which I focus) was always, according to Heidegger's own account, grounded in the essential doctrines of his philosophy: his political praxis during the Third Reich was articulated in the philosophico-political *texts* my book analyzes. Common to all these strategies, furthermore, is the unwillingness to recognize that after 1945 and until his death, Heidegger accepted his relationship with Nazism, with the "destiny of the West," with the German people as "the heart of all peoples," without abandoning one whit the generic foundation of the Nazi ideology that led him to join the movement, to aspire even to become its spiritual leader, pressure to censure in the harshest terms its deviationism after 1934, and to overlook forever its monstrosities. In effect, given that he converted "Being," after 1945, into "event" (*Ereignis*); that he construed language as "the house of Being," the place where a human being properly becomes human; that he affirmed that only the language of the Germans can rescue and save "Being," we can understand Heidegger's conception only as a radical discrimination at the highest level of thought—at the decisive level where factual history becomes ontological. Facing the danger entailed by the "planetary expansion of technology," Heidegger affirms in a posthumous text (the *Spiegel* interview) that *only* Nazism (the true initial Nazism, it alone) was on its way to confronting the essential problem of modern man. In that same text he reaffirms his contempt for democracy and for the systems that aspire to it. We hear not a word of censure regarding the Holocaust, nothing about the interests of journalists in Heidegger's opinion of Nazi crimes. If Heidegger reproached the Germans for anything, it was not extermination or war but their failure to philosophize profoundly.

Nor does the attempt to disassociate Heidegger's philosophy from its possible influences on other fields of serious inquiry, even the arts (Vattimo, Rorty), take into account that the history of culture (or reception and influence) is one thing and systematic philosophy quite another, and that only in terms of the latter is it possible to approach the vastness of the issue or of the potentially beneficial results of certain influences. Apart from this, even a misunderstanding may be fruitful.

To distinguish stages in the development of Heidegger's philosophy is also not very helpful. The attempt of Derrida, Vattimo, and Lacoue-Labarthe,[11] among others, to situate the commitment to Nazism at the time when Heidegger still affirmed "metaphysics" and "subjectivity" ("Nazism is a humanism": Lacoue-Labarthe) is not only an inversion of the problem, as Habermas has correctly noted, but an obvious contradiction.[12] Because to affirm that the Heideggerian overcoming of metaphysics provides us with the only instrument for combatting "technology" as well as anti-Semitism cannot possibly explain the fact that the author of that same instrument could never find a suitable word for censuring the most perverse and most "metaphysical" realization of subjectivity: that instead, as reported in his posthumously published interview, he praised Nazism in its initial version as a unique and wasted opportunity.

It is precisely in that context that I wish to underscore one of the most relevant systematic conclusions to which my study leads. It is erroneous, in my judgment, to criticize Heidegger (as is commonly done) for having constructed a philosophy incapable of founding an ethics and to suggest (as Levinas does) that therein lies the explanation for his adherence to Nazism. My study makes clear that the "incapacity" of Heidegger's philosophy to found an ethics has meaning only in terms of a *universally* valid ethics. On the contrary, the whole of the evolution of his philosophical options manifests as its invariant element a conviction in the spiritual superiority of Germans and thereby the foundation for an "ethics of masters" valid only for them. This is amply confirmed in Heidegger's rectoral address (1933); in such courses as "The Fundamental Questions of Philosophy" (1933) and "Introduction to Metaphysics" (1935); in the lectures on Nietzsche's philosophy (1936–40), Parmenides and Heraclitus (1943, 1944), and Hölderlin (1943); in his letters to Rudolf Stadelmann (1945); even in his posthumously published interview (1966). In all these, Heidegger dramatically places Germans face to face with their "mission," that of the only "metaphysical people," and appeals to their responsibility to save "the Treasure = all that is German" in order to save the liberal and rational West from the madness into which it has hurled itself and from which it could never escape on its own. The "natural" kindred "lineage" (*Stamm*) of the German language with Greek, which mediated the appearance of being, consequently became for Heidegger the foundation of an aristocratic national ethics, and his claims in that respect are extremely clear and radical.

From the viewpoint of political philosophy, the coverup strategy has consisted more than anything in arguing without having carefully read Heidegger's texts. Otto Pöggeler concedes the fact that Heidegger had a philosophically founded commitment to the regime—but only until 1936, whereupon he turned into something like an anti-Nazi. Thus Pöggeler believes he can refute my "thesis," according to which I supposedly maintain that Heidegger was "just another Nazi philosopher."[13] Such a "thesis" (which has also been attributed to me by Augstein, Ott, Nolte, Aubenque, Schwan, and my Italian critics)[14] I have never defended, because it would imply the nonsense of putting Heidegger on the same level as Alfred Rosenberg, Ernst Krieck, or Hans Heyse. If one cannot ignore the fact that, as a political and historical concept, "National Socialist" encompasses generic elements of its own, it would also be useless to separate it from the context of historico-political forces in Germany bent on amassing power and hegemony. So its meaning may produce such surprises as the following: while the "racist" Rosenberg converts his phrase "the soul speaks through the race" into a principle, Heidegger the "spiritualist" does not shrink from affirming in his rectoral address that "the spiritual world of a people is not the superstructure of a culture" but "the power to conserve the forces that spring from the soil and the blood."[15] What Pöggeler and other critics are unwilling to understand is that the transformation that Heidegger did in fact undergo toward 1936 was directed only against the hegemony of the official Nazi philosophers who based their own commitment on the biologization and technologization of thought and their application. Heidegger effected his own change not from an anti-Nazi stance but from the irreducible conviction that the "deviationist" option was betraying the true foundation, the inner truth, and the greatness of Nazism. For Pöggeler and other researchers to posit the break (in the sense they postulate) precisely at the time of the lectures on Nietzsche's philosophy seems to me a particularly mistaken judgment. Even over the protests of some students, Heidegger used to begin those lectures with the Nazi salute, and around (1938) he even went through channels to reinstate the obligatory Nazi salute repealed in 1936. Heidegger's transformation consists in changing accidental elements in order to keep the essential. Because if the sacralization of the German essence is what led him to join the Party, that is precisely what led him to see in biologism a degrading claim advanced in the name of the "metaphysical people." And that is what explains his unshakable faith in the *Führer* and his public support during his courses of 1943 and 1944, for the barbarism of the Nazi troops.

The critique based on the concealment and distortion of my text has also found a strategy among some historians. Regrettably, my long and detailed response to the critique published by Hugo Ott in the *Neue Zürcher Zeitung* never appeared because the newspaper denied me the right to reply. Likewise, the *Frankfurter Allgemeine Zeitung* denied me the opportunity to reply to the distorted critiques of P. Aubenque and A. Schwan. It did offer me such an opportunity after the publication of my critics' letters, but then refused on receiving the text of my reply. Ott (together with E. Nolte) raises an objection to my having nonsensically turned Heidegger into some sort of disciple of Abraham a Sancta Clara, having attributed "a decisive role" to the influence of the Augustinian monk in Heidegger's philosophical education.[16] Any unbiased reader will note that in drawing attention to the relationship of Heidegger and Abraham a Sancta Clara, I have effectively demonstrated there only *one* of the many preparatory influences that go to explain Heidegger's later development: to wit, his commitment around 1933 to the most radical anti-Semitic movement that we know of—one of the strands, in fact, of the complex populist and patriotic currents of the time.

The great commonplace in this regard (a more or less spontaneous mass demonstration on the part of my critics) is my sheer "ignorance" and its corresponding "discovery": the fact that I do not distinguish between the Sachsenhausen concentration camp and the place near Frankfurt am Main in the context of my interpretation of Heidegger's 1964 text about Abraham a Sancta Clara. A certain imprecision in the translation (despite the fact that it says that Sachsenhausen "designates" and *not* that it *is* a concentration camp near Frankfurt) could, in effect, give the impression that I was confused. But in the absence of a solid historical and philosophical argument, the critics opted for the incessant repetition of this "confusion"—which in the opinion of Nolte, disqualifies the whole of my book "forever." The compulsive insistence on my "error" really points to a sad truth. By pronouncing the name "Sachsenhausen" in 1964 (at a time when the whole country's attention was concentrated on the disturbing revelations of the Auschwitz tribunal, whose seat was in Frankfurt) and, what is more, by placing it in the mouth of one of the classic anti-Semitic preachers, Heidegger leaves no doubt that there is at least reason to consider whether he was not acting in a truly provocative manner (a matter, furthermore, that my text does not settle). But instead of considering the possibility of an *affaire Heidegger,* that option was totally and immediately abandoned in order to publicize its opposite, the *affaire Farías*. The *Frankfurter Allgemeine Zeitung* even went so far as to publish a special gloss arrogantly ridiculing anyone who did not know the difference between the two locations. Instead of asking whether it was possible—in 1964—to pronounce the name of the scene of the crime without wounding all those affected by it and thereby all of humanity, these critics chose to turn a discussion about the responsibility of a public speech into a polemic about the use of dictionaries.

Thus, for example; instead of

- appraising the perspectives that my work offers toward our understanding of the relationship of the young Heidegger to the Catholic, anti-Semitic world of Austria and Bavaria and all that that might contribute to an understanding of the rise of Nazism;
- arguing about the relevance of the antidemocratic and fascist options that I located in *Being and Time* (1927) in order to explain the decision of 1933;
- welcoming with interest the link I demonstrated between Heidegger and "patriotic" institutions (like the "Badische Heimat") in Heidegger's prefascist period, in order to study the development of chauvinism in the south of Germany and its influence on the rise of Nazism;
- recognizing that, for the first time, my study furnishes new and original data regarding Heidegger's relationship with the Association of German Universities, affording thereby the possibility of studying a key institution in German cultural and political life prior to and during Nazism;
- offering to collaborate in order to further the study of Heidegger's relations with the ministries and the NSDAP, for which my book offers previously unknown sources;
- examining my proposal to study Heidegger's political praxis, especially his populist project with regard to the Nazi student movement controlled by the SA until 1934;
- proposing various parameters within which to explain Heidegger's active participation in Nazi institutions at the highest level (the Academy for German Law, the Advanced School for German Politics), his disagreements with some party institutions (Amt Rosenberg) and his affinities with others (Goebbels's ministry), and his connections with the international fascist movement;
- explaining the grounds that Heidegger might have had for supporting German aggression during the war:

in short, instead of taking an interest in all these things and in the perspective that my book provides for understanding Nazism from the point of view of an exemplary case, my critics seemed able to focus only on my confusion about "Sachsenhausen" and on the need to tell the "world" that I do not know what any member of the German Automobile Club knows.

It is very interesting to observe the coincidences and the differences between my critics regarding two essential aspects of my study. My German detractors, without exception, totally ignore the reproach many have raised for a long time against Heidegger: his complicitous silence with regard to the Holocaust. R. Augstein, who reproaches me for confusing two such elementary notions as "national socialism" and "revolutionary conservativism" and who, in his article of 1987 (which followed the publication of my book in France), does criticize Heidegger's "silence" harshly, did not display any interest in interrogating the philosopher regarding the Holocaust during his historic 1966 interview. For E. Nolte and A. Schwan, the issue simply does not exist. Otto Pöggeler touches on the theme in a revealing but at the same time tangential and aesthetic manner. He reduces everything to a report about the clarification that Paul Célan requested of Heidegger. Pöggeler relates that Célan waited "for at least ten years," and that at Heidegger's request Célan even brought him a written account of his parents' death in a death camp; and Pöggeler concedes that, despite all this, Heidegger never uttered a word of condemnation. Instead, according to Pöggeler, Heidegger took "the sick man [*sic*]" (Célan) to "the place of health"(*lugar de la salud*), "to the places where Hölderlin had lived" (*a los lugares que había vivido Hölderlin*).[17] My French critics, on the other hand, even the most violent ones, more or less totally face the seriousness of the matter. The only exception is P. Aubenque, but in his case we are dealing with someone who has gone to the extreme of denying altogether the existence of a concentration camp in France.[18]

Another matter involves the differences and coincidences regarding my statement that for Heidegger the act of philosophizing, in its authentic and originary sense (which, for him, is an act that constitutes the human being as such), is possible only for Germans in their language, and that this constitutes discrimination and "philosophical racism" (R. Marten). This objection of mine has been disregarded by my French and Italian critics without exception and with the appropriate degree of circumspection. Among the philosophers of the "periphery," only Vattimo admitted and censured Heidegger's *Diktat,* without wanting, however, to attribute to it a significant role.[19] My German critics either totally elude the issue (Ott, Schwan, Pöggeler) or resolutely reaffirm the philosophical superiority of the German language (Nolte).[20]

Heidegger's philosophy is not a closed system that pretends to account for objective reality through corresponding concepts of permanent universal validity. It is, rather, an extreme historicism that seeks to found any possible objectivity by transcendentalizing history and at the same time by historicizing ontology. To that end, Heidegger conceives both, not according to generalizations that would render them comprehensible but from the viewpoint of events that are unique and determinative in their grandiose, absolute particularity. The historico-ontological *range* is what founds Being and its truth. The space where the ontologization of history and the historizing of Being are founded is the place where the act in which the question asked by Being (as well as the question that Being asks of itself) is constituted by and coincides with the event in which history becomes the transparency articulating that occurrence—thereby constituting itself as history in the full sense. Rather than being a "factor" acting "on" history and its immediate facticity, Heidegger's philosophy understands itself as the second decisive moment of the History of Being that allows history to *be* in the originary sense. It is precisely in its absolute contingency that it wants to be, at the same time, absolutely determining.

It is at this level of abstraction that the measure and the exact meaning of Heidegger's chauvinistic and discriminating ultranationalism can be discerned. The fundamental structure of the History of Being—that is, its essence (*Wesen*) and its truth, understood as disclosing (*desocultamiento*)—includes *within its own resources* (*de suyo*) the originary dis-closing movement of the Greeks as well as the correlative concealment initiated by the Judaeo-Christian-Latin historical counter-act and its own articulation in a language of distortion. The recovery that takes place in and through Heidegger's own thought is as originary as this double movement, inasmuch as it is thought in and through the language of Hölderlin, the language of the German essence. The congeniality that Heidegger postulates with unvarying insistence as "naturally given" between Greek and German is understood, therefore, not as a cultural or a linguistic or (even less) a biological phenomenon but rather as a decisive historico-ontological occurrence—a miracle as exceptional and unique as the Greek origin in which no one else can or ought to participate (at least as an individual subject). The superiority of the German people, the German spirit, German as the language guide of modern man is thereby founded in a vaster principle than any naturalist or spiritualist attempt could provide. This principle—the absolute vagueness of a "Being" that nothing and no one can determine—is founded at the same time on the most radical uniqueness conceivable: that only *one* language and *one* thought, that of *one* poet and *one* thinker, can open the way to the indeterminable founding moment. Once more, it is precisely a radical dehumanization (postulated as the "overcoming of metaphysics") that opens the door to the most arbitrary discrimination.

One last issue has to do with the alleged characteristics of my method. Pöggeler, Nolte, Ott, and Aubenque attribute to me a method that they call "associative," which consists in demonstrating the anti-Semitism of persons implicitly or explicitly associated with Heidegger in order finally to "accuse" the philosopher of "anti-Semitism." They affirm that my book is "full" of such associations but name only one. They claim that I find elements of anti-Semitism in a text about Abraham a Sancta Clara, written in Heidegger's youth, only by deducing them from the context; that the text itself contains no anti-Semitic passages in the sense that I am "looking for"; and that only thanks to this method am I able to demonstrate that Heidegger was "a Nazi philosopher" from "the cradle to the grave" (Pöggeler).[21] Or, even a Nazi *avant la lettre*. The truth in the case, however, is that the text itself includes decisive allusions to anti-Semitism. Heidegger devotes his article to a central figure of the Austrian and Bavarian Catholic anti-Semitic tradition, and if it is true that his text does not refer directly to Abraham's anti-Semitism, nevertheless, by calling him the teacher of the health of the people (*maestro de la salud del pueblo)*, the paradigm for overcoming a decadent culture, he is certainly alluding to the Augustinian preacher as a whole. He is stimulating around Abraham the cult of personality as such and as it was known publicly. What would we think nowadays of someone who would call Le Pen "the teacher of the people" *without* alluding explicitly to his racism? In the same text, Heidegger calls Karl Lueger, the mayor of Vienna, "unforgettable." Lueger (who meanwhile had died and could not possibly have attended the unveiling of the monument to Abraham, as Aubenque believes) was the leader of the anti-Semitic Christian-Socialist Party and, as mayor, had made the monument possible through a sizable grant. The young Heidegger, as my study shows, was even president of an association dedicated to the cult of Abraham which organized dramatized readings of *Judas,* one of the classics of anti-Semitism written by the Augustinian monk. And my allusion to the fact that at about the same time the young Adolf Hitler participated in a ceremony (in Vienna) in homage to Karl Lueger (as Hitler himself relates in *Mein Kampf,* not only with deep emotion but by way of alluding explicitly to its political function) is hardly, as my critics affirm, a fantastical free "association."

It demonstrates rather the obvious fact that all these personalities (Abraham, Lueger, Hitler, and Heidegger) are living parts of a historical whole that develops under an unequivocal political sign, even if each one has his own character and historical moment. Precisely because the goal of my work is to investigate the relationship of Heidegger to Nazism, it was my scholarly obligation to collect all the pertinent information that might render that relationship intelligible. What my critics are actually calling into question when they speak of my resorting to the "context" is nothing less than the unavoidable necessity of understanding a philosophical work, and *also* the biography of its author, from the point of view of the institutions mentioned in the text, as well as the historical ambience that makes its meaning and significance genuinely comprehensible. My method does not depend on "anecdotes" (always narrated from a particular or narrow point of view), nor does it make use of highly personal sources (such as "diaries," for example). The use of such materials leads—at best—to a description of "mentalities" lacking a certain objectivity.

Therefore, it seems to me contradictory as well as grotesque for Pöggeler to accuse me of "avoiding a political diagnosis" regarding the fact that Beaufret made Heidegger his teacher.[22] Is Pöggeler (as well as Nolte)[23] unaware of the solidarity between Beaufret and R. Faurisson, and of the former's explicit support of the latter's "revisionist" theses, which have been common knowledge for more than a year? Or rather, should Pöggeler and Nolte be the ones to do a "political diagnosis" of the fact that Beaufret—the only "ambassador" and authorized spokesman of Heidegger in France, to whom the philosopher addressed his "Letter on Humanism"—has denied the existence of gas chambers and has denounced them as a Jewish invention?

Assuming that my critics keep their enthusiasm for "political diagnoses," they should heed the observations of M. Frank, who has called attention to the fact that the French New Right, known for its violent racist and anti-Semitic stamp, grants Heidegger a far more important role than other extreme right ideologues, such as O. Spengler, A. Moeller van der Bruck, A. Gehlen, or K. Lorenz.[24] Faurisson himself has officially declared that his "predecessors in revisionism" are Heidegger and Beaufret.[25] A political diagnosis is in fact urgent, particularly since an entire book published to refute my conclusions and to defend Heidegger, continues as usual to accord Beaufret a decisive role.[26]

The problem of Heidegger's anti-Semitism is certainly a relevant question.[27] But despite the fact that the martyrdom of the Jews is without parallel in history, in this case it is also possible to make a distinction between principles and crystallizations. The Nazis did not articulate their racist and biologist ideology in a vacuum and without presuppositions. Nazism is the cruelest form of extermination known, but it is so precisely because of the degree to which it gave concrete form to a general discriminatory ideology. Where there is no discrimination, there can be no extermination; and where extermination proliferates, it does so as a determined form of the originating discrimination. In our long history, extermination has also been founded in the spirit (the autos-da-fé of the Middle Ages and the cruel "missions" in America and in obscenely materialist "arguments" (the social and ecological crimes of our times). The invariant element has always been the discrimination against some human beings to the advantage of others, postulated to be superior. This is precisely where the ultimate reason must be sought for my radical break with a philosophy that is inconceivable without such discrimination.

III

The sensitive and widespread reaction, first of international public opinion and, later, of specialists to the publication of my book is a fact that deserves to be separated from whatever options we may choose—above all, because that fact made it surprisingly evident that people are genuinely interested in our philosophical work and that they have always believed in its importance, even when we ourselves were not too sure that we were doing anything relevant. When a philosophical issue becomes the subject of international public opinion, the event implies the rehabilitation of what is commonly dismissed as "mass culture." Such a discussion affords a mutual and simultaneous rehabilitation, a democratization of relations. The many do not want to isolate or ignore the interests of the few, and the few have the opportunity to realize that their fundamental preoccupations are also shared by the many. In a way, this making public of a philosophy reminds us of the nobility of the act whereby, in other times, a philosopher preferred to take poison himself rather than to poison his people with vileness. But all this should not lead to easy transactions. The most significant aspect of the protest was the renewed and vital existence of a public opinion that came to life when it perceived under apparently new banners the features of the Nazi-fascist threat that brought humanity to the edge of a new barbarism.

If it is true that my book has contributed to all that then I can hand it over confidently to my Spanish and Latin American readers—because they (like Germans and all human beings) should know that if philosophy still has a function and a possibility, it can be no other than to humanize the human. This certainly includes thinking *about* Heidegger and his arrogant nationalist ontology but, at the same time, *against* him and, above all, *beyond* what lives in the essence of his philosophy. Thinking, in our countries (and it need not be "philosophical"), must, urgently, overcome not only the ambassadors of the "ontological metropolis" but also those who seek a liberation from the so-called identities (linking all humans as such), basing themselves on a philosophy that is indissolubly joined to the most inhuman crystallization of the ideology of the master. A liberation can occur only in a concrete historical context, and it is precisely then and there that "the liberated" can be nothing but human beings, each uniquely and universally such, united in solidarity.[28]

346 VICTOR FARÍAS

NOTES

1. R. Augstein, "Aber bitte nicht philosophieren," *Der Spiegel* 48 (1987). M. Haller confirms my interpretation in this sense in "Der Philosophenstreit zwischen Nazi-Rechtfertigung und postmoderner öko-philosophie," *Die Zeit*, January 29, 1988. See also the texts by O. Pöggeler and A. Schwan cited in notes 13 and 18. Despite the participation of J. P. Faye, J. M. Palmier, P. Bourdieu, F. Fédier, G. A. Goldschmidt, A. Finkielkraut, and others in numerous televised discussions, Pöggeler's conclusion refers derogatorily to those in France who are interested in my work as "T.V. philosophers."

2. Umberto Eco, "Il caso Heidegger," *L'Espresso*, May 29, 1988.

3. For Gianni Vattimo, see "Los Angeles sopra Berlino, Faccia a Faccia, Farías contro Vattimo," *L'Espresso*, April 24, 1988.

4. Jacques Derrida, "L'enfer des philosophes," interview with D. Eribon, *Le Nouvel Observateur*, November 6, 1987.

5. E. Martineau, *Le Quotidien* (Paris), November 22, 1987.

6. H. G. Gadamer, "L'imbroglio di Farías," *L'Espresso*, April 24, 1988; Spanish text in *Vuelta* (Mexico) 142 (September 1988).

7. Derrida, "L'enfer des philosophes." For an excellent critical reading of *De l'esprit*, see J. Lacoste, "Heidegger lu par Derrida," *La Quinzaine Littéraire*, December 16–31, 1988.

8. Hugo Ott, "Wege und Abwege," *Neue Zürcher Zeitung*, November 27, 1987.

9. See Jürgen Habermas, "Martin Heidegger: Nazi, forcément nazi," *Journal de Genève*, January 16, 1988, and also his foreword to German edition of my book, *Heidegger und der Nationalsozialismus* (Frankfurt, 1989): Rainer Marten, "Heideggers Geist," *Allmende* 20 (1988); Jean-Paul Faye, "Heidegger, l'état de l'être," *Lignes* 2 (January 1988); Lue Ferry and Alain Renaut, *Heidegger et les modernes* (Paris, 1988); Emmanuel Levinas, "Comme un consentement," *Le Nouvel Observateur* (January 22, 1988); Tristan Todorov, "Los intelectuales y la tentación del totalitarismo," *Vuelta* 142 (September 1988) and *Times Literary Supplement* (June 17–23, 1988); R. Rossanda, "Minimo dell'etica e massimo dell'indiferenza: Caso Heidegger," *Il manifesto*, June 21, 1988; Eco, "Il caso Heidegger"; Georges-Arthur Goldschmidt, "Heidegger, l'allemand et le ressentiment," *Le Monde*, January 13, 1988, and "Une vie, une oeuvre engagées dans le national-socialisme" *La Quinzaine Littéraire* 496 (November 1987); Christian Jambet, preface to my French edition *Heidegger et le nazisme* (Paris, 1987).

10. Richard Rorty, "Taking Philosophy Seriously," *New Republic,* April 11, 1988.

11. Philippe Lacoue-Labarthe, *La fiction du politique* (Paris, 1987), and "Heidegger: Les textes en appel," *Journal Littéraire* 117 (1988).

12. Habermas, foreword to my German edition.

13. Otto Pöggeler, "Besinnung oder Ausflucht? Heideggers ursprünglicheres Denken," in *Forum für Philosophie: Zerstörung des moralischen Selbstbewusstseins: Chance oder Gefahrdung*, ed. B. Homburg (Frankfurt, 1988), pp. 238–72.

14. For the polemic with the Italian critics, see my foreword to the Italian edition, *Heidegger e il Nazismo* (Torino, 1988). For Nolte's critique, see his "Ein Höhepunkt der Heidegger-Kritik? Victor Farías' Buch *Heidegger et le nazisme*," *Historische Zeitschrift* 247 (1988): 95–114. For Aubenque and Schwan, see the texts cited in note 18.

15. See "The Self-Assertion of the German University, "in *Martin Heidegger and National Socialism: Questions and Answers*, ed. Günther Neske and Emil Kettering (New York: Paragon, 1990), p. 9 (translation modified).

16. Ott, "Wegeund Abwege"; Nolte, "Ein Höhepunkt," p. 107.

17. Pöggeler, "Besinnung oder Ausflucht?" p. 272.

18. P. Aubenque, "Grosse Irrtümer über Heidegger" *Frankfurter allgemeine Zeitung* (January 25, 1988). A. Schwan supports Aubenque's critique without reservations in *Frankfurter Allgemeine Zeitung*, February 12, 1988. See also Aubenque, "Encore Heidegger et le Nazisme," *Le Débat*, January 1988, pp. 113–23.

19. Vattimo, "Los Angeles sopra Berlino."

20. Nolte, "Ein Höhepunkt."

21. Pöggeler. "Besinnung oder Ausflucht?"

22. Ibid., pp. 271–72.

23. Nolte, "Ein Höhepunkt, p. 96.

24. M. Frank, "Philosophie heute und jetzt," *Frankfurter Rundschau*, March 5, 1988. Frank alludes particularly to the ideologue Pierre Krebs.

25. Robert Faurisson, *Annales de histoire revisioniste* 4 (1988).

26. Gunther Neske, ed., *Antwort* (Pfullingen, 1988).

27. That Heidegger's radical anti-Semitism was apparent several years before his militant Nazism has been demonstrated by Ulrich Sieg's discovery of a 1929 letter in which Heidegger asserts that the task of fighting the growing "Judaization of the German spirit" is a historic mission of the thought and politics of the German universities. See Sieg, "Die Verjudung des deutschen Geistes," *Die Zeit*, no. 52 (December 22, 1989); Victor Farías, "El Antisemitismo de Heidegger," *El País*, January 19, 1990; and Henk Müller, "Antisemitisme Heidegger blijk uit brief," *De Volkskrant*, January 26, 1990.

28. Heidegger's relationship to National Socialism has been addressed in Spanish by Marcos García de la Huerta's valuable book, *La técnica y el Estado Moderno: Heidegger y el problema de la Historia* (Santiago de Chile, 1978).

15

The Purloined Letter

DOMINIQUE JANICAUD

> "And what is the difficulty now?" I asked. "Nothing more in the assassination way, I hope."
>
> "Oh no, nothing of that nature. The fact is, the business is *very* simple indeed, and I make no doubt that we can manage it sufficiently well ourselves; but then I thought Dupin would like to hear the details of it, because it is so excessively *odd*."
>
> "Simple and odd," said Dupin.
>
> "Why, yes; and not exactly that either. The fact is, we have all been a good deal puzzled because the affair is so simple, and yet baffles us altogether."
>
> "Perhaps it is the very simplicity of the thing that puts you at fault," said my friend.
>
> —Edgar Allan Poe, "The Purloined Letter"

> Just as when we are receptive to hearing the way in which Martin Heidegger discloses to us the play of truth in the word ἀλήθεια (*aletheia*, disclosure), we only find again a secret in which truth has always initiated her lovers, and from which they maintain that it is in what she hides that she *most truly* offers herself to them.
>
> —Jacques Lacan, Seminar on "The Purloined Letter"*

* Jeffrey Mehlman translates this: "As well, when we are open to hearing the way in which Martin Heidegger discloses to us in the word *aletheia* the play of truth, we rediscover a secret to which truth has always initiated her lovers, and through which they learned that it is in hiding that she offers herself to them *most truly*" (*The French Freud: Structural Studies in Psychoanalysis*, Yale French Studies [1972; Kraus Reprints, 1981], p. 52). —Transl.

Simple and odd—isn't this also the hermeneutic situation that Heidegger bequeathed regarding the links between his thought and National Socialism? A little phrase was published at the end of his *Introduction to Metaphysics* (1953) (Gilbert Kahn's translation had appeared in France as early as 1958).[1] In these few words, everything was already said, scandalously exposed to the public and yet (after initial protests)[2] supported and even "normalized" by the philosophical community. It would be futile to go on compiling innumerable archival documents and to give in to the anecdotal frenzy that took hold of so many people after Farías's study of Heidegger and Nazism appeared. Farías was like Poe's Prefect, who for weeks inspects, inch by inch, and by microscope, the furniture, partitions, draperies, and hangings of a particular town house of Minister D. In vain? Farías was less ineffectual than the Prefect, it will be said, since he aroused our suspicions and obliged us to "revisit" our evidence. No doubt about it; but if nothing was really understood at the end of the investigation, what would it all have come to except a displacement of the question? Nine years of Nazism instead of nine months? But which "Nazism," and why? In Heidegger's case, it was not enough to get our hands on the documents to determine what was at stake. In "The Purloined Letter" it was the reverse. To find the document, one had to understand the calculations of a superior mind. We shall discover bit by bit the relevance, the depth, the limits of the analogy. It appears already that in both cases, seeking the truth implies a paradoxical relation between the manifestation and its recognition ("the mystery . . . a little *too* self-evident," said Dupin): the police inquiry (the historiographers were nearly acting like that) is qualified—if not conditioned—by another dimension altogether, an intellectual or speculative one (Minister D. is a brilliant wit, a mathematician and a poet at the same time; the thinker in this respect is not presented). The corpse *in flagrante delicto*, which is to play the role of the letter for us, is those few words printed at the end of the *Introduction to Metaphysics*, in 1953, and which, in the sense given, do not seem to have been hidden from us but, on the contrary, openly offered (we shall see whether that is so):

> The works that are being peddled about nowadays as the philosophy of National Socialism but have nothing whatever to do with the inner truth and greatness of this movement (namely, the encounter between global technology and modern man) have all been written by men fishing in the troubled waters of "values" and "totalities."*

---

* Janicaud used the French translation by Kahn, with slight modifications. The English here is Manheim's (see note 1). —Transl.

First Reading

It seems simplest at first not to seek in these lines any justification more profound or subtle than a frank profession of faith in favor of Nazism. Heidegger was still a Nazi in 1935, and he said so *ex cathedra*. "Inner truth and greatness" are terms almost equivalent to "ideals": a profession of faith which thus concerns foundations and seems more serious than an approval of mere circumstance. The official "philosophers" of Nazism are not up to the heights of the movement. The movement deserves to be recognized and thought by, and at the heart of, Philosophy with a capital P (hence the inclusion of these lines in the *Introduction to Metaphysics*). Besides, the "movement" is a term used by the Nazis themselves to designate the NSDAP (Nationalsozialistische Deutsche Arbeiterpartei, "National Socialist German Workingmen's Party")—and we find Hitler using it in *Mein Kampf*.

On this hypothesis, Heidegger deserves at least some credit: he does not hide his cards. And all the less since he kept that expression in 1953, eight years after the collapse of Nazism and the revelation of its most hideous features. Frankness or provocation? Or, obliviousness?

Yet however frontal the readings may be, it should not ignore the context. This phrase is but a single incident, even if taken in its immediate context. Not only does the political allusion contribute nothing to the propositions of one of Heidegger's most complex and original texts (on the four limits of Being: becoming, appearance, thinking, and the ought), but it does not even add anything indispensable to the polemic it itself had just launched against the abuse of the concept of "value" in contemporary philosophy. Odd—the phrase is already relegated to this first level of reading because it is philosophically superfluous, even incongruous. Any professor permits himself a digression now and again in order to relax things, or picturesque allusions. But there is nothing innocent here. However, the anecdotal character of the preceding remarks has an almost frivolous side, which must have made the audience smile: "In 1928, there appeared the first part of a general bibliography of the concept of value. In it 661 titles are listed. No doubt the number has meanwhile swollen to one thousand."* Rather heavy irony, typically academic. Nothing lets us anticipate what is to follow (either syntactically or logically), apart from that sophomoric whimsy, in Heidegger's moving on to a violent attack on the ideologico-philosophical by-products of the regime, which would even reach the solemnity of a "quasi-profession of faith." Was the Master looking for an opportunity, no matter what? The sense of the arbitrary is perhaps only apparent. To consider only the rhetorical drift, Heidegger's

* Manheim, p. 166. —Transl.

stance seems—at that moment—to be the following: at the risk of an aside, let us discuss it seriously. Here is the fatal phrase introduced by a *vollends*, a "moreover"—in the way one slips in something important in a detached tone of voice, at the turn of an ordinary conversation (because one doesn't know how to "bring" the thing up?).

Now, the "thing" (the essential thing) does not present only one face. Until now our elementary reading has in its haste fastened only on the "profession of faith." The latter is, in fact, the background (or the "cover-up": let's not forget that everything is watched and noted in a regime where the least act of opposition so characterized leads to prison or the concentration camp) of a very sharp attack against the pseudophilosophy of National Socialism. Today it looks as if a "great philosopher" is vigorously attacking the likes of a Rosenberg or a Krieck, but then they did not hold high rank. More clearly still: in a State organized along the lines of Goebbels's propaganda, these philosophers defined the key to the ideological vault of a "world vision," presuming to impose new "values," instituting *a certain Nietzsche* as master thinker. Activist, imperialist, forcefully racist, the ideology was not offered as one Nietzschean interpretation among others. It was diffused (*herumgeboten*, recited), which means imposed for all practical purposes as the orthodox philosophy of the new regime. It was therefore not obvious that it could have been opposed with either ease or impunity. It is not for us to determine now whether (and to what extent) Heidegger's criticism was courageous. It is still difficult as this level of our reading to decide whether the "profession of faith" is, for its part, only the "cover" for an attack. But it appears indisputable that the reverse is not conceivable: the attack on the Party ideologues could not, in 1935, be the pretext of a "profession of faith." Whatever may have been Heidegger's inner adherence to the regime, the regime was firmly installed. Hitler held all power. The *Führerprinzip* was in place at all levels. Röhm and the SA had been eliminated. Unemployment began to be absorbed. The Saar plebiscite had been a complete success. Military service was reestablished. The *Reichswehr* was reinforced. Nazism was still at the beginning of its ascendant phase. The regime had no need of any kind of supplementary recognition from a Heidegger, who, besides, had "already gone over": his election as rector and his adherence of 1933 were still quite recent. Heidegger, for his part, had resigned the rectorship the preceding year, but we now know—remained a Party member. He in no way had to reaffirm his allegiance, which in such a regime was taken for granted; we have no evidence that it had been requested. The hypothesis of the priority of the "profession of faith" has no historical verisimilitude.

It has no contextual verisimilitude either. Let us reread the phrase. Will we find there, properly speaking, a personalized allegiance, an appeal to mobilization—comparable to the rectoral address or the 1933 declaration of affiliation? On the contrary, what is striking is the impersonal, almost detached tone, the use of academic privilege to judge what is great and what isn't, vis-à-vis History.

So there is no doubt that our first reading, if it is to be honest and complete (it still has not taken the parenthesis into account), must give priority to the look and the polemical content of the declaration. Now this polemic is intelligible only if we make an effort to put it back into the context of 1935. This effort in no way implies that we "approve" Heidegger's declaration or that we justify his keeping to it in 1953. It obliges us only— which is not negligible—to give up the temptation to stay with the simplistic leveling of any hurried first reading. I shall develop my reasons for this.

But if we have to hold both ends of the chain and not let either of the two sides of the declaration fall (Farías himself recognizes the situation of "internal opposition" that Heidegger assumed from 1934 onward), it is likewise interesting to note a reversal of circumstances between 1935 and 1953. As much as the polemical imperative appeared determinative in the situation of 1935 (without constituting, let us repeat, a sufficient justification because it was possible to remain silent on the point), it becomes to that extent, anachronistic in the situation after the war. The accent shifts, then, to *keeping* an acknowledgment of the "inner truth and greatness of this movement." In fact, this is what caused the question or scandal in 1953 and what keeps it alive. We cannot see any other sense to the declaration. Twenty years later, Heidegger becomes stubborn—in 1935, against the ideological firstcomers of Nazism; in 1953 against the now universally accepted opinion of the intrinsic and total perversity of the "movement." Are we now drawing on the context of 1953? I don't think so. Heidegger could not have been unaware of the commotion he would stir up by keeping the phrase in. Hartmut Buchner had warned him.[3] We know that now. He took shelter behind historical conformity (which has, as a subjective correlative, frankness and fidelity to self). But he could not have avoided taking responsibility for the polemical connotations of keeping it in (he seems to have made a deliberate choice). Why? It would have been so simple to delete it (as he did with an allusion to Hitler and Mussolini in the Schelling course, a deletion almost unnoticed until now).[4] Do subjective or emotional reasons explain the 1953 choice? It would show ignorance in Heidegger to accept such a banal hypothesis. There's a fundamental thought there. We shall have to dislodge it—hence the need for a second level of reading.

Second Reading

Before even making the effort to recover the genuinely Heideggerian sense of the expression "inner truth and greatness," all the while paying attention to the sense of the parenthesis, we must once again make allowance for the almost policelike element that encumbers the question of the parenthesis. Heidegger declared in 1966, in an interview with the staff of *Der Spiegel*, that this clarification was already in his manuscript, and, he said, it "corresponded exactly to the conception I had then [*damaligen Auffassung*] of technology."[5] In 1953, he had already written to the newspaper *Die Zeit* something to the same effect.[6] This justification invites a certain caution: Buchner had not seen this parenthesis in the manuscript,[7] and Petra Jaeger has noted (in the Heidegger archives at Marbach) that the litigious page is missing in the original manuscript, which can only reinforce "suspicions."[8] What *is* certain is that the explanatory parenthesis was not *uttered* in 1935[9] and that—even if he was already "thinking" it then—Heidegger had in no way made his thoughts on technology explicit for his student audience. What contradicts his retrospective self-justification—this time, *from the inside*—is the fact that the intelligibility of the parenthesis is not really possible until after what was published in the 1950s (first of all, in "The Question concerning Technology"). It would have required of his listeners, in 1935, an exceptional divinatory clairvoyance to have supposed that "those who knew how to hear" already understood the "profession of faith" by virtue of an unuttered parenthesis. On the other hand, with respect to content, the separation between the parenthesis and what immediately preceded it is obvious enough. While the words "inner truth and greatness" belong to the textual soil of the *Introduction to Metaphysics* (and are, strictly speaking, intelligible by reference to the course alone—still thinking, alas, of the *pathos* of 1933–34), the concept of "global technology" cannot be explicated under the same hermeneutic conditions. The parenthesis, therefore, is a foreign body in the text: there can be no doubt that it was conceived and added in 1953. But it is interesting to isolate the effect of "collage" that it introduces in a rather Gestaltist manner. Given the very ellipsis of the expression "inner truth and greatness," it is henceforth impossible to ignore that parenthesis. The enigma tends to settle on the parenthesis. As far as the new "police detectives" are concerned, didn't Heidegger show himself infinitely more clever than he would have been if he had expeditiously deleted the expression "inner truth and greatness"? From now on, thanks to this turn (too clever?) which seems to be part of the "stylization" of his past (as Habermas puts it), the reader's attention and interpretive effort are diverted from the contentiousness of Nazism to the global situation and its future. The "movement" becomes a particular instance in a global historical conjuncture or, better, an epochal conjunction where only Heideggerian thought is supposed to measure its impact. Doesn't the parenthesis succeed in hiding a truth that is *"too self-evident"* without actually hiding it, while *showing* something else?

What is shown, designated by this phrase (and its parenthesis) is now made explicable in Heidegger's own terms and according to Heidegger's own intentions. The "truth" is called inner in the sense of self-reference: that is, of simple coherence. We are no longer dealing with a truth adequated to transcendent "ideals" or autonomous "values." The Platonic legacy had already been reexamined down to the point of Nietzschean reversal. With section 44 of *Being and Time*, with the lecture "On the Essence of Truth" (the first version dates from 1930), with the text even of the *Introduction to Metaphysics*,[10] we know that truth (*Wahrheit*) is to be heard primordially as *Unverborgenheit* (disclosure), exposure or dispossession of being. Sophocles' tragedy *Oedipus Rex* is characterized as the "passion of disclosure," of Being, and, following both Hölderlin and Karl Reinhardt, hailed as a "tragedy of appearance."[11] But the context of the litigious phrase is not either that of a meditative deepening of the concept of truth or that of an explanation of a tragic gesture. It concerns, whether or not we deplore it, a political movement henceforth identified with the destiny of the German people. In what sense then, did Heidegger envisage a collective "inner truth"? The answer is that he envisaged it as what is the most proper (*"eigen/propre"* in the Hölderlinian sense). The most proper (*eigen*) is the capacity for *Eigentlichkeit*: that is, for authenticity at the heart of appropriating the possible. "Become what you are!" That Nietzschean phrase indicates the orientation of the "resoluteness" (*Entschlossenheit*) by which a person or a people assumes his or her or its historical situation, responds to the call (*Ruf*) of his or her or its freedom vis-à-vis death. In this resoluteness or decisive appropriation, the fundamental constitution of historicity does not leave the Existent absolutely isolated but leads it (back) to its historial task: "But if fateful *Dasein*, as Being-in-the-world, exists essentially in Being-with-Others, its historizing is a co-historizing and is determinative for it as *destiny* [*Geschick*]. This is how we designate the historizing of the community, of a people."*

Therefore, there is no doubt that what was recognized, even in 1935, in the "movement" was a reservoir of possibilities with regard to the appropriation of German existence. Heidegger makes a passing remark on language (which interpreters have not noticed until now) at the end of the first part of the *Introduction to Metaphysics*: "The organizations for the purification of the language and defense against its progressive barbarization are deserving of respect [*Beachtung*]. But such efforts merely demonstrate all the more clearly that we no longer know what is at stake in language."† The allusion is transparent: Heidegger simultaneously

---

* Martin Heidegger, *Being and Time*, trans. John Macquarrie and Edward Robinson (New York: Harper & Row, 1962), p. 436. —Transl.
† Manheim, p. 42. —Transl.

approves and criticizes the Nazi measures to eliminate words of foreign origin. He approves these measures to the extent that they move in the direction of the most proper (authentic) appropriation. He disapproves of them to the extent that they are simply "conformist" measures where the language itself is not listened to.

In so saying, we are not moving away from "inner truth." Refusing the language of the ideal, of values, or even of "intentions," Heidegger retains only the language of truth as "disclosure" of the most proper (authentic) possibilities and the unfolding of a destiny-laden historicity. Here indeed a very great honor is bestowed on this "movement," which supposed that it joined and brought together (like Italian fascism) all categories and classes of people in the same national impulse. All the more so since it deals with "greatness" also. From a purely syntactic point of view, we must take note that the *und* ("and") here, as very often with Heidegger (and in the very title, *Sein und Zeit*) is expletive. "Inner truth" *is* "greatness." It is disclosed as such: that is, manifests this "struggle against appearance" which is truth in the sense of homelessness. But why "greatness"? This eminently Nietzschean word is to be understood here in the sense in which Heidegger concludes the rectoral address with the quotation from Plato (*Republic* 497d): "All that is great stands in the storm." A few lines earlier, Heidegger was speaking about the "nobility and greatness of this rupture [*Aufbruch*]," and he had just affirmed: "We want our people to fulfill its genuinely historic mission. We want us ourselves."[12] We surely are dealing with a decisive appropriation of the people's possibilities favoring a breakthrough (the word *Entscheidung* is used on the same page) or a historical revolution (and, in Heidegger's mind, no doubt historical).

Whether or not we like this interpretation, whether or not it makes Heidegger the man out to be active or passive, is not our concern here. Essentially, it is important to understand and make understood what Heidegger had in mind as early as 1935. Heidegger saluted the Nazi movement in terms of historical and destinal possibilities. And it is in that sense that he would continue to qualify it in the *Spiegel* interview: "I saw that possibility."[13] It was obviously quite the reverse of a theoretical judgment. It was a perspectival choice (alas, a little too impulsive—*augenblicklich*) on a historical turning point: that is, on an occurrence that was mere finitude in time and that had no greatness to offer a future. Therefore it was truly an encounter (*Begegnung*), in the sense in which an essential myth conceals a founding (*Stiftung*) and an inception (*Anfang*). Greatness, according to Heidegger, is not principally a function of courage deployed by humans; it depends instead on the depth and radicality of what is truly beginning: that is, the decisive dimension where the sense of time and the relation to history are put back into play. The opposition of *Anfang* ("inception") and mere beginning (*Beginn*) runs throughout his work until it becomes penetrating. This celebration of *Anfang* is not absent from the *Introduction to Metaphysics:* "But what is great can only begin great. Its beginning is in fact the greatest thing of all."* This affirmation is made apropos of the pre-Socratic discovery of *physis*. But we cannot imagine that the word "*Grösse*" comes accidentally from Heidegger, given what he believes (like many Germans, victims of the promise of a "millenary Reich") to be a new era in German history. What is loudly proclaimed here is that there is a founding inception in this "movement."

To be sure, to speak of "greatness" implies also that one admits pettiness (and if there is *inner,* internal truth, it means that there is also "outer," external truth). There is not, then, in the phrase under consideration, any approval of the entire program proposed or all the measures already taken by Hitler's government. On the contrary, we have brought into focus a polemical aspect regarding the official ideology, which should not be underestimated. However (this point does not exonerate Heidegger), fascist regimes have used the rhetoric of grandeur ("greatness") and monumentality all too often. It is in the joining of the thinker's lofty and patronizing tone and grandiloquent bombast that "inner truth" collapses in derision and tears.

Nevertheless, whether there was an "encounter" (or a sketch of something like it) in such events attempting to form a destiny, we may readily admit by simple recall what a historical project might be like, whether utopian or not, whether blamable or mad. At this point, as in making an important compass sighting, we can no longer neglect the parenthesis because it indicates what elements (or partners) the encounter (*Begegnung*) takes place between: "modern man" vis-à-vis "global technology." To tell the truth, there is only one partner involved in what provokes or concerns Heidegger. It would be irrelevant to recall that technology is conceived (precisely in the postwar years when, in all likelihood, Heidegger was putting in his parenthesis) as a "mode of homelessness." The capacity of assuring the greatness of this mode of disclosure of beings, of taking on their risks and their reservations about openness: such, then, is the eventual "inner truth" of contemporary man. Such was, it seems, the aptitude of the "movement," at least such was what its beginning promised.

This, in its essentials, is the second reading. It takes up Heidegger's own retrospective interpretation, given in the *Spiegel* interview in 1966. This reading replaces the Nazi phenomenon, making the latter merely one of the forms of modern man's "response" to the call of technology (anticipated more than three centuries ago, since Galileo's mathematical

---

* Manheim, p. 13. —Transl.

physics and Descartes's methodology). Thus the incriminating phrase no longer contains anything scandalous. It becomes not only acceptable but almost banal, if not actually soothing, even if the language, still voluntarist in 1935, resists this retrospective "harmonizing" a little.

The *hic* of this last reading no longer lets us understand "advantage" accorded to National Socialism but refused to Communism and Americanism (except in the *Spiegel* interview, where, so to speak, the three figures float around as equals). This rather cowardly interpretation (clever but somewhat demagogic) was taken to be quite authoritative at first. It was accepted for lack of anything better. Now its inadequacy hits us in the face.

The question is focused, in short, on this difficulty: why recognize "inner truth and greatness" in National Socialism and not in Americanism and Bolshevism? Heidegger pretends to do so in 1966, but not in 1935! If we retain the "explanation" contributed by the parenthesis of 1953 ("namely the encounter between globally determined technology and modern man"), we are stranded upon the following reef: the parenthesis offers the appearance of intelligibility, but it explains nothing that *specifically* applies to National Socialism. We are no further along than we were. Indeed, if we take it strictly, the explanation applies equally well to Americanism and Communism. Isn't there—and to what a degree there is indeed!—an "encounter" with technology in America and the Soviet Union? Isn't this encounter clothed in a certain greatness; didn't it entail titanic or Faustian heroism? And doesn't it also propose a type of global man, two versions of the "worker" figure which, since 1932— the date of Ernst Jünger's publication—we know struck Heidegger as the last image, the final configuration of the realization of the metaphysics of the will to power?

If we accept the parenthesis, we find nothing that applies *specifically* to National Socialism. Its so-called "inner truth and greatness" bear down on the entire epoch. This is precisely what Heidegger was looking for in 1953: "to drown the fish," as the "mean-spirited" would say, and, by a successful and rather inspired optical illusion, to allow that enormous phrase to "pass." Wasn't it enough to change the context, to provide a new backdrop for the sake of "good form"? Of course, the explanation is valid. But it is not philosophically adequate. It reduces the addition to a mere opportunistic gesture, *which it is,* but to which it cannot be reduced if we admit—as I have proposed and as many a text proves—that the parenthesis finds its full hermeneutic justification *in what it says.* Which implies that the phrase has also an *unsaid* content (*un non-dit*) scarcely noticed until now—to which we shall now turn.

In what it says, the parenthesis has played its role to perfection only because it *effectively* refers back to historical interpretations of modernity, of Nietzscheanism, and of technicist nihilism. Heidegger conceals nothing. He does not lie. He says what he really thinks. National Socialism was for the German people a radically historicist manner of *confronting* the challenge of "total mobilization" that is, the world race to power. Just as Nietzsche formulates the metaphysics which is self-fulfilling (and will end as that of the "atomic age"), National Socialism has pursued an inevitable policy (according to Heidegger) and should also be commended—in some respects rising above the strife—for its "great-ness." Nietzschean nihilism fulfilled, transgression of the line . . .

However, what is the *unsaid* of the parenthesis? We understand it when we complete the radical historicism by adding the destinal element without which there would be no *appropriation* (besides, "inner truth" certainly reflects back on an innerness, an "own" or proper). Put more succinctly, if National Socialism brings with it a "positive possibility," it does so because it entails a *plus,* lacking in the other world-historical figures of technological man. Americanism and Communism are severely criticized on a number of points; even a (too) well-intentioned reading had come to believe that it could make this verdict of the "movement" acceptable. Otto Pöggeler himself, who hardly exhibits an excessive good will toward his former teacher, writes that the clarification furnished by the parenthesis is "completely negative."[14] In fact, the parenthesis is *doubly* ambiguous. To the ambiguity that fundamentally subtends tech-nology, according to the thinking of the late Heidegger (between techno-logical Apparatus and destinal Event), is added the ambiguity that con-cerns National Socialism *qua* National Socialism (the ambiguity in which specificity is covered over by the second reading).

To be precise, Pöggeler was not wrong to point out that the connota-tion of the parenthesis now leads to a negative judgment on National Socialism (Heidegger therefore rather cleverly reversed the positive con-notation of "inner truth and greatness"). But Pöggeler underestimates (at least in this particular passage) the margin of ambiguity that remains in Heidegger's proposition. A third reading becomes indispensable precisely to elucidate the displacement that took place between 1935 and 1953 (or 1966) with respect to National Socialism.

Third Reading

This third reading was supposed to unfold just before we had to intervene to explain the parenthesis. It seems good, therefore, that the parenthesis was planned to divert attention from that possibility. Which possibility? Precisely the one that provides for the specificity of the National Socialist possibility (according to Heidegger's conception of it in 1935). The partner is not modern man in general but the German, the new *possible* Existent (not to be confused with the regime's already defined ideological-political traits). The respondent is not "global technology" *in general* but that technology to the extent that it reveals its essence (in the privileged manner of Nietzsche's metaphysics) and shelters it (the possibility Heidegger was beginning to call *Ereignis*—"event"—after 1936). In the *Introduction to Metaphysics* itself, Americanism and Communism are explicitly criticized to the extent that they represent precisely a global leveling: "All things have sunk to the same level, a surface resembling a blind mirror that no longer reflects, that casts nothing back. The prevailing dimension became that of extension and number. . . . In America and Russia this development grew into a boundless etcetera of indifference and always-the-sameness—so much so that the quantity took on a quality of its own.* This presentation of the world situation, inseparable from the theory of the "pincers" (*étau*) at the heart of which Europe would be caught between the two superpowers, is found again even in the course on Parmenides, which dates from 1942–43. It is further significant that in our texts of 1935 and in the few lines that concern us, it is specified that Nietzsche missed the real midpoint (*Mitte*) of philosophy, an extremely Hegelian thought and expression (but one whose implications and inferences exceed absolute idealism, since "midpoint" [*milieu*] was henceforth interpreted in the Hölderlinian sense).[15] So it is to be in Germany, and in an explanation involving Germanic thought (Hölderlin and Nietzsche), that what might enable the existent beings (*l'existent*) to escape global technological leveling will be fashioned. This possibility is *the appropriation* of the *destinal*. Appropriation designates a task in a direct line from the "authenticity" preached in *Being and Time*—which has as a correlate the conjunction of people-language-history in the singular and proper form it could have only for Martin Heidegger and his compatriots: that is, Germanicism (*la germanité*). The word effectively designates what is not "exchangeable" either by will or force, unlike Americanism and Communism, which correspond to *world types*. A rereading of the Hölderlin courses of 1934–35 (*Germania, Der Rhein*)[16] helps to confirm to what extent the ideal (a word he never uses thus) of *appropriating* the destinal is rooted in the historical community of the Germanic people, especially in the language.[17] Later (in *On the Way to Language,* for example) popular support will be toned down, giving more emphasis to language, but language there is German, the language of Hölderlin and Heidegger—and not speech (*parole*) in general.

The least we can say is that the regime in place in Germany from 1933 to 1945 did not understand things in the sense of a demanding but

* Manheim, p. 38. —Transl.

rather modest inquiry into Hölderlin's *nationnel*. To be sure, Hitler had wreaths laid on Hölderlin's tomb; to be sure, official propaganda used and abused the theme of Germanicism and linguistic Germanization, but—naturally—it was never with the destinal arrogance of Heidegger's dream. They had enforced discipline, a persecutory and then an extermi-native racism, complaisant recourse to force for the sake of force and even "technological extravagance" (Hitler's own words). There was nothing astonishing in this. It was not the first time (nor, alas, the last) that a mystique degenerated into a politics. It was not the first time that an intellectual had been misled about the direction of a party and a political regime. It was not the first time that we had to distinguish (rightly or wrongly) between "inner truth and greatness" on the one hand and petty deeds, failings, and crimes on the other. Didn't L. Plioutch himself, coming off the train that led him out of captivity, still hail "the luminous ideals of Communism"? But Heidegger's case was more complex, and his relationship to ideology was different. We now know that his evolution after 1934 was in no way ever reduced to disillusionment in an ideology that could still be presented as an ideal.

Whatever may be the relevance of the *rapprochement,* it must not obscure the specific difficulty the third reading discloses. Not that the letter is still "purloined." On the contrary, the letter of the text is now reinscribed in a positive project not to be confused with either the first, too hastly reading (in the form of a mix between what the thinker thought possible and the politico-ideological reality) or the second, all-too-eager reading (making the bad memories and embarrassing revisions go away, favoring a more global and future-oriented interpretation). Two equally anachronistic readings motivated in diametrically opposed ways, both of which hinder, in identifying the "the inner truth and greatness of the movement," the encounter (for which Heidegger believed the time had come—had believed for at least several years) between Germanicism and a fresh appropriation of the destiny of the West. The "advantage" of the third reading is considerable: it helps us understand what the fundamental thought was (or what the "ideal" was, to put the matter suitably) to which he pinned his continued adherence. Adherence, an unsatisfactory term which, to be sure, corresponds formally to staying in the Party and paying one's dues (acts whose actual import is difficult to grasp in a totalitarian regime) and which covers over, after the first enthusiasm of 1933, an increasingly marked gap between the "possible" of the "Revo-lution" and the realities of the regime.

The specific difficulty to which we have alluded begins to emerge now. It does not concern either the contingent confusion between "inner truth and greatness" and the ideological Nazi iron triangle (authoritari-anism, imperialism, racism) or their tardy fusion with a historicist interpretation too broad and too glibly harmonized in hindsight. It delivers the ambiguity that our third reading has tried to fathom. It is therefore internal to Heidegger's mediating role during the years following 1933: "Every essential form of spiritual life is marked by ambiguity."* This remark at the beginning of *the Introduction to Metaphysics* applies to philosophy inasmuch as philosophy cannot provide—"in an immediate way"—the sufficient conditions for practical decisions, but also inasmuch as philosophy can and must reveal the "ways and perspectives" by which to gain that knowledge that bears on the destiny of a history-bound people. This almost literal recovery of Heidegger's own terms helps us understand that he opposed the inherent "ambiguity" of philosophy to the activities that claimed his direct involvement but that, correlatively, the ambiguity could not be denied to the "movement," once it acknowledged historical significance. The play between the "inner" and "outer," between greatness and the rest, already implies what requires thoughtful resolution, and will find it—for anyone, as for Heidegger himself—in the conflict between the "possible" and the brutality of the facts.

All Heidegger's efforts in his courses on Hölderlin (1934–35), but especially on Nietzsche (starting in 1936), were directed to rendering precise the terms of this ambiguity, to revealing its features, to declaring its stakes. If Nietzsche's interpretation of the will to power unmasked the fulfillment of Western metaphysics, then what it had announced—that is, the reign of the Superman—would be purely and simply the extension, the intensification, of the pursuit of global mastery. "Total mobilization" would be our sole, unique destiny: the thinker would have only to rise to the point of domination, to the vanguard of the bureaucrats of technology. Hölderlin indicates another possibility that Heidegger offered in 1934–35, but qualified as "no longer metaphysical" from 1941–42 on:[18] a thinking and poetic reception of what metaphysical destiny conceals but also keeps as a refuge (through the realization of nihilism and beyond),[19] Nietzsche or Hölderlin? Heidegger had pronounced in favor of the second as early as 1935, at the close of his course *Der Rhein*.[20] But ambiguity is never reduced to an alternative that would be unraveled by making a choice. For Heidegger, the thinker and poet are grappling with the "same," and history delivers, without separating them, the imperatives of the present and the signs of a different future.

The identification of this ambiguity between "total mobilization" and the preparation of what mobilization hides is not enough. We must now understand why Heidegger thematized in this way the juncture between thought and history, why he projected that ambiguity (which he thought epochal) into a "movement" (which he thought disastrous). What

---

* Manheim, p. 8. —Transl.

led him to that "error" (which is more an errance or straying, despite its internal "logic") is knotted in the radically *historical-destinal* character of thought. It remains for us to penetrate to the heart of this last circle. There lies the possibility of a breakthrough forbidden to Heidegger himself (or one that he wanted to interdict, covering over in silence the possibility of an ultimate confession); to learn why Heidegger could not go on to the end of his "self-analysis."

If an epilogue is still permitted, we shall not, like Poe, borrow it from Crébillon *fils* or even from the myth of Atrides. And yet these allusions are inseparably justified because this affair is tragic from beginning to end. Still, as is often the case in life, this tragic matter yields details dressed only in everyday pettiness. There is an unheard-of contrast between the stakes of history and Being, the provocative scope Heidegger knew how to give those stakes, and the meanness of the cosmetic deceptions of 1953 and 1966. There is a contrast no less unheard of (but more cruel) between the noble hauteur of the Hölderlin "possible" that Heidegger discerned in the depths of the "movement" and its own implacable shadowed face. Are these two steps measurable—or commensurate?

NOTES

1. Martin Heidegger, *Einführung in die Metaphysik* (Tübingen: Neimeyer, 1953), p. 153; trans. Ralph Manheim, *An Introduction to Metaphysics* (New York: Doubleday Anchor, 1961), p. 166.

2. The protests were chiefly those of Helmut Kuhn and Jürgen Habermas, whom Christian Lewalter answered in *Die Ziet*. See Jean-Michel Palmier, *Les écrits politiques de Heidegger* (Paris: L'Herne, 1968), pp. 279–82.

3. Hartmut Buchner, "Fragmentarisches," in *Erinnerungen an Martin Heidegger* (Pfullingen: Neske, 1977), p. 49.

4. I am indebted to Carl Ulmer, *Der Spiegel,* May 2, 1977, p . 10), for this detail.

5. Martin Heidegger, "Réponses et questions sur l'histoire et la politique," trans. J. Launay (Paris: Mercure de France, 1977), p. 41, from *Der Spiegel,* May 31, 1976, p. 204. (William J. Richardson, S.J., uses "planetary technicity" in his translation of the *Spiegel* interview in *Heidegger: The Man and the Thinker,* ed. Thomas Sheehan [Chicago: Precedent, 1981], 45–75).

6. *Die Zeit,* September 24, 1953, according to Thomas Sheenan, "Heidegger and the Nazis," *New York Review of Books,* June 16, 1988, p. 42.

7. See Buckner, "Fragmentarisches."

8. Petra Jaeger, "Nachwort der Herausgeberin," in Heidegger, *Gesamtausgabe,* 40:234.

9. Walter Bröcker's testimony in Otto Pöggeler, "Heideggers politisches

Selbstverständnis," in *Heidegger und die praktische Philosophie,* ed. Annemarie Gethmann-Siefert and Otto Pöggeler (Frankfurt: Suhrkamp, 1988), p. 59 n.11. Heidegger presumably would have said neither "NS" (which is found in the manuscript, according to Buchner) nor "this movement" (as found in the printed version) but "the movement" (*der Bewegung,* in the genitive).

10. Heidegger, *Einführung,* p. 77ff.

11. Ibid., p. 81ff.

12. Martin Heidegger, *Die Selbstbehauptung der deutschen Universität,* from French trans. G. Granel (Mauverzin: T.E.R., 1982), p. 22.

13. Heidegger, "Réponses et Questions," p. 22.

14. Pöggeler, "Heideggers politisches Selbstverständnis," p. 38.

15. See the closing to Heidegger, *Der Rhein,* in *Gesamtausgabe,* vol. 39.

16. See the French translation by François Fédier and Julien Hervier (Paris: Gallimard, 1988).

17. On the historical Being of the *Volk,* see Heidegger *Gesamtausgabe,* 39:20, and 31:49–52, 120, 143–44; on poetry as the *volk*'s original language, 31:214ff.

18. Heidegger, *Einführung; Hölderlins Hymne "Andenken," Gesamtausgabe,* 52: 99.

19. "Das Sein selbst entzeiht sich, der Entzug geschieht" (Being itself draws back, Retreat happens): Heidegger, *Nietzsche* (Pfullingen, 1961), 2:355.

20. Heidegger, *Der Rhein, Gesamtausgabe,* 39:294).

16

The Political Incompetence of Philosophy

HANS-GEORG GADAMER

The conflict that has pointedly attached itself in recent days to Heidegger's name is actually an ancient one. How does a philosopher relate to political and social realities? How do his problems and insights help him to come to terms with reality? To the discussion that took place over Farías's book on Heidegger, I contributed my own views in November 1987, in a text that appeared in its fullest form in German under the title "Zurück von Syrakus" (Return from Syracuse). The title alludes to Plato's disillusionment during two trips to Syracuse, in Sicily, by invitation of the "Tyrant." The mission was meant to introduce the young ruler to Plato's basic tenets regarding perfect government and the perfect social order. It was a complete failure. Plato was barely able to escape with his life and return home. Later, other great disappointments awaited him in the circle of his students and friends. Dion, the leader of a victorious expedition to Syracuse and a close companion, was suddenly murdered by his friends.

Plato's political adventure in Sicily is almost symbolic in its implications. It makes one wonder. Of course, Heidegger's political commitment in 1933 cannot be judged by the same standard as Plato's Sicilian venture. The Platonic academy, to which Dion and others among Plato's friends belonged, had from the start a much stronger sociopolitical character than any academy or university (or general intellectual pursuit) in modern society. This inclines us to wonder all the more whether philosophy may not be the decisive factor. The philosopher's view, which probes the ultimate generalities and foundations of all questions, seems less aptly predisposed to probe the concrete circumstances and practicalities of

social and political life. Perhaps we should examine just what is fundamental here in the light of philosophy itself. What actually is the cognitive
value of philosophy if it gives twisted and extravagant answers to important and vital questions?

Some years ago the French sociologist Bourdieu, an important and
intelligent man, took a critical stance toward Heidegger's philosophy,
traced it back to the conservative tradition and the pseudorevolutionary
thought of the Rightists—the followers of the "Revolution of the Right"
in the Weimar Republic. Bourdieu's interpretation is interesting, but it
makes an assumption I cannot accept (even from a sociologist): namely,
that philosophy exists only as a particular worldly institution, which we
must first observe critically from various sociotheoretical viewpoints if
we are to unmask it and its cognitive claims.

I have a strange feeling when I see such questions directed toward
philosophy. They give the impression that there exists a special sort of
human being who pursues philosophy. That is not true. Everybody
"pursues" philosophy but usually makes a worse job of it than the so-
called philosopher. For me, this alone seriously compromises the entire
investigation—after all, it is an awkward and ominous fact that the
sociologist does not direct his criticism against everybody, not even
against himself, but only against the so-called philosopher. Human beings
everywhere pose philosophical questions that no one is in a position to
answer—concerning the future, death, the meaning of life, happiness,
and so on. There is evidently a passion for philosophical questioning that
exists in all human beings, not just the professional philosopher.

Proceeding thus, I am hardly following a particular philosophy. This
"world"-concept of philosophy—to use a Kantian expression—refers to
a natural human state that has from the very start made us receptive also
to the answers offered by religion. By contrast, the academic concept of
philosophy is not very interesting. Compared with the passion for thinking and the restless questioning inherent in human beings, the academic
concept—like everything that pertains to academic affairs—is a decidedly
secondary matter.

It is true, of course, that the basic problems addressed by human
beings include the question of the future of one's own social relationships,
concern for personal happiness. The question of what constitutes the
"right" life has been posed ever since Socrates, who was not a professor
of philosophy. Socrates posed his question so persistently, in fact, that I
feel sure he also believed that ultimately every human asks the same
question but also secretly avoids addressing it, constantly distances
himself from it through the answers he gives in lieu of putting himself to
the test. When we recognize this, we realize immediately how the passion

for questioning, whether it concerns the future of mankind or the happiness of the individual or the terrible mystery of death, constantly confronts our ignorance. The same holds for the origins of mankind, which have predetermined all of us in ways we did not choose. The same holds for the past, which not even a god can undo. All this is accompanied by "a process of socialization," as people call it today, which molds us, leads us from the pure instincts of early childhood, trains and regulates our lives, and finally forms us in the understanding and use of language. In view of all this, we must, I think, ask ourselves why a professor of philosophy, driven to ask the sort of philosophical question that no science can answer, should be considered especially qualified to penetrate and solve daily problems better than others. I always wonder why the philosopher (in the particular academic sense of the term) should be expected to have unique insight and expected even to bear a special responsibility. Shouldn't the clergyman, the doctor, the schoolteacher, the judge, even the journalist exercise a far greater influence on events, and therefore bear a far greater responsibility for the present and future?

We may recall that Heidegger was once asked: "Why don't you write an ethics?" When a young Frenchman, Beaufret, asked him this question after the war, Heidegger tried to answer in a detailed way. But the gist of his reply was that the question was essentially unanswerable. How can it be the task of a philosopher to construe an ethical system that proposes or prescribes a social order or recommends a new way of molding morals or general public convictions about concrete matters? These actually involve processes of human learning and socialization that are already under way, forming an *ethos*, long before people ever confront the radical questions associated with philosophy. "Ethics" presupposes a lived system of values.

The conflict lies within man himself, in his questions and musings, not between specialized and expert knowledge and its bearing on the social realities of practical life. As human beings, we have turned away so far from the natural order of things that we follow no natural *ethos*. The word *ethos*, in Greek, signifies the manner of life that nature bestows on both humans and animals. Among animals, the power of habituation and instinctive direction is so dominant that it overwhelmingly determines their behavior.

I once observed this myself. It was a bad summer. A pair of swallows had built their nest on our balcony. Their second brood had come very late. And now the migratory urge proved to be even stronger than the brooding instinct: the parent birds deserted their poor little offspring, left them behind to die of hunger. We later found their bones in the nest, reminders of how the order of nature dominates the behavior of other living creatures.

We humans have no such unambiguous instincts to direct us. We have "freedom of choice," or at least we seem to ourselves to have it, and we call it by that name. The Greeks used the expression *prohairesis* for it. The freedom to behave in a self-chosen way presupposes the ability to ask questions, to see possibilities even when they may not be able to be realized. Of course, anyone who does not have the imagination to see possibilities will not easily fall into error. So I would say, not only of Heidegger and so-called philosophers but of human beings in general, that every one of them is subject to error and falls prey (above all) to his or her own secret wishes for happiness and the shimmering dreams of fulfillment. These depend on the assessment of one's own circumstances and relations with other human beings. We are all in danger of misjudging ourselves and of clinging to illusions. Even physicians are too close to themselves to treat their own ailments, as are the accused to undertake their own defense. It is true of all knowledge that its practical application requires a special gift that does not rely on merely technically acquired information. One of the imbalances of the knowledge-oriented culture of modern times is that we do not recognize this special structure of practical knowledge. When the philosopher (in the academic sense), to whom we ascribe a certain competence in formulating supposedly insoluble problems, has the good fortune of finding answers to them, he may be considered wise—but not rightly because of his philosophical competence, which could never protect him from error or misunderstanding (especially in his own affairs).

We may of course say that the philosopher does bear a certain responsibility inasmuch as he does have influence, whether he cares to or not, as a teacher or intellectual guide. But we cannot deny that someone from another field may prove to be a better philosopher than a so-called professional philosopher, especially when his own specialty has to do with the real problems of economic, social, and political life. It would be sheer self-deception to believe that it was his special competence alone and not his own "philosophy" as a thinking human being that taught him to think in a practical way. Conversely, we may be quite impressed by a person who, thanks to his philosophical powers, exhibits a certain superiority—a superiority, I may say, that I recognized in Heidegger. Such power can also lead us astray: I will not deny that Heidegger's powerful intellectual influence in his own time led many a person to make incorrect judgments in practical and political matters. But in thought as in life, we each assume our own responsibility. If we have learned as philosophers (in the academic sense of the term again) to pose questions that deeply concern each of us—even without being able to find conclusive answers— then, with Jaspers, we may call this a "clarification of existence." It illuminates the boundaries of knowledge, but it is entirely different from the ability to anticipate which practical goals will be manageable and realistic.

And thus a case such as that of Heidegger may come about. Here was a man whose thinking held a half-century in its spell, a man who radiated an incomparable power of suggestion, who as a thinker discovered the "care-structure" of existence in all the behavior of humans toward one another and the world, and (inextricably bound to it) man's tendency toward self-destruction. Yet this man could also, in his own behavior, lose himself in delusions. Heidegger himself recognized this and admitted it through his later silence. Certainly it was not as if he did not continue to hold firm to his own ways as a thinker and teacher. His lectures through the years, which have since been published in part, attest to this. For himself he remained committed to his vision of the "right way" for mankind, even after he realized that National Socialism and Hitler's leadership were anything *but* a step toward the new beginning that hovered before him as the real task of mankind.

We should not be surprised that a man who possesses superior powers of thought may also err. Whoever thinks, envisions possibilities. Whoever envisions possibilities with great clarity may also see what he wants to see—which may not actually exist at all. Like many others, Heidegger was clearly aware of the abuses and decline of his own social and political surroundings, especially of the German university life of the time. There were incalculable forces at work in the collapse of World War I society and the imported democracy, for which the Germans were so ill prepared. It is a matter of record how many strains and failures, acts of violence, secret slayings, attempted coups, and cases of corrupt rigging occurred in the Weimar Republic. Even after the government was consolidated, the Germans could not really look forward to an open future, since the peace treaty and its imposed economic burdens thwarted any reasonable prospects. The English later realized how these things contributed to the extreme radicalization of a nation of unemployed. Heidegger saw all that. But he saw it writ large in world history, and he envisioned an inevitable radical reversal of direction. He believed he saw such a reversal in 1933. We should scarcely be surprised that such extravagance can be found in a great thinker. On the contrary, I am more surprised that philosophers are constantly being confronted by the question of ethics. The need to ask another person what is honorable or decent or humane strikes me as a distress signal or possibly a sign of the impoverishment of our existing society—even when we seek such answers from a so-called philosopher. This simply shows that our society has lost its bearings.

Naturally, this is not the fault of one who asks something of another. Such inquiry is understandable. But there is an indissoluble relationship between, on the one hand, the "imprint" that human beings receive—from their earliest days and from everything they experience in society—in their own nature and in their historical context and, on the other hand, the problem of what is good, which must always be solved concretely if one wants to improve things.

How else can we possibly ask what is truly good? The first requirement is that the question must be addressed to oneself and that in asking about the good one must not think only of oneself. In any case, one can certainly not take another's place or prompt another to adopt recommendations, proposals, advice, or prescriptions for action that he does not himself see or understand. There is no conciliatory ethics. When Beaufret, the young Frenchman, asked when Heidegger might write an ethics, his reason was simply that he had found in *Being and Time* such a forceful and radical potential for posing intellectual questions that he believed Heidegger must be able to help mankind in its threatened state after the devastations of World War II. It was surely not a specific philosophical task that Heidegger was being asked to perform. The imperatives of discretion are directed toward every human being. But this was precisely what Germany lacked. It had known no revolution, no overthrow of authority, and it was used to subordination. Thus, our political immaturity became our destiny.

The extraordinary depoliticization of Germany in this period prompted Max Weber to coin the term "ethics of responsibility"—as if responsibility did not lie at the heart of all ethics! In any case, ethics is not a question merely of attitude; it also means correct behavior and, therefore, the acceptance of responsibility for the consequences of one's deeds and omissions. The "ethics of principle" that people saw in Kant (erroneously, by the way) was in reality the expression of the German political weakness and lack of political solidarity. This weakness became a malady of the authority-oriented bourgeois society of nineteenth-century Germany. It was apparently also a weakness of the Protestant religion, whose secularization had been supported by the religious fervor of its beliefs and then rigidified in matters of principle and conscience. So I would say basically that we each discover eventually within ourselves the responsibility that we all must bear. Some time ago I had occasion to read Franz Kafka's *The Trial* again. There one finds a wonderful but rather oppressive description of how so-called "guiltlessness" entails guilt. Perhaps in such situations the "philosopher" may be able to help us formulate our questions better—those that affect us all. But the philosopher helps us only in the sense that he or she understands and is able to show us how thoroughly we must confront our own tasks: their resolution cannot depend on others alone. Guilt and responsibility never belong solely to others.

VII

17

Heidegger's French Connection and the Emperor's New Clothes

TOM ROCKMORE

In France, the intellectual debate on Heidegger's Nazism began in the pages of *Les Temps Modernes,* the well-known French intellectual journal founded by Sarte and his colleagues when France was liberated from the Nazis, and later edited by him for many years. The first phase includes texts by Karl Löwith, Alfred de Towarnicki, Eric Weil, Alphonse De Waelhens, and Maurice de Gandillac, preceded by an unsigned editorial note. Here, just before the appearance of the "Letter on Humanism," in which Heidegger rejects Sartrean existentialism as well as humanism, the unnamed editor (in all probability, Sartre) draws a comparison between Heidegger and Hegel: in the same way that Hegel's later thought led him to compromise with Prussia, so Heidegger the philosopher and Heidegger the political activist prove to be one and the same. Heidegger's political choice follows from his existential thought. But just as a close analysis of Hegel's position would remove any doubts about the validity of dialectical thought as such, a similar analysis would demonstrate the independence of an existential view of politics and would place it at the antipodes of Nazism.[1]

There are no fewer than three subphases of this discussion: the initial publication of articles by Löwith, Gandillac, and Towarnicki, followed some time later by articles by Weil and De Waehlens, and ending with responses by Löwith and De Waelhens. Gandillac, probably the first French philosopher to come into contact with Heidegger after the war, went on to an important career at the Sorbonne. Löwith, a former student and later a colleague of Heidegger, spent the war in exile. He is well known for his own work as well as for his interesting study of why and how Heidegger achieved such philosophical importance.[2] Weil, a Jew and an assistant to Cassirer, himself a Jew, emigrated at an early date to France, where he achieved considerable distinction as an original thinker, above all for an important analysis of the nature of philosophical categories.[3] De Waelhens was a well-known Belgian scholar of phenomenology, author of important studies on Heidegger, Husserl, and Merleau-Ponty. Towarnicki, a journalist, is still active.

As in the more recent debates, the discussion proceeds here as a series of dialectically interrelated analyses of the some phenomenon seen from diverse points of view. Both Gandillac and Towarnicki embroider into their own accounts various themes from the so-called official view of Heidegger's Nazism, due finally to Heidegger himself. Gandillac offers a short account of a visit to Heidegger's home, in which he makes two interesting points.[4] He reports with sympathy Heidegger's view that Hitlerism was the historic manifestation of a so-called structural disease of human being as such, a notion that clearly anticipates Heidegger's later effort to link the topics of technology and Nazism; here Heidegger refuses to implicate the fall of the Germanic community, whose true sense of liberty he hopes to awaken. We are also told several times in the article that Heidegger was seduced like a child by the exterior aspects of Hitlerism, that he was persuaded to enroll in the Nazi party by his children, and so on. These two themes signify that Heidegger was unaware of, and hence not responsible for, his own political actions; at the same time they hold open the possibility, which Heidegger never renounced, of the future flowering of the German people in an authentic form of Nazism.

Towarnicki's version of the official view is at least partly false.[5] He mistakenly suggests that Heidegger was elected rector unanimously. He quotes Heidegger to the effect that the death of Röhm opened his eyes to the true nature of Nazism, which he later criticized in his courses on Nietzsche. We know, of course, that Heidegger continued to affirm his belief in an authentic form of National Socialism. Towarnicki's article ends with an affirmation, in the form of a direct quotation, of Heidegger's emotional insistence on France's spiritual importance to the world. Since Heidegger also justified his turn toward Nazism by the way of a similar concern with the spiritual welfare of the German people, however, the remark seems less than uplifting.

Löwith's discussion, written outside Germany in 1939—hence at the beginning of the war that was to devastate Europe—is still surprisingly complete.[6] It includes many of the topics that dominate the later debate: the relation between Heidegger's turn toward Nazism and his famous description of resoluteness in paragraph 74 of *Being and Time,* the role of the *Rektoratsrede,* the praise of Schlageter, his relationship to the students of Freiburg, Jünger's influence, and the like. Löwith's analysis can be summarized as follows: (1) *Being and Time* offers a theory of historical existence; (2) Heidegger was able to turn toward Nazism by interpreting his own thought; (3) his turning is squarely based on an essential principle of his thought: namely, that existence, reduced to itself, relies only on itself in the face of nothing; (4) this principle enabled Heidegger to reconcile and identify his thought with the radical political situation in which it arose.

Löwith's is a clear attempt to understand Heidegger's Nazism as following from his philosophical position, and to understand that position as the expression of the historical situation—in Hegelian terms, as the times comprehended in thought. He opposes two points favored by most of Heidegger's subsequent defenders. He denies that Heidegger's philosophy can be understood except in terms of its social and political context; hence, he contradicts in advance the well-known textualist approach, widely favored in French circles, in which the analysis of Heidegger's writings is insulated from their wider social and political influences. He further denies the "official" reading of Heidegger's turn to National Socialism—later developed by Fédier, by Aubenque, and, from a different perspective, by Derrida and Lacoue-Labarthe—which minimizes, even excuses, the turn toward Nazism as merely unfortunate and temporary.

At the outset of the French debate the opposition between Löwith and Gandillac and Towarnicki already fixes the basic readings of Heidegger's Nazism as either necessary or contingent. Within and without the French context, all later versions of the debate hardly alter these two options in any fundamental way. Obviously, they are incompatible. Löwith in fact specifically opposes Towarnicki, who treats Heidegger's link to National Socialism as merely temporary, regrettable, and unmotivated by his underlying philosophical position; he also opposes Gandillac's assertion that Heidegger was unaware of what he did.

The disagreement led to a debate. Weil describes Towarnicki's article as a plea for Heidegger, or rather as a plea by Heidegger. He opposes the necessitarian thesis, whereas De Waelhens defends the contingency view. Weil criticizes Heidegger's failure to assume responsibility for his acts; he further criticizes Heidegger for being the sole important philosopher to support Hitler.[7] But he denies the necessitarian thesis, since even on Heideggerian grounds the link between Heidegger's thought and National Socialism is illegitimate. Weil argues that "Heideggerian existentialism" is defective in leading to a decision in general, not to a particular decision. He claims that Heidegger falsified his own thought in pretending *a contrario* that a political decision could be derived from his apolitical thought.

His deconstruction of the necessitarian reading is peculiar. It is peculiar not because it conflates Heideggerian phenomenology and existentialism, which Heidegger later denied, or because it denies that Heidegger is privileged as an interpreter of his own thought. Rather, it is peculiar in its failure to respond to the claim that a clear political decision follows from Heidegger's view of authenticity. Alphonse De Waelhens, who also identifies Heidegger's thought as an existential phenomenology, suggests that Heidegger's fidelity to his own position is less significant than its intrinsic relation to National Socialism.[8]

De Waelhens's attack on the necessitarian thesis is remarkable for two reasons. First, he maintains that before we can criticize Heidegger's thought, we must settle the issue of who really understands Heidegger. Even such later defenders as Derrida, who acknowledge that Heidegger's Nazism is central to his philosophical thought, insist that only someone deeply steeped in it (by inference: an unconditional adherent) is competent to measure its defects. Second, De Waelhens formulates a quasi-transcendental argument to demonstrate that Heidegger could not have based his actions on his philosophy. He maintains that the author of *Being and Time* could not accept fascism, because it is incompatible with his ideas, above all with historicity. He answers Löwith's version of the necessitarian thesis by arguing that Löwith possessed an insufficient grasp of Heidegger's texts.

Since Weil and De Waehlens both deny a more than casual link between Heidegger's philosophic thought and Nazism, each must construe Heidegger's politics and political actions as an instance of Heidegger's infidelity to his position. But since Heidegger quickly abandoned real Nazism in favor of his own ideal version (which he never relinquished), Weil and De Waehlens do not defuse the necessitarian thesis: they do not demonstrate that the relation between Heidegger's philosophy and his Nazism is a contingent one. At best they show only that, on the basis of this thought, Heidegger's turn toward real Nazism was mistaken, as he later acknowledged. But they do not show that he was mistaken in turning toward National Socialism as he wished it to exist—in accord with the futural perspective of his own position.

De Waehlens is more radical than Weil. His claim is not that Heidegger misunderstood his own thought but rather that the individual Heidegger is without philosophical interest. He was answered by Löwith, who does not respond to the issue of who is capable of judging Heidegger.[9] The omission is important, since it is always possible to claim that any criticism is based on an insufficient awareness of the position in question. Löwith, who restates his belief that Heidegger's Nazism is a necessary consequence of his philosophy of existence, notes how curious it is to defend Heidegger against his own conscious political engagement. In his rejoinder, De Waelhens maintains that his own demonstration that Heidegger's political action did not, and could not, follow him from his philosophical position is only an illustration of the fact that one cannot deduce a political stance from a philosophy.[10]

De Waelhens's rejoinder is controversial. The principle he invokes effectively suppresses any analysis of the relation between thought and action. It also contradicts the entire ethical tradition, whose unexpressed premise is that reasons can be causes. But it is easy to show that this principle is false for at least two reasons. First, throughout history—for example, at present in Eastern Europe and in the Middle East—millions of people have been moved by ideas to political action. This is a point De Waehlens can accept only by denying that such ideas are philosophical. Second, Waelhens's politically charged request to abandon any analysis of the link between Heidegger's philosophy and his politics presupposes the very efficacy of philosophy that he is concerned to deny.

The initial phase of the French discussion of Heidegger's relation to Nazism is calm and scholarly. It is interesting as a clear statement of the necessitarian and contingent readings, and as an anticipation of later proposed deconstructions of the necessitarian thesis on *a priori* grounds. These include an *a priori* impossibility argument and the related claim that opposed criticisms are simply uninformed. Interestingly, the versions of the necessitarian argument due to Weil and De Waelhens eschew any analysis of Heidegger's texts in favor of general statements. This is particularly true of De Waehlens, since his two main claims—namely, his *a priori* argument against the possibility of an intrinsic link between philosophy and politics, and his assertion that criticism is based on insufficient knowledge—each respond in general to all objections but fail to consider the merits of any particular objection.

This initial debate sets the stage for all later discussions in France of the relation between Heidegger's philosophical thought and his Nazism. The second phase differs widely from the first. It is less compact and, for that reason, more difficult to delimit. It occurred roughly from 1948, when the French first edition of Lukács's book appeared, to the publication of Jean-Michel Palmier's study in 1968, the year of the French student uprising. It includes articles by François Fédier, Jean-Paul Faye, François Bondy, Alfred Grosser, Robert Minder, Aimé Patri, and others, and contributions to such journals as *Médiations* and *Critique*. It is more international, since it refers more often to materials published in languages other than French. The discussion is increasingly heated, often overheated, even strident on occasion, which takes it beyond the polite nature of traditional scholarly debate. The excited character of the debate reflects the political stakes of the critique, or defense, of Heidegger's form of National Socialism.

The remarkable change in tone is due to a variety of factors. In the initial phase of the discussion, some participants, including Löwith and Weil, were not native French. But those who intervened in the next stage of the debate were mainly of French origin. It is a fact that French intellectual debates tend to be noisy and strident. In the meantime, Heidegger's "Letter on Humanism" had become influential as well. As a result, Heidegger became a commanding presence in French intellectual life, the horizon of which came to be increasingly determined by his thought. As Heidegger displaced Hegel in the role of master thinker, French scholars sometimes acted as if they were as much engaged in defending French thought as in defending Heidegger's position. The publication of works by Guido Schneeberger, Adorno, and Hühnerfeld meant that Heidegger's philosophy, not only his personal reputation, was now at risk. Finally, France was approaching a political crisis that would nearly paralyze the country for a number of months from March 1968 on.

Since the entire translation of *Being and Time* appeared in France only in the mid-1980s, the French Heidegger discussion revolves mainly around the "Letter on Humanism." This text is Heidegger's response to a letter addressed to him, on November 10, 1945, by Jean Beaufret. Heidegger replied on November 23 of that year and then reworked his response for publication. The response, which took the form of an open letter to a figure on the French philosophical scene, just when Heidegger was in eclipse because of his association with the Nazis, is both philosophical and strategic in character. For instance, there was an obvious strategic value in Heidegger's claim of a turning (*Kehre*) in his position, by implication a turning away from his earlier view (which was also a turning away from Nazism). The concept of the turning seemed a tacit, even graceful admission of an earlier complicity, combined with a suggestion of a fresh start. It also suggested a reasonable alternative to Sartre, to many an objectionable French guru. All these characteristics quickly raised Heidegger's stock in French intellectual thought and may even have been calculated to do so.

In his "Letter," Heidegger implicitly admits his culpability in his stated desire to turn over a new leaf. Beaufret took a more extreme line, which developed only slowly. As early as 1945, when he was close to Marxism, he described Heidegger's adherence to National Socialism as the result of a naiveté linked to a bourgeois character.[11] But he rapidly abandoned his youthful flirt with revolutionary thought, common in France. His letter to Heidegger mentions his concern with the relation of ontology to ethics. But he later provides a curious answer to his own question in two ways: (1) by denying a more than casual relation between Heidegger and National Socialism, itself a form of the contingency thesis;[12] and (2) above all by turning to the revisionist view of history that simply denies the existence of Nazi concentration camps![13] As a result, the link between Heidegger and National Socialism becomes unproblematic because, in a word, Nazism was not Nazism! In this most extreme deconstruction of the necessitarian thesis, one could without hesitation acknowledge that Heidegger's philosophy led him to Nazism, since Nazism would no longer be problematic.

We may deal separately with the works by Lukács and Palmier. Lukács, the great Marxist philosopher and literary scholar, is the author of *History and Class Consciousness*, in which he almost single-handedly created the Hegelian approach to Marxism so widely influential in later Marxist discussion. His study of Marxism and existentialism, a polemical work written during his Stalinist phase, dismisses existentialism from an orthodox Marxist perspective.[14] It uses Engels's view of the relation between thought and being as the watershed question of all philosophy, in order to reject the possibility of existentialism as a third way between idealism and materialism. For Lukács, existentialism is only a form of subjective idealism linked to the defense of bourgeois class interests. In passing, he attacks Heidegger's position as prefascist. He develops this criticism at length in an appendix, "Anhang: Heidegger Redivivus" (responding to Heidegger's "Letter on Humanism," the document that cemented Heidegger's relation to French philosophy), which was added to the German edition of his book.[15]

Lukács's work affected the French discussion of Heidegger only marginally, through its influence on Merleau-Ponty and Sartre. It was later answered in part by Merleau-Ponty, who, in a famous discussion, identified Lukács as the founder of so-called Western Marxism.[16] Lukács clearly influenced Sartre's later turn to Marxism. Some two decades later, Palmier defended Heidegger against various attacks, perhaps for the first time in the French discussion through a detailed textual analysis.[17] Palmier's study, appearing after a sharp exchange between Fédier and Faye, was intended as an initial approach to Heidegger's writings from April 1933 to February 1934: that is, during Heidegger's period as rector. But by casting his net so narrowly, Palmier (perhaps unintentionally) takes this period, which he recognizes as belonging to Heidegger's principal *oeuvre*, out of context; he renders it difficult to perceive any continuity between it and the later evolution of Heidegger's thought. Possibly for this reason, Palmier's serious study attracted little attention in the later debate.[18]

The conceptual and chronological limits of the second phase of the discussion are the books by Lukács and Palmier. To characterize the period, we do well to turn to the polemic between Fédier and Faye. It differs from the initial phase of the discussion, which, of course, began with a defense of Heidegger. Here, the opening shot was fired by an opponent and was immediately met by a defender determined to repulse any assault on the house of Being.

This second battle of the conceptual war concerning Heidegger was launched by Jean-Paul Faye, in 1961, through the publication in French translation of certain Heideggerrian texts, including the "Rektoratsrede" and the homage to Schlageter. In a short presentation of Heidegger's texts, Faye notes the violence of Heidegger's revolutionary language, particularly in the rectoral speech, as well as its link to Nazi terminology.[19] In a later article, Faye reproduces Heidegger's statement on the essence of authentic Nazism, taken from *An Introduction to Metaphysics*, and Heidegger's endorsement in a letter to *Die Zeit* (dated 24 September 1953) of the effort by Christian E. Lewalter (published in the same journal on August 13 to explain away Heidegger's concern with Nazism. Here, Faye develops his earlier discussion by insisting on the close relation between the views of Heidegger and Ernst Krieck.[20] Faye also takes the occasion, prodded by Aimé Patri, to correct his earlier translation of certain Heideggerean texts.

Faye's articles did not break new ground. Their main contribution was to make available material that cast doubt on the contingency analysis. François Fédier's initial intervention in the discussion occurred some five years after Faye's articles. His ire was directed mainly toward other targets; he turned on Faye only when the latter responded to his impassioned defense of Heidegger against all comers. Since that time, Fédier has maintained his visible role—which now, after the death of Beaufret, his former teacher, is his alone—as the self-appointed official spokesman for the contingency thesis, determined to deconstruct the necessitarian analysis in all its various forms.

Fédier's initial article was prompted by attacks on Heidegger by Guido Schneeberger, Theodor Adorno, and Paul Hühnerfeld. His self-described intent is not to answer a polemic but to examine the presuppositions of hostile arguments. In each instance, Fédier proves to his own satisfaction that the critic is methodologically incapable of comprehending Heidegger's Nazism without acknowledging the "main facts" of the case.[21] He does not examine later evidence—with the exception of the *Spiegel* interview—but he argues that an analysis of Heidegger's courses between 1934 and 1944 demonstrates Heidegger's opposition to Nazism. It also shows why, in 1933, Heidegger hoped for the achievement of something other than what Nazism became. But in view of Heidegger's consistent commitment to an ideal form of Nazism, it is doubtful that his understanding of real National Socialism varied significantly after he joined the Nazi party.

None of the works to which Fédier responds here is either due to a French author or published in French. Fédier's discussion is a form of the contingency thesis—in particular, of the claim that Heidegger's critics do not know his writings. His effort is innovative perhaps only as the first attempt in French circles to respond to any foreign criticism of Heidegger. Fédier's defense *tous azimuths* does not even consider the nascent French effort to come to grips with the problem. He was quickly answered by three French writers—Patri, Minder, and Faye—and shot back a rapid rejoinder.

Fédier is defended by Patri. In his short paper, he argues in support of Fédier and against Faye, to the effect that on linguistic grounds there is no relation between Heidegger and Nazism, since the adjective *völkisch* was already used by Fichte, who was not an SS.[22] This defense, which attacks the necessitarian thesis on the grounds that the critic is misinformed, was immediately refuted in another short paper by Minder. Minder shows that even a cursory examination of Heidegger's language supposes an acceptance of some fundamental principles of the Third Reich.[23] He further notes, as Farías and especially Ott later argue in detail, that Heidegger was strongly influenced by a rustic, politically reactionary form of Catholicism.

The latter point, a historicist form of the necessitarian thesis, contradicts Heidegger's later thought following the famous turning. The claim that anyone, including the author of the *Fundamentalontologie*, is *not* in part a product of the surrounding environment denies Heidegger's own view that we are all determined by the modern world, by technology, ultimately by metaphysics, even by Being. In response, Faye returns to the attack with a perceptive comment on nascent right wing Heideggereanism.[24] He notes ironically that a Parisian sect is presently devoted to protecting its masters in the way that the ASPCA is devoted to protecting animals. He discusses the history of the term *völkisch* and its relation to racism, in particular its relation to anti-Semitism, which is later developed by Bourdieu; and he mentions the difference, crucial in his eyes, between being in the world and transforming it.

Faye's article was perceived as it was in part intended: as a provocation. Nevertheless, in his article he commits a strategic error: he argues that he has the knowledge Fédier says he lacks. The argument cannot be won on such terms, however; it is always possible to maintain that the critic knew certain things but not others, and that those other things were surely relevant, indeed crucial. In short, one can always claim that a critic is not sufficiently informed. The insight was not lost on Fédier, who quickly responded that *après tout* Faye was uninformed, in any case unable to criticize Heidegger because he did not know German sufficiently well. Fédier has continued to employ this technique in his later attempts to defend the "sacred" cause. In his response, Fédier concedes that Heidegger did use certain incriminating expression over a ten-month period, but he denies that Heidegger's thought was compromised as a result. In a demonstration of why no translation is safe from deconstruction, which anticipates Derrida's use of this method in his best days, Fédier even asserts that a "real translation" of the rectoral address will remove the vestiges of Nazism which Faye has injected into it. He claims (a point later developed at length in a book) that Heidegger was mistaken in 1933, but at the time it was impossible to understand the future evolution of National Socialism. In closing, he criticizes Heidegger's triple failure to foresee the consequences of Nazism, to measure the powerlessness of thought with respect to Nazism, and to grasp that thought could not modify what was already under way.[25] The latter two points are versions of Heidegger's own idea of the weakness of thought, as distinguished from philosophy, advanced in the "Letter on Humanism" and elsewhere.

Fédier's argument is the basic statement of the contingentist attack on the necessitarian analysis. More than twenty years later, one can no longer in good faith doubt the existence of a form of right-wing Heideggerianism determined to save Heidegger at all costs, even by denying the self-evident. Except for Beaufret, Gandillac, De Waelhens, and to a lesser extent such secondary figures as Patri, at this early stage Fédier was virtually alone as the keeper of the grail of Being.

Obviously, Fédier's strategy partly depends on De Waelhens's attack (a pioneer move in the French-language discussion) on the necessitarian thesis on the grounds of insufficient evidence. Now De Waelhens's claim that the critic must be uninformed was entirely unconvincing; certainly it was not convincing with respect to such a truly knowledgeable observer as Löwith. If he does not perfect this strategy, Fédier at least develops it into a coherent defense, just as in chess the difference between isolated moves and a viable defense consists in the united articulation of the various elements. Fédier's countermove contains elements that make it difficult, perhaps impossible, to show a durable (or even transitory) link between Heidegger and Nazism: among them, the gambit that Heidegger was naive but not culpable, since he did not or could not know the nature of Nazism; the intimation that the critic is inadequately informed about Heidegger's views, about the German language, and so on; the suggestion that a simple statement of the facts suffices to separate the real Heidegger from the mythic target of his critics. In different ways, each of these elements returns in the third phase of the French debate on Heidegger and National Socialism.

Fédier's strategy to defend Heidegger relies on the inherently problematic status of translation. Any translation can be attacked on the grounds that it fails finally to convey the exact meaning: that, strictly speaking, it fails as a precise rendering, for, as the Italians say, *tradurre tradire*: to translate is to betray. The claim that translation is an impossible task is strategically important in the Heidegger discussion. It enables one to maintain that any criticism is based on an insufficient grasp of the German texts, on a failure to capture in another language the meaning expressed in the original language. This strategem is insufficient to disconfirm what has actually taken place, but it enables defenders of the faith to refute any criticism—even when it is known by all to be true—by directing attention not to the text but to its translation.

The third and most recent phase of the French debate began when Farías's study flared up like an intellectual supernova in the fall of 1987. One must distinguish between the immediate reaction to his book in French circles and the more measured but often heated discussion that is still under way.[26] Obviously, the immediate French reaction to Farías's work was part of an almost instant response which, it is fair to say, swept over Western Europe. The major newspapers and many magazines in all the major European countries carried articles concerning this study, often with a kind of concealed amusement directed at its French reception.

Two examples from the West German press and one from an Italian daily are typical. The writer of an article in a well-known liberal German daily, apparently unaware of the preceding discussion, comments that the question of the influence of Heidegger's thought will henceforth be raised in France as well as in Germany.[27] In a respected German intellectual weekly, another author concludes that Heidegger's letter to Jean Beaufret led to French postmodernism; but none of the postmodernists, all staunchly antitotalitarian, can be simply assimilated to Heidegger in a political manner.[28] Both articles are cautious and, in the best German sense, *sachlich*, more concerned to report than to pass judgment.

We find a much sharper reaction in Italian newspaper articles by two well-known Italian philosophers: Roberto Maggiori, an anti-Heideggerian; and Gianni Vattimo, a Heideggerian. In response to Vattimo's review of the Farías book, Maggiori criticizes his view that the whole *affaire Heidegger* is directed against certain Parisian thinkers. In a sharp response, which recalls Beaufret's estimate of Heidegger as a conceptual giant among pygmies, Vattimo dismisses Farías's work as of little historical consequence.[29]

The sharp exchange between Maggiori and Vattimo is similar to the often much sharper character of the French discussion. The immediate reaction, what in French is aptly called *réaction à chaud,* was precisely that: heated—in fact, overheated to a degree unusual even in French intellectual circles. This phase of the controversy, more symptomatic of the depth of feeling than of any depth of insight into the problem, was uncharacteristically played out in the pages of the daily papers and weekly magazines, in art and literary journals, on television—in short, through forms of communication not often associated with the measured tread of philosophical debate. It involved such well-known figures on the French intellectual scene as Derrida, Finkielkraut, E. de Fontenay, Baudrillard, Levinas, Aubenque, Blanchot, Bourdieu, Renaut, Ferry, and Daix, as well as many lesser figures; it involved as well such foreign scholars as Gadamer. What had earlier been a philosophical debate, a disagreement between scholars concerning a well-known difficult German thinker, quickly became an intellectual free-for-all in which opinions, even frank accusations, were voiced in rapid fashion. This guaranteed a *succès de scandale* for a book that rapidly became a *cause célèbre*.

The amplitude of the immediate reaction—which lasted for weeks in some quarters—may be indicated by a simple list, in no particular order, of newspapers and journals that ran articles (sometimes numerous articles) on the topic: *Art Press, La Quinzaine Littéraire, Le Monde, Le Matin, Libération, La Croix, Le Quotidien de Paris, Le Figaro, Le Magazine Littéraire, Le Canard Enchaîné,* and others. Christian Jambet, a former *nouveau philosophe,* set the tone in his preface to the French edition of Farías's work. His sharply worded preface begins with a reference to the traditional belief in the virtue of philosophy for life, before moving on to Heidegger's identification of authentic existence with a mere semblance, a mere representative of the politics of extermination. Jambet ends with a statement intended to sum up Heidegger's thought in a reference to a well-known film, *Nuit et brouillard* (Night and fog), on the Nazi concentration camps: "Heidegger has the merit of making ontology the question of our time. But how can we accept that philosophy, born of Socrates' trial for leading a just life, ends in the twilight where Heidegger wanted to see the end of the gods, but which was only the time of Night and Fog?"[30]

In his preface, opposing Heidegger to the entire philosophical tradition, Jambet raises the question of the specific difference between them in their treatment of the relation between thought and absolute evil. But he does not address the theme, highly relevant in the French context, of the specific link between Heidegger's philosophy and French thought. Certainly, this topic is partially responsible for the inflamed, passionate character of the immediate French reaction. Hugo Ott, the Freiburg historian, caught the mood extremely well in the opening comment of his review of Farías's book: "In France a sky has fallen in—*the sky of the philosophers.*"[31]

A small selection will indicate the sheer breadth of opinion in the immediate French response to Farías's study. Georges-Arthur Goldschmidt, a French refugee from German Nazism, welcomes Farías for swelling the meager ranks of those bothered by Heidegger's Nazi past; he regards Farías's book as impeding the normal business of the Parisian

Heideggerians, henceforth obliged to confront the issues.[32] In response, Emmanuel Martineau, the author of the pirated translation of *Being and Time* and a friend and student of Beaufret, admits that Beaufret became part of Heideggerian fascism, which he regards as matched by a hysterical anti-Heideggerian fascism. He accuses Goldschmidt of falling prey not to the hate of Nazi cruelty but purely and simply to the hatred of thought.[33]

Alain Finkielkraut complains that to insist on the connection between *Being and Time* and *Mein Kampf* conceals the risk of promoting a fascist reaction against philosophy.[34] In response to Finkielkraut, Goldschmidt suggests that in France there is little real knowledge of Nazism; there is also an inability to see, through Fichte's central relation to Heidegger, a kind of Nazism rooted in German thought.[35] Jean Baudrillard observes that the so-called necrological discussion concerning Heidegger has no intrinsic philosophical meaning but only betrays a transition from the stage of history to the stage of myth in which events we cannot grasp on the plane of reality give rise to a convulsion indicative of a loss of reality.[36]

Martineau's view of the incompetence of Heidegger's critics is further developed by Jacques Derrida in an interview. According to Derrida, at that time about to publish a book concerned with Heidegger and politics, Farías's so-called discoveries were not at all new to anyone seriously interested in Heidegger, and Farías's interpretation was so insufficient as to raise the question of whether he had devoted more than an hour to reading Heidegger. But Derrida also concedes the necessity to show the deep link between Heidegger's thought and actions to the possibility and reality of what he called all the Nazisms.[37] Farías's response, the enumeration of a list of facts supposedly brought to the attention of scholars for the first time, seems vaguely unsatisfactory.[38]

A more radical reply to Farías is furnished by Pierre Aubenque, the well-known Aristotle scholar, whose bitter article denies all the essential points, including the very relevance of Farías's book, the intellectual honesty of his analysis, the need for a study of this kind, and the lack of a significant connection between Heidegger's thought and Nazism.[39] Aubenque's analysis is supported by Pascal David, who ends a review of Farías's study with a quotation from Abraham a Santa Clara—the Augustinian anti-Semite whom Farías regards as influential on Heidegger—to the effect that God loves fools, not foolishness.[40]

Aubenque refers approvingly to Derrida, but their respective readings of Heidegger's Nazism place them in different camps. Although infinitely more clever, Aubenque's version of the contingency thesis is finally close to Fédier's unyielding defense, which simply denies that there is a problem worthy of consideration. By comparison, Derrida is

more innovative, since he deconstructs the opposition between representatives of the necessitarian and contingentist analyses. In essence, he
proposes that we acknowledge the intrinsic link between Heidegger and
Nazism, while still insisting that only the anointed few can comprehend it
correctly.

   In effect, Derrida concedes the main point of the necessitarian
approach, but he restricts its development by maintaining the contingentist insistence that only the orthodox critic of Heidegger can measure the
problem. An analogy may be found in the claim made by a former
Stalinist that only Stalin's victims can legitimately judge his crimes. This
new standard of criticism couples an admission of the problem—which is
no longer straightforwardly denied by any observer except Fédier—with
the insistence on expert knowledge of Heidegger's thought as a precon-
dition for valid discussion of his Nazism. It represents a significant
evolution in the scholarly French discussion, narrowing considerably the
gap between the discussants, since the point at issue becomes not
whether there was a real or durable link between Heidegger and Nazism
(something that perhaps only Aubenque still denies) but rather how to
understand the link—in particular how to understand its significance for
Heidegger's philosophy.

   In philosophy in general, because of the length of the gestation
period required, debates normally unfold slowly over periods measured
at least in years, more often in decades or centuries. In French circles,
where the half-life of a theory is always short, debate unfolds more
quickly, since to publish slowly is to risk commenting on a topic only as
it disappears into history. With the exception of Palmier's study, until the
publication of Farías's work no book wholly or even mainly centered on
the theme of Heidegger and Nazism had ever appeared in France. After
Farías, the lacuna was filled—and at a speed extraordinary even by the
standards of French intellectual discussion. From the publication of
Farías's book in October 1987 until the following May, a steady—if
steadily diminishing—stream of articles poured out, and in an extraordinary burst of scholarly creativity no less than six book-length studies
devoted to Heidegger's thought and politics appeared.[41] In most cases,
these books reflected the new consensus that there *was* a problem, but
they differed widely as to its description and analysis.

   The order in which the six books appeared presumably corresponds
roughly to the order of their composition. We may begin with the three
rather different studies due to Bourdieu, Lyotard, and Fédier. Bourdieu's
account of Heidegger's political ontology, following Heidegger's interest
in ontology, is the second edition of a text originally published in 1975,
rewritten and adapted to the current state of the discussion. Lyotard's
study exemplifies the desire, or at least the felt need, of every well-known

Parisian intellectual to comment on any major topic. Fédier's work is a further example of his continued effort, now deprived of any semblance of scholarly credibility, to maintain the contingentist thesis in its original, now outmoded form. These three disparate works nicely illustrate the range of the next strand in the scholarly discussion.

In a short introduction to his short study, Boudieu, a well-known Marxist sociologist, indicates that his analysis has been updated in the footnotes and by the addition of three chapters analyzing Heideggerian language. Referring to the first edition of his book, Bourdieu remarks that despite the image of sociology, a close reading of Heidegger's work already revealed such themes as his anti-Semitism, his refusal to break with Nazism, and his ultrarevolutionary conservative tendencies, as well as his disappointment in not having been recognized for his revolutionary aspirations as the philosophical *Führer* of Germany. Bourdieu indicates that the prior debate on Heidegger and his politics was impeded by Heidegger's construction of a wall between anthropology and ontology, although we must now examine the intrinsic blindness of these "professionals of lucidity."[42]

Bourdieu was prescient in regard to Heidegger's anti-Semitism, which has only recently been established.[43] He raises an important second-order question of how so-called professionals of lucidity are able to respond to a situation of this kind. His view reveals the politically conservative thrust of purely textual analysis favored in the current French discussion by Derrida and other so-called deconstructionists. Bourdieu maintains that even Heidegger's strongest critics have missed some of the signs regarding his Nazism, since they accept the form of immanent textual hermeneutics on which others—that is, Heidegger's epigones—insist. An approach of this kind can be only partially successful. In fact, it is a dangerous practice when rigorously applied, since it sanitizes what is unsavory and turns attention away from the political dimension of the texts in question. A striking example of this tendency appears in the French discussion, e.g., in writings by Beaufret, Lefebvre, Châtelet, and Axelos, who see a textual convergence between Heidegger and Marx.[44]

Bourdieu insists that we must abandon the separation between a political and a philosophical interpretation in order to institute a double reading (*lecture double*) for Heideggerian texts characterized by an intrinsic ambiguity. He aims to break out of the circle formed by an exclusively immanent reading of the text, doubly confined—within the text and to professional philosophers, possibly even confined to philosophers professing allegiance to Heidegger. He treats Heidegger as representative of certain extremely conservative revolutionary tendencies that appeared in Germany between the two world wars. And he agrees in part with

Heidegger's French defenders who discern two basically different stages in his thought. According to Bourdieu, Heidegger II constitutes a series of commentaries on Heidegger I; nothing is abandoned, but, in Bourdieu's words, the celebrated author now absolutizes his practical choices in philosophical language. He regards Heidegger's denial of a relation between his and any other position as an exercise in negative political ontology. On Bourdieu's view, only those sensitive to the situation beyond the internal approach to textual interpretation can finally decode it.[45]

Bourdieu goes too far in claiming that Heidegger refused to explain his relation to Nazism because to do so would have been to admit that the essential thought never thought the essential. His error is to trivialize Heidegger's position by reducing it to an unconscious component which it later explicitly erects as a philosophical standard. But when we consider Heidegger's texts in the context of his thought, and his thought in the social and political context, we do have direct access to a dimension of life and work that is not accessible to those who limit themselves to a more imminent textual approach. In this sense, Bourdieu undermines various forms of immanent hermeneutics, including the celebrated view of intertextuality. It further reveals a strategy favored by some right-wing Heideggerians, reasons for its success, and a way in which (as his own essay demonstrates) we may surpass its limits.

Bourdieu's book is a rare, impressive effort to understand the political dimension of Heidegger's thought against the historical background. His account is limited mainly by relying quite heavily on an early essay with only minor changes added to take account of more recent discussion. Although both Lyotard and Fédier make greater efforts to confront the latest research, their books are distinctly less impressive. Like Bourdieu, Lyotard refuses to amalgamate Heidegger's thought and his politics.[46] But compared with Bourdieu's book, Lyotard's essay appears hasty and unsatisfactory. Bourdieu's work is saturated with references to the English and German discussion; it is particularly rich in allusions to the constitution of the Weimar ethos against the nineteenth-century German background. With the exception of the obligatory tipping of the hat to Freud and Kant, Lyotard is exclusively concerned with French sources—which is not surprising, since he holds that the problem is essentially French.

Despite Habermas's effort to portray Lyotard and his colleagues as cryptoconservatives,[47] Lyotard's approach offers a fashionable, postmodernist form of liberalism. The term *les juifs* in the title refers not only to Jews but to all those who in Europe have always been assimilated to them. This slight volume is divided into two chapters, titled "The 'Jews'" and "Heidegger." Lyotard, who seems to like quotation marks, believes that the Heidegger problem is a "French" problem.[48] He holds that "the Jews," those outcasts of society, demonstrate that man's misery is constitutive of his being.[49] Lyotard insists on the need to think through the Heidegger problem (*penser l'affaire Heidegger*) without accepting the modish views either that Nazism can be deduced from *Being and Time* or that *Being and Time* arose from an ethos that was already Nazi or pre-Nazi. After announcing that both Farías and Derrida are correct, Lyotard asserts that the real problem, unforgettable but forgotten, is Heidegger's thought that a real opportunity existed through collaboration with Nazism.[50]

Lyotard is close to Bourdieu with respect to the famous turning, which he describes in difficult language as "the amnesiac meditation of what will occur in Heideggerian 'politics.' "[51] He suggests that *Being and Time* makes possible but does not require Heidegger's political engagement—as witness the political reading Heidegger gave of his own thought during the rectoral episode. The remainder of the book offers a serial critique of the views of other French commentators, including Derrida, Lacoue-Labarthe, and Nancy. They all fail to grasp that in his turn toward Being and (by inference) away from the Jews, or "Jews," Heidegger's thought is still hostage to the Law [*la Loi*].[52]

Lyotard's discussion is perhaps most enlightening in the undeveloped suggestion that although *Being and Time* is not a political book, Heidegger read it politically as the basis for his turn toward Nazism.[53] His suggestion that Heidegger's thought is basically flawed because of its relation to the Law—by extension, in its dependency on the nondifferentiated other, or other than itself—calls attention to a possible relation to the German idealist tradition; but it is too vague to render clearly, much less to evaluate. This is not the defect of Fédier's work, which could hardly be clearer in its intent, or weaker in its arguments.

Fédier's book is the latest expression of his unremitting faith as an orthodox Heideggerian, not swayed or even chastened by new information or the intervening debate.[54] Thus, it is the last such study by the last prominent representative of this angle of vision, a sort of living dinosaur. Like that of the mythical author in Camus's *La Peste,* the entire bibliography of certain writers is composed of multiple versions of a single text, which they write again and again in different forms. Fédier's work follows in detail the meanders of his initial defense of the master in articles published more than two decades ago. Then, he called attention to Heidegger's biography in order to undertake an apology in a Socratic manner. Here, the *rappel des faits,* meant to exonerate Heidegger, is not due to Fédier and does not follow but precedes the discussion. François Vezin, in a "bibliographical essay" (*essai biographique*) which begins the work and which opens and closes with comments on the tranquil little city of Messkirch where Heidegger was born and is buried, declares that the period of the rectorate is no more than a parenthesis in Heidegger's life.[55]

As a form of the contingentist analysis, Fédier's book defends Heidegger by attacking his detractors, Farías in particular. In a difficult defense, the author takes extreme measures. Two examples are worth remarking: (1) the tortured distinction between anti-Judaism and anti-Semitism,[56] and (2) the defense of the German bishops for their 1933 decision to remove the interdiction preventing Roman Catholics from adhering to National Socialism. In his introduction, Fédier describes his book as an apology intended to dispose of the charges.[57] Like a good defense lawyer, he begins by exaggerating the crime in order to show that his client could not possibly be guilty of it. According to Fédier—who is perhaps thinking of Adorno—Farías holds that Heidegger never said nor thought essentially anything other than Nazism, a charge that Fédier affirms to be a calumny.[58]

This defense is quite problematic, since neither Farías nor anyone else has ever criticized Heidegger as broadly as Fédier pretends. Fédier concentrates mainly on the rectoral period. He claims that it is permissible to accuse Heidegger of adhesion to Nazism in 1933–34 but slanderous to describe the adhesion as total, since he never adhered to biological racism. Fédier's main argument is that it was not possible in 1933 to foresee the future of National Socialism. He asserts that the definitive form of Nazism was not known prior to September 1, 1939.[59] Jaspers, who makes a similar observation, remarks that it was already clear in 1933 that Nazism meant at least lawlessness, encroachment on the rights of Jews, the confiscation of positions, and the like.[60] In fact, the situation was already sufficiently clear in 1933 to a great many, including such Jewish philosophers as Cassirer, Marcuse, Weil, and Löwith, for them to choose exile. Even Fédier is not convinced by this argument, since he concedes that when Heidegger took up the cause of National Socialism, it already carried with it the signs of an essential perversity.[61]

The first part of Fédier's discussion, "Un pseudo-événement," is a long attack on Farías's book for its inquisitorial tone, its obfuscation, its unconscious appeal to Freudian mechanisms of condensation and displacement, its failure to respect the rules of honest scientific procedure, and more. Alone, at this late date when so much is known, when Derrida claims incorrectly that everything is known, Fédier explains the existence of Farías's study as a sheer invention (*montage*) of which almost no page resists serious study. In the second part of the discussion, "Heidegger et la politique," Fédier analyzes the problem raised by the rectoral period, a problem that he attributes to Heidegger's impatience.[62]

In his defense, Fédier makes the following points: the rectoral address shows not an acceptance of Nazism but only a concern to defend academic science in the university; Heidegger later distinguished himself in his opposition to Nazism; the source of his action lies in a philosophical error leading to a need to modify his position; and Heidegger's later silence is to be respected, given the "martyrdom" he endured.[63] But the rectoral address shows an explicit concern (which Heidegger there stresses but later minimizes to utilize the university for the purpose of achieving a goal shared with the Nazis: the realization of the historical destiny of the German people. And Heidegger's later silence is neither honorable nor acceptable.

Fédier's most interesting point is his claim, made in passing, that a philosophical error requires a modification of the position affected. In different ways this same theme is developed in three other books on Heidegger and politics: those by Derrida, Lacoue-Labarthe, and Ferry and Renaut. Derrida requires no introduction. Lacoue-Labarthe, Derrida's former student, is a well-known Heidegger specialist who has worked closely in the past with Jean-Luc Nancy, another of Derrida's close associates.[64] Ferry and Renaut are two young antiestablishment philosophers who have collaborated also on several other works. Derrida's book, which coincidentally appeared almost immediately after Farías's study, caused a stir in Heidegger circles. Lacoue-Labarthe's work is an effort to think through the problem in a manner similar to Derrida's analysis itself apparently dependent on Lacoue-Labarthe's earlier writing. The study by Ferry and Renaut is an attack on French right-wing Heideggerianism as a form of antihumanism due ultimately to Heidegger himself.

Derrida's influential, unorthodox form of Heideggerianism is paradoxically an important form of Heideggerian orthodoxy, especially in France. His thought is deeply marked by, in fact inconceivable without, the encounter with Heidegger, on whose position he has commented in numerous writings.[65] His book can be read from at least two perspectives: as a Heideggerian analysis of Heidegger, and as an indirect but pointed response to the theme of Heidegger and politics.[66] It employs an approach strikingly similar to forms of orthodox Marxism.[67]

As a defense of the importance of Heidegger's thought which at the same time acknowledges its clear and undeniable link to Nazism, Derrida's strategy is reminiscent of the orthodox Marxism of Althusser and his associates, which argued for a conceptual break situated within Marx's thought. According to Althusser, Marx's thought decomposes into two chronologically separable positions: an initial philosophy that is not yet science, and a later break with philosophy in accord with a science that eclipses philosophy.[68] Althusser, though obliged by the tardy publication of Marx's early writings to acknowledge the philosophical tenor of Marx's early position, defends the nonphilosophical, allegedly superior scientific character of the later theory: that is, the supposedly mature form that Marx's theory took after it broke with philosophy. In a similar manner, Derrida correlates Heidegger's initial critique of metaphysics with his supposedly still-metaphysical philosophy, which then later gives way to an antimetaphysical view of thinking beyond philosophy itself. According to Derrida, Heidegger turned, as a metaphysician, to Nazism, which he then renounced in his move away from metaphysics and beyond philosophy.

Derrida's Heidegger interpretation takes shape as a meditation on the terms *Geist, geistig,* and *geistlich* in Heidegger's thought. He points out that, in *Being and Time,* Heidegger warns against the use of *Geist,* which he puts in quotation marks; but twenty-five years later, in an essay on Trakl, Heidegger employs the term without quotation marks. Derrida's hypothesis is that, for Heidegger, the term refers to supposedly metaphysical concepts such as unity [*l'Un*] and gathering [*Versammlung*]. He believes that, for Heidegger, spirit is neither *pneuma* nor *spiritus,* but finally a flame more orginary than either the Christian or the Platonico-metaphysical concept. Even in 1933, Heidegger rejected the reduction of spirit to reason in order to spiritualize Nazism, as can be seen in the role assigned to spirit in the rectoral address. It follows that Heidegger's Nazism was metaphysical, and that he overcame it when he overcame the metaphysical element in his own thought.[69]

This defense is problematic for various reasons. First, it is at least arguable that in his self-described Heideggerian effort to think the unthought, Derrida exaggerates the importance of a concept that Heidegger never thematizes precisely, because it is not fundamental but only ancillary to (possibly even insignificant for) his position. Second, Derrida trivializes Heidegger's commitment to Nazism as having been due to a residually metaphysical turn of mind. In effect, he reduces a practical political engagement to a philosophical commitment from which it apparently followed but with which it cannot reasonably be equated. A form of thought that leads to a particular political approach, no matter what kind, cannot be conflated with its consequences. Obviously, metaphysics does not as such necessarily lead to Nazism, since there are many metaphysicians who did not become Nazis. Third, Heidegger supposedly gave up metaphysics as a result of the turning in his thought, but there is no reason to believe that he also gave up Nazism. Fourth, Derrida is obviously incorrect in suggesting that when Heidegger employs the term *Geist* without quotation marks in 1953 (in the article on Trakl), he has overcome *both* metaphysics and Nazism, for in the very same year he republished *An Introduction to Metaphysics,* in which he publicly reaffirmed his commitment to a Nazism. Fifth, as part of his supposed overcoming of metaphysics, Heidegger turned away at most from real

Nazism. But there is no evidence that he ever accepted it without reservations, and he never turned away from an ideal or idealized Nazism.

Lacoue-Labarthe presents a clearer, even more extreme, less acceptable form of Derrida's argument. Lacoue-Labarthe's consideration of *la question* precedes Farías's book. In a recent collection he includes two earlier papers concerning Heidegger and politics, which obviously influenced both his and Derrida's later discussions of Heidegger and politics: "La transcendance fini^e/t dans la politique" from 1981, and "Poétique et politique" from 1984.[70] In the former, which examines the possibility of a Heideggerian politics, he studies the rectoral speech in order to show its link to the destruction of the history of ontology and, by extension, its link to the effort to rethink the problem of the meaning of being. Here he makes two points: (1) the rectoral speech is not an occasional document but a reflection on science, which is metaphysics as such; and (2) the speech is intended as a philosophical foundation of the political. He reads Heidegger's political engagement in 1933 as metaphysical, and its basic result as the collapse of his fundamental ontology. In the latter paper, which examines why the poetical dimension arose within political discourse, he argues that Heidegger's effort at the leadership (*Führung*) of National Socialism was essentially spiritual.[71]

There is an obvious, striking continuity between the views of Derrida and Lacoue-Labarthe: both insist on the metaphysical nature of Heidegger's turning toward Nazism and the spiritual component of Heidegger's view of politics. But there is an even more important difference in Lacoue-Labarthe's stress on the link between the political and the philosophical in Heidegger's thought, in virtue of which his philosophical project is compromised by its political consequences. The admission that Heidegger's fundamental ontology was irreparably compromised by his turn to Nazism derives from the acknowledgment—now rarely denied, and explicitly affirmed by Heidegger—that his initial enthusiasm for National Socialism followed from his philosophical position. It is significant for an understanding of the link between Heidegger's thought and Nazism. It points to a conclusion that Lacoue-Labarthe does not draw and that Heidegger denies in his description of the rectoral episode as meaningless (*bedeutungslos*): that is, that the later evolution of his position is determined by his relation to Nazism.

This unstated but important consequence of Lacoue-Labarthe's article needs to be emphasized. In his treatment of the political as fiction, he mainly develops other themes from his earlier analysis of the relation of poetry and politics, less menacing for the faith of a Heideggerian. Much of the French discussion is concerned to defend Heidegger at all costs; hence, it is not concerned to present the full record. But Lacoue-Labarthe mentions items rarely evoked in the French debate: anti-

Semitism, the views of Löwith and Jaspers, Heidegger's denunciation of Baumgarten, his comparison between the Holocaust and agricultural technology, and so on. In view of his identifying Heidegger as incontestably the best thinker of our time, it is significant that Lacoue-Labarthe does not hesitate to denounce in a clear way Heidegger's failure to decry the Holocaust. As he points out, in Heidegger's conception of history as the unfolding of metaphysics, the Holocaust supposedly constitutes a metaphysical event.[72]

Lacoue-Labarthe's work is an obviously sincere, nonideological effort to understand Heidegger's turn towards Nazism. But it is insufficiently critical, as a single important example will show. In a passage that Lacoue-Labarthe cites, Heidegger compares agricultural technology to the Nazi gas chambers.[73] Lacoue-Labarthe criticizes the inadequacy of Heidegger's dreadful comparison, but since he remains within the Heideggerian orbit, he is unable to perceive the full implication of the remark in at least two respects: (1) in his quasi-Heideggerian claim that this phenomenon somehow reveals the essence of the West,[74] which Heidegger allegedly failed to perceive, which in its own turn presupposes the Heideggerian view that technology is the extension of metaphysics; and (2) in his inability to draw the consequence of his own indictment of Heidegger's failure, on the basis of fundamental ontology, to comprehend Nazism.

In his book, Lacoue-Labarthe modifies his earlier analysis. Heidegger's political engagement in 1933, he says, was grounded in the hegemony of the spiritual and the philosophical over the political (a stance in obvious agreement with *Being and Time* and coherent with all his earlier thought) which cannot be explained as an error but must be viewed as a consequence.[75] But Lacoue-Labarthe no longer insists on the significance of the rectoral speech; he argues instead for a caesura (*césure*) in Hölderlin's sense. Heidegger's understanding of the political is found not in his texts from 1933, even in the rectoral address, but in writings after the break with Nazism, specifically those on technology. Here, Lacoue-Labarthe makes two important points: (1) he suggests that there is a beginning of the *Verwindung* of nihilism in Hölderlin's thought, since, for Heidegger, art opens the possibility of the historicity of *Dasein*; and (2) he argues that Heidegger's discourse on art illuminates Nazism as a national aestheticism.[76]

These suggestions are independent of each other and require separate discussion. Lacoue-Labarthe is correct in holding that Heidegger never abandoned his concern with the destiny of the German people, and that he later linked this interest to the alethic qualities of poetry. But this point is inconsistent in two ways with Lacoue-Labarthe's own analysis: (1) he insists on a break in Heidegger's position, although this interpretation requires him to acknowledge Heidegger's continued preoccupation with the destiny of Dasein; and (2) as a further consequence, he is obliged to acknowledge the kind of conceptual kinship between Heidegger's philosophical thought and Nazism which he denies in his critique of Adorno's claim that Heidegger's thought was Nazi to its core.[77] It is additionally inaccurate to regard Heidegger's discussion of art or technology as illuminating the essence of Nazism. One may concede a certain perverse aestheticism in Nazi ideology, for instance in the writings of Albert Speer, the Nazi architect. But one must resist the idea that the massive political phenomenon of German fascism is solely, or mainly or essentially, aesthetic.

Lacoue-Labarthe's analysis—patient, sober, careful, informed, considerate of other points of view—exhibits virtues unsurpassed in the present French Heidegger debate. His comprehension and tolerance are replaced in Ferry and Renaut's work by an accusatory, pamphletory, confrontational style, more characteristic of recent French philosophy. These authors attack the separations among various forms of French Heideggerianism as distinctions without a difference, which they paradoxically regard as an effort to surpass mere polemics.[78] They deny the antihumanist assumption, shared by Derrida and Lacoue-Labarthe, of a break in Heidegger's thought. Their book carries further their earlier work on contemporary antihumanism, mainly by being centered on French varieties of Heideggerianism.[79]

Ferry and Renaut are most original in their effort to develop Lyotard's view of the link between the defense of Heidegger and French philosophy. They draw attention to the parallel between the French controversy about Marxist antihumanism in the 1970s and the current Heidegger controversy. They discern a link between Heidegger's antihumanism, which they define as the rejection of modernity, and the supposed *erreur par excellence* of contemporary French philosophy. They find the error instantiated in Lacoue-Labarthe's strange, even wild comment that "Nazism is a humanism."[80]

After commenting on the significance of Farías's book in the context of the French debate, Ferry and Renaut indict contemporary French philosophy, referring to the common source of the different forms of French Heideggerianism. They isolate three variants: the so-called zero degree, represented by Beaufret, which simply denies any relation between Heidegger and Nazism; Heideggerian orthodoxy, which, by playing Heidegger II off against Heidegger I, admits that in 1933 the master was not yet free of the metaphysics of subjectivity; and Derridean or unorthodox, Heideggerianism, which relies on Heidegger's purported later deconstruction of the concept of spirit. In the final analysis, there is no difference between Derridean and orthodox Heideggerianism since the Derridean approach at best, offers innovations at a strategic level only.[81]

The main contribution of Ferry and Renault is to help clarify links between the various factions of the French debate on Heidegger and politics. The connection, for instance, between French postmodernism, or antihumanism, and Heidegger's Nazism is politically suggestive. They construe Heidegger's conception of modernity as the reign of technology, and his adherence to the possibility of a good form of National Socialism as, implicitly, both postmodernist and antimodernist. They criticize Heidegger's general incapacity to appreciate subjectivity as being due to his inability to think of humanism in a nonmetaphysical way, to his inattention to the plural and diversified character of modernity, and to his inconsistent rejection of a humanist vision of man in developing his notion of *Dasein* in terms of the analysis of Being. They also invoke the humanism of Heidegger's view of man as transcendental in order to criticize Nazi biologism and racism.[82]

These criticisms are well taken. Heidegger does identify humanism with metaphysics, although in the "Letter on Humanism" he indicates, in passing, the alternative of a more authentic form linked to his evolving conception of postmetaphysical, nonphilosophical thinking. The relation of postmodernism and antihumanism in the work of such recent French thinkers as Derrida, Lyotard, Foucault, and Lévi-Strauss, among others, is too well known to require detailed commentary here. Ferry and Renaut's most original point exposes Heidegger's inability to differentiate the various forms of modernity, which facilitated the notion that Nazism was humanism of a different, supposedly acceptable kind. The indictment of the French identification with Heidegger's rejection of Cartesian subjectivity—manifest in the ongoing effort to decenter the concept—is well taken. Perhaps the most important result of their work is to indicate the essential poverty of Heidegger's conception of the subject as transcendence, a constant theme in his writings from the dissertation on Duns Scotus to his mature texts.[83]

The French discussion of Heidegger's philosophy and politics has recently witnessed a confrontation between the views of Fédier and Nicolas Tertulian, the well-known Lukács specialist.[84] The primary lesson of our survey concerns, of course, the delicate relation between thought and the context in which it arises. We do not know how a philosophical theory takes shape; but we do know that it can be neither reduced to nor separated from the operative elements of its context, including its social, political, and historical aspects as well as the network of competing views it opposes. Heidegger worked repeatedly at creating his own legend—for instance, by forging a unique and exclusive connection between his own position and pre-Socratic thought. But we cannot possibly understand his developing career or his philosophy without reference to the complex background of theology, German neo-Kantianism, medieval Aristotelianism, and the general concern in Germany between the two world wars to promote the self-image of the German people. Kant's own thought—his conception of the noumenon, for example—arguably provides the root metaphor for Heidegger's idea of Being as present under the mode of absence, which dominates Heidegger's mediation on ontology.

The French debate offers an interesting case study of the delicate relation between thought and context. With the exceptions already noted, French philosophers still insist on the discontinuity between Heidegger's early and later position—in order, apparently, to save his thought and French philosophy. But the truth is that Heidegger turned against only one form of Nazism, not Nazism as such. To fail to grasp this point, to obscure the difference between Heidegger's rejection of real National Socialism (the actual political phenomenon) and his continued faithfulness to the supposedly misunderstood essence and greatness of Nazism is to overlook the emperor's new clothes.

Since French thinkers are not less intelligent or less well informed than philosophers elsewhere, we need to explain their apparent incapacity to see that the emperor *has* no clothes. The delusion surely rests with the peculiarly persistent, unhealthy degree of identification of contemporary French thought with Heidegger's position—which forms its very horizon. The paradox and predicament are plain enough: to the extent that Heidegger's thought forms the horizon of contemporary French philosophy, it cannot examine Heidegger's link to Nazism without putting itself into question: that is, without simultaneously rejecting the Heideggerian position. In a word, Heidegger's French connection prevents French thinkers from perceiving the emperor's new clothes.

The French example is unusual. Heidegger's domination opens certain possibilities inhering as it were in his position, but it also raises obstacles to any attempt to question its own (Heideggerian) horizon. The situation is useful to the extent that French philosophy remains within the Heideggerian orbit, but it is also philosophically dangerous. For philosophy has long been steadfast in its refusal to accept undemonstrated assumptions; in its insistence on self-examination in order to clarify, demonstrate, or eliminate what it happens to presuppose, to advance by reviewing its own presuppositions.

The recent efforts of dissident French thinkers to reflect on the so-called French position, to reexamine the roots of French Heideggerianism, is certainly a healthy sign. Despite Heidegger's oft-cited claim that when French philosophers begin to think, they think in German, French thought will surely be more robust and will surely develop along new lines when it finally dissects its Heideggerianism. At present it is still difficult for a French thinker to do so because of the tentacular nature of Heidegger's grip on French thought.

The French discussion is an extreme example of the problem posed by the reception of Heidegger's Nazism. Philosophers, not just Heideggerians, have been remarkably slow to confront Heidegger's Nazism. The failure to do so is significant for the reception of Heidegger, for the study of his thought, and for philosophy itself. Ever since its beginnings in ancient Greece, a flattering view of philosophy has been making the rounds. According to this view, philosophy is the source of reason in the highest sense, productive of truth, intrinsically linked to goodness. Yet Heidegger failed to come to grips with Nazism, the main instance of evil in our time—eminent philosopher though he was. His own thought led him to Nazism. If the true is good and Nazism is evil, then by implication Nazism is also false, certainly false as a political option. Judged by that standard, Heidegger's thought is neither useful nor true. The result is a paradox, for how can a great philosopher be a proponent of Nazism? Unless we simply overlook Nazism, turn away from one of the central political problems of our epoch, it is impossible to hold that great philosophy preserves the link between truth and goodness and to describe Heidegger as a great philosopher. We cannot ignore the puzzle.

To understand the link, we must relate theorizing to its own time. Since the ancient Greeks, philosophers have often held that thought is in but not *of* time, that philosophy somehow evades the limits of its own historical moment. Heidegger presupposes the notion in his distinction between philosophy (productive of theoretical knowledge) and a mere world view, or *Weltanschauung* (the expression of a coherent conviction about the present state of the world). In fact, he himself relies on this distinction in his critique of "theories"—such as Nazism—that are mere "world views."

Obviously, theory *does* rise above its own time. That cannot be denied. But to admit as much is not to escape the limitations of history; it is rather to grasp its fresh possibilities. Heidegger's theory is, in many ways, certainly new and insightful, a distinctly novel advance. But it builds on and transforms earlier views—as it must. It is also a reflection of certain deeply held contemporary beliefs linked to the actual situation of Germany between two world wars, beliefs to which Heidegger gave philosophical expression. And it is even true that Heidegger's thought forms a "world view" or *Weltanschauung*, in fact, in Heidegger's own sense, the "philosophy" of the Weimar Republic.

A different point needs to be made about the frequent failure in the Heidegger reception to come to grips with his Nazism. In its most extreme form, this failure includes the effort to withhold evidence, perhaps the occasional falsification of documents, the denial of the evident, the appeal to special standards for a great philosopher (supposedly different from the standards for the ordinary Nazi). It is admittedly misleading, simplistic, and just plain false to claim that every reluctance to examine Heidegger's Nazism is due to bad faith. Nevertheless, such reluctance does threaten our understanding of Heidegger's thought. In the defense of Heidegger, it has often been argued that politics and philosophy are separable. But this is certainly not true for Heidegger: his political commitment and his thought are clearly inseparable. It is obvious that new ideas cannot be understood at once, since a new way must be found to comprehend a position that differs significantly from others already in place. No original thinker is ever grasped without an intervening process of reception. Claims to instant, even rapid, comprehension of novel bodies of thought are likely to be based on misunderstanding. But neither Heidegger nor anyone else can finally be understood if an essential element in his position is omitted or ignored. In Heidegger's case, his Nazism is certainly an essential ingredient; without it, his position is literally incomprehensible.

The failure to come to grips with Heidegger's Nazism is further important for philosophy. The only difference between the reception of Heidegger's position and that of others lies in the public controversy his Nazism has generated. Since we cannot start afresh, *ex nihilo*, and since we cannot just vault over the entire tradition, we are obliged to come to grips with prior thought. In short, appropriating the history of philosophy, our way of doing so, is central to the philosophical pursuit itself. But if our reading of the tradition offers us merely what we always wanted to believe, then it is useful only as a source of reassurance. In that case, the failure to come to grips with Heidegger's Nazism identifies the incapacity of philosophy from time to time to make good on its promise to pursue truth and, accordingly, to be useful.

NOTES

1. See "Deux documents sur Heidegger," *Les Temps Modernes* 1, no. 4 (1946): 713n.

2. See Karl Löwith, *Heidegger: Denker in dürftiger Zeit* (Freiburg, 1953).

3. See Eric Weil, *Logique de la philosophie* (Paris: Vrin, 1974).

4. See Maurice de Gandillac, "Entretien avec Martin Heidegger," *Les Temps Modernes* 1, no. 4 (1946): 713–16.

5. See Alfred de Towarnicki, "Visite à Martin Heidegger," *Les Temps Modernes* 1, no. 4 (1946): 717–24.

6. See Karl Löwith, "Les implications politiques de la philosophie de l'existence chez Heidegger," *Les Temps Modernes* 2, no. 14 (1947): 343–60.

7. See Eric Weil, "Le cas Heidegger," *Les Temps Modernes* 2, no. 22 (1947): 128–38.

8. See Alphonse de Waelhens, "La philosophie de Heidegger et le nazisme," *Les Temps Modernes* 2, no. 35 (1947): 115–27.

9. See Karl Löwith, "Réponse à M. de Waelhens," *Les Temps Modernes* 3, no. 35 (1948): 370–73.

10. See Alphonse De Waelhens, "Réponse à cette réponse," *Les Temps Modernes* 3, no. 35 (1948): 374–77.

11. See Jean Beaufret, *Introduction aux philosophies de l'existence,* série Médiations (Paris: Denoël/Gonthier), p. 30; rpt. as *De l'existentialisme à Heidegger* (Paris: Vrin, 1986), p. 25.

12. See, e.g., Jean Beaufret, "En chemin avec Heidegger," in *Cahiers de l'Herne: Heidegger,* ed. Michel Haar (Paris: L'Herne, 1983), pp. 205–33. See also his statement in Beaufret, *Entretiens avec F. de Towarnicki* (Paris: Presses Universitaires de France, 1984), p. 87: "Heidegger n'a jamais rien fait qui ait pu motiver les allégations formulés contre lui," and the examination of his philosophy from a political perspective represents "la conspiration des médiocres au nom de la médiocrité." Essentially the same defense is offered later by Gianni Vattimo in his claim that Heidegger's thought is more important than that of his accusers.

13. See *Annales d'Histoire Révisionniste,* no. 3 (Autumn–Winter 1987): 204–5. For a discussion of the link between Beaufret and Robert Faurisson, see Michel Kajman, *Le Monde,* January 22, 1988, pp. 1, 18. The following passage (cited in Jean-François Lyotard, *The Différend: Phrases in Dispute,* trans. Georges Van Den Abbeele [Minneapolis: University of Minnesota Press, 1988], p. 3) provides an idea of Faurisson's view: "I have analyzed thousands of documents. I have tirelessly pursued specialists and historians with my questions. I have tried in vain to find a single former deportee capable of proving to me that he had really seen, with his own eyes, a gas chamber." This form of historical revisionism is fundamentally different from the more benign discussion in German intellectual circles where the controversy concerns not the existence but rather the interpretation of the final solution. See *"Historikerstreit": Die Dokumentation der Kontroverse um die Einzigartigkeit der national-sozialistischen Judenvernichtung* (Zurich: 1987). For a philosophical reaction to Faurisson, see Lyotard, *The Différend,* pp. 3–4.

14. See Georg Lukács, *Existentialisme ou Marxisme?* (Paris: Nagel, 1948).

15. See Georg Lukács, *Existentialisme oder Marxismus?* (Berlin: Aufbau, 1951).

16. See Maurice Merleau-Ponty, *Les aventures de la dialectique* (Paris: Gallimard, 1955), chap. 2, "Le Marxisme 'occidental,' " pp. 43–80.

17. See Jean-Michel Palmier, *Les écrits politiques de Heidegger* (Paris: L'Herne, 1968).

18. Palmier argues that Heidegger made two basic mistakes: he thought that through the Nazi party he could realize an intuition he perceived in Ernst Jünger's book, *Der Arbeiter;* and he thought that within Nazism he could develop a philosophical dimension, since he had deluded himself into perceiving within it a spiritual potentiality. See Jean-Michel Palmier, "Heidegger et le national-social-

isme," in Haar, *Cahier de l'Herne: Heidegger*, pp. 409–46, with a summary of Palmier's criticism, pp. 443–444.

19. See Jean-Paul Faye, "Heidegger et la révolution," *Médiations*, no. 3 (Autumn 1961): 151–59.

20. See Jean-Paul Faye, "Attaques Nazies contre Heidegger," *Médiations*, no. 5 (Summer 1962): 137–51.

21. See François Fédier, "Trois attaques contre Heidegger," *Critique*, no. 234 (November 1966): 883–904. The discussion begun by Fédier, followed by a series of responses and rejoinders, ended with contributions by Bondy and Fédier. See François Bondy, "Une lettre de Heidegger à François Bondy," *Critique*, no. 251 (April 1968): 433–35; and François Fédier, "Le Point," *Critique*, no. 251 (April 1968): 435–37.

22. See Aimé Patri, "Serait-ce une querelle d'allemands?" *Critique*, no. 237 (February 1967): 296–97.

23. See Robert Minder, "Langage et nazisme," *Critique*, no. 237 (February 1967): 284–87.

24. See Jean-Paul Faye, "La lecture et l'énoncé," *Critique*, no. 237 (February 1967): 288–95.

25. See François Fédier, "A propos de Heidegger: Une lecture dénoncée," *Critique*, no. 242 (June 1967): 672–86.

26. The most recent French book on this topic, a sober, mature study, differs from the more passionate but less objective works published in the wake of Farías's book. See Dominique Janicaud, *L'ombre de cette pensée: Heidegger et la question politique* (Grenoble: Jérôme Millon, 1990).

27. See the *Frankfurter Rundschau* (Donnerstag), no. 245 (October 22, 1987): "Bis zuletzt ein Nazi: Heidegger im grellen Licht / Eine Pariser Sensation" (p. 11).

28. See *Die Zeit*, no. 46 (November 6, 1987): "Wie braun war Heidegger? Die postmodernen Grossfurthsen und ihr deutscher Ahnherr."

29. See Gianni Vattimo, "Il pensiero di Heidegger più forte di chi lo accusa," *La Stampa*, November 14, 1987.

30. Christian Jambet, preface to Victor Farías, *Heidegger et le nazisme* (Paris: Verdier, 1987), p. 14.

31. Hugo Ott, "Wege und Abwege: Zu Victor Farias' kritischer Heidegger-Studie", *Neue Zürcher Zeitung* (Freitag), no. 275 (November 27, 1987): "In Frankreich ist ein Himmel eingestürzt—*le ciel des philosophes*" (p. 67).

32. See Georges-Arthur Goldschmidt, "Heidegger, militant et penseur nazi," *Le Matin*, October 15, 1987, p. 16.

33. See Emmanuel Martineau, "De la haine de la pensée aux 'faurisonner-ies,' " *Le Matin*, October 26, 1987.

34. See Alain Finkielkraut, "Heidegger: La question et le procès," *Le Monde*, January 5, 1988, p. 2.

35. See Georges-Arthur Goldschmidt, "Heidegger: L'Allemand et le ressentiment," *Le Monde*, January 13, 1988.

36. See Jean Baudrillard, "Nécrospective autour de Martin Heidegger," *Libération*, January 27, 1988, pp. 1–2.

37. See Jacques Derrida, "Un entretien avec Jacques Derrida. Heidegger, l'enfer des philosophes," *Le Nouvel Observateur,* November 6, 1988.

38. See Victor Farías, "Victor Farías: pas d'accord avec Jacques Derrida," *Le Nouvel Observateur,* November 27–December 3, 1987, p. 47.

39. See Pierre Aubenque, "Encore Heidegger et le nazisme," *Le Débat,* January–February 1988, pp. 113–23. This issue, which provides a good point of entry into the recent French discussion of Heidegger and Nazism, contains a diverse collection of articles by P. Aubenque, H. Crétella, M. Deguy, F. Fédier, G. Granel, S. Moses, and A. Renaut under the heading of "Heidegger, la philosophie et le nazisme," as well as a collection of twelve texts headed "Martin Heidegger: Textes politiques 1933–1934."

40. See Pascal David, *"Heidegger et le nazisme:* A propos du livre de V. Farías de même intitulé," *Les Etudes Philosophiques,* April–June 1988, pp. 257–63.

41. See *Heidegger: Questions ouvertes* (Paris: Osiris, 1988), a diverse collection of articles presented at a seminar organized by the Collège International de Philosophie. Under the heading of "Histoire, Politique," there is a series by J. Rolland, Eliane Escoubas, P. Lacoue-Labarthe, J. Derrida, M. Abensour, and E. Levinas on various aspects of the theme of Heidegger and Nazism. For a review covering the works by Fédier, Bourdieu, Lacoue-Labarthe, Renaut and Ferry, and Lyotard, see Jean-Michel Palmier, "Heidegger et le national-socialisme," *Magazine Littéraire,* no. 255 (June 1988): 89–93.

42. See Pierre Bourdieu, *L'ontologie politique de Martin Heidegger* (Paris: Minuit, 1988), pp. 7–8. On the importance of Heidegger's refusal of an anthropological reading of his thought, see Martin Heidegger, *La lettre à Jean Wahl,* cited in ibid., p. 114.

43. On this point, see Bourdieu, *L'ontologie politique,* p. 59 (referring to Toni Cassirer's well-known comment) and 61n (discussing the influence of H. von Treitschke on later German thought, including the German academy). Heidegger's anti-Semitism has been established with the belated publication of his letter to Victor Schwoerer, dated October 2, 1929: see Ulrich Sieg, "Die Verjudung des deutschen Geistes," *Die Zeit,* no. 52 (December 22, 1989): 50. See also a letter of Husserl to Dietrich Mahnke, dated May 4, 1933: "Vorangegangen ist der von ihm [Heidegger] vollzogene Abbruch des Verkehrs mit mir (und schon bald nach seiner Berufung) und in den letzen Jahren sein immer stärker zum Ausdruck kommender Antisemistismus—auch gegenüber seiner Gruppe begeisterter jüdischer Schüler und in der Fakultät" (cited by Hugo Ott in Annemarie Gethmann-Siefert and Otto Pöggler, eds., *Heidegger und die praktische Philosophie* [Frankfurt: Suhrkamp, 1988], p. 69); this contradicts the widespread view, represented by Pöggeler (ibid., p. 17), that the story of Heidegger's anti-Semitism is at best apocryphal.

44. See Bourdieu, *L'ontologie politique,* pp. 67, 107–8.

45. Ibid., pp. 10, 102, 115, 117, 118.

46. See Jean-François Lyotard, *Heidegger et "les juifs"* (Paris: Galilée, 1988), pp. 97–101.

47. See Jürgen Habermas, "Die Moderne-ein unvollendetes Projekt," in

Habermas, *Kleine politische Schriften I–IV* (Frankfurt: Suhrkamp, 1981), pp. 444–64.

48. "L'affaire Heidegger est une affaire 'française' " (Lyotard, *Heidegger et "les juifs,"* p. 16).

49. See ibid., pp. 52; 71, "judéo-christianisme"; 73, "société"; 103, "politique"; 146, "faute"; 153, "Célan," etc.

50. See ibid., pp. 87, 90, 109, 95.

51. "La méditation anamnésique de ce qui aura eu lieu dans la 'politique' heideggerienne" (ibid., p. 103).

52. See ibid., pp. 110, 111, 115–20, 148.

53. Lyotard here contradicts such French commentators as Aubenque, who directly deny the political nature of Heidegger's work. For Aubenque's denial, see his "Encore Heidegger," pp. 118–19.

54. See François Fédier, *Heidegger: Anatomie d'un scandale* (Paris: Robert Laffont, 1988).

55. "Le rectorat n'a cependant rien d'une parenthèse dans la vie de Heidegger et il vaut la peine de lire les 'textes politiques' de la période de 1933–1934" (ibid., p. 22).

56. See ibid., p. 67.

57. Or, as he says, "lever l'accusation portée contre Heidegger" (ibid., p. 30).

58. See ibid., p. 31.

59. See ibid., pp. 31–33, 37, 162.

60. See Karl Jaspers, *Notizen zu Martin Heidegger*, ed. Hans Saner (Munich: Piper, 1989), p. 185.

61. Fédier, *Heidegger,* p. 185.

62. See ibid., pp. 114, 115, 147, 116, 136, 152.

63. See ibid., pp. 198–99, 234, 237, 240.

64. Among the French Heideggerians, Lacoue-Labarthe has been most persistent in pursuing the problem raised by Heidegger's Nazism in all its many variations. Heidegger's later view of the role of poetry in the disclosure of truth led to his encounter with Paul Célan; for a recent effort to study the role of poetry based on that encounter, see Philippe Lacoue-Labarthe, *La poésie comme expérience* (Paris: Christian Bourgois, 1986.)

65. A short list of Derrida's writings on or about Heidegger includes *La vérité en peinture, Ousia, Grammé*, "Geschlecht: Différence sexuelle, différence ontologique," "La main de Heidegger (Geschlecht II)."

66. The latter aspect has not been lost on orthodox or Derridean Heideggerians. It is significant that his study has in fact been praised by Heideggerians for its Heideggerian quality. For instance, David Farrell Krell, in a long review arguably intended, in part, to defend Heidegger against Farías's criticism, makes this point: "Spiriting Heidegger: A Discussion of *De l'esprit: Heidegger et la question* by Jacques Derrida," in *Research in Phenomenology* 18 (1988): 205–30.

67. For an effort to deny the importance of the distinctions between the Derridean approach and so-called orthodox Heideggerianism in France, see Luc

404   TOM ROCKMORE

Ferry and Alain Renaut, *Heidegger et les modernes* (Paris: Grasset, 1988), p. 99ff.

68. See Louis Althusser, *For Marx,* trans. Ben Brewster (New York: Vintage Books, 1970).

69. See Martin Heidegger, "Die Sprache im Gedicht: Eine Erörterung von Georg Trakis Gedicht" (1953), in *Unterwegs zur Sprache* (Pfullingen: Neske, 1959); *Jacques Derrida, De l'esprit: Heidegger et la question* (Paris: Galilée, 1987), pp. 11, 12, 24, 156, 155, 64, 66.

70. See Philippe Lacoue-Labarthe, *L'imitation des modernes: Typographies II* (Paris: Galilée, 1986).

71. See ibid., p. 184.

72. See Philippe Lacoue-Labarthe, *La fiction du politique: Heidegger, l'art et la politique* (Paris: Christian Bourgois, 1987), pp. 14, 75.

73. See ibid., p. 58.

74. See ibid., p. 59.

75. See ibid., pp. 28, 35, 38, 39, 43.

76. See ibid., pp. 64, 86, 87, 91, 115.

77. See ibid., p. 150.

78. Ferry and Renaut, *Heidegger et les modernes,* p. 12.

79. See Luc Ferry and Alain Renaut, *La pensée 68: Essai sur l'antihumanisme contemporain* (Paris: Gallimard, 1985).

80. Ferry and Renaut, *Heidegger et les modernes,* pp. 40, 10, 12; Lacoue-Labarthe, *La fiction du politique,* p. 58.

81. See Ferry and Renaut, *Heidegger et les modernes,* p. 117.

82. See ibid., pp. 149, 155, 227, 170, 172, 224–25.

83. See Heidegger, "Die Kategorien- und Bedeutungslehre des Duns Scotus," in *Martin Heidegger: Frühe Schriften* (Frankfurt: Klostermann, 1972), p. 141: "Es felht dem Mittelalter, was gerade einen Wesenszug des modernen Geistes ausmacht; die Befreiung des Subjekts von der Gebundenheit an die Umgebung, die Befestigung im eigenen Leben."

84. See Nicolas Tertulian, "Trois témoignages: Löwith, Jaspers, Marcuse," *La Quinzaine Littéraire,* no. 496 (November 1–15, 1987): 10–11; "A propos de Heidegger, la manipulation des textes a tout de même des limites," *La Quinzaine Littéraire,* no. 515 (September 1–15, 1988): 18–21; "Quand le discours heideggerien se mue en prise de position politique," *La Quinzaine Littéraire,* no. 523 (November 1–5, 1988); 26; "Esquives, abandons et nouvelles inexactitudes: Un tournant dans les recherches sur Heidegger, *La Quinzaine Littéraire,* no. 526 (January 16–25, 1989): 19–21; Nicolas Tertulian, "Heidegger et le national-socialisme. Aspects et points de vue," in *Tramonto dell'occidente?* ed. Gian Mario Cazzaniga, Domenico Losurdo, and Livio Sichirollo (Napoli: Istituto per gli Studi Filosofici, 1989), pp. 165–206.

18

Discarding and Recovering Heidegger

JOSEPH MARGOLIS

What, ultimately, is the connection between politics and philosophy? Is power subject to rational direction, or is rational direction the self-deceiving idealization of the exertion of power? Are they relatively independent of each other, or are they the disjoined mirrorings of a deeper single process? One senses the trap of answering and the scandal of refusing to answer. But given the enormities of the Second World War, the events that led to it, the breaching of all political constraints which that trauma seems to have made commonplace down to Vietnam, Afghanistan, Cambodia, Ethiopia, Lebanon, Iran, Northern Ireland, the Hungarian uprising, the Dubček spring, Ecuador, El Salvador, Guatemala, Nicaragua, Tienanmen Square, Israel, South Africa, Angola, Uganda, Sri Lanka, Argentina, and on and on, we can no longer pretend to understand ourselves directly. We cannot still cling to the stately vision of a rational politics well within our understanding, which the mere complexities of practical life somehow thwart in an engineering sense again and again. The truth must go deeper.

I

The shortest argument linking philosophy and politics that could reasonably claim comprehensiveness for the entire history of the Western world, seen from the vantage of our own age, is the following. If we deny the transparency of the real world, admit the preformation of man's cognizing powers by the contingencies of cultural life, then (1) the ancient disjunction between *theoretical* and *practical* reasoning must also be denied; and if we treat such reasoning (and all accompanying action) horizontally, if we regard the self as a historicized construction, deny all discernible invariance normative for knowledge and practice, then (2) a disjunction between (the discovery of) *truth* and (the exercise of) *power* is impossible to maintain; and if these concessions range over the institutional life of entire societies, then (3) science and philosophy entail an ineliminable *political* structure inseparable from their own achievements, and politics may claim a certain *legitimative* parity with science.

This argument is disturbing to contemporary minds, who find in it no working reference to the changeless norms of reason, the final truths of inquiry, the fixed goods of man, the assured neutrality of knowledge and understanding. So be it: they are right. It would not be farfetched to say that nearly every major current of philosophical inquiry of the last fifty years, particularly the influential ones of our own day, has been committed to one version or another of these three themes. They mark in a way the reversal of the most ancient philosophical canon of the West. No doubt they have been championed in a "strong" sense by Marx and Nietzsche—in the sense of a "strong" philosophy that would be the analogue of what the literary critic Harold Bloom has memorably characterized as "strong" poetry: the "misprision" or "transumption" of the work of strong precursors (poets or critics) in order to clear a receptive space for one's own voice, which later poets and critics also deliberately deform for a similar purpose.[1] That sense emphasizes the social "production" of knowledge—in both first-order and second-order respects.

Under that circumstance, no mere isolated voice can ensure its own dominance, poetic or philosophical, by virtue of its solo utterance. The power of a new vision or new mapping of the world is a function of the gathering bias of entire societies or of certain of their more attentive and potent aggregates responding to such a dawning. This is so much so that the rise of a distinctly "strong" poetic or political voice which, by its own magnetic presence, compels a sort of *clinamen* of thought and action is often regarded as a mark of prophecy or titanic wisdom. The important thing is that it disallows any strong disjunction between *argument* and *rhetoric,* or any reliably temperate connection between the two that might support invariant human norms.

No philosopher of the twentieth century, possibly no philospher of the entire Western tradition, counts more compellingly as a "strong" voice, in the sense given—in the sense uniting the point of Bloom's conception with that of the short argument favoring the inseparability of philosophy and politics—than Martin Heidegger. What is so extraordinary about Heidegger's career is this: first, his life instantiates his own conception of the relationship between philosophy and politics; second, that conception is the most influential contemporary source of the short argument with which we began; and third, that argument has proved to be the nerve of nearly all the dominant or salient views of what, at the present time, the relationship between philosophy and politics is said to be.

In this triple sense Heidegger *is* the "strong" theorist he truly is. It's no good dismissing him in accord with the embarrassed hindsight of those who rightly deplore his intransigent Nazism; and it's no good dismissing his conception on the grounds of its intolerable use in (his) reading (of) Hitler's and Nazi Germany's destiny and in promoting the universalizable lesson of his own version of the short argument. It is also, let us not forget, no good laundering his philosophical conception by simply detaching it from its thick historical context, as if (contrary to Heidegger's own pronouncement) philosophical theories enjoy timeless validity apart from the social *praxis* from which they issue. Not at all strangely, Bloom's conception of the politics of poetry—itself a mere instance of a deeper fashion of thought affecting the interpreting of texts—ultimately derives, via the influence of Paul de Man, from Heidegger's persuasive vision. That it has affected in a serious way theorists of remarkably different political tastes, however, may be easily discerned in the "strong" views of Jacques Derrida and Michel Foucault and, respectively, by their mediation, in Philippe Lacoue-Labarthe and Jean-François Lyotard. There you have an inkling of the peculiar force and importance of Heidegger's thought.

To put matters this way is to oblige Western philosophy (and much more than philosophy) to face up to the truth that a great many of the perceptive minds of our age (concerned to understand the connection) have been following Heidegger right up to the present day; that most of these would not see at all how to disentangle themselves from Heidegger's tentacular influence; that it may be impossible at present to disconnect any genuinely advanced line of thinking bridging philosophy and politics from Heidegger's large vision; and that that influence ranges over the entire spectrum of divergent political and philosophical conviction, including many views opposed to Heidegger's own Nazi turn of mind. To say that Western thought is indebted to, influenced by, Heidegger, possibly even ignorant of the full meaning of his presence, is to impose an obligation on the intellectuals of our age. They must define that influence—for good or ill; and they must determine, for all the questions that fall within the space of that influence, what remains tenable in their own recovery, particularly regarding the connection between philosophy and politics.

It is more than difficult to name another contemporary thinker who occupies a comparable role. Foucault seems a very tepid second. Jacques

Derrida is hardly a second at all. Ludwig Wittgenstein was always *hors de combat,* though he obviously counts as a "strong" philosopher. Theodor Adorno, Jürgen Habermas, Hans-Georg Gadamer are very small beer by comparison. G. E. Moore, Bertrand Russell, Rudolf Carnap, John Dewey, William James, W. V. O. Quine are almost never more than mildly interesting "philosophico-political" figures at best. Also, by an unexpected turn of fate, Heidegger as a "strong" thinker has managed to gather together many of the forces of the philosophical-political connection that never played itself out, in a comparable way, in the time of Hegel, Marx, and Nietzsche. That is surely extraordinary.

We may now recast, in its most provocative form, the thesis at stake: we are all, largely, infected by Heideggerian themes, whether we wish to be or not; and many of us are appalled or worried by that unshakable fact. How, we may ask, can we disengage what is conceptually acceptable in Heidegger from what we reject as his philosophical Nazism? Failing that, how can we convincingly displace his own executive themes by politically more acceptable ones of at least comparable range and plausibility? The second question can be answered only by a philosophical voice of Heidegger's own rank. The first is a manageable one, but to answer it profitably, we must have a better sense of what it is about Heidegger's thought that marks it as compelling. After all, on the argument, we are not so much concerned to dissect Heidegger's personal use of the link he himself affirms between philosophy and politics as we are to dissect our own infected thinking and that of anyone drawn to our short argument. For, through an influence we need not have been aware of, we ourselves have been brought, partially at least, either under Heidegger's spell or under those same forces of contemporary experience that found, in Heidegger, a more perceptive and more deliberate voice than that of any other contemporary philosopher. Whatever was inchoate but potentially compelling in that experience, Heidegger seems to have directly sensed (seems to have guessed) would be irresistible enough to command a responsiveness, beyond but also through the crudities of Nazism, affecting even those who would finally be Nazism's sworn ruin. There you have the deeper mystery.

It must not be supposed that in claiming Heidegger as one of the "strong" *political* thinkers of our age, in the sense intended, we are endorsing any of his specific philosophical or political claims. His larger notions must be at least sufficiently plausible to have attracted the kind of sustained influence he has had. But his piecemeal claims may well be defective, even untenable. That may not ultimately matter as much as the devotees of reason suppose, though the admission cannot fail to be disturbing. The history of philosophy, even the history of the connection between philosophy and politics, bears this out. One could easily say, for instance, that in his arguments John Locke was a most uncompelling philosopher just at the moment his novel form of empiricism gained such a decisive march on the so-called rationalism of the European continent; and his politico-economic thesis of mixing labor with land as somehow justifying the acquisitive zeal of Europe vis-à-vis the New World was hardly slowed by any detailed exposé of its transparent opportunism. This, of course, is no more than a very tame example of the pertinence of the themes of the short argument. But it helps to set our sights.

In any case, as much as we may applaud the decisions of the Nuremburg trials, we cannot shake the feeling that the victors and the judges were implicated as much as the criminals there convicted, and we cannot sufficiently assure ourselves that the justice of the victors rested on conceptual grounds that reliably and neutrally defeated the short argument with which we began. To acknowledge that much is to admit the penetrating influence of Heidegger well beyond his own distasteful career. That is hardly to say that Heidegger's theories vindicated Nazism or were, ultimately, even designed to do so; or that, in acknowledging Heidegger's influence, we find ourselves obliged to soften any verdict on the man, the philosopher, or the Nazi. It says rather that the concepts of justice, just war, political right, science, the truth of theory, philosophical legitimation, the interpretation of history are all placed at permanent risk by Heidegger—in a way that quite straightforwardly subverts the confidence of the older canons of those sorts that were so laboriously called into play, with a dose of bad faith, by the victors of the war. Nor is it to condemn Nuremburg. It is only to confront us with the predicament of our own making. It is, of course, a predicament that has found its way into the sciences just as compellingly. The plain truth is: we have not yet found a clear conceptual stance, *committed to some version of our short argument,* by which to draw the bond between philosophy and politics congruent with our own political tastes. The positive force of Heidegger's thought is collected at least in the ubiquitous notion that all conceptual work is historically perspectived, horizoned, interested, prejudiced, contexted, resourceful, and transient. It is hard to see how to give that notion up in opposing Heidegger or in vindicating Nuremburg.

II

The force of Heidegger's thought lies in a myth—in a double myth, in fact—that represents the movement of his philosophy from its early enunciation in *Being and Time* to the later essays, at least up to the "Letter on Humanism." Much of what can be said here is so well known that its repetition may seem quite primitive. But its full significance has certainly eluded easy capture, and it is that significance that we need to isolate. So let us risk the tale again.

Most proximately, the source of Heidegger's myth is found in Nietzsche. But Heidegger transforms the spirit in which Nietzsche proclaims the (mythic) diremption of the ultimate Void in which an active and cognizing agent (man) unaccountably finds himself confronted by an intelligible if recalcitrant world. Nietzsche fears a madness in approaching the Void conceptually, in directly subverting more and more deeply the saving illusions of human life. Truth itself and objectivity prove to be the systematic artifacts of those same reflexive illusions. We flee the Void, he thinks, but we are forever attracted to it, since the nagging intuition that There Is Nothing invades our every perspectived argument against determinate claims. Nietzsche moves on then to undermine the false claims of Christianity and Socratism—until, of course, he is co-opted by his own sly enemies. Their claims are false because, to win the contest they invent, they must (and do) presume an invariance foreign to the Void and the obvious flux of the world, and because by that maneuver a suitable conformity can, for a time, be effectively imposed on others. *Ressentiment* is the price of that endeavor, fearful of the uncluttered freedom of those great souls who may have glimpsed the Truth. So there is an obvious symbiosis, in Nietzsche's view, between the stabilities of truth and the stabilities of power: *neither* can be construed in any naively "positive" way. The "real world" *has* no changeless structure to which our own efforts at truth or power can legitimately claim a rational allegiance. You can see, therefore, that there is much more than a mere adumbration of our short argument in Nietzsche. By contrast, Heidegger makes us *love* the void of Being (*Sein*), the utterly unstructured source of all structured beings (*Seiende*). It is in a way the home of homes.

In the first version of Heidegger's myth, *Dasein* (which is more than man, but which man is the mortal instance of—since *Dasein* is itself a part of the myth of *Sein*) is the active power that essentially concerns itself with every contingently manifested order of determinate things (*Seiende*) *and* with their privileged disclosure from *Sein* to *Dasein*. Heidegger appears sanguine, here, about the prospects of an effective science, of the interpretation of history, of the understanding of man himself, of man's active purposiveness, even of his metaphysics—all within the articulated conceptual space drawn from the apparently benign void of Being. The myth serves to warn us of the unconditional contingency and horizonal bias of every disclosed world; but our own world is at least the salient world we share. It yields an operative objectivity, but not invariance or necessity. Furthermore, since Heidegger speaks (in *Being and Time*) of the essential structure *of Dasein* (of what he calls its "ontic-ontological" nature), it becomes impossible for him to deny, consistently, a certain essentialism as well to the world disclosed to *Dasein*. *"Understanding of Being* [Heidegger says] *is itself a definite characteristic of Dasein's Being*. Dasein is ontically distinctive in that it *is* ontological."[2] In the context of *Being and Time*, Heidegger finds the natural sciences straightforward enough, provided we do not mistake the "ontic" and "ontological" structure of what we mean by "world" (*Welt*); for "worldhood" (*Weltlichkeit*) is itself "an ontological concept, and stands for the structure of *one* of the constitutive items of Being-in-the world [*In-der-Welt-sein*]": that is, is itself an *existentiale*.[3] In a word, the sciences are phenomenologically contexted; but, once thus understood, the activity of *Dasein* (through the activity of historical man), which catches up again the duality of the ontic and ontological and the alternation of emphases on the naturalistic and the phenomenological, produces no untoward worries about the viability of the sciences—or of metaphysics, properly harnessed. On the contrary, Heidegger's educational vision, following on the themes of the *Rektoratsrede*, clearly assigns a continuing function to the sciences.

Somewhere in his early work, however, already incipient in *Being and Time* and now confirmed, through a number of changes, in the recently published *Beiträge*, Heidegger was already attracted to some version of the *Kehre* theme. (There are of course many "turnings" in his philosophical career.) At the end of that process, for instance in the "Letter on Humanism" and in "The End of Philosophy," Heidegger repudiates altogether that sanguine activism of the world said to have been disclosed to *Dasein*, in his sweeping repudiation of the entire range of technologized thinking that seemed (to him) to install in the most soulless way the fixity of the categories of our *praxis*. (That final "turning" also entails a rejection of historical Nazism.) He therefore displaces *Dasein* and leads us to the full doctrine of *Gelassenheit*, in which the best advice to man is simply to accept in a certain passive way this or that particular order of *Seiende* that originates one-sidedly from *Sein*. The fateful feature of Heidegger's late thought is that the disclos*ing* is somehow more beneficial for man's existence than any knowledge of the apparent order of what is thus disclos*ed*. Purpose and commitment ultimately lose their point. To dwell in any disclosed world is inevitably to follow the way of technologized life. But, of course, to oppose it is also to abandon all science and philosophy and politics and rational life itself. (Or so it seems.) It is surely the expression of a failed personal history that Heidegger once believed (chiefly but not only as a Nazi) could be reversed by an apocalyptic event—one not altogether unlike what he thought he perceived in the rise of Hitler's star. In any case, he moves here to a postphilosophical stance, a putative wisdom that discursive reason cannot penetrate.

In the very opening of "The End of Philosophy" (1966), Heidegger decisively warns his reader: "Questions are paths toward an answer. If the answer could be given it would consist in a transformation of thinking, *not* in a propositional statement about a matter at stake."[4] The essay construes itself explicitly as a critique of *Being and Time* and introduces "a thinking which can be neither metaphysics nor science."[5] It may be the most explicit essay in which Heidegger's fatigue over the victory of "technology" and "science" (and therefore of metaphysics as well) is acknowledged. But the "thinking" he has reference to is the same that dominates, more sanguinely, the earlier "Letter on Humanism" (1947), published shortly after the War. There he catches up his reading of the pre-Socratics and the full theme of the *Kehre*—passing beyond the metaphysics of *Dasein* to his theme of "ek-sistence" (existing "ecstatically"), the *Gelassenheit* addressed to Being as Void, to the "nihilating" power of all structured Being and beings, the ultimate "nothing" that is no longer an affirmable ground for any particular structure: "The nihilating in Being is the essence of what I call the nothing. Hence because it thinks Being, thinking thinks the nothing."[6] This is surely beyond the activism of any politics or philosophy.

Now, the important consideration for our present purpose is that during the extended interval of the developing conception of the *Kehre* (with all its changes)—certainly, philosophically, in a well-known essay on Parmenides[7] and, politically, already in the *Rektoratsrede* and in his many exhortations thereafter in the university world—Heidegger hit on a remarkable compromise that would redeem political activism (for him) in a new way. He came to believe (he may have believed this to the end of his days) that the appropriate receptivity of man (*not* his final passivity, the passivity of the last essays), faced with the momentous disclosures of *Being*—the kind of visionary revelation only a gifted figure like Hitler had the power to receive and transmit, a vision that somehow focused the imminent destiny of an entire people—could also be suitably transformed into a *destinal and collective activism*. Here, the disclosure of Being *is* explicitly, even determinately, political, whereas in *Being and Time* the linkage between philosophy and politics is fairly clearly confined to the lines of our short argument. In the *Rektoratsrede*, metaphysics has a destinal voice; in *Being and Time*, there is, generally, no line of demarcation between thought and existence: hence, between philosophy and politics. But in *Being and Time*, though there is a touch of the destinal, *Dasein* tends to straddle the solipsistic and the most solipsistic possibilities of social existence.

Thus, in the rectoral address (1933: "Die Selbstbehauptung der Universität"), Heidegger explicitly links the corrections (the "self-determination") of German science and philosophy to the destiny of the

German *Volk,* itself identified by the educational *Führer* of the people (Heidegger) attentive to its collective historical role—"led by the relentlessness of that spiritual order that expresses itself through the fate of the German nation."[8] This, then, also involves a version of the doctrine of the *Kehre,* one that unites the theme of Heidegger's pre-Socratic studies with his novel metaphysical (conceptually idealized) Nazism. For what Heidegger has in mind is at once the collectively focused longing and drive of a nation bent on realizing in historical time its true essence (*Wesenwille*), which it can ultimately accomplish only "metaphysically," by returning to the original revelatory beginning (*Anfang*) of any suitably pursued inquiry—say, of some ancient Greek or contemporary German science.[9] There *is,* therefore, an activist version of the *Kehre,* but it is pure Nazism. By contrast, the rejection of historical Nazism is, as in the later essays, linked to the joint repudiation of technology and metaphysical thought.

Heidegger was, at first, entirely prepared to play John the Baptist to Hitler's Jesus (after the fact), until he came to believe that Hitler, too, had somehow missed the world-historical calling of the German people— on whose fate the fate of the entire Western world essentially depended. And so, perhaps at first unwillingly, Heidegger came to realize that he alone must be the true custodian of *that* destinal role in which, within the flux of history, a "strong" voice—at once philosophically astute and politically charismatic—could conceivably lead the German people (which history or Being had in a way chosen to take up its appointed collective life). In that way, Germany—and the Western world—would, once and for all, break through the nihilism of all the usual liberal, rational, positivist, optimistic, calculating thought that, at the end of his life, he felt had provisionally won the decisive victory. Nevertheless, toward the end of his life, Heidegger repudiates all technological, political, and metaphysical thinking; the optimistic disjunctions of his own Nazi vision thereupon become untenable as well. (But to say that is to say nothing about political repentance, of course. There is no evidence that Heidegger ever abandoned *his* version of Nazism, despite its inconsistency with his own late brand of "nonphilosophical" thinking.)

All this is madness, you may say, and you would be right. But it does afford a clue to separating Heidegger's own utterly bizarre reading of his own philosophical vision from that same vision. (It is, however, emphatically *not* to say—and not to decide—just how separable or inseparable Heidegger the philosopher and Heidegger the political activist finally are.) The argument confirming the point rests on two notions. Let us have them before us straight off to avoid confusion. First, the conception of the relation between *Sein* and *Dasein* (*alētheia*) and, second, the conception of the self-disclosing power of *Sein* received but not in any way

affected by the active inquiry of man (*Gelassenheit*)—the two themes of
Heidegger's philosophy—are never more, can never be more, than *holistic* visions, myths of *the context of all contexts* of life that for that very
reason *cannot* entail or subtend or legitimate any of the specific distributed acts and claims of any particular society. On the Heideggerian view,
it is true, there can be no disjunction between thought and commitment.
But *what* some particular society (Germany) should do here and now
Heidegger cannot tell by consulting his own philosophical tale (although,
by consulting it, he did not shrink from pronouncements in its name—for
example, as the spiritual *Führer* of the German university world). There
is no science or ethic or politics or poetry or practice that *follows* in any
sense whatsoever from *either* of his two myths—unless it is to love the
Void, to love structureless *Sein*. (And, indeed, that *is*, finally, Heidegger's
entirely vacant ethic.) Otherwise, there is only the play of competing
projects within the contingent world of formed things (*Seiende*)—things
no more than salient to equally contingent human agents, both discovered
in the flux of history. Humans, in this sense, must fend as they can. They
are adrift in the world.

That way of thinking confirms with a certain grandeur a "neutral"
space for the *agon* of human thought and struggle. It is a vision that could
not, however, actually have served Heidegger's large aspiration as the
Führer of the entire university world of Germany. It had to be superseded
if his philosophical vision was ever to be made congruent with the
supreme educator's role he came to assign himself—certainly no later
than the moment of assuming the rectorship at Freiburg. That is, the
neutrality to be marked here is *not* the neutrality of philosophy vis-à-vis
politics, but the larger (at least apparent) neutrality of the vision of *Being
and Time* vis-à-vis Heidegger's discovery of Germany's "metaphysical"
destiny in Nazism.

What Heidegger must have realized was that neither the myth of
Sein/Dasein nor the myth, incipient in his lectures on the pre-Socratics,
of fruitful fulgurations caught from a self-sufficient Source by a Parmenides or a Heraclitus could possibly justify his pronouncements on the
destinal history of his beloved Germany. (The *polemos* lecture on Heraclitus follows immediately Heidegger's resignation from the rectorate in
the summer of 1934.) He had to "find" a richer figure, one that could
combine the developing theme of *Gelassenheit* with the theme of a
personal freedom entirely within the gathering force of a collective
history. That figure had to fuse in one nature an idealized patriotism
reaching beyond politics to the very soul of a people, an indubitable
German genius or, better, an inspiration from the authentic sources of
German greatness, an awareness of destinal history grounded in the true
meaning of the French Revolution, and a charismatic presence. He found

such a figure, of course, in the poet Hölderlin. But in a way, in addition to that incarnation, he found it also in a contemporary political leader (Hitler) and, perhaps dawningly, in a philosophical leader (himself).

The point is that Heidegger *needed*—needed in a philosophical sense *for* his own political purpose—a conception of history and collective life that could *overcome* the *political neutrality* (or political alienation) of *each* of his mythic visions. *He could incorporate what he required only by cheating philosophically.* (This, of course, is not to say that philosophy *is* politically neutral, or to say that *any* part of Heidegger's own philosophy is politically neutral or separable from his own political motivation, however inchoate.) If the maneuver he hit on were merely an idiosyncratic bit of cleverness, not much would be served by exposing it here. The fact is that Heidegger found the supreme trick by which to transform the irresistible short argument (his version, to be sure, of the opening argument which, we said, dominates our tacit grasp of the connection between philosophy and politics) into the most effective possible defense of philosophical and political fascism. He accomplishes this, illicitly of course, by making history destinal if not specifically telic (great nations must respond to the challenge of history or lose their place on the world stage) and by construing the structureless void of ultimate Being as *actually* (somehow) *yielding* determinate instruction regarding the collective destinies of certain "apt" peoples. The result is a kind of historicized Platonism that channels the seeming neutrality of the themes of our initial "short" argument into the determinate purposes of a world-historical people brought charismatically to an awareness of its appointed role. (This is, perhaps, the meaning of *Geist* [as flame, *pneuma*] that Derrida labors to recover. But if it is, then it is inseparable from Heidegger's "philosophical" Nazism.)[10]

The lean conclusion to be drawn from all this is that Heidegger's variant of the Nazi reading of German destiny requires—and could almost convincingly supply—a replacement for his first philosophical myth and a decisive supplement for something distantly resembling the second. The maneuver fails because, first, it violates the very notion of radical historicity that Heidegger uniquely fashioned—for instance against Hegel (and of course against Marx); and because, second, it transforms a mythic, holistic, structureless space (*Sein*) into a space or plenum of Being that includes at least the adequately determinate signs of historical direction and normative value. So the structure of the "third" option— the full-blown Nazi metaphysics that is centered in the rectoral address, the *Introduction to Metaphysics,* the lectures on the Greeks, Hölderlin, and Nietzsche and that bleeds (both prospectively and retrospectively) into the space of the two master myths of Heidegger's entire career—is defined by the following elements: (a) historicizing metaphysics; (b) ontologizing history; (c) construing their identity in teleological and practical terms (politically, spiritually, educationally); (d) assigning the locus of the emergent truth of that identity to the uniquely "metaphysical" career of the German *Volk;* and (e) assigning the discovery of that truth to a gifted voice attuned to its disclosure within the continuity of the Greek and the German (ultimately, Heidegger himself). The invention is a piece of bombast, of course, opportunistic and dirty at best, politically and philosophically a cheat, but awfully sly and artful conceptually—and difficult to isolate.

There is the clue we promised: Separate the philosophical sham of this third—this specifically Nazi—addition from either or both of the myths that give determinate form to Heidegger's work, and you will have recovered the autonomous part of his compelling vision (of the relation between philosophy and politics) to which at the present time no one appears to have a satisfactory alternative. It is for that reason that *we* cannot (yet) escape being potential Heideggerians ourselves, and for that reason that we must not permit ourselves to be *Heidegger's* own sort of Heideggerian. We may of course resist. We may repudiate Heidegger and his theme. But we need to know what doing so entails and how it may be legitimated. Two clues suggest themselves. The first clue: Heidegger thought to "destroy" the history of ontology by his attention to the "meaning of Being." This is the grand purpose of *Being and Time.* But now the disclosure about Being is inseparable from the analysis of *Dasein,* which is itself a specific individuated being (*Seiendes*) that should have figured in the "destruction" of ontology (the classical tradition reaching, say, from Aristotle to Kant). On the one hand, the entire novelty of Heidegger's new beginning implicates an inexpungeable element of the tradition he means to attack; on the other, the privileged disclosure of German destiny is *somehow* bound either to the exploratory powers of *Dasein* or, later, to the fulgurations caught from Being itself by some gifted poet or leader who functions as a historical conduit. The second clue: The privileged instruction of Heidegger's entire Nazi vision draws its energy from what, in a technical sense, must be noumenal rather than phenomenal—and therefore beyond discursive or categorical thinking. It is, for that reason, profoundly illicit, on Heidegger's own Kantianized conviction, and yet content with its "destructive" achievement. Heidegger quite blithely moves to recover a putatively "higher" truth that cannot possibly be disconnected from the other. Concede these two clues: you cannot fail to grasp what is entailed in escaping from Heidegger's conceptual tentacles; and by the same token you cannot fail to grasp what (very much diminished) could possibly be saved of Heidegger's philosophy—from his own philosophical and political opportunism.

III

Some will say the proposed separation is a fraud. Perhaps. But there can be no question that the "short" argument given *is* quite distinct from Heidegger's Nazi reading of the developing versions of his "second" myth—which, like the first, provides a global context for just that argument. So there is a fair sense in which Heidegger may be rightly regarded as one of the principal authors *of* the generic form *of* the short argument. What is decisive is hardly local to Heidegger's own fate, however. The fact is that the philosophical vision associated with either of Heidegger's myths *creates a vacuum for thought and action* that could (and did) invite a Nazi reading. The supreme problem Heidegger posed, the problem every alert mind of our age is still struggling to resolve, concerns how to shape a coherent and plausible view of theoretical and practical reason under the condition of a radical history. Notice, please, that the separation recommended is *not* the separation of philosophy and politics. Under the terms of our short argument—of which Heidegger is as much an architect as anyone—there can be no such disjunction. The disjunction separates Heidegger's philosophical Nazism from both his myths in the sense that it cannot be made to follow from either, not in the sense that Heidegger ever formulated his philosophical views without an eye to their political use or ever formulated his political convictions without an eye to their philosophical congruity.

Some favor what we may call *archism*, the notion that human reason can discern the invariant principles of effective thought and action—in a praxical or political sense—in a way that escapes the flux of history. This is the irony of Habermas's vision, for instance: that is, the irony of one who would inherit the negative dialectics of the Frankfurt school. It is plainly self-contradictory insofar as reason is said to be historically formed and transformed. Others favor the clever discovery, within the very movement of history, of the normative near-invariances of human life that no new turn of open history, no matter how radical, could possibly disconfirm. That vision, espoused for instance by Gadamer, is hardly more than a magical doctrine, a doctrine we may pejoratively name *traditionalism*. It sometimes takes the form of openly redeeming a model from past history (again by an essentialism *manqué*), as it does for instance in the political vision of Alisdair MacIntyre. It is no more than an archism, and it is equally self-defeating.

Still others favor the response of *reactivism*—or of a reactivism that verges on *opportunism*. This is Foucault's way: at first merely subversive of *any* would-be "normalization," anarchical, desperate, avoiding archisms at any cost; and then, finally, approaching his own death, intrusively, arbitrarily, irrationally optimistic and "humane." Not only are the two moments of Foucault's political vision inconsistent with each other; the first hardly sustains a continuous life for any but the most marginalized souls, and the second is a flat betrayal of what might have linked Foucault's attraction with what, in Nietzsche and Heidegger, helped to form what we are here calling the short argument. It is, in brief, the dilemma of the poststructuralist, who veers finally toward liberalism—as do Jean-François Lyotard and the French feminists, whenever they believe they must have a sustained political program.

Still others favor the response of opportunism that verges on *quietism*, or quietism itself, the principled fatigue of those who find that once we abandon all archisms, the world cannot sustain *any* rational direction at all, any reflexive legitimation. They fall back to the "local," to the neighborly practices of their own known world. They are the "postmodern" pluralists prepared to accommodate every (or, preferably, their own) local practice as far as possible. This, for instance, is the blend of philosophy and politics that Richard Rorty recommends, blithely indifferent to the lucky leisure that permits him to invest in such a liberal affection, blithely indifferent to the demand, arising from the misery of vast populations, to justify such an insouciance. There is a sense in which such thinkers as Rorty and Lyotard are irresponsible if not inconsistent, and inconsistent to the extent that they are liberal or humane, whereas Foucault is trapped by the logic of his extreme historicism (apparently inspired in part by Heidegger).[11] Once we regard such a solution as a solution for a mass society within a space of competing mass societies, we cannot fail to see its bankruptcy. It calls for a know-nothing mentality that smokes its pipe or sips its liqueur in the shade. None but the fortunate can afford its comfort.

Heidegger's own solution oscillates between the extreme quietism of the *Gelassenheit* doctrine (as in "The End of Philosophy") and the active fascism of the *Rektoratsrede*. Stalinism may be similarly seen as the Marxian version of a fascist response; and Marxism de-essentialized, de-teleologized, de-deterministic, inclines toward a reactive opportunism like Foucault's.

These are the principal specimen solutions of our day. They are all conceptual and political failures. No one has a convincing reconciliation of philosophy and politics to offer. And that means that we cannot convincingly retreat from Heidegger's implicit problematic. Of course, we are not bound to Heidegger. The only time Heidegger himself engages the issue is when he is imbued with the most objectionable Nazi sentiment. Nevertheless, on the argument, *no* contemporary philosopher who has framed that problematic is "stronger" than Heidegger. That is the reason so many thinkers, who have either risked appearing as fascists or are frank fascists themselves, have with some justice rallied to remind us (we who might be happier being mindless about our own intellectual debt) that we cannot simply discard Heidegger as a Nazi—though he most certainly was one: let no one now deny it—without addressing as well the troubled relation between thought and action (between philosophy and politics), that we cannot comprehend *in the way we now do* without Heidegger's magisterial influence. Anyone who does not see that is either illiterate or a knave. So there is an important piece of courage that the defenders of Heidegger exhibit at considerable risk to themselves. Unfortunately, nearly all of them have blundered badly in presenting their case. Perhaps it was inevitable, but the world will not forgive them.

If, by the terms of the short argument, we may isolate the symbiosis of the theoretical and the practical, the radical historicity of human existence, the socially constructed nature of selves, the intransparency of the real world, the absence of exceptionless invariances of any cognitional or normative sort, the horizonal and preformative process of inquiry and action, the intelligible incommensurabilities and discontinuities of theory and cultural life, the self-transformational capacities of man, the inescapability of existential commitment, the inseparability of first- and second-order claims, the impossibility of originary and totalized thinking, then we must admit that we cannot avoid the Heideggerian setting of the interconnection between philosophy and politics.

In a deep sense, it *is* that perceived connection that has produced the characteristic orientations we were sampling just a moment ago, and it is that same connection that has produced the vacuum we are now obliged to fill. At the risk of an abuse of terms, the union of the themes we have just mentioned is now plausibly collected as the new *pragmatism* of our age: that is to say, not any particular American pragmatism—certainly not the modernist or postmodernist or poststructuralist versions we were just counting as failures—but a family of philosophical proposals, strongly shaped by Heidegger, that range through the phenomenological and Marxian and deconstructivist and other alternatives that converge on the salient themes just tallied.

The problematic of pragmatism so construed, the explication of the legitimated relationship between philosophy and politics, is in a way the supreme philosophical puzzle of our age. We are faced with immense forms of planetary power of our own making, faced with our own capacity to alter and destroy our world and possibly other worlds in our vicinity; and we see that we are very nearly incapable of formulating a just vision of how to give reasonable order and direction to our life all the while the exercise of power palpably reduces the future prospects of making any effective commitment regarding its control.

Heidegger is no help at all in this regard. Where he speaks to the point, he is a Nazi; where he is not a Nazi, he has nothing to say—except, of course, in focusing in his incomparable way our grasp of the conceptual space within which a suitable *praxis* might be invented. We were at that same point at the very beginning of his work as a philosopher. We are hardly further now, except that we understand the difficulty we face (and share responsibly) in a way that only World War II and what has happened in its wake could keep us from ignoring.

Here, we must reclaim our sense of what is needed. On the one hand, the answer to our question concerns the responsibility of intellectuals. When, as with Aristotle, the entire range of practical reason was thought to join together a science of the invariant structures of the world (including human nature) and the application of its findings under the contingencies of perceived life, the responsibility of philosophers proved (of course) quite straightforward. The irony is that now there is no invariant social world to justify the self-absorption of autonomous philosophy. Philosophy is a radically historicized undertaking: *therefore, not even politically neutral*. We find ourselves on the threshold of an utterly novel kind of philosophical work. That is the point of Heidegger's distinction, whatever unlovely forms it favored. Now, more than half a century later, his notion still remains obscure. We may (and should) reject his Nazism; but we cannot reject his philosophical discoveries if, by doing that, we suppose we can recover the political neutrality of philosophy.

On the other hand, deliberate political commitment can no longer claim the saving invariances of the old order. It now entails a radical improvisation at every turn. So philosophy acquires an even deeper practical function than it once could claim, for the need to weigh the reasonableness of *any* significant intervention is now an inseparable part of our existential condition. Politics has become fully "philosophical"— in the same way that science has—by replacing the space of a separable *theory* with the inseparable intimacy of its own *history* and by demanding a sense of rational direction nevertheless. The threatening chaos of the philosophy of politics is no more startling than the chaos of the philosophy of science or the philosophy of art. They are, of course, all tarred with the same brush.

Once we see this, we see the essential danger. The most touching aspect of contemporary philosophies of science concerns our fathoming the structure (whatever it is, if indeed there is a structure) that might ensure, in spite of the flux of history, the steady progress of the sciences. We *are* beginning to understand the elusive saliencies of reasoning in the sciences, but it will surely cost us all the delusions of the past. The same is true, even more compellingly, in our political world, for the pretense, there, of invariant structures requires a deeper self-delusion. Furthermore, where the physical sciences postulate an order of nature free, or relatively free, of inherent historical structures like those of the cultural world—although the *science* of such an order *is* inseparable from its history, and although that world *is* posited (and "found") only within that history—we finally face ourselves in politics. The vagaries of interpreting the meaning of history take such a baffling turn that the very idea of a disciplined politics is permanently risked.

Two symptoms say it all. First, Heidegger's fascist elaboration of his own metaphysics is extremely difficult to detect or disallow at the very moment of recovering what we may rightly regard as salvageable in his philosophy. Second, the cryptofascist readings of literature that have so scandalously appeared in the early writings of Paul de Man, converging more or less independently with the hermeneutic themes of Heidegger's own vision, force us to bear in mind that the inconstancy of human culture signifies that the old notions of interpretive objectivity are no longer compelling. Of course, we cannot endorse the mere trickery of manipulated meanings, but we have not yet arrived at a notion of interpretive rigor robust enough to stand by the short argument with a thoroughly new confidence.

Philosophy, like politics itself, is not separable from ideology. But it cannot be merely a creature of political power either. It requires a sense of critique that, perhaps only in a dialectical way, can hope to isolate the extremes of untenable commitment, interpretation, judgment, theory, principle, and the like. It is not that the rigor of the old interpretive and legitimative practices are beyond our present competence. It is rather that they are no longer convincing. We have hardly lost what we never actually had. Here, too, the responsibility of intellectuals and the philosophical complication of politics come together.

That, ultimately, is Heidegger's best instruction. It is also, unpleasantly, what he obscures—and deforms. But, in exposing Heidegger's untenable Nazi version of his own instruction, we may claim to have offered a small example of the competence and pertinence of philosophy under the terms of the short argument. We have also, of course, sketched a larger map of the principal misreadings of political life. The better future of philosophy is bound to follow that instruction.

NOTES

1. See Harold Bloom, *A Map of Misreading* (New York: Oxford University Press, 1975), Intro. and chap. 1.
2. Martin Heidegger, *Being and Time*, trans. (from 7th ed.) John Macquarrie and Edward Robinson (New York: Harper & Row, 1962), p. 32 (p. 12, German pagination).

3. Ibid., p. 92 (pp. 63–64, German pagination; emphasis added). Cf. the whole of § 14.

4. Martin Heidegger, "The End of Philosophy and the Task of Thinking," trans. Joan Stambaugh, in *Martin Heidegger: Basic Writings*, ed. David Farrell Krell (New York: Harper & Row, 1977), p. 373 (emphasis added).

5. Ibid., p. 378.

6. Martin Heidegger, "Letter on Humanism," trans. Frank A. Capuzzi and J. Glenn Gray, in Krell, *Heidegger: Basic Writings*, p. 258.

7. See Martin Heidegger, "Moira," in *Early Greek Thinking*, trans. David Farrell Krell and Frank A. Capuzzi (New York: Harper & Row, 1975).

8. Quoted in Victor Farías, *Heidegger and Nazism*, ed. Joseph Margolis and Tom Rockmore, trans. (French) Paul Burrell with Dominic Di Bernardi, and (German) Gabriel R. Ricci (Philadelphia: Temple University Press, 1989), p. 99. Cf. *Being and Time*, § 74, for passages closest to the theme of the rectoral address.

9. Cf. Farías, *Heidegger and Nazism*, p. 101, for citation from the address.

10. See Jacques Derrida, *De l'esprit: Heidegger et la question* (Paris: Galilée, 1987), p. 10.

11. See Michael Foucault, "The Return of Morality," trans. Thomas Levin and Isabelle Lorenz, in *Politics, Philosophy, Culture: Interviews 1977–1984*, ed. Lawrence D. Kritzman (New York: Campman & Hall, 1988), pp. 253–54.

Contributors

JOHN D. CAPUTO is Professor of Philosophy at Villanova University and Distinguished Adjunct Professor at Fordham University.

FRED DALLMAYR is the Dee Professor of Government at Notre Dame University.

VICTOR FARÍAS is Professor of Latin American Studies at the Free University, Berlin, Germany.

HANS-GEORG GADAMER is Professor Emeritus of Philosophy at the University of Heidelberg, Germany.

DOMINIQUE JANICAUD is Professor of Philosophy at the University of Nice, France.

THEODORE KISIEL is Professor of Philosophy at Northern Illinois University.

LESZEK KOLAKOWSKI is Research Professor of All Souls College, Oxford University, and Professor in the Committee on Social Thought, University of Chicago.

DOMENICO LOSURDO is Professor of Philosophy at the University of Urbino, Italy.

HANS-CHRISTIAN LUCAS is Research Director in the Hegel Archives at the University of Bochum, Germany.

JOSEPH MARGOLIS is Laura H. Carnell Professor of Philosophy at Temple University.

REINER MARTEN is Professor of Philosophy at the University of Freiburg, Germany.

HUGO OTT is Professor of History at the University of Freiburg, Germany.

OTTO PÖGGELER is Professor of Philosophy and Director of the Hegel Archives at the University of Bochum, Germany.

TOM ROCKMORE is Professor of Philosophy at Duquesne University.

JACQUES TAMINIAUX is Professor of Philosophy at the University of Louvain, Belgium, and at Boston College.

NICOLAS TERTULIAN is Professor of Philosophy at Ecole Pratique des Hautes Études in Paris, France.

REINER SCHÜRMANN is Professor of Philosophy at the New School for Social Research.

MICHAEL E. ZIMMERMANN is Professor of Philosophy at Tulane University.

Index

Abraham a Sancta Clara, 28–31, 36, 196, 339, 343–44, 385
Academic freedom, Heidegger's rejection of, 214–16, 238–39, 251n.28
Action proper, 189
Adorno, Theodor, 378, 380, 390, 395, 408
Adventure, Jünger's work on, 70–71
Adventurous Heart, The, 70
Aeschylus, 325–26, 330n.13
Aestheticism, metaphysics and, 74–77
Aesthetik des Schreckens, Die, 76–77
"Age of the World Picture, The" (lecture), 67
Agricultural technology, Heidegger's comparision of, with Holocaust (the Technology lecture), 56, 110, 157–59, 265–68
Ahistorical vision of philosophy, 3–5
Akademiker, Der, 15, 36–37
Alexander of Jugoslavia, 160n.19
Alioth, Max, 116
Allgemeine Psychologie, 41
Althusser, Louis, 391–92
America: Heidegger's view of, 133–34, 137–39; role of, in western philosophy, 115–18
"Americanism," 57, 75, 86n.19, 133–34; Heidegger's rejection of, 223–25, 292; "inner truth" and, 357–59; "Romanism" and, 148–50. *See also* Democracy
Anaxagoras, 170
Anaximander, 4, 170

"Anhang: Heidegger Redivivus," 379
Antigone, 98
Anti-Oedipus, 248
Anti-Semitism, Heidegger and, 27–36, 43, 55–56; of Abraham a Sancta Clara, 28–31; in Catholic Church, 343; Farías's charges of, 46, 343–45, 347n.27; heightened by German defeat at Stalingrad, 153–54. *See also* Holocaust
Aquinas, Thomas, 100–101
Arbeiter, Der, 53, 64–65, 147, 217, 289–91, 400n.18
Archilochus, 170
Archism, 417–19
Architecture, aesthetics of, 118–19
Archives, 47n.7; as evidence in "Heidegger case," 13–14, 16–18; Farías's access to, 334–35; of Heidegger in Japan, 21. *See also names of specific archives*
Arendt, Hannah, 55, 133, 188–91, 200, 225, 239, 310n.16
"Argumentum e silentio," 138
Aristotle, 126, 170, 200–202; Heidegger influenced by, 130–31; Heidegger's work on, 43, 174–78; on man as "rational animal," 66; *praxis* and, 191–92. *See also names of specific works*
Arithmetic, philosophy of, 124
Arminius and "Geist," 115–16
Arnold, Matthew, 115

Syberberg, Hans Jürgen, 72–73
Syracuse, Plato in, 364

Taoism, 117–18
Tat, Die, 35
Technē, 80; Heidegger on, 66; in *Contributions to Philosophy*, 318–19, 323–24; *praxis* and, 191–92, 194, 199, 204
Technology: character of work in, 68; *Gestalt* of worker and, 59–63; "inner truth" of National Socialism and, 353–55; Heidegger discussion of, 5, 52, 64–71, 80–84, 178–79, 302–3; politics and, 136–37
Technology lecture ("The Question concerning Technology"), 56, 110, 157–59, 265–68
Temps Modernes, Les, 11, 373
Tertulian, Nicolas, 396–97
Tezuka, Tomio, 21–23
Theaetetus, 215
Theology: Heidegger on, 33–35; philosophy and, 22–25
Theoria, 198, 202
Theresa of Avila, 105
Thessalonians, Letter to (New Testament), 121–22
Theweleit, Klaus, 78
"Thorn in the Flesh, The," 107
Thucydides, 201–3
Tietjen, Hartmut, 16–18
Time: Aristotelian concept of, 175–79; dimensions of, 127; phenomenology and, 122–25; philosophy and, 2–3, 122–25
Time and Free Will, 123
Tocqueville, Alexis de, 116
"Total Mobilization," 40, 53, 289–90, 361–62
Towarnicki, Alfred de, 373–75
Toynbee, Arnold, 117
Trakl, Georg, 37, 171, 299–301, 305, 393
Translation of Heidegger's work, problems with, 7
Trial, The, 369
Triumph of the Will, The, 72
Troeltsch, Ernst, 121
Twenty-Third Psalm, 96–97, 111n.11
"Twenty-three questions" of *Fragebogen*, 93

Über Abraham a Sancta Clara, 49n.27
"Über das Wesen deutscher Wissenschaft," 174
Ulmer, Karl, 210
Ultimate power, ideal of, 155
University of Freiburg, 237–247; academic and national politics at, 32–33; Heidegger's inaugural address at, 45; Heidegger's rectorship at, 54; Heidegger's resignation from, 11, 243; postwar investigation of, 94–95; rejection of Ott's biography by, 50n.35
University reform: Heidegger's role in, 43–45; National Socialism and, 54–55
Untimely Meditations, 128, 204
Ursprung des Kunstwerks, Der, 203–4
Utopianism, Being and, 183–84

Valéry, Paul, 304
Value theory, Heidegger's rejection of, 6
van Gogh, Vincent, 293
Vattimo, Gianni, 333–34, 336–37, 341, 383–84
Vezin, François, 389–90
Vienna School, 117–18, 120
Volkgemeinschaft, 56
Volk philosophy, 220–21; artistic power of, 72–73; *Contributions to Philosophy* and, 318–19, 329n.7; *Geist* and, 81–82; *Gestalt* of worker and, 60–61; Heidegger's political ideology and, 21, 34, 55, 241–42, 293–94, 381
Vollrath, Ernst, 239
von Ficker, Ludwig, 37
von Gebsattel, Victor Freiherr, 95–100, 111n.10
von Hevesy, Paul, 138
von Kralik, Richard, 37
von Oertzen, W., 78
von Schirach, Baldur, 153
von Thaden, Nikolaus, 233
Vorhandenheit, 199, 295–96

Wagner, Richard, 79–80
Wallenstein, 28
War, 141; *Gestalt* of worker and, 61–62; peace and, 69–70
War and Warrior, 39